# CI
# CA
# TE
# RA

# 3

# MINORU
# FURUYA

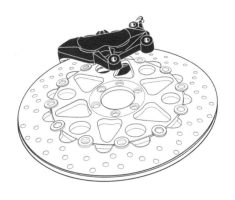

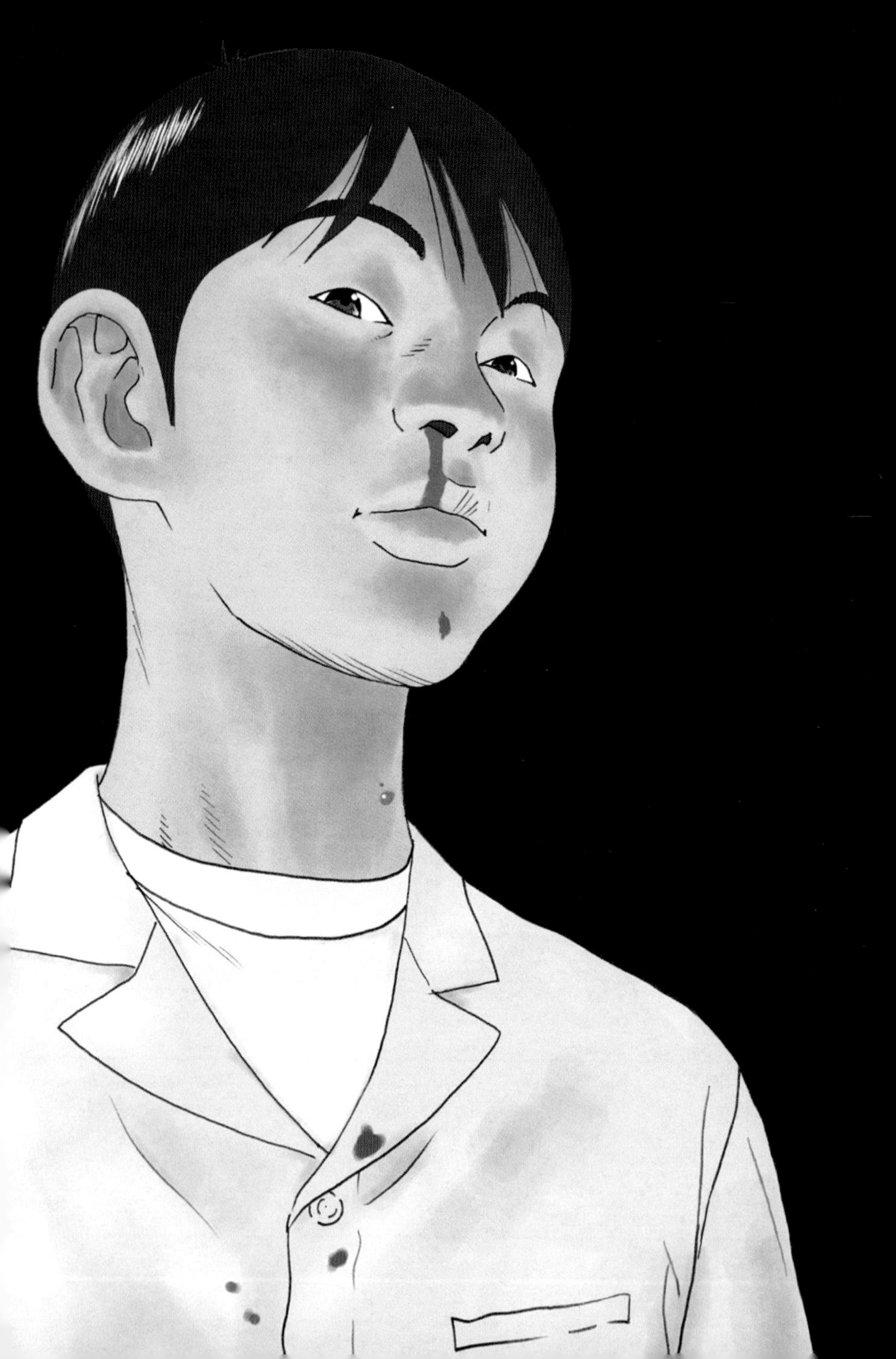

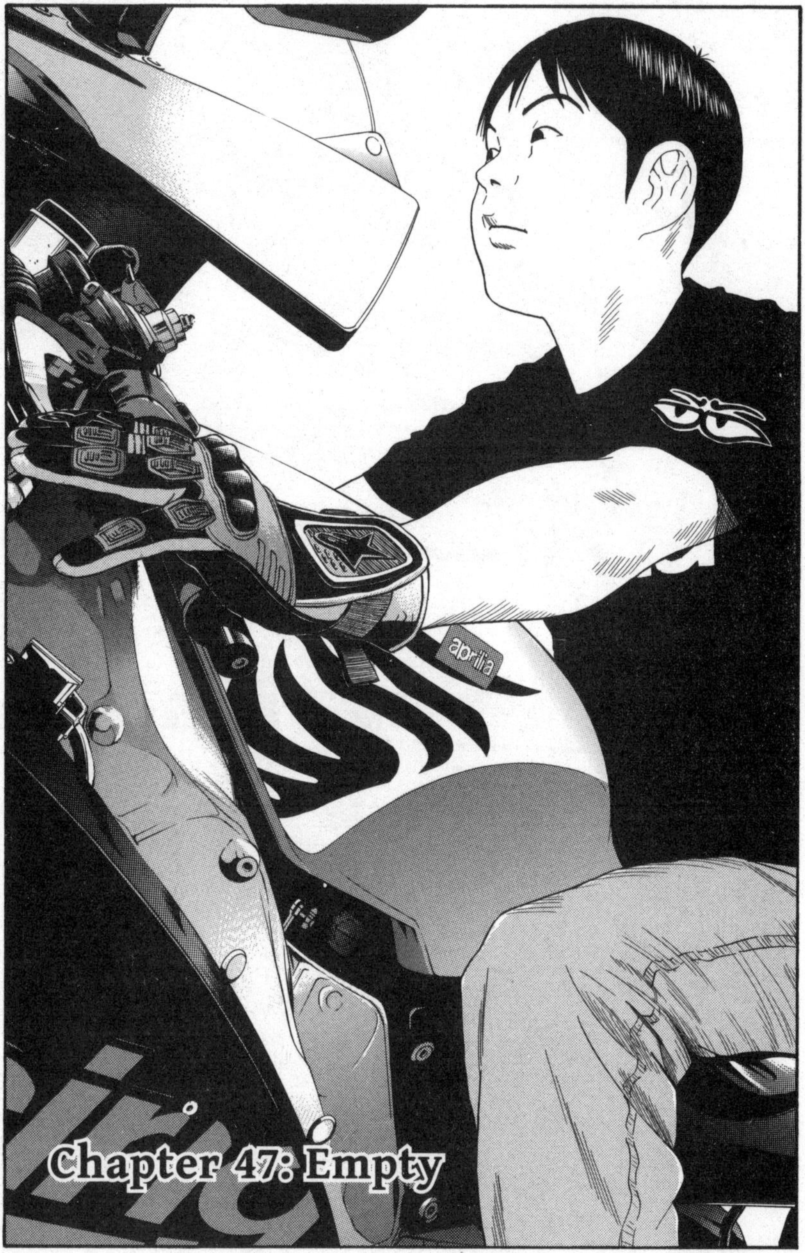

Chapter 47: Empty
aprilia

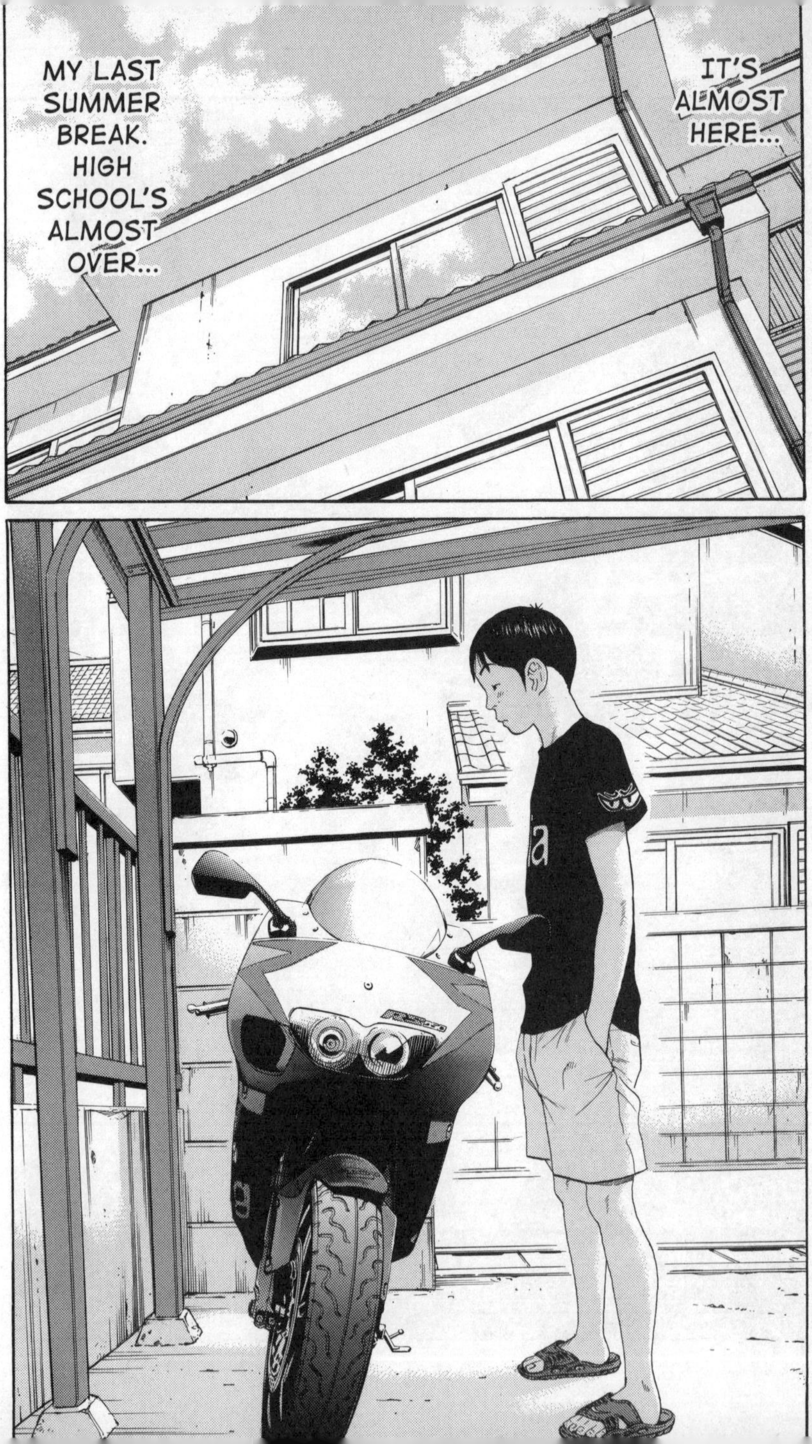
IT'S ALMOST HERE...
MY LAST SUMMER BREAK. HIGH SCHOOL'S ALMOST OVER...

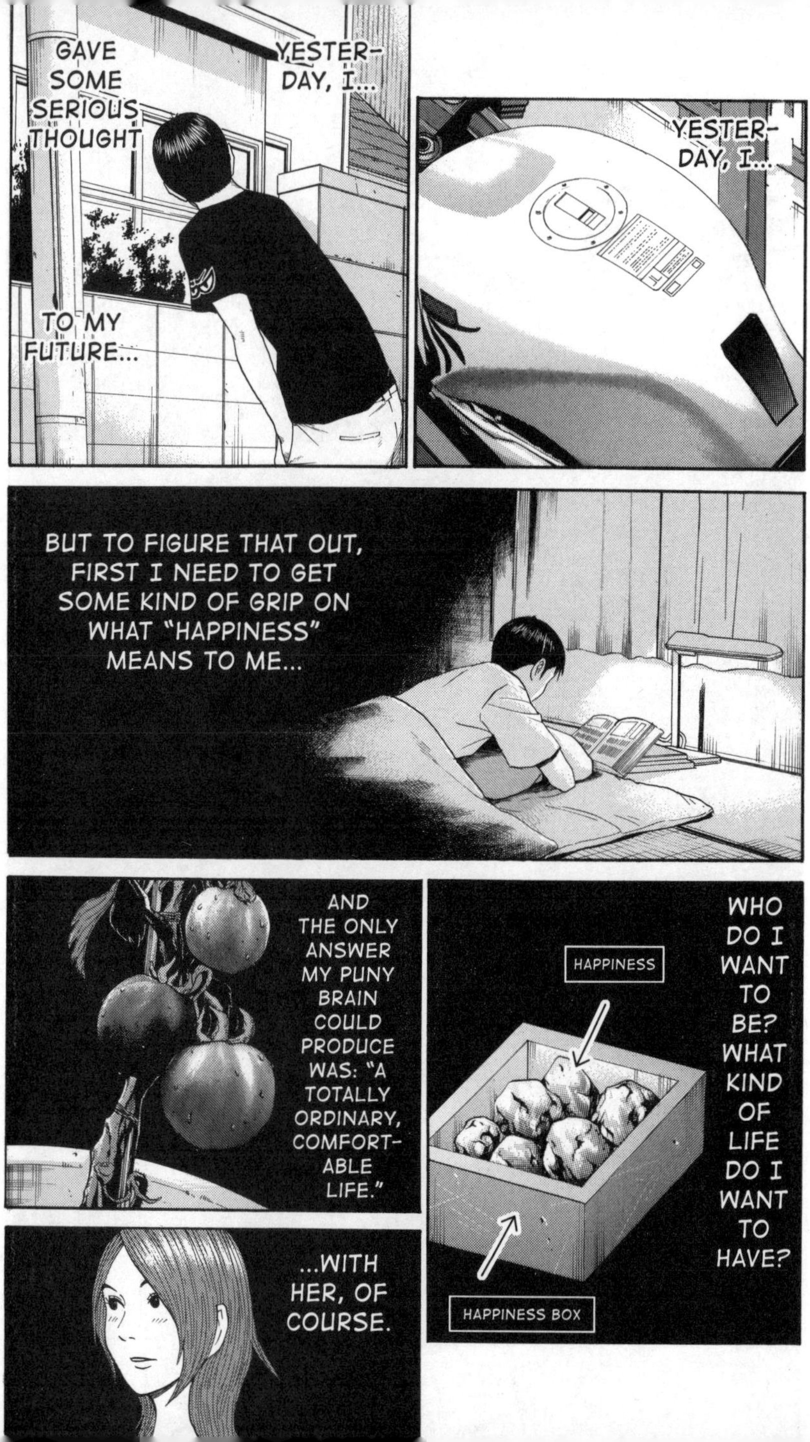
YESTER-DAY, I...
YESTER-DAY, I...
GAVE SOME SERIOUS THOUGHT
TO MY FUTURE...
BUT TO FIGURE THAT OUT, FIRST I NEED TO GET SOME KIND OF GRIP ON WHAT "HAPPINESS" MEANS TO ME...
WHO DO I WANT TO BE? WHAT KIND OF LIFE DO I WANT TO HAVE?
HAPPINESS
HAPPINESS BOX
AND THE ONLY ANSWER MY PUNY BRAIN COULD PRODUCE WAS: "A TOTALLY ORDINARY, COMFORT-ABLE LIFE."
...WITH HER, OF COURSE.

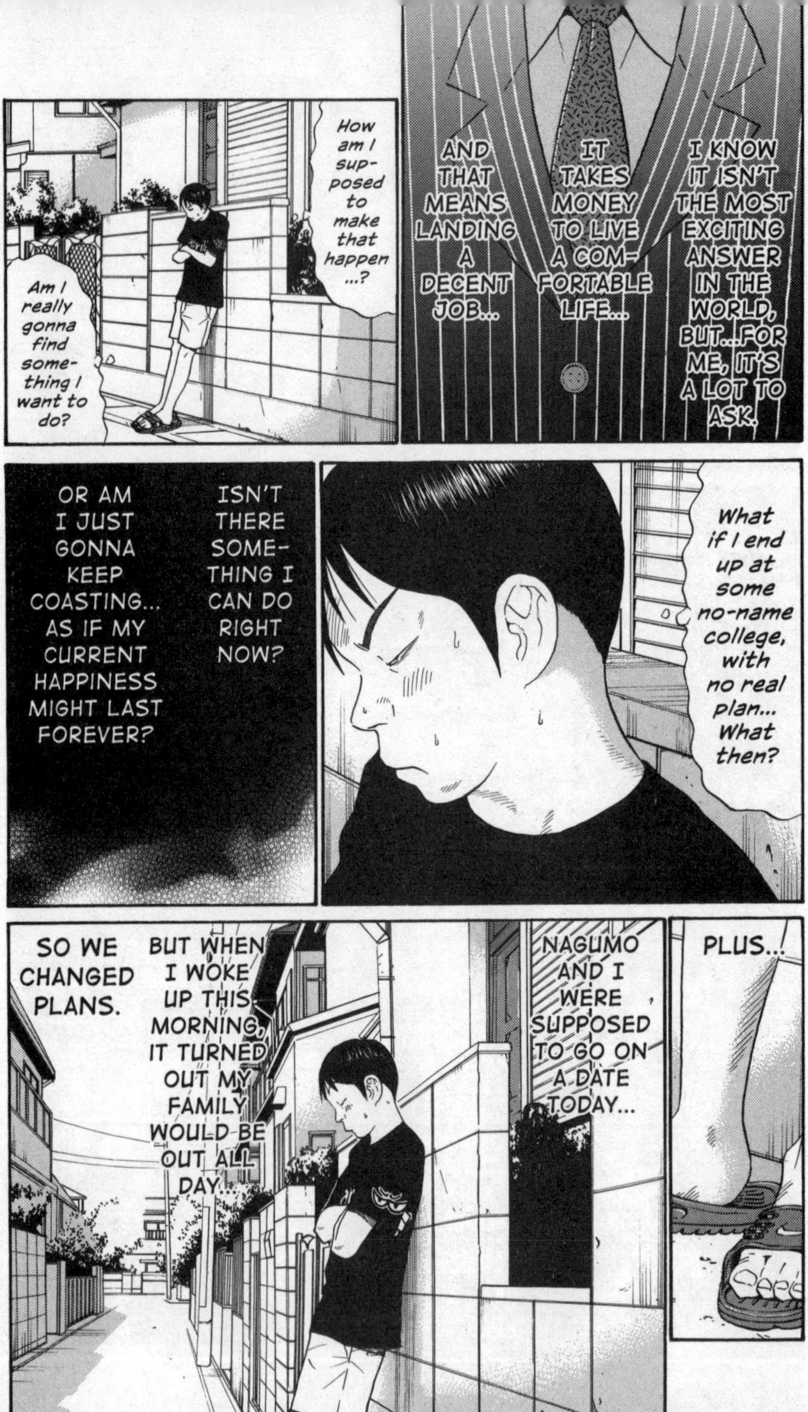
I KNOW IT ISN'T THE MOST EXCITING ANSWER IN THE WORLD, BUT...FOR ME, IT'S A LOT TO ASK.
IT TAKES MONEY TO LIVE A COMFORTABLE LIFE...
AND THAT MEANS LANDING A DECENT JOB...
How am I supposed to make that happen...?
Am I really gonna find something I want to do?
What if I end up at some no-name college, with no real plan... What then?
ISN'T THERE SOMETHING I CAN DO RIGHT NOW?
OR AM I JUST GONNA KEEP COASTING... AS IF MY CURRENT HAPPINESS MIGHT LAST FOREVER?
PLUS...
NAGUMO AND I WERE SUPPOSED TO GO ON A DATE TODAY...
BUT WHEN I WOKE UP THIS MORNING, IT TURNED OUT MY FAMILY WOULD BE OUT ALL DAY.
SO WE CHANGED PLANS.

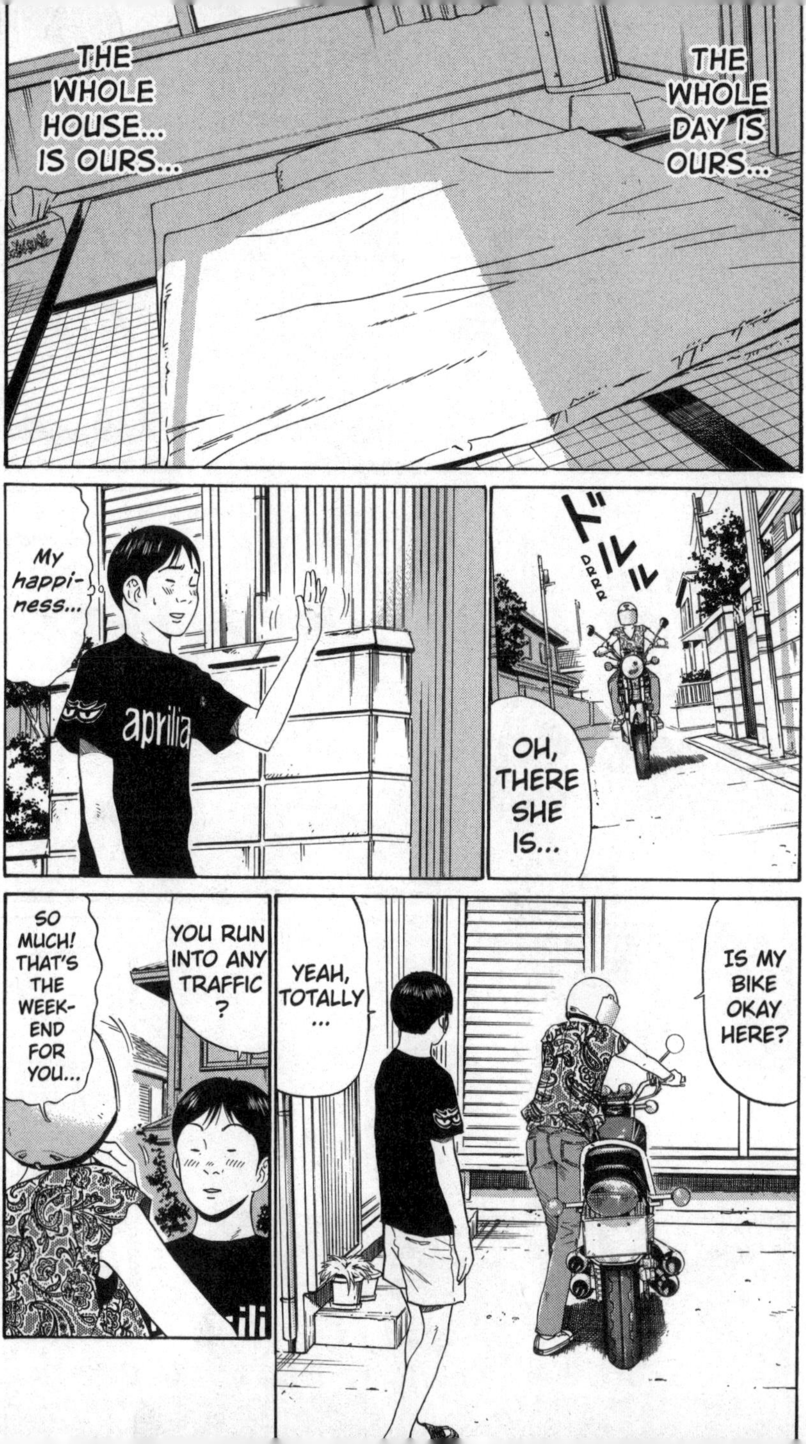
THE WHOLE DAY IS OURS...
THE WHOLE HOUSE... IS OURS...
ドルルル
DRRR
OH, THERE SHE IS...
My happi-ness...
aprilia
IS MY BIKE OKAY HERE?
YEAH, TOTALLY...
YOU RUN INTO ANY TRAFFIC?
SO MUCH! THAT'S THE WEEK-END FOR YOU...

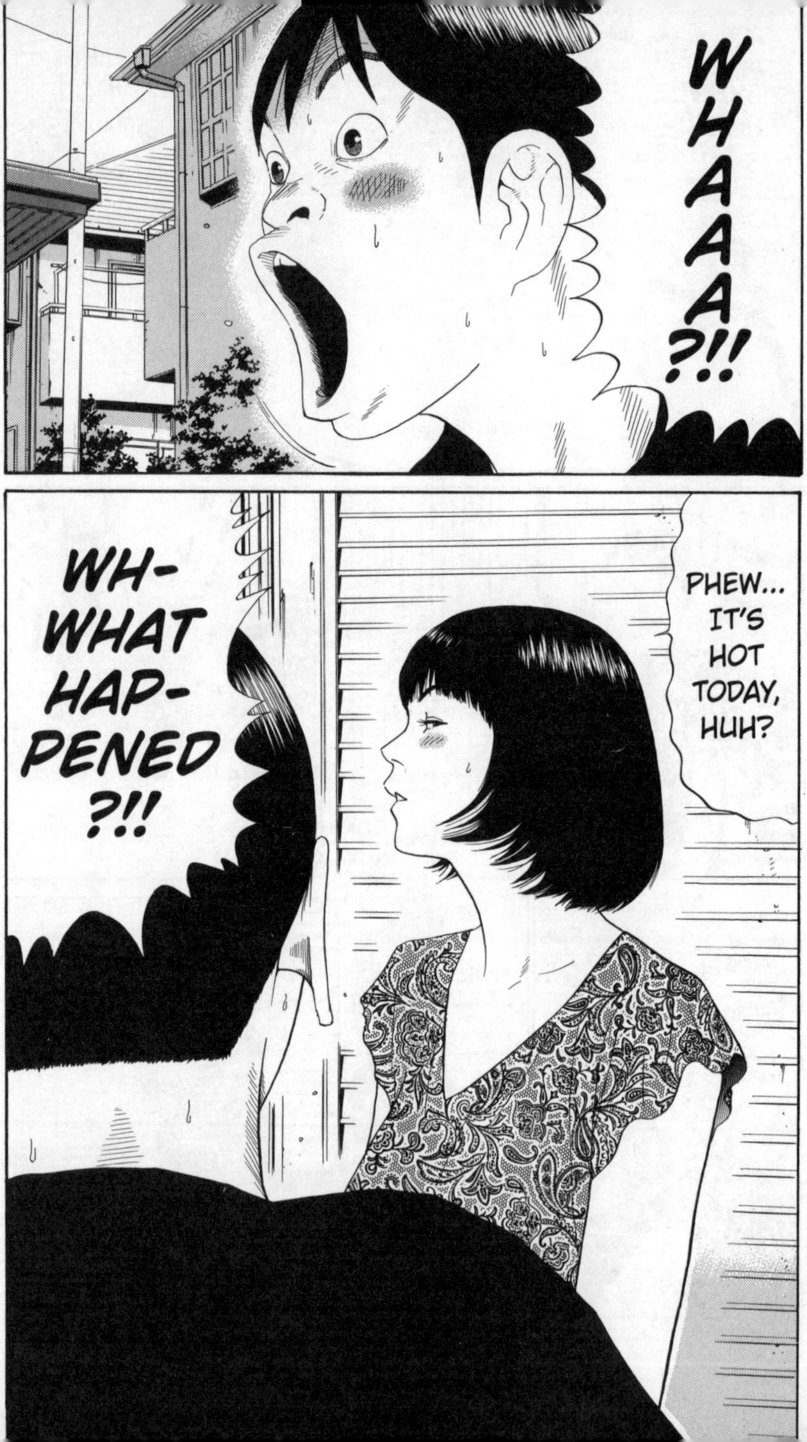
WHAAAA?!!
PHEW... IT'S HOT TODAY, HUH?
WH-WHAT HAP-PENED?!!

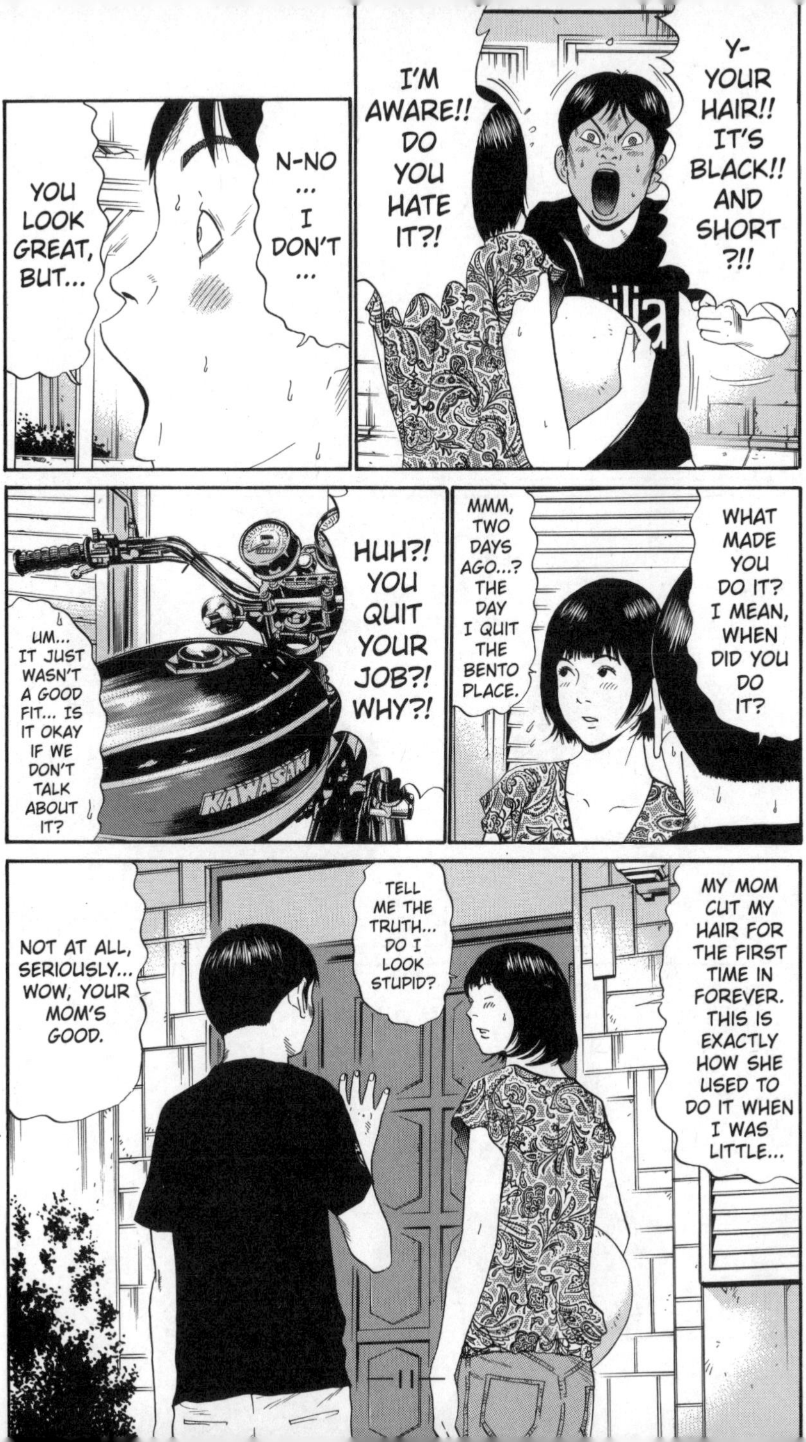
Y- YOUR HAIR!! IT'S BLACK!! AND SHORT?!!
I'M AWARE!! DO YOU HATE IT?!
N-NO ... I DON'T ...
YOU LOOK GREAT, BUT...
WHAT MADE YOU DO IT? I MEAN, WHEN DID YOU DO IT?
MMM, TWO DAYS AGO...? THE DAY I QUIT THE BENTO PLACE.
HUH?! YOU QUIT YOUR JOB?! WHY?!
UM... IT JUST WASN'T A GOOD FIT... IS IT OKAY IF WE DON'T TALK ABOUT IT?
KAWASAKI
MY MOM CUT MY HAIR FOR THE FIRST TIME IN FOREVER. THIS IS EXACTLY HOW SHE USED TO DO IT WHEN I WAS LITTLE...
TELL ME THE TRUTH... DO I LOOK STUPID?
NOT AT ALL, SERIOUSLY... WOW, YOUR MOM'S GOOD.

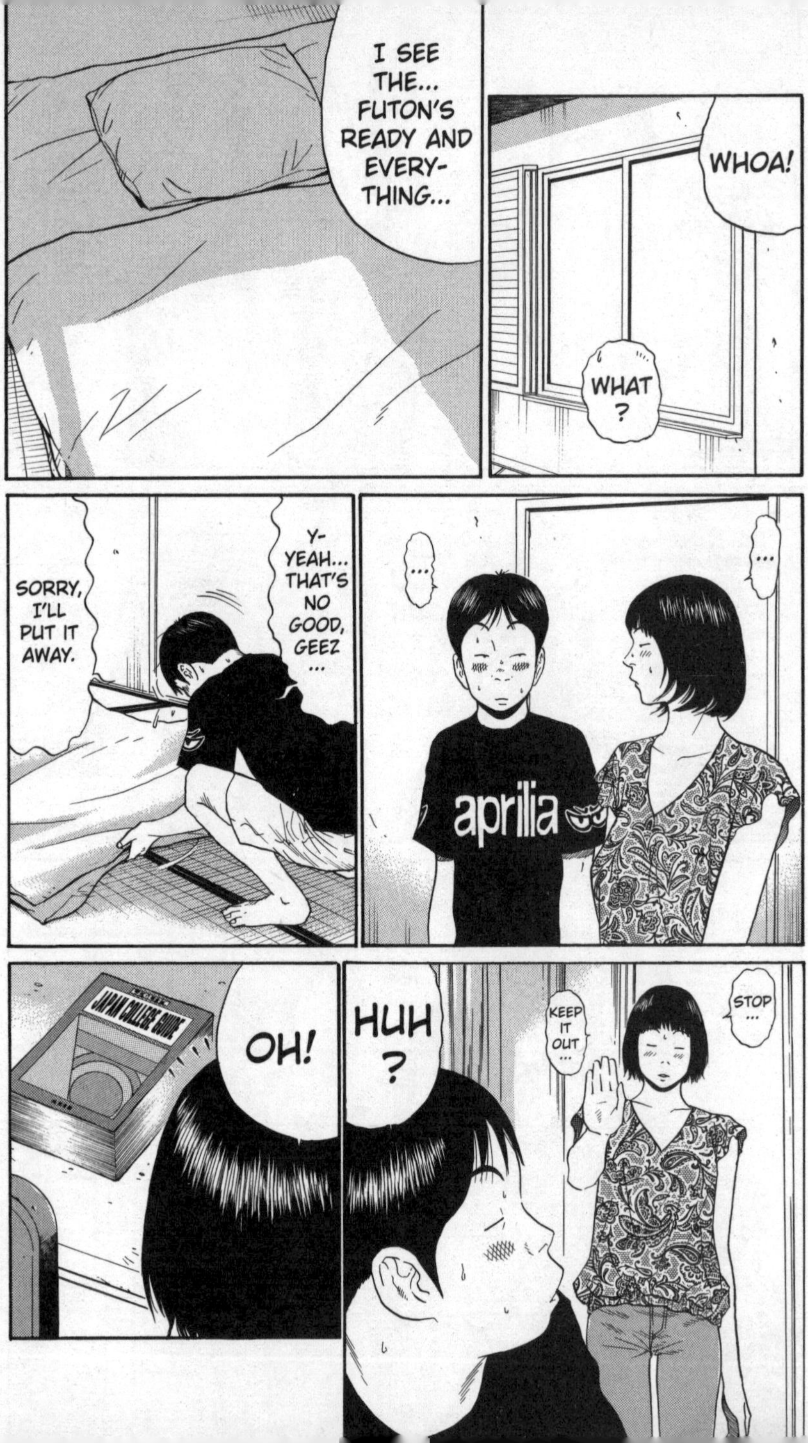
WHOA!
WHAT ?
I SEE THE... FUTON'S READY AND EVERY-THING...
...
...
Y-YEAH... THAT'S NO GOOD, GEEZ ...
SORRY, I'LL PUT IT AWAY.
STOP ...
KEEP IT OUT ...
HUH ?
OH!
JAPAN COLLEGE GUIDE

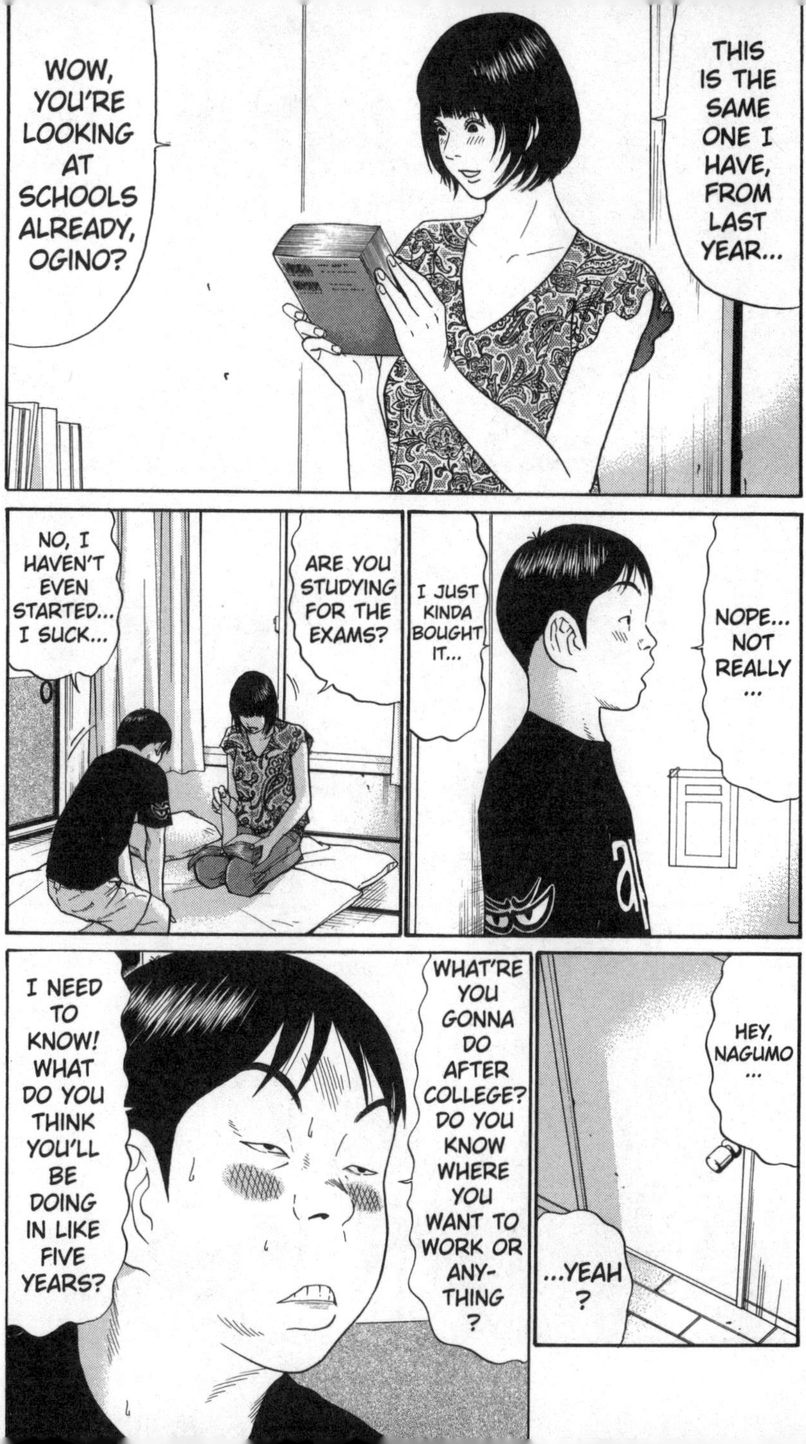
THIS IS THE SAME ONE I HAVE, FROM LAST YEAR...
WOW, YOU'RE LOOKING AT SCHOOLS ALREADY, OGINO?
NOPE... NOT REALLY ...
I JUST KINDA BOUGHT IT...
ARE YOU STUDYING FOR THE EXAMS?
NO, I HAVEN'T EVEN STARTED... I SUCK...
HEY, NAGUMO ...
...YEAH ?
WHAT'RE YOU GONNA DO AFTER COLLEGE? DO YOU KNOW WHERE YOU WANT TO WORK OR ANY-THING ?
I NEED TO KNOW! WHAT DO YOU THINK YOU'LL BE DOING IN LIKE FIVE YEARS?

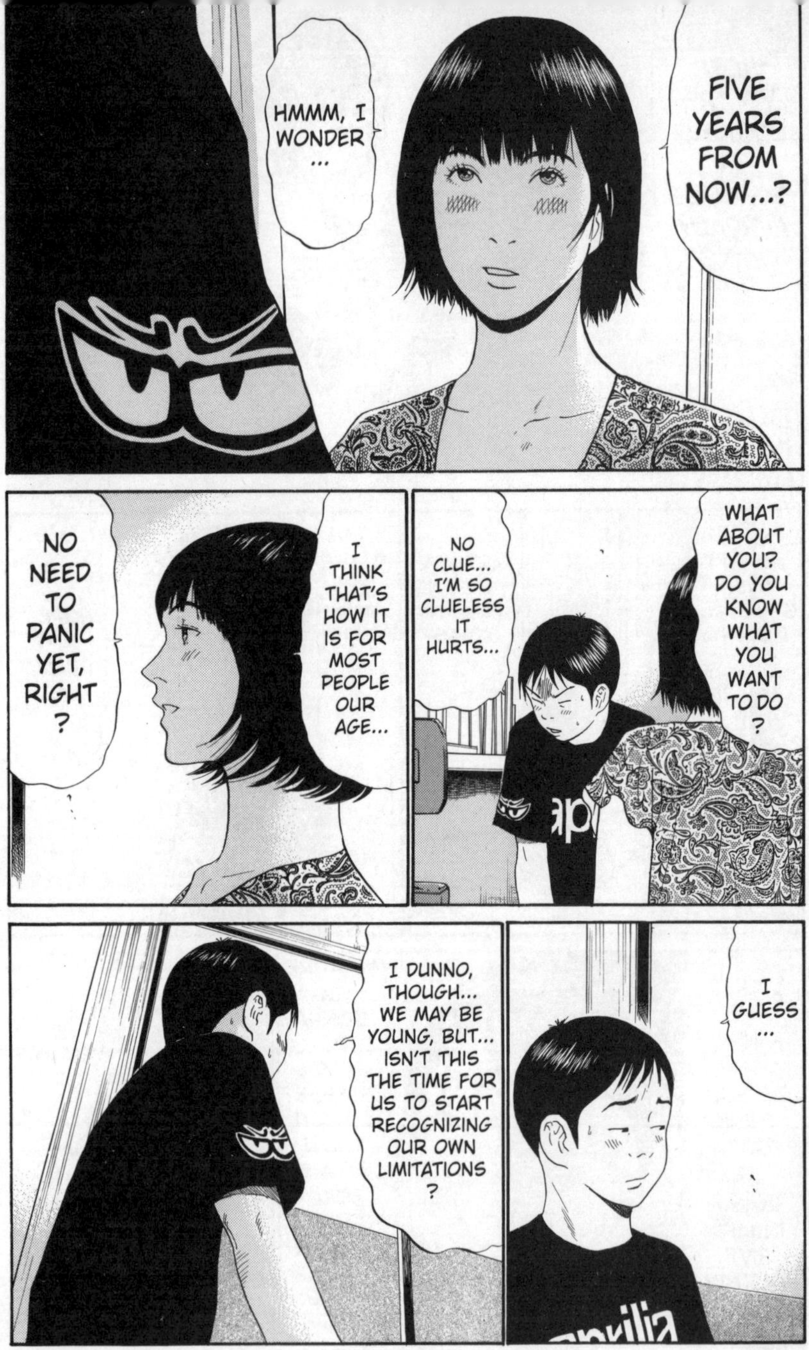
FIVE YEARS FROM NOW...?
HMMM, I WONDER...
WHAT ABOUT YOU? DO YOU KNOW WHAT YOU WANT TO DO?
NO CLUE... I'M SO CLUELESS IT HURTS...
I THINK THAT'S HOW IT IS FOR MOST PEOPLE OUR AGE...
NO NEED TO PANIC YET, RIGHT?
I GUESS...
I DUNNO, THOUGH... WE MAY BE YOUNG, BUT... ISN'T THIS THE TIME FOR US TO START RECOGNIZING OUR OWN LIMITATIONS?

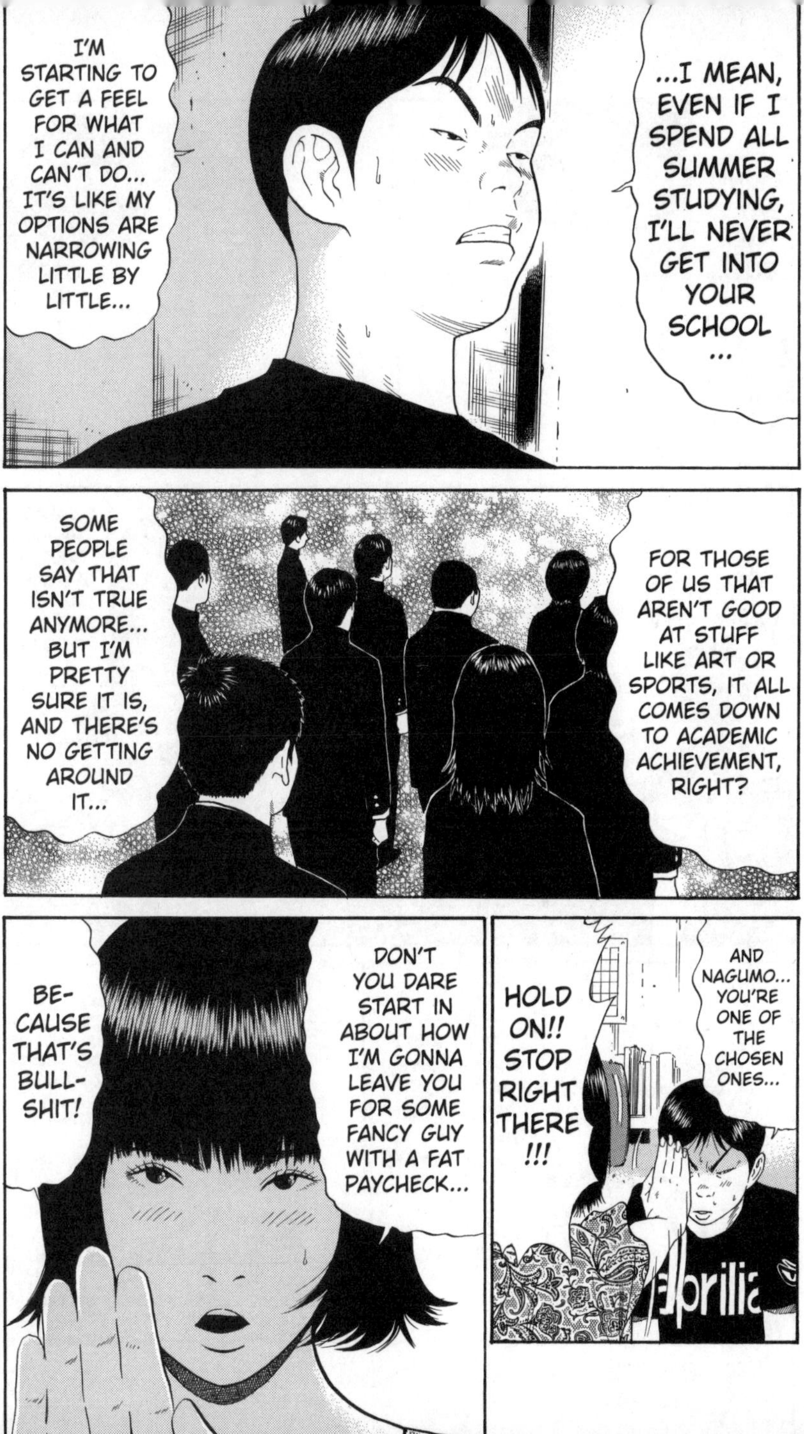
...I MEAN, EVEN IF I SPEND ALL SUMMER STUDYING, I'LL NEVER GET INTO YOUR SCHOOL ...
I'M STARTING TO GET A FEEL FOR WHAT I CAN AND CAN'T DO... IT'S LIKE MY OPTIONS ARE NARROWING LITTLE BY LITTLE...
FOR THOSE OF US THAT AREN'T GOOD AT STUFF LIKE ART OR SPORTS, IT ALL COMES DOWN TO ACADEMIC ACHIEVEMENT, RIGHT?
SOME PEOPLE SAY THAT ISN'T TRUE ANYMORE... BUT I'M PRETTY SURE IT IS, AND THERE'S NO GETTING AROUND IT...
AND NAGUMO... YOU'RE ONE OF THE CHOSEN ONES...
HOLD ON!! STOP RIGHT THERE !!!
DON'T YOU DARE START IN ABOUT HOW I'M GONNA LEAVE YOU FOR SOME FANCY GUY WITH A FAT PAYCHECK...
BE-CAUSE THAT'S BULL-SHIT!

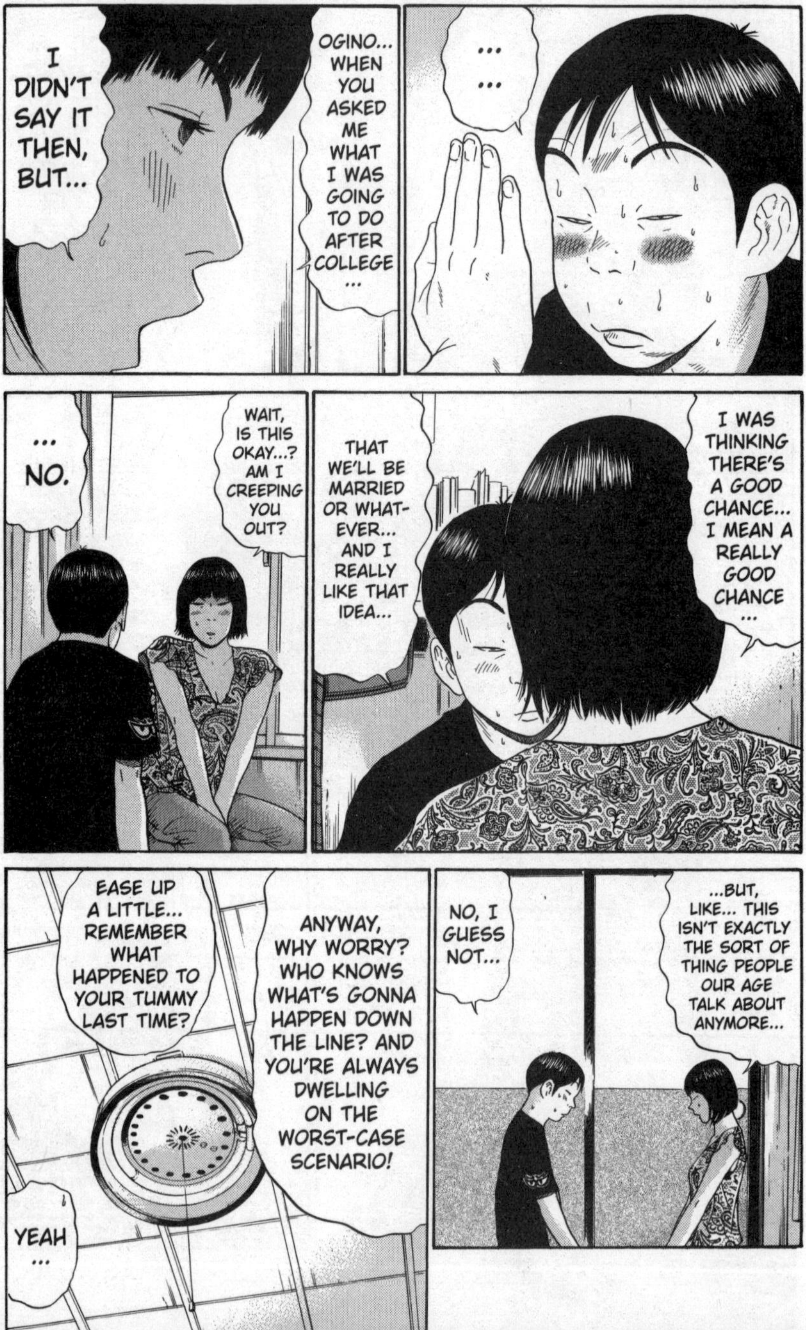
... ...
OGINO... WHEN YOU ASKED ME WHAT I WAS GOING TO DO AFTER COLLEGE ...
I DIDN'T SAY IT THEN, BUT...
I WAS THINKING THERE'S A GOOD CHANCE... I MEAN A REALLY GOOD CHANCE ...
THAT WE'LL BE MARRIED OR WHAT-EVER... AND I REALLY LIKE THAT IDEA...
WAIT, IS THIS OKAY...? AM I CREEPING YOU OUT?
... NO.
...BUT, LIKE... THIS ISN'T EXACTLY THE SORT OF THING PEOPLE OUR AGE TALK ABOUT ANYMORE...
NO, I GUESS NOT...
ANYWAY, WHY WORRY? WHO KNOWS WHAT'S GONNA HAPPEN DOWN THE LINE? AND YOU'RE ALWAYS DWELLING ON THE WORST-CASE SCENARIO!
EASE UP A LITTLE... REMEMBER WHAT HAPPENED TO YOUR TUMMY LAST TIME?
YEAH ...

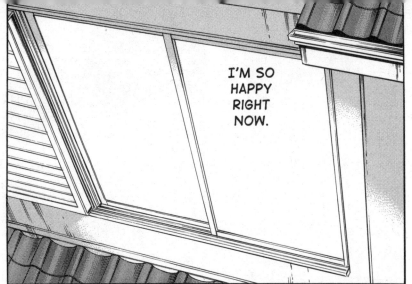

I'M SO HAPPY RIGHT NOW.
I'VE GOT LITERALLY NOTHING
TO COMPLAIN ABOUT...

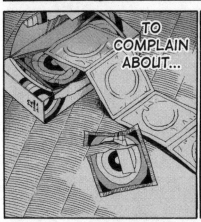

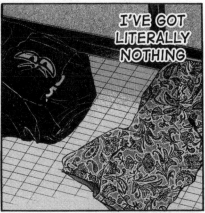

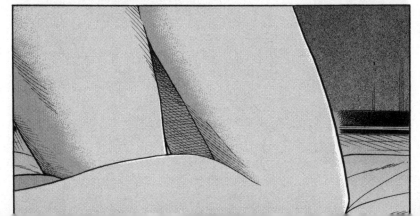

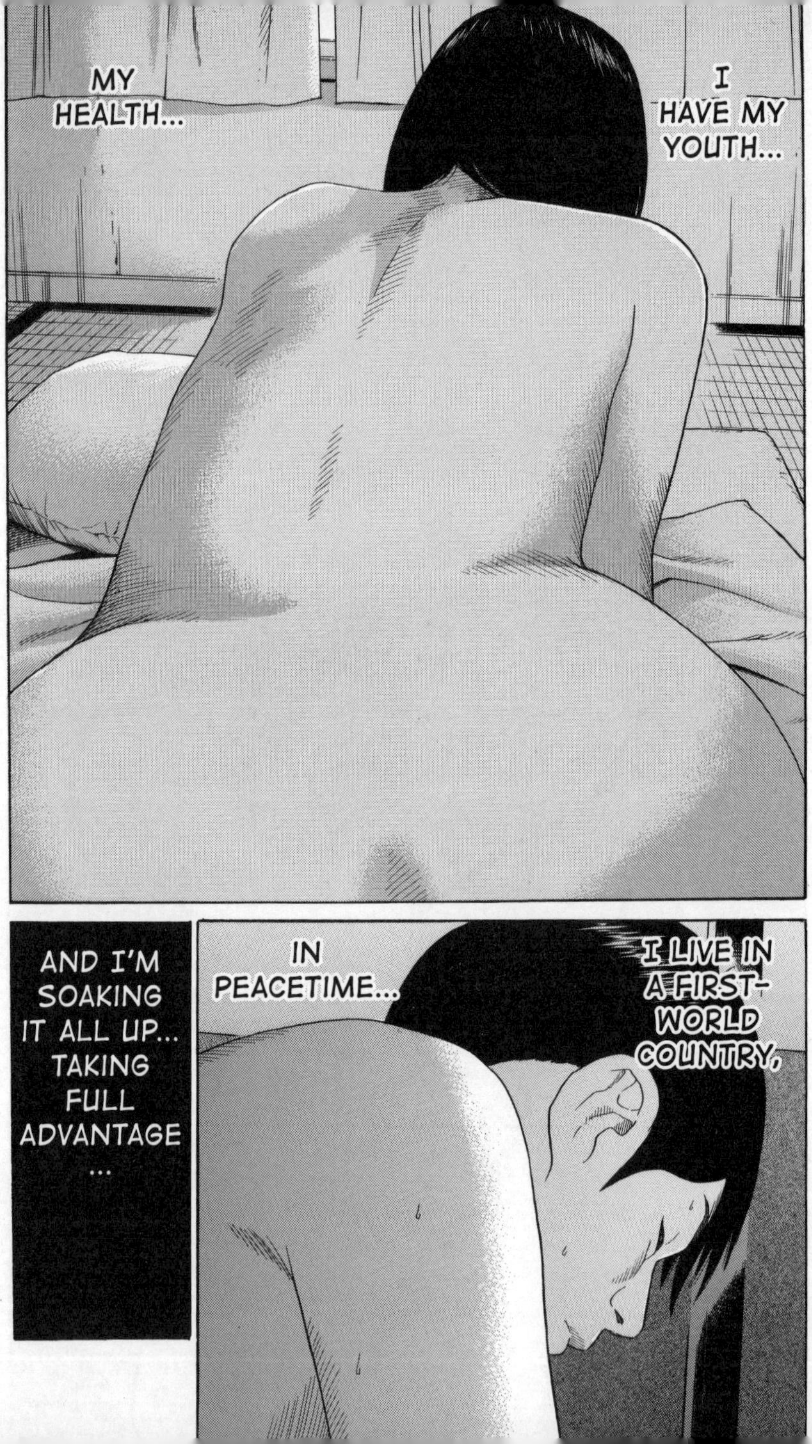
I HAVE MY YOUTH...
MY HEALTH...
I LIVE IN A FIRST-WORLD COUNTRY,
IN PEACETIME...
AND I'M SOAKING IT ALL UP... TAKING FULL ADVANTAGE ...

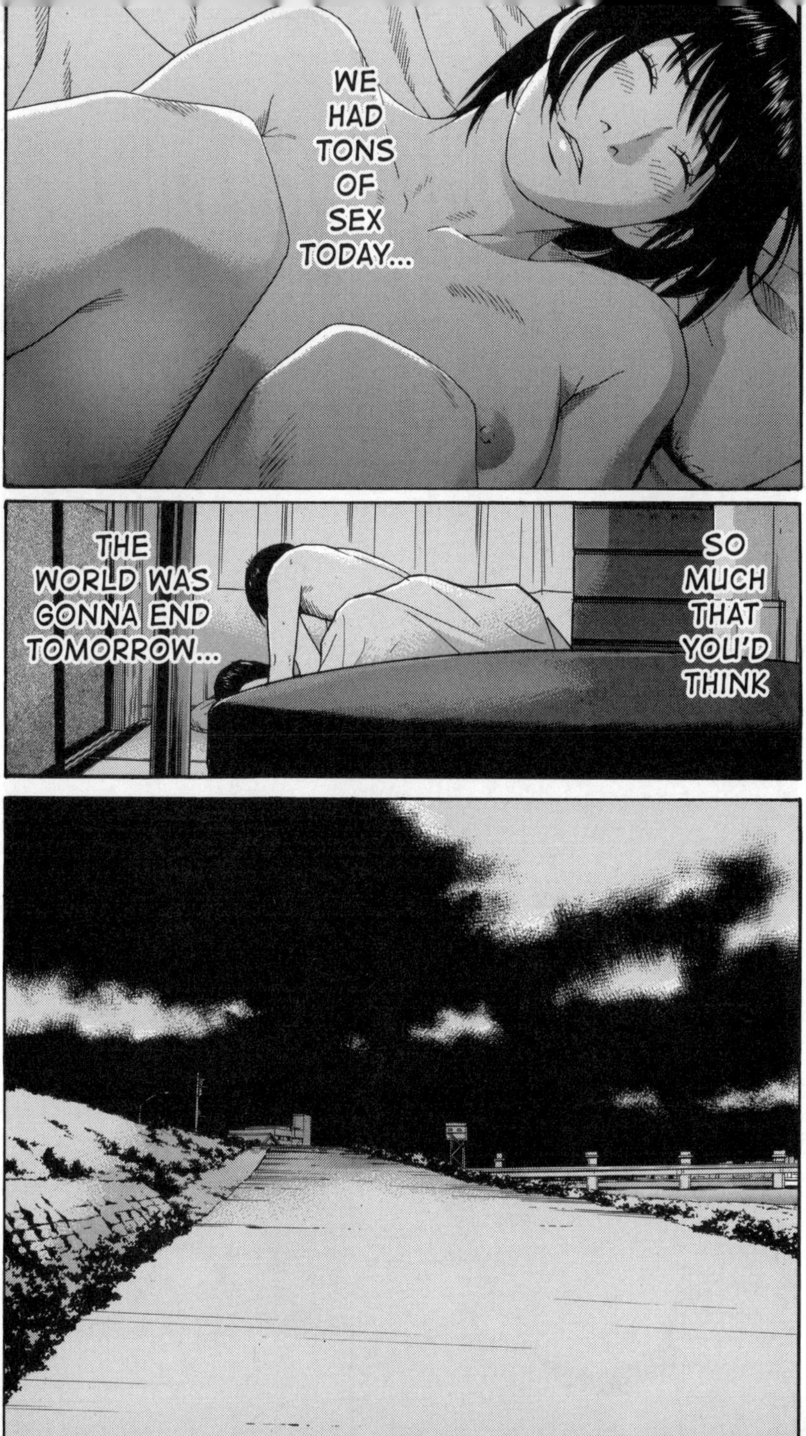
WE HAD TONS OF SEX TODAY...
SO MUCH THAT YOU'D THINK
THE WORLD WAS GONNA END TOMORROW...

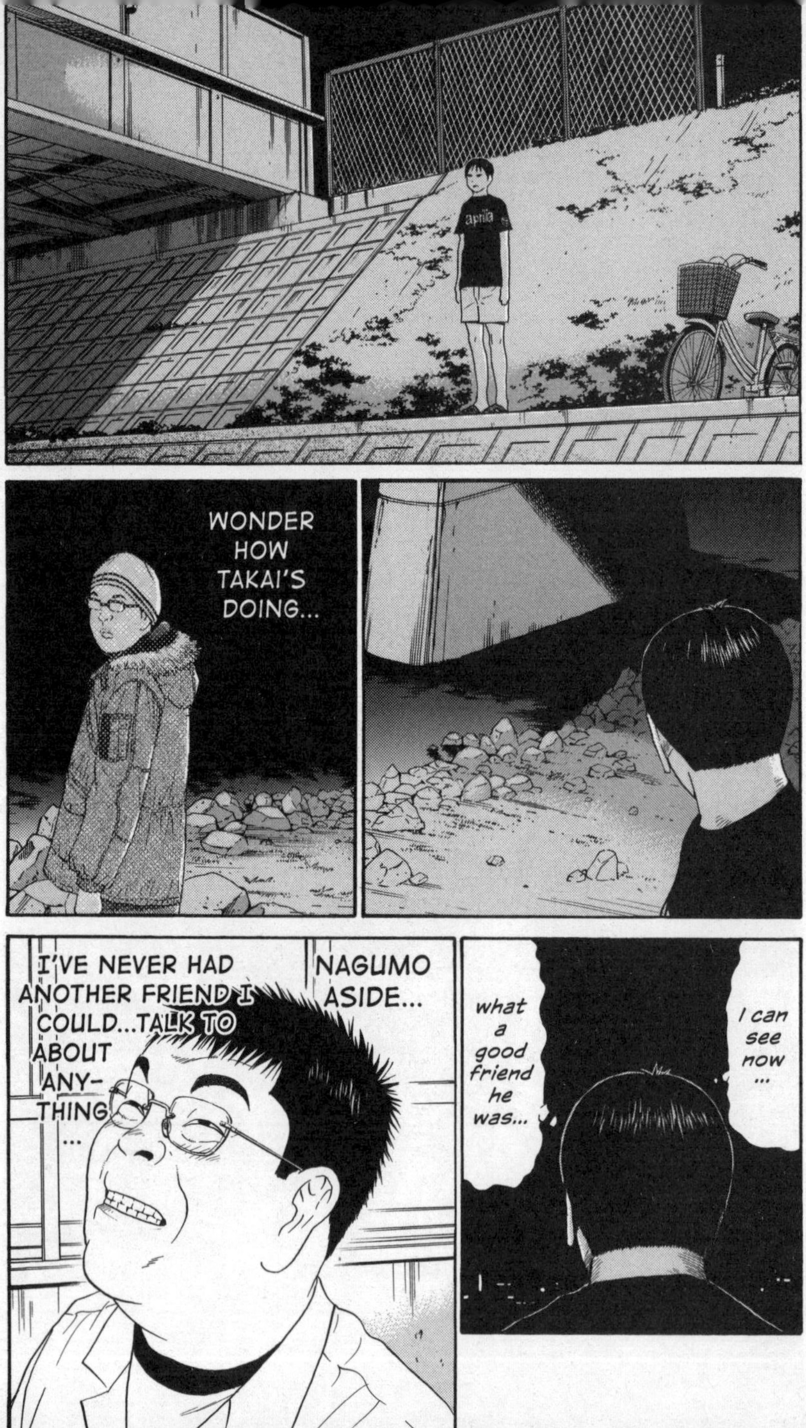
aprilia
WONDER HOW TAKAI'S DOING...
I can see now...
what a good friend he was...
NAGUMO ASIDE...
I'VE NEVER HAD ANOTHER FRIEND I COULD...TALK TO ABOUT ANY-THING...

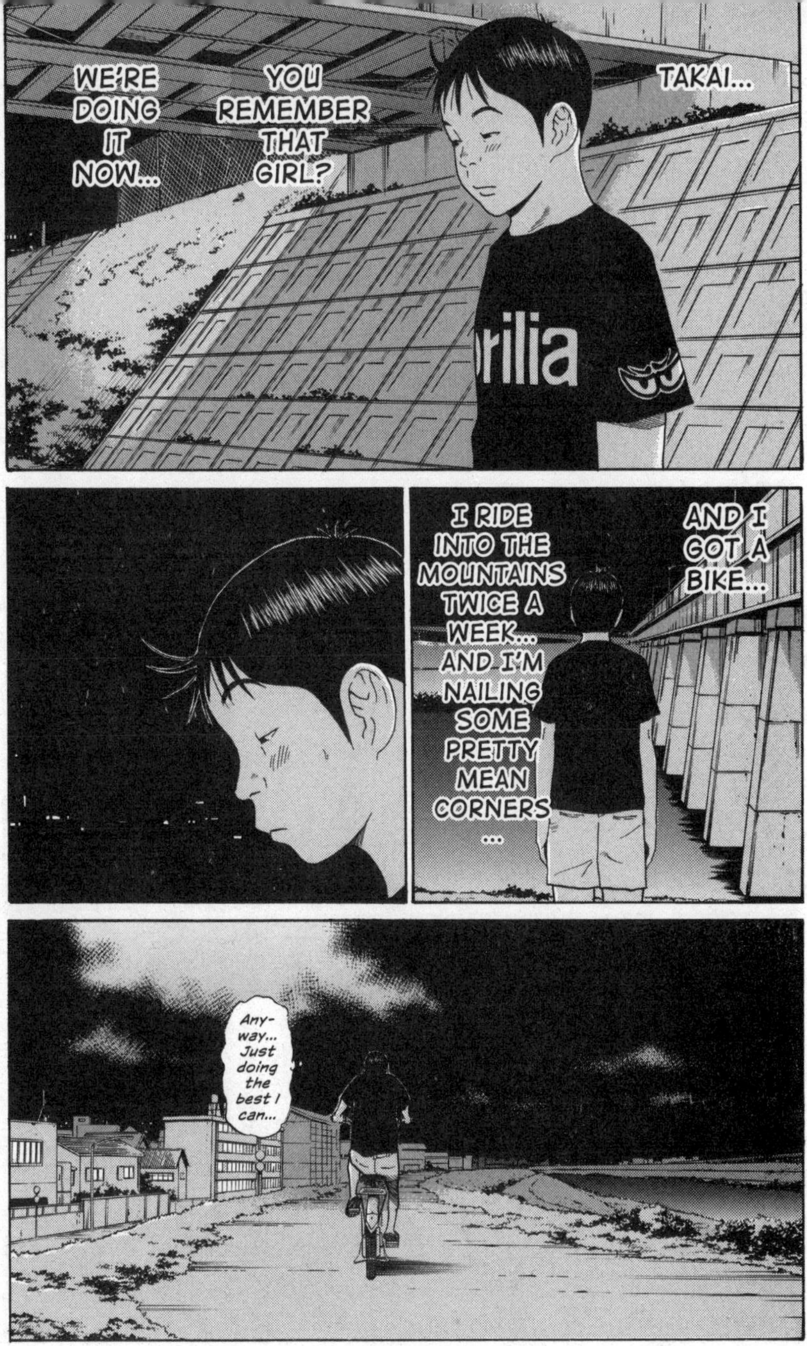
TAKAI...
YOU REMEMBER THAT GIRL?
WE'RE DOING IT NOW...
AND I GOT A BIKE...
I RIDE INTO THE MOUNTAINS TWICE A WEEK... AND I'M NAILING SOME PRETTY MEAN CORNERS...
Any-way... Just doing the best I can...

# 欲

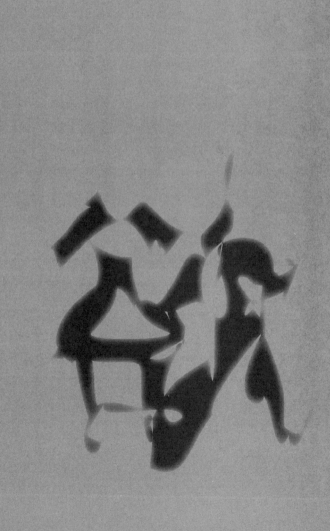

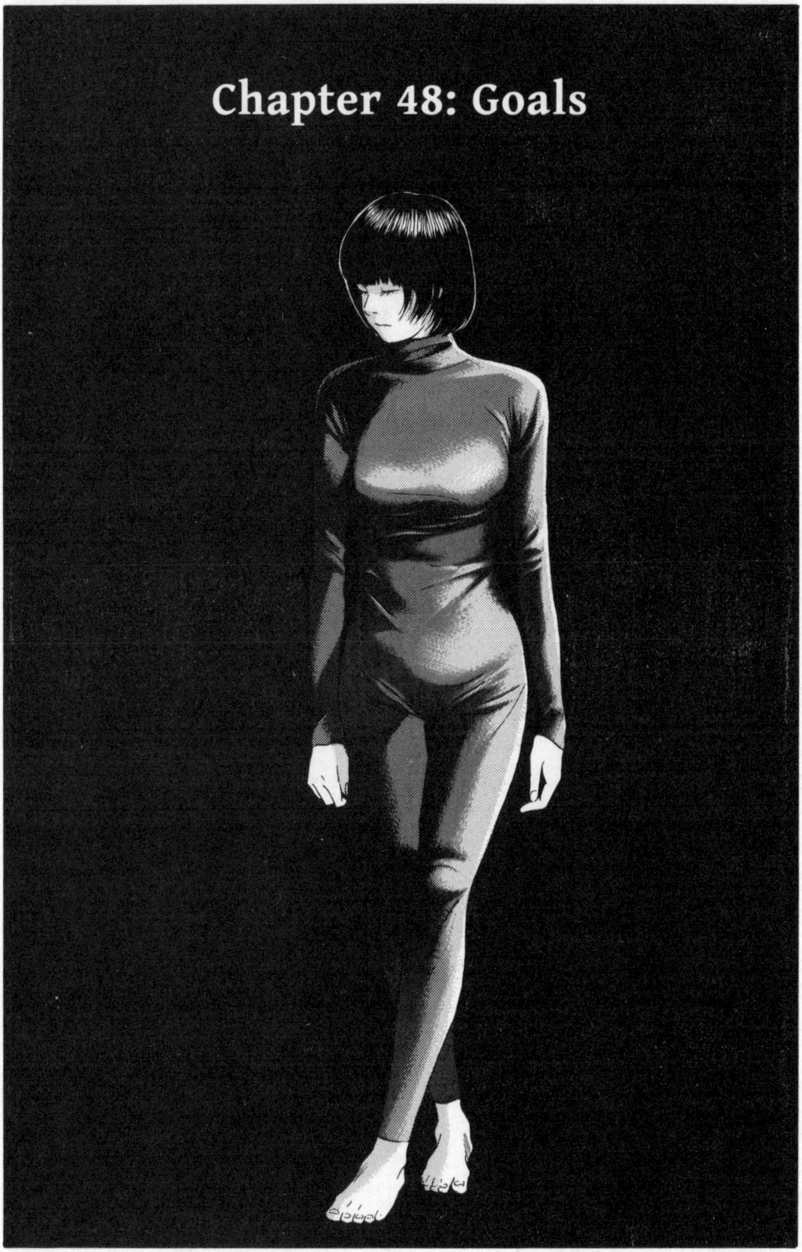
Chapter 48: Goals

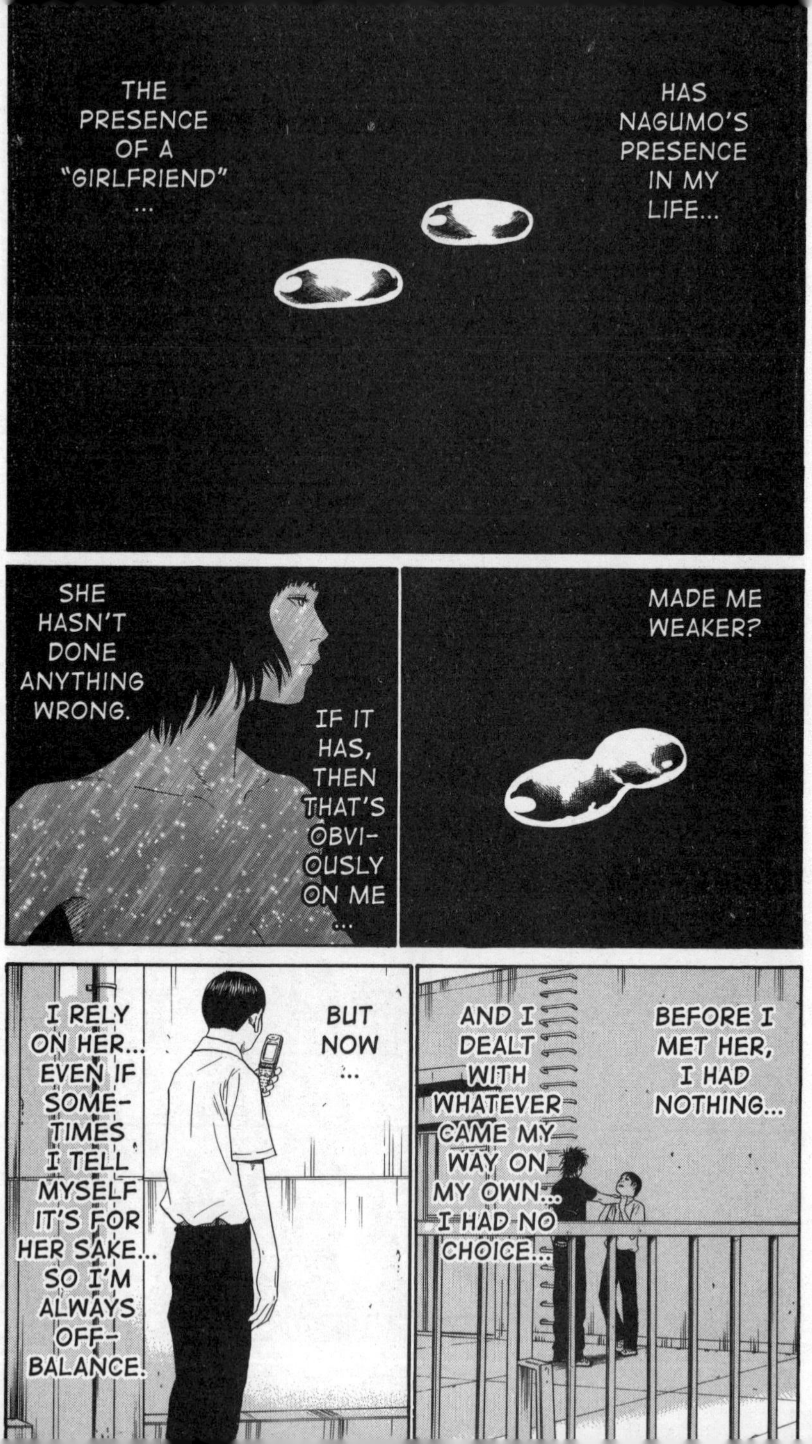
HAS NAGUMO'S PRESENCE IN MY LIFE...
THE PRESENCE OF A "GIRLFRIEND"...
MADE ME WEAKER?
SHE HASN'T DONE ANYTHING WRONG.
IF IT HAS, THEN THAT'S OBVIOUSLY ON ME...
BEFORE I MET HER, I HAD NOTHING...
AND I DEALT WITH WHATEVER CAME MY WAY ON MY OWN... I HAD NO CHOICE...
BUT NOW...
I RELY ON HER... EVEN IF SOMETIMES I TELL MYSELF IT'S FOR HER SAKE... SO I'M ALWAYS OFF-BALANCE.

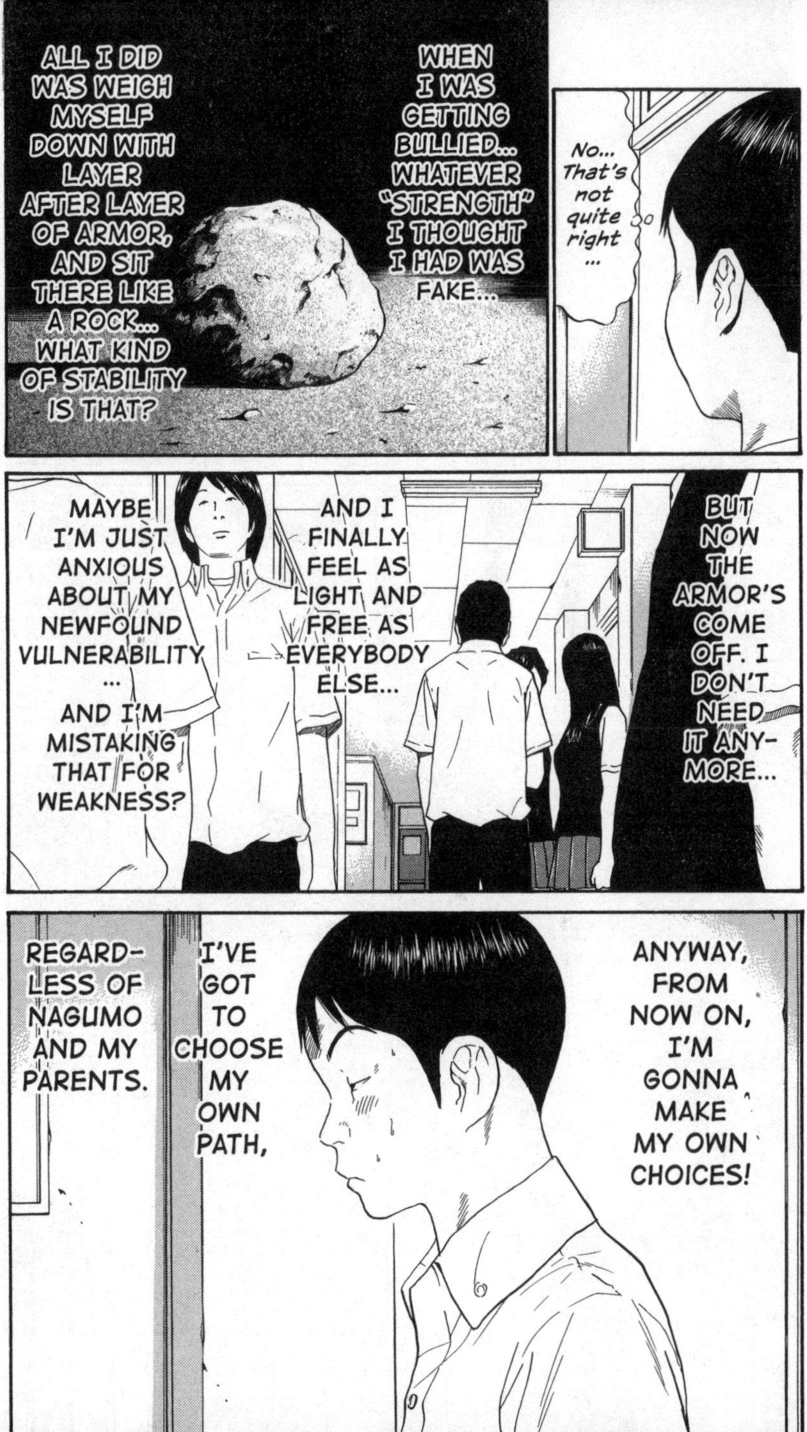
No... That's not quite right ...
WHEN I WAS GETTING BULLIED... WHATEVER "STRENGTH" I THOUGHT I HAD WAS FAKE...
ALL I DID WAS WEIGH MYSELF DOWN WITH LAYER AFTER LAYER OF ARMOR, AND SIT THERE LIKE A ROCK... WHAT KIND OF STABILITY IS THAT?
BUT NOW THE ARMOR'S COME OFF. I DON'T NEED IT ANY-MORE...
AND I FINALLY FEEL AS LIGHT AND FREE AS EVERYBODY ELSE...
MAYBE I'M JUST ANXIOUS ABOUT MY NEWFOUND VULNERABILITY ...
AND I'M MISTAKING THAT FOR WEAKNESS?
ANYWAY, FROM NOW ON, I'M GONNA MAKE MY OWN CHOICES!
I'VE GOT TO CHOOSE MY OWN PATH,
REGARD-LESS OF NAGUMO AND MY PARENTS.

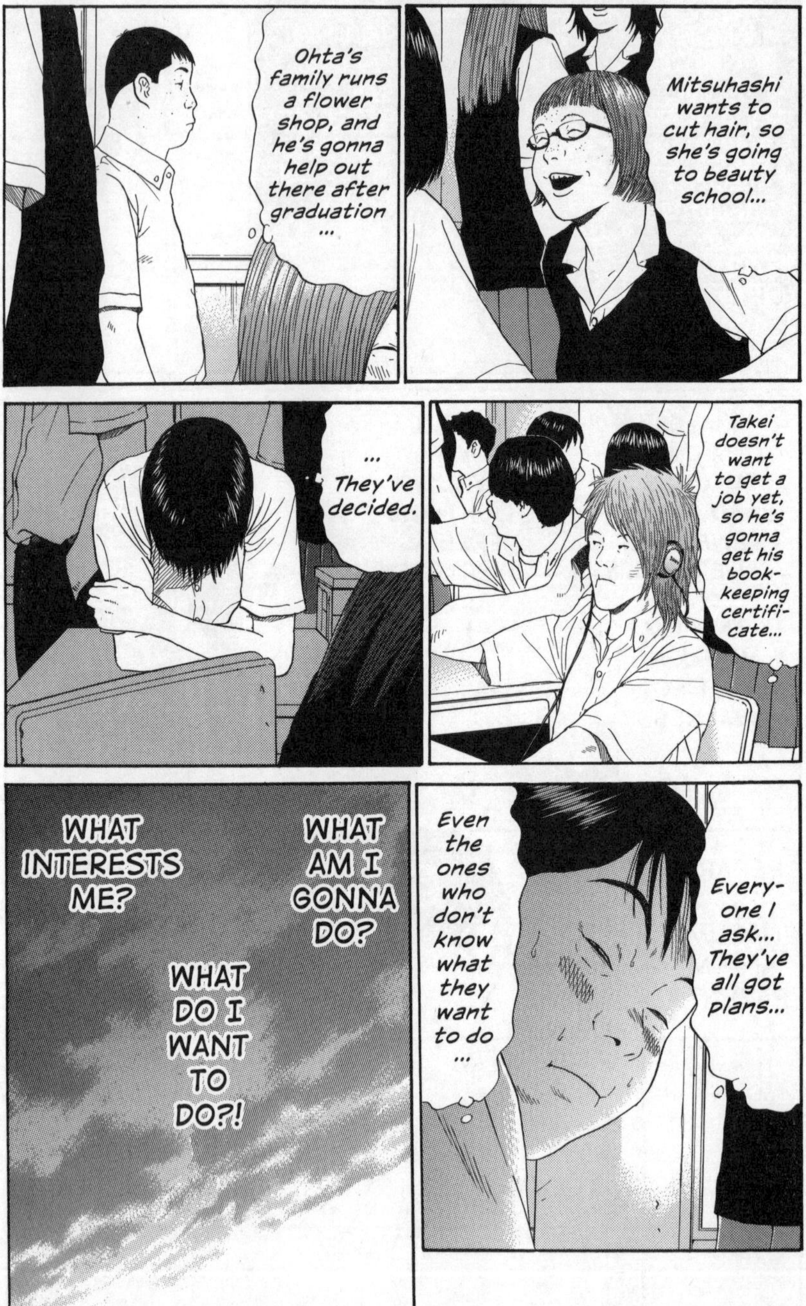
Mitsuhashi wants to cut hair, so she's going to beauty school...
Ohta's family runs a flower shop, and he's gonna help out there after graduation ...
Takei doesn't want to get a job yet, so he's gonna get his book-keeping certifi-cate...
... They've decided.
Every-one I ask... They've all got plans...
Even the ones who don't know what they want to do ...
WHAT AM I GONNA DO?
WHAT INTERESTS ME?
WHAT DO I WANT TO DO?!

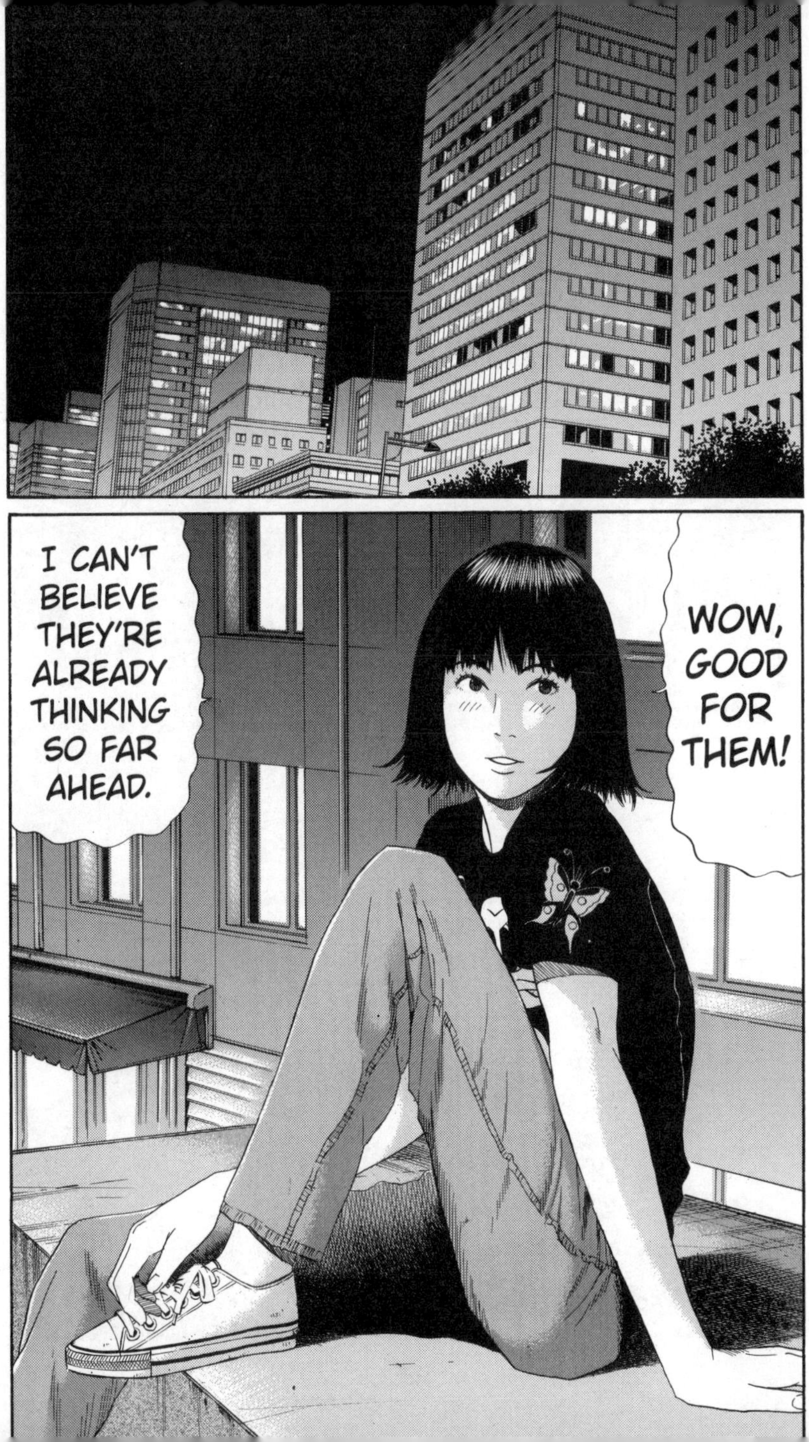
WOW, GOOD FOR THEM!
I CAN'T BELIEVE THEY'RE ALREADY THINKING SO FAR AHEAD.

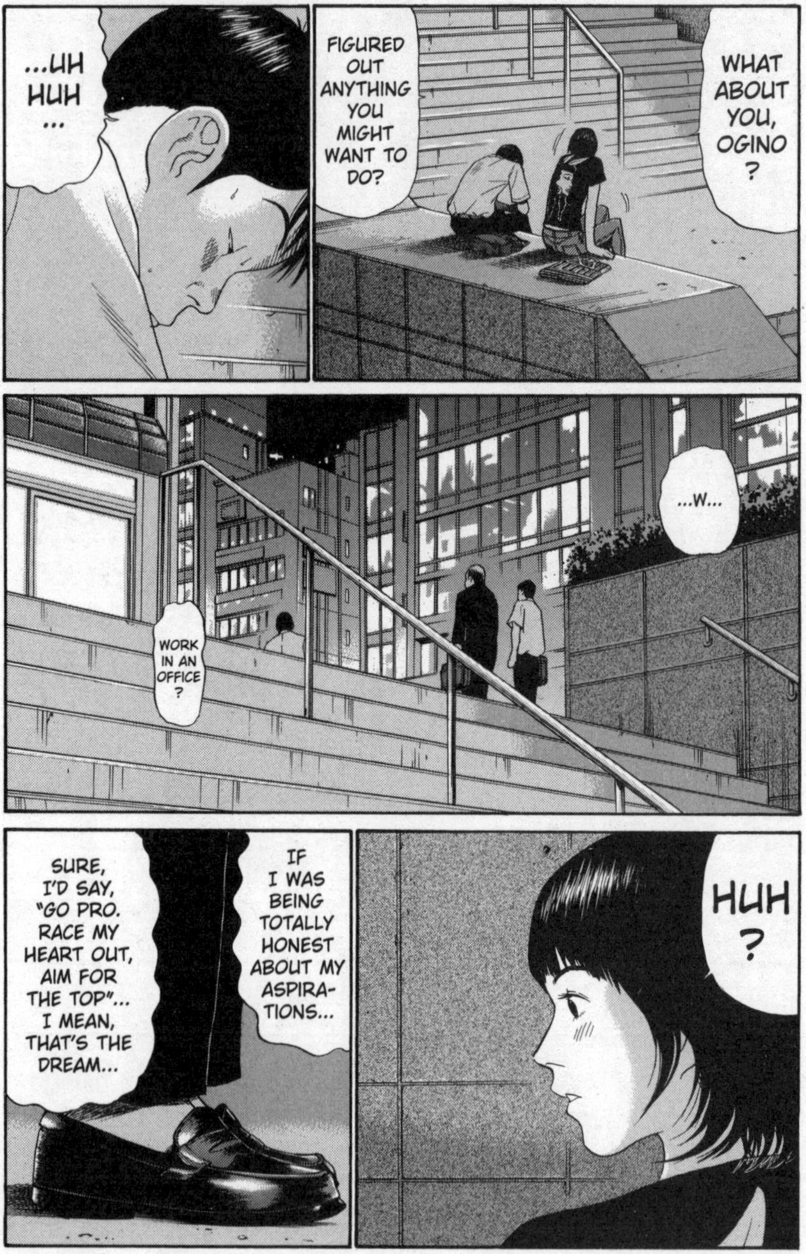
WHAT ABOUT YOU, OGINO?
FIGURED OUT ANYTHING YOU MIGHT WANT TO DO?
...UH HUH...
...W...
WORK IN AN OFFICE?
HUH?
IF I WAS BEING TOTALLY HONEST ABOUT MY ASPIRATIONS...
SURE, I'D SAY, "GO PRO. RACE MY HEART OUT, AIM FOR THE TOP"... I MEAN, THAT'S THE DREAM...

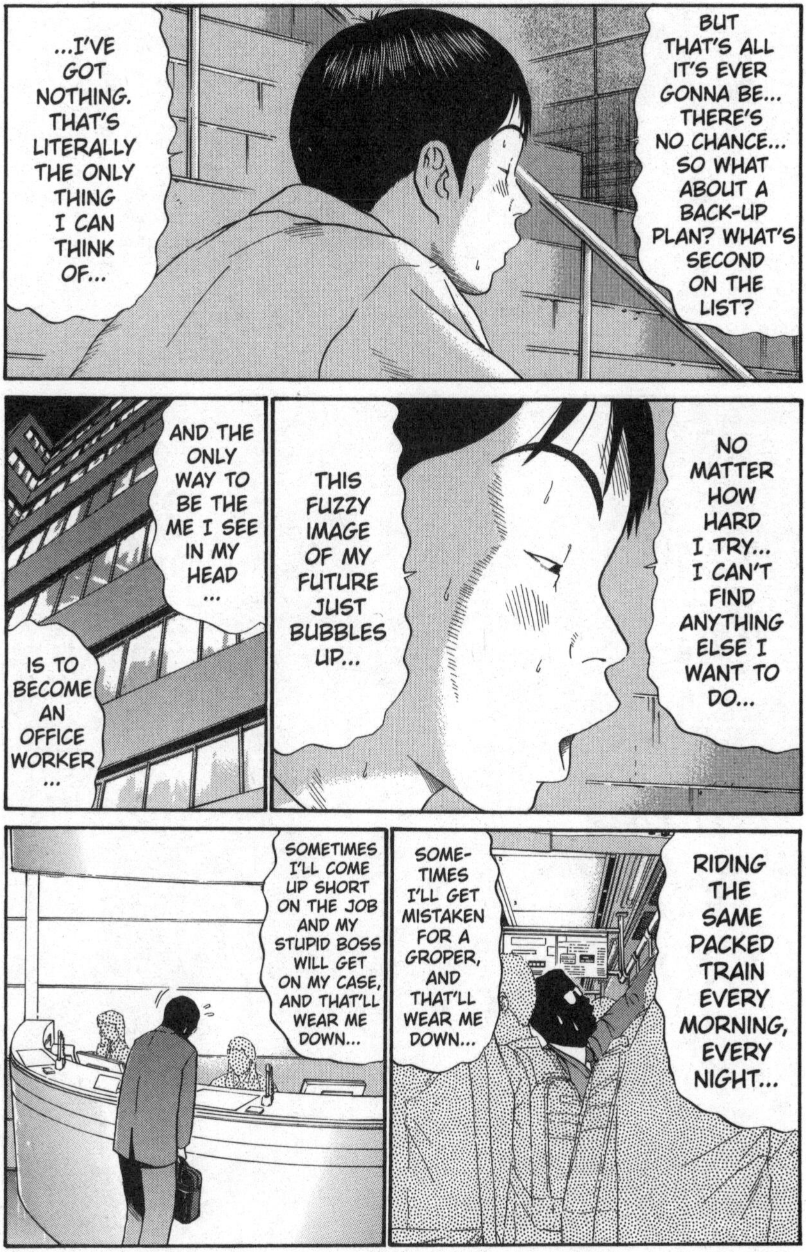
BUT THAT'S ALL IT'S EVER GONNA BE... THERE'S NO CHANCE... SO WHAT ABOUT A BACK-UP PLAN? WHAT'S SECOND ON THE LIST?
...I'VE GOT NOTHING. THAT'S LITERALLY THE ONLY THING I CAN THINK OF...
NO MATTER HOW HARD I TRY... I CAN'T FIND ANYTHING ELSE I WANT TO DO...
THIS FUZZY IMAGE OF MY FUTURE JUST BUBBLES UP...
AND THE ONLY WAY TO BE THE ME I SEE IN MY HEAD ...
IS TO BECOME AN OFFICE WORKER ...
RIDING THE SAME PACKED TRAIN EVERY MORNING, EVERY NIGHT...
SOME-TIMES I'LL GET MISTAKEN FOR A GROPER, AND THAT'LL WEAR ME DOWN...
SOMETIMES I'LL COME UP SHORT ON THE JOB AND MY STUPID BOSS WILL GET ON MY CASE, AND THAT'LL WEAR ME DOWN...

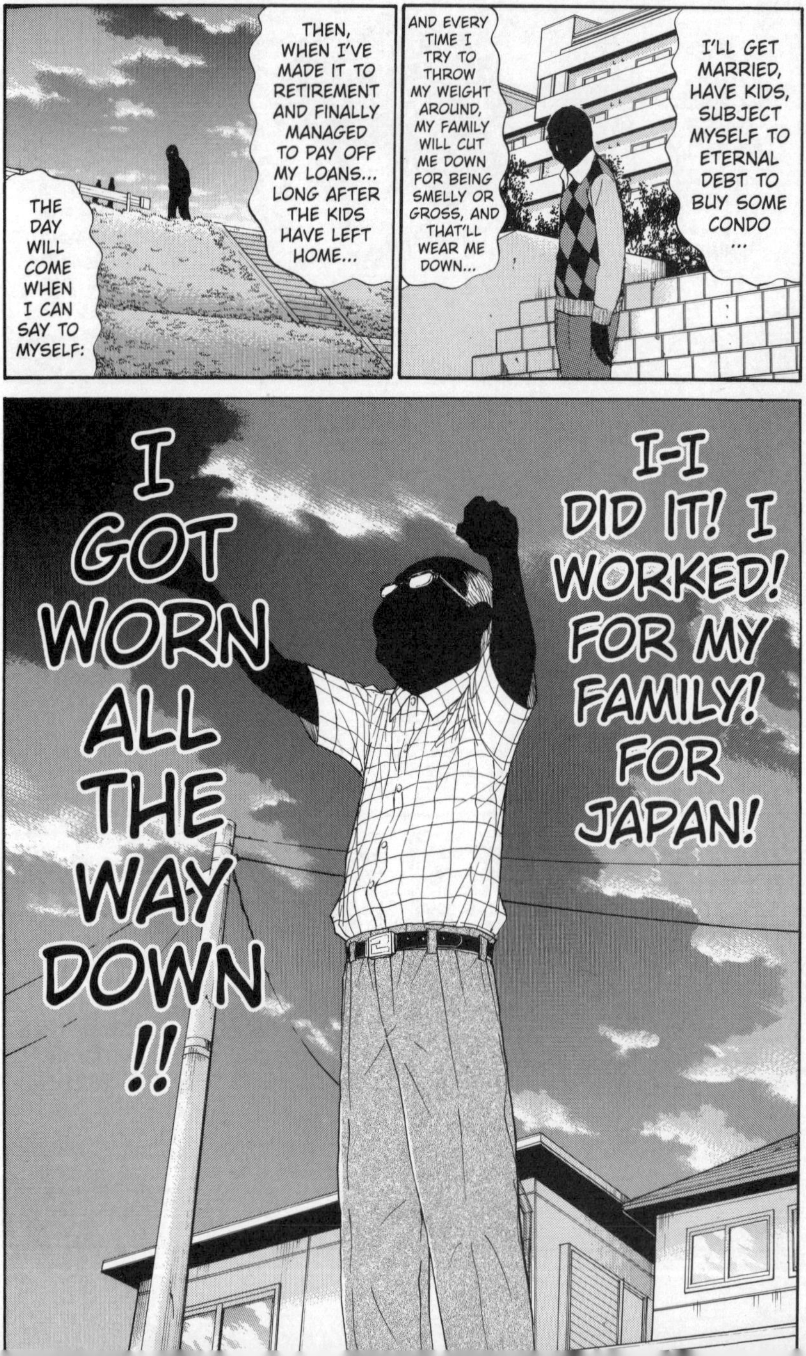
I'LL GET MARRIED, HAVE KIDS, SUBJECT MYSELF TO ETERNAL DEBT TO BUY SOME CONDO ...
AND EVERY TIME I TRY TO THROW MY WEIGHT AROUND, MY FAMILY WILL CUT ME DOWN FOR BEING SMELLY OR GROSS, AND THAT'LL WEAR ME DOWN...
THEN, WHEN I'VE MADE IT TO RETIREMENT AND FINALLY MANAGED TO PAY OFF MY LOANS... LONG AFTER THE KIDS HAVE LEFT HOME...
THE DAY WILL COME WHEN I CAN SAY TO MYSELF:
I-I DID IT! I WORKED! FOR MY FAMILY! FOR JAPAN!
I GOT WORN ALL THE WAY DOWN !!

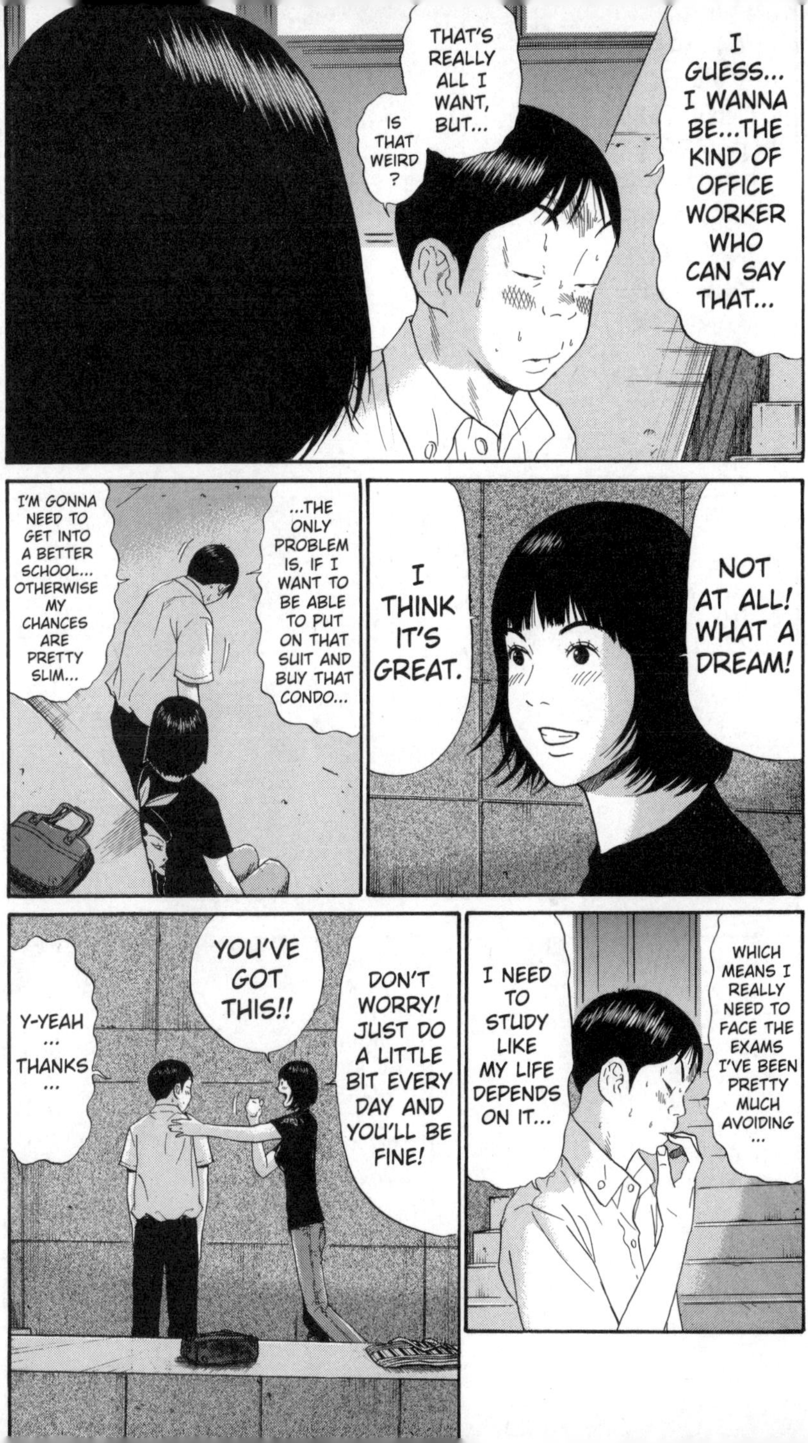
I GUESS... I WANNA BE...THE KIND OF OFFICE WORKER WHO CAN SAY THAT...
THAT'S REALLY ALL I WANT, BUT...
IS THAT WEIRD?
NOT AT ALL! WHAT A DREAM!
I THINK IT'S GREAT.
...THE ONLY PROBLEM IS, IF I WANT TO BE ABLE TO PUT ON THAT SUIT AND BUY THAT CONDO...
I'M GONNA NEED TO GET INTO A BETTER SCHOOL... OTHERWISE MY CHANCES ARE PRETTY SLIM...
WHICH MEANS I REALLY NEED TO FACE THE EXAMS I'VE BEEN PRETTY MUCH AVOIDING...
I NEED TO STUDY LIKE MY LIFE DEPENDS ON IT...
DON'T WORRY! JUST DO A LITTLE BIT EVERY DAY AND YOU'LL BE FINE!
YOU'VE GOT THIS!!
Y-YEAH... THANKS...

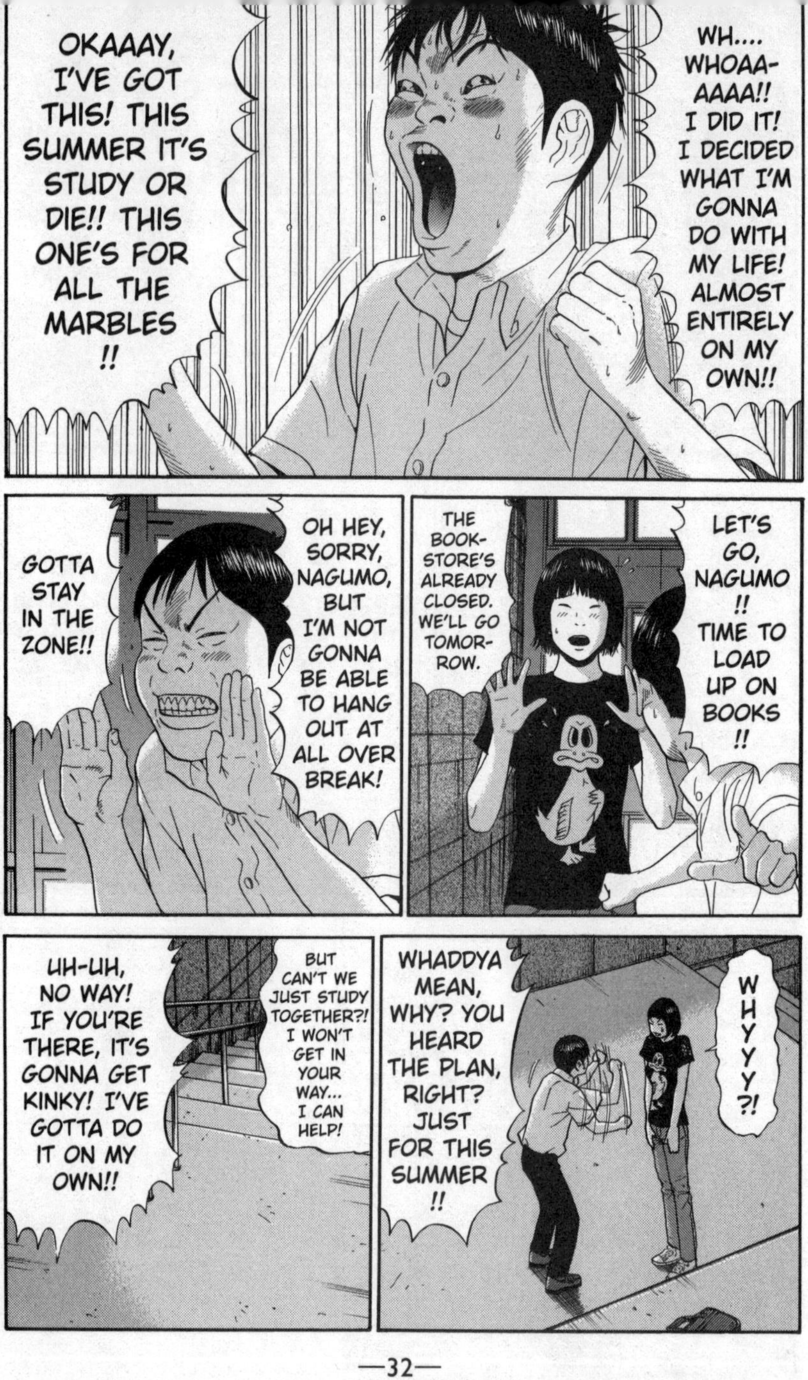
WH.... WHOAA-AAAA!! I DID IT! I DECIDED WHAT I'M GONNA DO WITH MY LIFE! ALMOST ENTIRELY ON MY OWN!!
OKAAAY, I'VE GOT THIS! THIS SUMMER IT'S STUDY OR DIE!! THIS ONE'S FOR ALL THE MARBLES!!
LET'S GO, NAGUMO!! TIME TO LOAD UP ON BOOKS!!
THE BOOK-STORE'S ALREADY CLOSED. WE'LL GO TOMOR-ROW.
OH HEY, SORRY, NAGUMO, BUT I'M NOT GONNA BE ABLE TO HANG OUT AT ALL OVER BREAK!
GOTTA STAY IN THE ZONE!!
WHYYY?!
WHADDYA MEAN, WHY? YOU HEARD THE PLAN, RIGHT? JUST FOR THIS SUMMER!!
BUT CAN'T WE JUST STUDY TOGETHER?! I WON'T GET IN YOUR WAY... I CAN HELP!
UH-UH, NO WAY! IF YOU'RE THERE, IT'S GONNA GET KINKY! I'VE GOTTA DO IT ON MY OWN!!

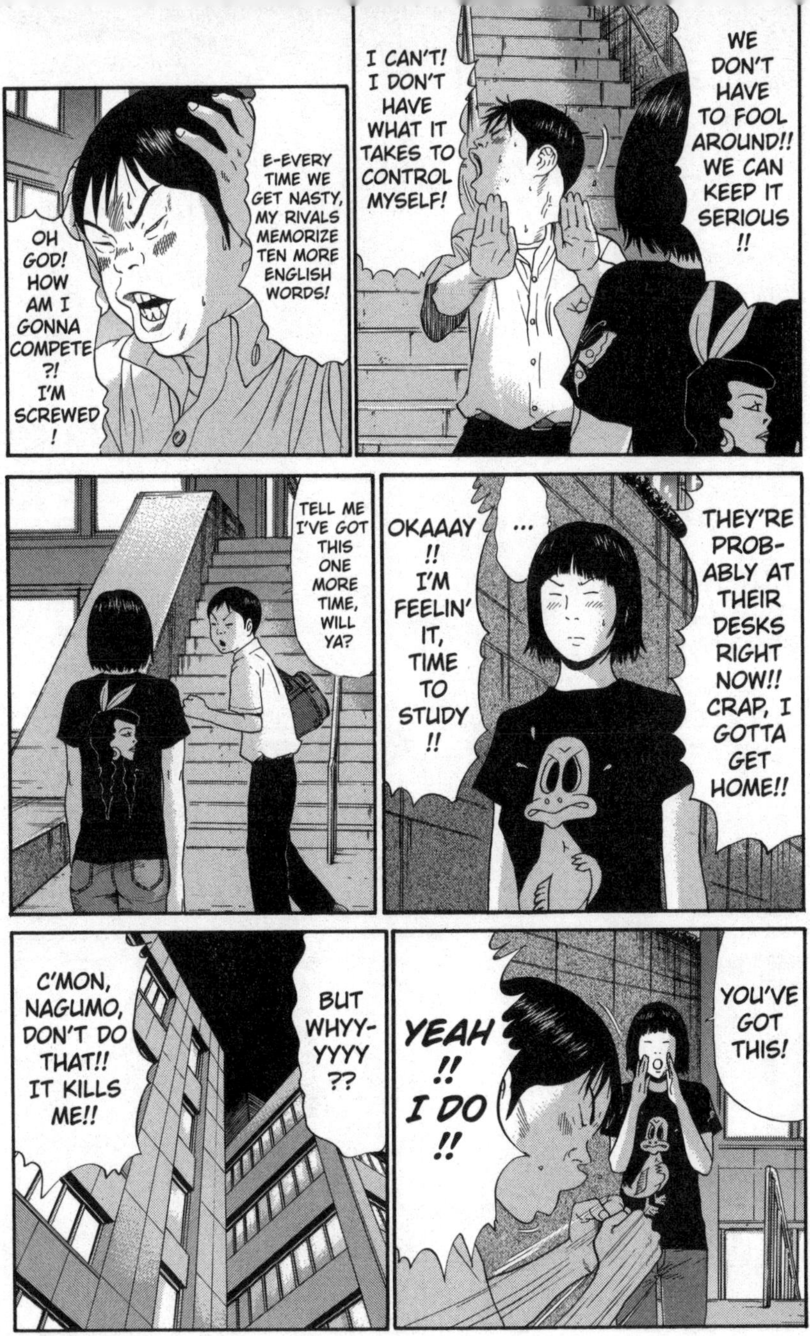
WE DON'T HAVE TO FOOL AROUND!! WE CAN KEEP IT SERIOUS !!
I CAN'T! I DON'T HAVE WHAT IT TAKES TO CONTROL MYSELF!
E-EVERY TIME WE GET NASTY, MY RIVALS MEMORIZE TEN MORE ENGLISH WORDS!
OH GOD! HOW AM I GONNA COMPETE ?! I'M SCREWED !
THEY'RE PROB-ABLY AT THEIR DESKS RIGHT NOW!! CRAP, I GOTTA GET HOME!!
...
OKAAAY !! I'M FEELIN' IT, TIME TO STUDY !!
TELL ME I'VE GOT THIS ONE MORE TIME, WILL YA?
YOU'VE GOT THIS!
YEAH !! I DO !!
BUT WHYY-YYYY ??
C'MON, NAGUMO, DON'T DO THAT!! IT KILLS ME!!

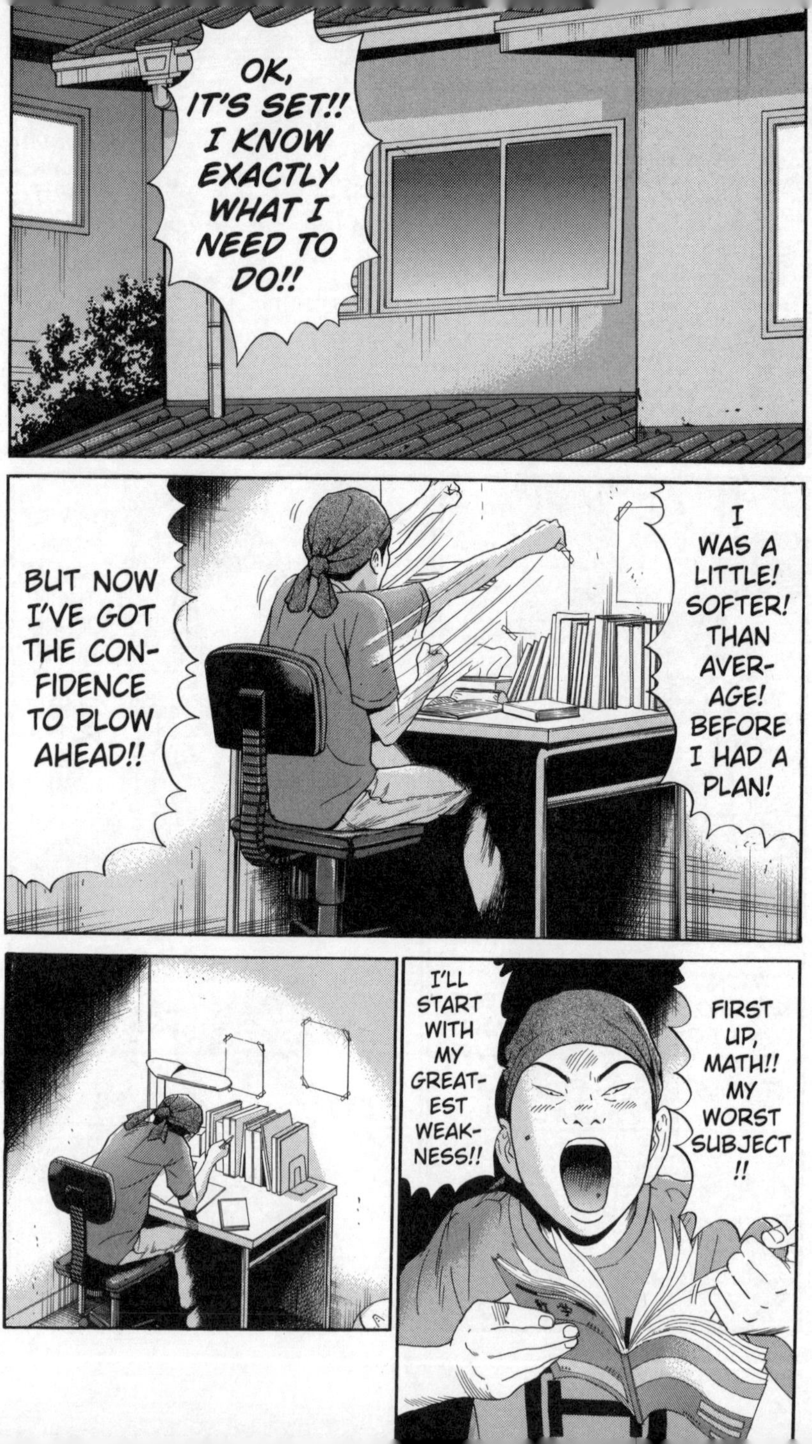
OK, IT'S SET!! I KNOW EXACTLY WHAT I NEED TO DO!!
I WAS A LITTLE! SOFTER! THAN AVER-AGE! BEFORE I HAD A PLAN!
BUT NOW I'VE GOT THE CON-FIDENCE TO PLOW AHEAD!!
FIRST UP, MATH!! MY WORST SUBJECT!!
I'LL START WITH MY GREAT-EST WEAK-NESS!!

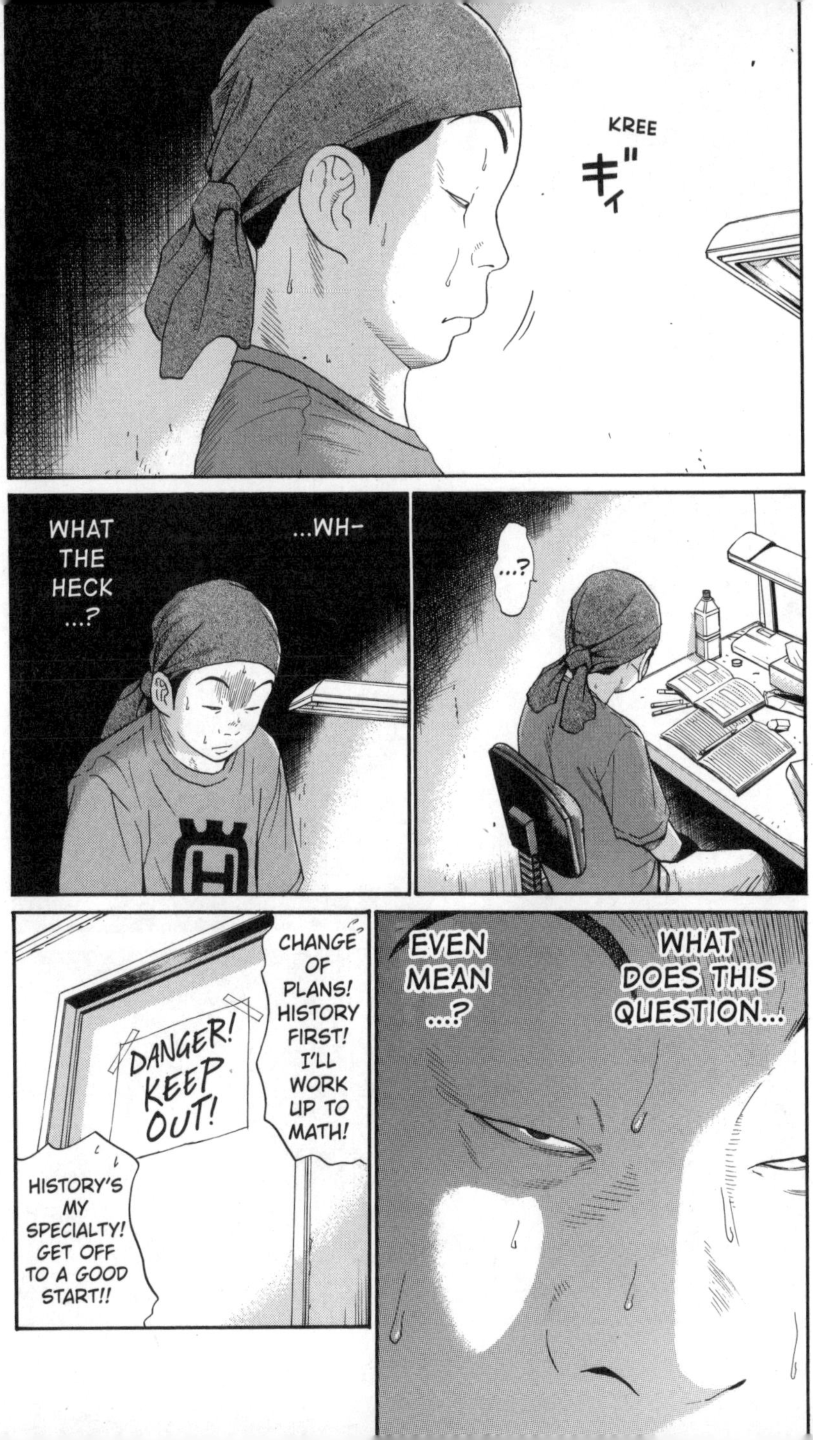
KREE
ギィ
...?
...WH-
WHAT THE HECK ...?
WHAT DOES THIS QUESTION...
EVEN MEAN ...?
CHANGE OF PLANS! HISTORY FIRST! I'LL WORK UP TO MATH!
DANGER! KEEP OUT!
HISTORY'S MY SPECIALTY! GET OFF TO A GOOD START!!

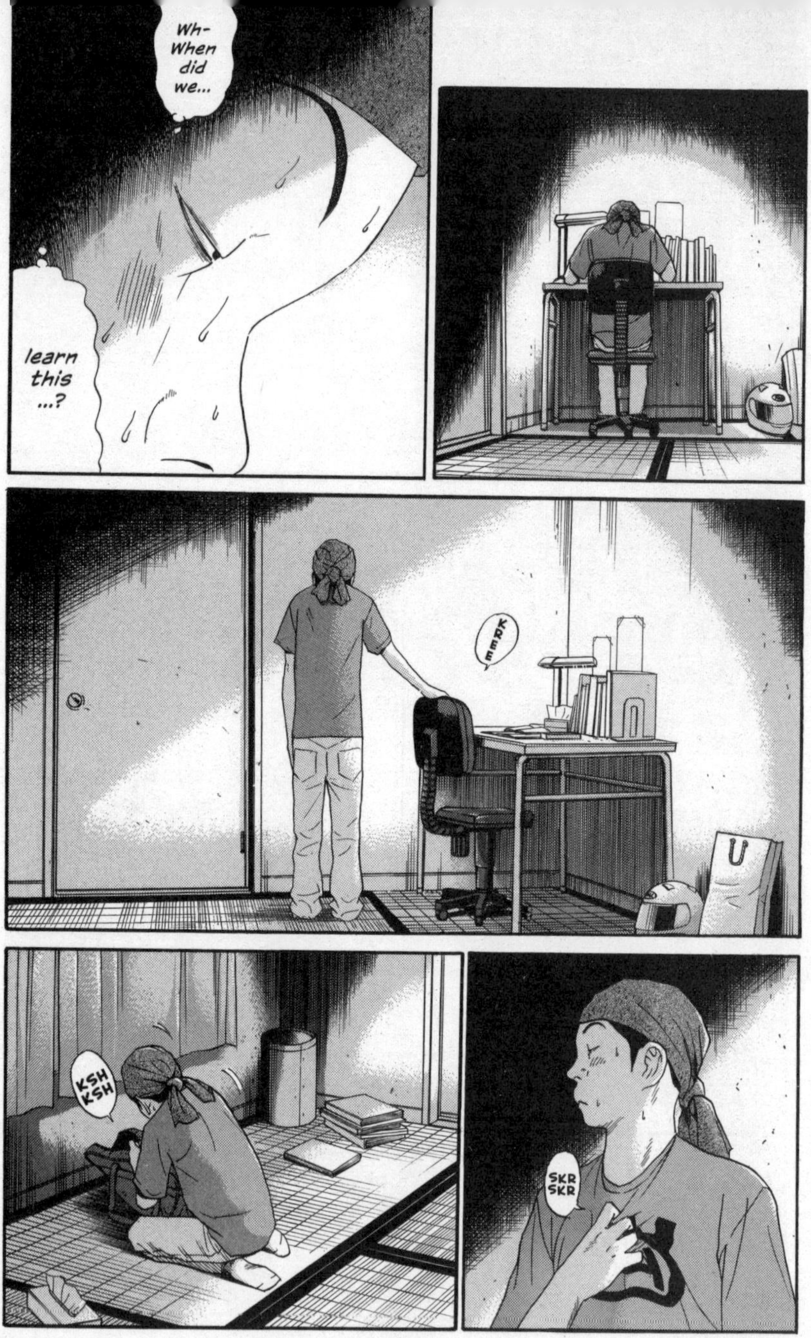

Wh- When did we...
learn this ...?
KREE
SKR SKR
KSH KSH

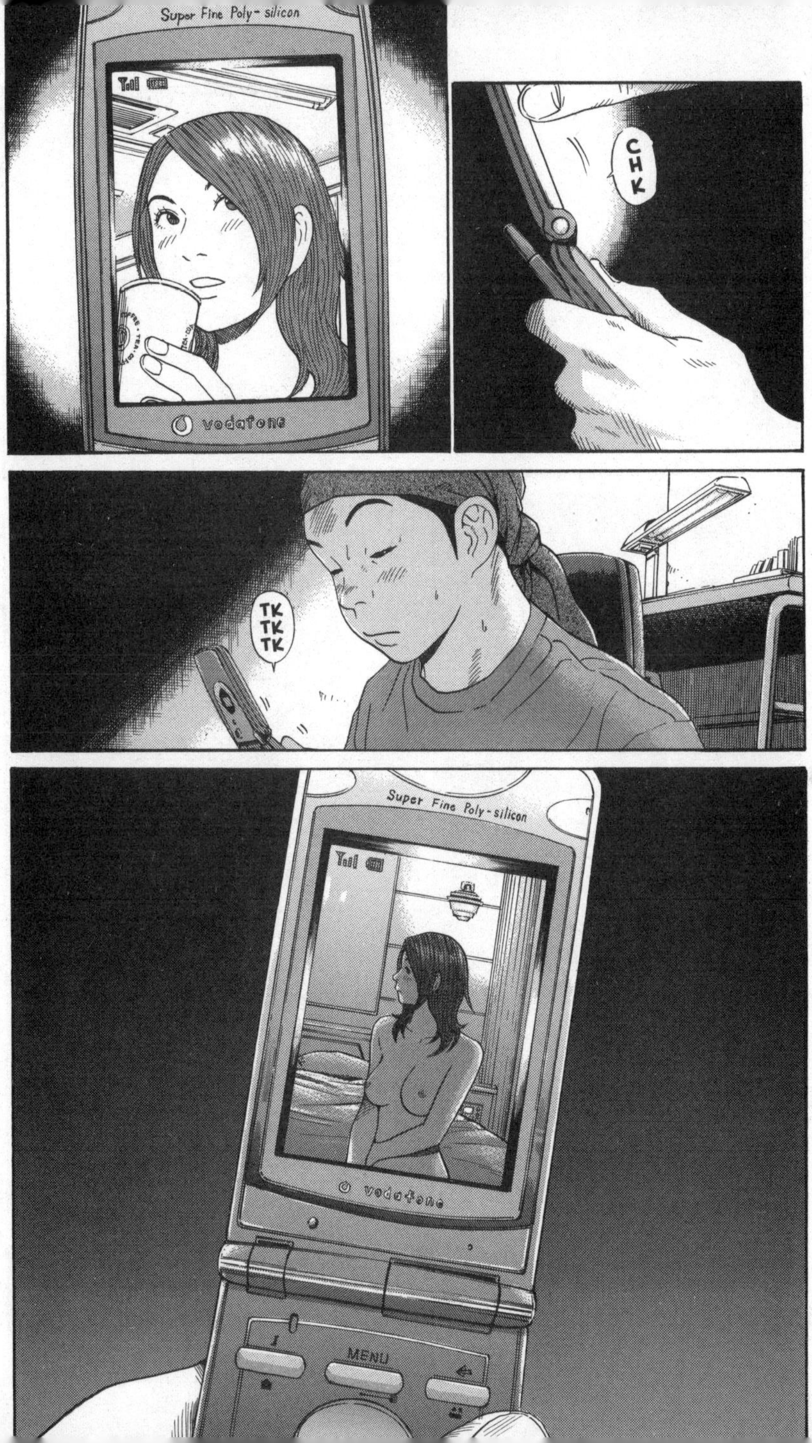
CHK
Super Fine Poly-silicon
vodafone
TK TK TK
Super Fine Poly-silicon
vodafone
MENU

HERE
COMES
CAPIROSSI
ON THE
OUTSIDE!

...OH...
HEY,
NAGUMO
?

SORRY...
WERE
YOU
ASLEEP
?

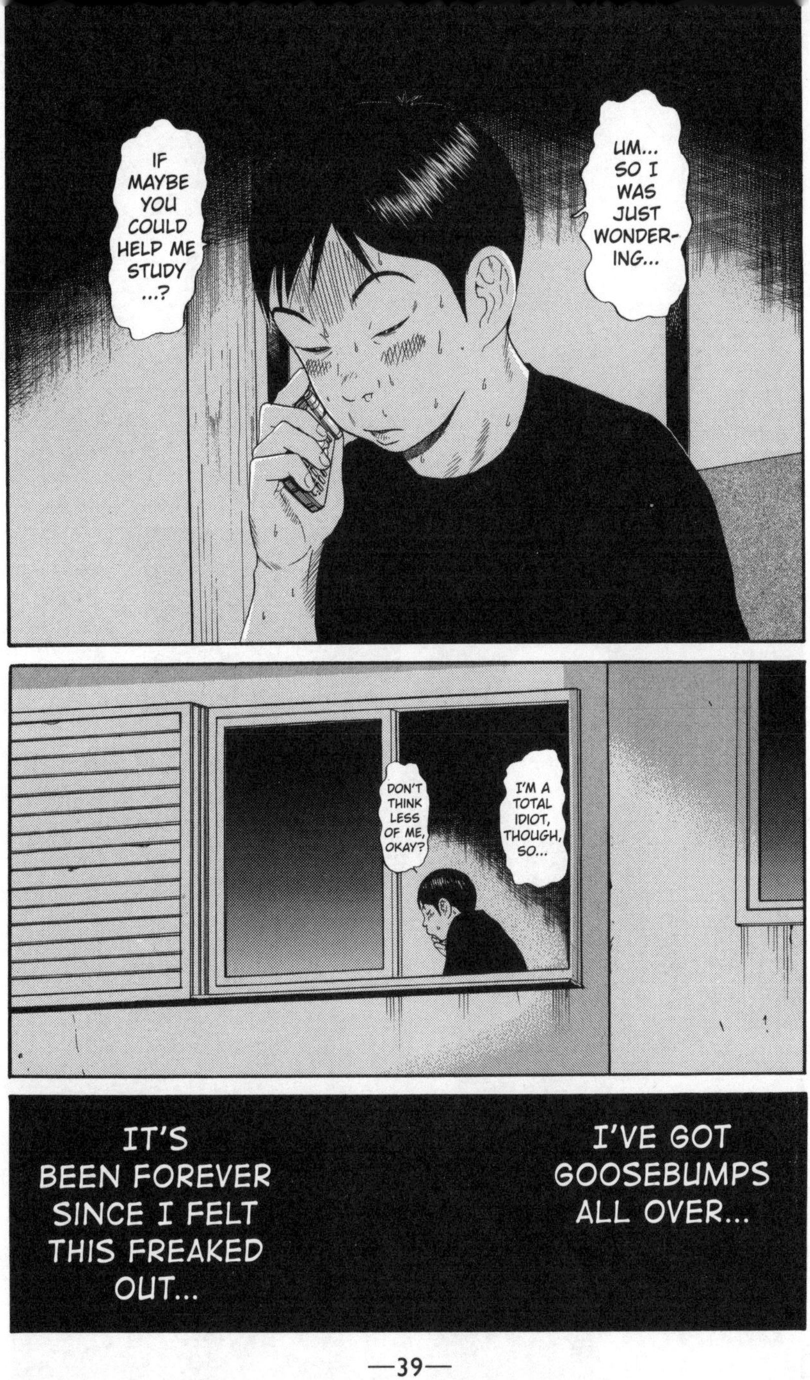
UM... SO I WAS JUST WONDER-ING...
IF MAYBE YOU COULD HELP ME STUDY ...?
I'M A TOTAL IDIOT, THOUGH, SO...
DON'T THINK LESS OF ME, OKAY?
I'VE GOT GOOSEBUMPS ALL OVER...
IT'S BEEN FOREVER SINCE I FELT THIS FREAKED OUT...

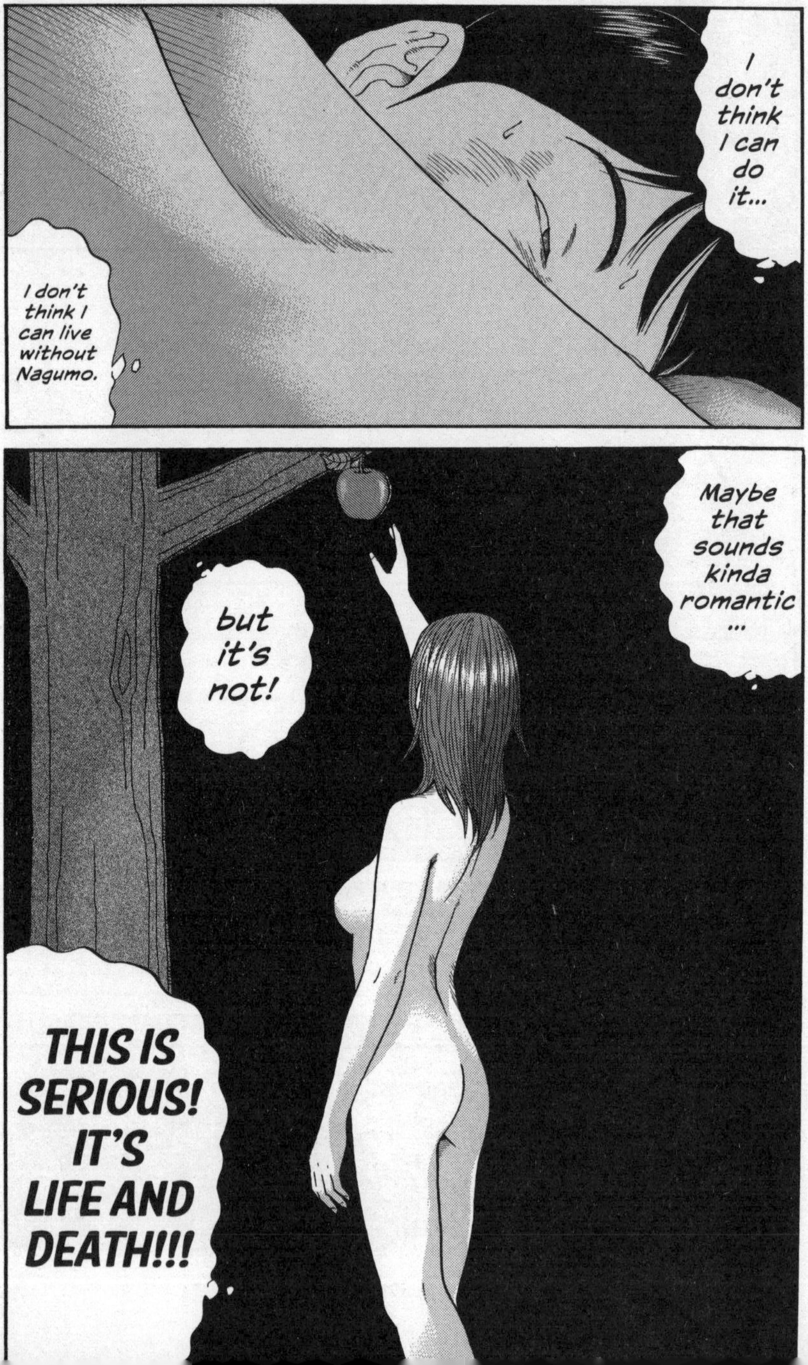
I don't think I can do it...
I don't think I can live without Nagumo.
Maybe that sounds kinda romantic...
but it's not!
THIS IS SERIOUS! IT'S LIFE AND DEATH!!!

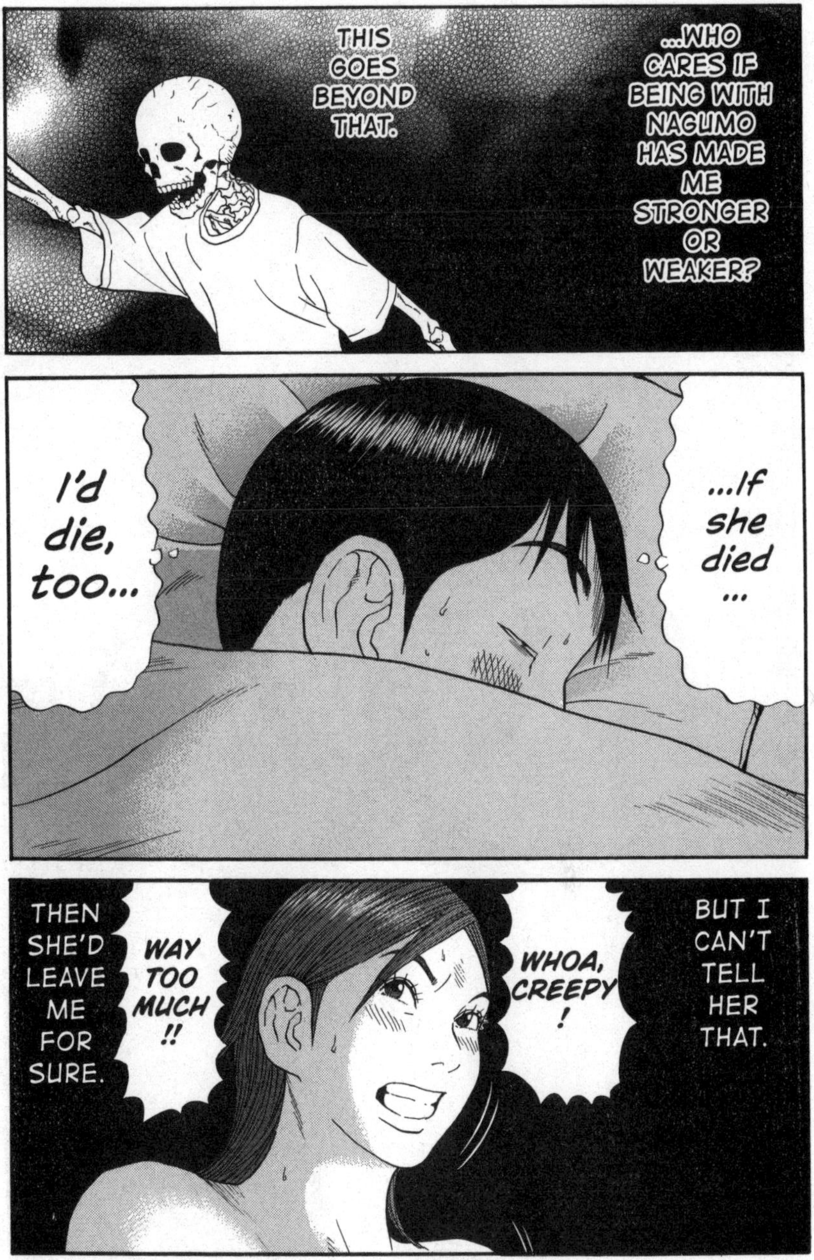
...WHO CARES IF BEING WITH NAGUMO HAS MADE ME STRONGER OR WEAKER?
THIS GOES BEYOND THAT.
...If she died...
I'd die, too...
BUT I CAN'T TELL HER THAT.
WHOA, CREEPY!
WAY TOO MUCH!!
THEN SHE'D LEAVE ME FOR SURE.

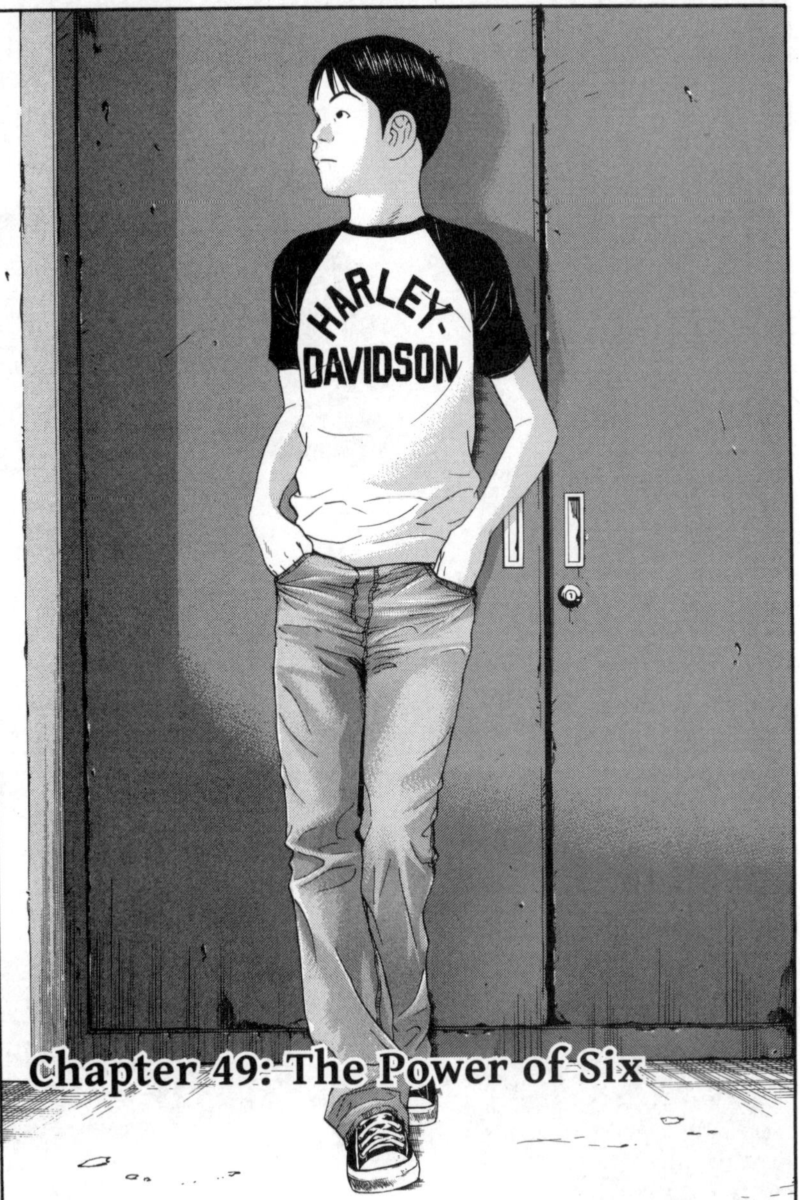
HARLEY-
DAVIDSON

# Chapter 49: The Power of Six

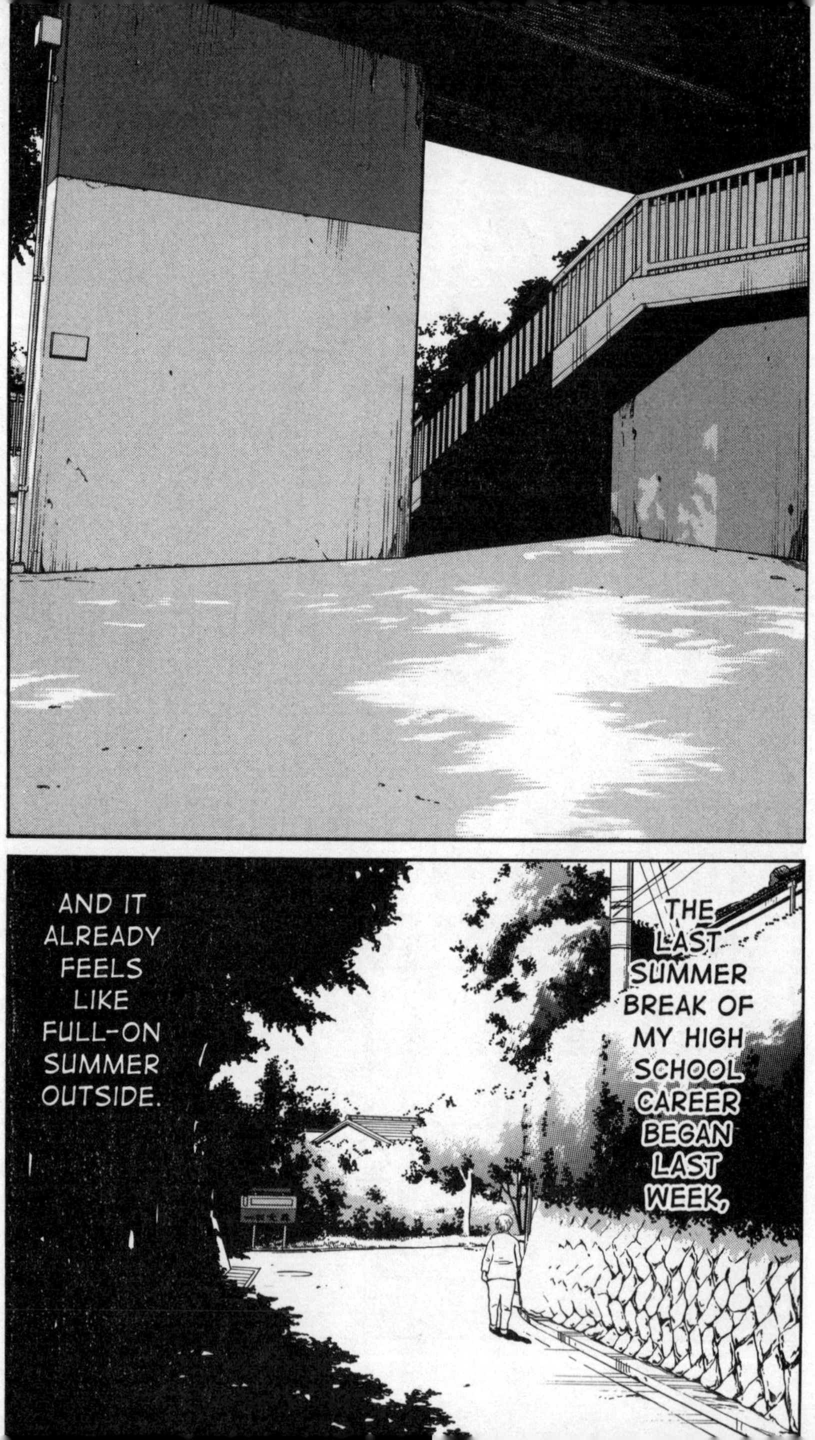
THE LAST SUMMER BREAK OF MY HIGH SCHOOL CAREER BEGAN LAST WEEK,
AND IT ALREADY FEELS LIKE FULL-ON SUMMER OUTSIDE.

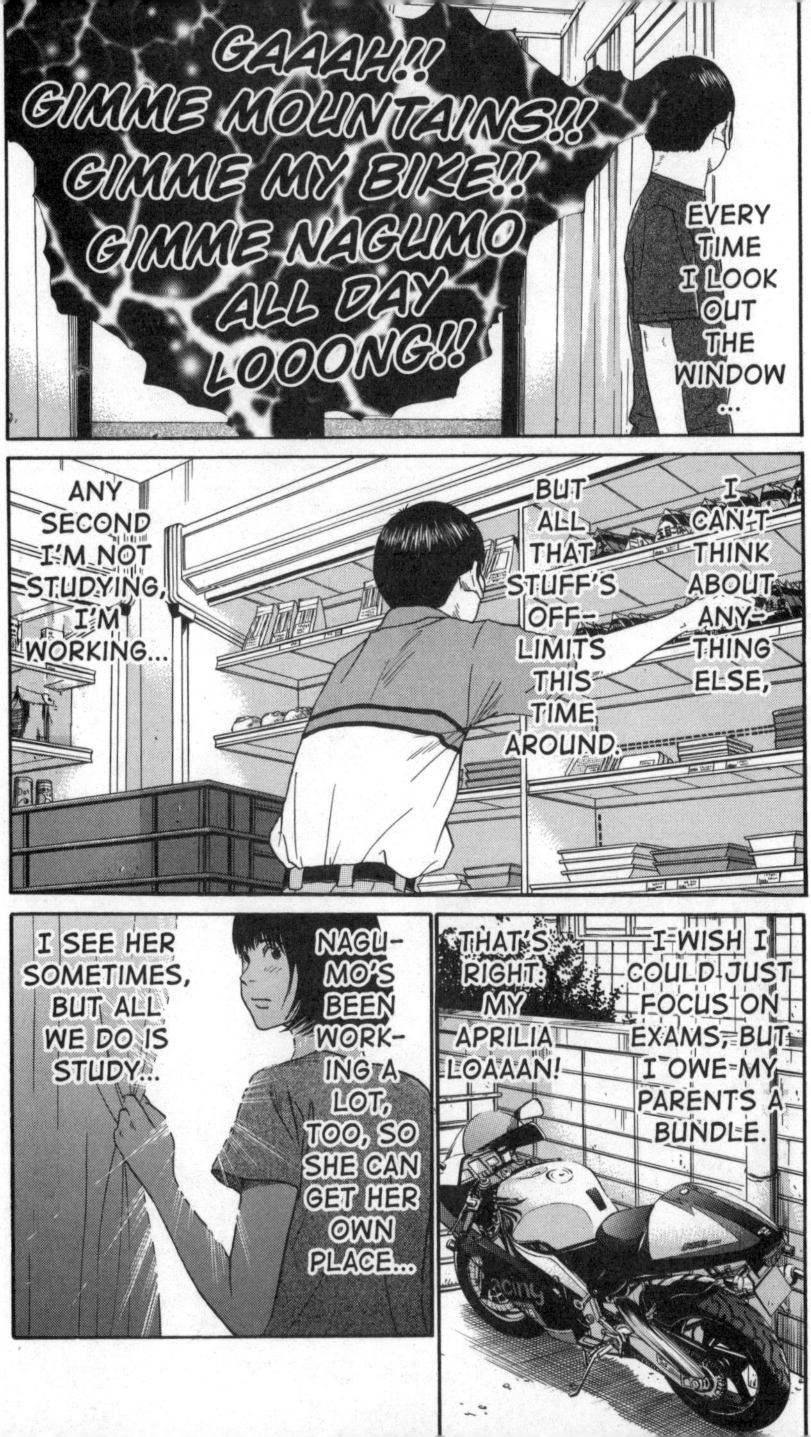
EVERY TIME I LOOK OUT THE WINDOW...
GAAAH!! GIMME MOUNTAINS!! GIMME MY BIKE!! GIMME NAGUMO ALL DAY LOOONG!!
I CAN'T THINK ABOUT ANYTHING ELSE,
BUT ALL THAT STUFF'S OFF-LIMITS THIS TIME AROUND.
ANY SECOND I'M NOT STUDYING, I'M WORKING...
I WISH I COULD JUST FOCUS ON EXAMS, BUT I OWE MY PARENTS A BUNDLE.
THAT'S RIGHT: MY APRILIA LOAAAN!
NAGUMO'S BEEN WORKING A LOT, TOO, SO SHE CAN GET HER OWN PLACE...
I SEE HER SOMETIMES, BUT ALL WE DO IS STUDY...

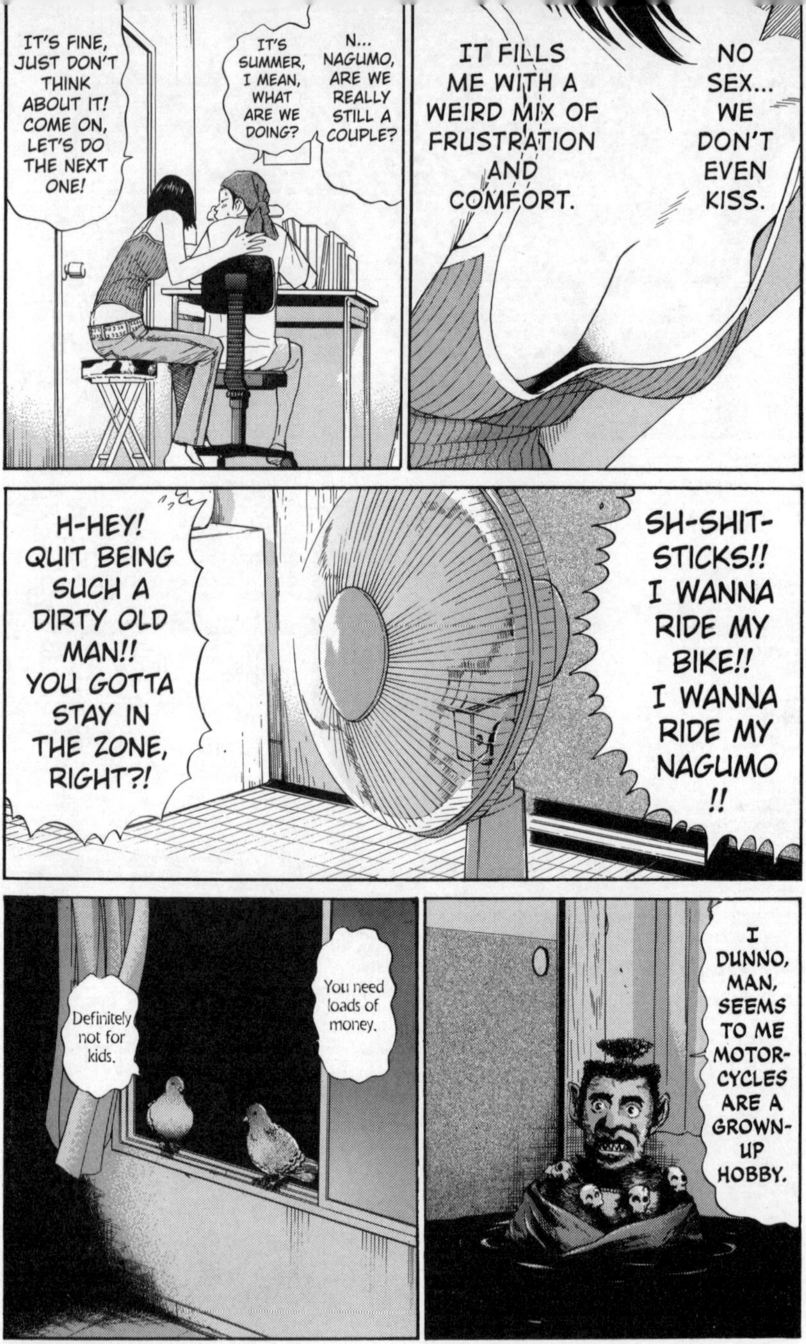
NO SEX... WE DON'T EVEN KISS.
IT FILLS ME WITH A WEIRD MIX OF FRUSTRATION AND COMFORT.
N... NAGUMO, ARE WE REALLY STILL A COUPLE?
IT'S SUMMER, I MEAN, WHAT ARE WE DOING?
IT'S FINE, JUST DON'T THINK ABOUT IT! COME ON, LET'S DO THE NEXT ONE!
SH-SHIT-STICKS!! I WANNA RIDE MY BIKE!! I WANNA RIDE MY NAGUMO !!
H-HEY! QUIT BEING SUCH A DIRTY OLD MAN!! YOU GOTTA STAY IN THE ZONE, RIGHT?!
I DUNNO, MAN, SEEMS TO ME MOTOR-CYCLES ARE A GROWN-UP HOBBY.
You need loads of money.
Definitely not for kids.

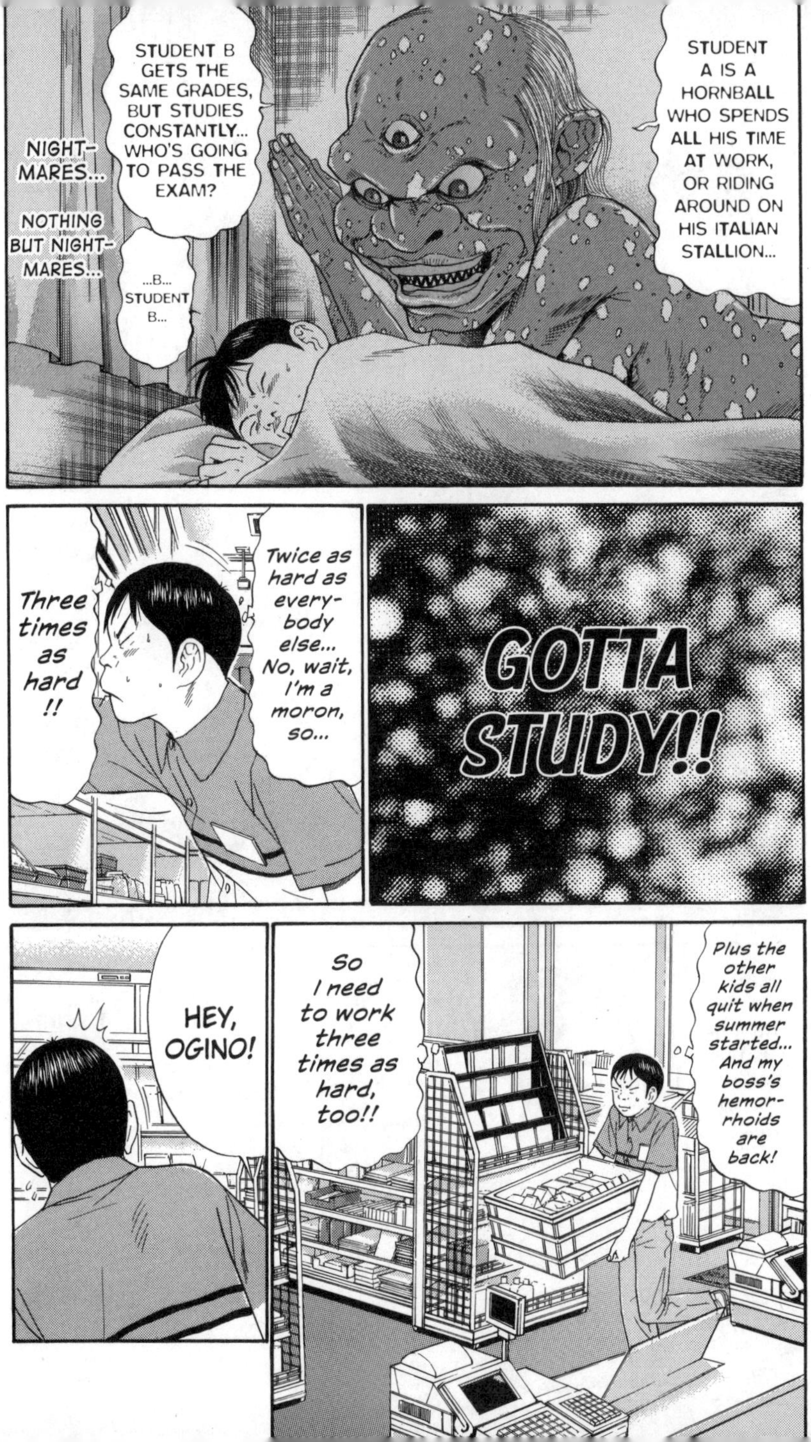
STUDENT A IS A HORNBALL WHO SPENDS ALL HIS TIME AT WORK, OR RIDING AROUND ON HIS ITALIAN STALLION...
STUDENT B GETS THE SAME GRADES, BUT STUDIES CONSTANTLY... WHO'S GOING TO PASS THE EXAM?
...B... STUDENT B...
NIGHT-MARES...
NOTHING BUT NIGHT-MARES...
GOTTA STUDY!!
Twice as hard as every-body else... No, wait, I'm a moron, so...
Three times as hard !!
Plus the other kids all quit when summer started... And my boss's hemor-rhoids are back!
So I need to work three times as hard, too!!
HEY, OGINO!

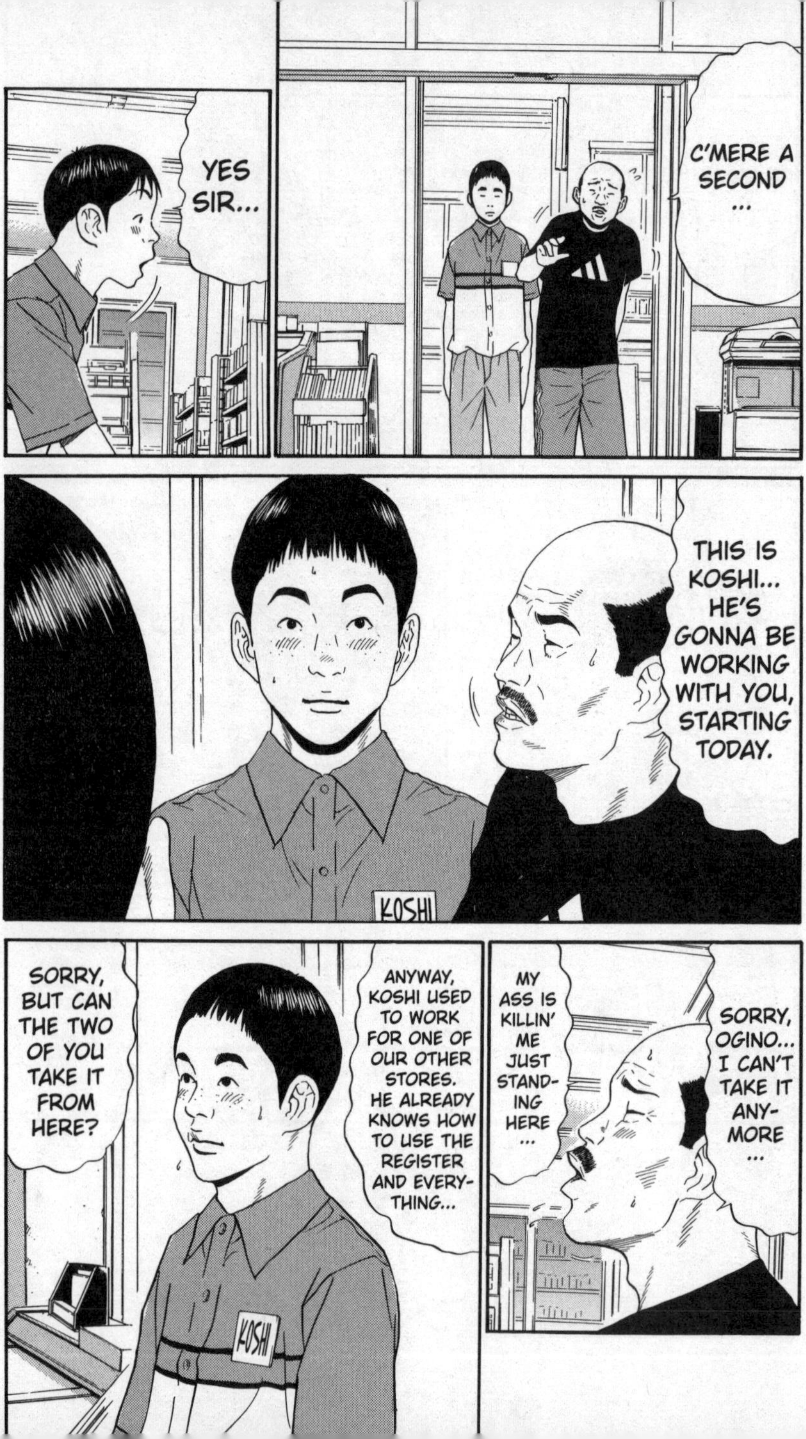
C'MERE A SECOND ...
YES SIR...
THIS IS KOSHI... HE'S GONNA BE WORKING WITH YOU, STARTING TODAY.
KOSHI
SORRY, OGINO... I CAN'T TAKE IT ANYMORE ...
MY ASS IS KILLIN' ME JUST STANDING HERE ...
ANYWAY, KOSHI USED TO WORK FOR ONE OF OUR OTHER STORES. HE ALREADY KNOWS HOW TO USE THE REGISTER AND EVERYTHING...
SORRY, BUT CAN THE TWO OF YOU TAKE IT FROM HERE?
KOSHI

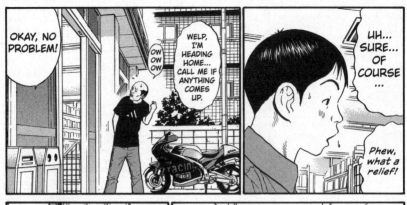

UH... SURE... OF COURSE ...
Phew, what a relief!
WELP, I'M HEADING HOME... CALL ME IF ANYTHING COMES UP.
OW OW OW
OKAY, NO PROBLEM!
UM... HI... I'M KOSHI.
KOSHI
HI... I'M OGINO.
...SO, DOES HE LIVE AROUND HERE?
THE BOSS? UH HUH ...
RIGHT BEHIND THE STORE ...

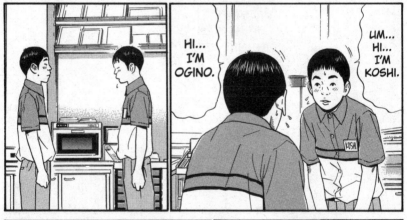

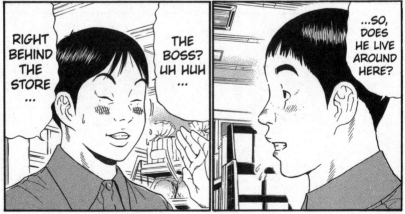

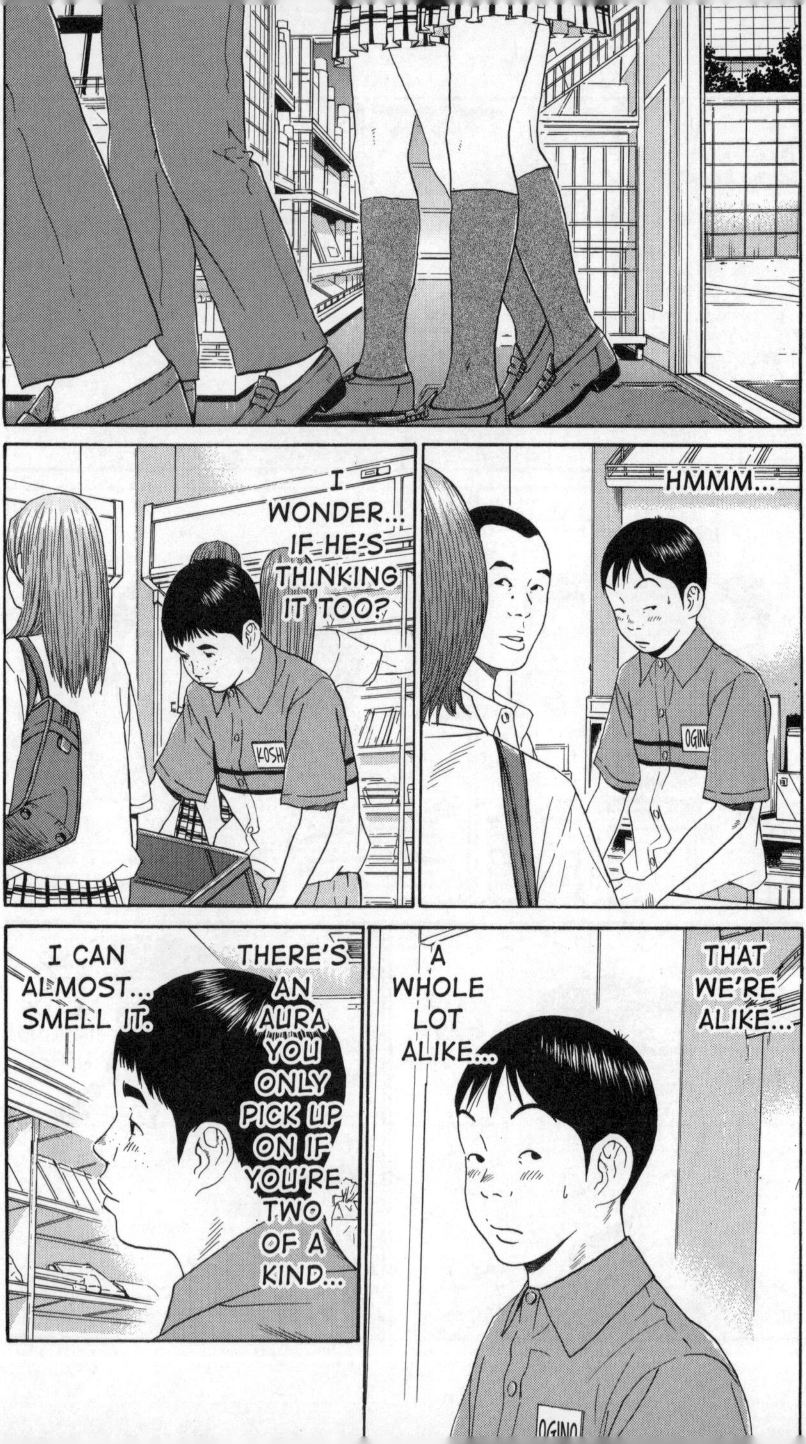
HMMM...
I WONDER... IF HE'S THINKING IT TOO?
THAT WE'RE ALIKE...
A WHOLE LOT ALIKE...
THERE'S AN AURA YOU ONLY PICK UP ON IF YOU'RE TWO OF A KIND...
I CAN ALMOST... SMELL IT.

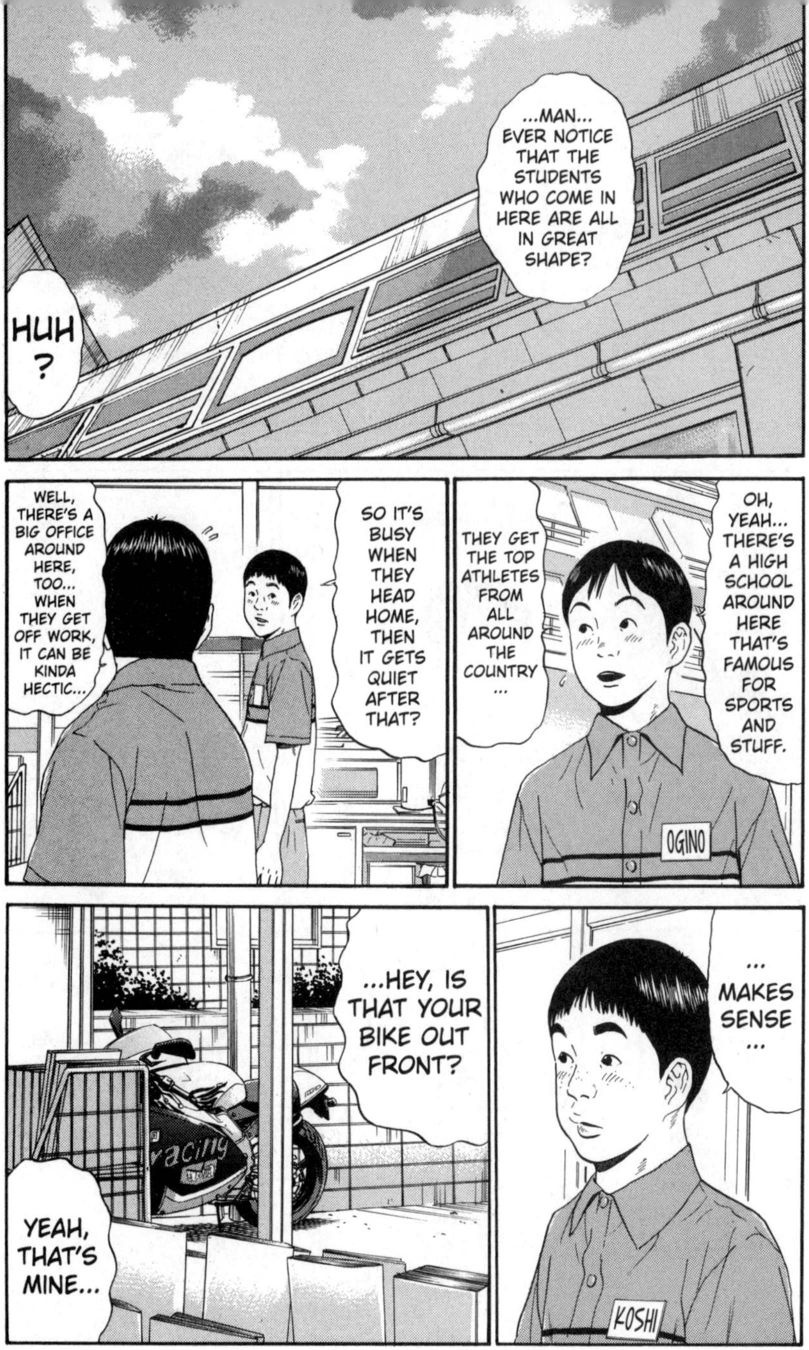
...MAN... EVER NOTICE THAT THE STUDENTS WHO COME IN HERE ARE ALL IN GREAT SHAPE?
HUH ?
OH, YEAH... THERE'S A HIGH SCHOOL AROUND HERE THAT'S FAMOUS FOR SPORTS AND STUFF.
THEY GET THE TOP ATHLETES FROM ALL AROUND THE COUNTRY ...
OGINO
SO IT'S BUSY WHEN THEY HEAD HOME, THEN IT GETS QUIET AFTER THAT?
WELL, THERE'S A BIG OFFICE AROUND HERE, TOO... WHEN THEY GET OFF WORK, IT CAN BE KINDA HECTIC...
... MAKES SENSE ...
KOSHI
...HEY, IS THAT YOUR BIKE OUT FRONT?
YEAH, THAT'S MINE...

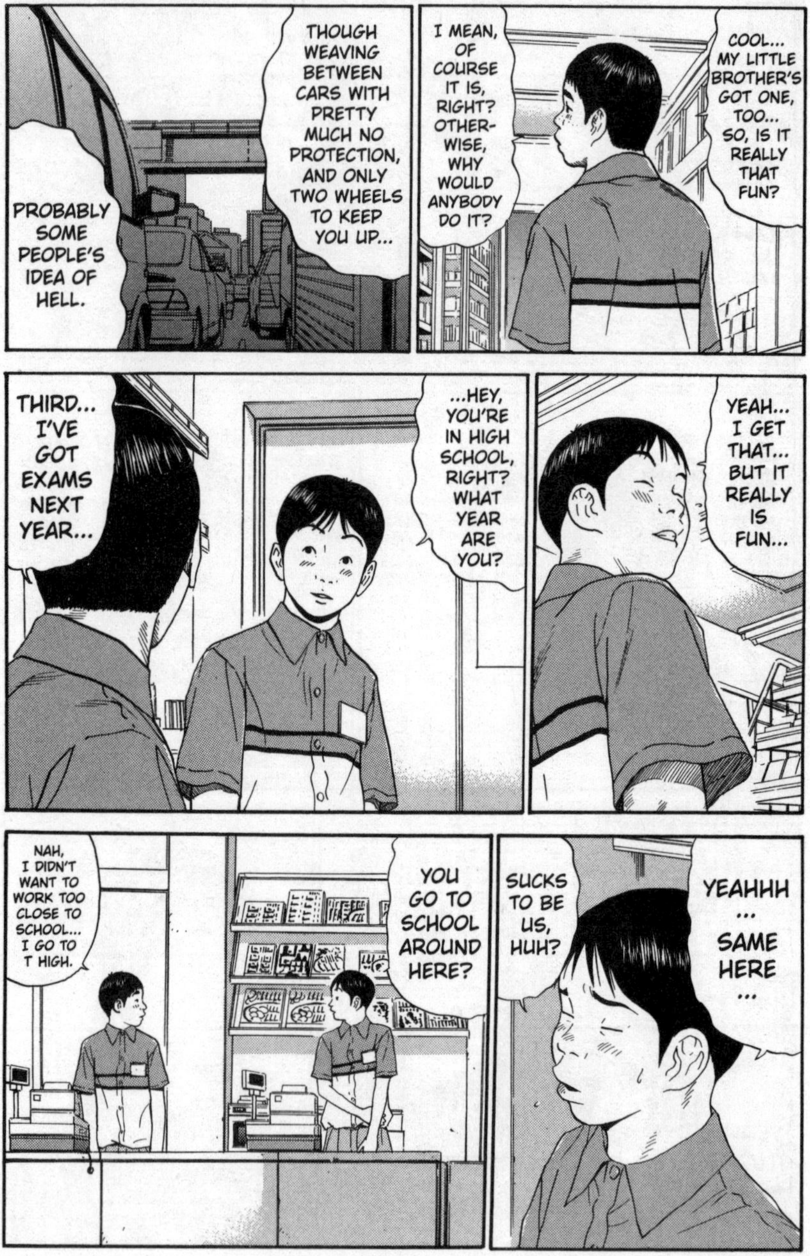
COOL... MY LITTLE BROTHER'S GOT ONE, TOO... SO, IS IT REALLY THAT FUN?
I MEAN, OF COURSE IT IS, RIGHT? OTHER-WISE, WHY WOULD ANYBODY DO IT?
THOUGH WEAVING BETWEEN CARS WITH PRETTY MUCH NO PROTECTION, AND ONLY TWO WHEELS TO KEEP YOU UP...
PROBABLY SOME PEOPLE'S IDEA OF HELL.
YEAH... I GET THAT... BUT IT REALLY IS FUN...
...HEY, YOU'RE IN HIGH SCHOOL, RIGHT? WHAT YEAR ARE YOU?
THIRD... I'VE GOT EXAMS NEXT YEAR...
YEAHHH ... SAME HERE ...
SUCKS TO BE US, HUH?
YOU GO TO SCHOOL AROUND HERE?
NAH, I DIDN'T WANT TO WORK TOO CLOSE TO SCHOOL... I GO TO T HIGH.

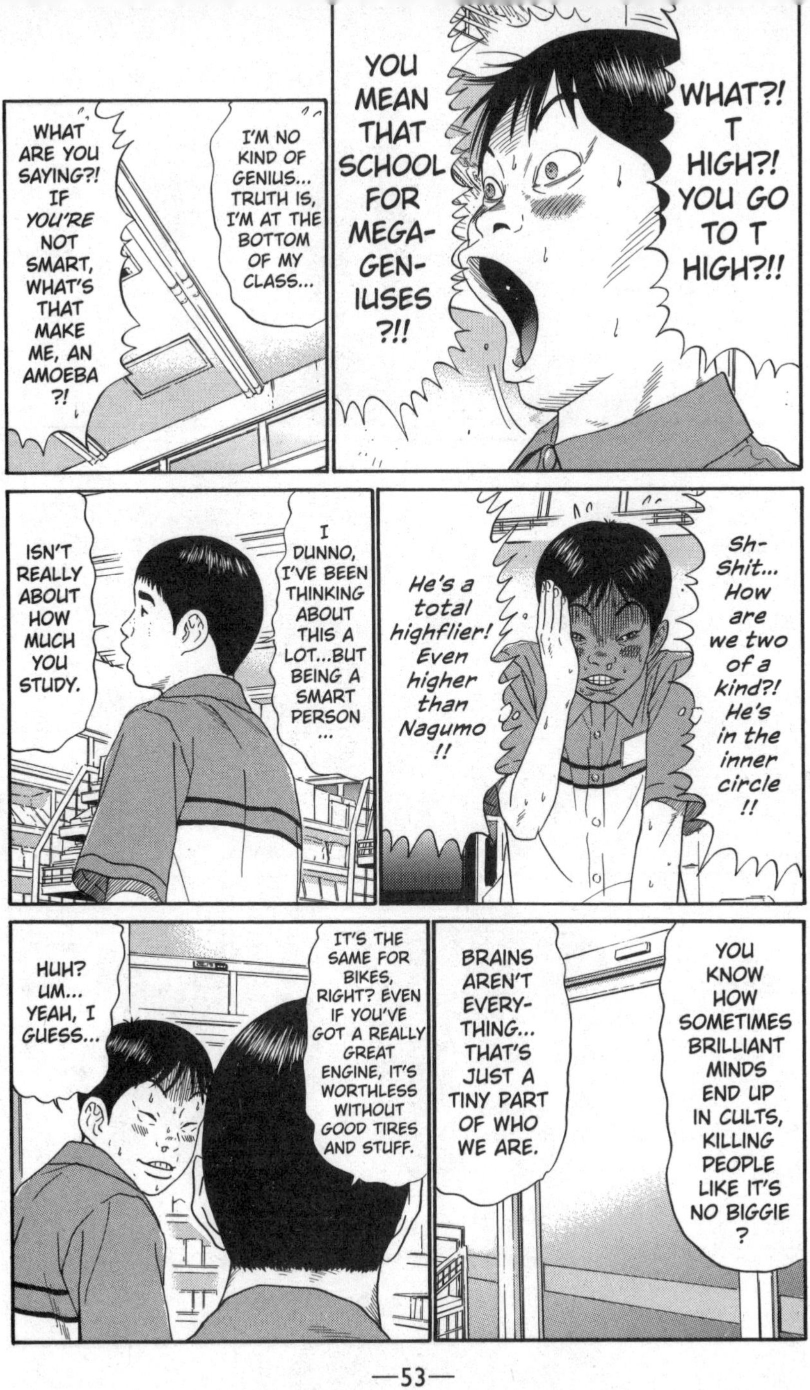
WHAT?! T HIGH?! YOU GO TO T HIGH?!!
YOU MEAN THAT SCHOOL FOR MEGA-GENIUSES?!!
I'M NO KIND OF GENIUS... TRUTH IS, I'M AT THE BOTTOM OF MY CLASS...
WHAT ARE YOU SAYING?! IF *YOU'RE* NOT SMART, WHAT'S THAT MAKE ME, AN AMOEBA?!
*Sh-Shit... How are we two of a kind?! He's in the inner circle!!*
*He's a total highflier! Even higher than Nagumo!!*
I DUNNO, I'VE BEEN THINKING ABOUT THIS A LOT...BUT BEING A SMART PERSON...
ISN'T REALLY ABOUT HOW MUCH YOU STUDY.
YOU KNOW HOW SOMETIMES BRILLIANT MINDS END UP IN CULTS, KILLING PEOPLE LIKE IT'S NO BIGGIE?
BRAINS AREN'T EVERYTHING... THAT'S JUST A TINY PART OF WHO WE ARE.
IT'S THE SAME FOR BIKES, RIGHT? EVEN IF YOU'VE GOT A REALLY GREAT ENGINE, IT'S WORTHLESS WITHOUT GOOD TIRES AND STUFF.
HUH? UM... YEAH, I GUESS...

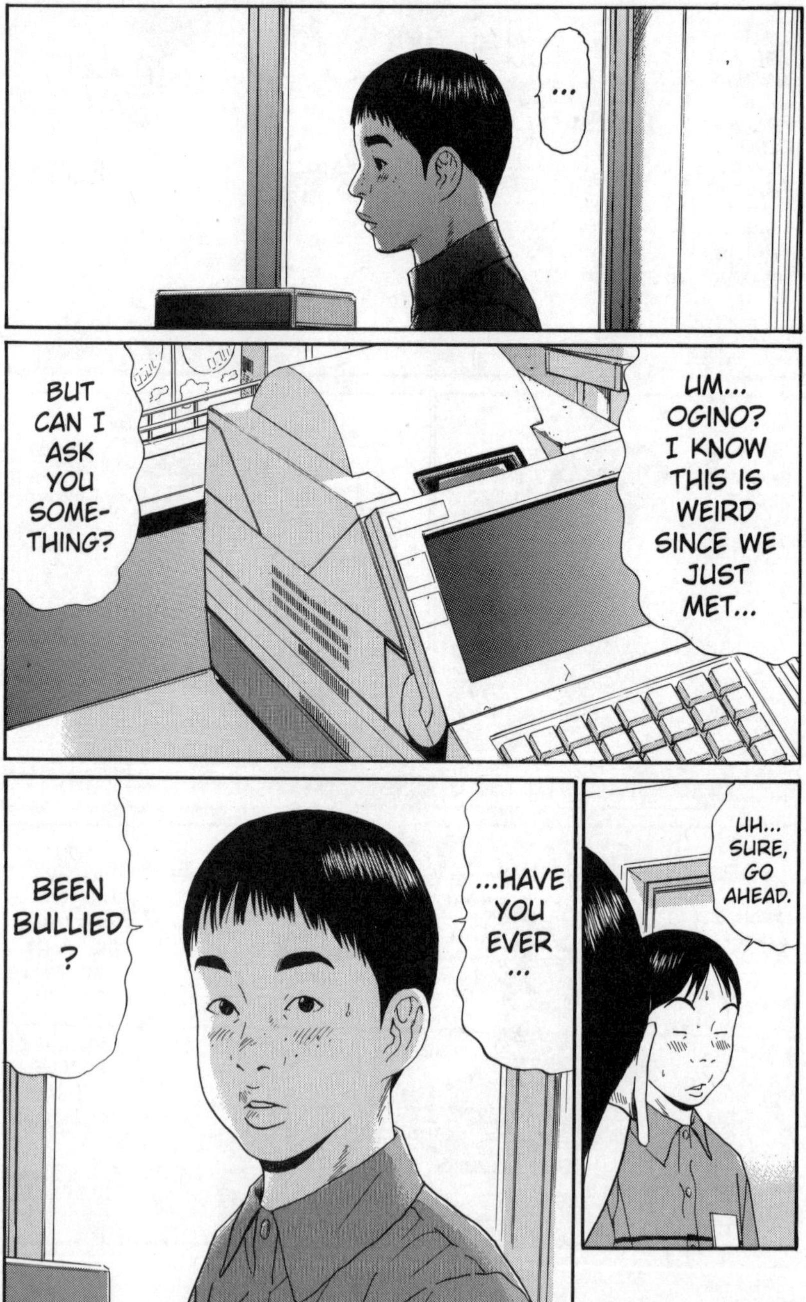
...
UM... OGINO? I KNOW THIS IS WEIRD SINCE WE JUST MET...
BUT CAN I ASK YOU SOMETHING?
UH... SURE, GO AHEAD.
...HAVE YOU EVER...
BEEN BULLIED?

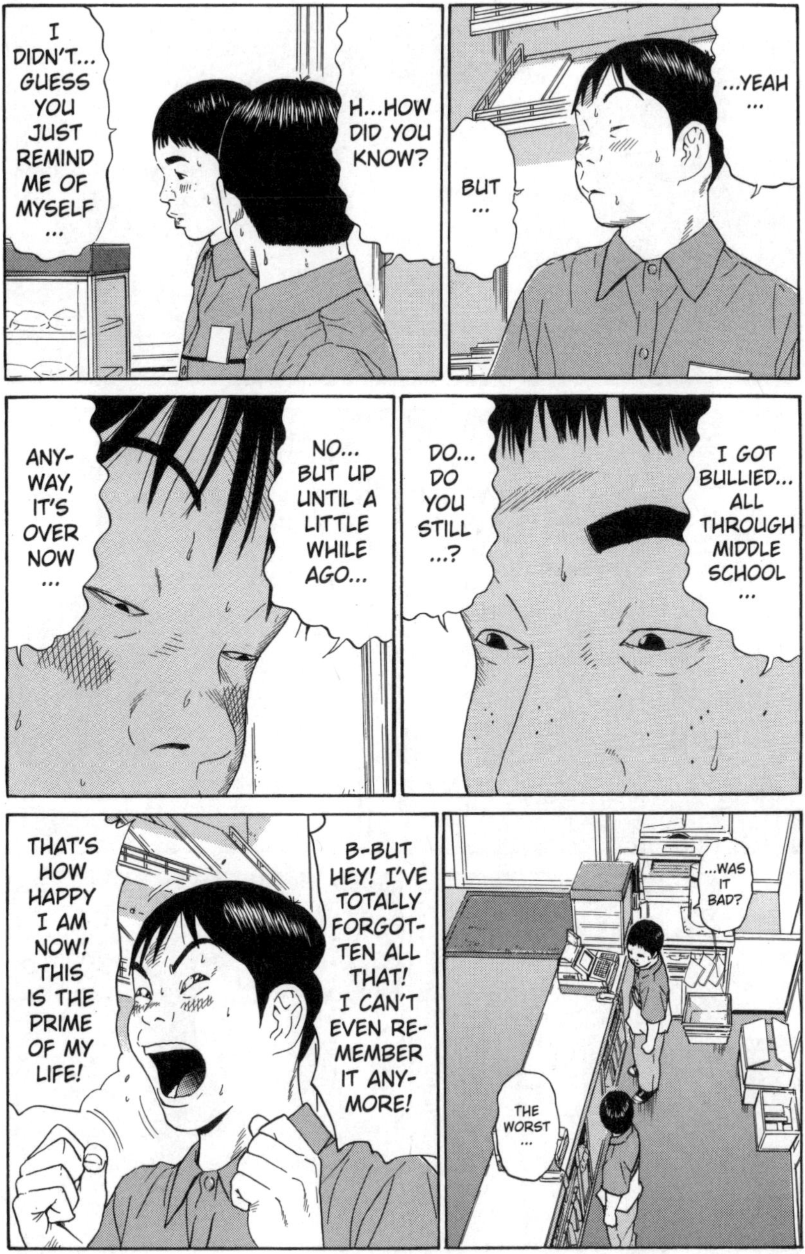
...YEAH ...
BUT ...
H...HOW DID YOU KNOW?
I DIDN'T... GUESS YOU JUST REMIND ME OF MYSELF ...
I GOT BULLIED... ALL THROUGH MIDDLE SCHOOL ...
DO... DO YOU STILL ...?
NO... BUT UP UNTIL A LITTLE WHILE AGO...
ANY-WAY, IT'S OVER NOW ...
...WAS IT BAD?
THE WORST ...
B-BUT HEY! I'VE TOTALLY FORGOT-TEN ALL THAT! I CAN'T EVEN RE-MEMBER IT ANY-MORE!
THAT'S HOW HAPPY I AM NOW! THIS IS THE PRIME OF MY LIFE!

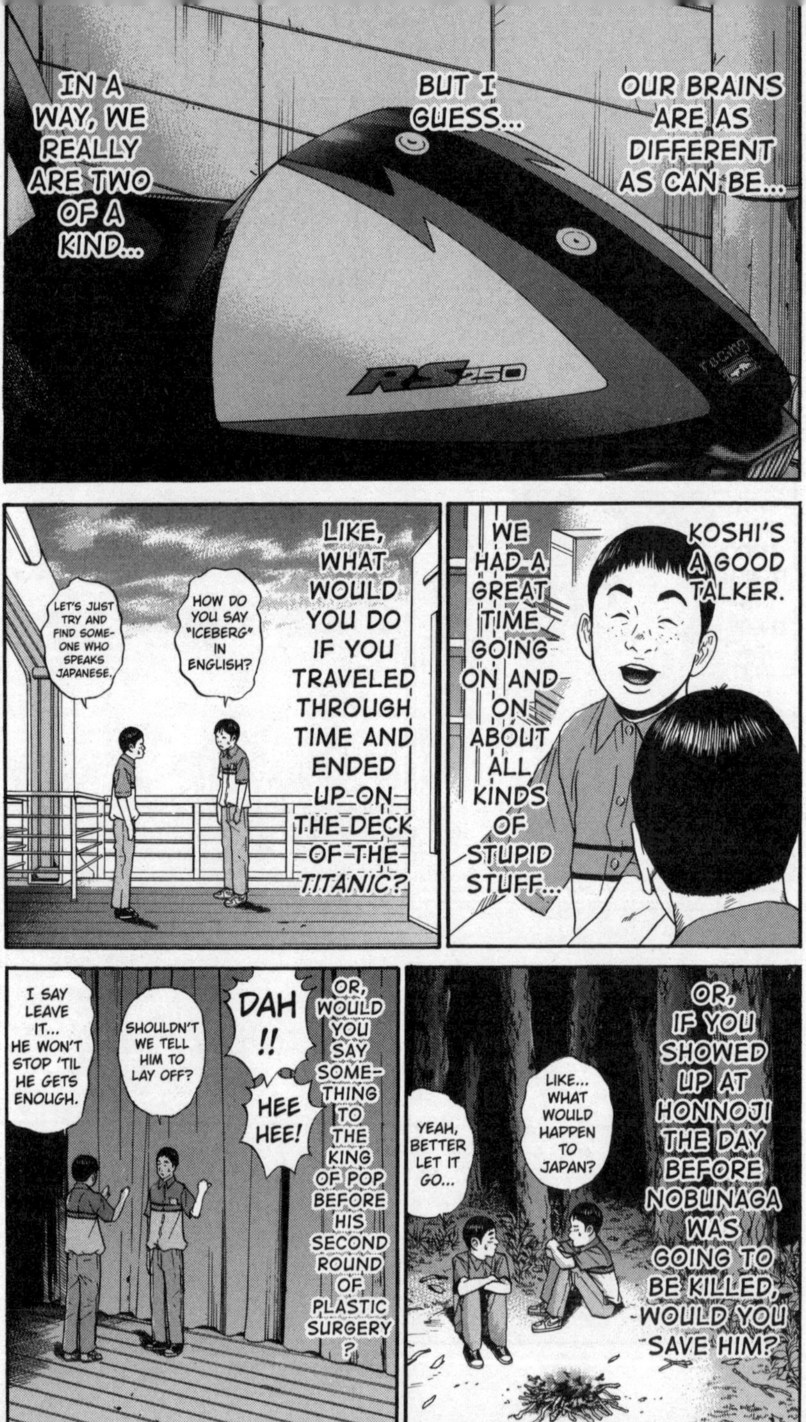

OUR BRAINS ARE AS DIFFERENT AS CAN BE...
BUT I GUESS...
IN A WAY, WE REALLY ARE TWO OF A KIND...
RS250
KOSHI'S A GOOD TALKER.
WE HAD A GREAT TIME GOING ON AND ON ABOUT ALL KINDS OF STUPID STUFF...
LIKE, WHAT WOULD YOU DO IF YOU TRAVELED THROUGH TIME AND ENDED UP ON THE DECK OF THE *TITANIC*?
HOW DO YOU SAY "ICEBERG" IN ENGLISH?
LET'S JUST TRY AND FIND SOME-ONE WHO SPEAKS JAPANESE.
OR, IF YOU SHOWED UP AT HONNOJI THE DAY BEFORE NOBUNAGA WAS GOING TO BE KILLED, WOULD YOU SAVE HIM?
LIKE... WHAT WOULD HAPPEN TO JAPAN?
YEAH, BETTER LET IT GO...
OR, WOULD YOU SAY SOME-THING TO THE KING OF POP BEFORE HIS SECOND ROUND OF PLASTIC SURGERY?
DAH!!
HEE HEE!
SHOULDN'T WE TELL HIM TO LAY OFF?
I SAY LEAVE IT... HE WON'T STOP 'TIL HE GETS ENOUGH.

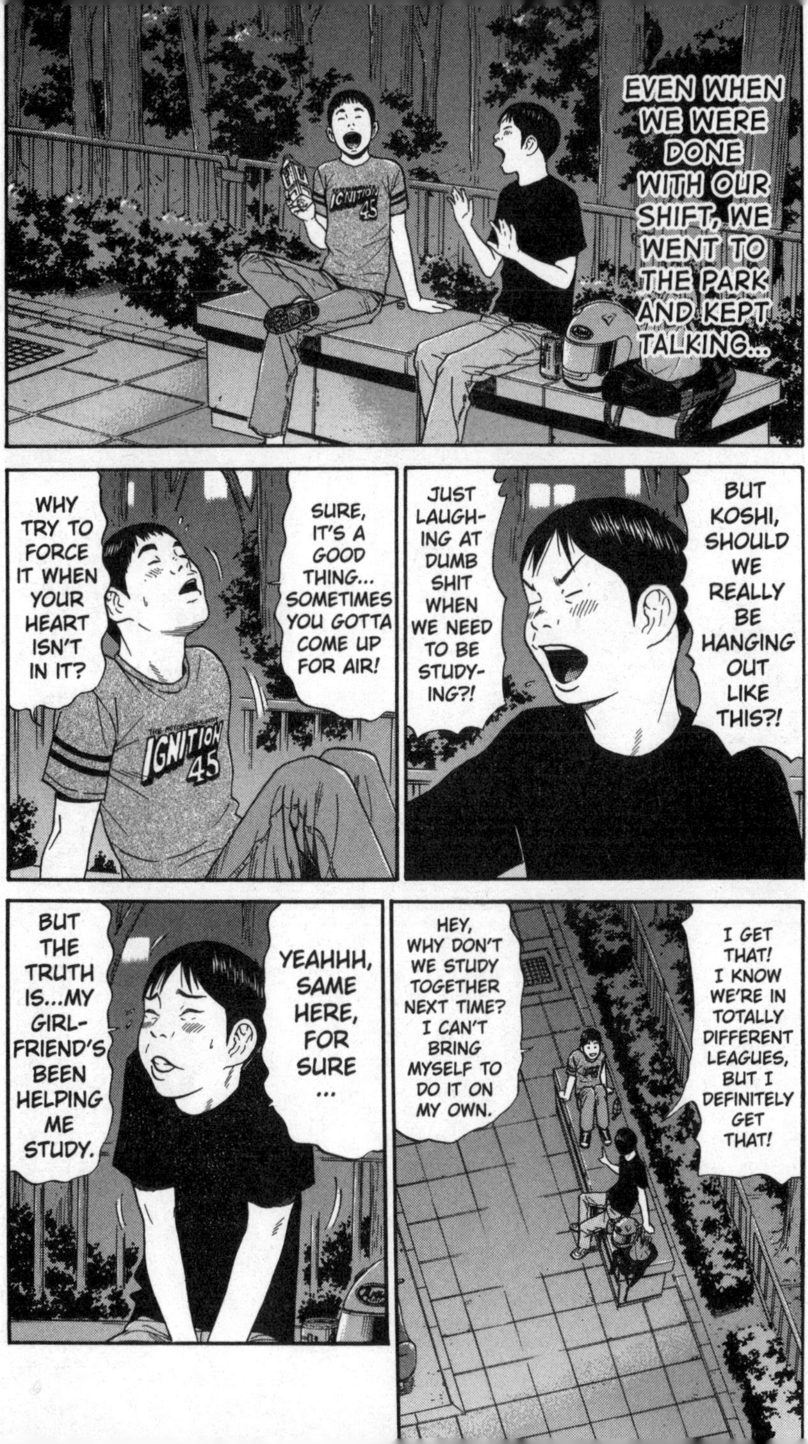

EVEN WHEN WE WERE DONE WITH OUR SHIFT, WE WENT TO THE PARK AND KEPT TALKING...
BUT KOSHI, SHOULD WE REALLY BE HANGING OUT LIKE THIS?!
JUST LAUGHING AT DUMB SHIT WHEN WE NEED TO BE STUDYING?!
SURE, IT'S A GOOD THING... SOMETIMES YOU GOTTA COME UP FOR AIR!
WHY TRY TO FORCE IT WHEN YOUR HEART ISN'T IN IT?
IGNITION 45
I GET THAT! I KNOW WE'RE IN TOTALLY DIFFERENT LEAGUES, BUT I DEFINITELY GET THAT!
HEY, WHY DON'T WE STUDY TOGETHER NEXT TIME? I CAN'T BRING MYSELF TO DO IT ON MY OWN.
YEAHHH, SAME HERE, FOR SURE...
BUT THE TRUTH IS...MY GIRLFRIEND'S BEEN HELPING ME STUDY.

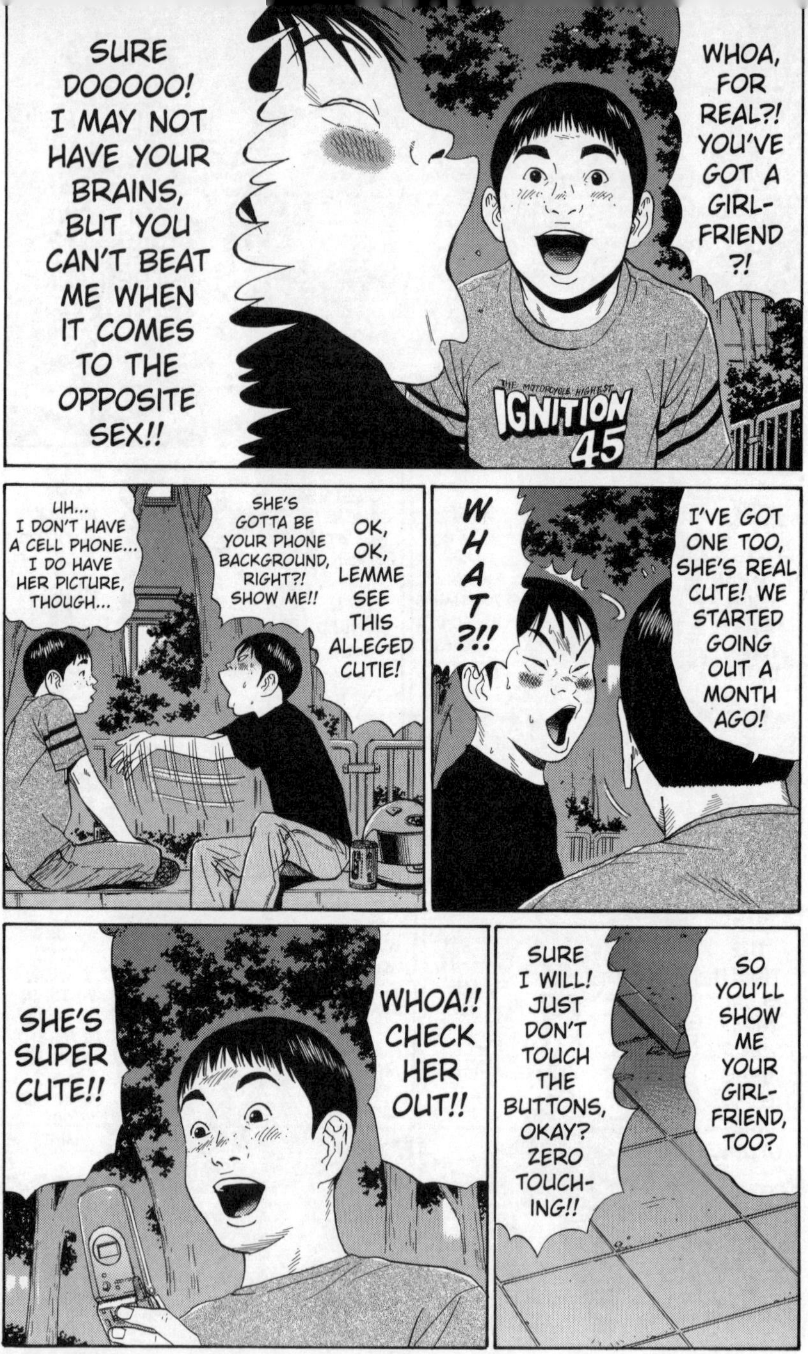
WHOA, FOR REAL?! YOU'VE GOT A GIRL-FRIEND ?!
SURE DOOOOO! I MAY NOT HAVE YOUR BRAINS, BUT YOU CAN'T BEAT ME WHEN IT COMES TO THE OPPOSITE SEX!!
IGNITION 45
I'VE GOT ONE TOO, SHE'S REAL CUTE! WE STARTED GOING OUT A MONTH AGO!
WHAT ?!!
OK, OK, LEMME SEE THIS ALLEGED CUTIE!
SHE'S GOTTA BE YOUR PHONE BACKGROUND, RIGHT?! SHOW ME!!
UH... I DON'T HAVE A CELL PHONE... I DO HAVE HER PICTURE, THOUGH...
SO YOU'LL SHOW ME YOUR GIRL-FRIEND, TOO?
SURE I WILL! JUST DON'T TOUCH THE BUTTONS, OKAY? ZERO TOUCH-ING!!
WHOA!! CHECK HER OUT!!
SHE'S SUPER CUTE!!

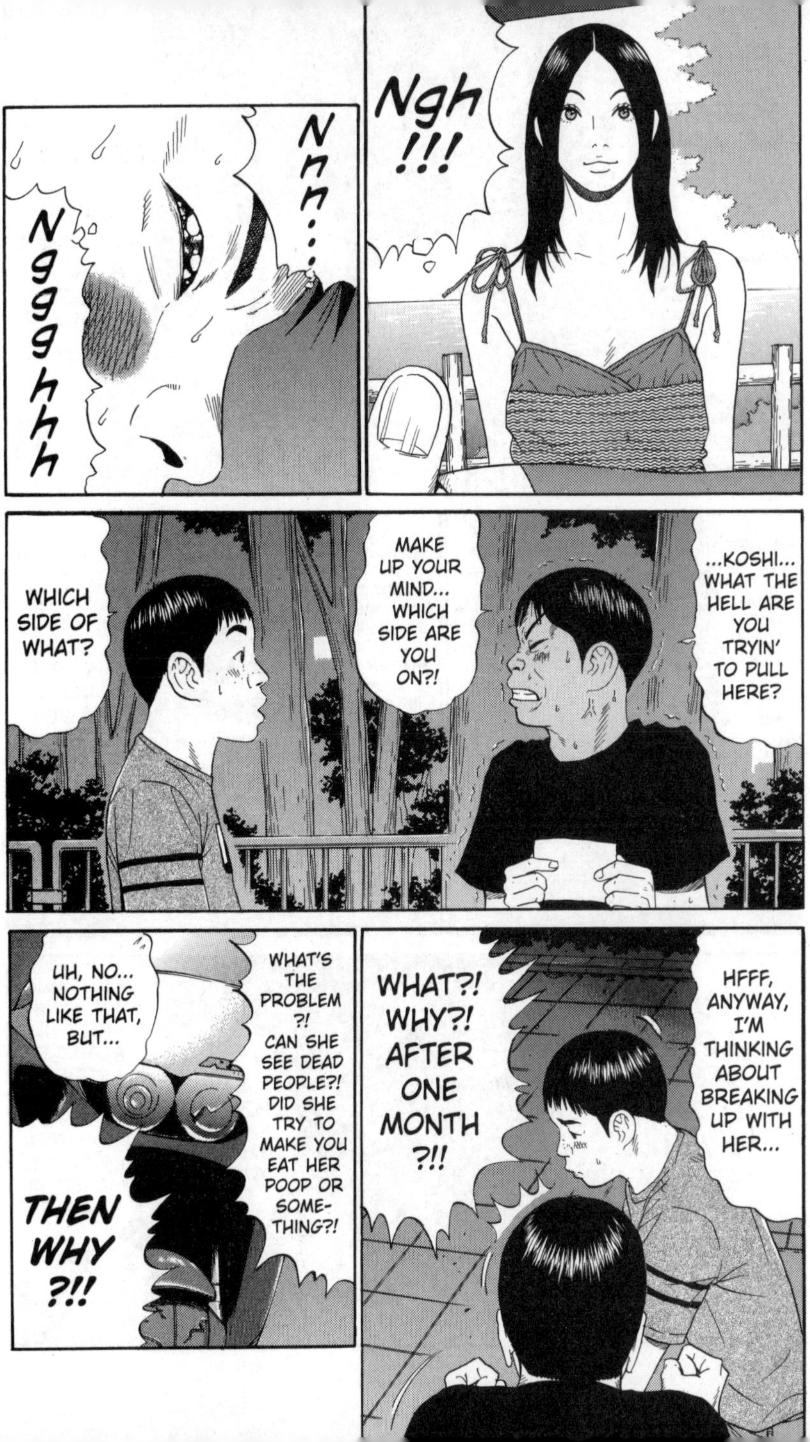
Ngh!!!
Nnn...
Nggghhh
...KOSHI... WHAT THE HELL ARE YOU TRYIN' TO PULL HERE?
MAKE UP YOUR MIND... WHICH SIDE ARE YOU ON?!
WHICH SIDE OF WHAT?
HFFF, ANYWAY, I'M THINKING ABOUT BREAKING UP WITH HER...
WHAT?! WHY?! AFTER ONE MONTH?!!
WHAT'S THE PROBLEM?! CAN SHE SEE DEAD PEOPLE?! DID SHE TRY TO MAKE YOU EAT HER POOP OR SOME-THING?!
UH, NO... NOTHING LIKE THAT, BUT...
THEN WHY?!!

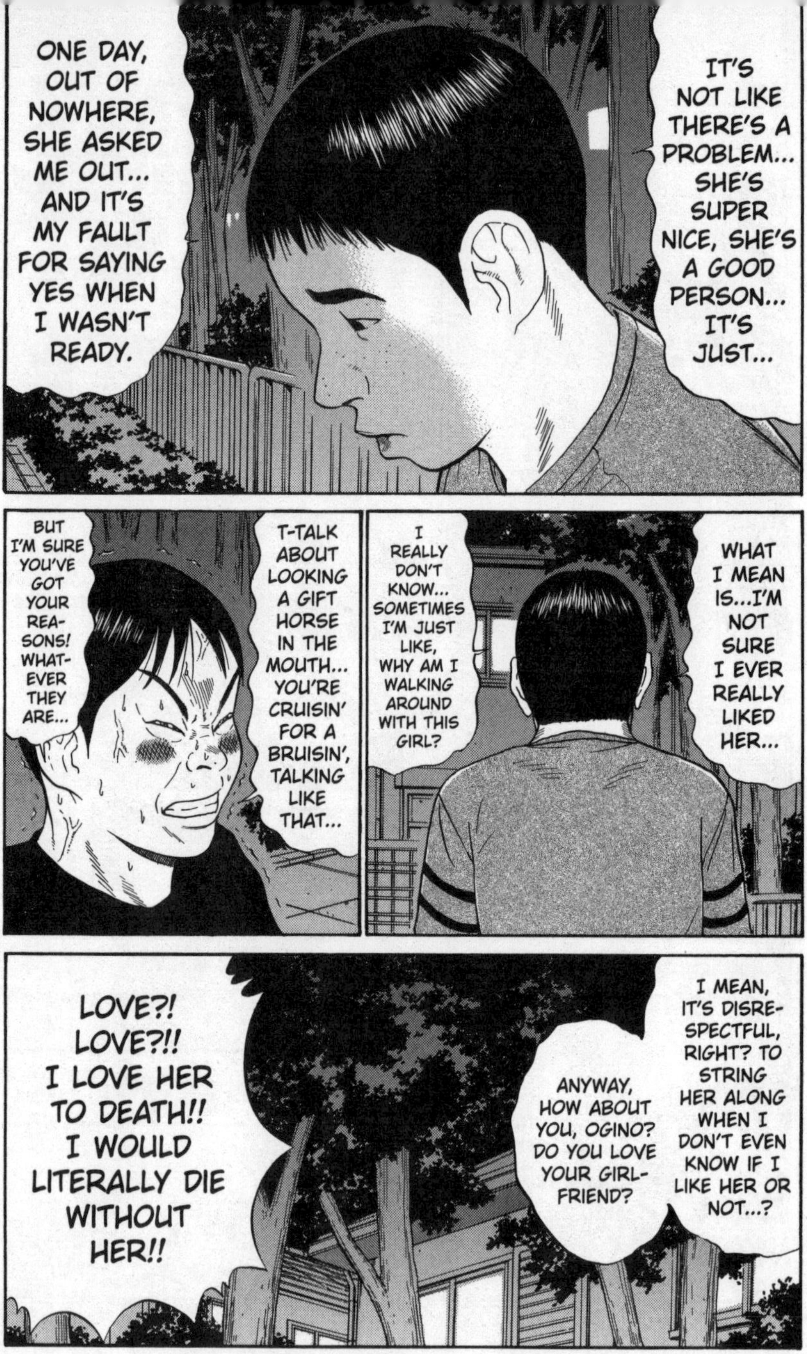
IT'S NOT LIKE THERE'S A PROBLEM... SHE'S SUPER NICE, SHE'S A GOOD PERSON... IT'S JUST...
ONE DAY, OUT OF NOWHERE, SHE ASKED ME OUT... AND IT'S MY FAULT FOR SAYING YES WHEN I WASN'T READY.
WHAT I MEAN IS...I'M NOT SURE I EVER REALLY LIKED HER...
I REALLY DON'T KNOW... SOMETIMES I'M JUST LIKE, WHY AM I WALKING AROUND WITH THIS GIRL?
T-TALK ABOUT LOOKING A GIFT HORSE IN THE MOUTH... YOU'RE CRUISIN' FOR A BRUISIN', TALKING LIKE THAT...
BUT I'M SURE YOU'VE GOT YOUR REA-SONS! WHAT-EVER THEY ARE...
I MEAN, IT'S DISRE-SPECTFUL, RIGHT? TO STRING HER ALONG WHEN I DON'T EVEN KNOW IF I LIKE HER OR NOT...?
ANYWAY, HOW ABOUT YOU, OGINO? DO YOU LOVE YOUR GIRL-FRIEND?
LOVE?! LOVE?!! I LOVE HER TO DEATH!! I WOULD LITERALLY DIE WITHOUT HER!!

# Chapter 50: A Better Environment

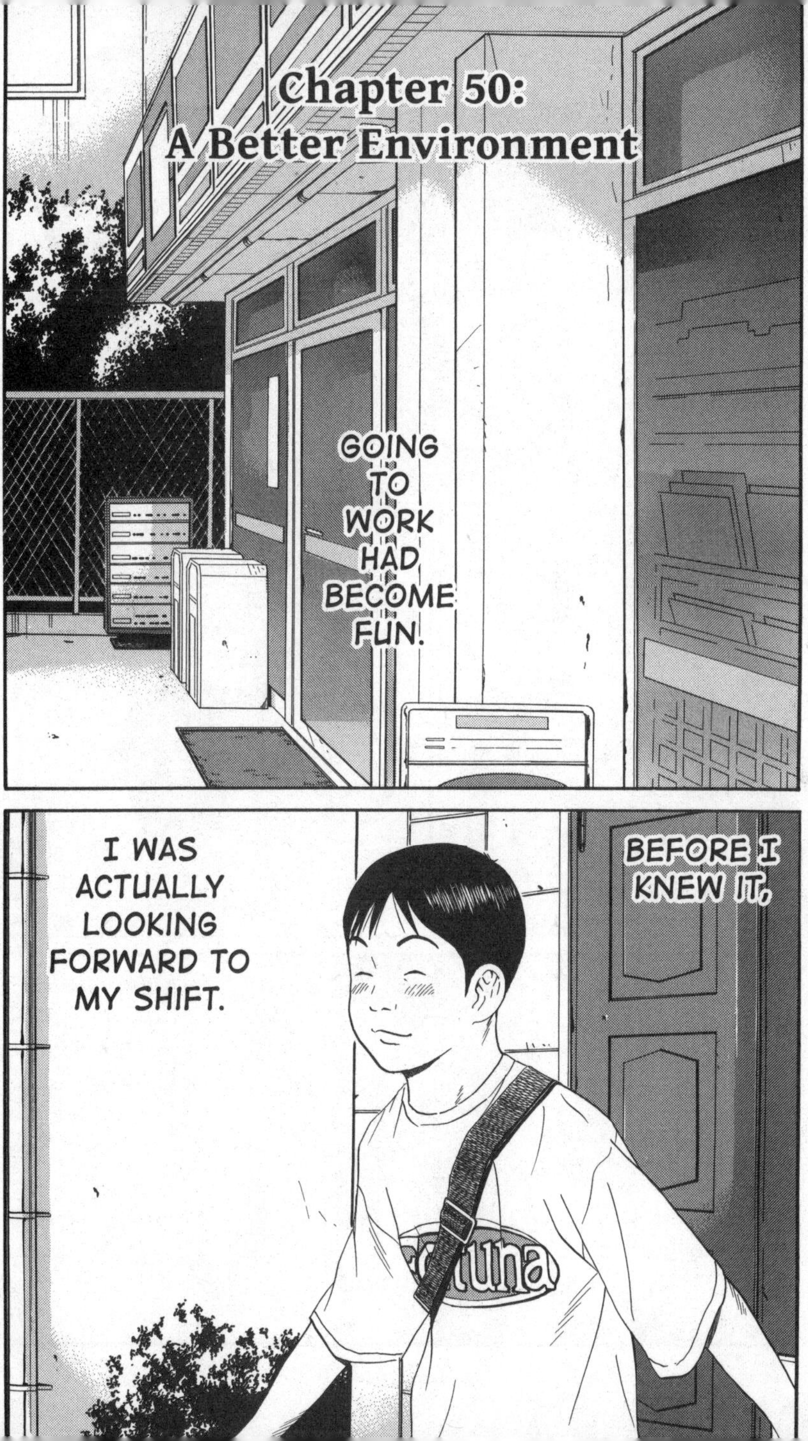
GOING TO WORK HAD BECOME FUN.
BEFORE I KNEW IT,
I WAS ACTUALLY LOOKING FORWARD TO MY SHIFT.

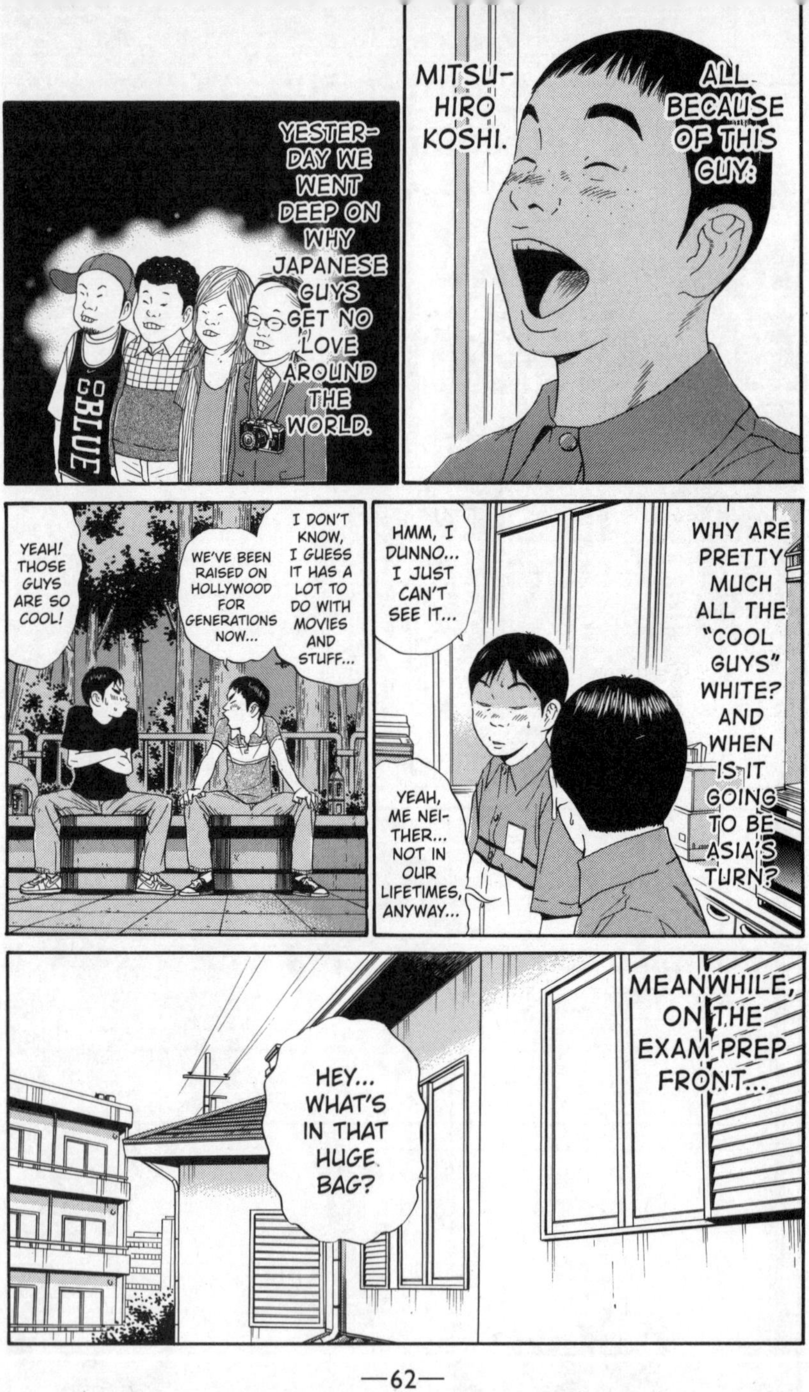
ALL BECAUSE OF THIS GUY:
MITSU-HIRO KOSHI.
YESTER-DAY WE WENT DEEP ON WHY JAPANESE GUYS GET NO LOVE AROUND THE WORLD.
GO BLUE
WHY ARE PRETTY MUCH ALL THE "COOL GUYS" WHITE? AND WHEN IS IT GOING TO BE ASIA'S TURN?
HMM, I DUNNO... I JUST CAN'T SEE IT...
YEAH, ME NEI-THER... NOT IN OUR LIFETIMES, ANYWAY...
I DON'T KNOW, I GUESS IT HAS A LOT TO DO WITH MOVIES AND STUFF...
WE'VE BEEN RAISED ON HOLLYWOOD FOR GENERATIONS NOW...
YEAH! THOSE GUYS ARE SO COOL!
MEANWHILE, ON THE EXAM PREP FRONT...
HEY... WHAT'S IN THAT HUGE BAG?

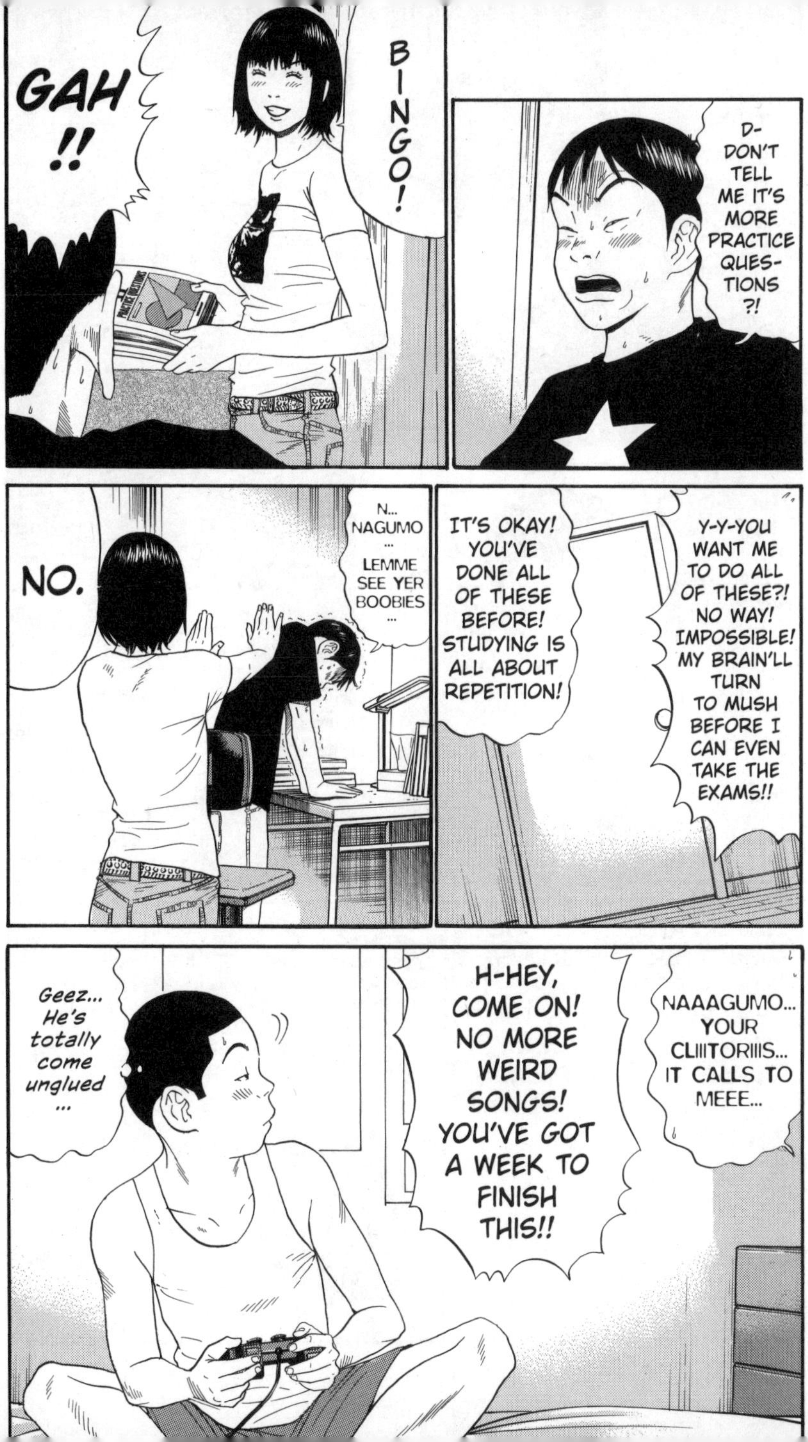
D-DON'T TELL ME IT'S MORE PRACTICE QUES-TIONS?!
BINGO!
GAH!!
Y-Y-YOU WANT ME TO DO ALL OF THESE?! NO WAY! IMPOSSIBLE! MY BRAIN'LL TURN TO MUSH BEFORE I CAN EVEN TAKE THE EXAMS!!
IT'S OKAY! YOU'VE DONE ALL OF THESE BEFORE! STUDYING IS ALL ABOUT REPETITION!
N... NAGUMO ... LEMME SEE YER BOOBIES ...
NO.
NAAAGUMO... YOUR CLIIITORIIIS... IT CALLS TO MEEE...
H-HEY, COME ON! NO MORE WEIRD SONGS! YOU'VE GOT A WEEK TO FINISH THIS!!
*Geez... He's totally come unglued ...*

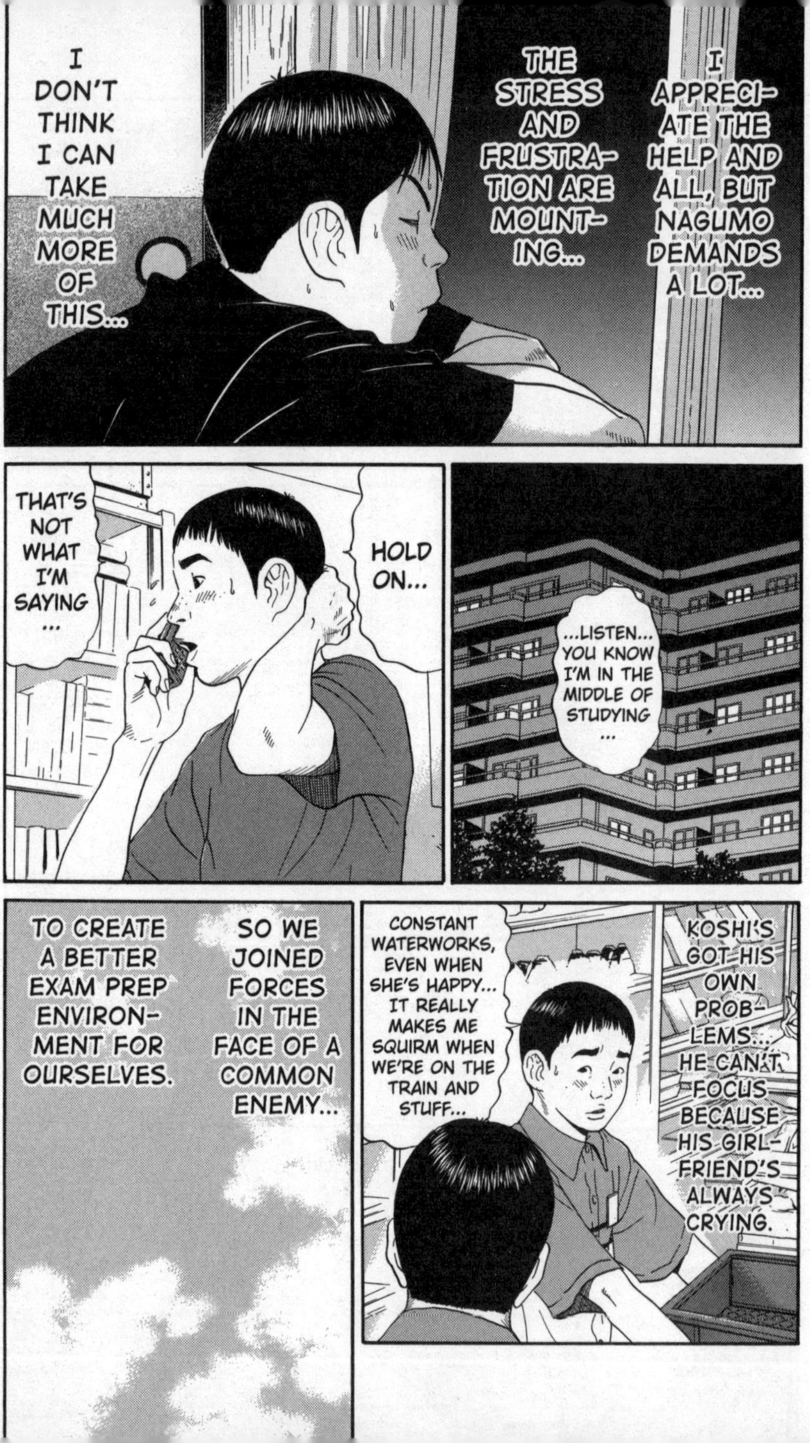
I APPRECIATE THE HELP AND ALL, BUT NAGUMO DEMANDS A LOT...
THE STRESS AND FRUSTRATION ARE MOUNTING...
I DON'T THINK I CAN TAKE MUCH MORE OF THIS...
...LISTEN... YOU KNOW I'M IN THE MIDDLE OF STUDYING...
HOLD ON...
THAT'S NOT WHAT I'M SAYING...
KOSHI'S GOT HIS OWN PROBLEMS... HE CAN'T FOCUS BECAUSE HIS GIRLFRIEND'S ALWAYS CRYING.
CONSTANT WATERWORKS, EVEN WHEN SHE'S HAPPY... IT REALLY MAKES ME SQUIRM WHEN WE'RE ON THE TRAIN AND STUFF...
SO WE JOINED FORCES IN THE FACE OF A COMMON ENEMY...
TO CREATE A BETTER EXAM PREP ENVIRONMENT FOR OURSELVES.

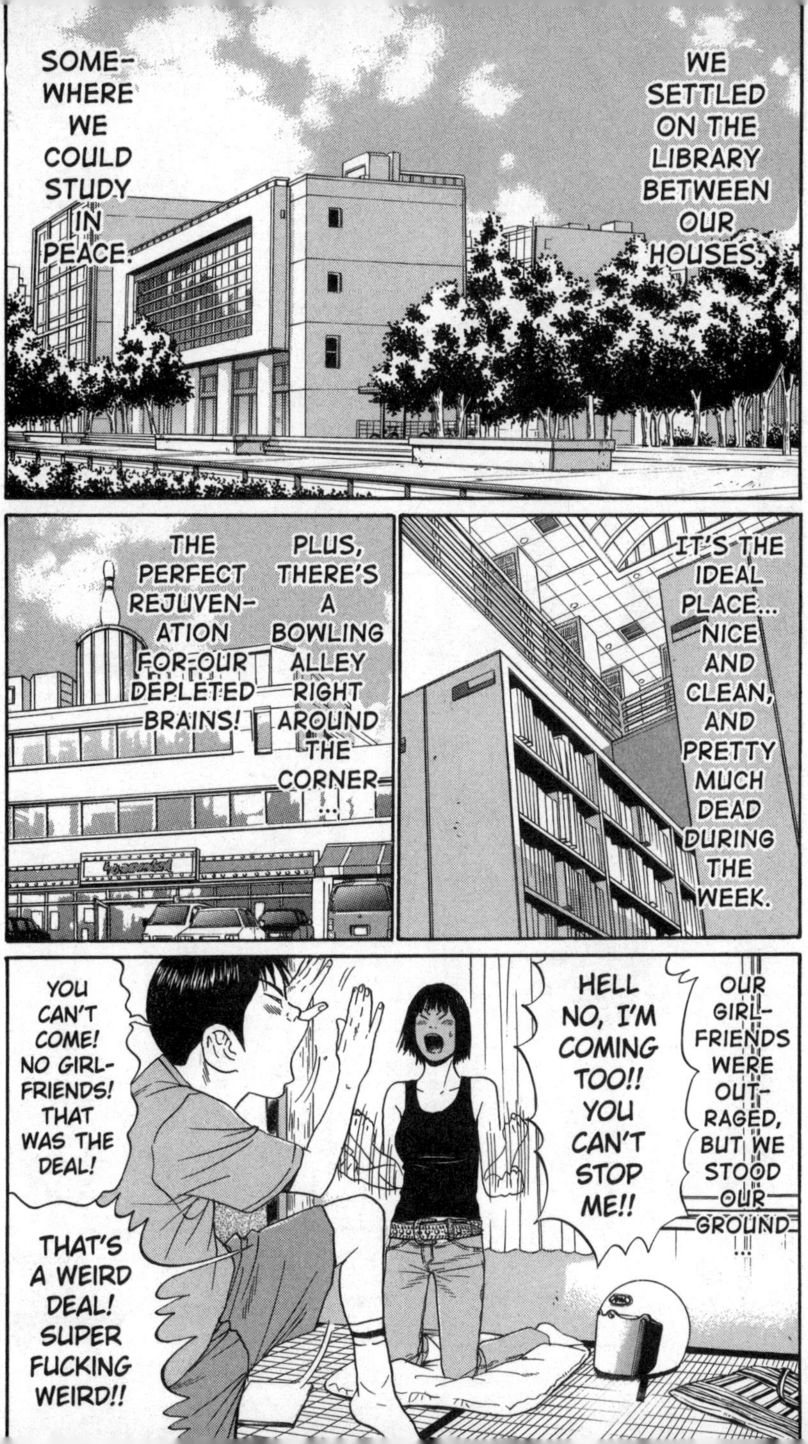
WE SETTLED ON THE LIBRARY BETWEEN OUR HOUSES.
SOMEWHERE WE COULD STUDY IN PEACE.
IT'S THE IDEAL PLACE... NICE AND CLEAN, AND PRETTY MUCH DEAD DURING THE WEEK.
PLUS, THERE'S A BOWLING ALLEY RIGHT AROUND THE CORNER...
THE PERFECT REJUVENATION FOR OUR DEPLETED BRAINS!
OUR GIRLFRIENDS WERE OUTRAGED, BUT WE STOOD OUR GROUND...
HELL NO, I'M COMING TOO!! YOU CAN'T STOP ME!!
YOU CAN'T COME! NO GIRLFRIENDS! THAT WAS THE DEAL!
THAT'S A WEIRD DEAL! SUPER FUCKING WEIRD!!

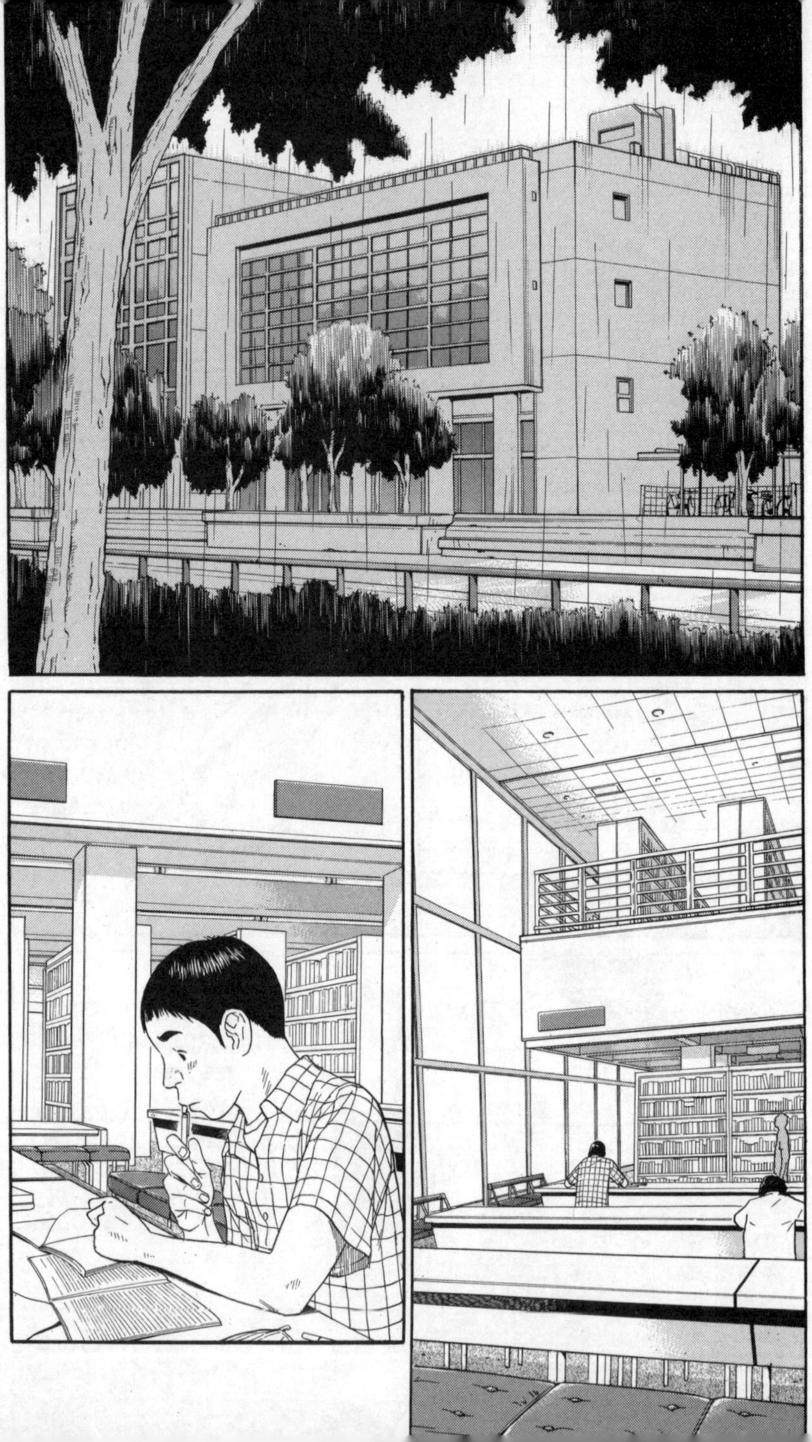

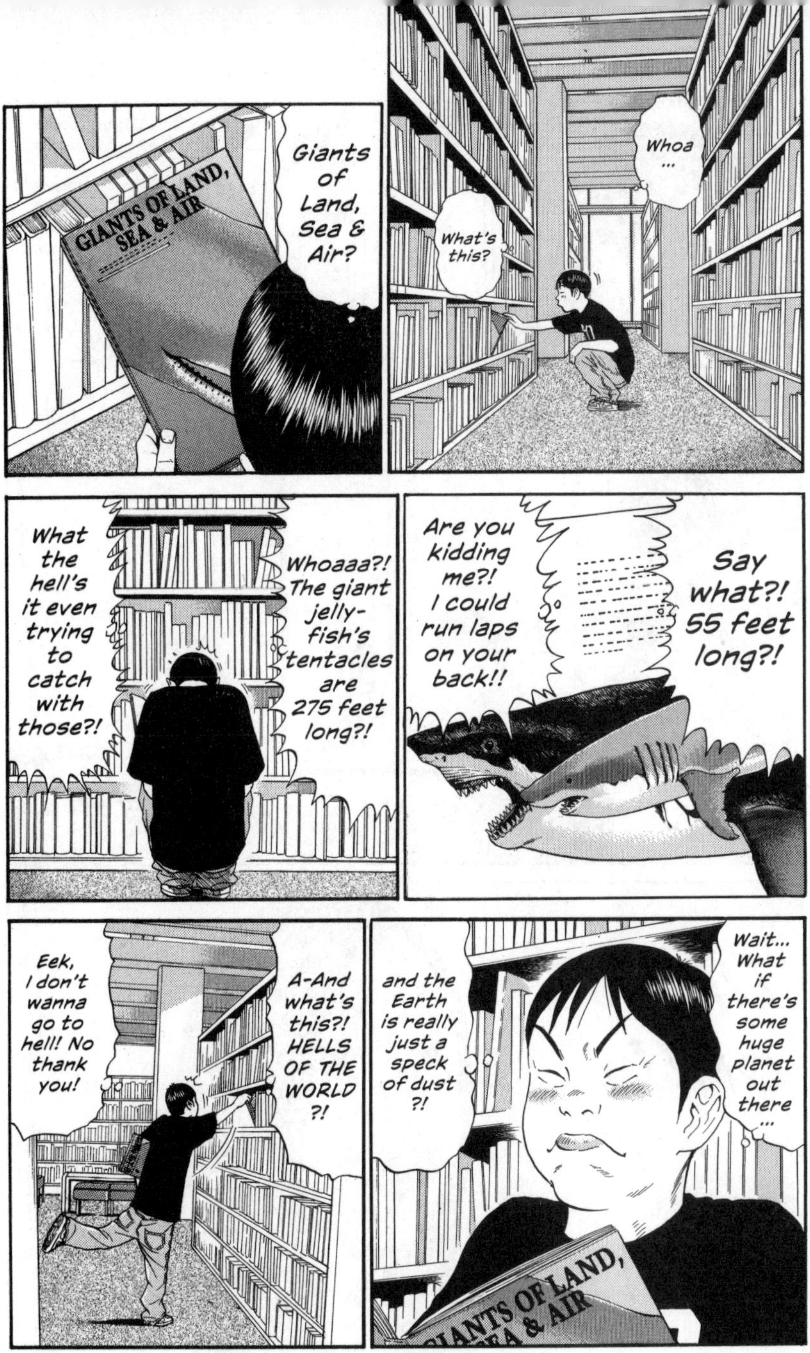
Whoa ...
What's this?
Giants of Land, Sea & Air?
GIANTS OF LAND, SEA & AIR
Say what?! 55 feet long?!
Are you kidding me?! I could run laps on your back!!
Whoaaa?! The giant jellyfish's tentacles are 275 feet long?!
What the hell's it even trying to catch with those?!
Wait... What if there's some huge planet out there...
and the Earth is really just a speck of dust?!
GIANTS OF LAND, SEA & AIR
A-And what's this?! HELLS OF THE WORLD?!
Eek, I don't wanna go to hell! No thank you!

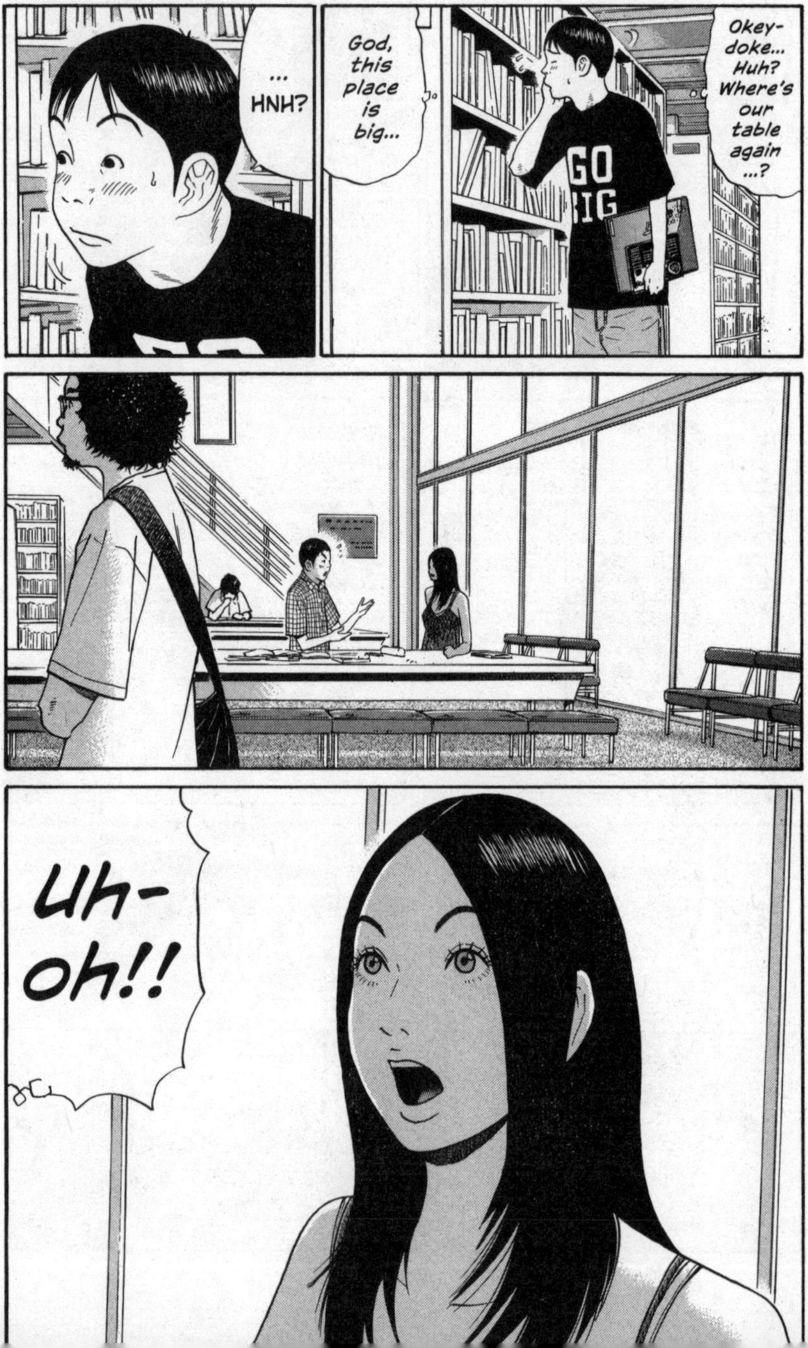
Okey-doke... Huh? Where's our table again ...?
God, this place is big...
... HNH?
Uh-oh!!

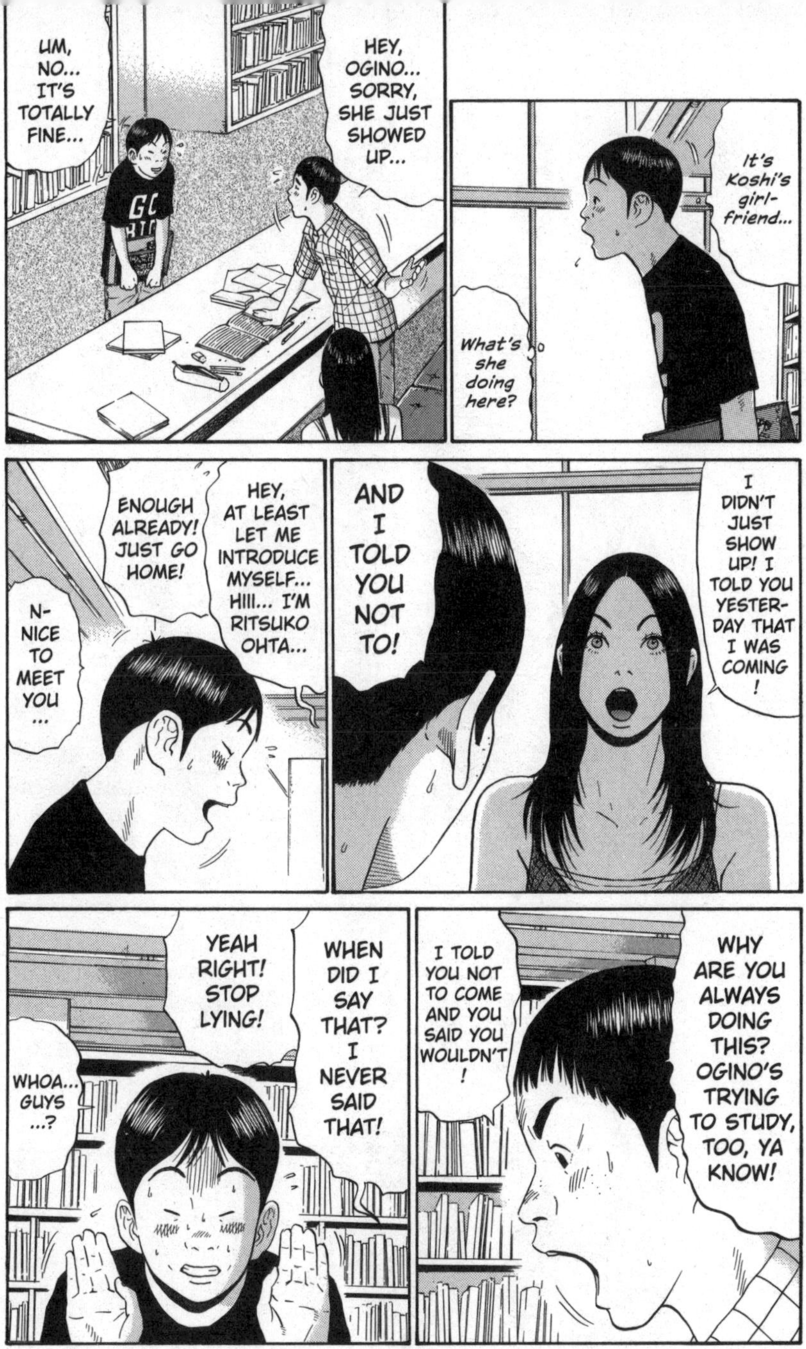
It's Koshi's girlfriend...
What's she doing here?
HEY, OGINO... SORRY, SHE JUST SHOWED UP...
UM, NO... IT'S TOTALLY FINE...
I DIDN'T JUST SHOW UP! I TOLD YOU YESTERDAY THAT I WAS COMING!
AND I TOLD YOU NOT TO!
HEY, AT LEAST LET ME INTRODUCE MYSELF... HIII... I'M RITSUKO OHTA...
ENOUGH ALREADY! JUST GO HOME!
N-NICE TO MEET YOU...
WHY ARE YOU ALWAYS DOING THIS? OGINO'S TRYING TO STUDY, TOO, YA KNOW!
I TOLD YOU NOT TO COME AND YOU SAID YOU WOULDN'T!
WHEN DID I SAY THAT? I NEVER SAID THAT!
YEAH RIGHT! STOP LYING!
WHOA... GUYS...?

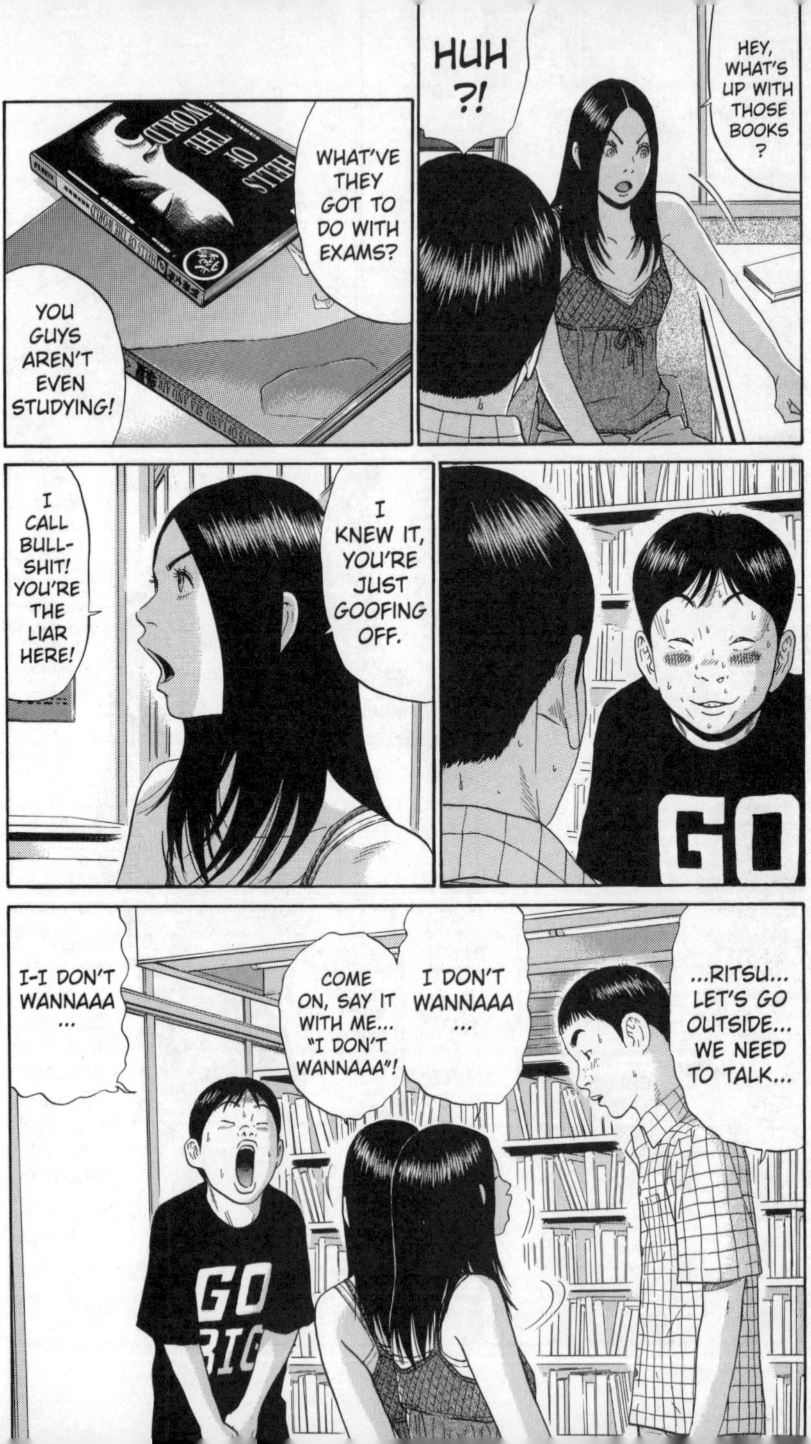
HEY, WHAT'S UP WITH THOSE BOOKS ?
HUH ?!
WHAT'VE THEY GOT TO DO WITH EXAMS?
HELLS OF THE WORLD
YOU GUYS AREN'T EVEN STUDYING!
GO
I KNEW IT, YOU'RE JUST GOOFING OFF.
I CALL BULL-SHIT! YOU'RE THE LIAR HERE!
...RITSU... LET'S GO OUTSIDE... WE NEED TO TALK...
I DON'T WANNAAA ...
COME ON, SAY IT WITH ME... "I DON'T WANNAAA"!
I-I DON'T WANNAAA ...
GO BIG

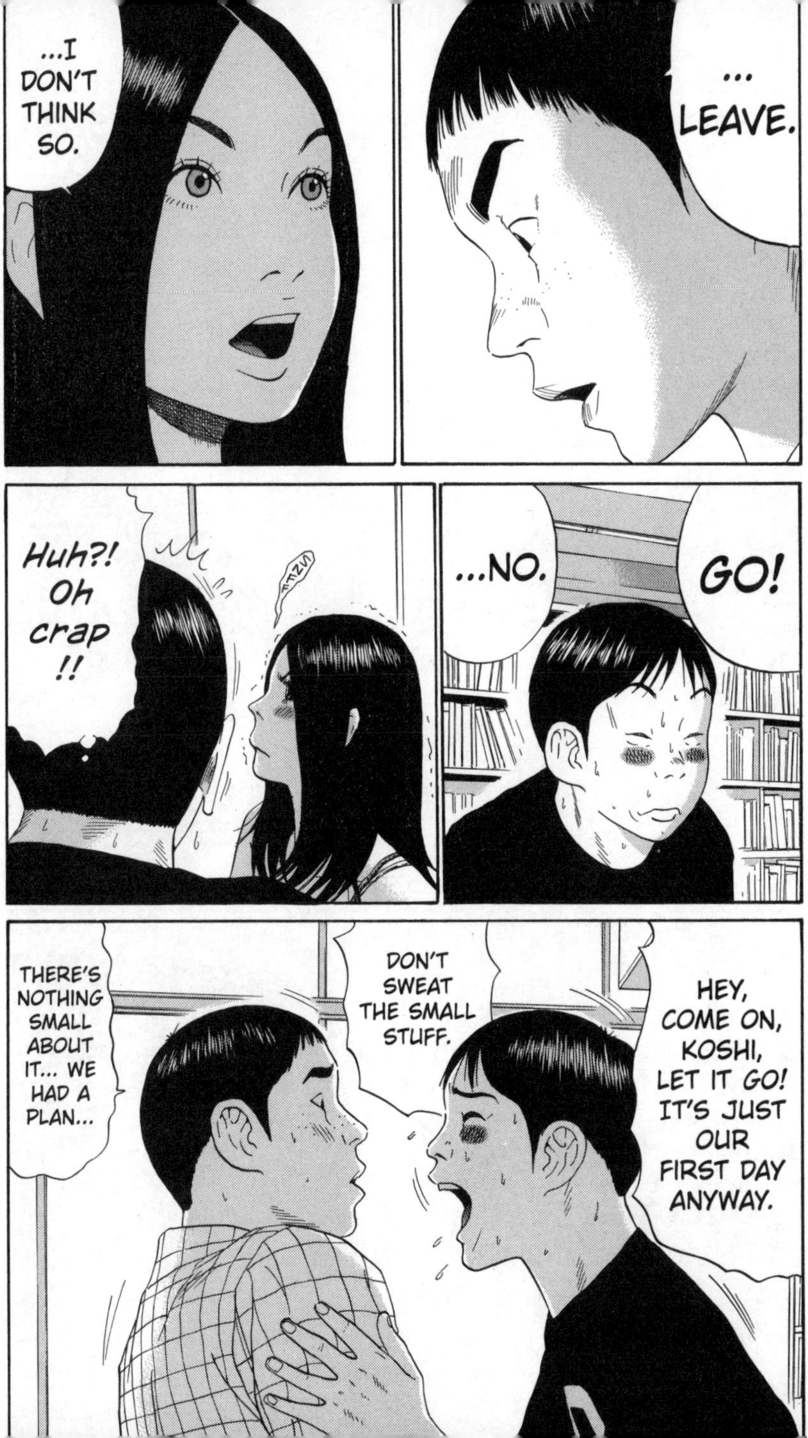
... LEAVE.
...I DON'T THINK SO.
GO!
...NO.
Huh?! Oh crap !!
HEY, COME ON, KOSHI, LET IT GO! IT'S JUST OUR FIRST DAY ANYWAY.
DON'T SWEAT THE SMALL STUFF.
THERE'S NOTHING SMALL ABOUT IT... WE HAD A PLAN...

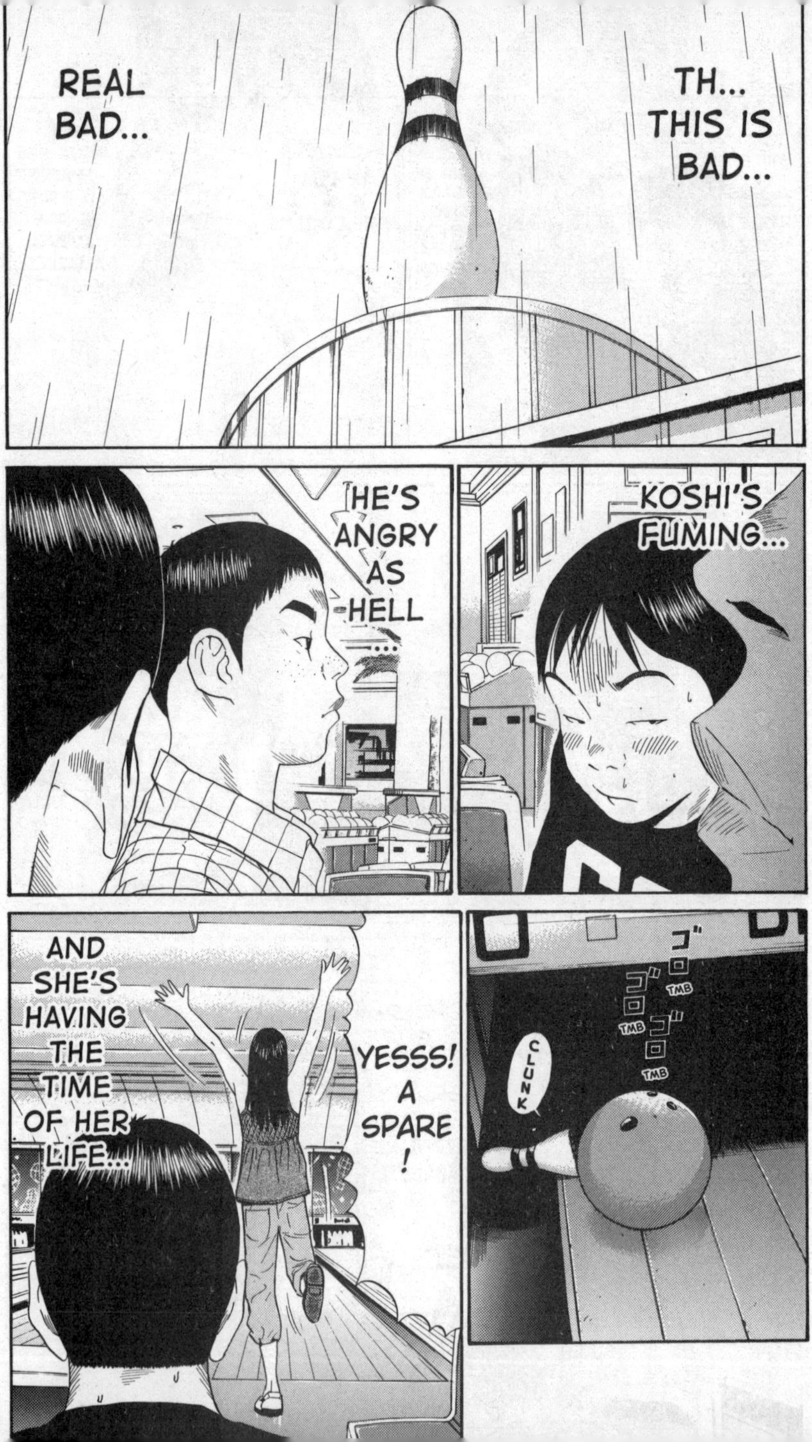
TH... THIS IS BAD...
REAL BAD...
KOSHI'S FUMING...
HE'S ANGRY AS HELL ...
ゴロ
TMB
ゴロ
TMB
ゴロ
TMB
CLUNK
YESSS! A SPARE!
AND SHE'S HAVING THE TIME OF HER LIFE...

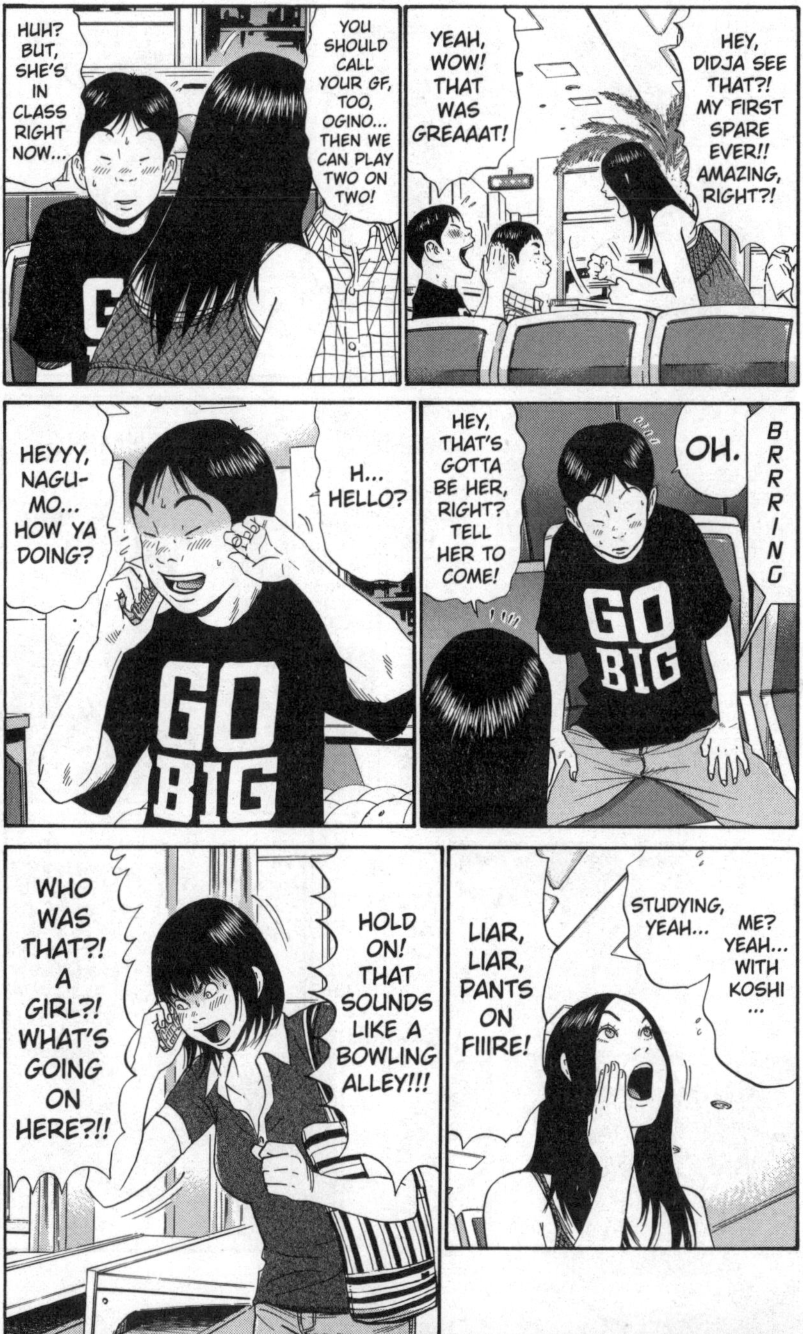
HEY, DIDJA SEE THAT?! MY FIRST SPARE EVER!! AMAZING, RIGHT?!
YEAH, WOW! THAT WAS GREAAAT!
YOU SHOULD CALL YOUR GF, TOO, OGINO... THEN WE CAN PLAY TWO ON TWO!
HUH? BUT, SHE'S IN CLASS RIGHT NOW...
BRRRING
OH.
HEY, THAT'S GOTTA BE HER, RIGHT? TELL HER TO COME!
GO BIG
H... HELLO?
HEYYY, NAGUMO... HOW YA DOING?
GO BIG
ME? YEAH... WITH KOSHI ...
STUDYING, YEAH...
LIAR, LIAR, PANTS ON FIIIRE!
HOLD ON! THAT SOUNDS LIKE A BOWLING ALLEY!!!
WHO WAS THAT?! A GIRL?! WHAT'S GOING ON HERE?!!

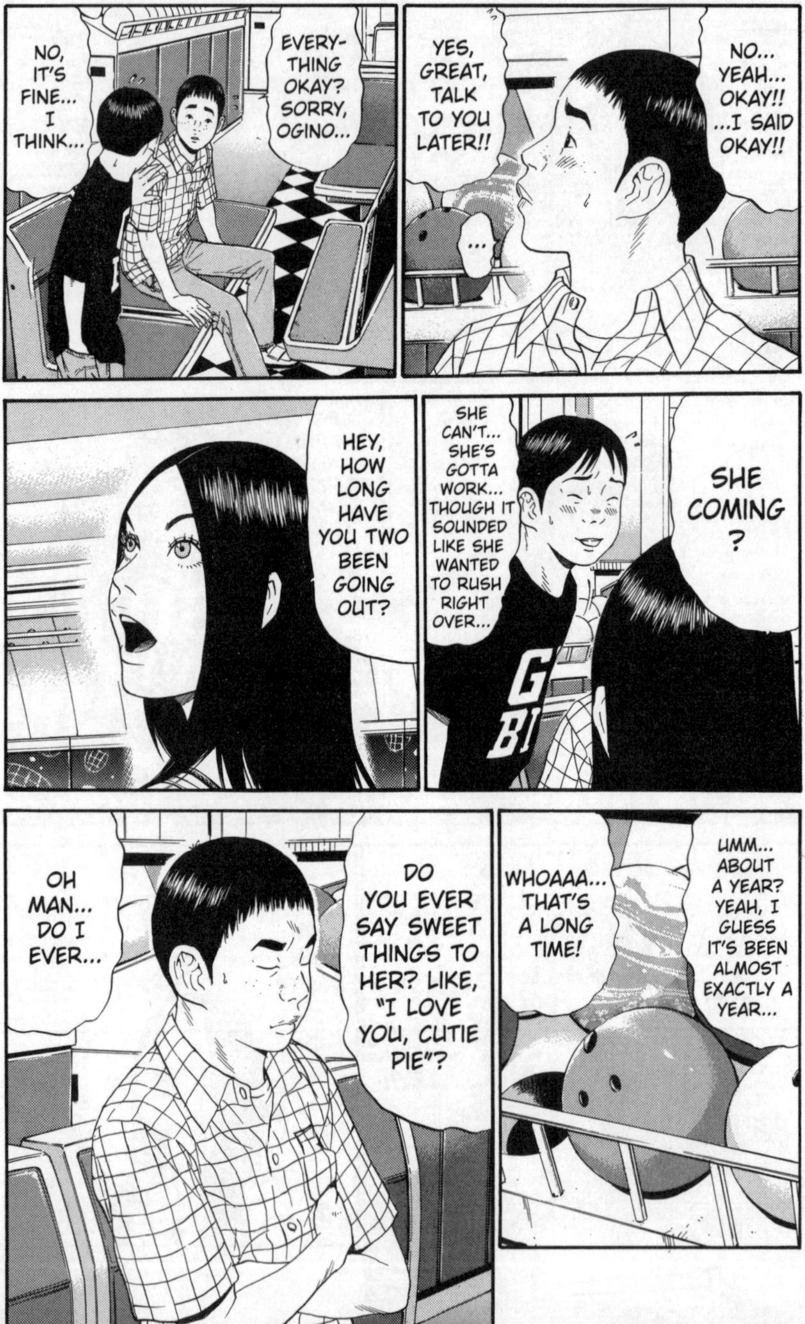
NO... YEAH... OKAY!! ...I SAID OKAY!!
YES, GREAT, TALK TO YOU LATER!!
...
EVERY-THING OKAY? SORRY, OGINO...
NO, IT'S FINE... I THINK...
SHE COMING?
SHE CAN'T... SHE'S GOTTA WORK... THOUGH IT SOUNDED LIKE SHE WANTED TO RUSH RIGHT OVER...
HEY, HOW LONG HAVE YOU TWO BEEN GOING OUT?
UMM... ABOUT A YEAR? YEAH, I GUESS IT'S BEEN ALMOST EXACTLY A YEAR...
WHOAAA... THAT'S A LONG TIME!
DO YOU EVER SAY SWEET THINGS TO HER? LIKE, "I LOVE YOU, CUTIE PIE"?
OH MAN... DO I EVER...

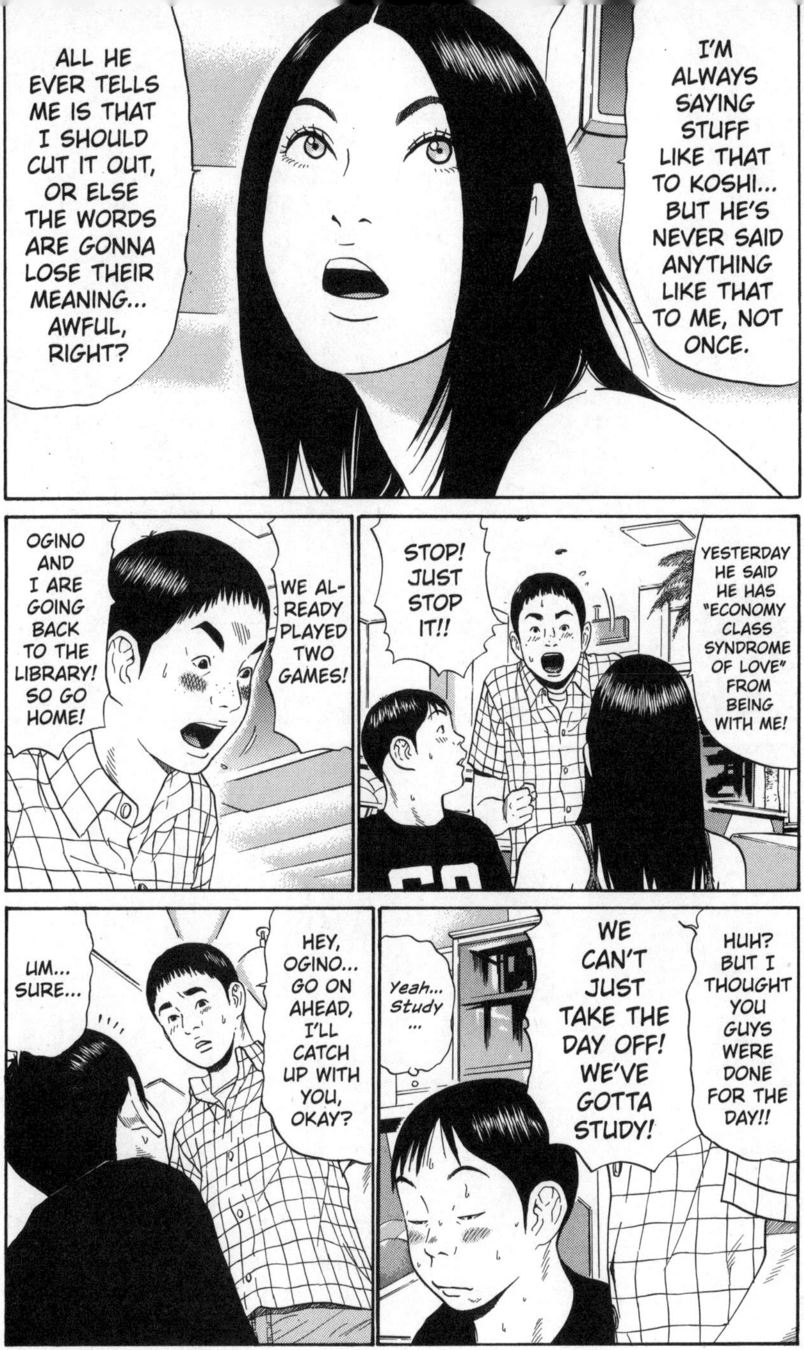
I'M ALWAYS SAYING STUFF LIKE THAT TO KOSHI... BUT HE'S NEVER SAID ANYTHING LIKE THAT TO ME, NOT ONCE.
ALL HE EVER TELLS ME IS THAT I SHOULD CUT IT OUT, OR ELSE THE WORDS ARE GONNA LOSE THEIR MEANING... AWFUL, RIGHT?
YESTERDAY HE SAID HE HAS "ECONOMY CLASS SYNDROME OF LOVE" FROM BEING WITH ME!
STOP! JUST STOP IT!!
WE AL-READY PLAYED TWO GAMES!
OGINO AND I ARE GOING BACK TO THE LIBRARY! SO GO HOME!
HUH? BUT I THOUGHT YOU GUYS WERE DONE FOR THE DAY!!
WE CAN'T JUST TAKE THE DAY OFF! WE'VE GOTTA STUDY!
Yeah... Study ...
HEY, OGINO... GO ON AHEAD, I'LL CATCH UP WITH YOU, OKAY?
UM... SURE...

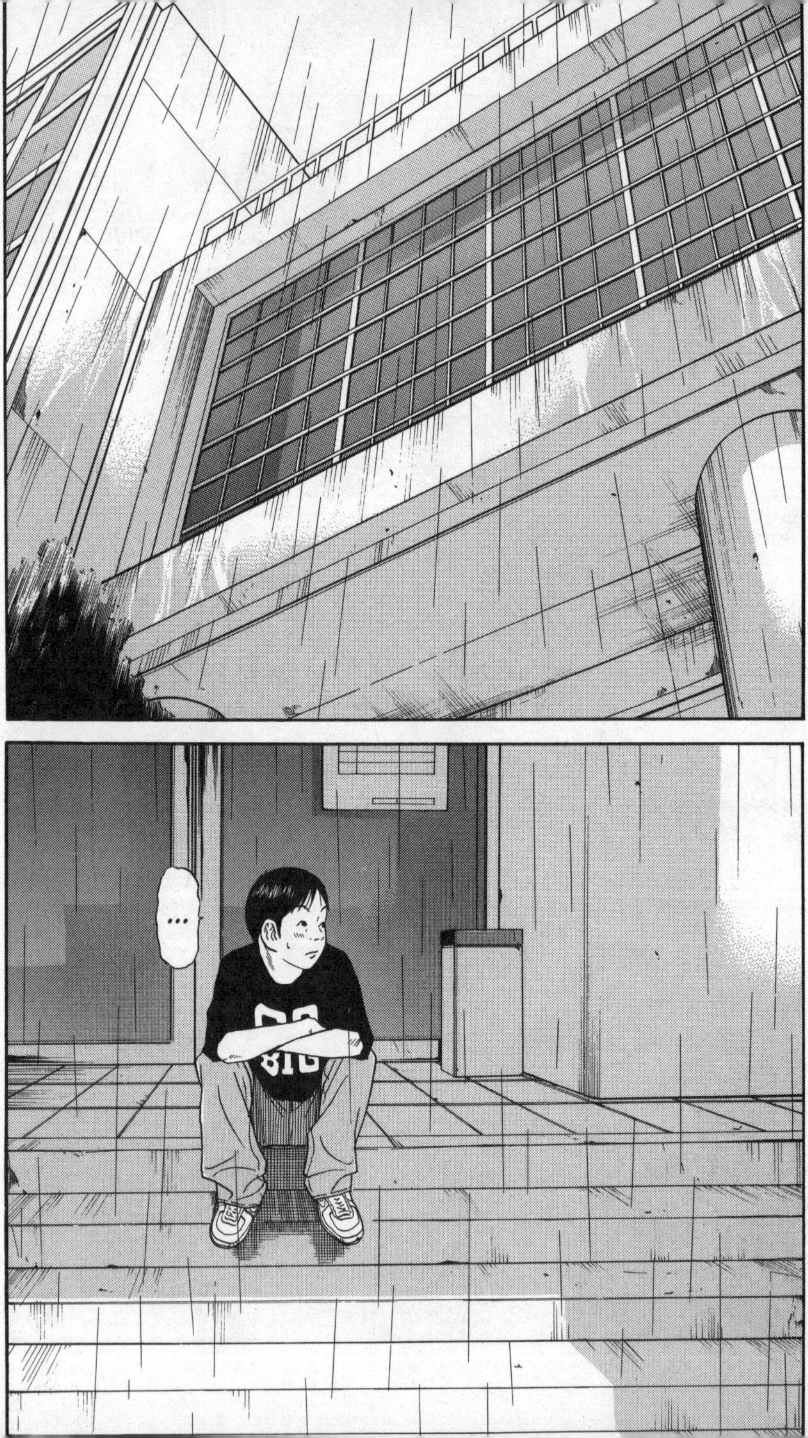
…

...Guess they're really going at it...
He... wouldn't break up with her in a place like this... Would he?
If he did, it'd kinda be my fault... More than kinda...
IS THAT ...?
...
GO BIG

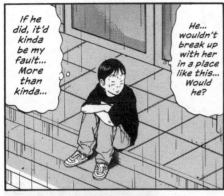

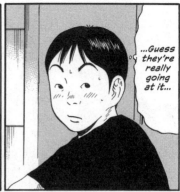

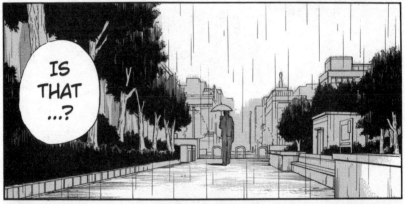

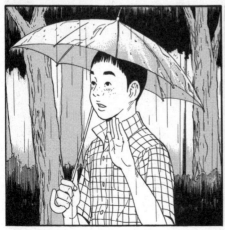

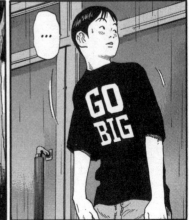

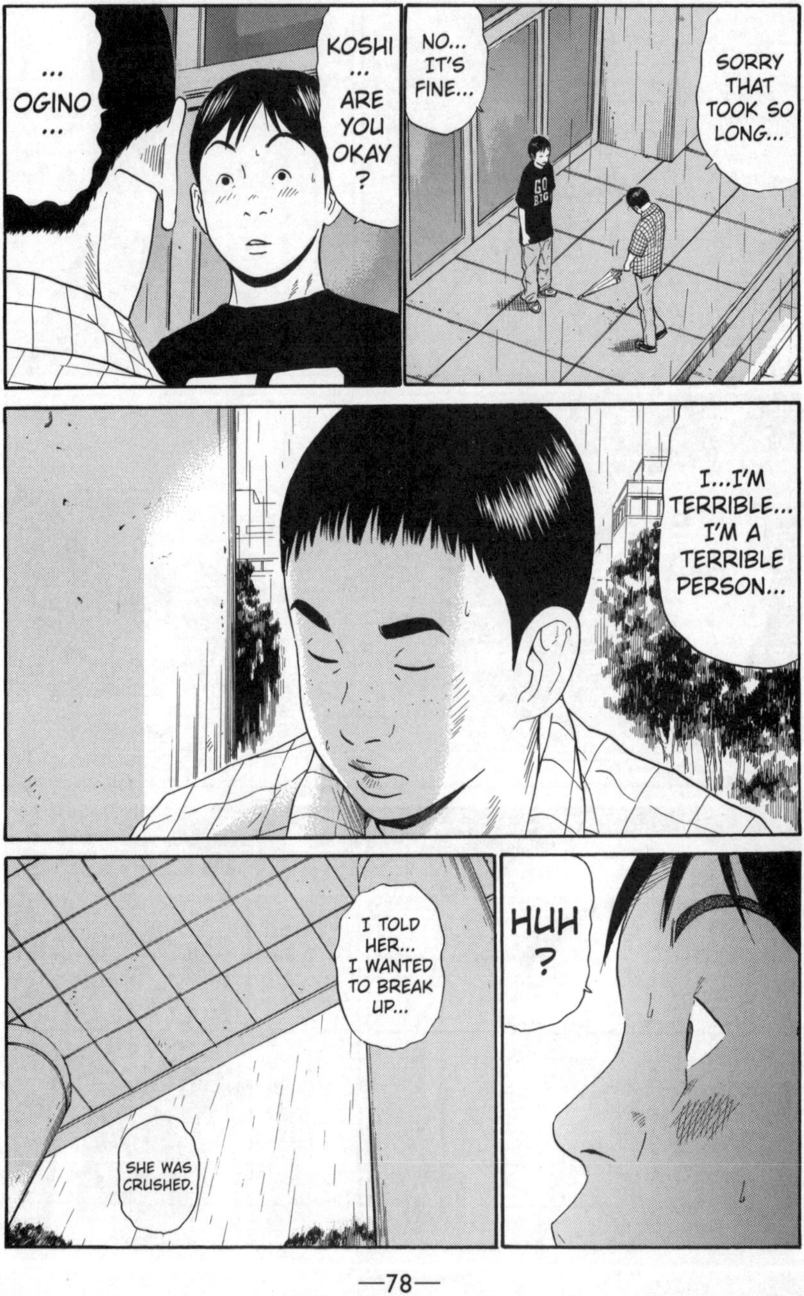
SORRY THAT TOOK SO LONG...
NO... IT'S FINE...
KOSHI... ARE YOU OKAY?
... OGINO ...
I...I'M TERRIBLE... I'M A TERRIBLE PERSON...
HUH?
I TOLD HER... I WANTED TO BREAK UP...
SHE WAS CRUSHED.

# Chapter 51: The Mission

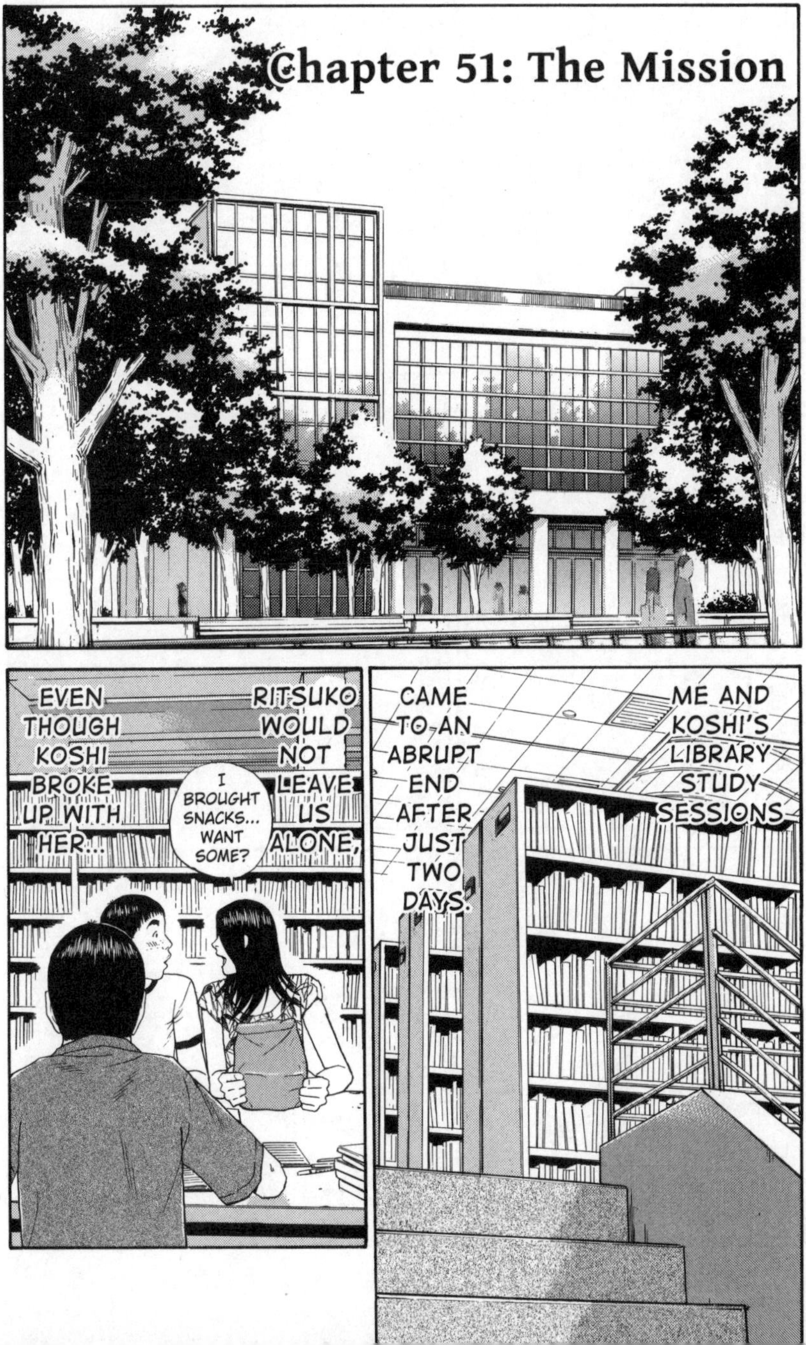
ME AND KOSHI'S LIBRARY STUDY SESSIONS
CAME TO AN ABRUPT END AFTER JUST TWO DAYS.
RITSUKO WOULD NOT LEAVE US ALONE,
I BROUGHT SNACKS... WANT SOME?
EVEN THOUGH KOSHI BROKE UP WITH HER...

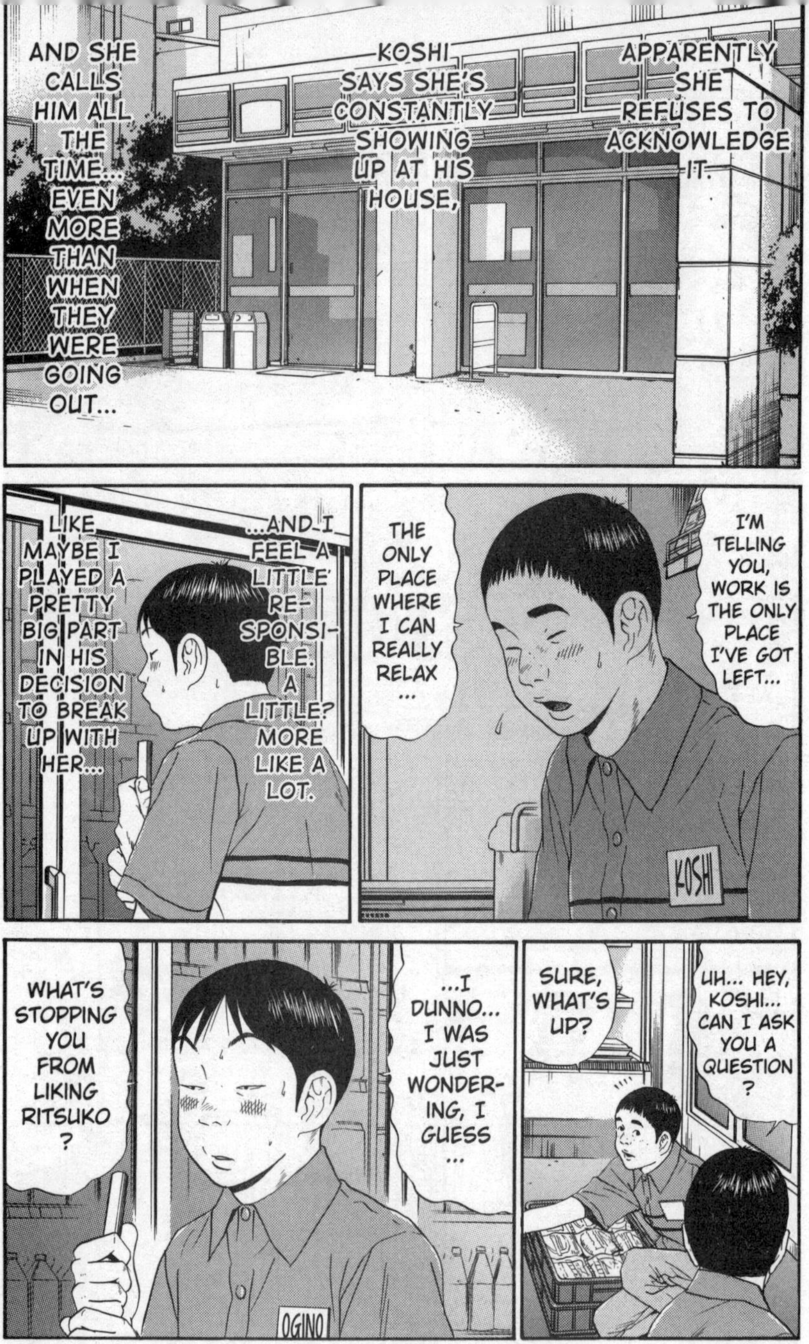
APPARENTLY SHE REFUSES TO ACKNOWLEDGE IT.
KOSHI SAYS SHE'S CONSTANTLY SHOWING UP AT HIS HOUSE,
AND SHE CALLS HIM ALL THE TIME... EVEN MORE THAN WHEN THEY WERE GOING OUT...
I'M TELLING YOU, WORK IS THE ONLY PLACE I'VE GOT LEFT...
THE ONLY PLACE WHERE I CAN REALLY RELAX ...
KOSHI
...AND I FEEL A LITTLE RE-SPONSIBLE. A LITTLE? MORE LIKE A LOT.
LIKE MAYBE I PLAYED A PRETTY BIG PART IN HIS DECISION TO BREAK UP WITH HER...
UH... HEY, KOSHI... CAN I ASK YOU A QUESTION ?
SURE, WHAT'S UP?
...I DUNNO... I WAS JUST WONDER-ING, I GUESS ...
WHAT'S STOPPING YOU FROM LIKING RITSUKO ?
OGINO

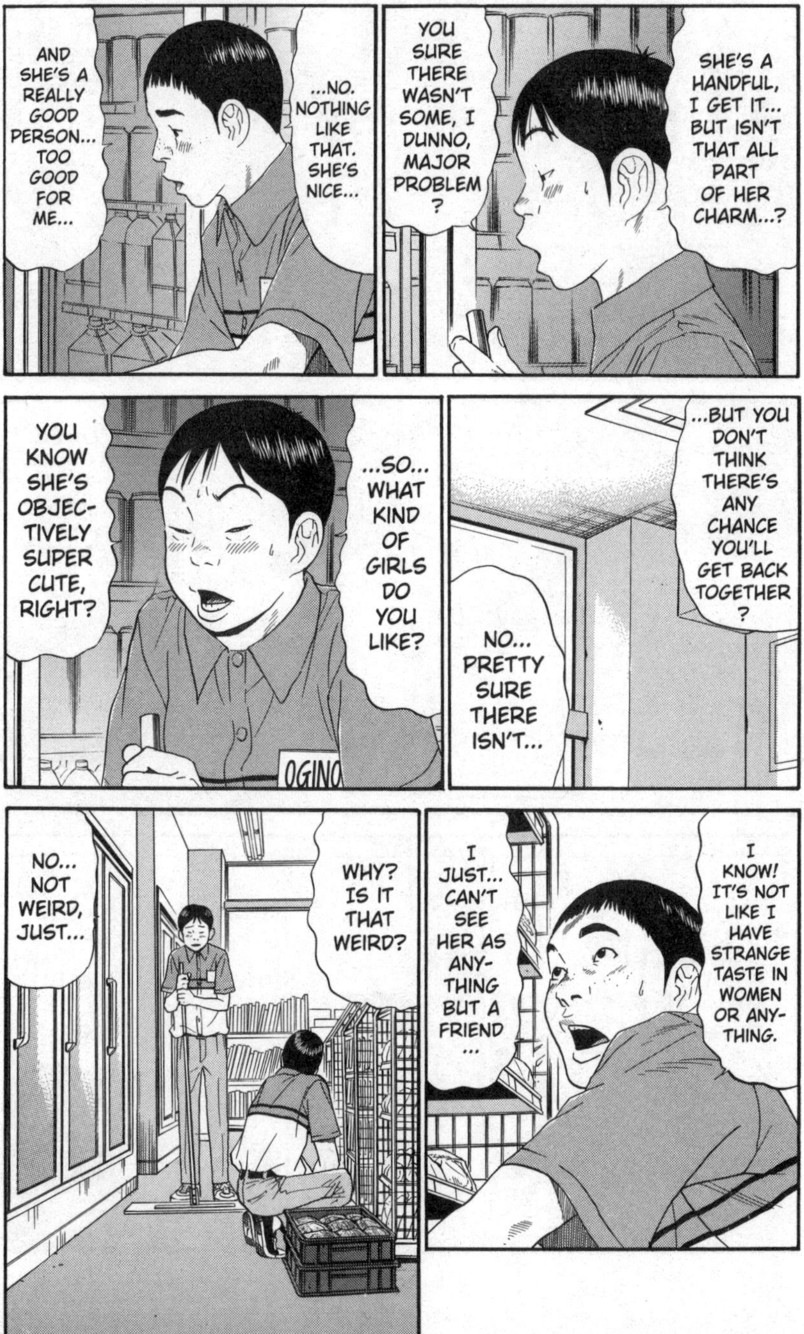
SHE'S A HANDFUL, I GET IT... BUT ISN'T THAT ALL PART OF HER CHARM...?
YOU SURE THERE WASN'T SOME, I DUNNO, MAJOR PROBLEM?
...NO. NOTHING LIKE THAT. SHE'S NICE...
AND SHE'S A REALLY GOOD PERSON... TOO GOOD FOR ME...
...BUT YOU DON'T THINK THERE'S ANY CHANCE YOU'LL GET BACK TOGETHER?
NO... PRETTY SURE THERE ISN'T...
...SO... WHAT KIND OF GIRLS DO YOU LIKE?
YOU KNOW SHE'S OBJECTIVELY SUPER CUTE, RIGHT?
OGINO
I KNOW! IT'S NOT LIKE I HAVE STRANGE TASTE IN WOMEN OR ANY-THING.
I JUST... CAN'T SEE HER AS ANY-THING BUT A FRIEND...
WHY? IS IT THAT WEIRD?
NO... NOT WEIRD, JUST...

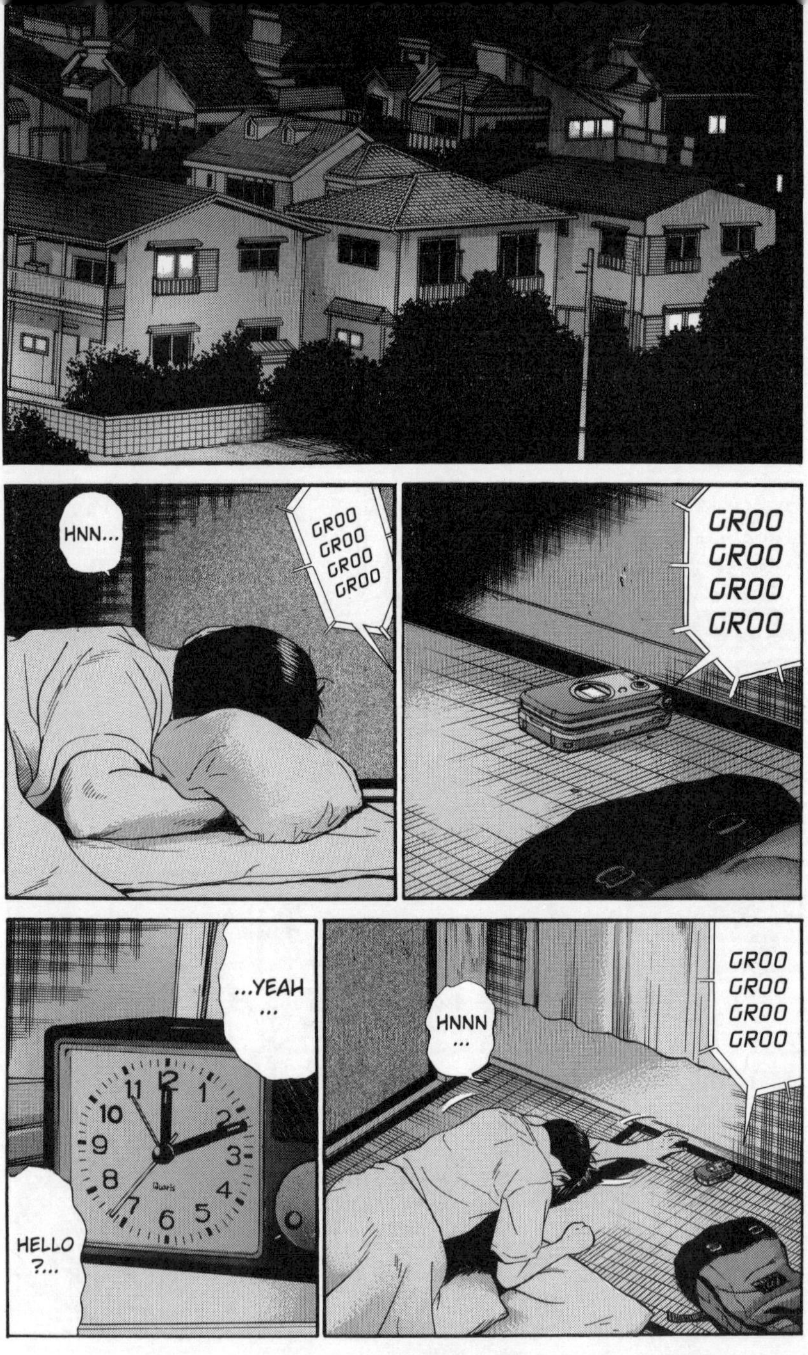
GROO
GROO
GROO
GROO
GROO
GROO
GROO
GROO
HNN...
GROO
GROO
GROO
GROO
HNNN
...
...YEAH
...
HELLO
?...

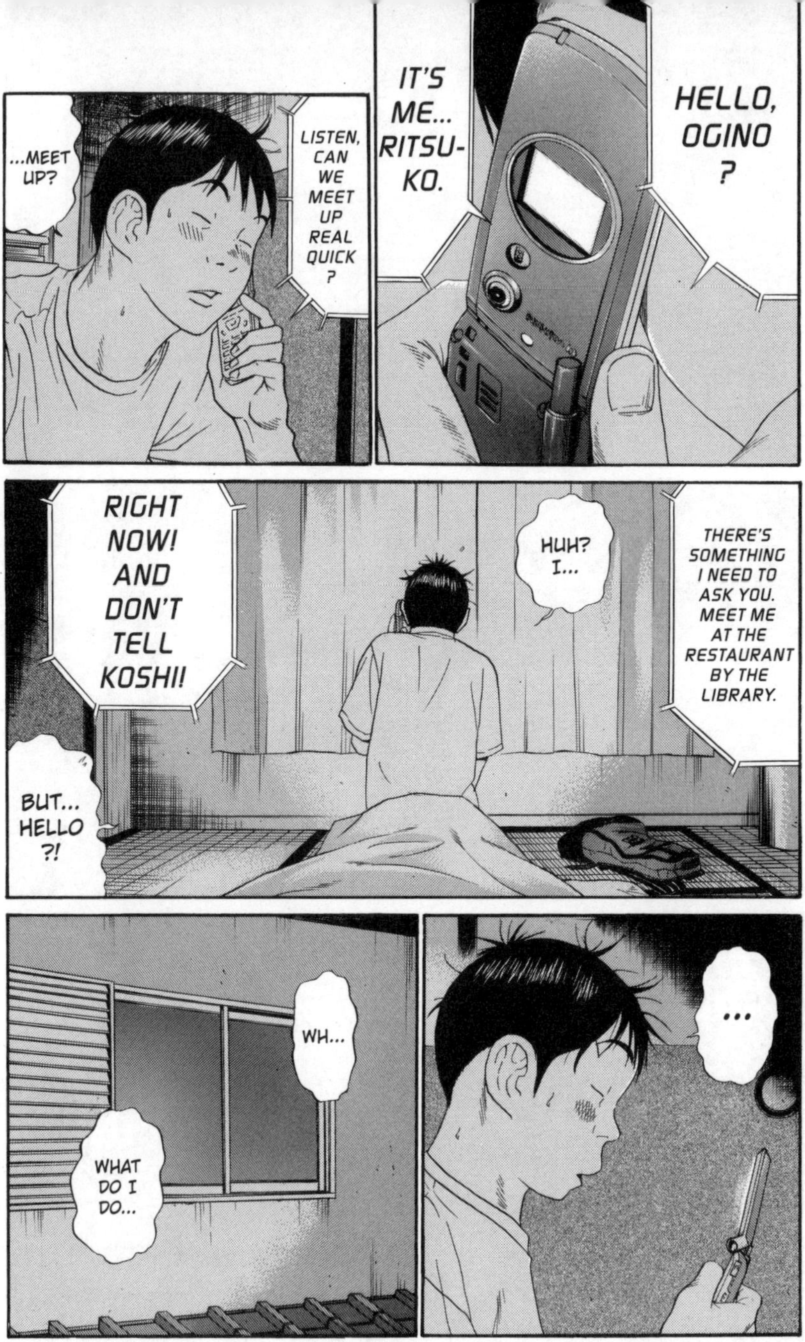
HELLO, OGINO ?
IT'S ME... RITSU-KO.
LISTEN, CAN WE MEET UP REAL QUICK ?
...MEET UP?
THERE'S SOMETHING I NEED TO ASK YOU. MEET ME AT THE RESTAURANT BY THE LIBRARY.
HUH? I...
RIGHT NOW! AND DON'T TELL KOSHI!
BUT... HELLO ?!
...
WH...
WHAT DO I DO...

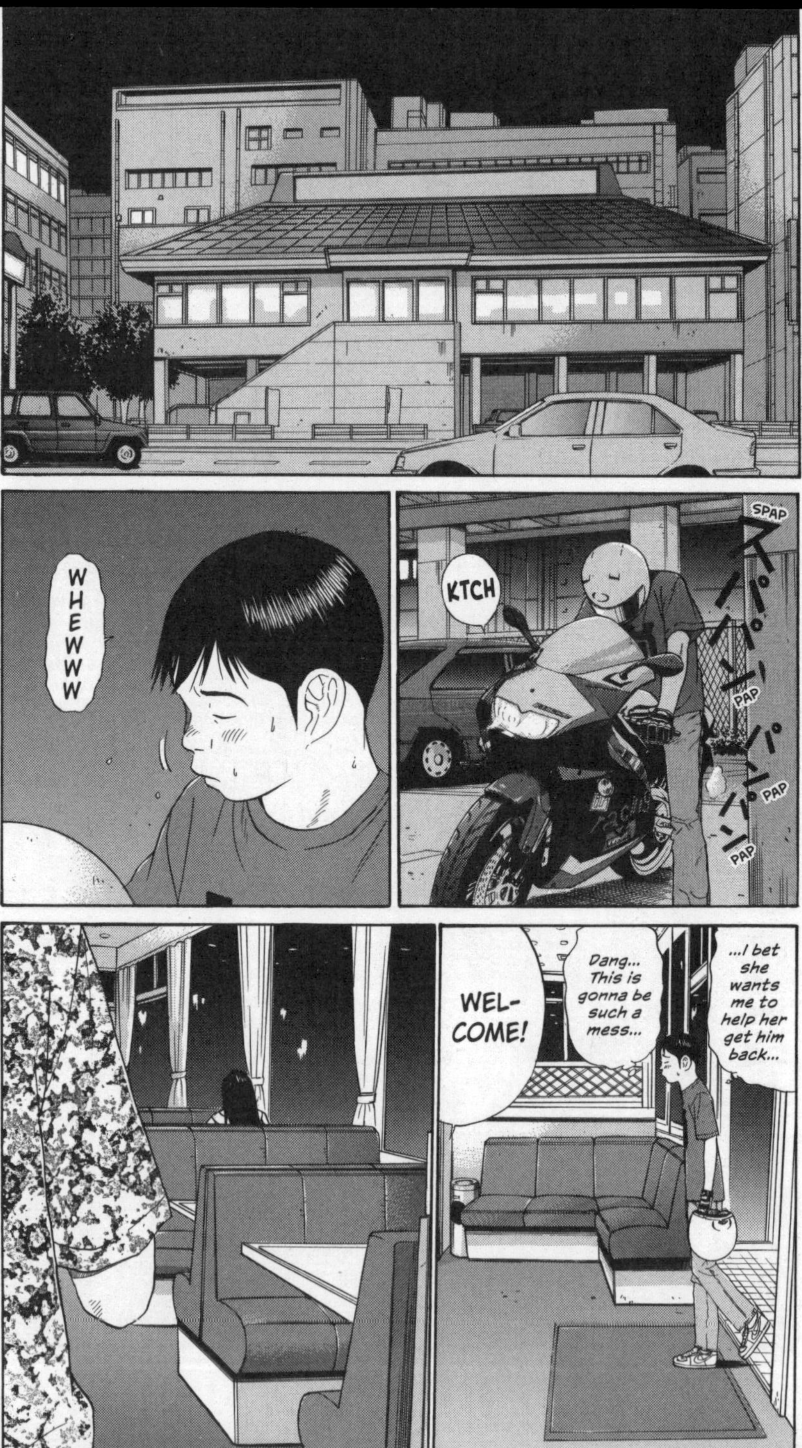
KTCH
SPAP
PAP
PAP
PAP
WHEWWWW
...I bet she wants me to help her get him back...
Dang... This is gonna be such a mess...
WEL-COME!

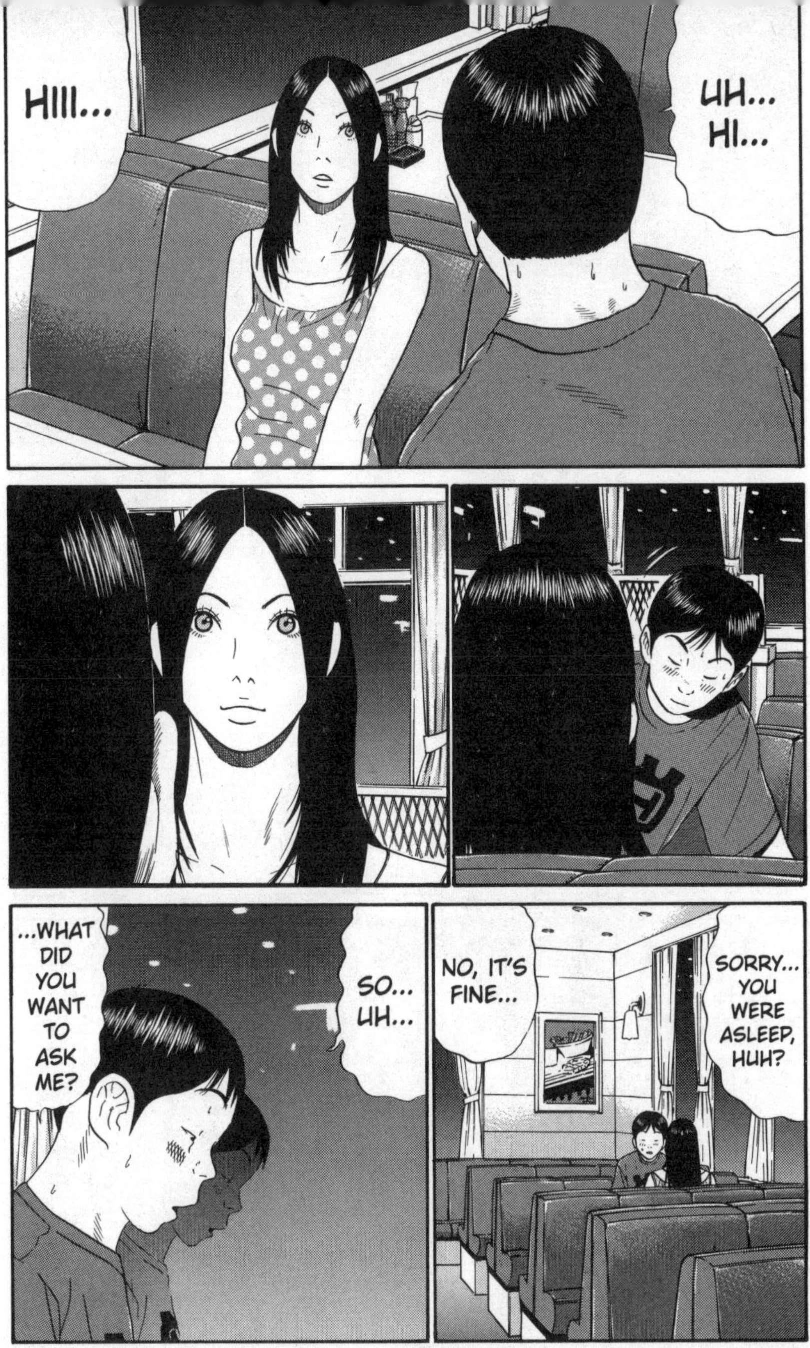
UH... HI...
HIII...
SORRY... YOU WERE ASLEEP, HUH?
NO, IT'S FINE...
SO... UH...
...WHAT DID YOU WANT TO ASK ME?

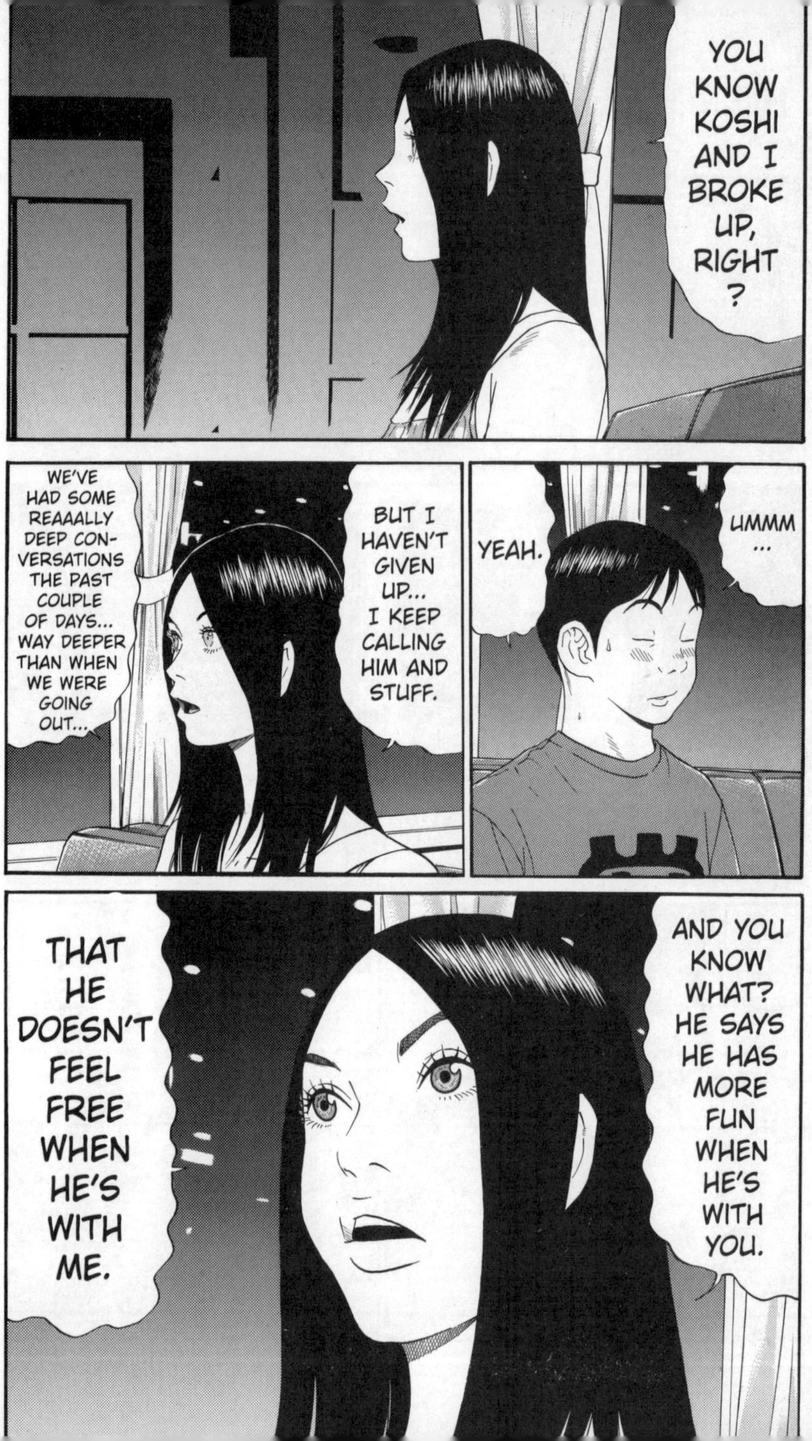
YOU KNOW KOSHI AND I BROKE UP, RIGHT?
UMMM...
YEAH.
BUT I HAVEN'T GIVEN UP... I KEEP CALLING HIM AND STUFF.
WE'VE HAD SOME REAAALLY DEEP CON-VERSATIONS THE PAST COUPLE OF DAYS... WAY DEEPER THAN WHEN WE WERE GOING OUT...
AND YOU KNOW WHAT? HE SAYS HE HAS MORE FUN WHEN HE'S WITH YOU.
THAT HE DOESN'T FEEL FREE WHEN HE'S WITH ME.

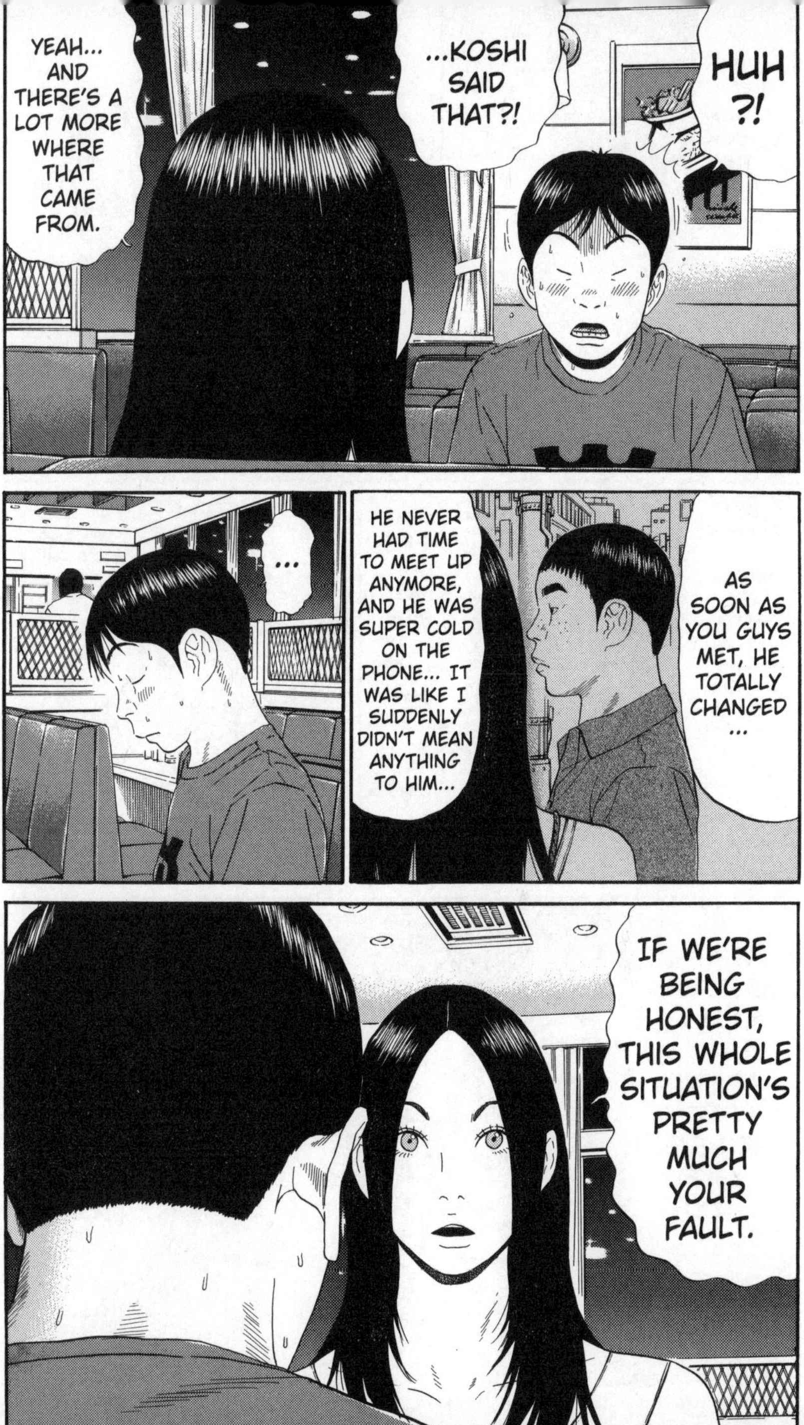
HUH ?!
...KOSHI SAID THAT?!
YEAH... AND THERE'S A LOT MORE WHERE THAT CAME FROM.
AS SOON AS YOU GUYS MET, HE TOTALLY CHANGED ...
HE NEVER HAD TIME TO MEET UP ANYMORE, AND HE WAS SUPER COLD ON THE PHONE... IT WAS LIKE I SUDDENLY DIDN'T MEAN ANYTHING TO HIM...
...
IF WE'RE BEING HONEST, THIS WHOLE SITUATION'S PRETTY MUCH YOUR FAULT.

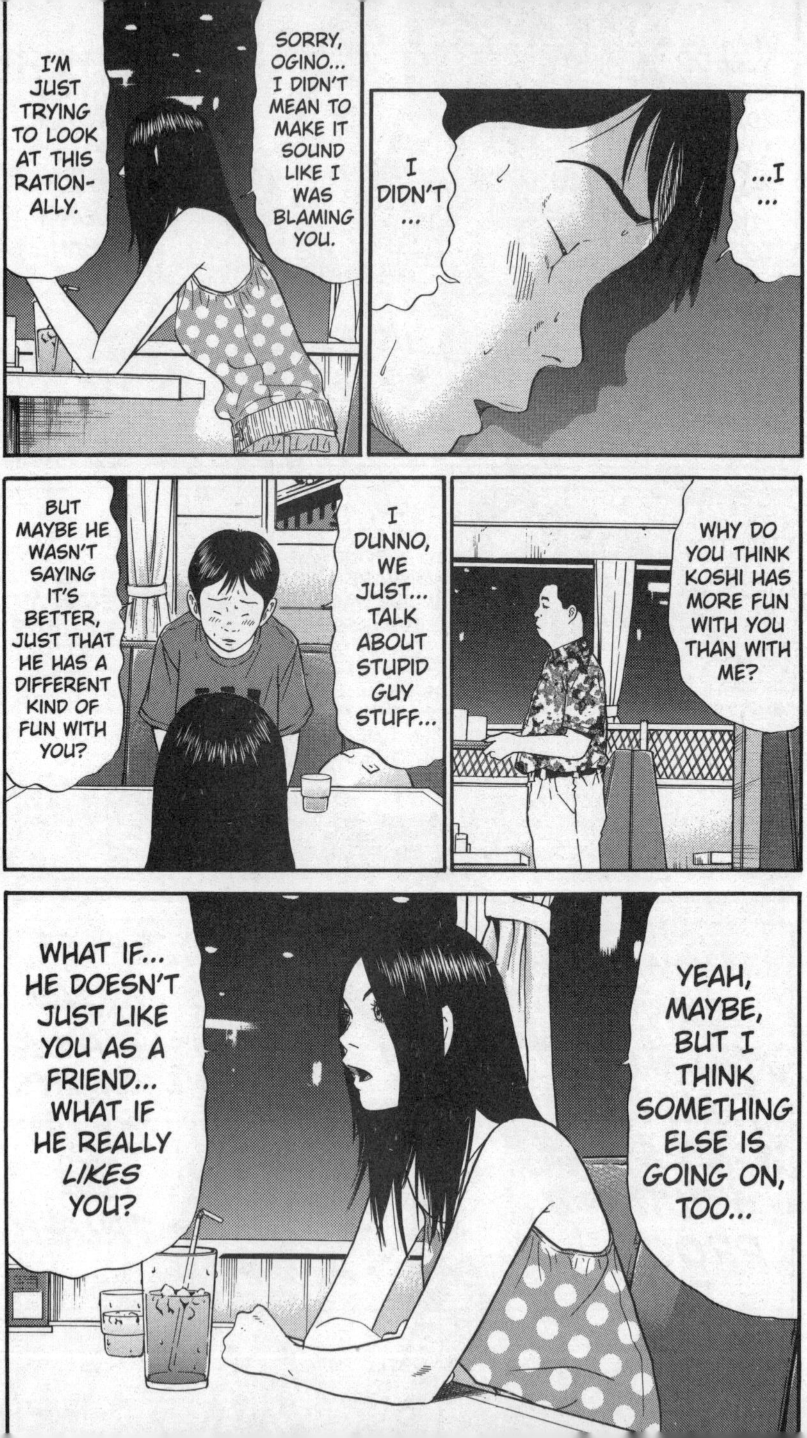
...I ...
I DIDN'T ...
SORRY, OGINO... I DIDN'T MEAN TO MAKE IT SOUND LIKE I WAS BLAMING YOU.
I'M JUST TRYING TO LOOK AT THIS RATION-ALLY.
WHY DO YOU THINK KOSHI HAS MORE FUN WITH YOU THAN WITH ME?
I DUNNO, WE JUST... TALK ABOUT STUPID GUY STUFF...
BUT MAYBE HE WASN'T SAYING IT'S BETTER, JUST THAT HE HAS A DIFFERENT KIND OF FUN WITH YOU?
YEAH, MAYBE, BUT I THINK SOMETHING ELSE IS GOING ON, TOO...
WHAT IF... HE DOESN'T JUST LIKE YOU AS A FRIEND... WHAT IF HE REALLY *LIKES* YOU?

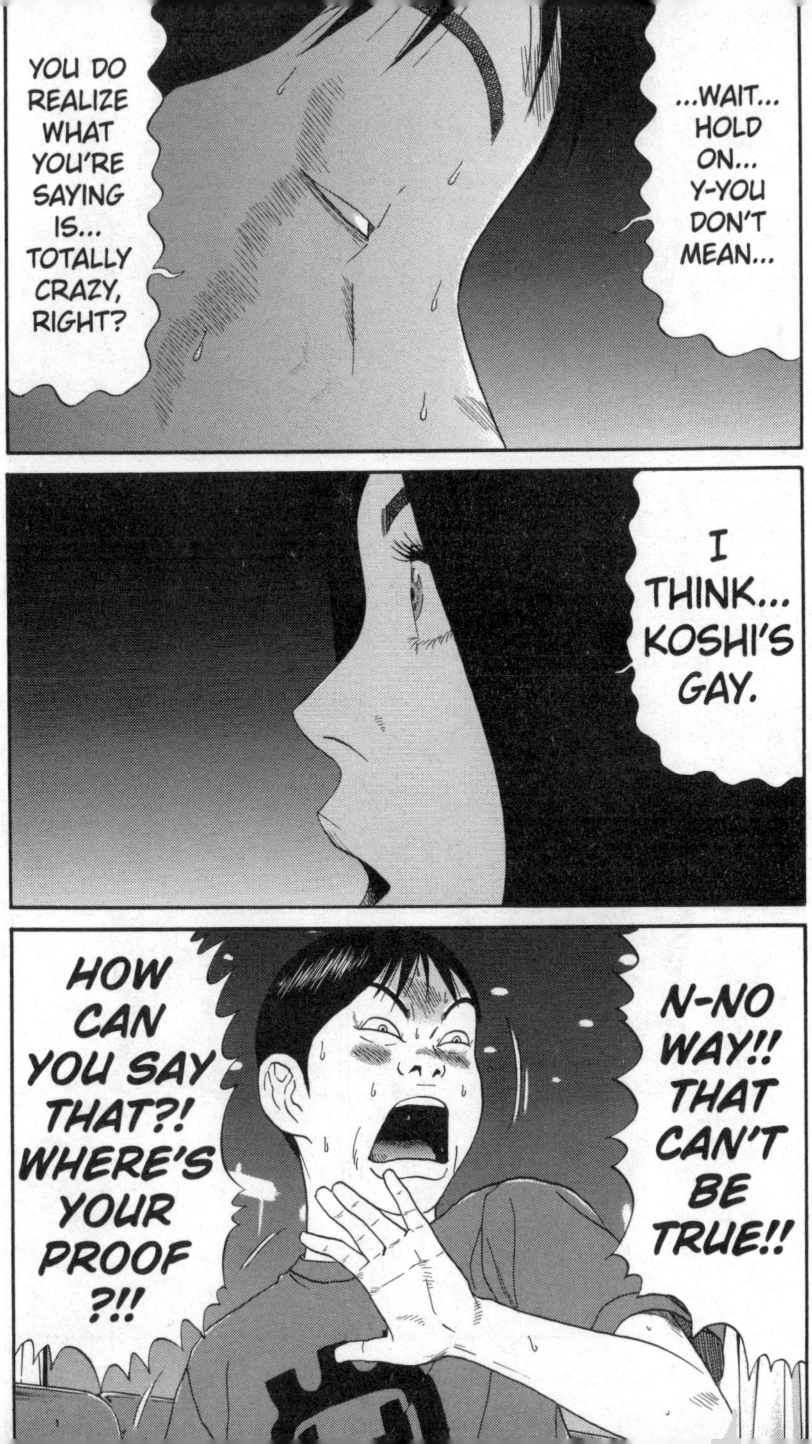
...WAIT... HOLD ON... Y-YOU DON'T MEAN...
YOU DO REALIZE WHAT YOU'RE SAYING IS... TOTALLY CRAZY, RIGHT?
I THINK... KOSHI'S GAY.
N-NO WAY!! THAT CAN'T BE TRUE!!
HOW CAN YOU SAY THAT?! WHERE'S YOUR PROOF?!!

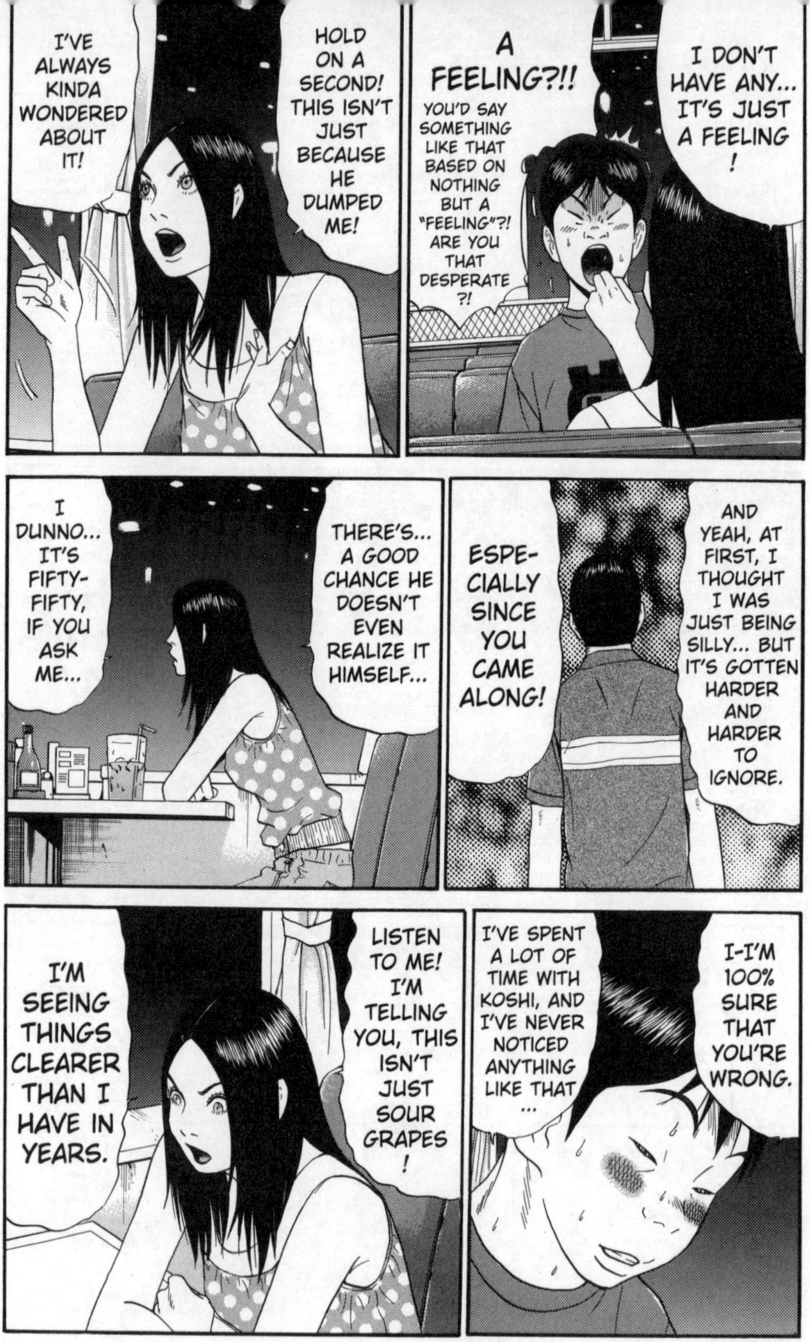
I DON'T HAVE ANY... IT'S JUST A FEELING!
A FEELING?!!
YOU'D SAY SOMETHING LIKE THAT BASED ON NOTHING BUT A "FEELING"?! ARE YOU THAT DESPERATE?!
HOLD ON A SECOND! THIS ISN'T JUST BECAUSE HE DUMPED ME!
I'VE ALWAYS KINDA WONDERED ABOUT IT!
AND YEAH, AT FIRST, I THOUGHT I WAS JUST BEING SILLY... BUT IT'S GOTTEN HARDER AND HARDER TO IGNORE.
ESPECIALLY SINCE YOU CAME ALONG!
THERE'S... A GOOD CHANCE HE DOESN'T EVEN REALIZE IT HIMSELF...
I DUNNO... IT'S FIFTY-FIFTY, IF YOU ASK ME...
I-I'M 100% SURE THAT YOU'RE WRONG.
I'VE SPENT A LOT OF TIME WITH KOSHI, AND I'VE NEVER NOTICED ANYTHING LIKE THAT...
LISTEN TO ME! I'M TELLING YOU, THIS ISN'T JUST SOUR GRAPES!
I'M SEEING THINGS CLEARER THAN I HAVE IN YEARS.

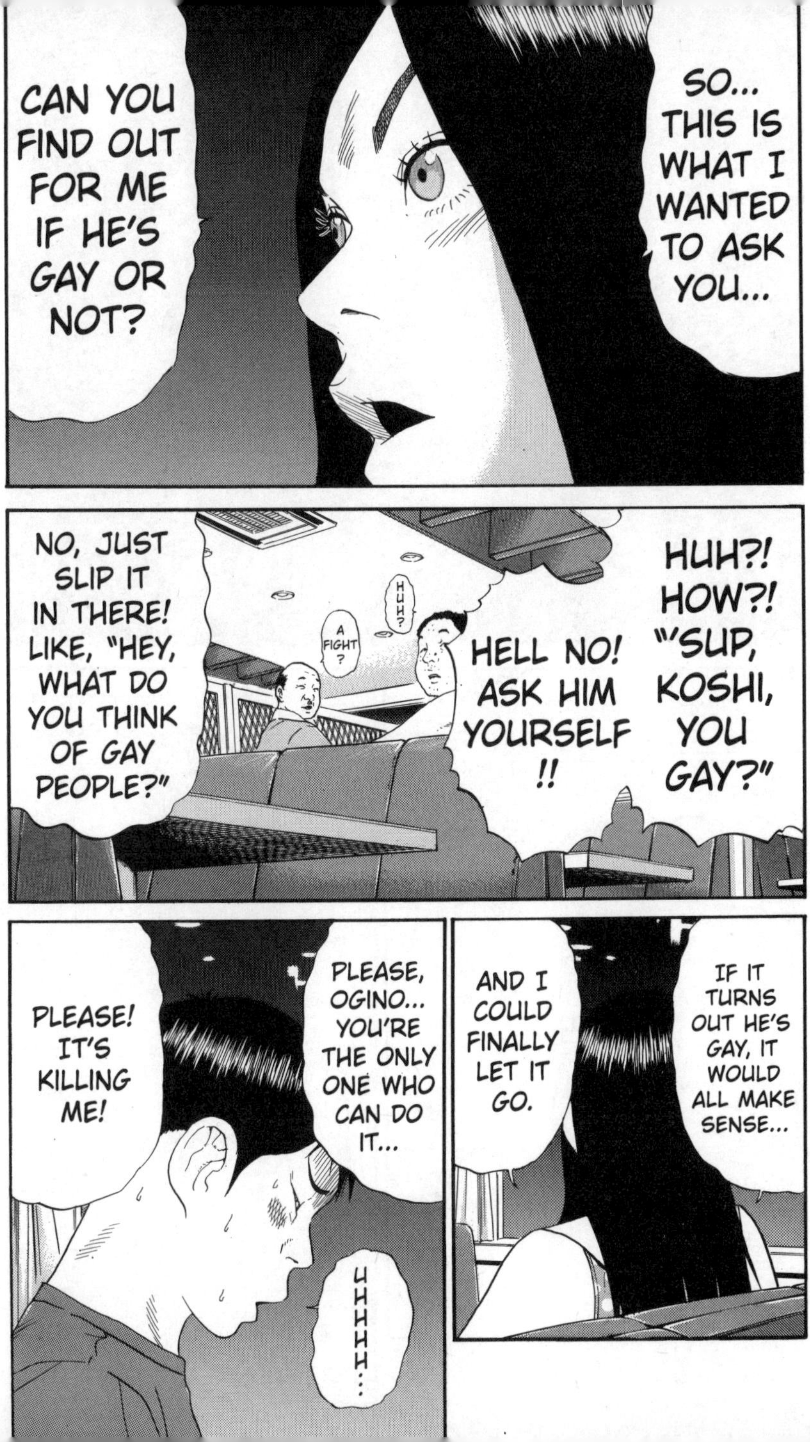
SO... THIS IS WHAT I WANTED TO ASK YOU...
CAN YOU FIND OUT FOR ME IF HE'S GAY OR NOT?
HUH?! HOW?! "SUP, KOSHI, YOU GAY?"
HELL NO! ASK HIM YOURSELF !!
HUH?
A FIGHT?
NO, JUST SLIP IT IN THERE! LIKE, "HEY, WHAT DO YOU THINK OF GAY PEOPLE?"
IF IT TURNS OUT HE'S GAY, IT WOULD ALL MAKE SENSE...
AND I COULD FINALLY LET IT GO.
PLEASE, OGINO... YOU'RE THE ONLY ONE WHO CAN DO IT...
PLEASE! IT'S KILLING ME!
UHHHH...

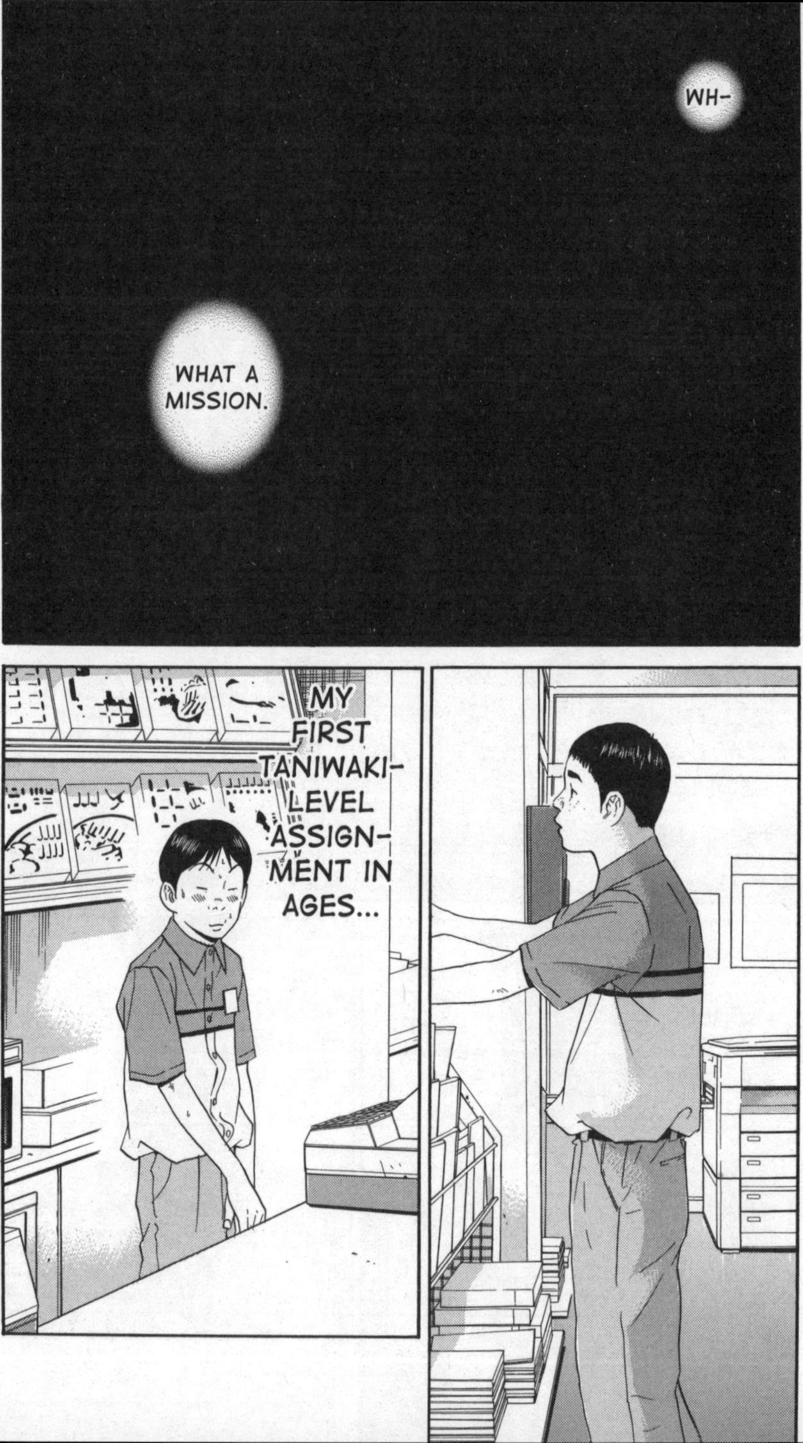
WH-
WHAT A MISSION.
MY FIRST TANIWAKI-LEVEL ASSIGNMENT IN AGES...

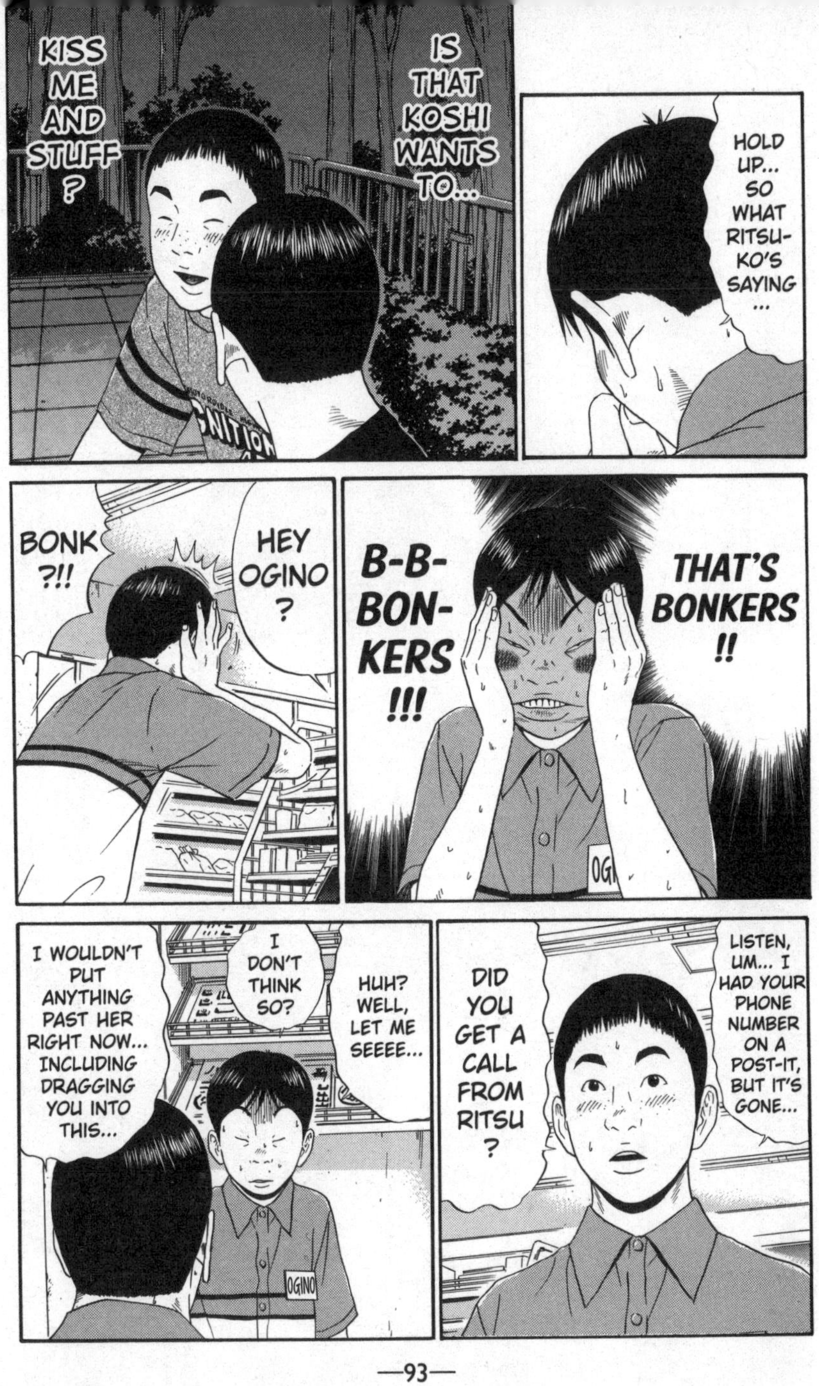
HOLD UP... SO WHAT RITSU-KO'S SAYING...
IS THAT KOSHI WANTS TO...
KISS ME AND STUFF?
THAT'S BONKERS!!
B-B-BON-KERS!!!
HEY OGINO?
BONK?!!
LISTEN, UM... I HAD YOUR PHONE NUMBER ON A POST-IT, BUT IT'S GONE...
DID YOU GET A CALL FROM RITSU?
HUH? WELL, LET ME SEEEE...
I DON'T THINK SO?
I WOULDN'T PUT ANYTHING PAST HER RIGHT NOW... INCLUDING DRAGGING YOU INTO THIS...

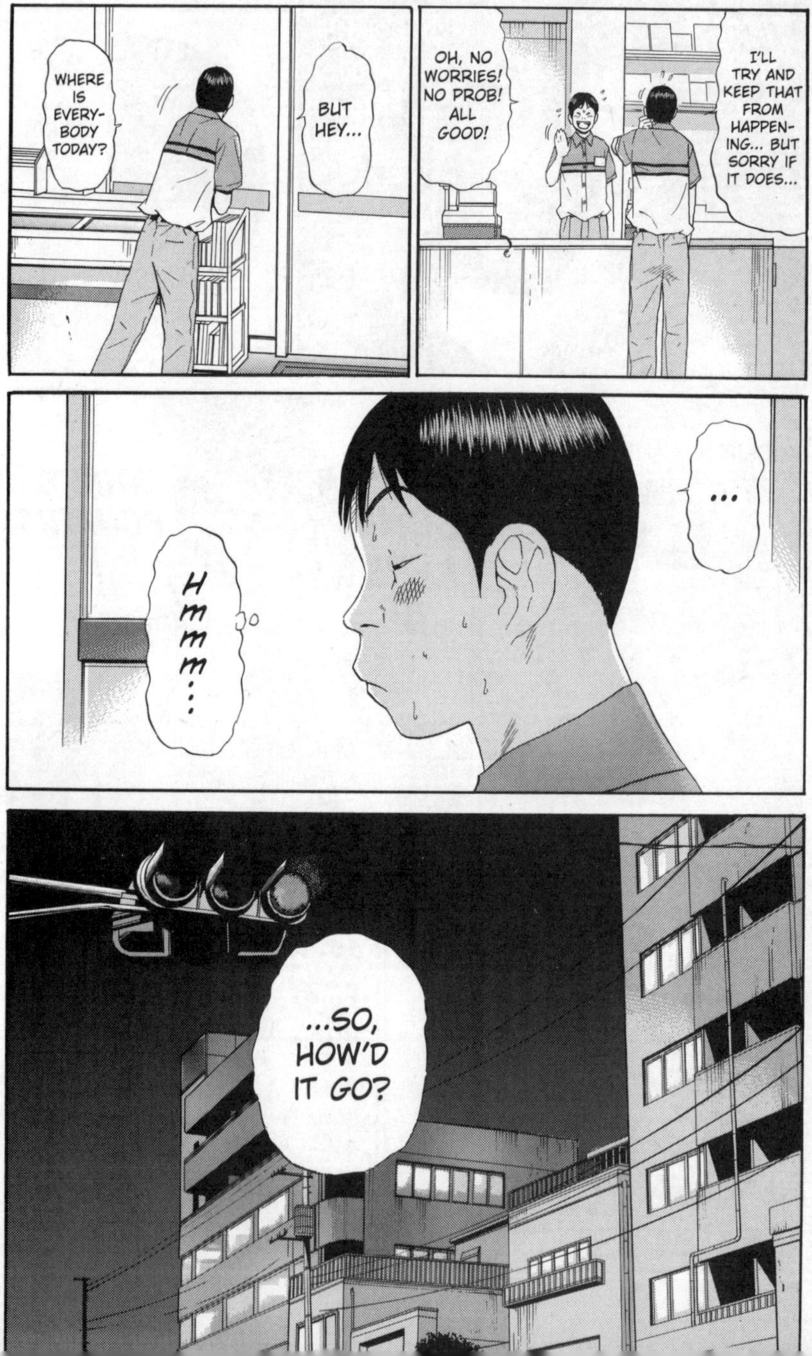
I'LL TRY AND KEEP THAT FROM HAPPEN-ING... BUT SORRY IF IT DOES...
OH, NO WORRIES! NO PROB! ALL GOOD!
BUT HEY...
WHERE IS EVERY-BODY TODAY?
...
Hmmm...
...SO, HOW'D IT GO?

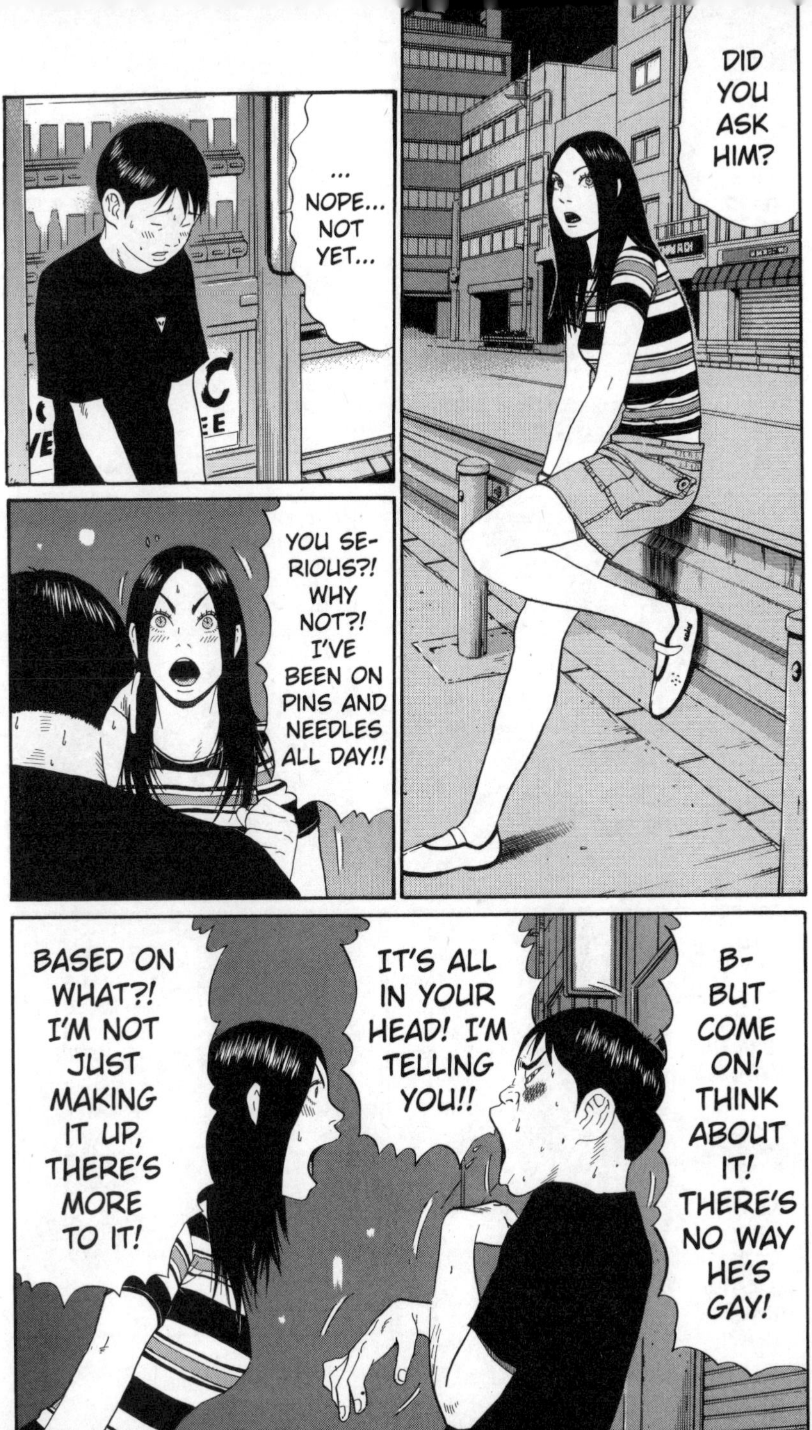
DID YOU ASK HIM?
... NOPE... NOT YET...
YOU SERIOUS?! WHY NOT?! I'VE BEEN ON PINS AND NEEDLES ALL DAY!!
B- BUT COME ON! THINK ABOUT IT! THERE'S NO WAY HE'S GAY!
IT'S ALL IN YOUR HEAD! I'M TELLING YOU!!
BASED ON WHAT?! I'M NOT JUST MAKING IT UP, THERE'S MORE TO IT!

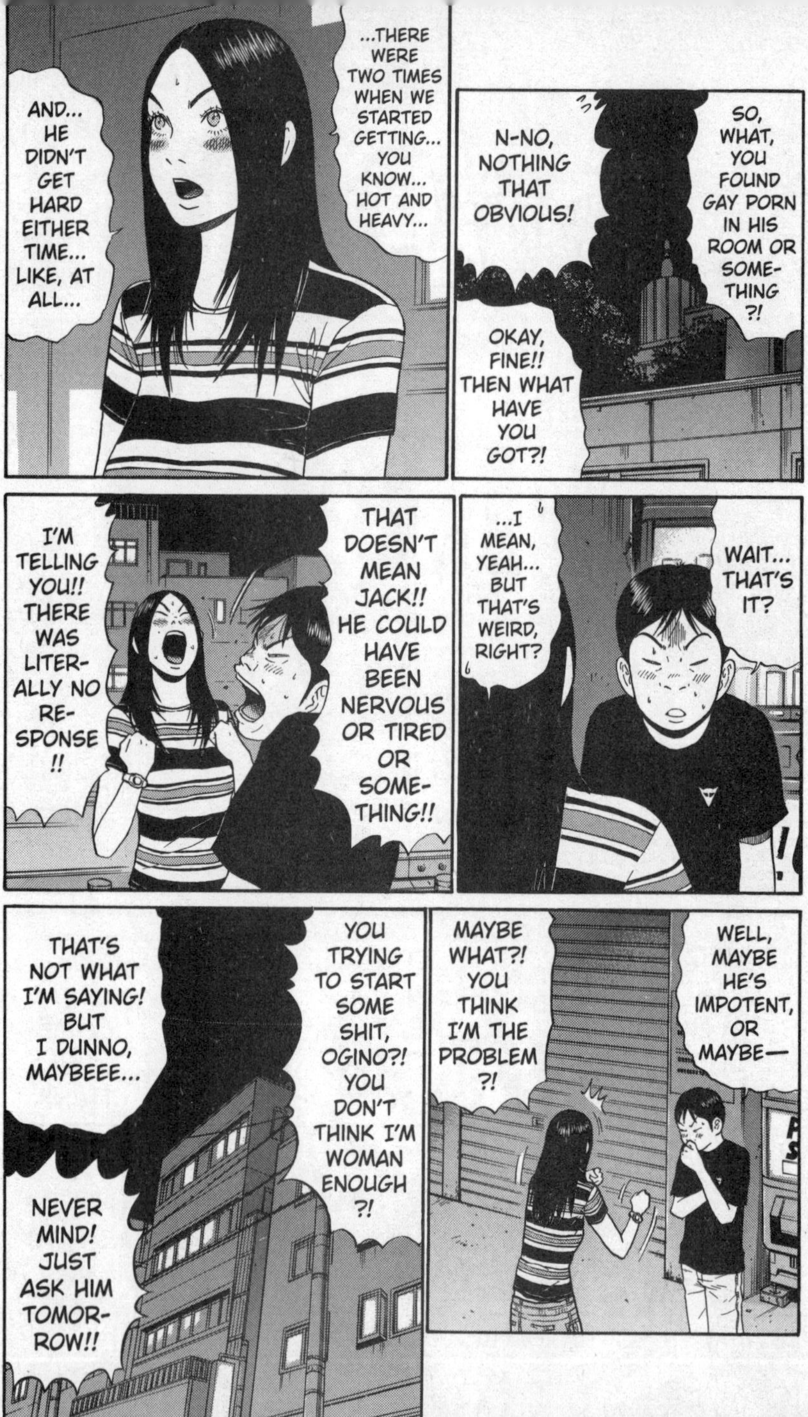
SO, WHAT, YOU FOUND GAY PORN IN HIS ROOM OR SOMETHING?!
N-NO, NOTHING THAT OBVIOUS!
OKAY, FINE!! THEN WHAT HAVE YOU GOT?!
...THERE WERE TWO TIMES WHEN WE STARTED GETTING... YOU KNOW... HOT AND HEAVY...
AND... HE DIDN'T GET HARD EITHER TIME... LIKE, AT ALL...
WAIT... THAT'S IT?
...I MEAN, YEAH... BUT THAT'S WEIRD, RIGHT?
THAT DOESN'T MEAN JACK!! HE COULD HAVE BEEN NERVOUS OR TIRED OR SOME-THING!!
I'M TELLING YOU!! THERE WAS LITER-ALLY NO RE-SPONSE !!
WELL, MAYBE HE'S IMPOTENT, OR MAYBE—
MAYBE WHAT?! YOU THINK I'M THE PROBLEM ?!
YOU TRYING TO START SOME SHIT, OGINO?! YOU DON'T THINK I'M WOMAN ENOUGH ?!
THAT'S NOT WHAT I'M SAYING! BUT I DUNNO, MAYBEEE...
NEVER MIND! JUST ASK HIM TOMOR-ROW!!

CI

GUA

TE

RA

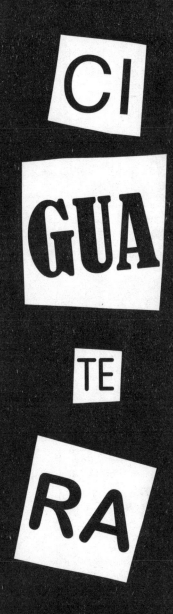

# Chapter 52: Double Agent

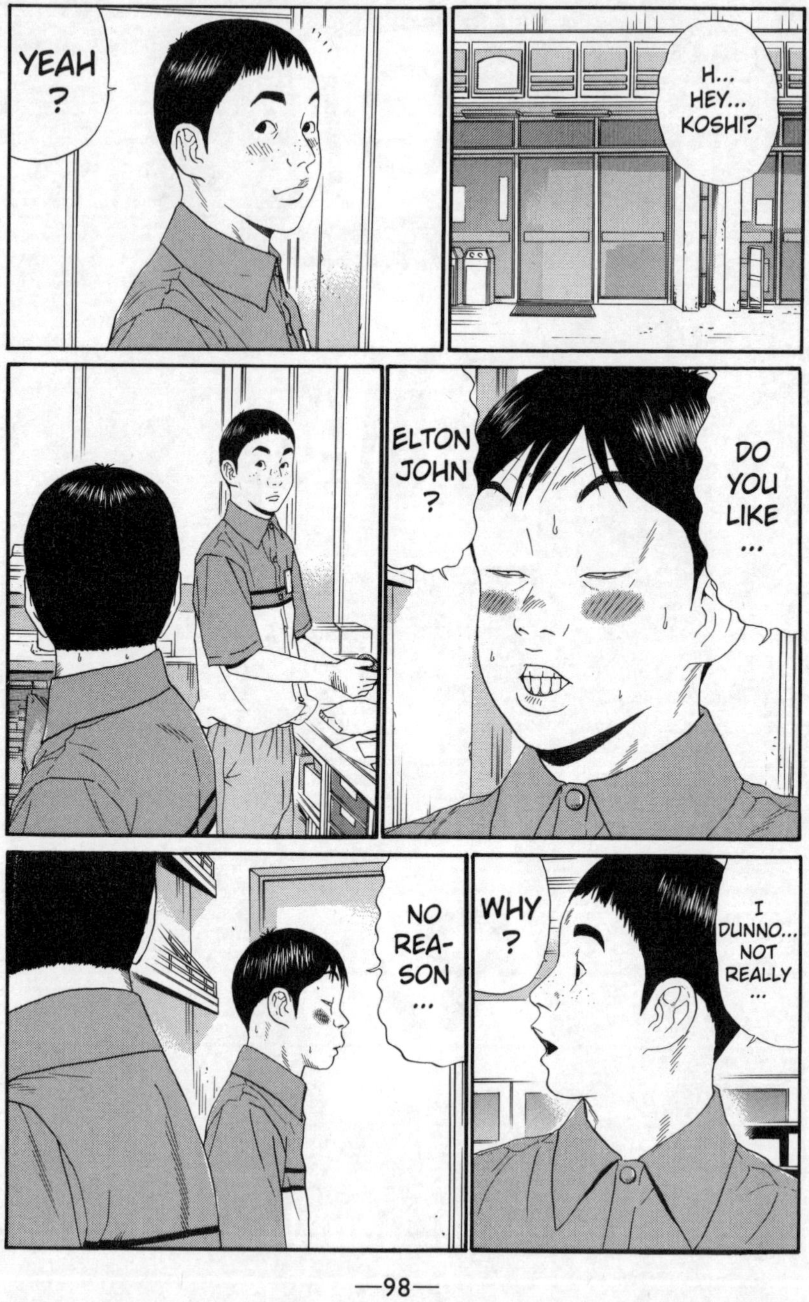
H... HEY... KOSHI?
YEAH ?
DO YOU LIKE ...
ELTON JOHN ?
I DUNNO... NOT REALLY ...
WHY ?
NO REA-SON ...

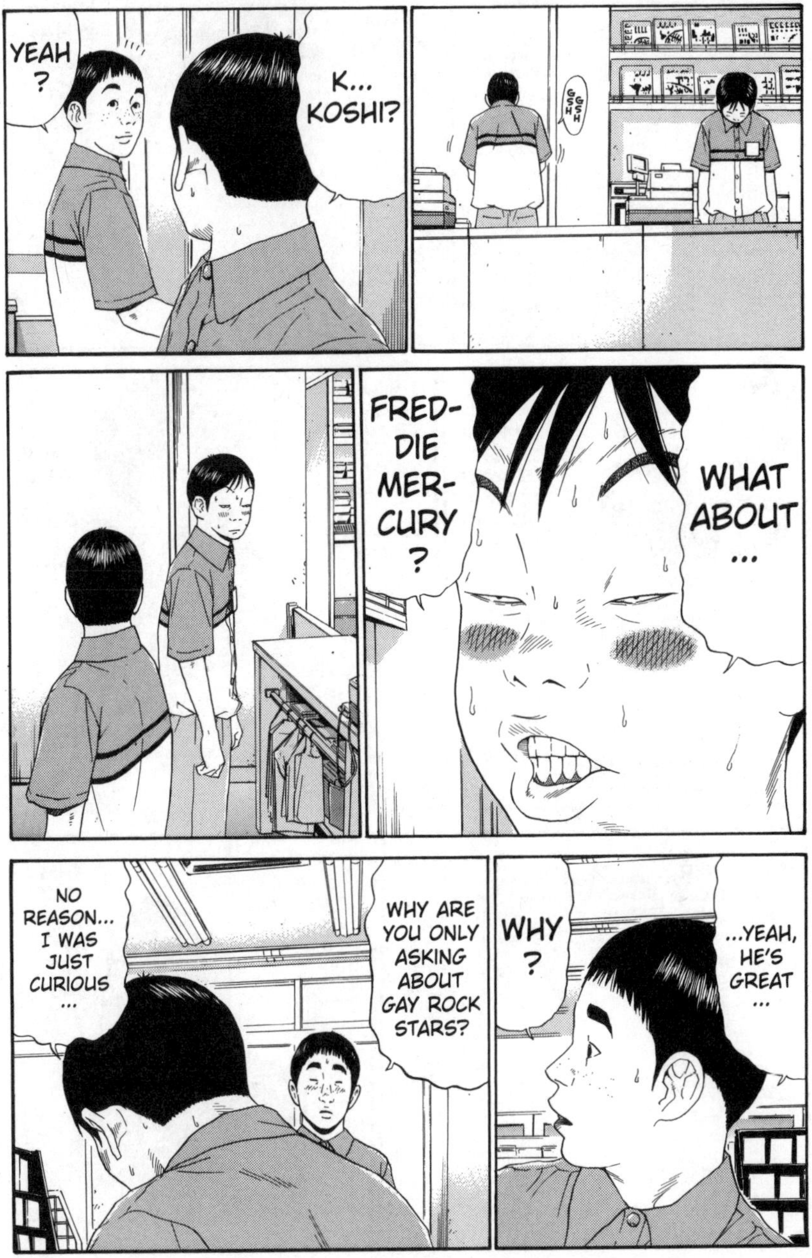
GSH GSH
K... KOSHI?
YEAH ?
WHAT ABOUT ...
FRED-DIE MER-CURY ?
...YEAH, HE'S GREAT ...
WHY ?
WHY ARE YOU ONLY ASKING ABOUT GAY ROCK STARS?
NO REASON... I WAS JUST CURIOUS ...

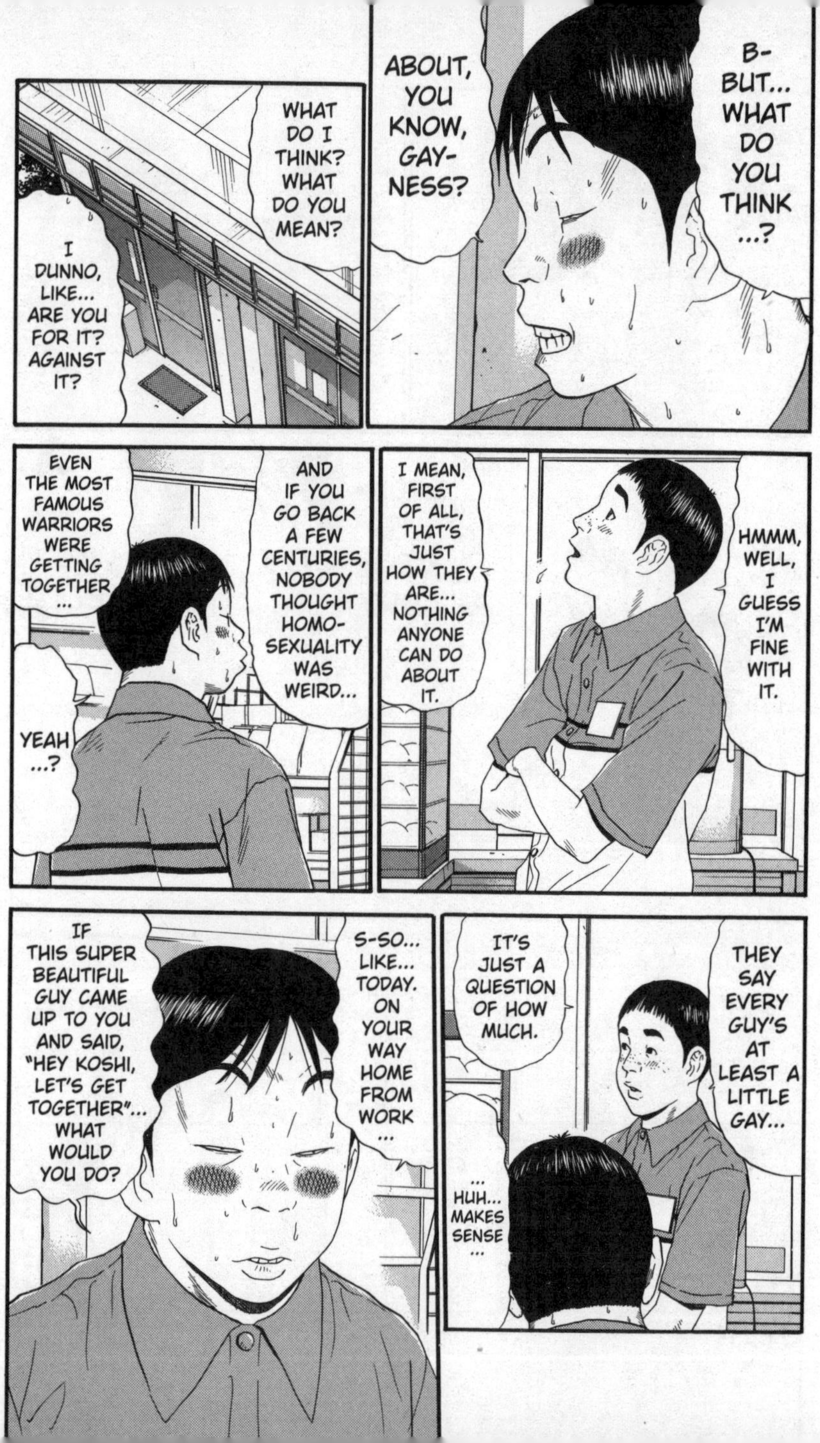
B-BUT... WHAT DO YOU THINK...?
ABOUT, YOU KNOW, GAY-NESS?
WHAT DO I THINK? WHAT DO YOU MEAN?
I DUNNO, LIKE... ARE YOU FOR IT? AGAINST IT?
HMMM, WELL, I GUESS I'M FINE WITH IT.
I MEAN, FIRST OF ALL, THAT'S JUST HOW THEY ARE... NOTHING ANYONE CAN DO ABOUT IT.
AND IF YOU GO BACK A FEW CENTURIES, NOBODY THOUGHT HOMO-SEXUALITY WAS WEIRD...
EVEN THE MOST FAMOUS WARRIORS WERE GETTING TOGETHER...
YEAH...?
THEY SAY EVERY GUY'S AT LEAST A LITTLE GAY...
IT'S JUST A QUESTION OF HOW MUCH.
...HUH... MAKES SENSE...
S-SO... LIKE... TODAY. ON YOUR WAY HOME FROM WORK...
IF THIS SUPER BEAUTIFUL GUY CAME UP TO YOU AND SAID, "HEY KOSHI, LET'S GET TOGETHER"... WHAT WOULD YOU DO?

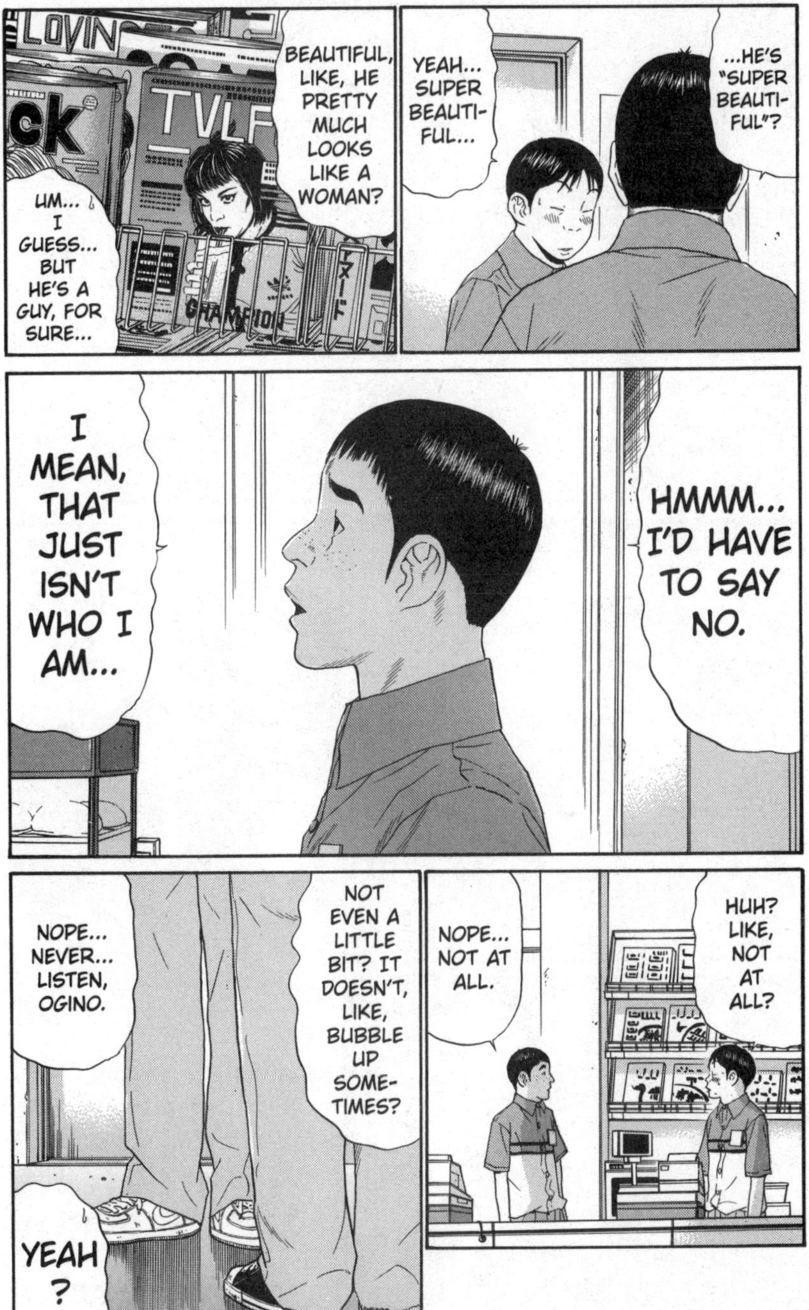
...HE'S "SUPER BEAUTIFUL"?
YEAH... SUPER BEAUTIFUL...
BEAUTIFUL, LIKE, HE PRETTY MUCH LOOKS LIKE A WOMAN?
UM... I GUESS... BUT HE'S A GUY, FOR SURE...
HMMM... I'D HAVE TO SAY NO.
I MEAN, THAT JUST ISN'T WHO I AM...
HUH? LIKE, NOT AT ALL?
NOPE... NOT AT ALL.
NOT EVEN A LITTLE BIT? IT DOESN'T, LIKE, BUBBLE UP SOMETIMES?
NOPE... NEVER... LISTEN, OGINO.
YEAH?

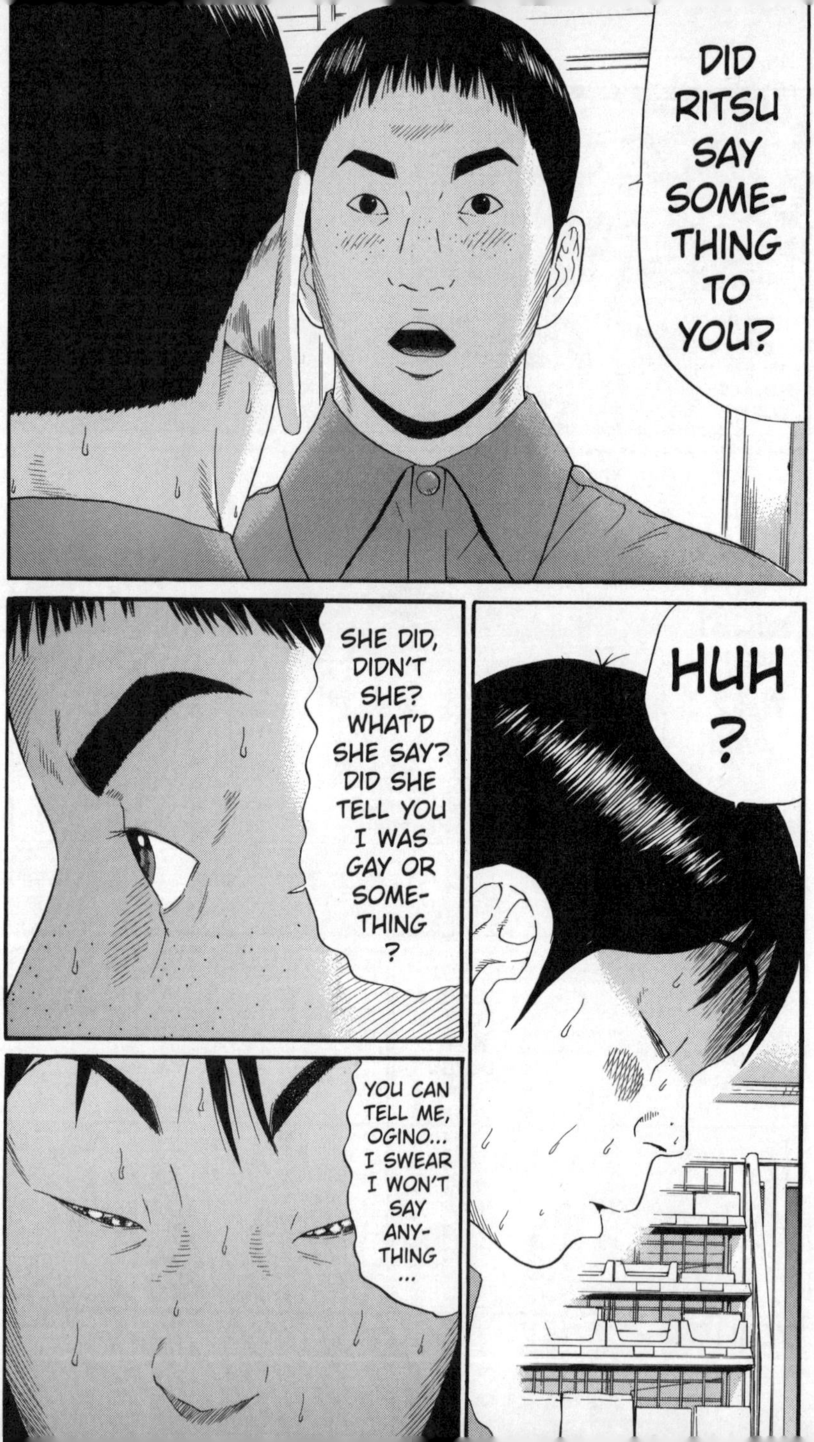
DID RITSU SAY SOME-THING TO YOU?
HUH ?
SHE DID, DIDN'T SHE? WHAT'D SHE SAY? DID SHE TELL YOU I WAS GAY OR SOME-THING ?
YOU CAN TELL ME, OGINO... I SWEAR I WON'T SAY ANY-THING ...

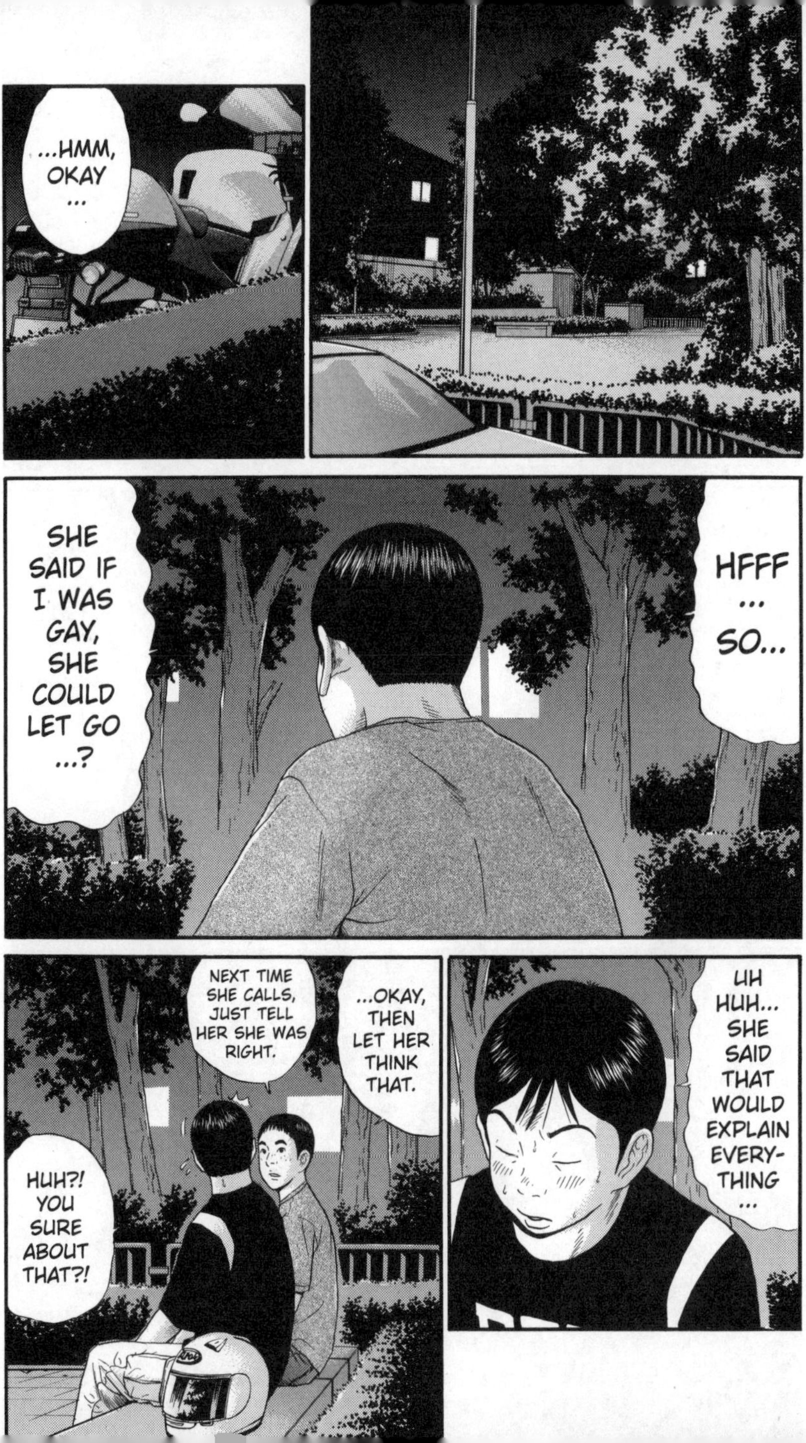
...HMM, OKAY ...
HFFF ... SO...
SHE SAID IF I WAS GAY, SHE COULD LET GO ...?
UH HUH... SHE SAID THAT WOULD EXPLAIN EVERY-THING ...
...OKAY, THEN LET HER THINK THAT.
NEXT TIME SHE CALLS, JUST TELL HER SHE WAS RIGHT.
HUH?! YOU SURE ABOUT THAT?!

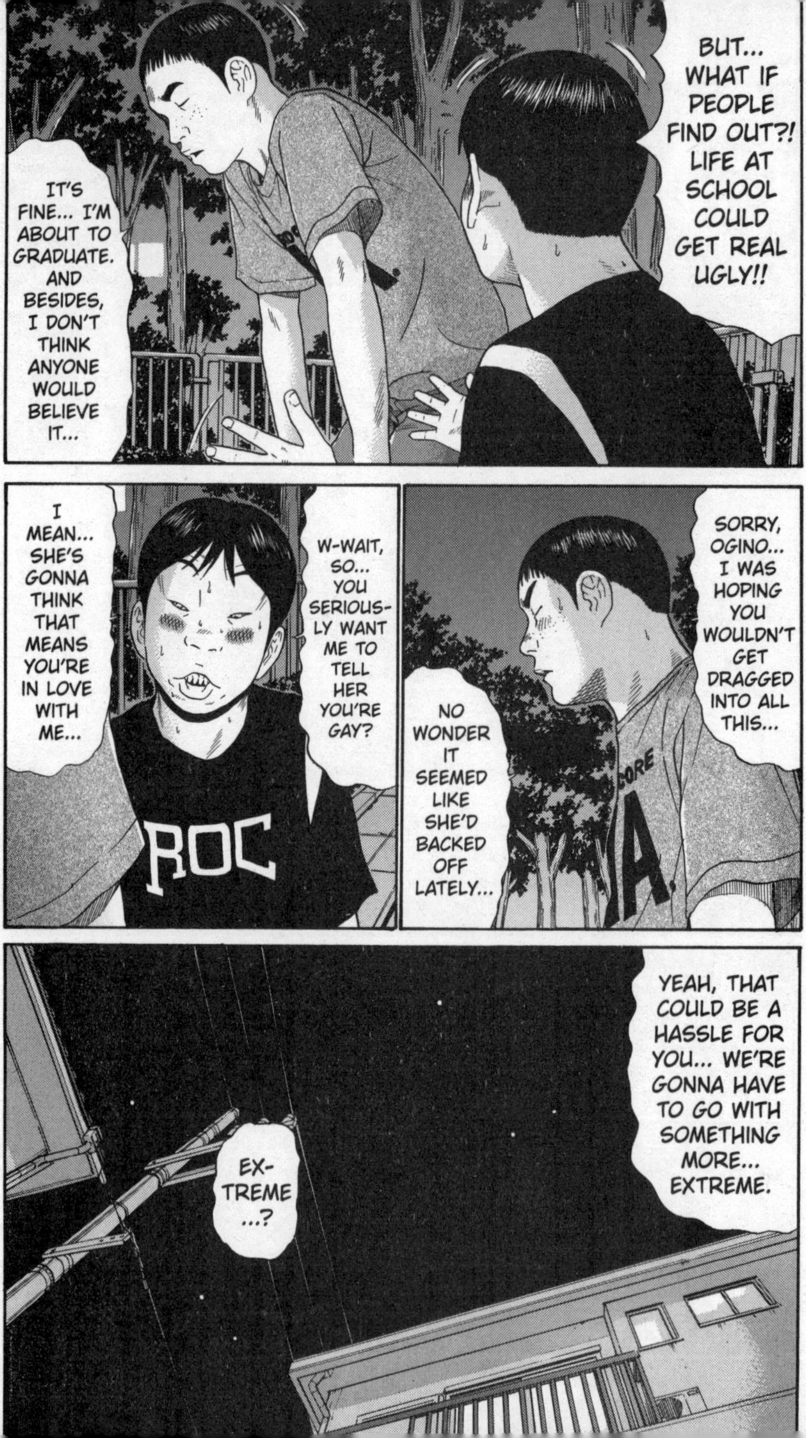
BUT... WHAT IF PEOPLE FIND OUT?! LIFE AT SCHOOL COULD GET REAL UGLY!!
IT'S FINE... I'M ABOUT TO GRADUATE. AND BESIDES, I DON'T THINK ANYONE WOULD BELIEVE IT...
SORRY, OGINO... I WAS HOPING YOU WOULDN'T GET DRAGGED INTO ALL THIS...
NO WONDER IT SEEMED LIKE SHE'D BACKED OFF LATELY...
W-WAIT, SO... YOU SERIOUSLY WANT ME TO TELL HER YOU'RE GAY?
I MEAN... SHE'S GONNA THINK THAT MEANS YOU'RE IN LOVE WITH ME...
YEAH, THAT COULD BE A HASSLE FOR YOU... WE'RE GONNA HAVE TO GO WITH SOMETHING MORE... EXTREME.
EX-TREME ...?

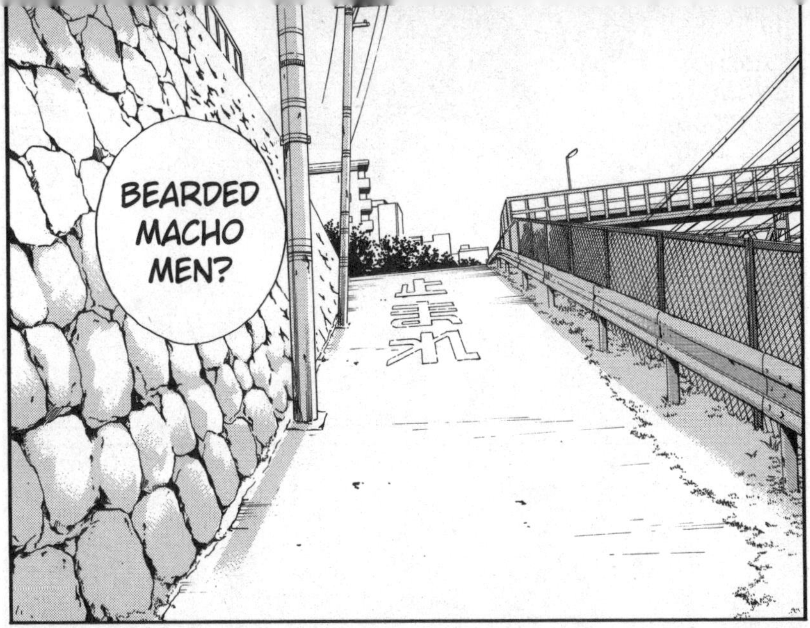
BEARDED MACHO MEN?
止まれ
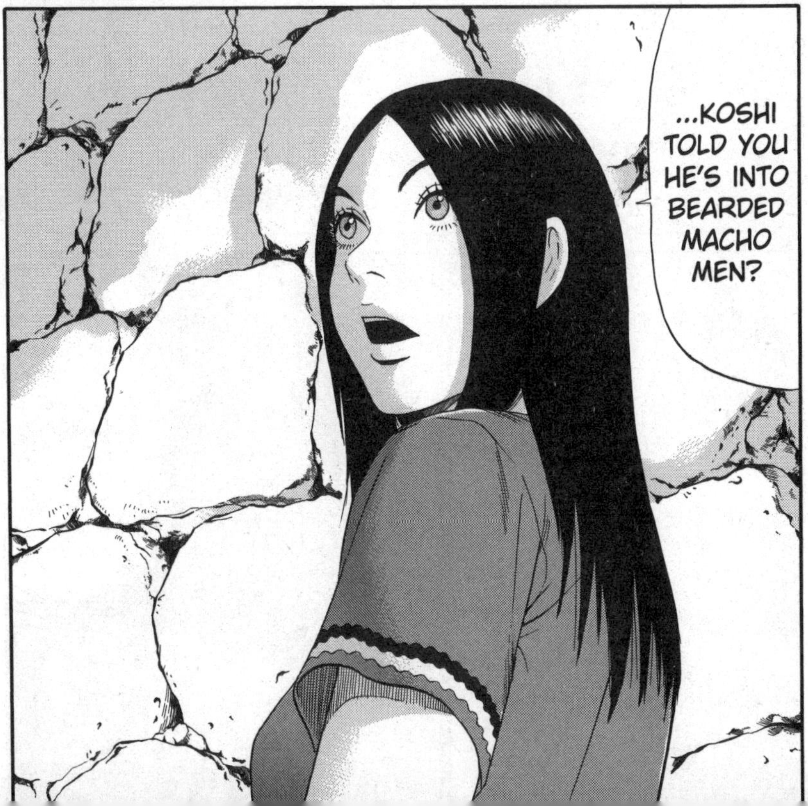
...KOSHI TOLD YOU HE'S INTO BEARDED MACHO MEN?

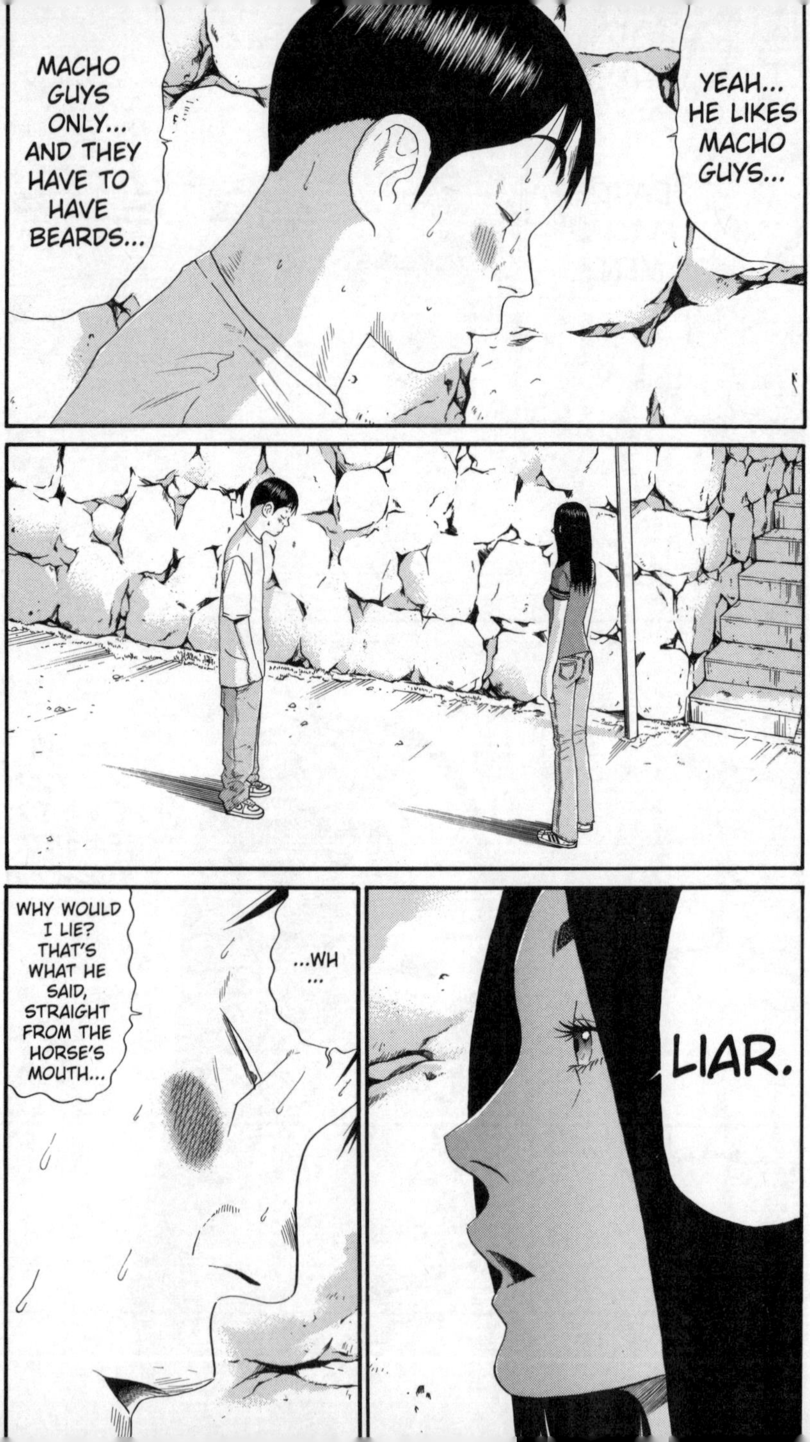
YEAH... HE LIKES MACHO GUYS...
MACHO GUYS ONLY... AND THEY HAVE TO HAVE BEARDS...
LIAR.
...WH ...
WHY WOULD I LIE? THAT'S WHAT HE SAID, STRAIGHT FROM THE HORSE'S MOUTH...

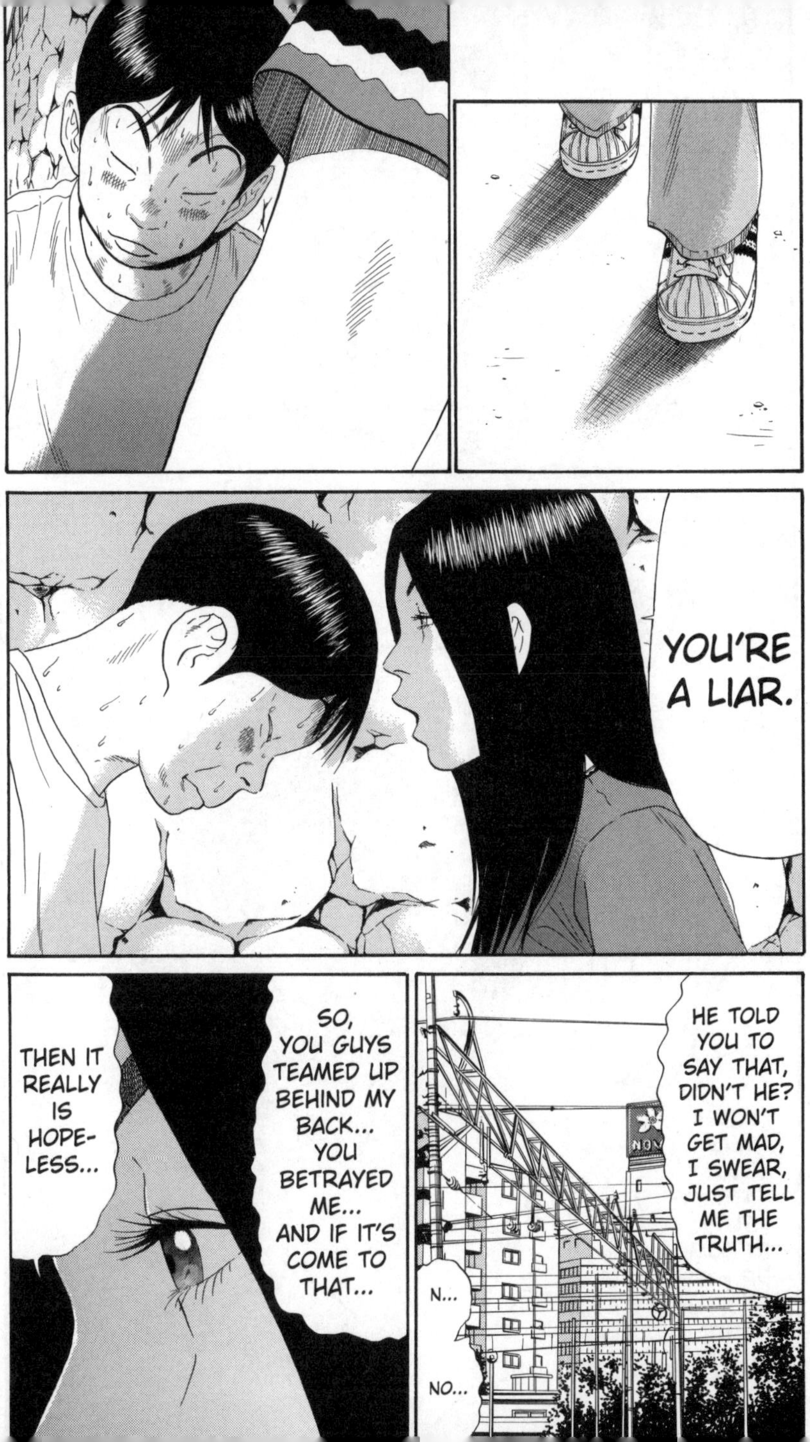
YOU'RE A LIAR.
HE TOLD YOU TO SAY THAT, DIDN'T HE? I WON'T GET MAD, I SWEAR, JUST TELL ME THE TRUTH...
N...
NO...
SO, YOU GUYS TEAMED UP BEHIND MY BACK... YOU BETRAYED ME... AND IF IT'S COME TO THAT...
THEN IT REALLY IS HOPE-LESS...

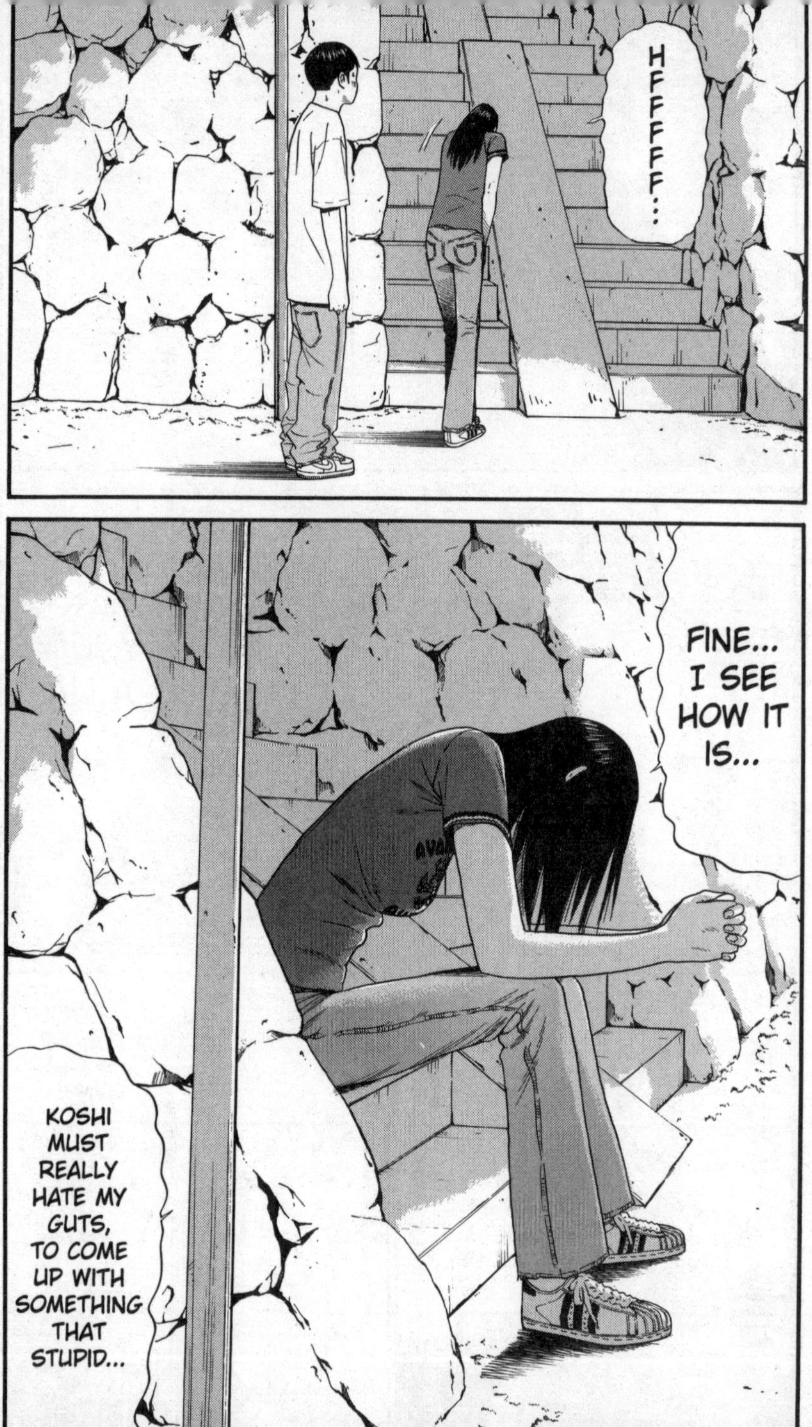
HFFFFFF...
FINE... I SEE HOW IT IS...
KOSHI MUST REALLY HATE MY GUTS, TO COME UP WITH SOMETHING THAT STUPID...

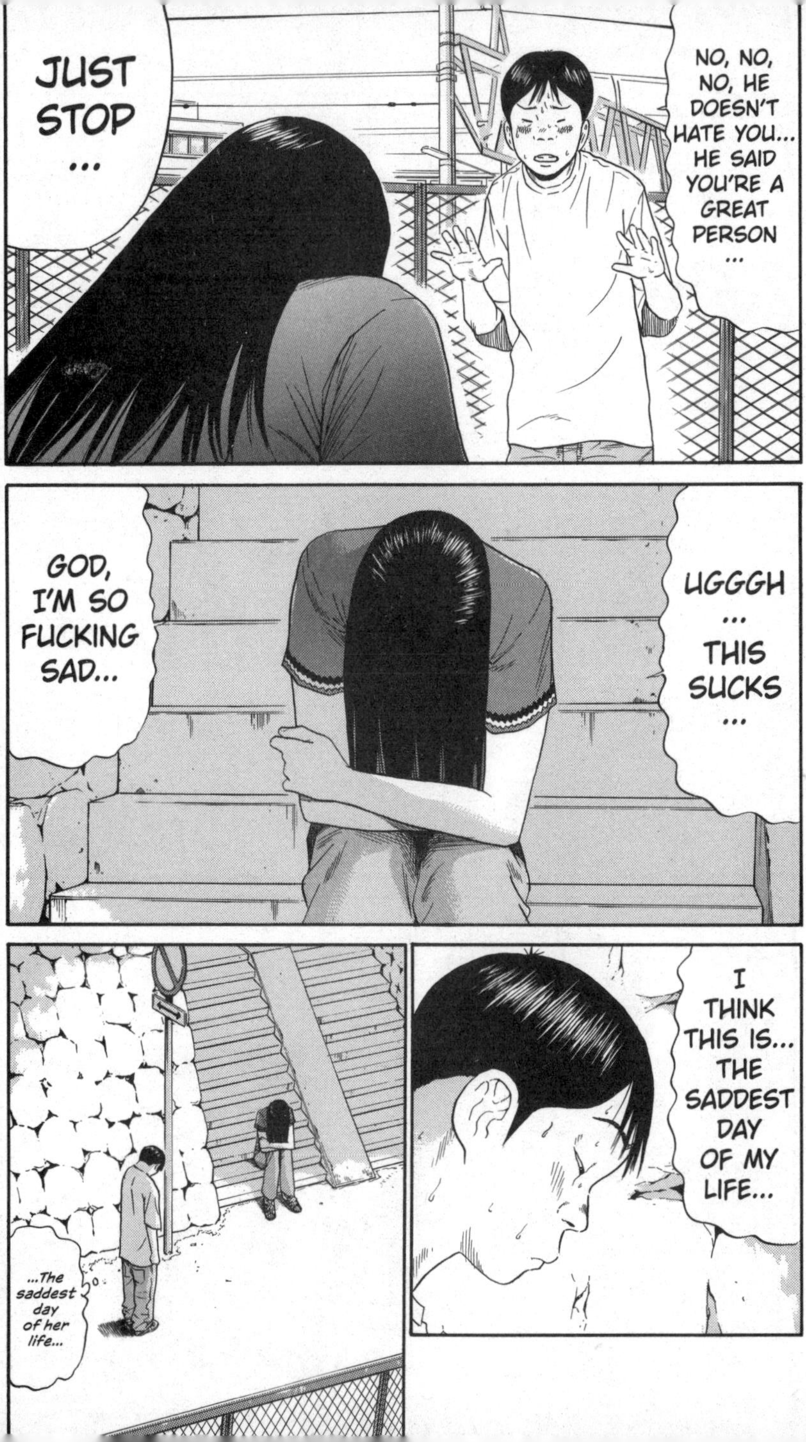
NO, NO, NO, HE DOESN'T HATE YOU... HE SAID YOU'RE A GREAT PERSON ...
JUST STOP ...
UGGGH ... THIS SUCKS ...
GOD, I'M SO FUCKING SAD...
I THINK THIS IS... THE SADDEST DAY OF MY LIFE...
...The saddest day of her life...

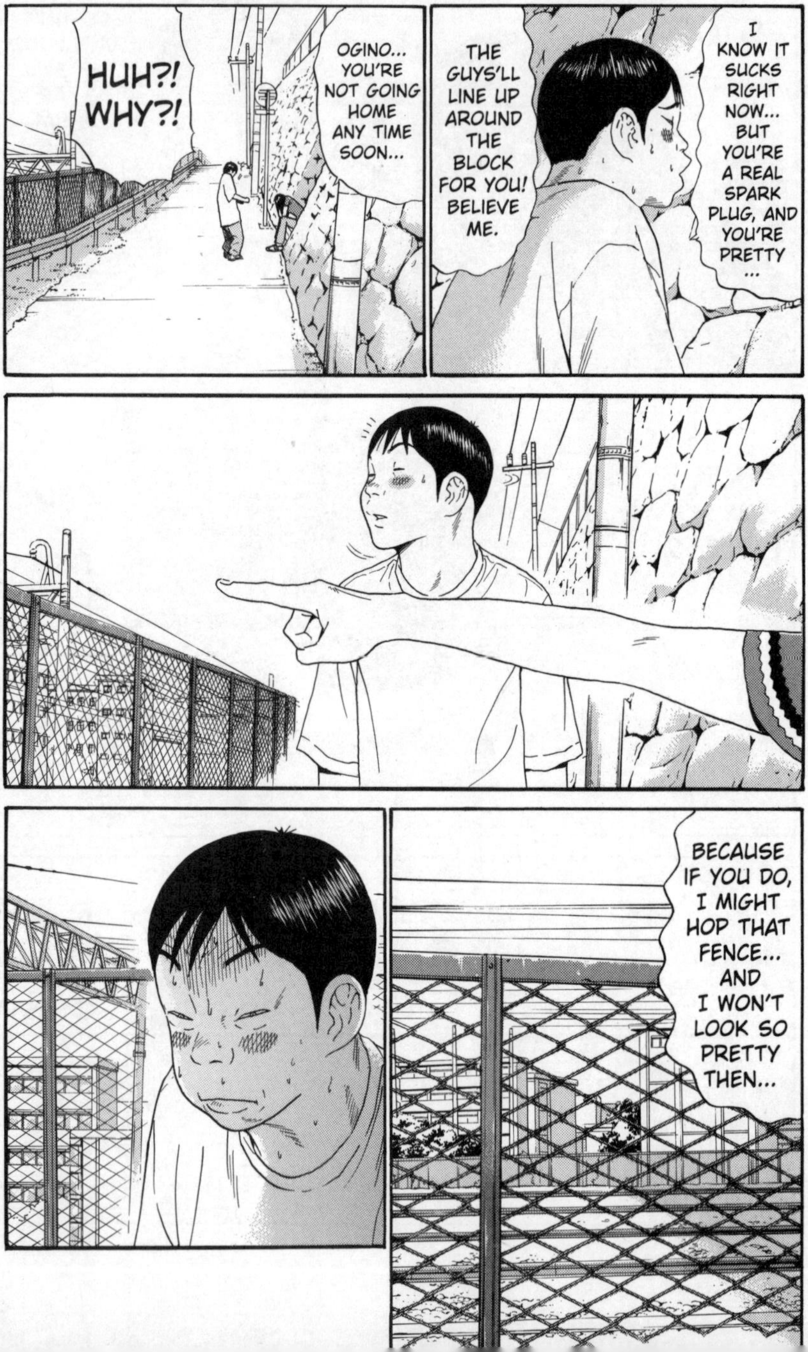
I KNOW IT SUCKS RIGHT NOW... BUT YOU'RE A REAL SPARK PLUG, AND YOU'RE PRETTY ...
THE GUYS'LL LINE UP AROUND THE BLOCK FOR YOU! BELIEVE ME.
OGINO... YOU'RE NOT GOING HOME ANY TIME SOON...
HUH?! WHY?!
BECAUSE IF YOU DO, I MIGHT HOP THAT FENCE... AND I WON'T LOOK SO PRETTY THEN...

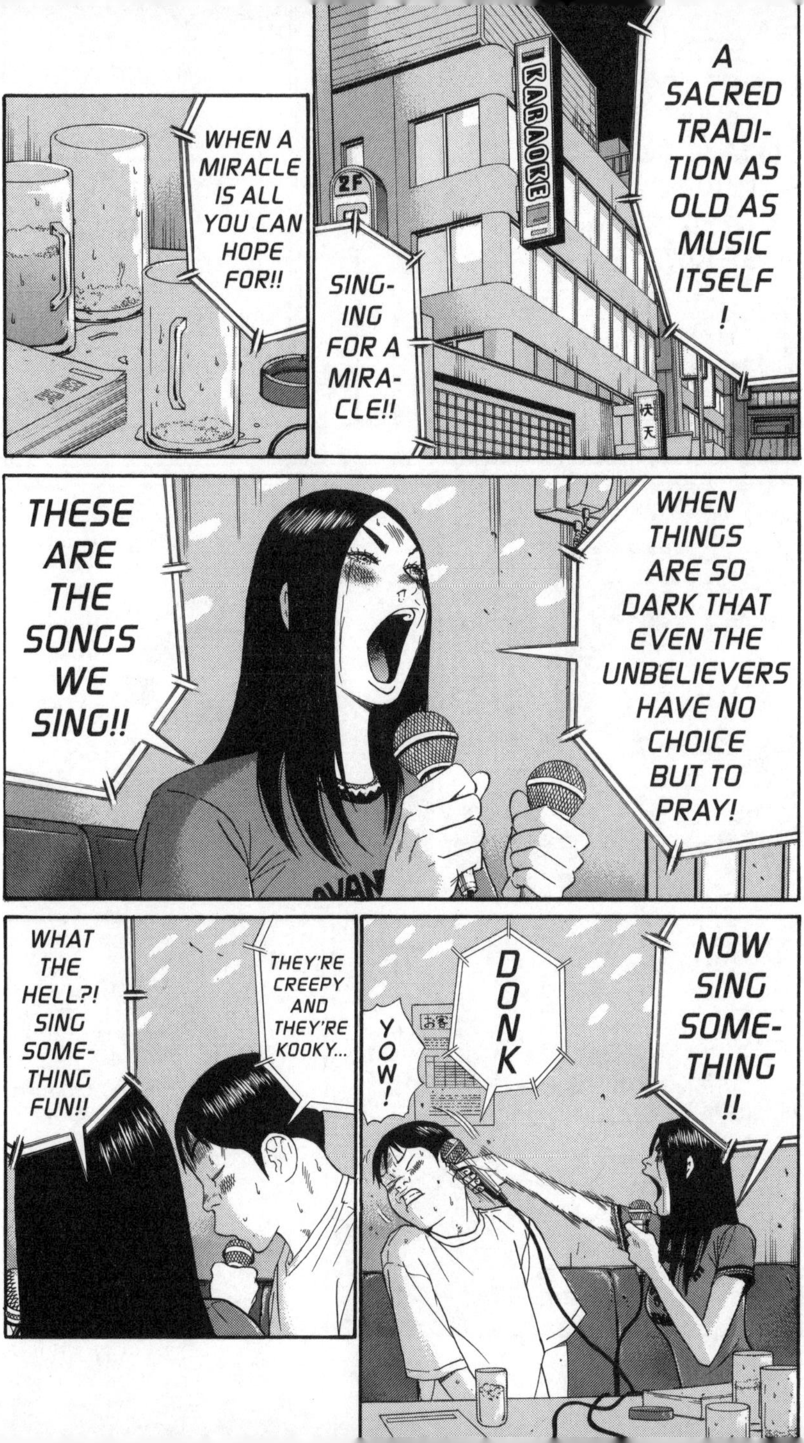

A SACRED TRADITION AS OLD AS MUSIC ITSELF!
SINGING FOR A MIRACLE!!
WHEN A MIRACLE IS ALL YOU CAN HOPE FOR!!
WHEN THINGS ARE SO DARK THAT EVEN THE UNBELIEVERS HAVE NO CHOICE BUT TO PRAY!
THESE ARE THE SONGS WE SING!!
NOW SING SOMETHING!!
DONK
YOW!
THEY'RE CREEPY AND THEY'RE KOOKY...
WHAT THE HELL?! SING SOMETHING FUN!!

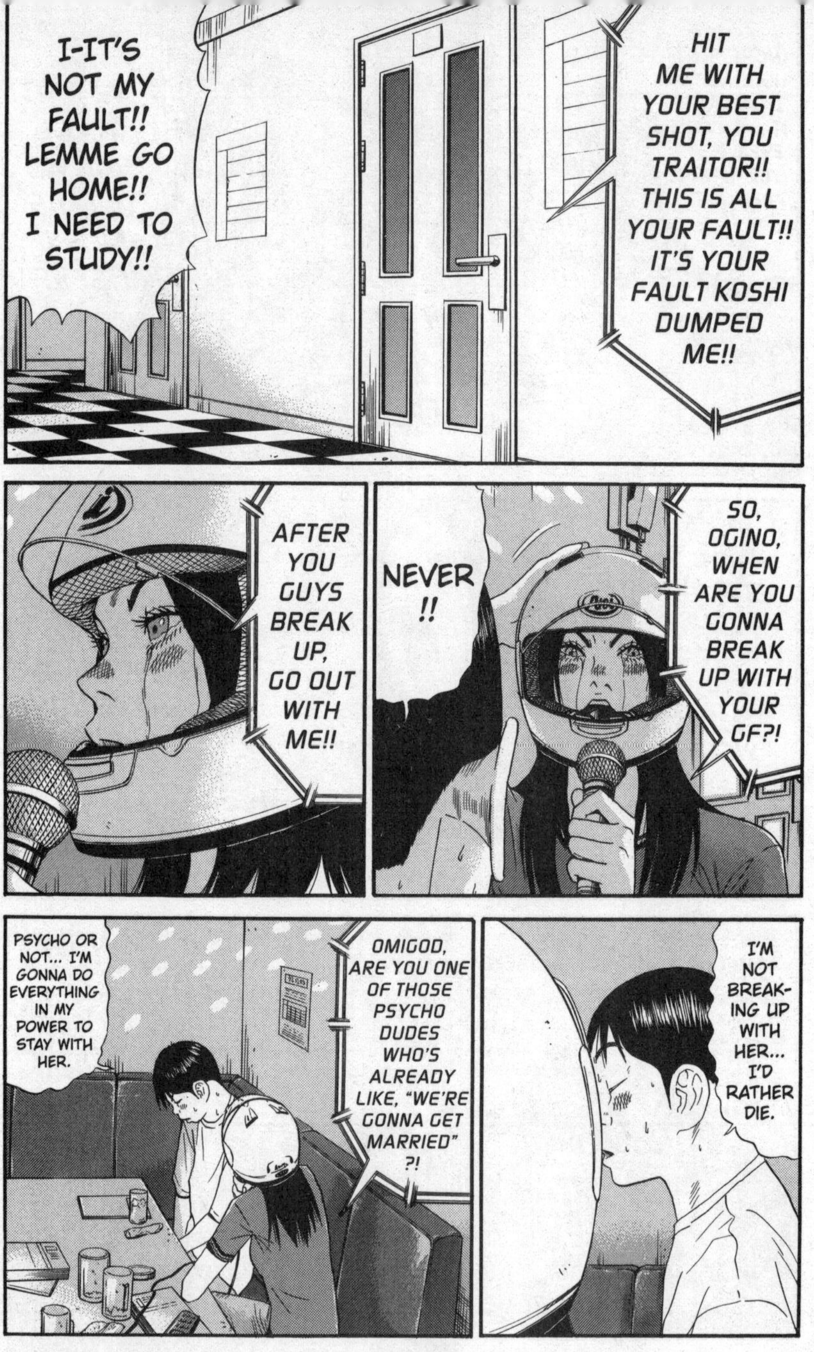
HIT ME WITH YOUR BEST SHOT, YOU TRAITOR!! THIS IS ALL YOUR FAULT!! IT'S YOUR FAULT KOSHI DUMPED ME!!
I-IT'S NOT MY FAULT!! LEMME GO HOME!! I NEED TO STUDY!!
SO, OGINO, WHEN ARE YOU GONNA BREAK UP WITH YOUR GF?!
NEVER!!
AFTER YOU GUYS BREAK UP, GO OUT WITH ME!!
I'M NOT BREAKING UP WITH HER... I'D RATHER DIE.
OMIGOD, ARE YOU ONE OF THOSE PSYCHO DUDES WHO'S ALREADY LIKE, "WE'RE GONNA GET MARRIED"?!
PSYCHO OR NOT... I'M GONNA DO EVERYTHING IN MY POWER TO STAY WITH HER.

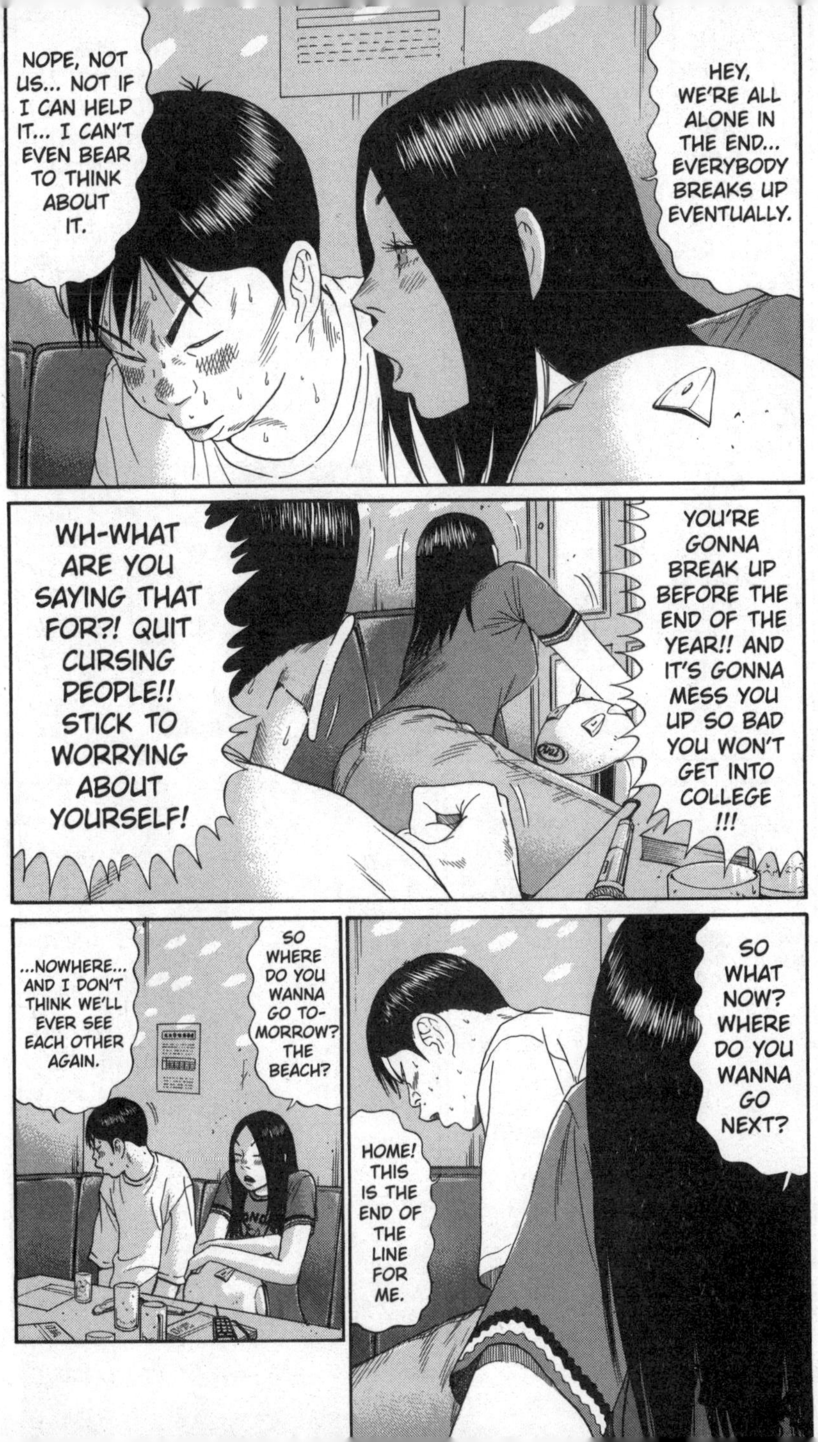
HEY, WE'RE ALL ALONE IN THE END... EVERYBODY BREAKS UP EVENTUALLY.
NOPE, NOT US... NOT IF I CAN HELP IT... I CAN'T EVEN BEAR TO THINK ABOUT IT.
YOU'RE GONNA BREAK UP BEFORE THE END OF THE YEAR!! AND IT'S GONNA MESS YOU UP SO BAD YOU WON'T GET INTO COLLEGE!!!
WH-WHAT ARE YOU SAYING THAT FOR?! QUIT CURSING PEOPLE!! STICK TO WORRYING ABOUT YOURSELF!
SO WHAT NOW? WHERE DO YOU WANNA GO NEXT?
HOME! THIS IS THE END OF THE LINE FOR ME.
SO WHERE DO YOU WANNA GO TO-MORROW? THE BEACH?
...NOWHERE... AND I DON'T THINK WE'LL EVER SEE EACH OTHER AGAIN.

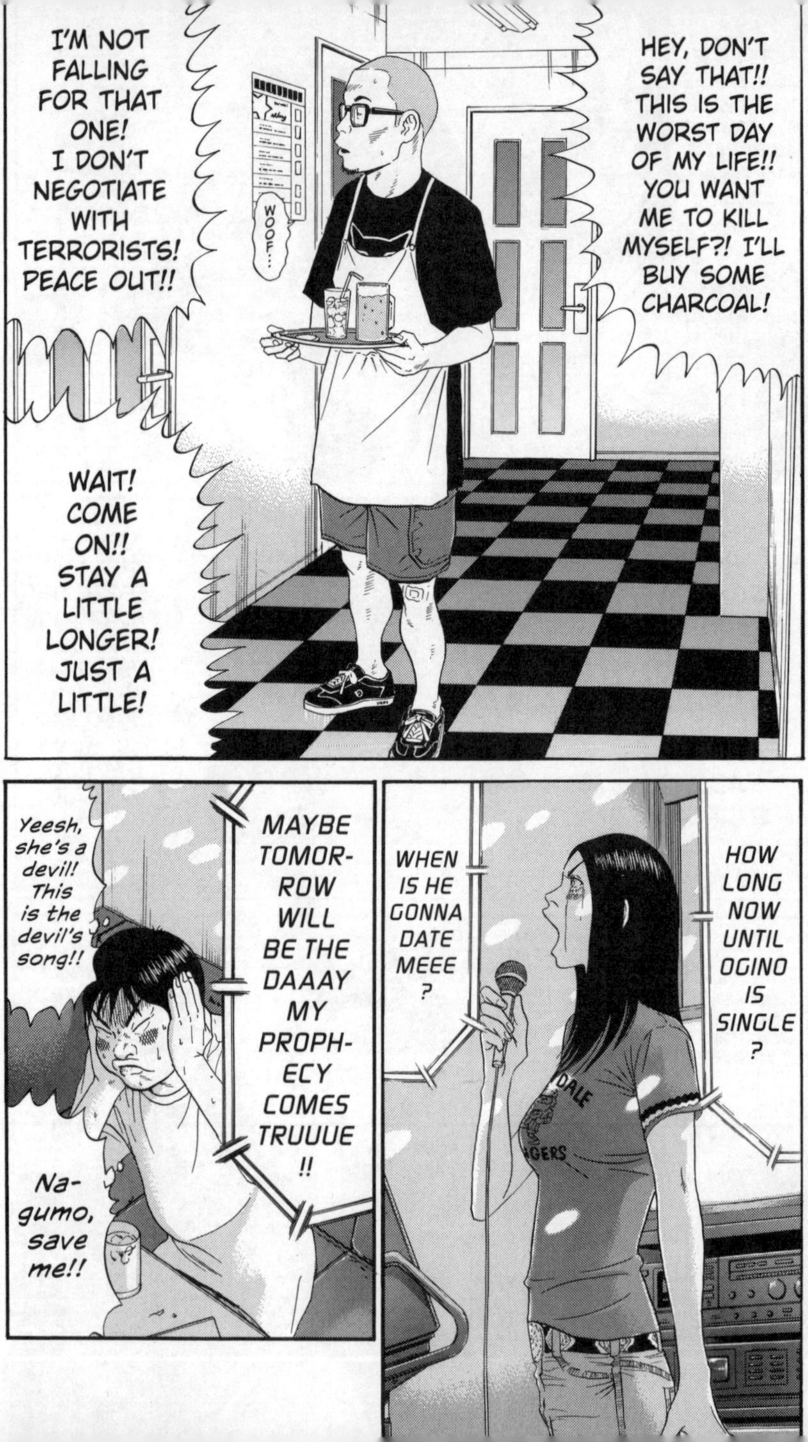
HEY, DON'T SAY THAT!! THIS IS THE WORST DAY OF MY LIFE!! YOU WANT ME TO KILL MYSELF?! I'LL BUY SOME CHARCOAL!
I'M NOT FALLING FOR THAT ONE! I DON'T NEGOTIATE WITH TERRORISTS! PEACE OUT!!
WOOF...
WAIT! COME ON!! STAY A LITTLE LONGER! JUST A LITTLE!
HOW LONG NOW UNTIL OGINO IS SINGLE?
WHEN IS HE GONNA DATE MEEE?
MAYBE TOMOR-ROW WILL BE THE DAAAY MY PROPH-ECY COMES TRUUUE!!
Yeesh, she's a devil! This is the devil's song!!
Na-gumo, save me!!

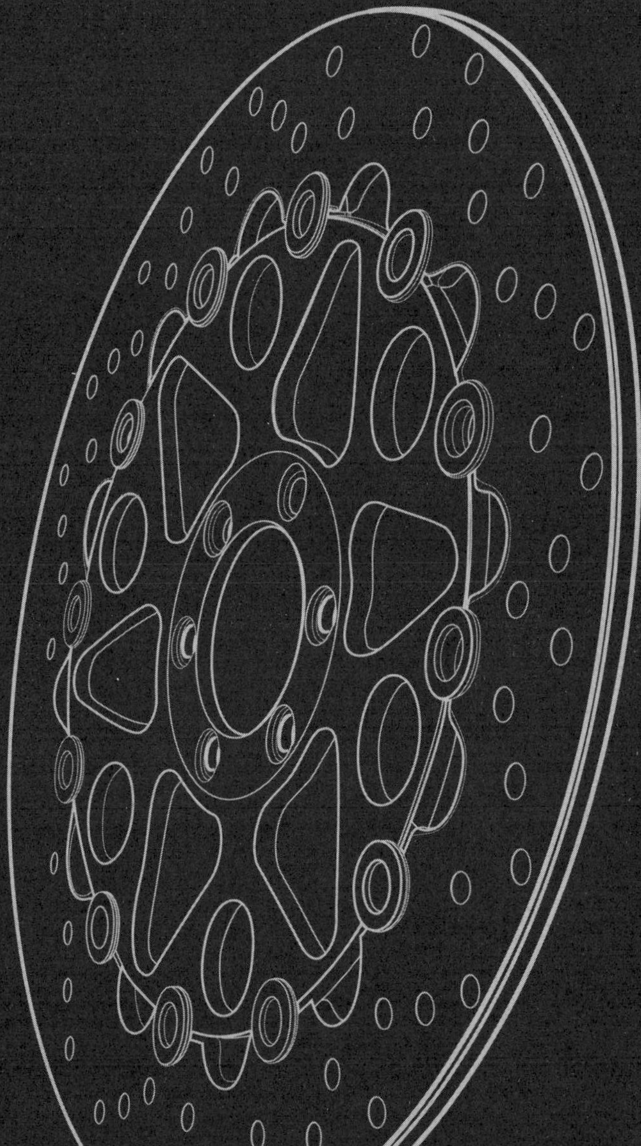

# Chapter 53: Terrible

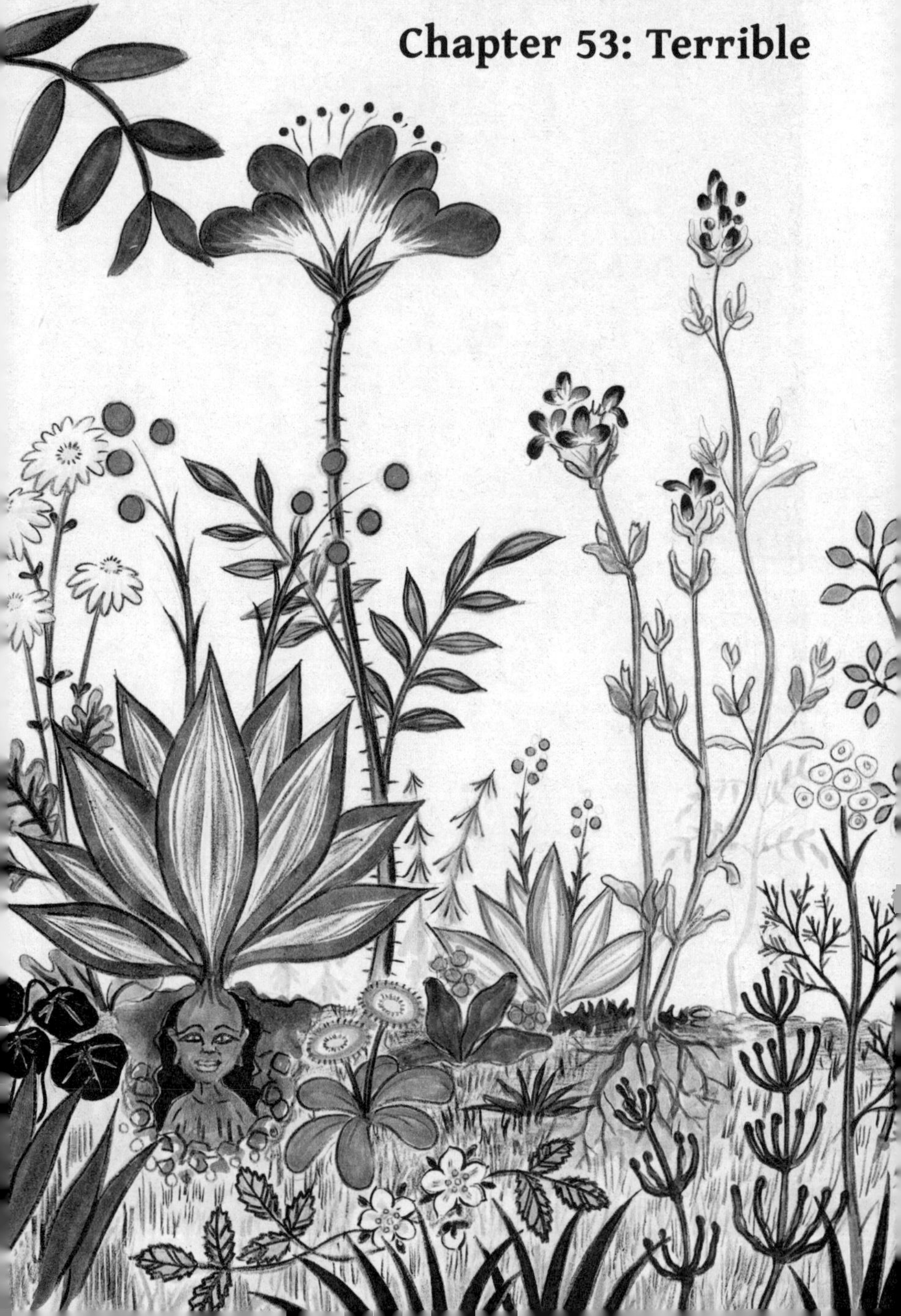

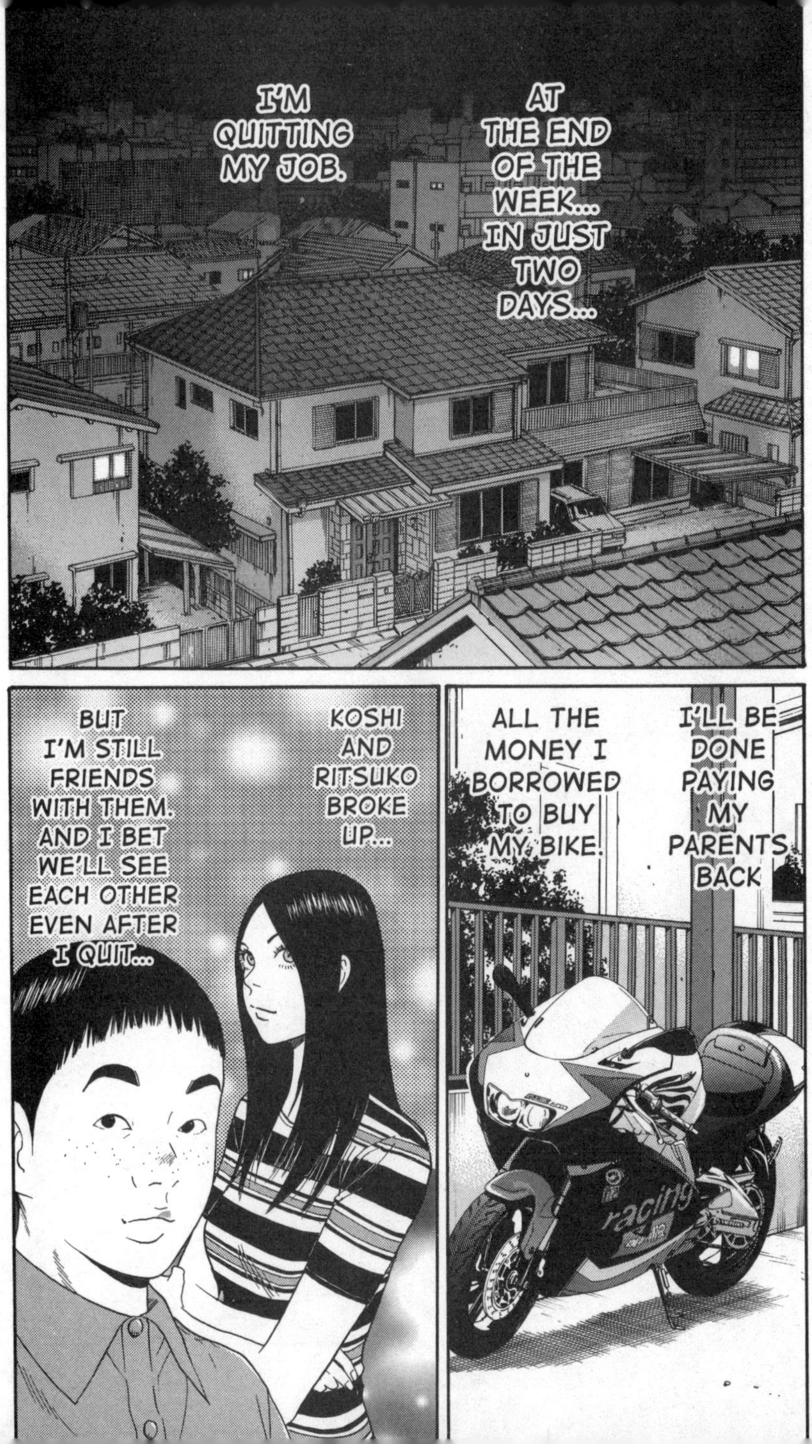
AT THE END OF THE WEEK... IN JUST TWO DAYS...
I'M QUITTING MY JOB.
I'LL BE DONE PAYING MY PARENTS BACK
ALL THE MONEY I BORROWED TO BUY MY BIKE.
KOSHI AND RITSUKO BROKE UP...
BUT I'M STILL FRIENDS WITH THEM. AND I BET WE'LL SEE EACH OTHER EVEN AFTER I QUIT...
racing

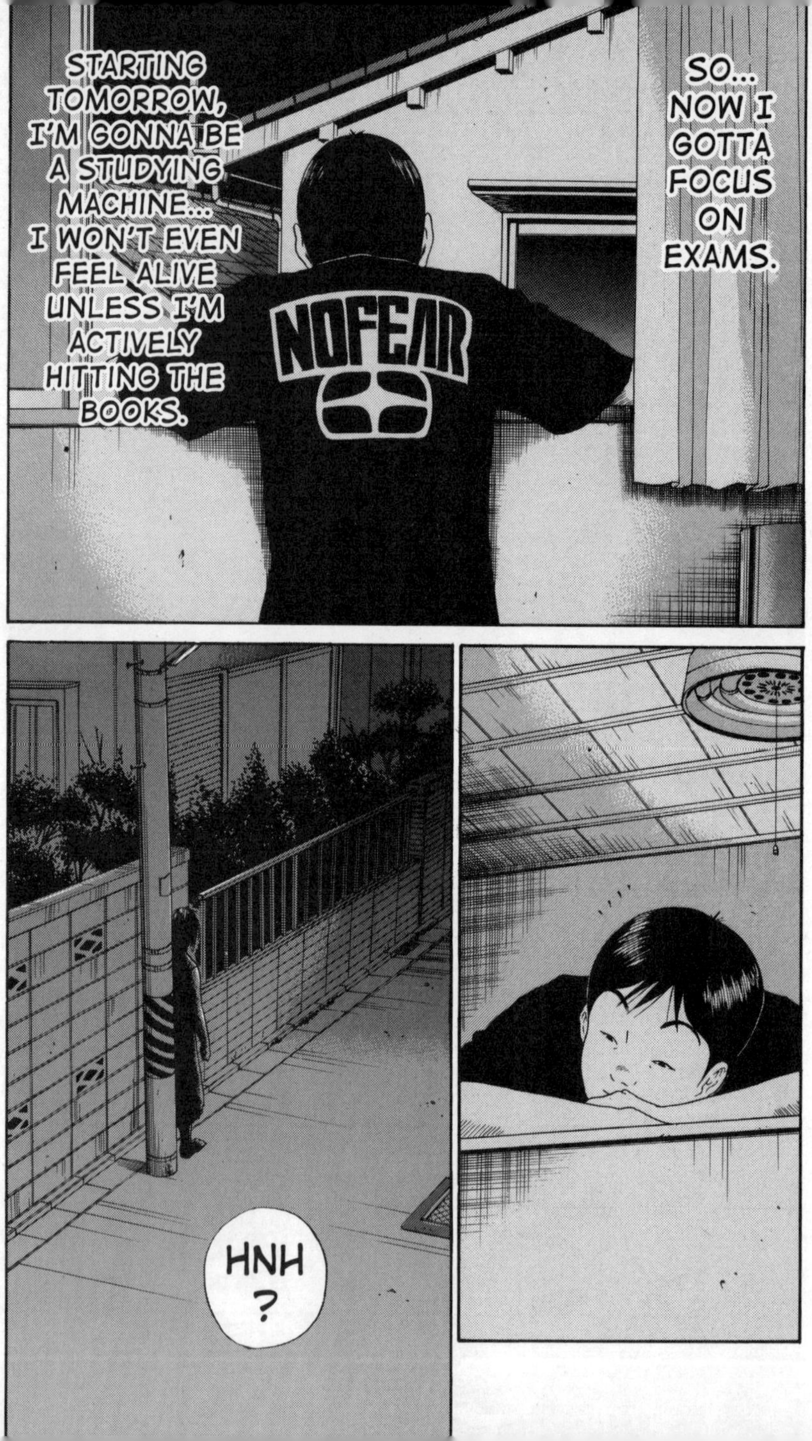
SO... NOW I GOTTA FOCUS ON EXAMS.
STARTING TOMORROW, I'M GONNA BE A STUDYING MACHINE... I WON'T EVEN FEEL ALIVE UNLESS I'M ACTIVELY HITTING THE BOOKS.
HNH ?

Who's that...?

... Peep-ing?

What are they up to at this time of night?

NOFEAR

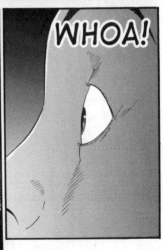

WHOA!

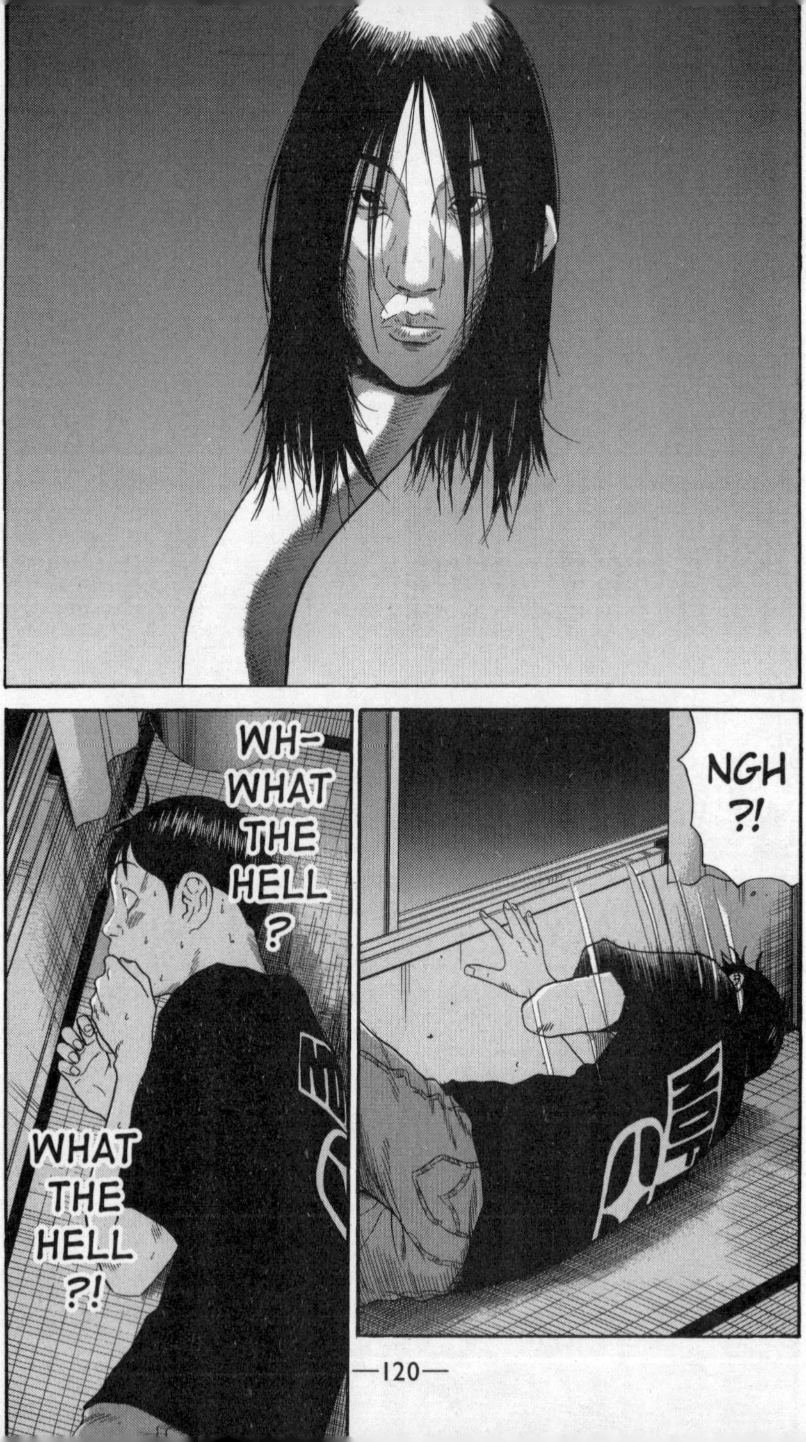
NGH ?!
WH- WHAT THE HELL ?
WHAT THE HELL ?!

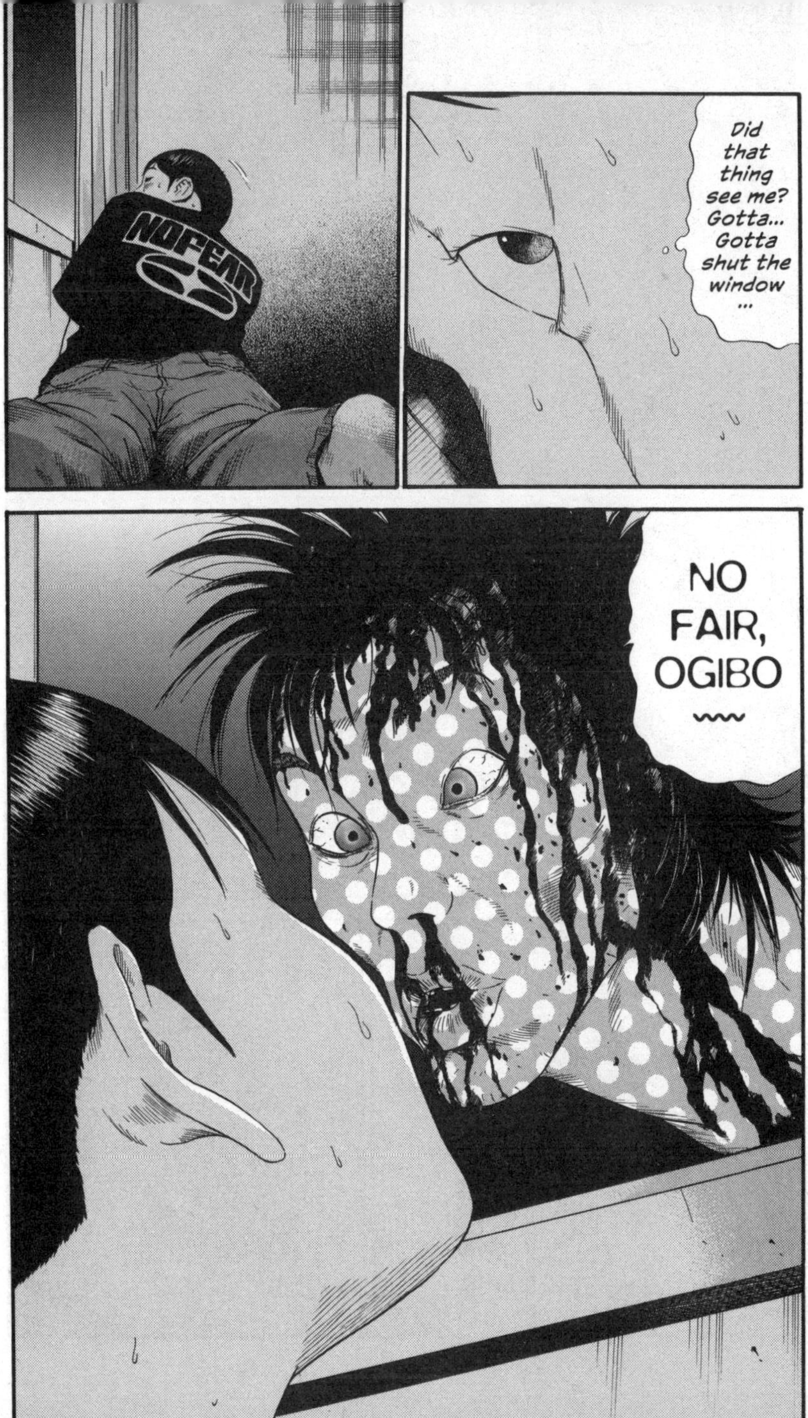
Did that thing see me? Gotta... Gotta shut the window ...
NOFEAR
NO FAIR, OGIBO ~~~

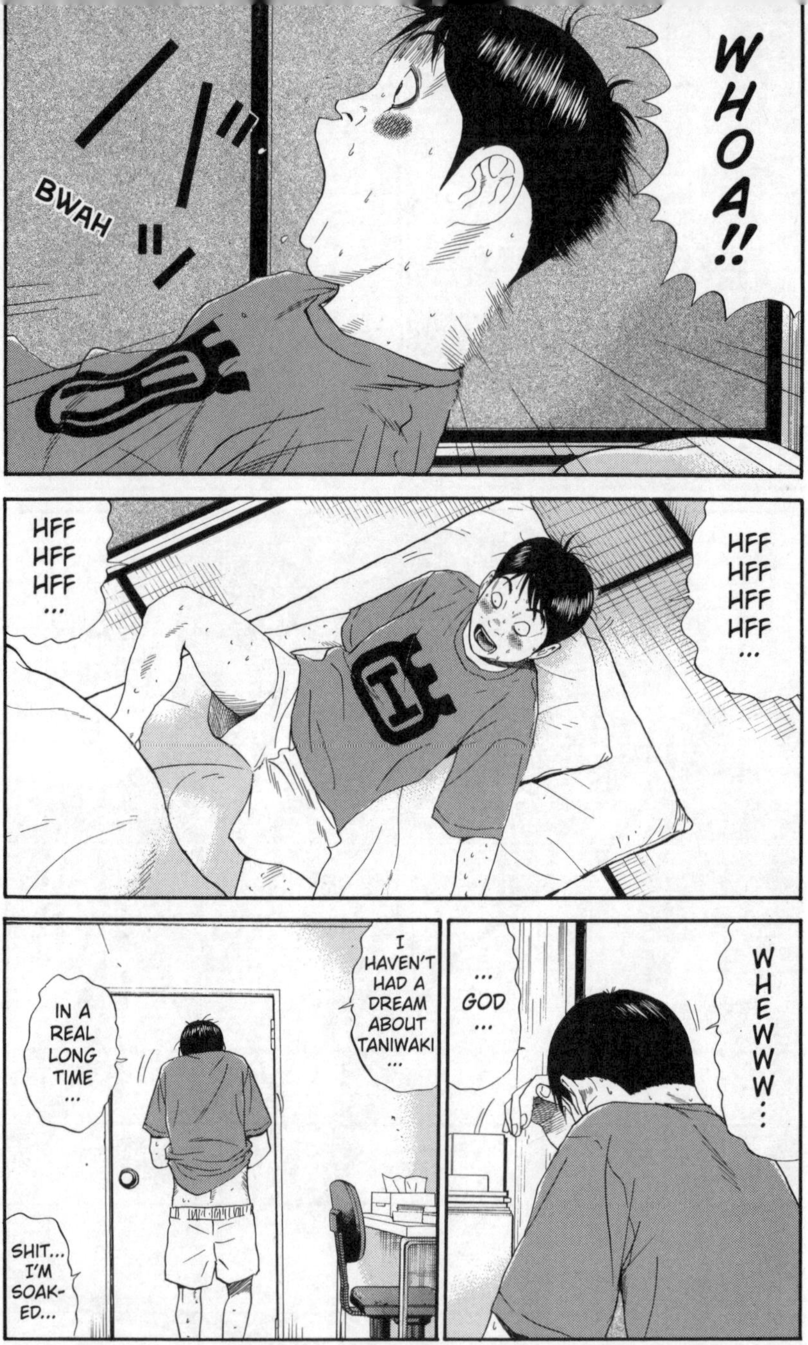
WHOA!!
BWAH
HFF HFF HFF HFF...
HFF HFF HFF...
WHEWWW...
...GOD...
I HAVEN'T HAD A DREAM ABOUT TANIWAKI...
IN A REAL LONG TIME...
SHIT... I'M SOAK-ED...

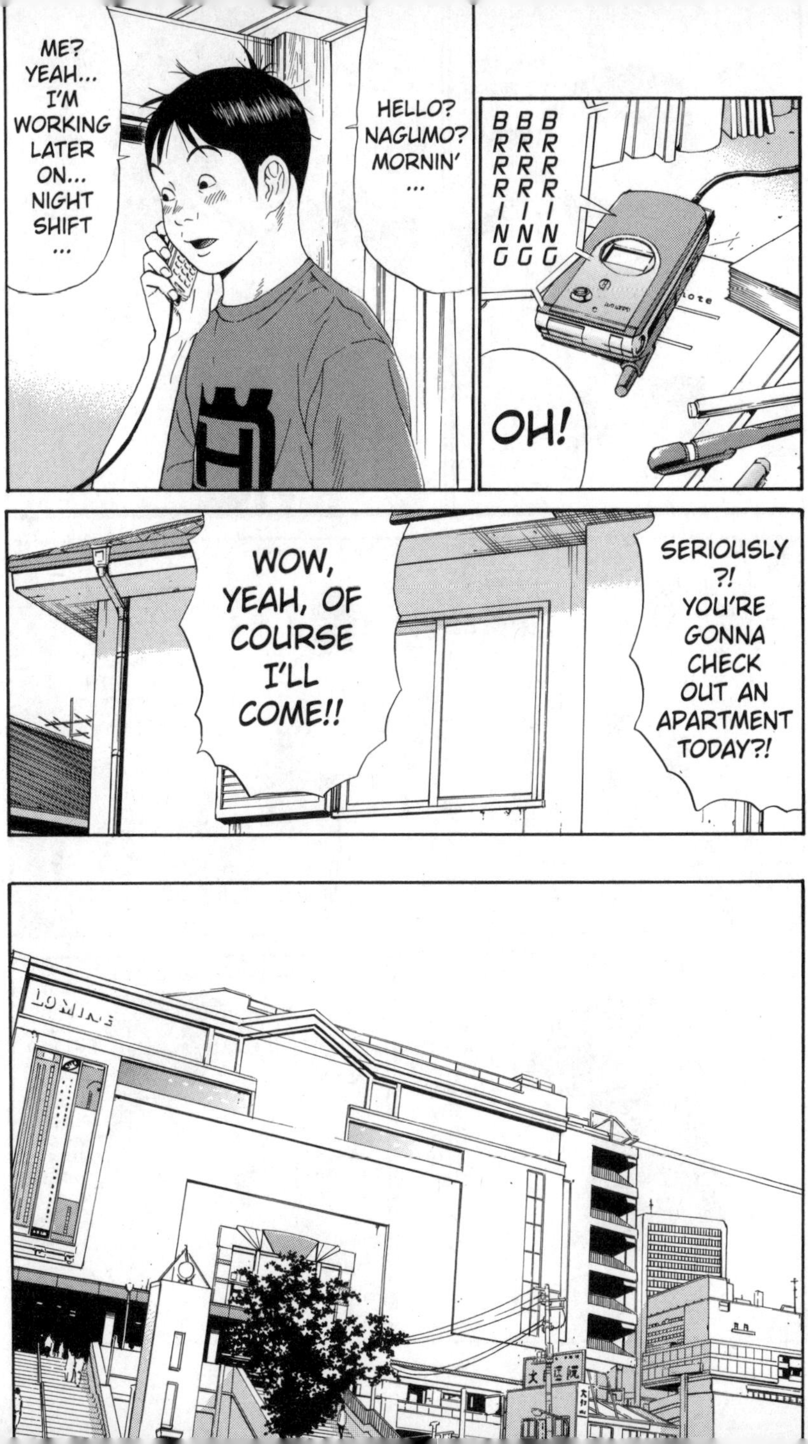

BRRRING
BRRRING
BRRRING
OH!
HELLO? NAGUMO? MORNIN' ...
ME? YEAH... I'M WORKING LATER ON... NIGHT SHIFT ...
SERIOUSLY?! YOU'RE GONNA CHECK OUT AN APARTMENT TODAY?!
WOW, YEAH, OF COURSE I'LL COME!!
LOMING

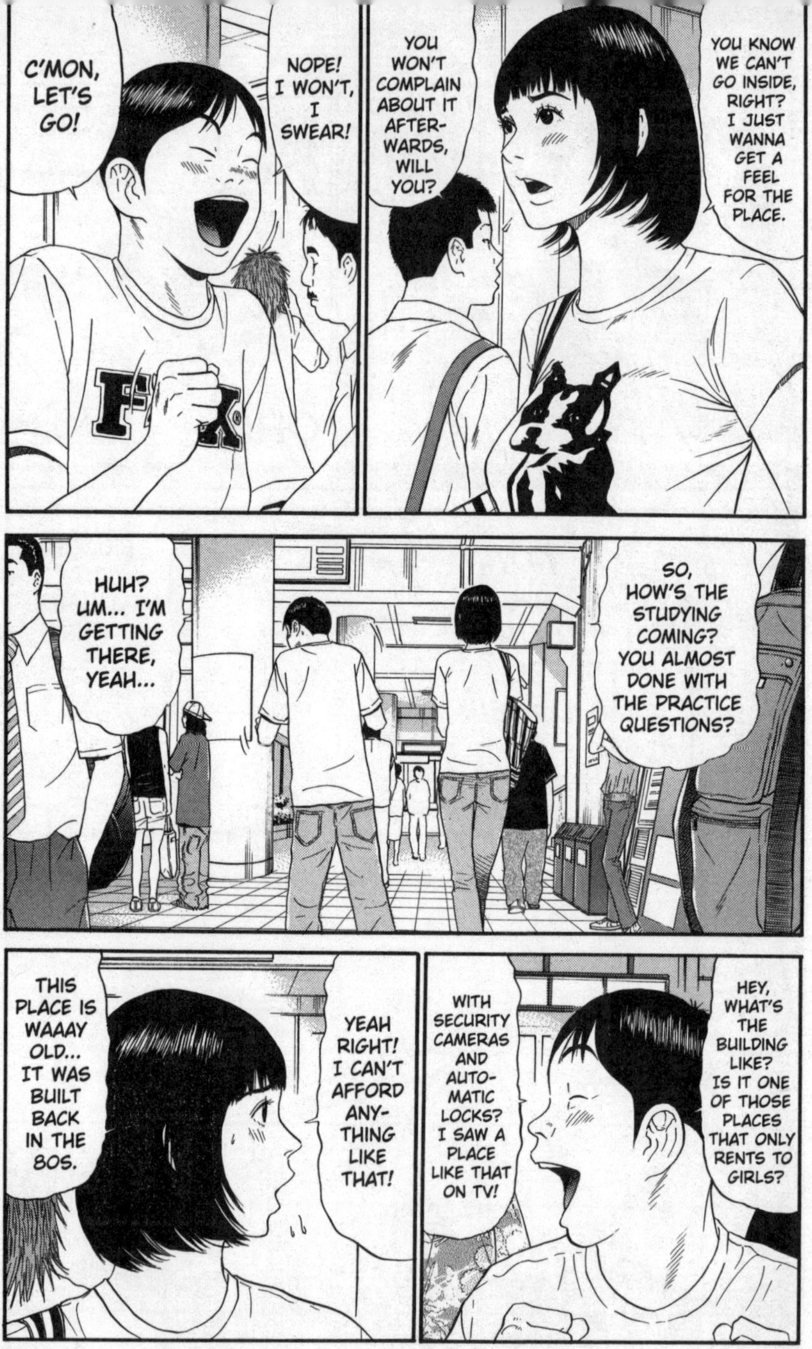
YOU KNOW WE CAN'T GO INSIDE, RIGHT? I JUST WANNA GET A FEEL FOR THE PLACE.
YOU WON'T COMPLAIN ABOUT IT AFTER-WARDS, WILL YOU?
NOPE! I WON'T, I SWEAR!
C'MON, LET'S GO!
SO, HOW'S THE STUDYING COMING? YOU ALMOST DONE WITH THE PRACTICE QUESTIONS?
HUH? UM... I'M GETTING THERE, YEAH...
HEY, WHAT'S THE BUILDING LIKE? IS IT ONE OF THOSE PLACES THAT ONLY RENTS TO GIRLS?
WITH SECURITY CAMERAS AND AUTO-MATIC LOCKS? I SAW A PLACE LIKE THAT ON TV!
YEAH RIGHT! I CAN'T AFFORD ANY-THING LIKE THAT!
THIS PLACE IS WAAAY OLD... IT WAS BUILT BACK IN THE 80S.

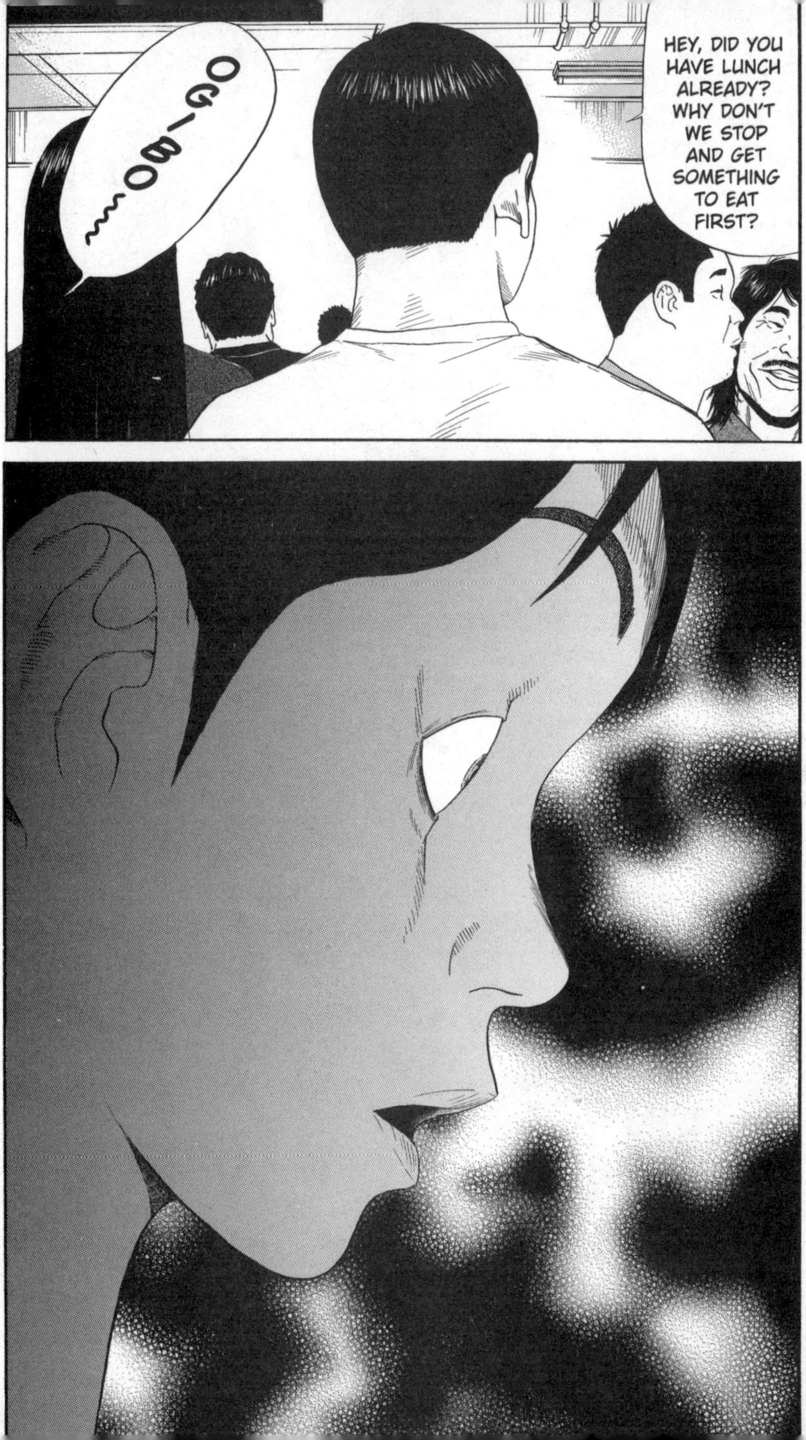
HEY, DID YOU HAVE LUNCH ALREADY? WHY DON'T WE STOP AND GET SOMETHING TO EAT FIRST?
OG-BO~~

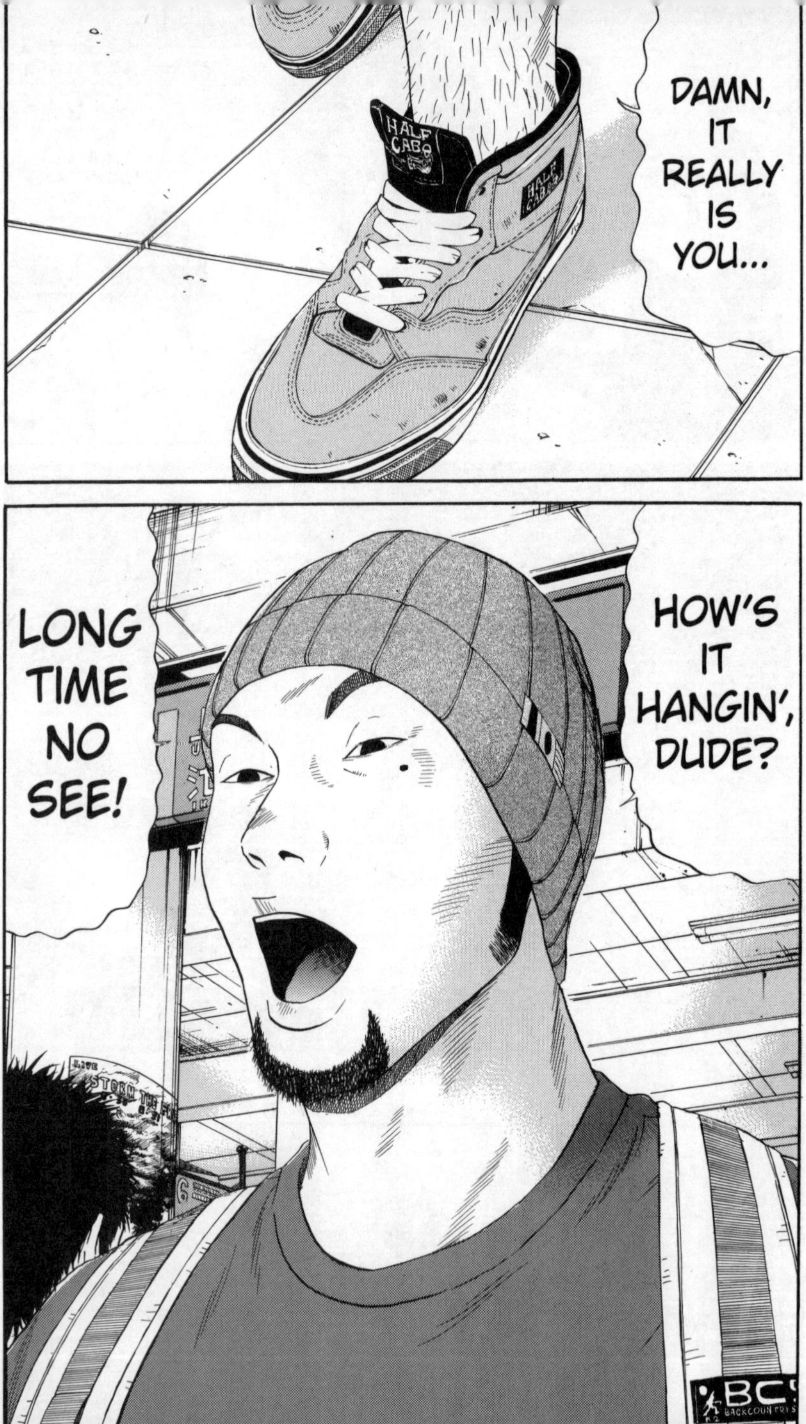
DAMN, IT REALLY IS YOU...
HOW'S IT HANGIN', DUDE?
LONG TIME NO SEE!

H... HEY...

HEYYYY, I'M AN OLD CLASSMATE OF OGINO'S!

... HELLO.

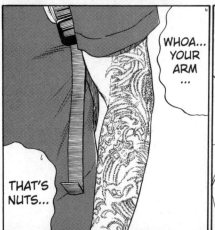

WHOA... YOUR ARM...

THAT'S NUTS...

...UM... YEAH...

LOOK AT YOU, OGI! YOU GUYS ON A DATE?

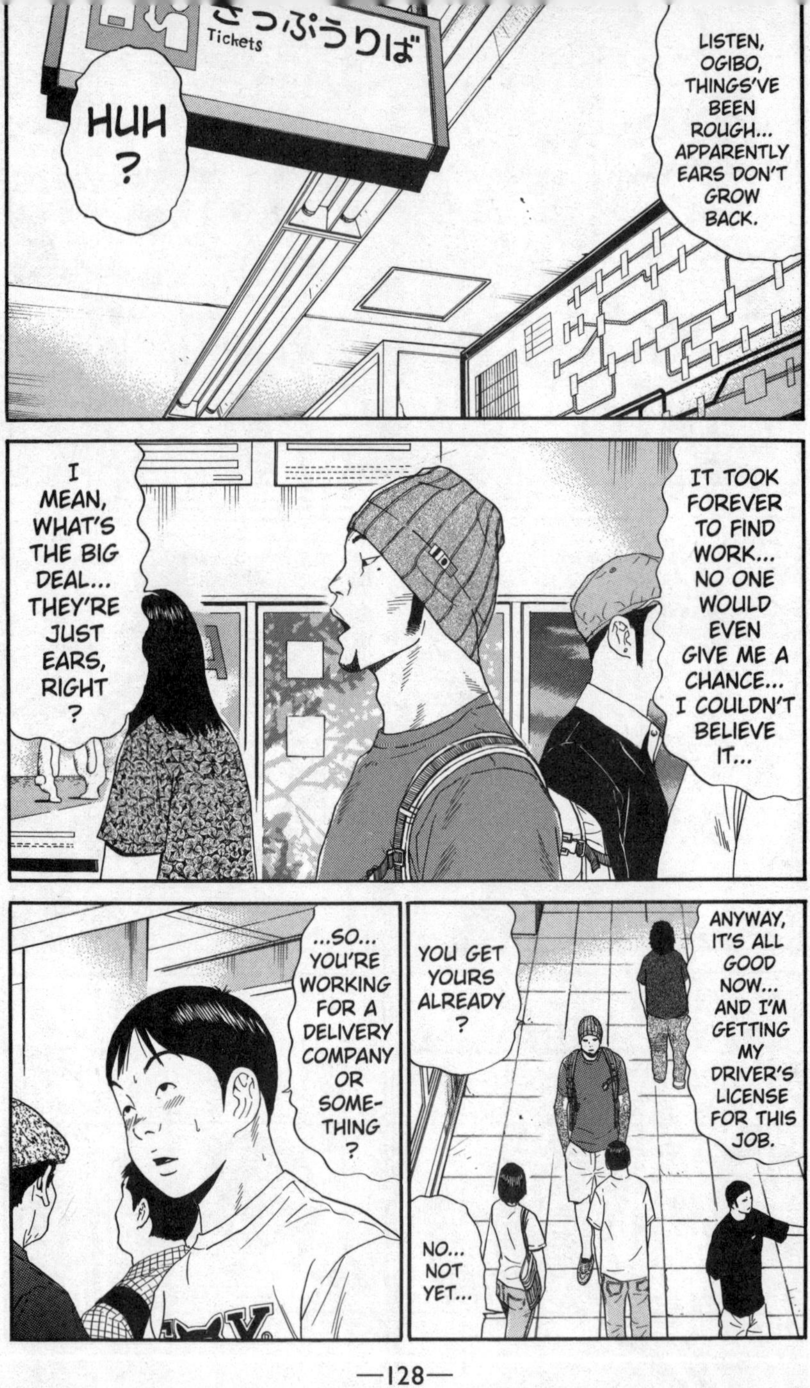

LISTEN, OGIBO, THINGS'VE BEEN ROUGH... APPARENTLY EARS DON'T GROW BACK.
Tickets
HUH ?
IT TOOK FOREVER TO FIND WORK... NO ONE WOULD EVEN GIVE ME A CHANCE... I COULDN'T BELIEVE IT...
I MEAN, WHAT'S THE BIG DEAL... THEY'RE JUST EARS, RIGHT ?
ANYWAY, IT'S ALL GOOD NOW... AND I'M GETTING MY DRIVER'S LICENSE FOR THIS JOB.
YOU GET YOURS ALREADY ?
NO... NOT YET...
...SO... YOU'RE WORKING FOR A DELIVERY COMPANY OR SOME-THING ?

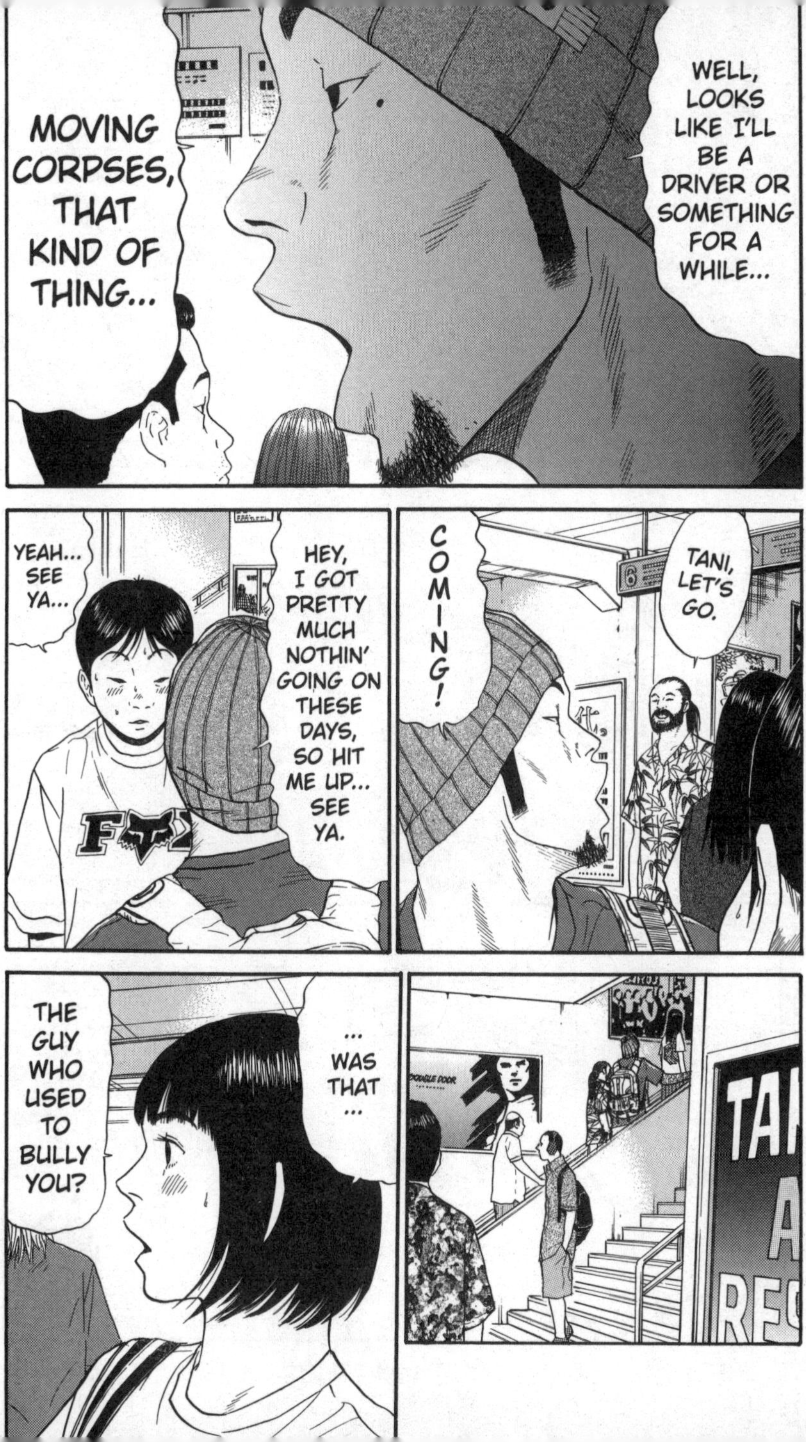
WELL, LOOKS LIKE I'LL BE A DRIVER OR SOMETHING FOR A WHILE...
MOVING CORPSES, THAT KIND OF THING...
TANI, LET'S GO.
COMING!
HEY, I GOT PRETTY MUCH NOTHIN' GOING ON THESE DAYS, SO HIT ME UP... SEE YA.
YEAH... SEE YA...
... WAS THAT ...
THE GUY WHO USED TO BULLY YOU?

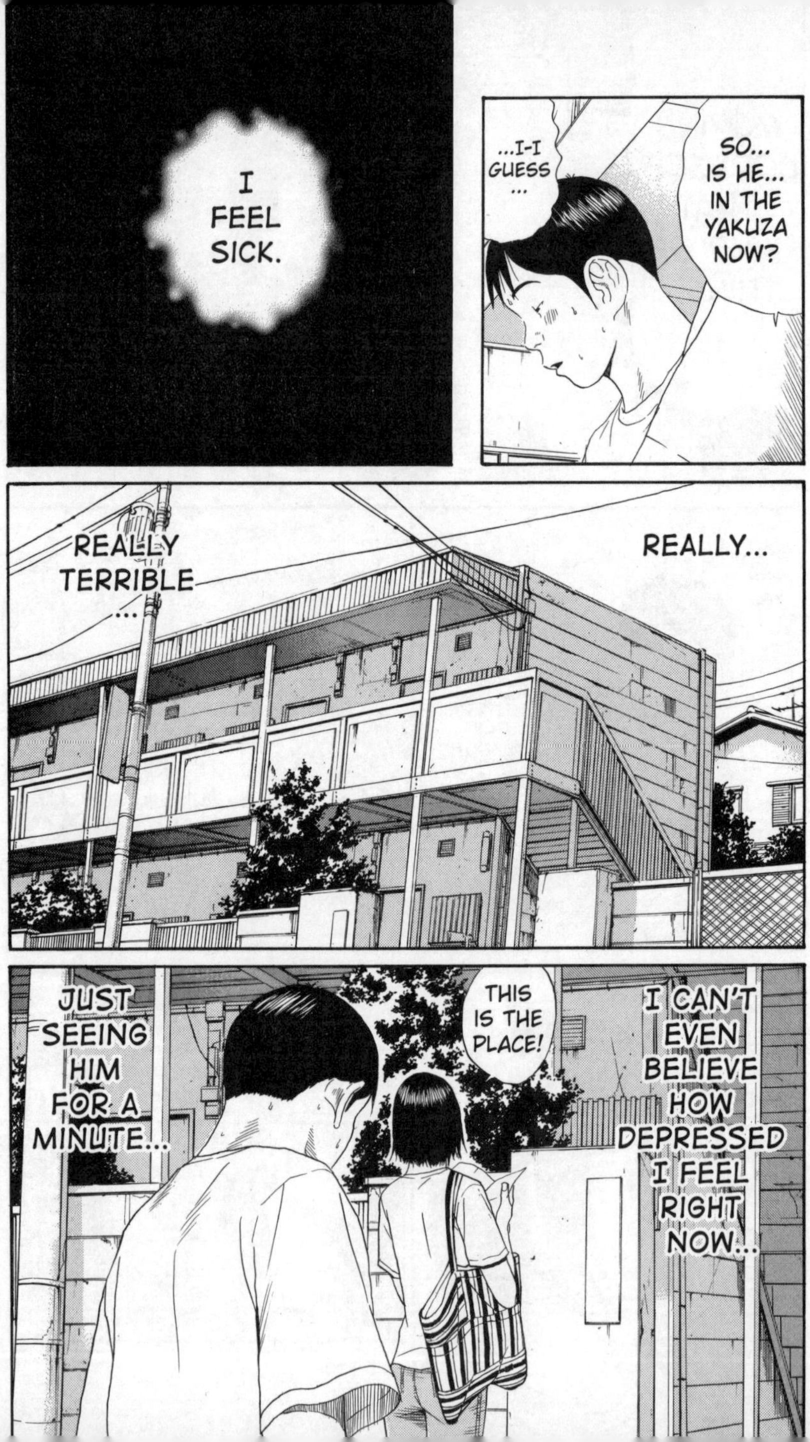
SO... IS HE... IN THE YAKUZA NOW?
...I-I GUESS...
I FEEL SICK.
REALLY...
REALLY TERRIBLE...
I CAN'T EVEN BELIEVE HOW DEPRESSED I FEEL RIGHT NOW...
THIS IS THE PLACE!
JUST SEEING HIM FOR A MINUTE...

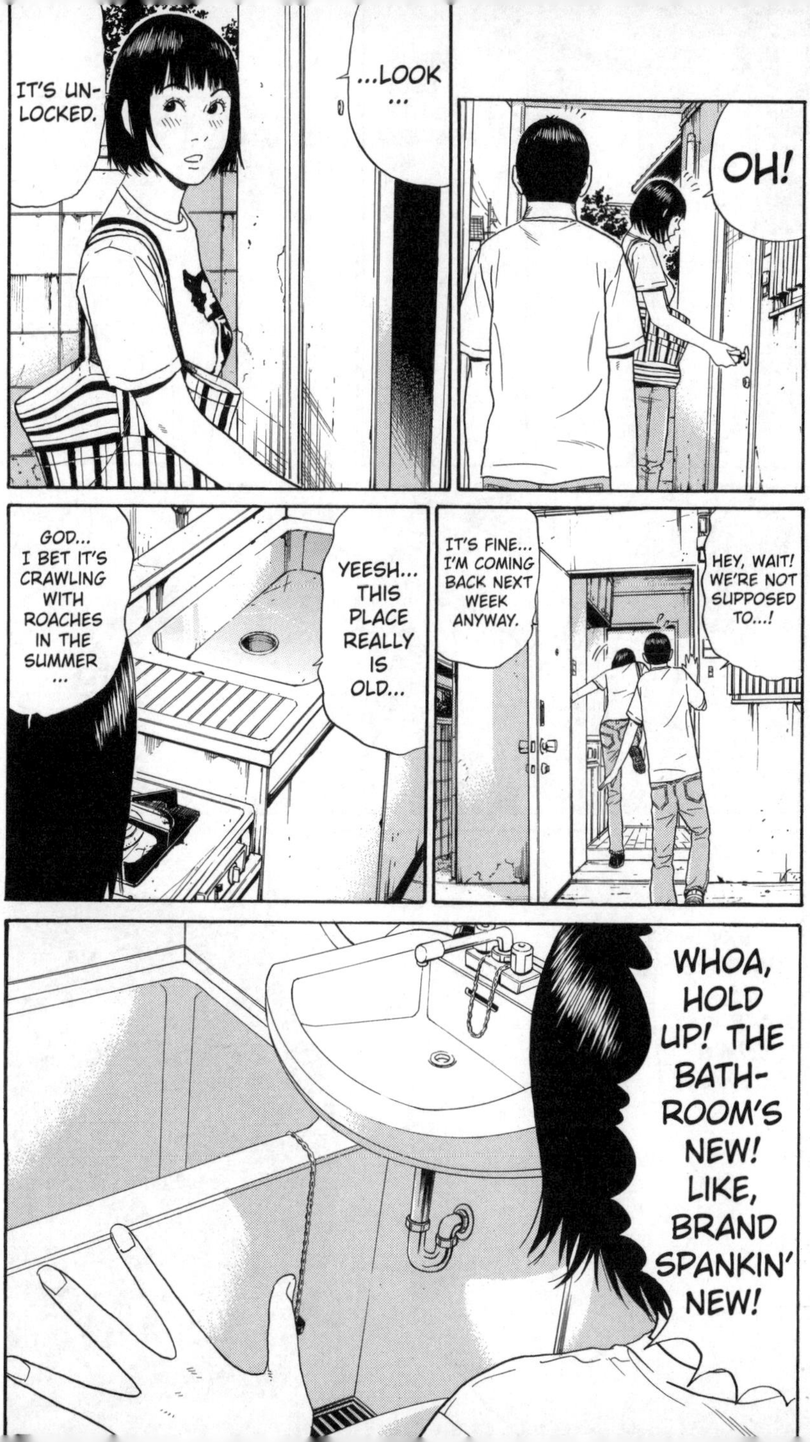
OH!
...LOOK ...
IT'S UN-LOCKED.
HEY, WAIT! WE'RE NOT SUPPOSED TO...!
IT'S FINE... I'M COMING BACK NEXT WEEK ANYWAY.
YEESH... THIS PLACE REALLY IS OLD...
GOD... I BET IT'S CRAWLING WITH ROACHES IN THE SUMMER ...
WHOA, HOLD UP! THE BATH-ROOM'S NEW! LIKE, BRAND SPANKIN' NEW!

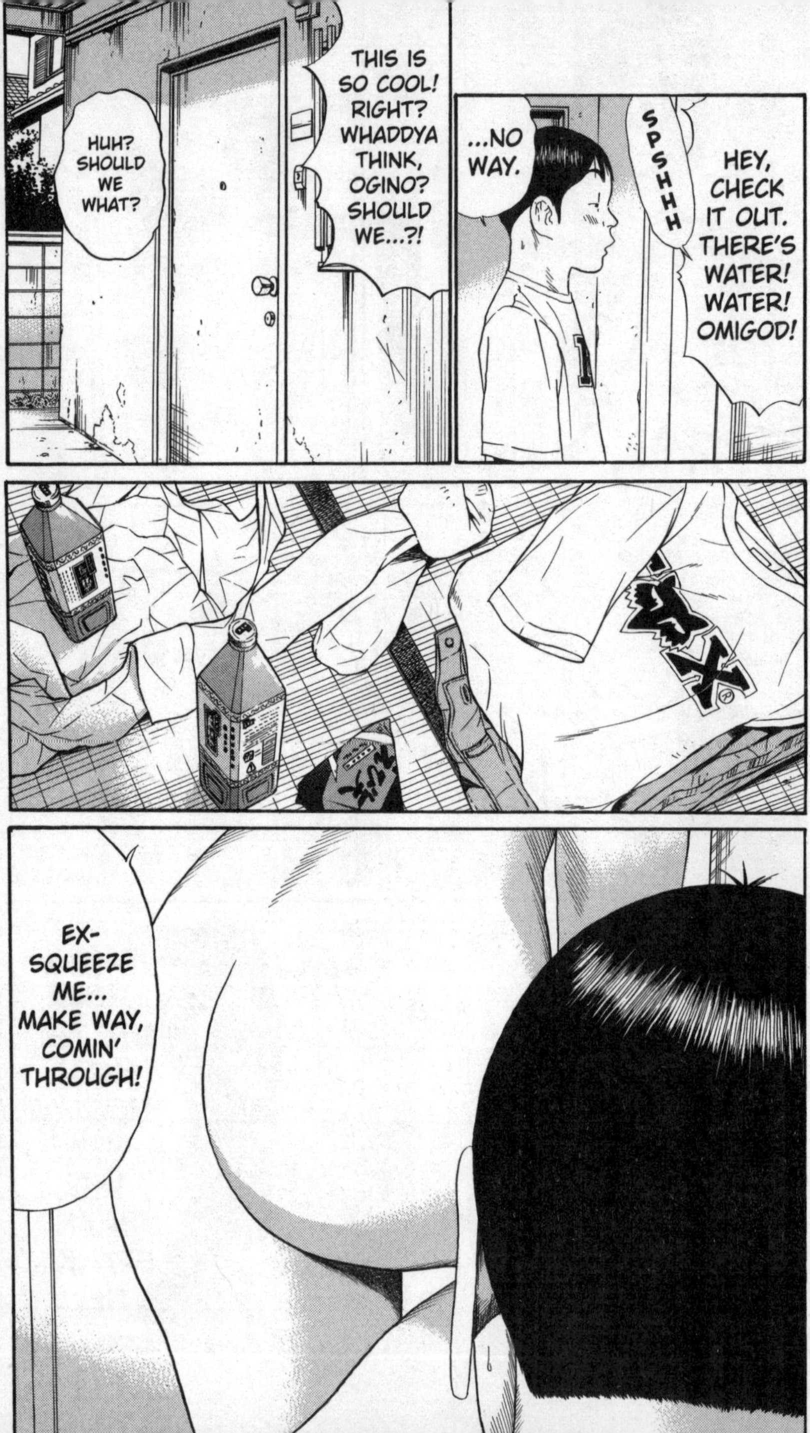
HEY, CHECK IT OUT. THERE'S WATER! WATER! OMIGOD!
SPSHHH
...NO WAY.
THIS IS SO COOL! RIGHT? WHADDYA THINK, OGINO? SHOULD WE...?!
HUH? SHOULD WE WHAT?
EX-SQUEEZE ME... MAKE WAY, COMIN' THROUGH!

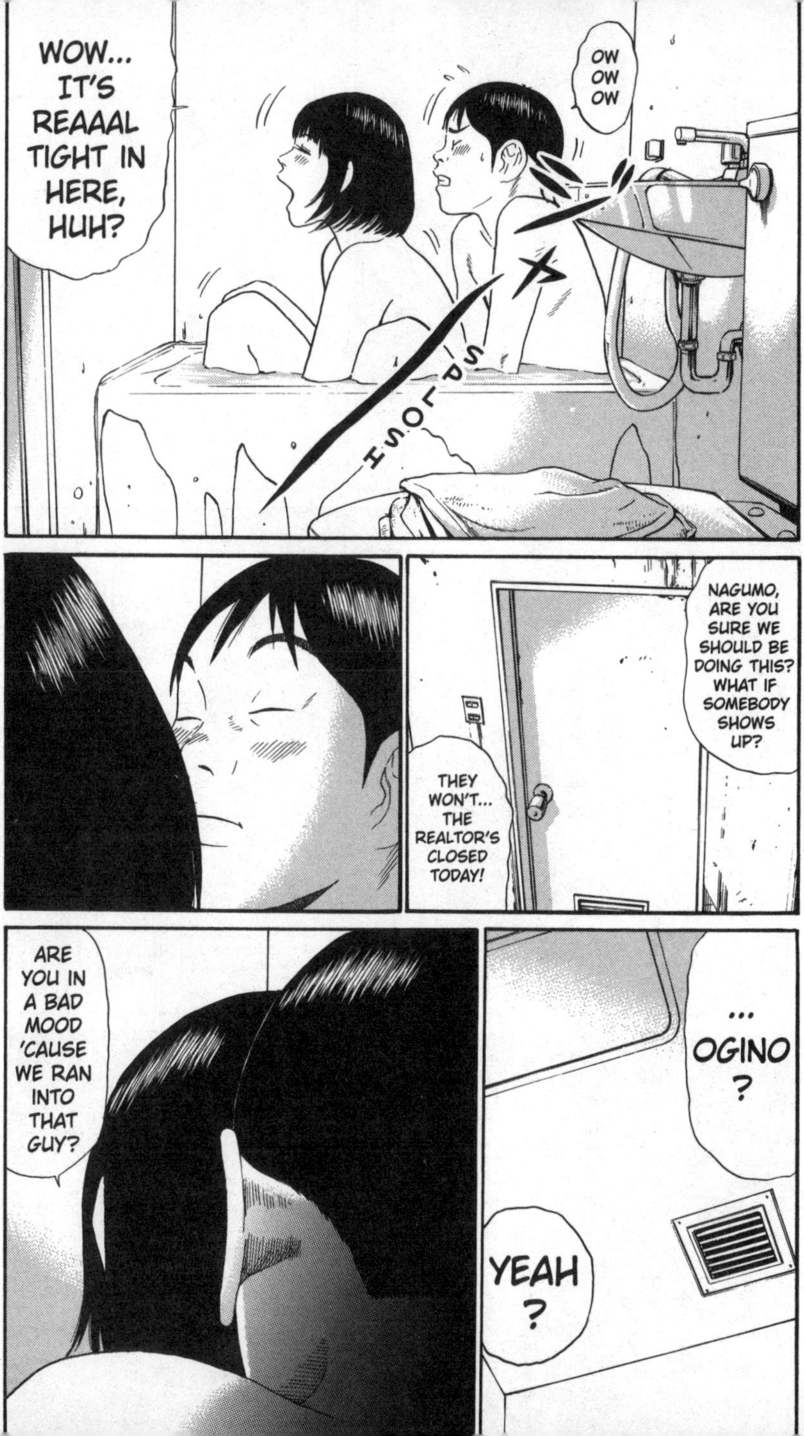
OW OW OW
WOW... IT'S REAAAL TIGHT IN HERE, HUH?
SPLOSH
NAGUMO, ARE YOU SURE WE SHOULD BE DOING THIS? WHAT IF SOMEBODY SHOWS UP?
THEY WON'T... THE REALTOR'S CLOSED TODAY!
... OGINO?
YEAH?
ARE YOU IN A BAD MOOD 'CAUSE WE RAN INTO THAT GUY?

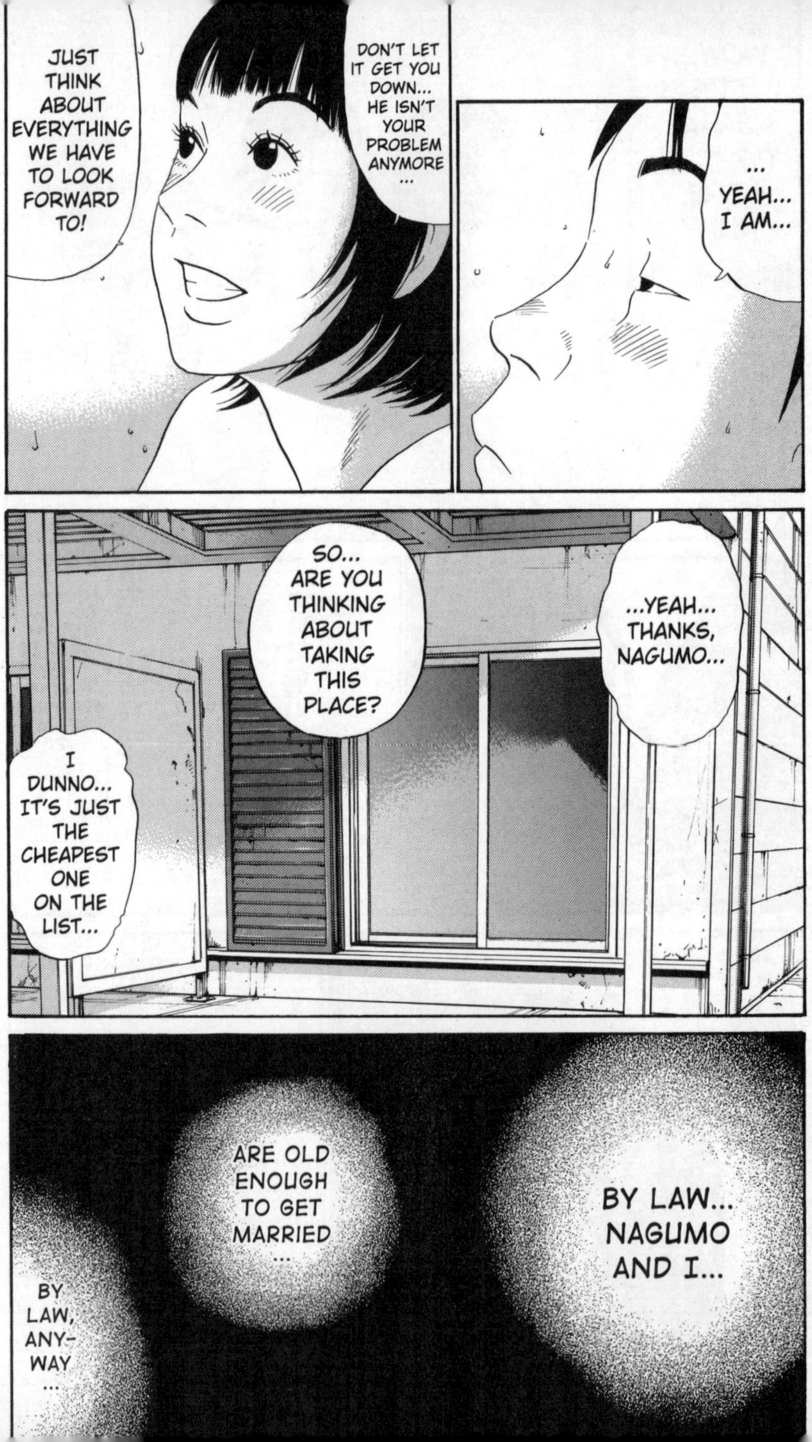
... YEAH... I AM...
DON'T LET IT GET YOU DOWN... HE ISN'T YOUR PROBLEM ANYMORE ...
JUST THINK ABOUT EVERYTHING WE HAVE TO LOOK FORWARD TO!
...YEAH... THANKS, NAGUMO...
SO... ARE YOU THINKING ABOUT TAKING THIS PLACE?
I DUNNO... IT'S JUST THE CHEAPEST ONE ON THE LIST...
BY LAW... NAGUMO AND I...
ARE OLD ENOUGH TO GET MARRIED ...
BY LAW, ANY-WAY ...

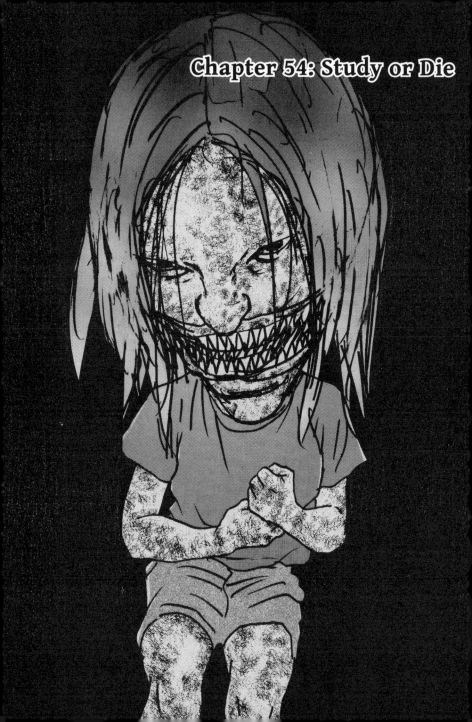

Chapter 54: Study or Die

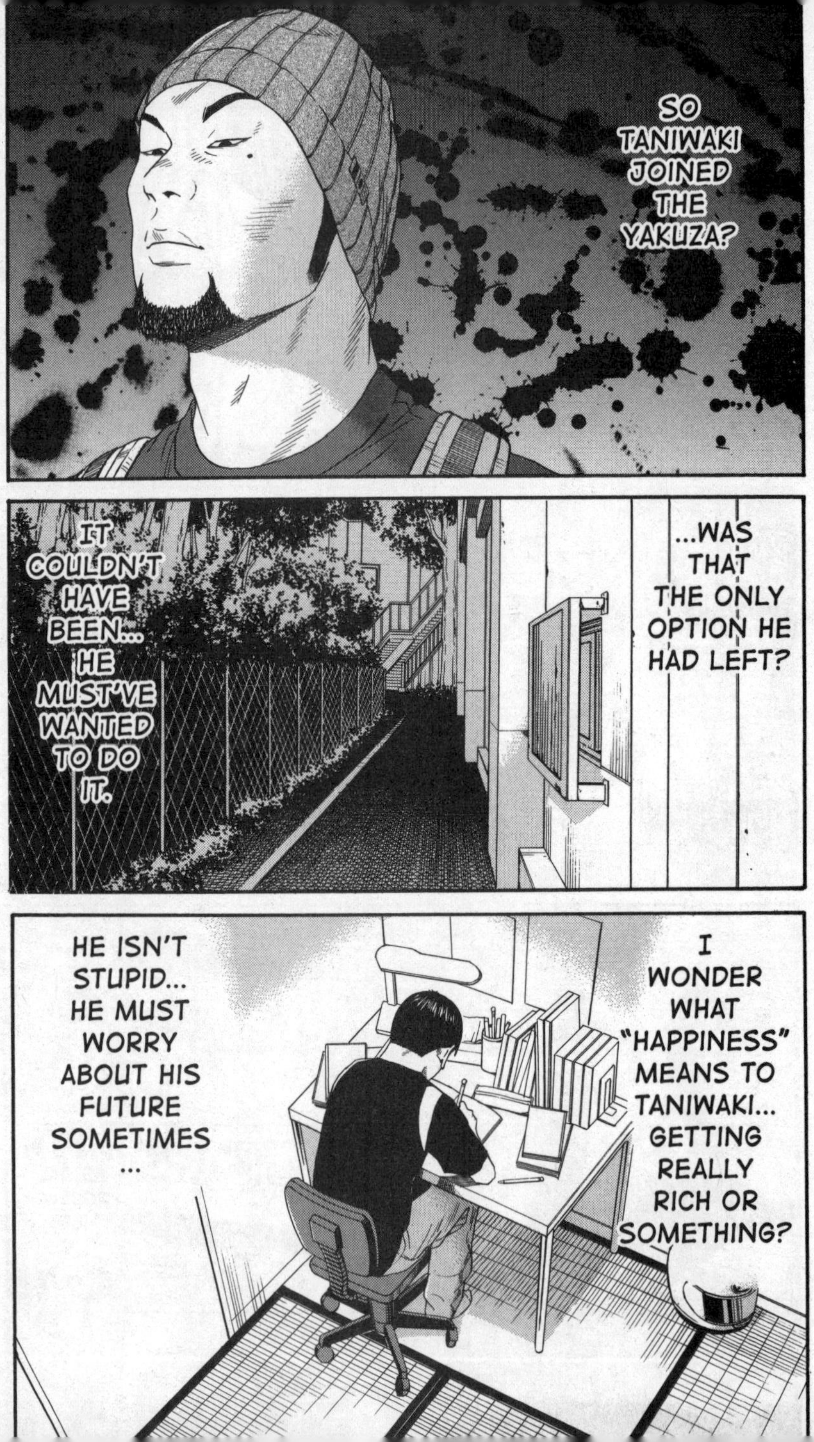
SO TANIWAKI JOINED THE YAKUZA?
...WAS THAT THE ONLY OPTION HE HAD LEFT?
IT COULDN'T HAVE BEEN... HE MUST'VE WANTED TO DO IT.
I WONDER WHAT "HAPPINESS" MEANS TO TANIWAKI... GETTING REALLY RICH OR SOMETHING?
HE ISN'T STUPID... HE MUST WORRY ABOUT HIS FUTURE SOMETIMES...

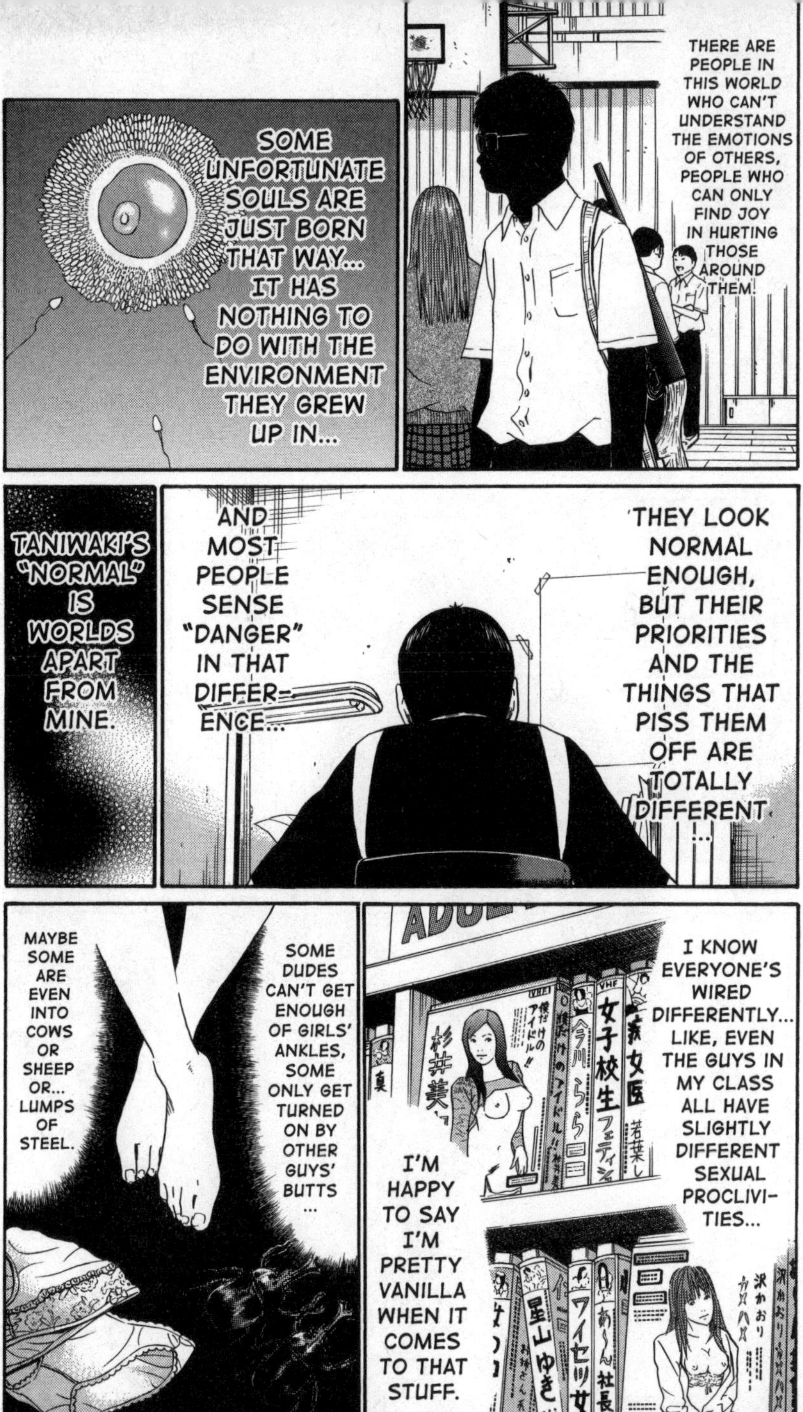
THERE ARE PEOPLE IN THIS WORLD WHO CAN'T UNDERSTAND THE EMOTIONS OF OTHERS, PEOPLE WHO CAN ONLY FIND JOY IN HURTING THOSE AROUND THEM.
SOME UNFORTUNATE SOULS ARE JUST BORN THAT WAY... IT HAS NOTHING TO DO WITH THE ENVIRONMENT THEY GREW UP IN...
THEY LOOK NORMAL ENOUGH, BUT THEIR PRIORITIES AND THE THINGS THAT PISS THEM OFF ARE TOTALLY DIFFERENT...
AND MOST PEOPLE SENSE "DANGER" IN THAT DIFFER-ENCE...
TANIWAKI'S "NORMAL" IS WORLDS APART FROM MINE.
I KNOW EVERYONE'S WIRED DIFFERENTLY... LIKE, EVEN THE GUYS IN MY CLASS ALL HAVE SLIGHTLY DIFFERENT SEXUAL PROCLIVI-TIES...
I'M HAPPY TO SAY I'M PRETTY VANILLA WHEN IT COMES TO THAT STUFF.
SOME DUDES CAN'T GET ENOUGH OF GIRLS' ANKLES, SOME ONLY GET TURNED ON BY OTHER GUYS' BUTTS...
MAYBE SOME ARE EVEN INTO COWS OR SHEEP OR... LUMPS OF STEEL.

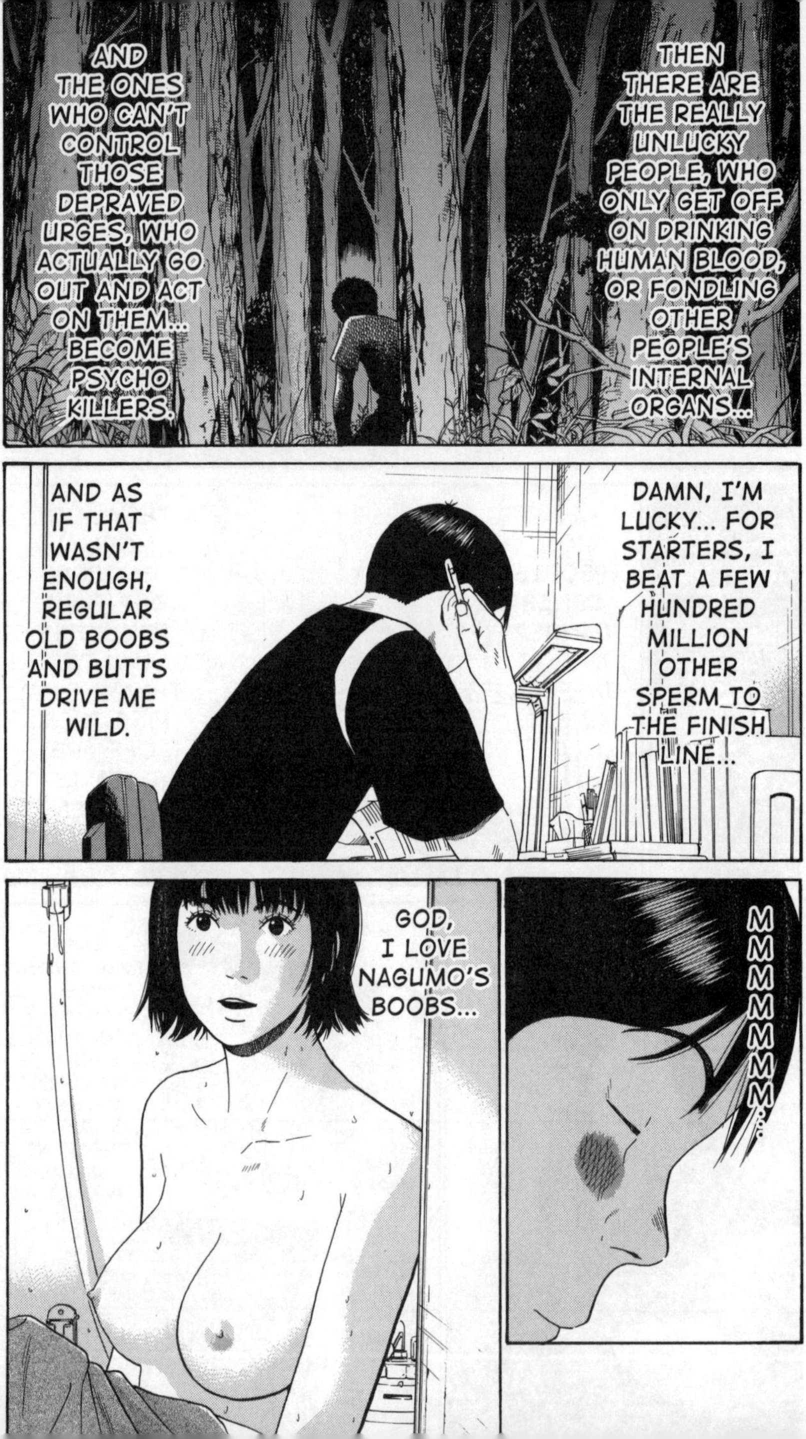
THEN THERE ARE THE REALLY UNLUCKY PEOPLE, WHO ONLY GET OFF ON DRINKING HUMAN BLOOD, OR FONDLING OTHER PEOPLE'S INTERNAL ORGANS...
AND THE ONES WHO CAN'T CONTROL THOSE DEPRAVED URGES, WHO ACTUALLY GO OUT AND ACT ON THEM... BECOME PSYCHO KILLERS.
DAMN, I'M LUCKY... FOR STARTERS, I BEAT A FEW HUNDRED MILLION OTHER SPERM TO THE FINISH LINE...
AND AS IF THAT WASN'T ENOUGH, REGULAR OLD BOOBS AND BUTTS DRIVE ME WILD.
MMMMMMM...
GOD, I LOVE NAGUMO'S BOOBS...

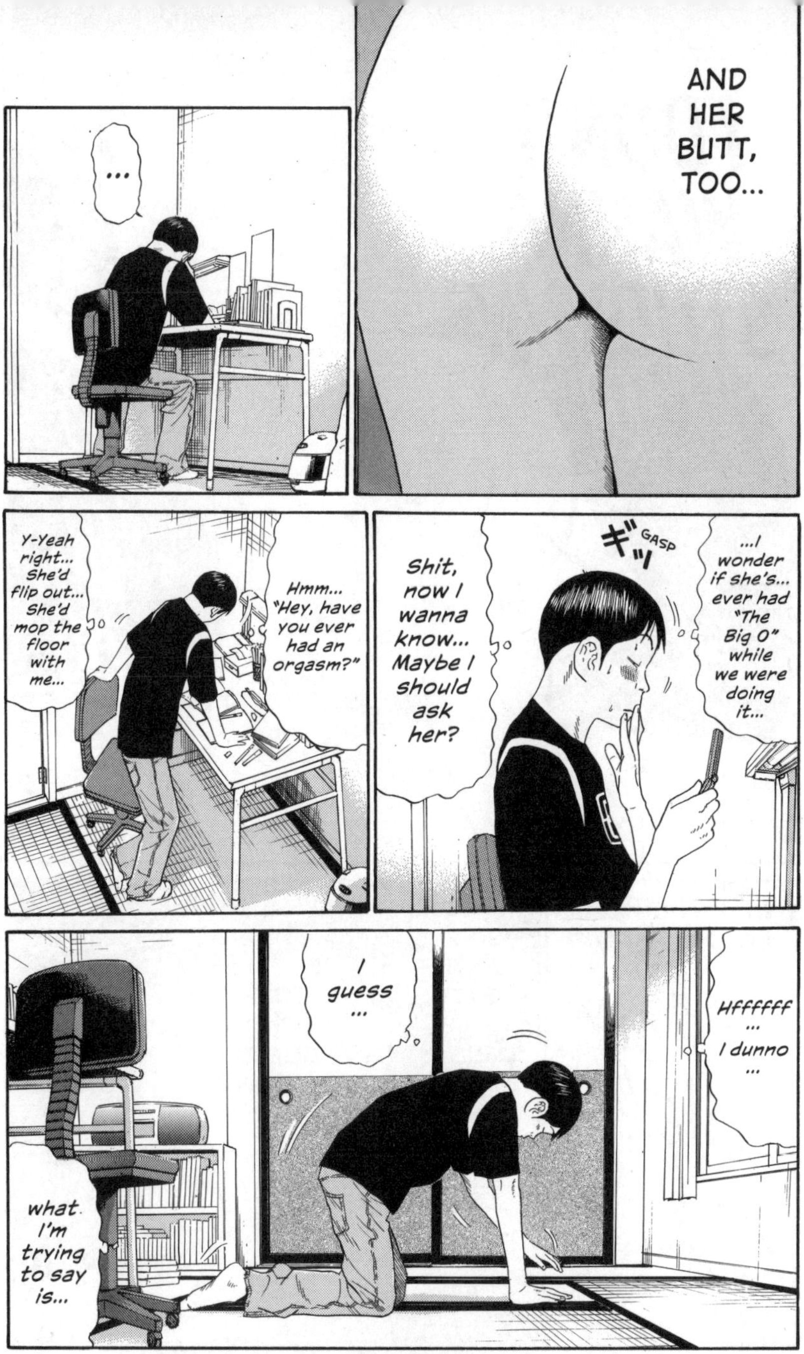

AND HER BUTT, TOO...
...
ギッ GASP
...I wonder if she's... ever had "The Big O" while we were doing it...
Shit, now I wanna know... Maybe I should ask her?
Hmm... "Hey, have you ever had an orgasm?"
Y-Yeah right... She'd flip out... She'd mop the floor with me...
Hffffff ... I dunno ...
I guess ...
what I'm trying to say is...

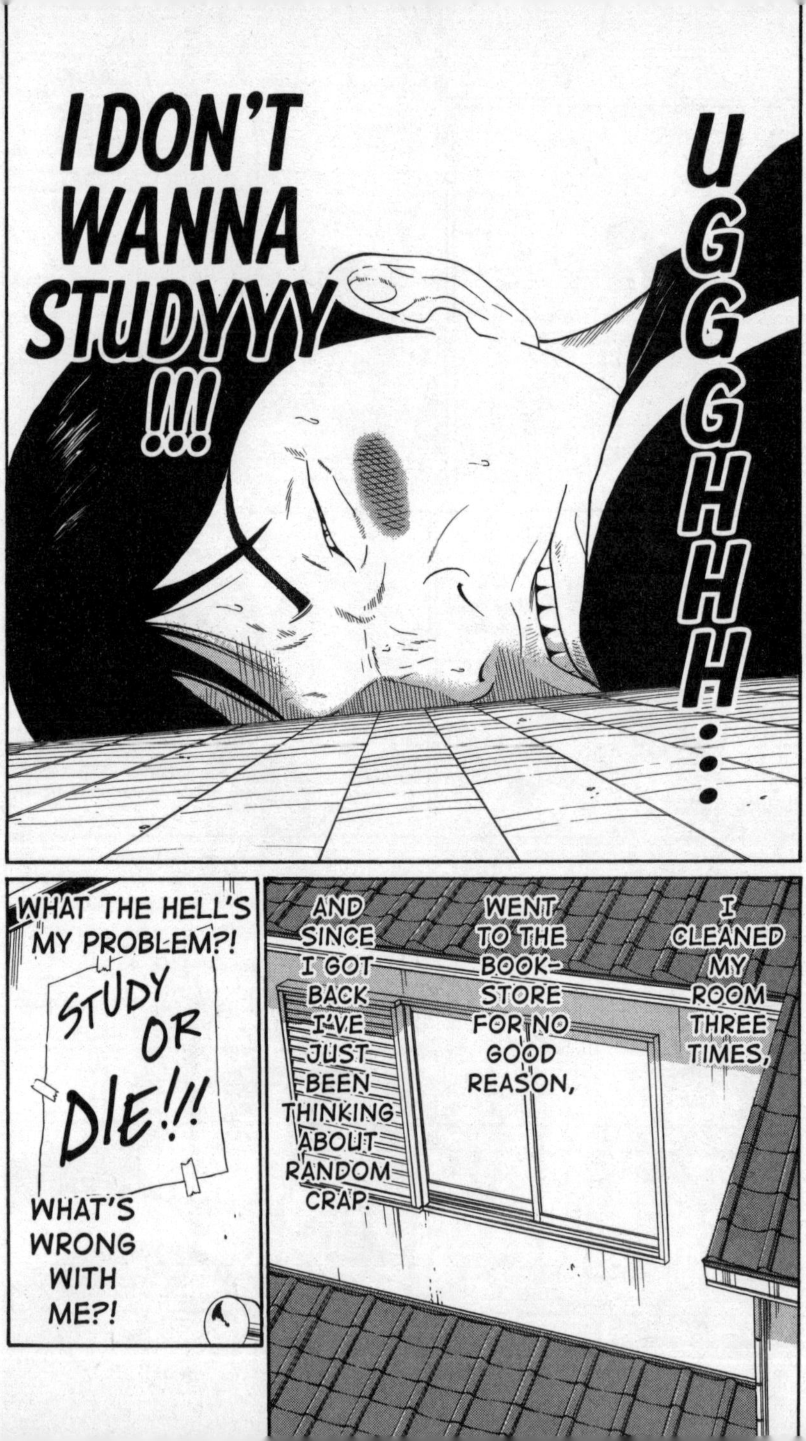
UGGGHHHH...
I DON'T WANNA STUDYYY!!!
I CLEANED MY ROOM THREE TIMES,
WENT TO THE BOOK-STORE FOR NO GOOD REASON,
AND SINCE I GOT BACK I'VE JUST BEEN THINKING ABOUT RANDOM CRAP.
WHAT THE HELL'S MY PROBLEM?!
STUDY OR DIE!!!
WHAT'S WRONG WITH ME?!

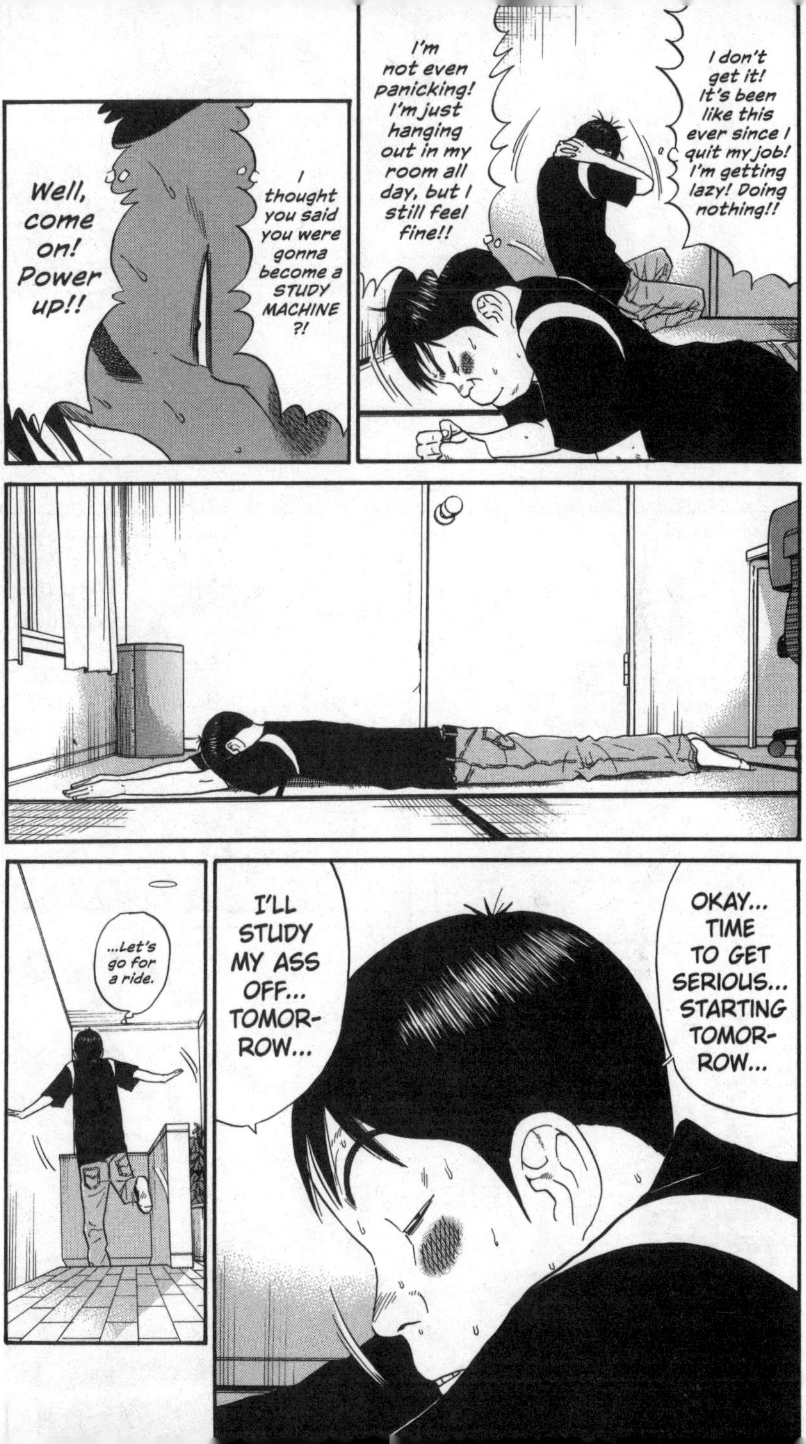
I don't get it! It's been like this ever since I quit my job! I'm getting lazy! Doing nothing!!
I'm not even panicking! I'm just hanging out in my room all day, but I still feel fine!!
I thought you said you were gonna become a STUDY MACHINE?!
Well, come on! Power up!!
OKAY... TIME TO GET SERIOUS... STARTING TOMOR-ROW...
I'LL STUDY MY ASS OFF... TOMOR-ROW...
...Let's go for a ride.

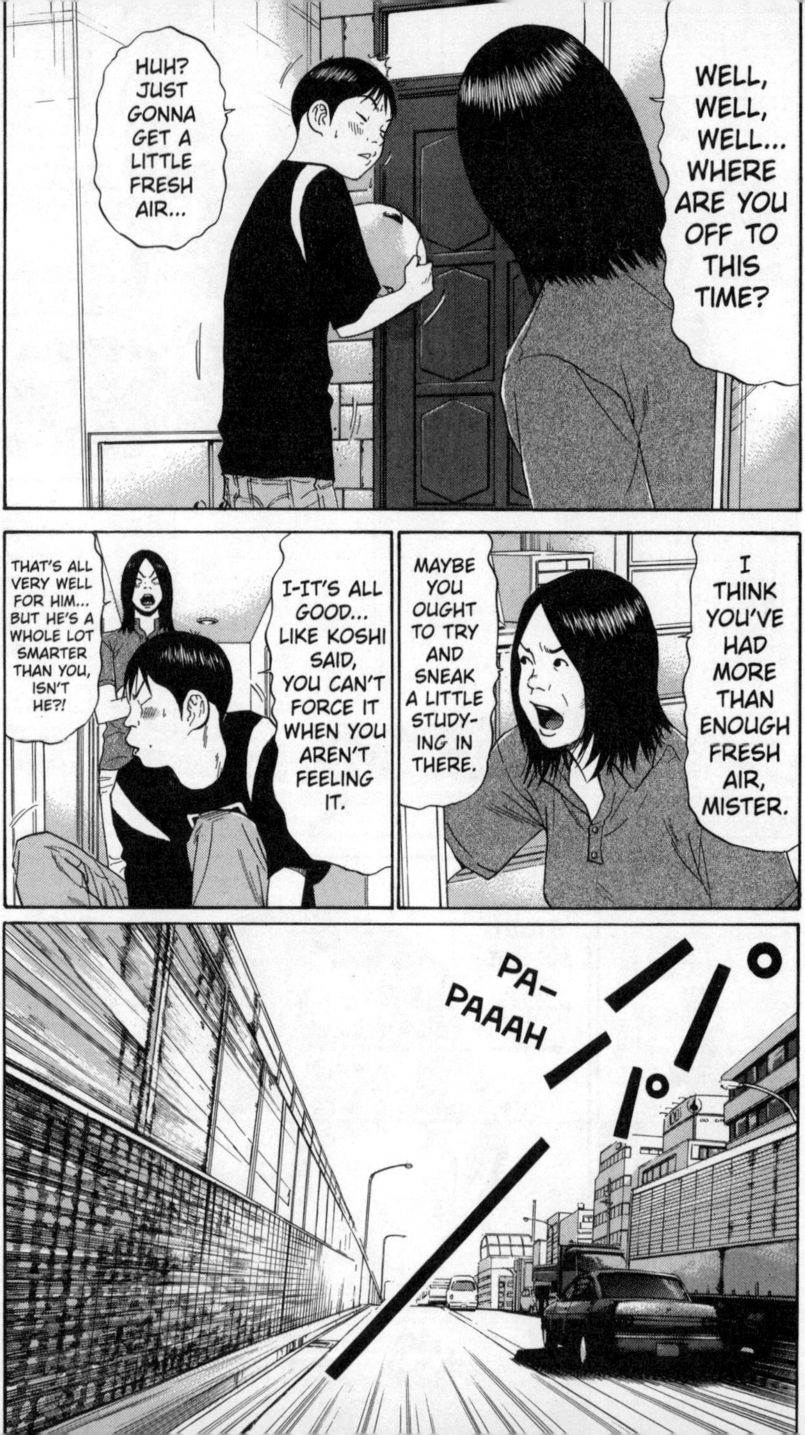
WELL, WELL, WELL... WHERE ARE YOU OFF TO THIS TIME?
HUH? JUST GONNA GET A LITTLE FRESH AIR...
I THINK YOU'VE HAD MORE THAN ENOUGH FRESH AIR, MISTER.
MAYBE YOU OUGHT TO TRY AND SNEAK A LITTLE STUDYING IN THERE.
I-IT'S ALL GOOD... LIKE KOSHI SAID, YOU CAN'T FORCE IT WHEN YOU AREN'T FEELING IT.
THAT'S ALL VERY WELL FOR HIM... BUT HE'S A WHOLE LOT SMARTER THAN YOU, ISN'T HE?!
PA-PAAAH

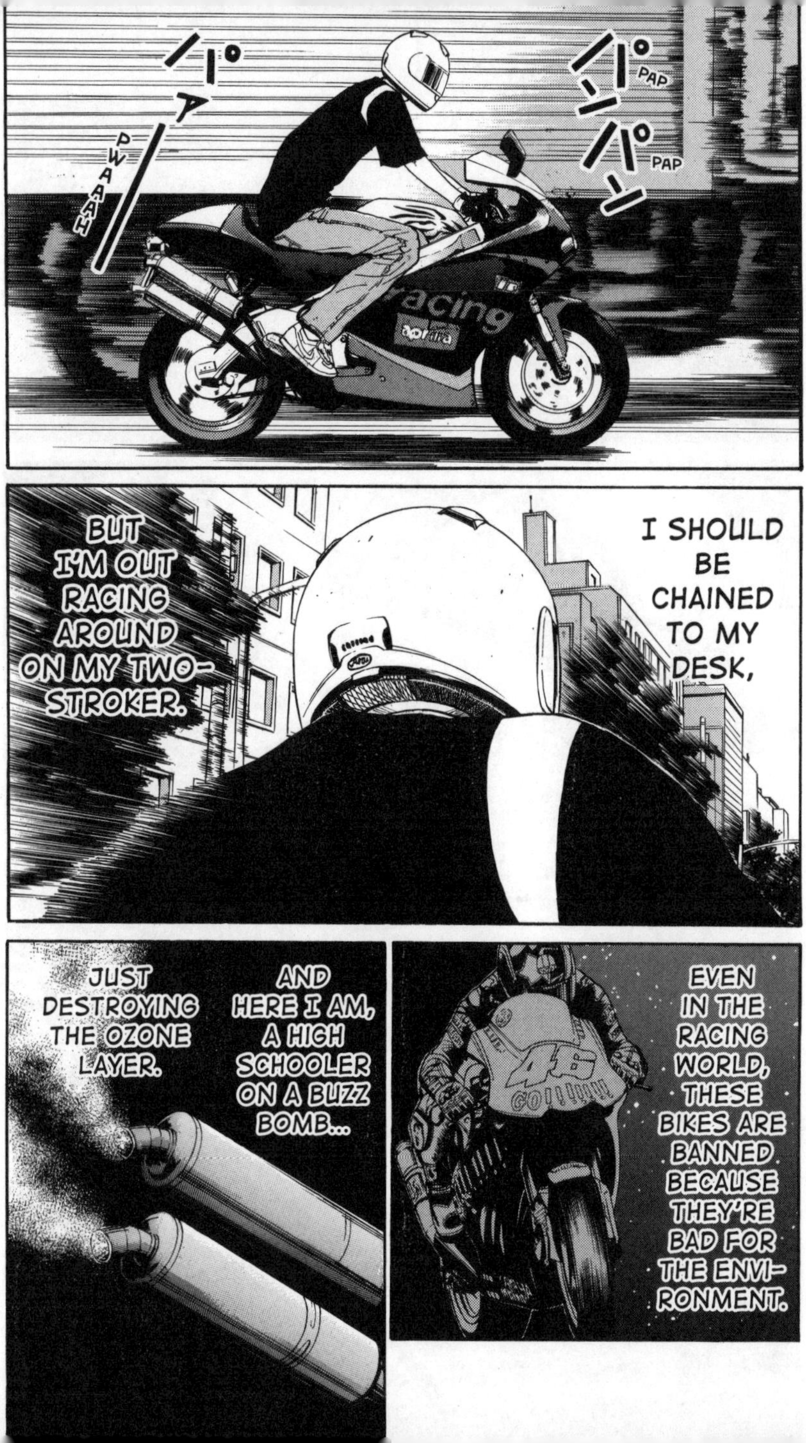
PAP
PAP
PWAAAAH
I SHOULD BE CHAINED TO MY DESK,
BUT I'M OUT RACING AROUND ON MY TWO-STROKER.
EVEN IN THE RACING WORLD, THESE BIKES ARE BANNED BECAUSE THEY'RE BAD FOR THE ENVIRONMENT.
AND HERE I AM, A HIGH SCHOOLER ON A BUZZ BOMB...
JUST DESTROYING THE OZONE LAYER.

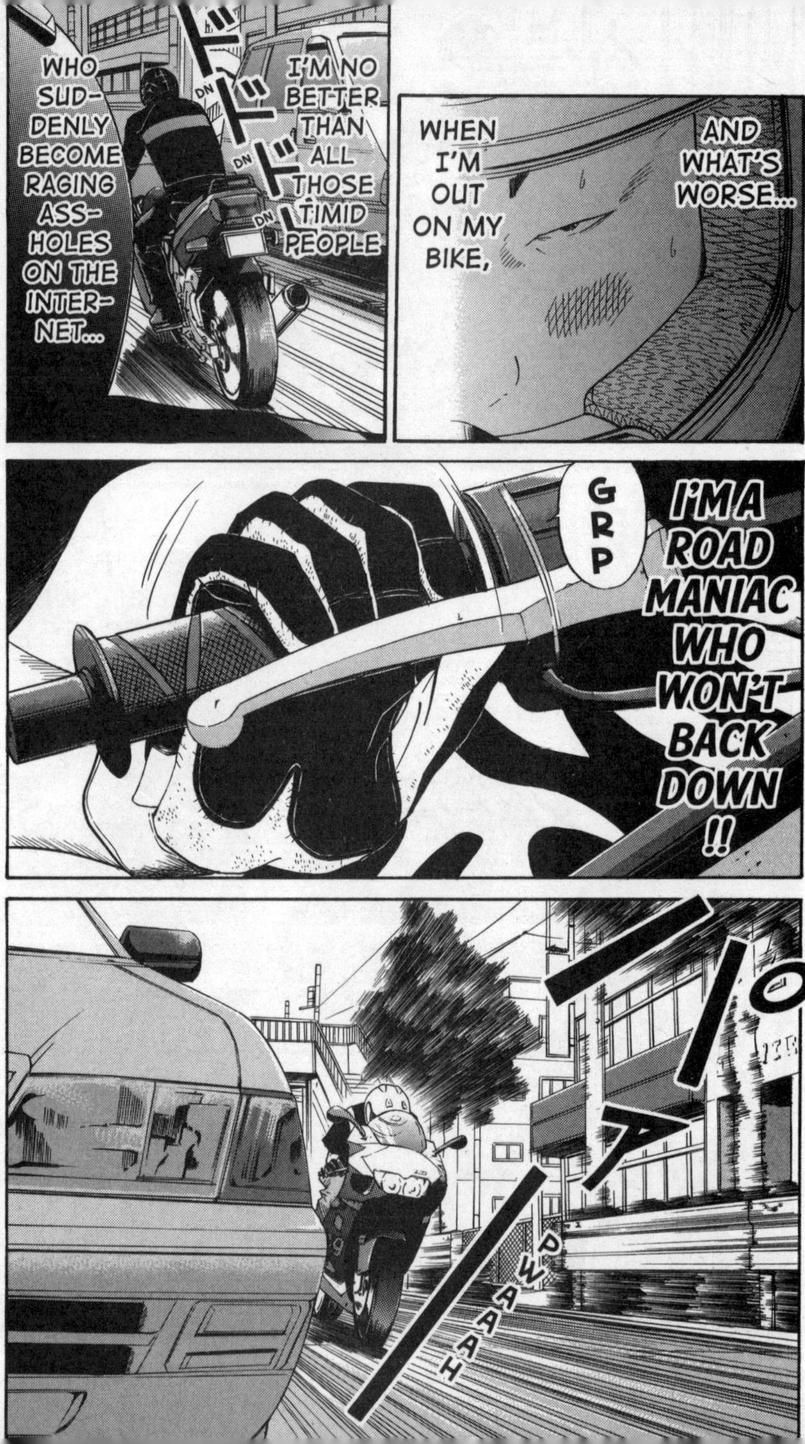
AND WHAT'S WORSE...
WHEN I'M OUT ON MY BIKE,
DN
DN
DN
I'M NO BETTER THAN ALL THOSE TIMID PEOPLE
WHO SUD-DENLY BECOME RAGING ASS-HOLES ON THE INTER-NET...
I'M A ROAD MANIAC WHO WON'T BACK DOWN !!
GRP
PWAAAAH

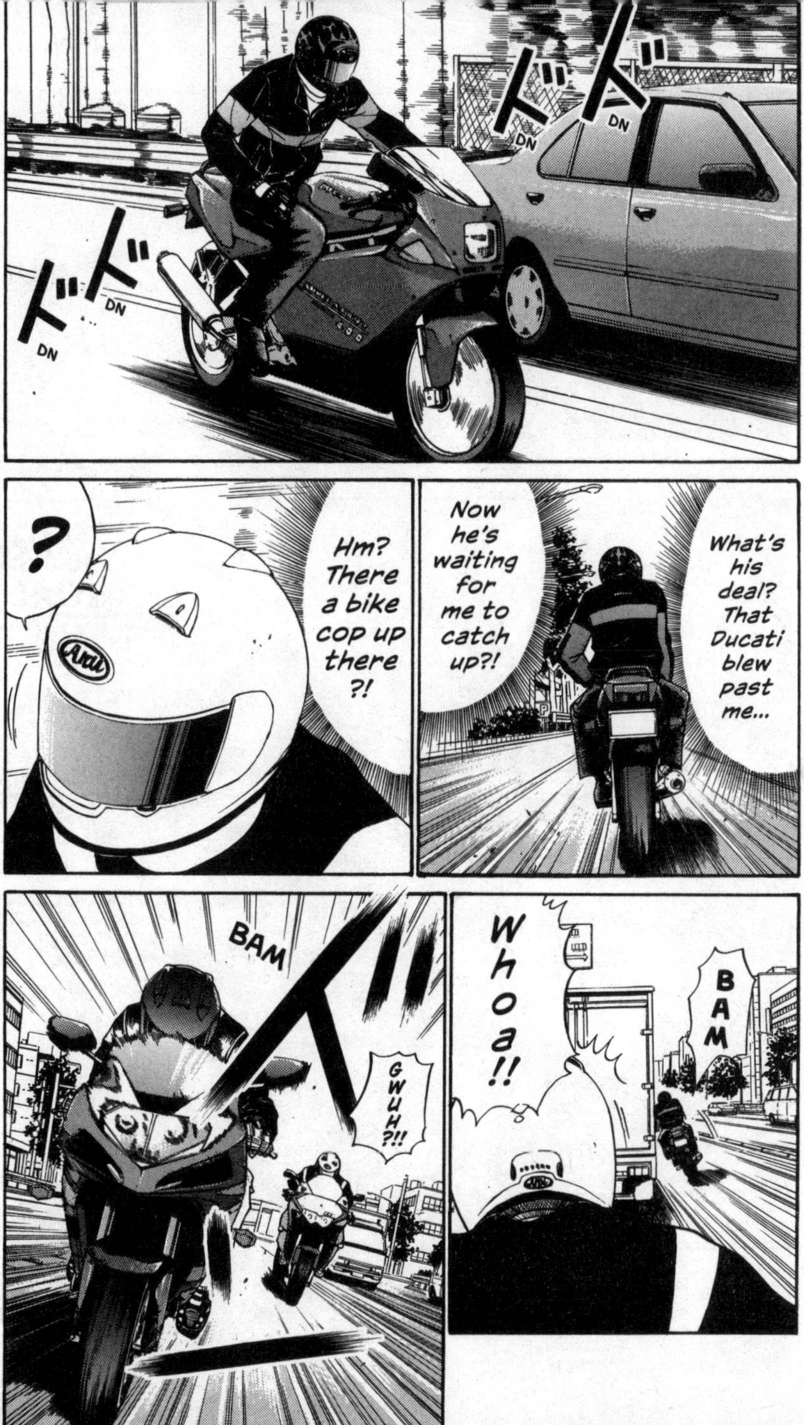
ドド
DN
DN
ドド
DN
DN
What's his deal? That Ducati blew past me...
Now he's waiting for me to catch up?!
Hm? There a bike cop up there?!
?
BAM
Whoa!!
BAM
ド
GWUH?!!

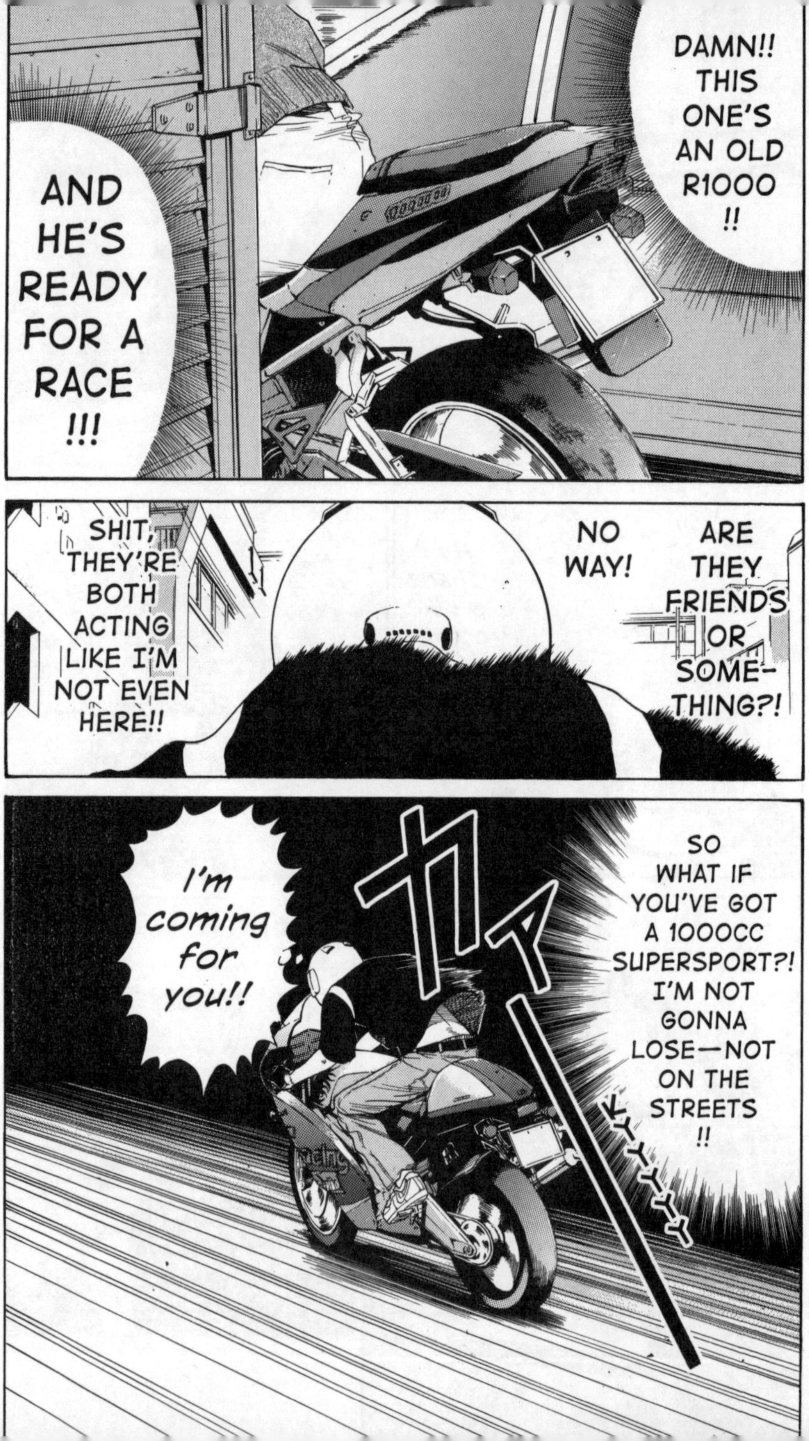
DAMN!! THIS ONE'S AN OLD R1000 !!
AND HE'S READY FOR A RACE !!!
ARE THEY FRIENDS OR SOME-THING?!
NO WAY!
SHIT, THEY'RE BOTH ACTING LIKE I'M NOT EVEN HERE!!
SO WHAT IF YOU'VE GOT A 1000CC SUPERSPORT?! I'M NOT GONNA LOSE—NOT ON THE STREETS !!
I'm coming for you!!

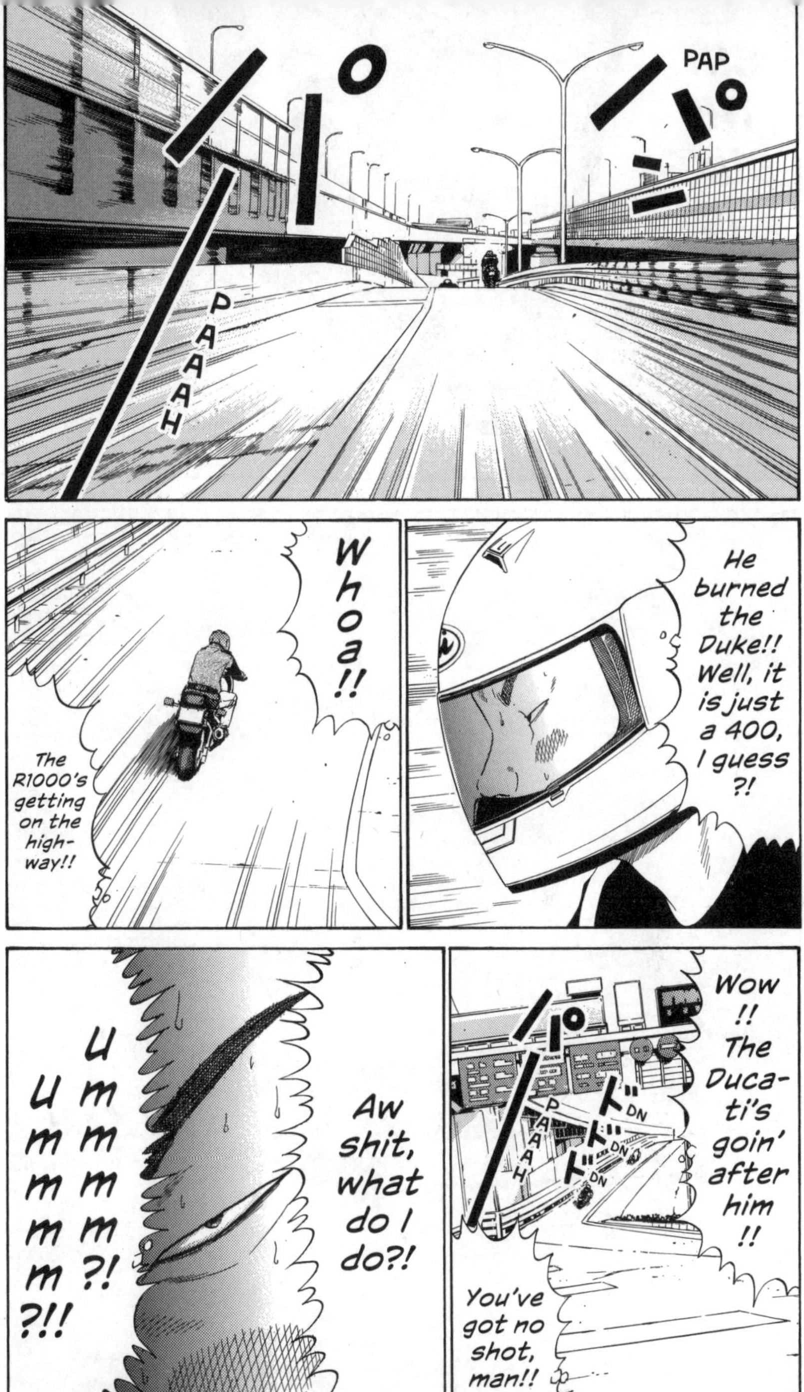
PAP
PAAAAH
He burned the Duke!! Well, it is just a 400, I guess?!
Whoa!!
The R1000's getting on the highway!!
Wow!! The Ducati's goin' after him!!
PAAAH
DN
DN
DN
You've got no shot, man!!
Aw shit, what do I do?!
Ummmm?!
Ummmmm?!!

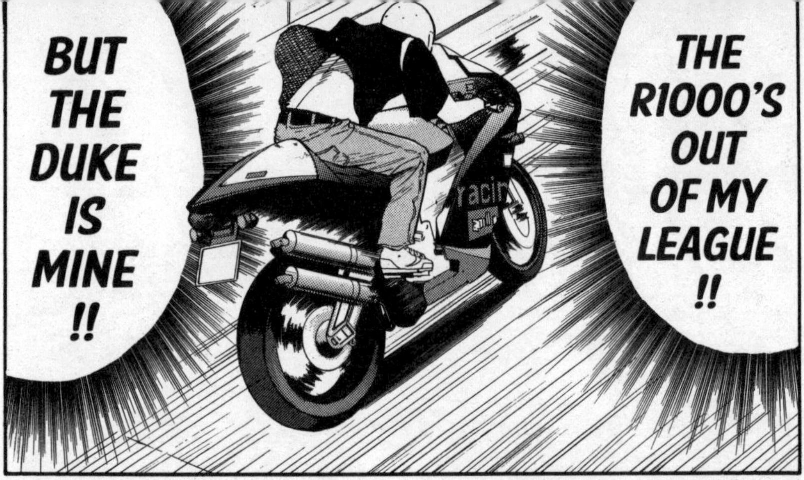
THE R1000'S OUT OF MY LEAGUE !!
BUT THE DUKE IS MINE !!

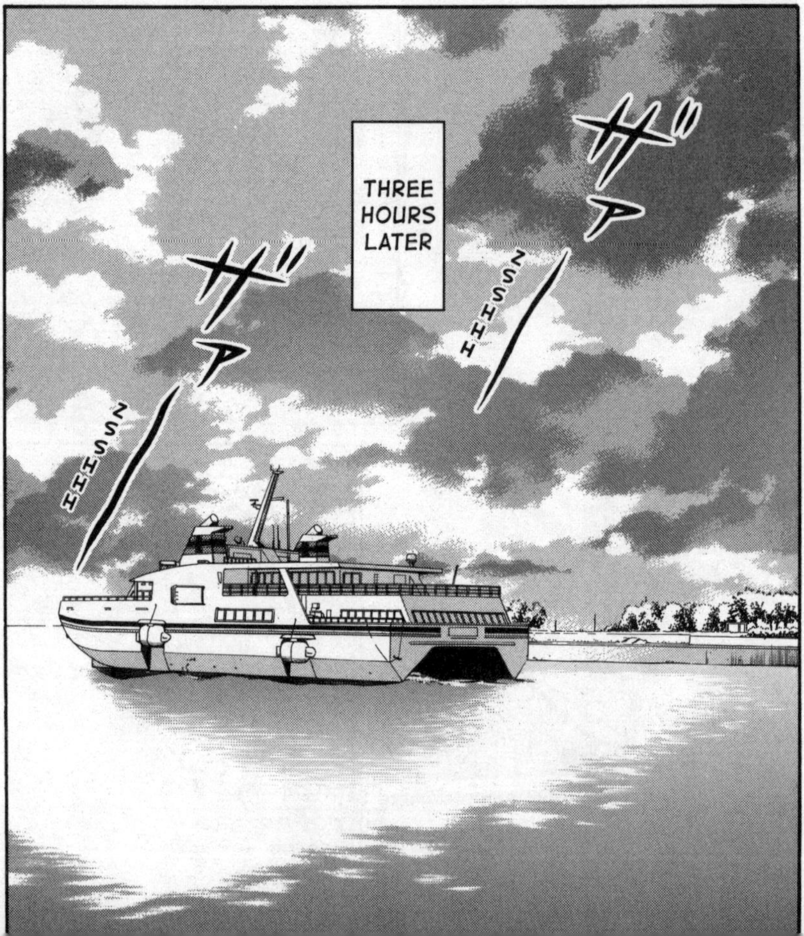
THREE HOURS LATER
ザァ
ZSSHHH
ザァ
ZSSHHH

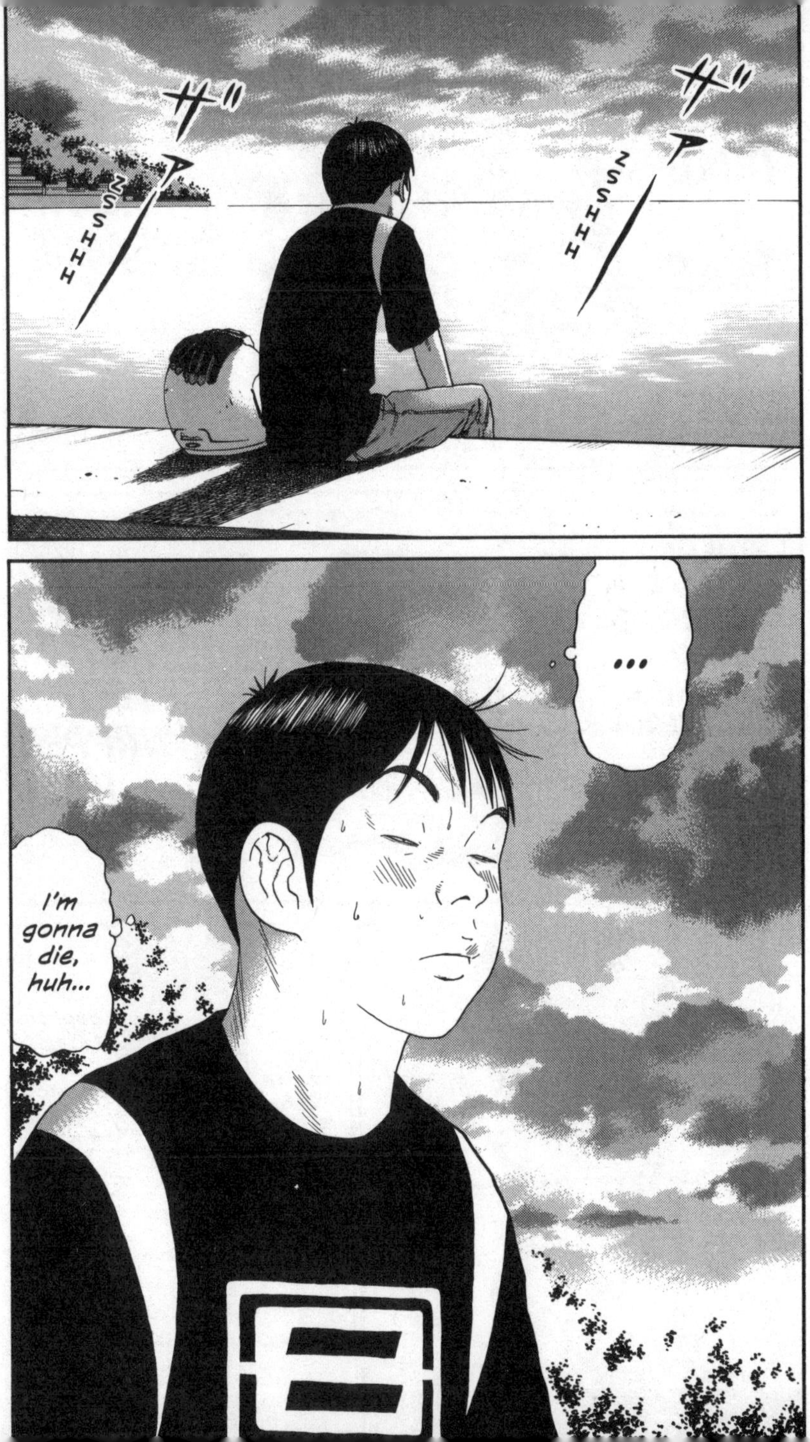
ZSSHHH
ZSSHHH
...
I'm gonna die, huh...

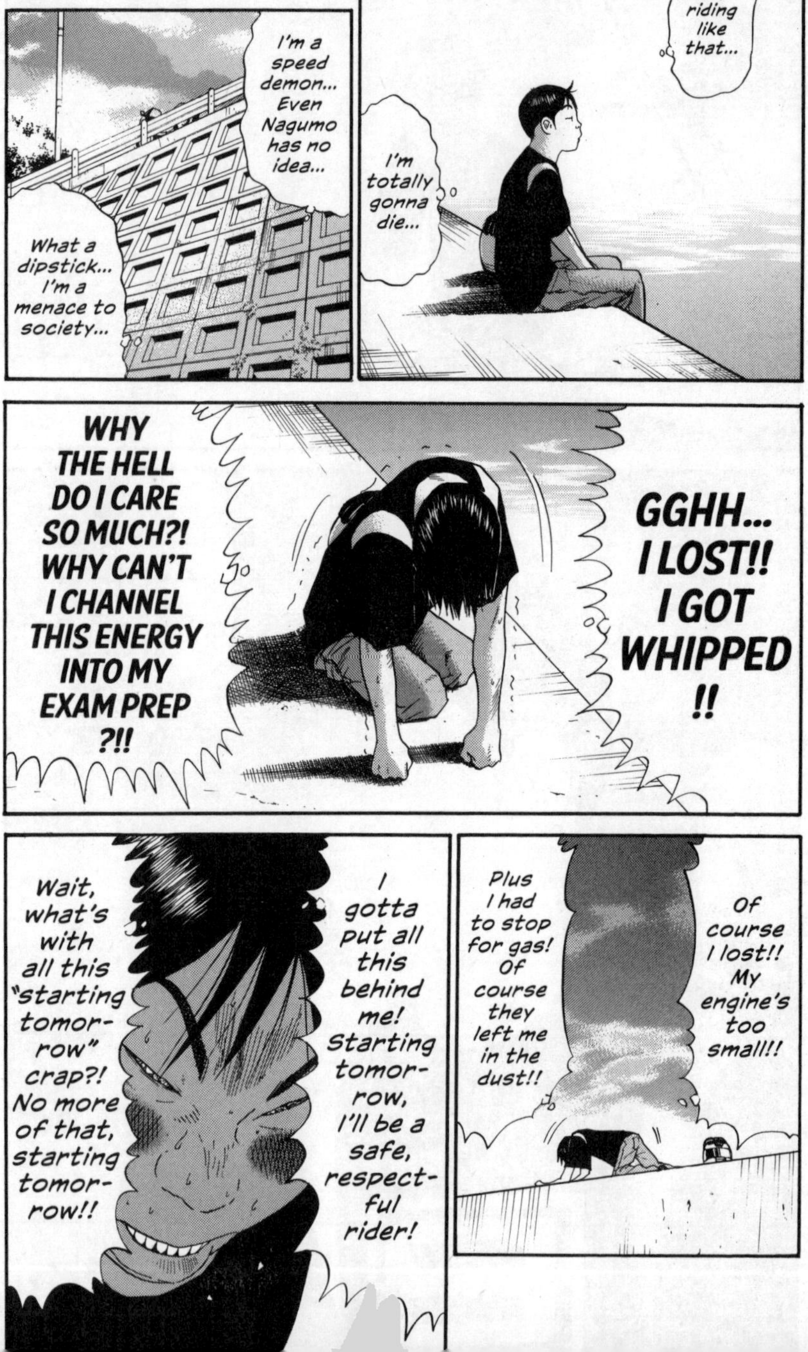
If I keep riding like that...
I'm totally gonna die...
I'm a speed demon... Even Nagumo has no idea...
What a dipstick... I'm a menace to society...
GGHH... I LOST!! I GOT WHIPPED !!
WHY THE HELL DO I CARE SO MUCH?! WHY CAN'T I CHANNEL THIS ENERGY INTO MY EXAM PREP ?!!
Of course I lost!! My engine's too small!!
Plus I had to stop for gas! Of course they left me in the dust!!
I gotta put all this behind me! Starting tomorrow, I'll be a safe, respectful rider!
Wait, what's with all this "starting tomorrow" crap?! No more of that, starting tomorrow!!

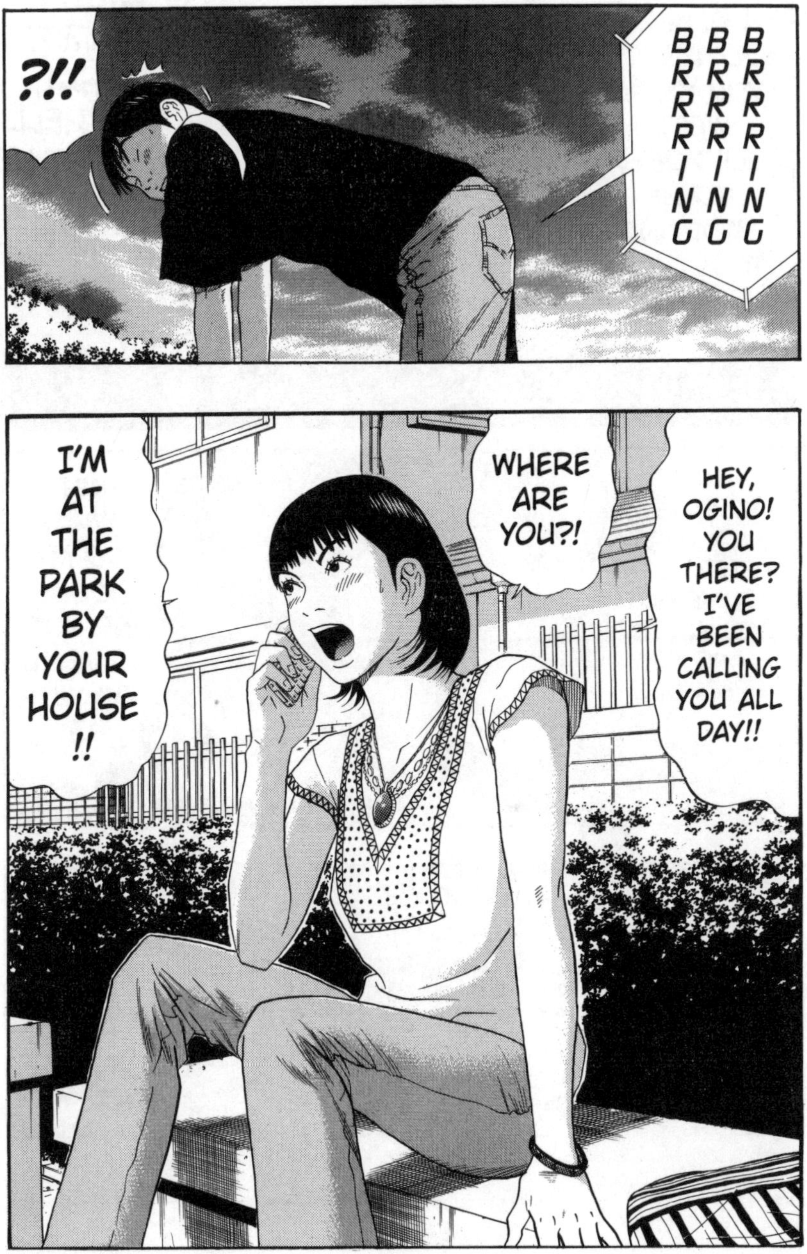
BRRRING
BRRRING
BRRRING
?!!
HEY, OGINO! YOU THERE? I'VE BEEN CALLING YOU ALL DAY!!
WHERE ARE YOU?!
I'M AT THE PARK BY YOUR HOUSE!!

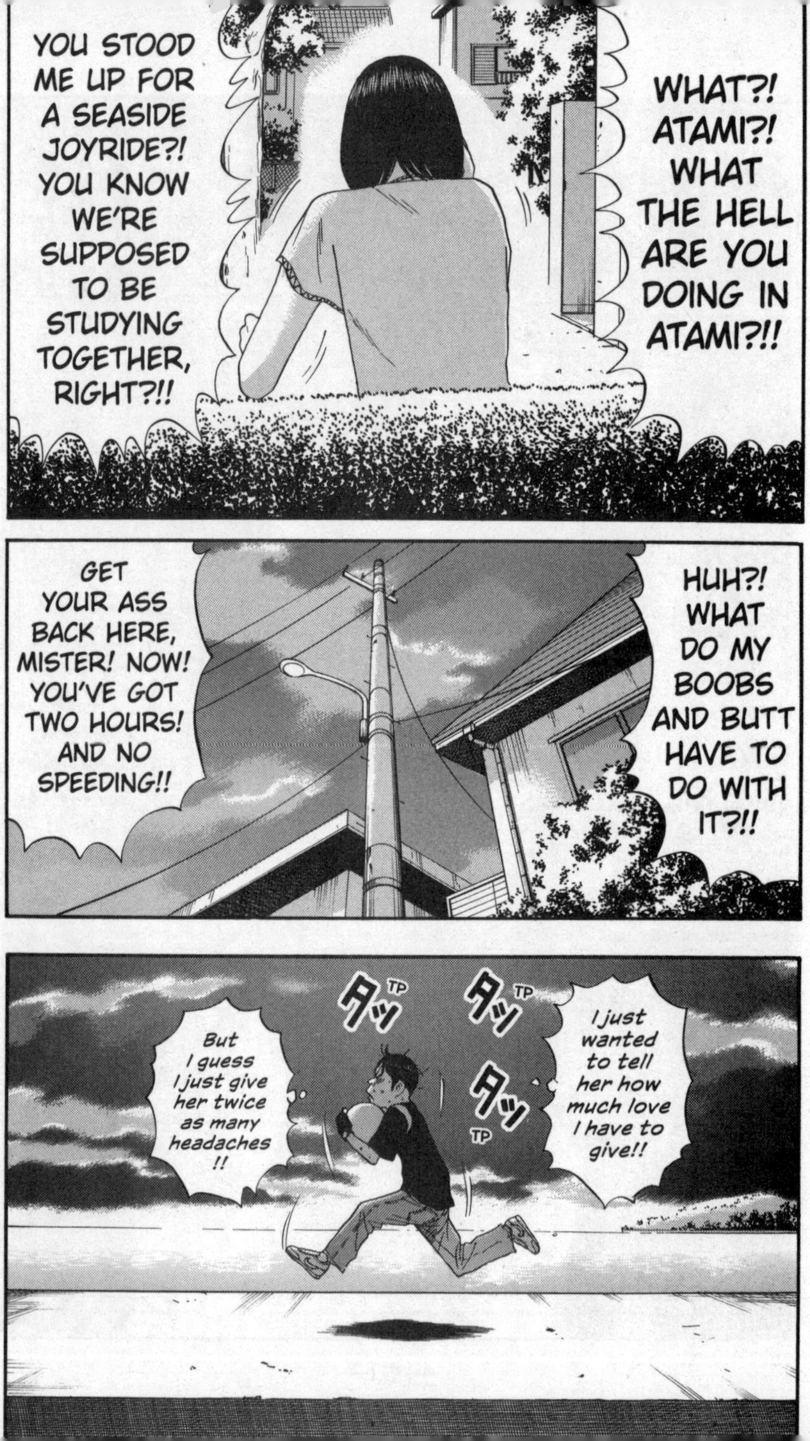
WHAT?! ATAMI?! WHAT THE HELL ARE YOU DOING IN ATAMI?!!
YOU STOOD ME UP FOR A SEASIDE JOYRIDE?! YOU KNOW WE'RE SUPPOSED TO BE STUDYING TOGETHER, RIGHT?!!
HUH?! WHAT DO MY BOOBS AND BUTT HAVE TO DO WITH IT?!!
GET YOUR ASS BACK HERE, MISTER! NOW! YOU'VE GOT TWO HOURS! AND NO SPEEDING!!
タッ TP
タッ TP
タッ TP
I just wanted to tell her how much love I have to give!!
But I guess I just give her twice as many headaches!!

# Chapter 55: Living Alone

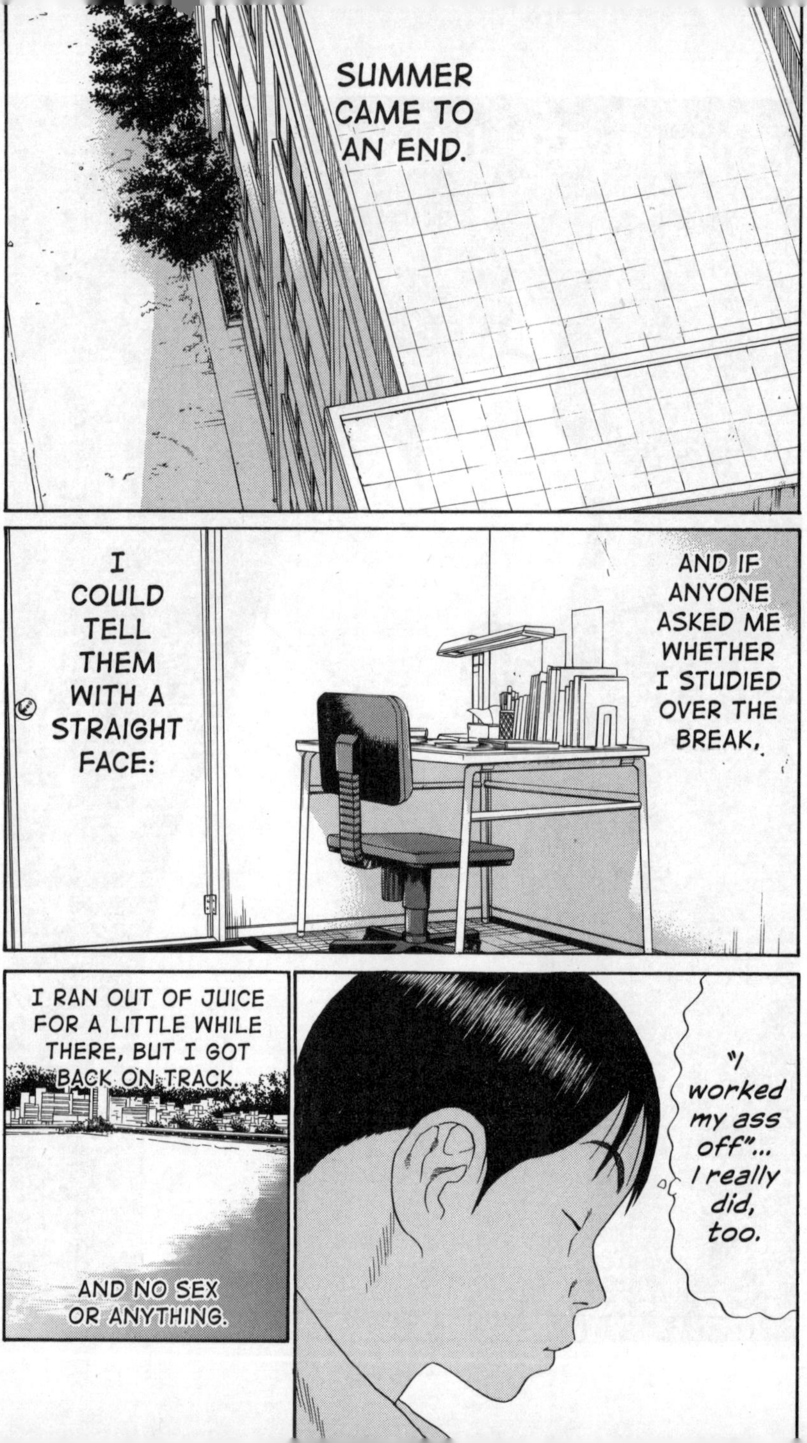

SUMMER CAME TO AN END.
AND IF ANYONE ASKED ME WHETHER I STUDIED OVER THE BREAK,
I COULD TELL THEM WITH A STRAIGHT FACE:
"I worked my ass off"... I really did, too.
I RAN OUT OF JUICE FOR A LITTLE WHILE THERE, BUT I GOT BACK ON TRACK.
AND NO SEX OR ANYTHING.

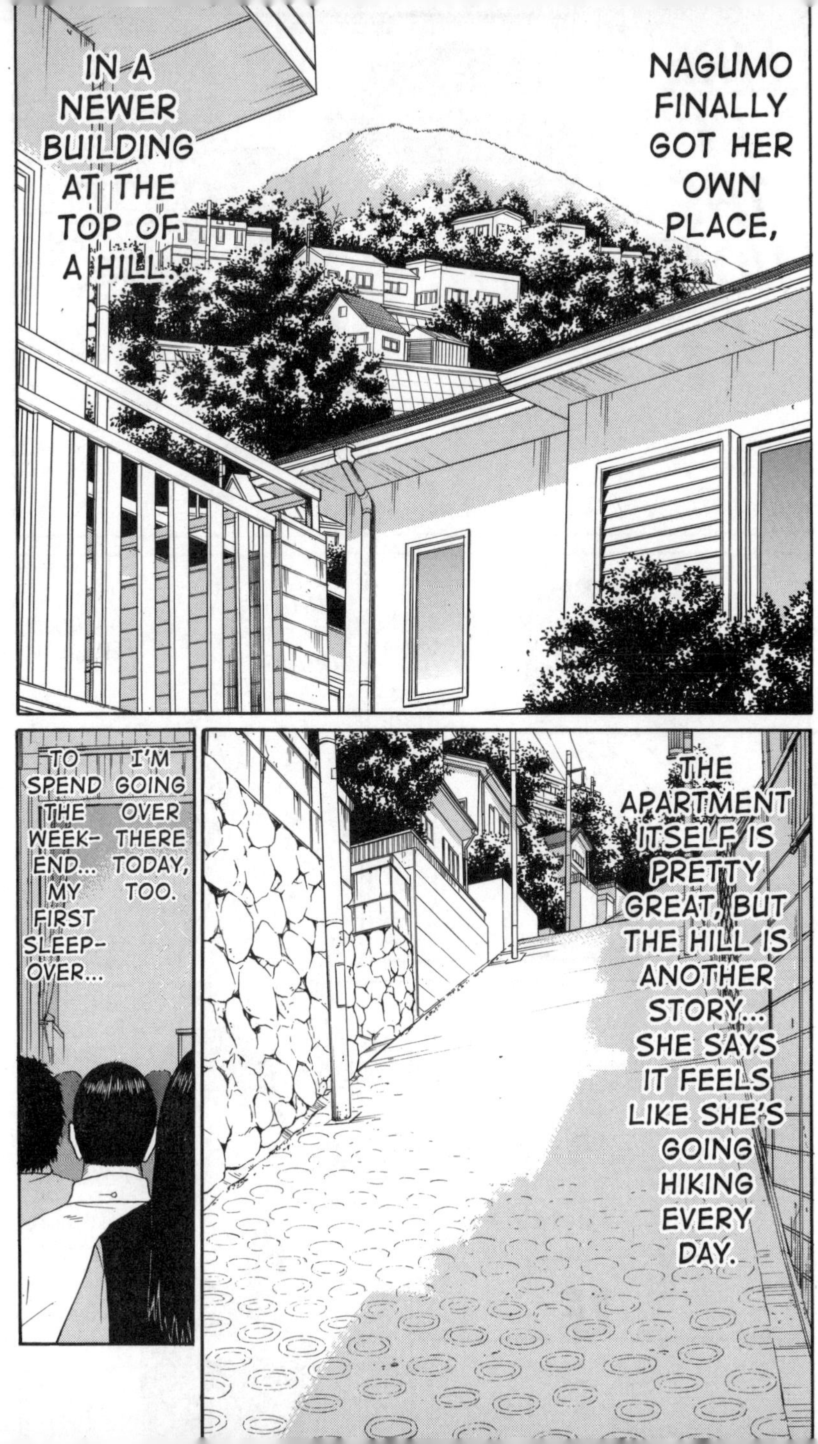
NAGUMO FINALLY GOT HER OWN PLACE,
IN A NEWER BUILDING AT THE TOP OF A HILL.
THE APARTMENT ITSELF IS PRETTY GREAT, BUT THE HILL IS ANOTHER STORY... SHE SAYS IT FEELS LIKE SHE'S GOING HIKING EVERY DAY.
I'M GOING OVER THERE TODAY, TOO.
TO SPEND THE WEEKEND... MY FIRST SLEEPOVER...

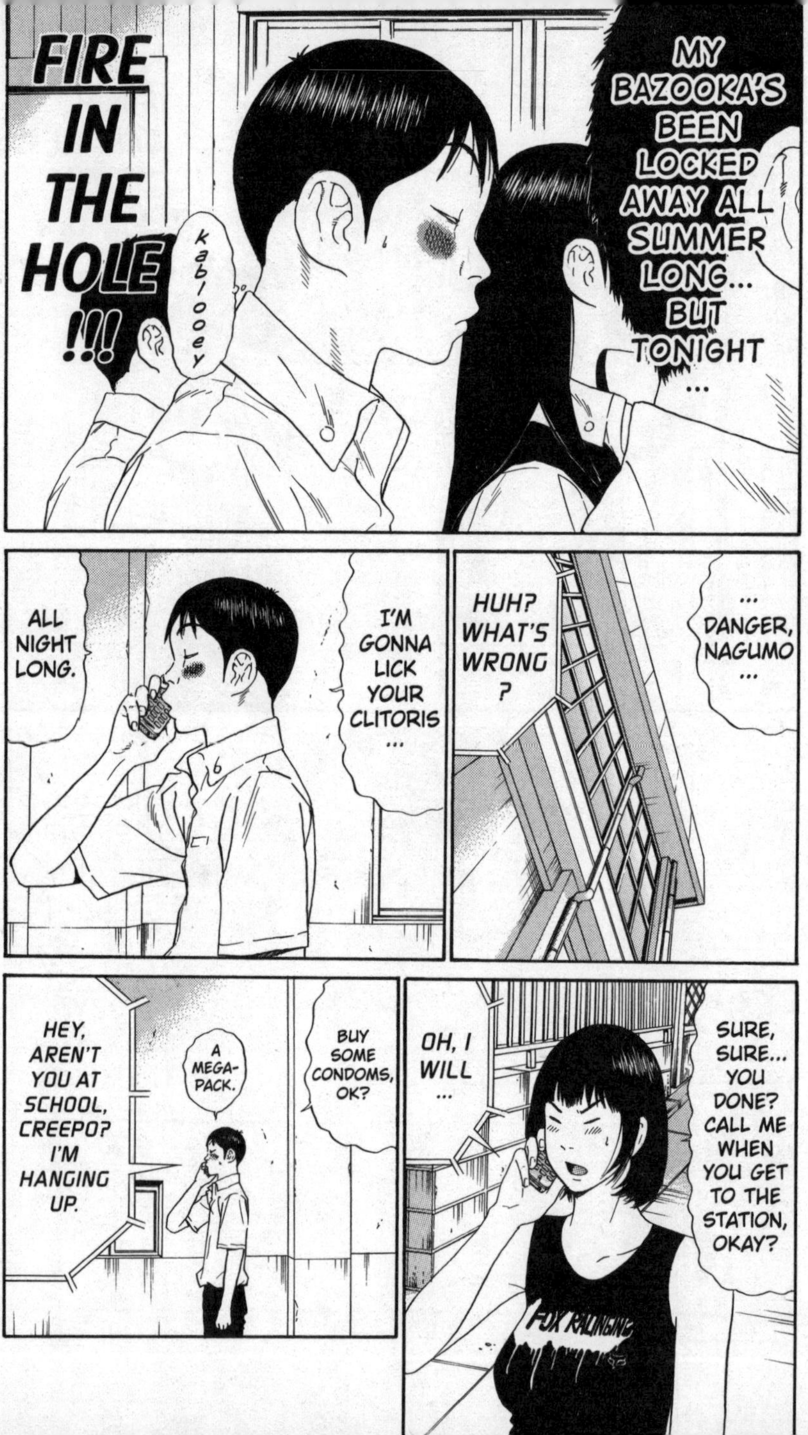
MY BAZOOKA'S BEEN LOCKED AWAY ALL SUMMER LONG... BUT TONIGHT ...
FIRE IN THE HOLE !!!
kablooey
... DANGER, NAGUMO ...
HUH? WHAT'S WRONG ?
I'M GONNA LICK YOUR CLITORIS ...
ALL NIGHT LONG.
SURE, SURE... YOU DONE? CALL ME WHEN YOU GET TO THE STATION, OKAY?
OH, I WILL ...
BUY SOME CONDOMS, OK?
A MEGA-PACK.
HEY, AREN'T YOU AT SCHOOL, CREEPO? I'M HANGING UP.

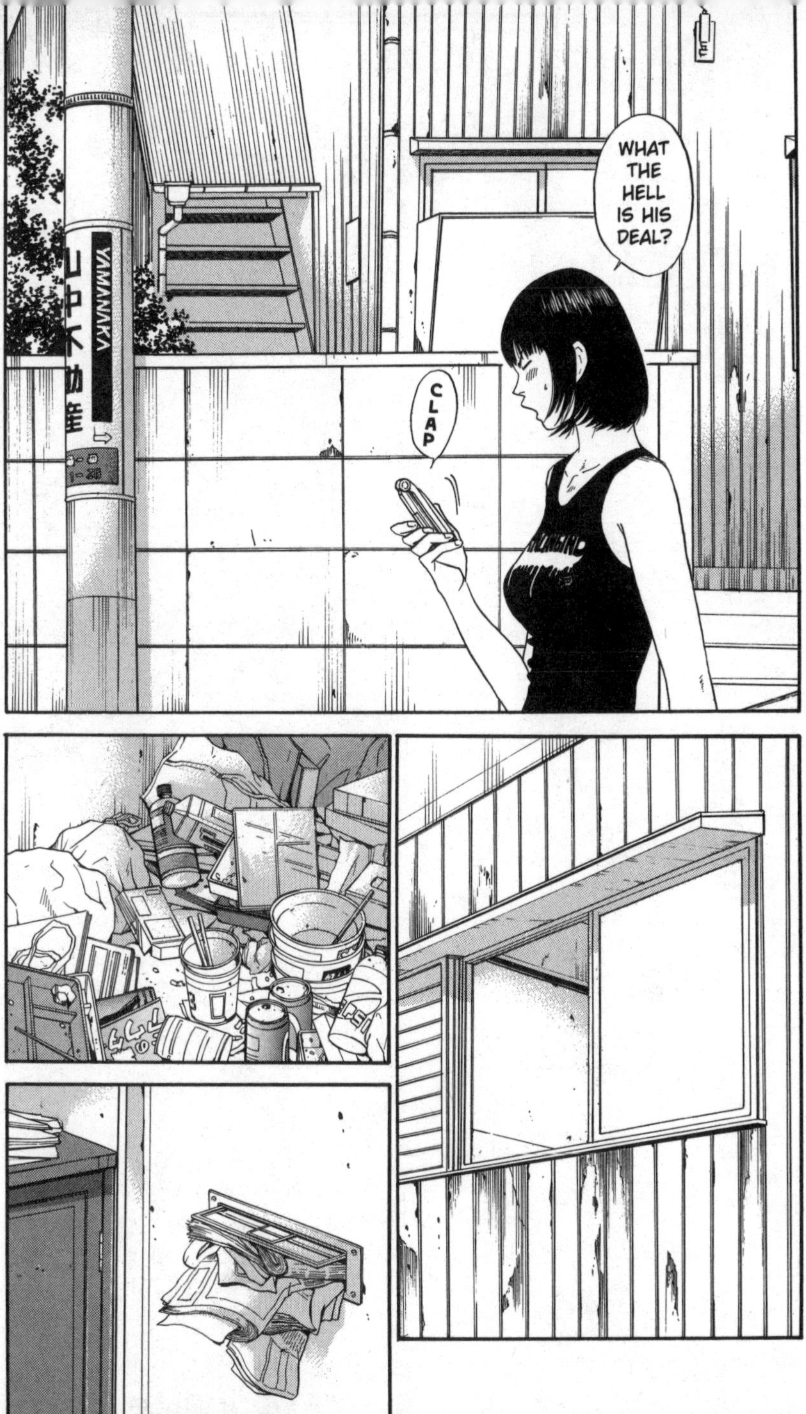
WHAT THE HELL IS HIS DEAL?
CLAP
YAMANAKA
山中不動産

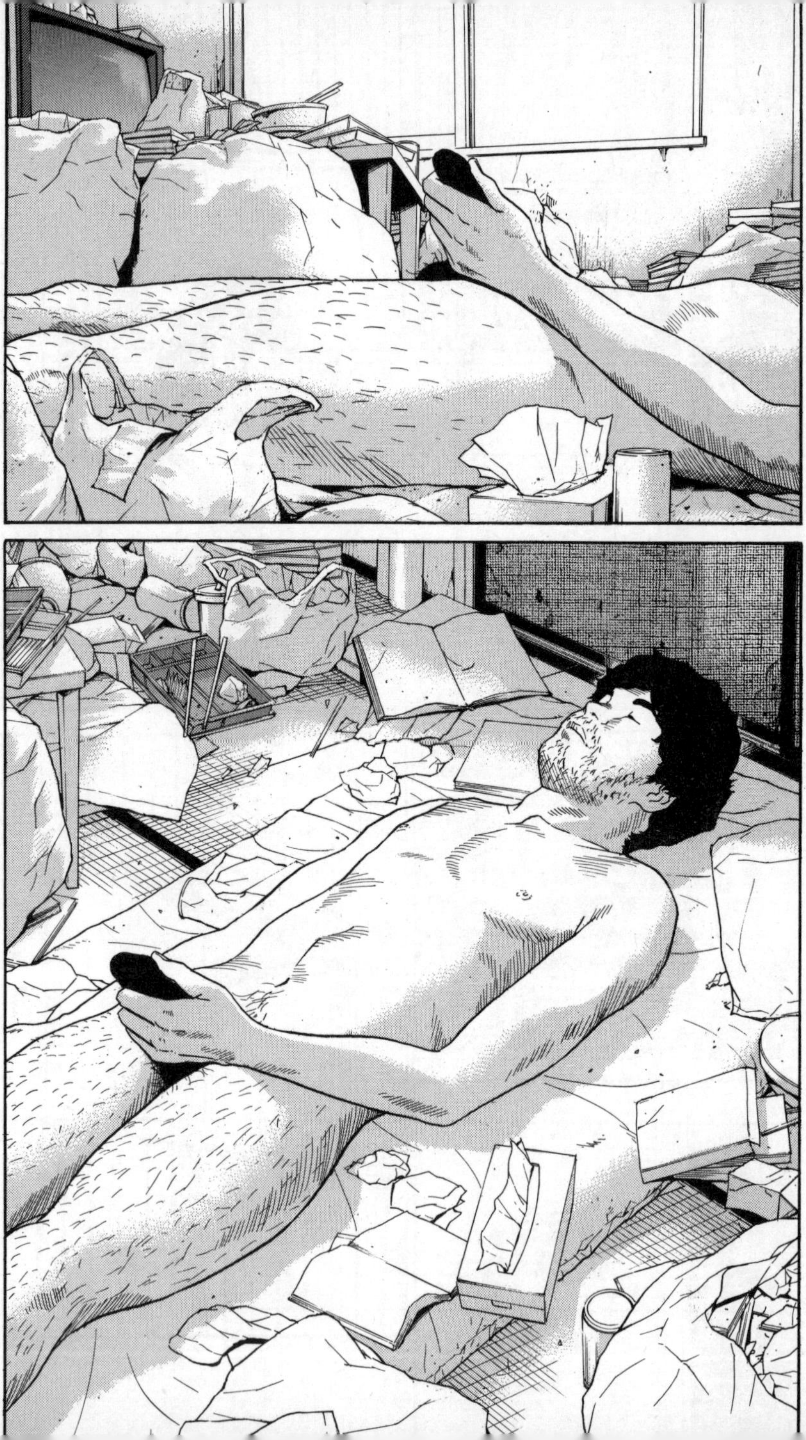

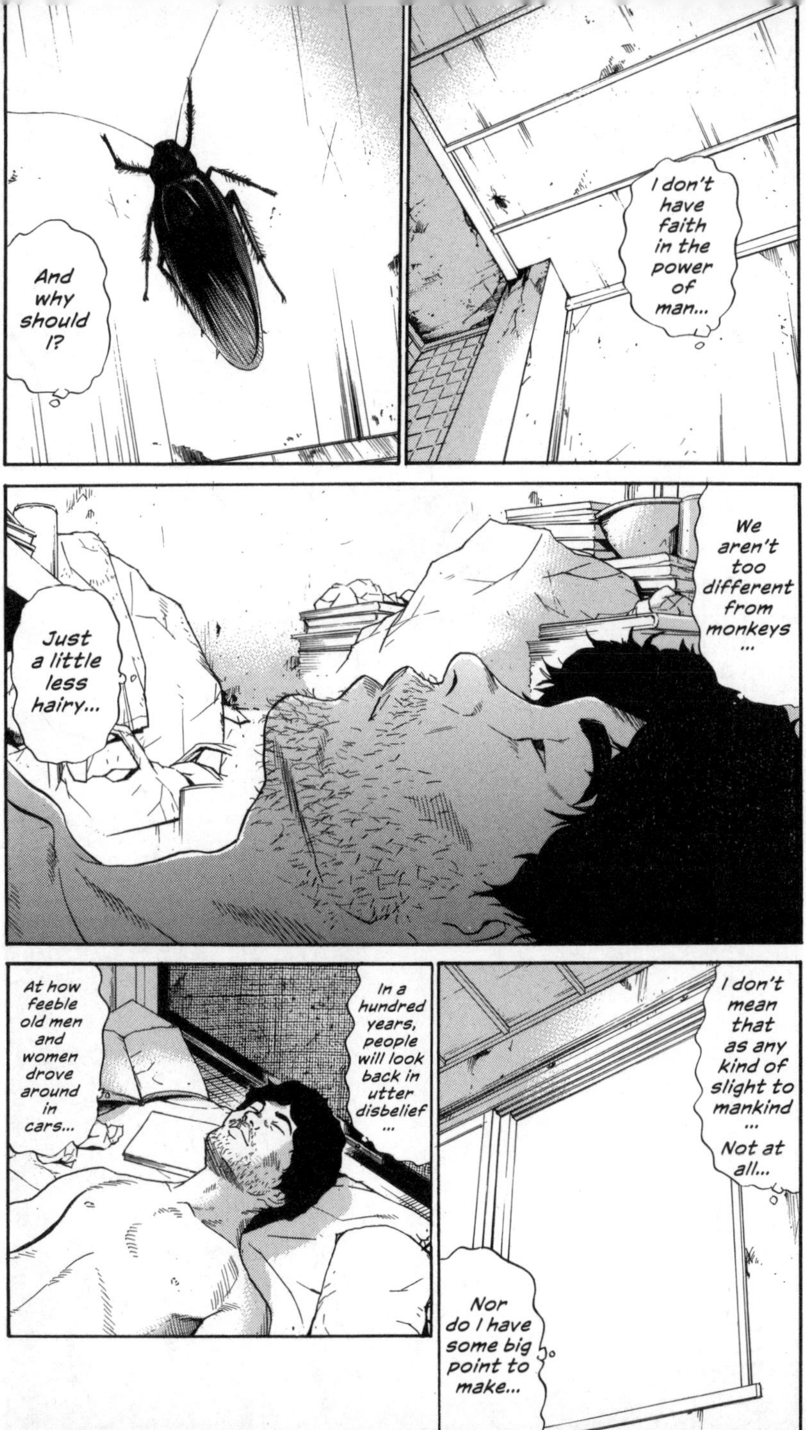
I don't have faith in the power of man...
And why should I?
We aren't too different from monkeys...
Just a little less hairy...
I don't mean that as any kind of slight to mankind...
Not at all...
Nor do I have some big point to make...
In a hundred years, people will look back in utter disbelief...
At how feeble old men and women drove around in cars...

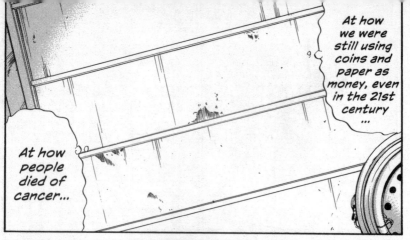

At how
we were
still using
coins and
paper as
money, even
in the 21st
century
...

At how
people
died of
cancer...

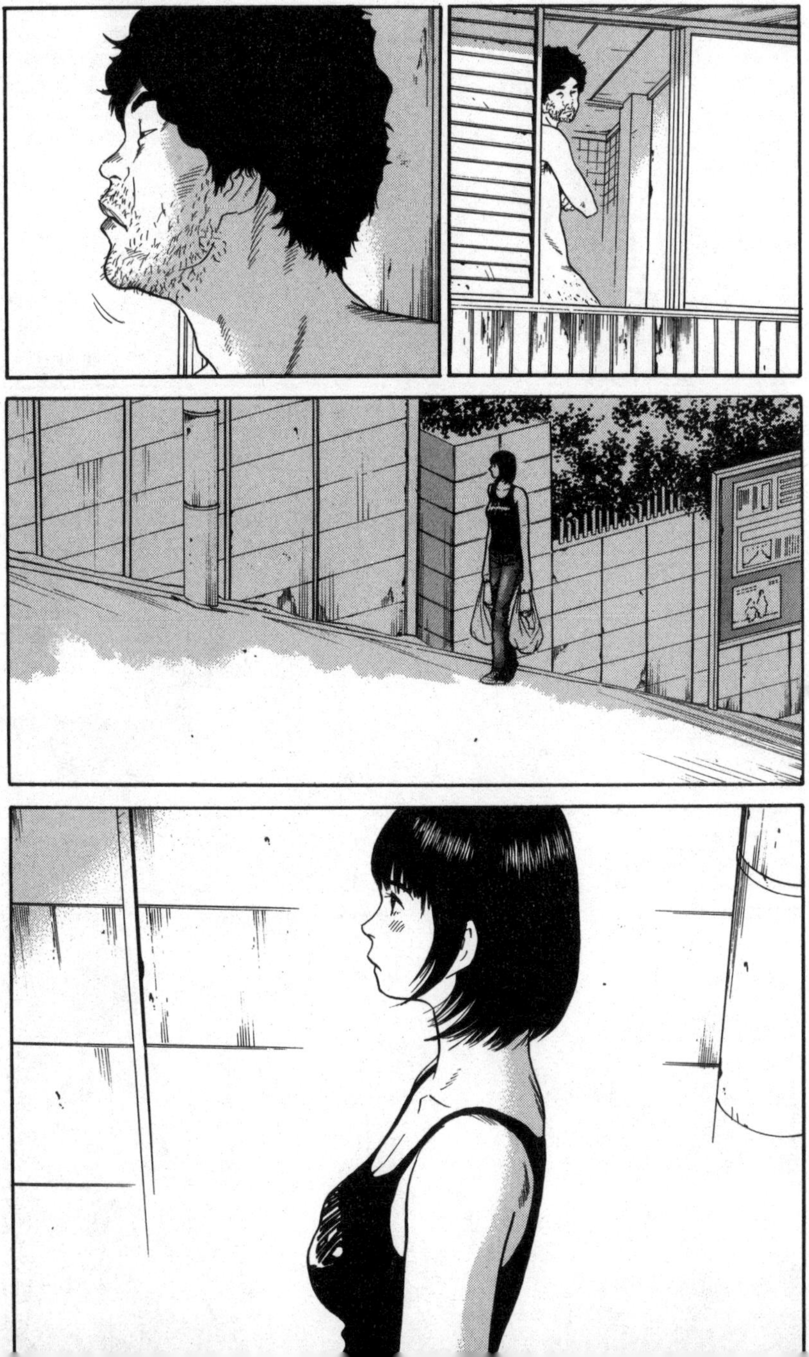

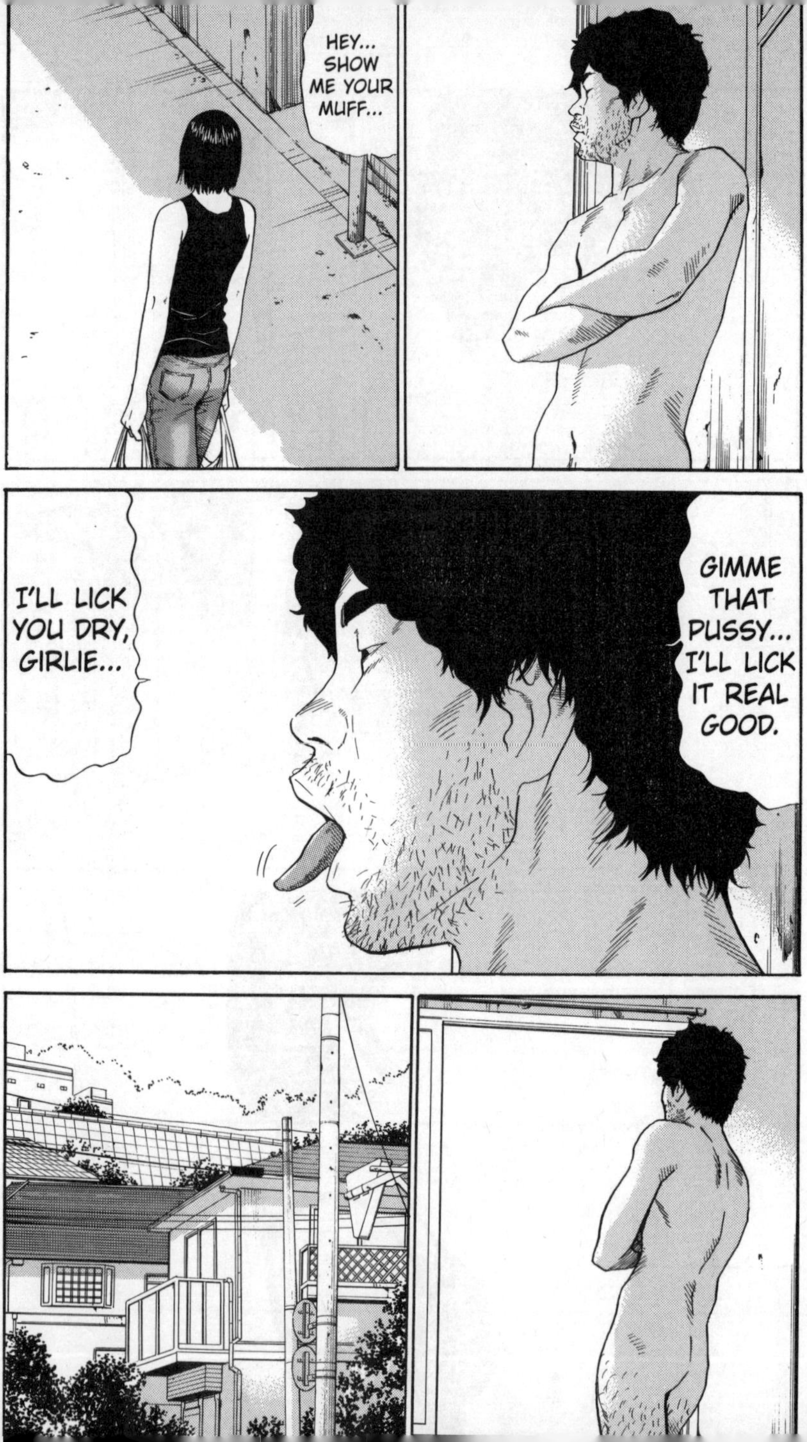
HEY... SHOW ME YOUR MUFF...
GIMME THAT PUSSY... I'LL LICK IT REAL GOOD.
I'LL LICK YOU DRY, GIRLIE...

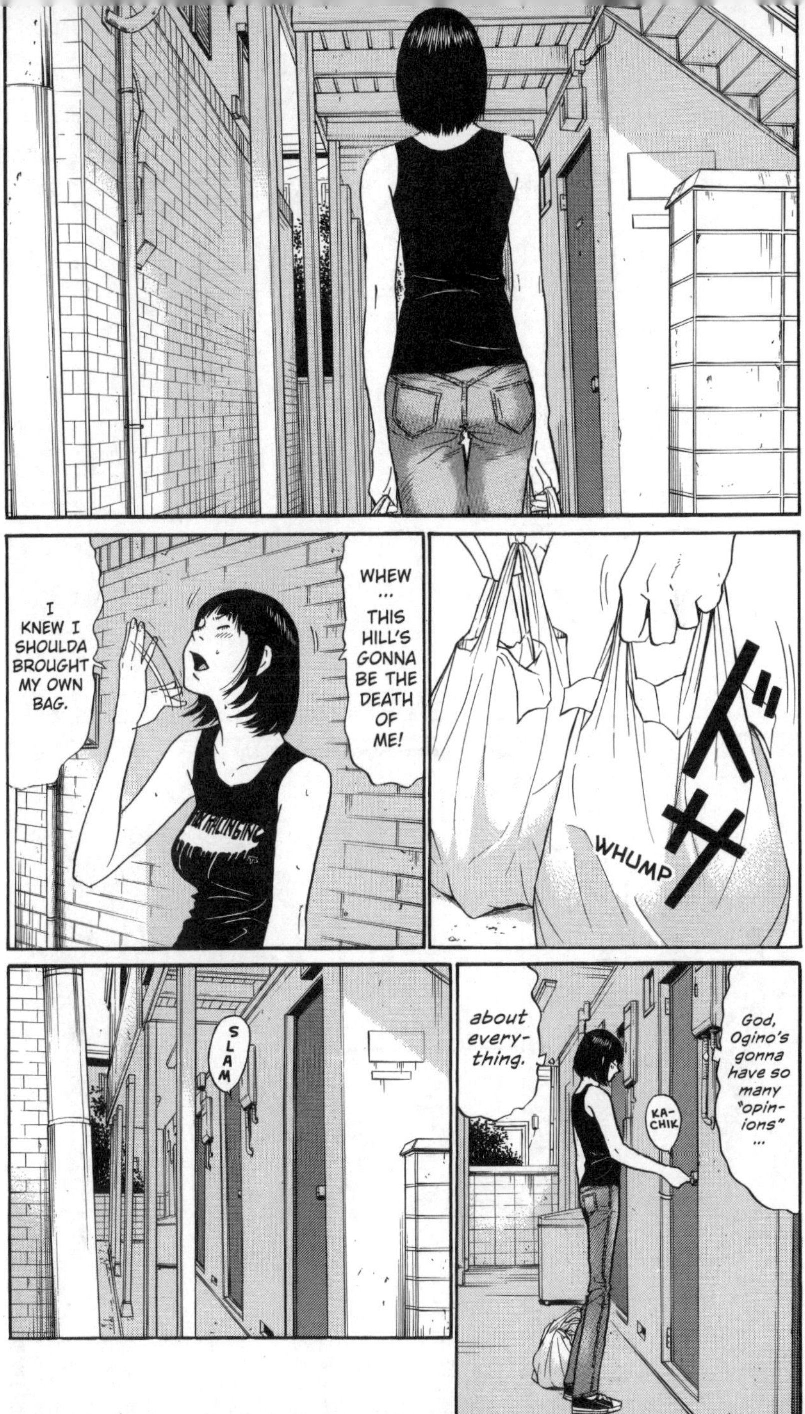
ドサ
WHUMP
WHEW ... THIS HILL'S GONNA BE THE DEATH OF ME!
I KNEW I SHOULDA BROUGHT MY OWN BAG.
God, Ogino's gonna have so many "opinions" ...
KA-CHIK
about every-thing.
SLAM

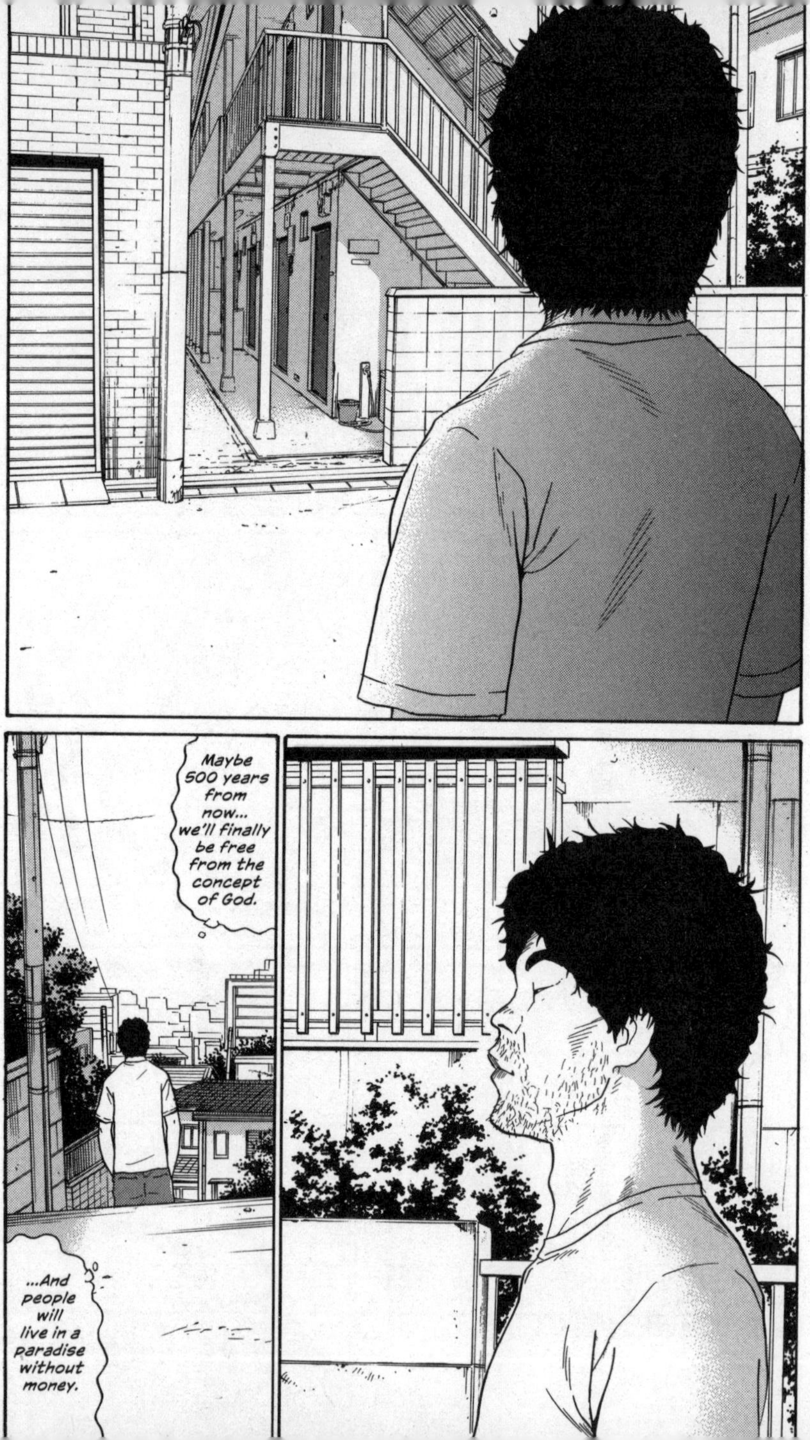
Maybe 500 years from now... we'll finally be free from the concept of God.
...And people will live in a paradise without money.

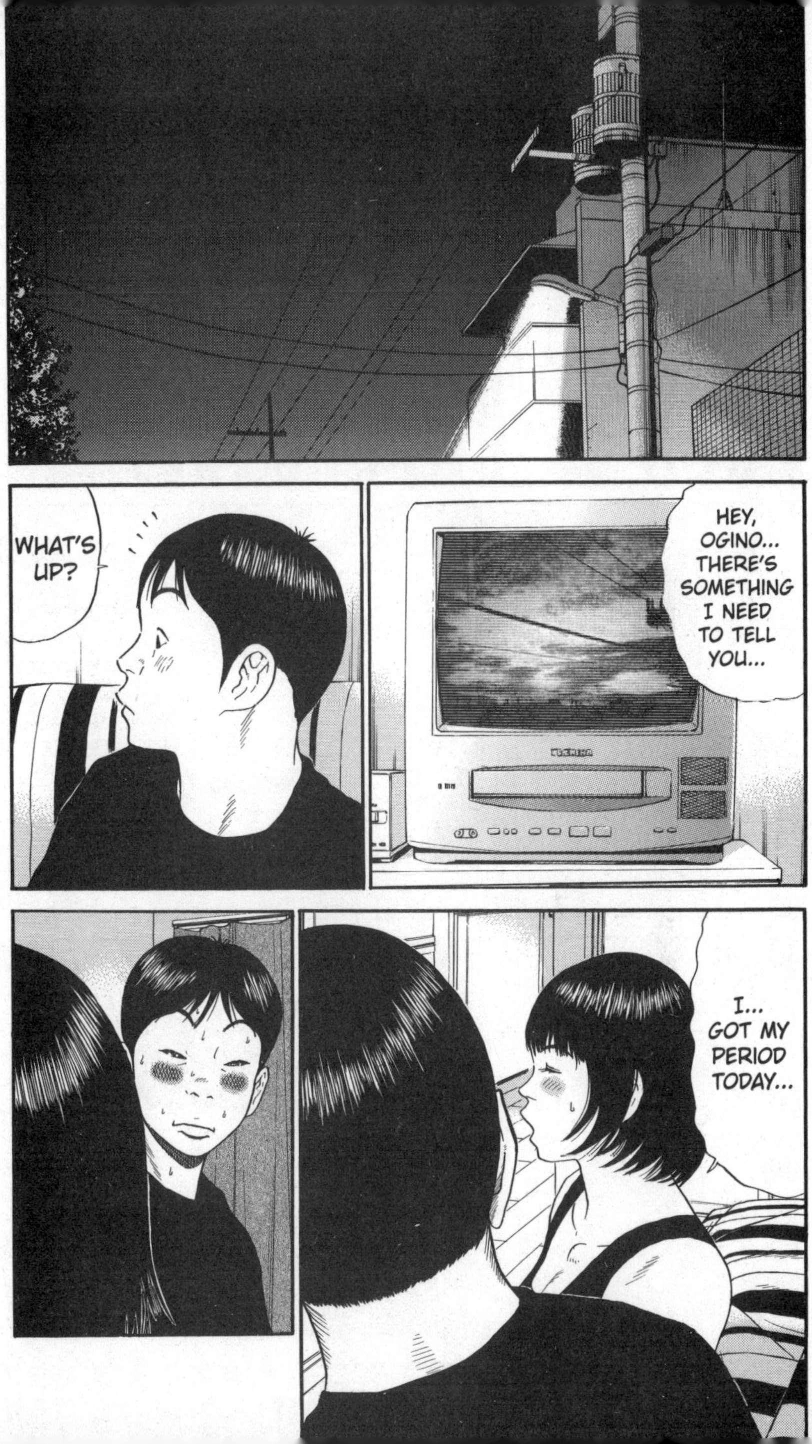
HEY, OGINO... THERE'S SOMETHING I NEED TO TELL YOU...
WHAT'S UP?
I... GOT MY PERIOD TODAY...

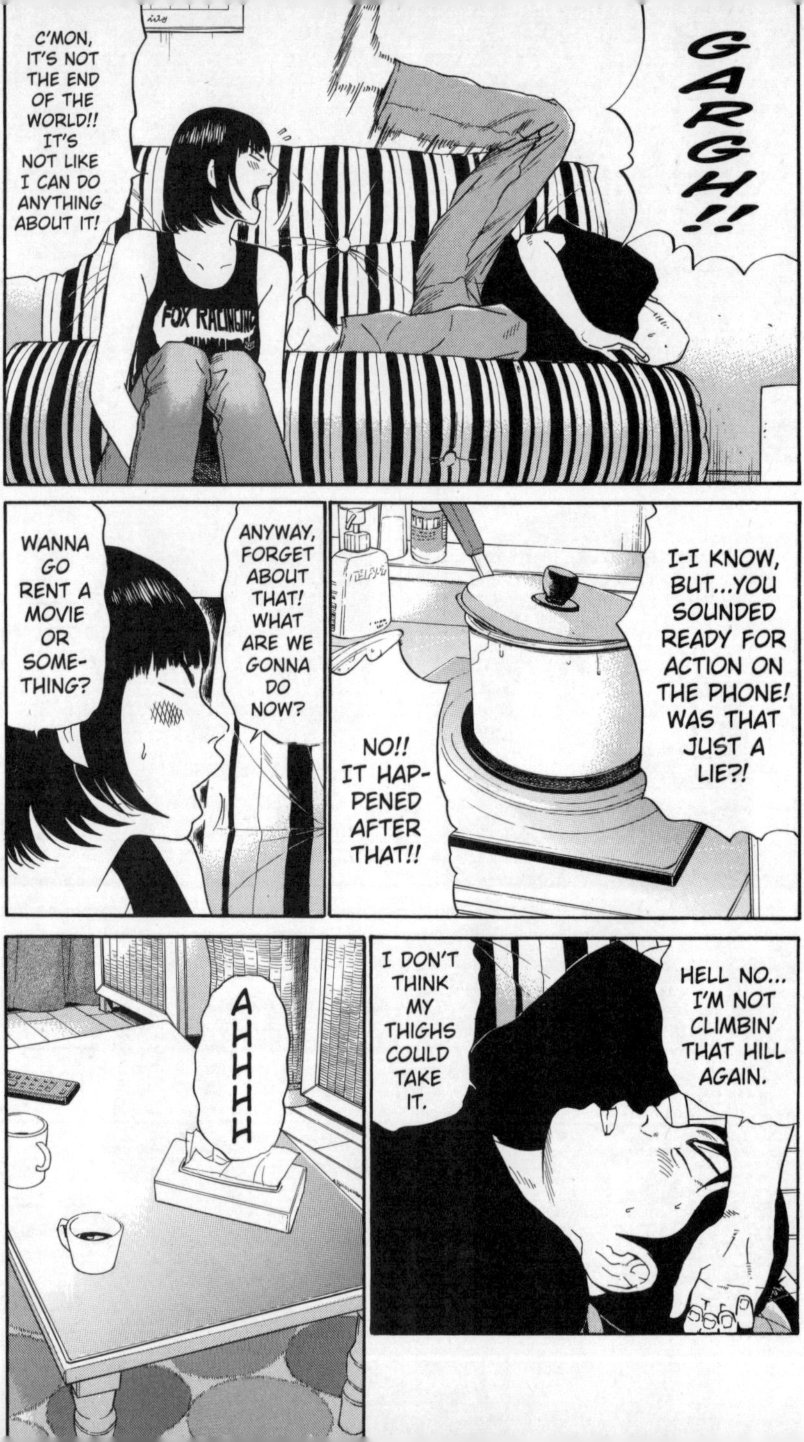
GARGH!!
C'MON, IT'S NOT THE END OF THE WORLD!! IT'S NOT LIKE I CAN DO ANYTHING ABOUT IT!
I-I KNOW, BUT...YOU SOUNDED READY FOR ACTION ON THE PHONE! WAS THAT JUST A LIE?!
NO!! IT HAP-PENED AFTER THAT!!
ANYWAY, FORGET ABOUT THAT! WHAT ARE WE GONNA DO NOW?
WANNA GO RENT A MOVIE OR SOME-THING?
HELL NO... I'M NOT CLIMBIN' THAT HILL AGAIN.
I DON'T THINK MY THIGHS COULD TAKE IT.
AHHHH

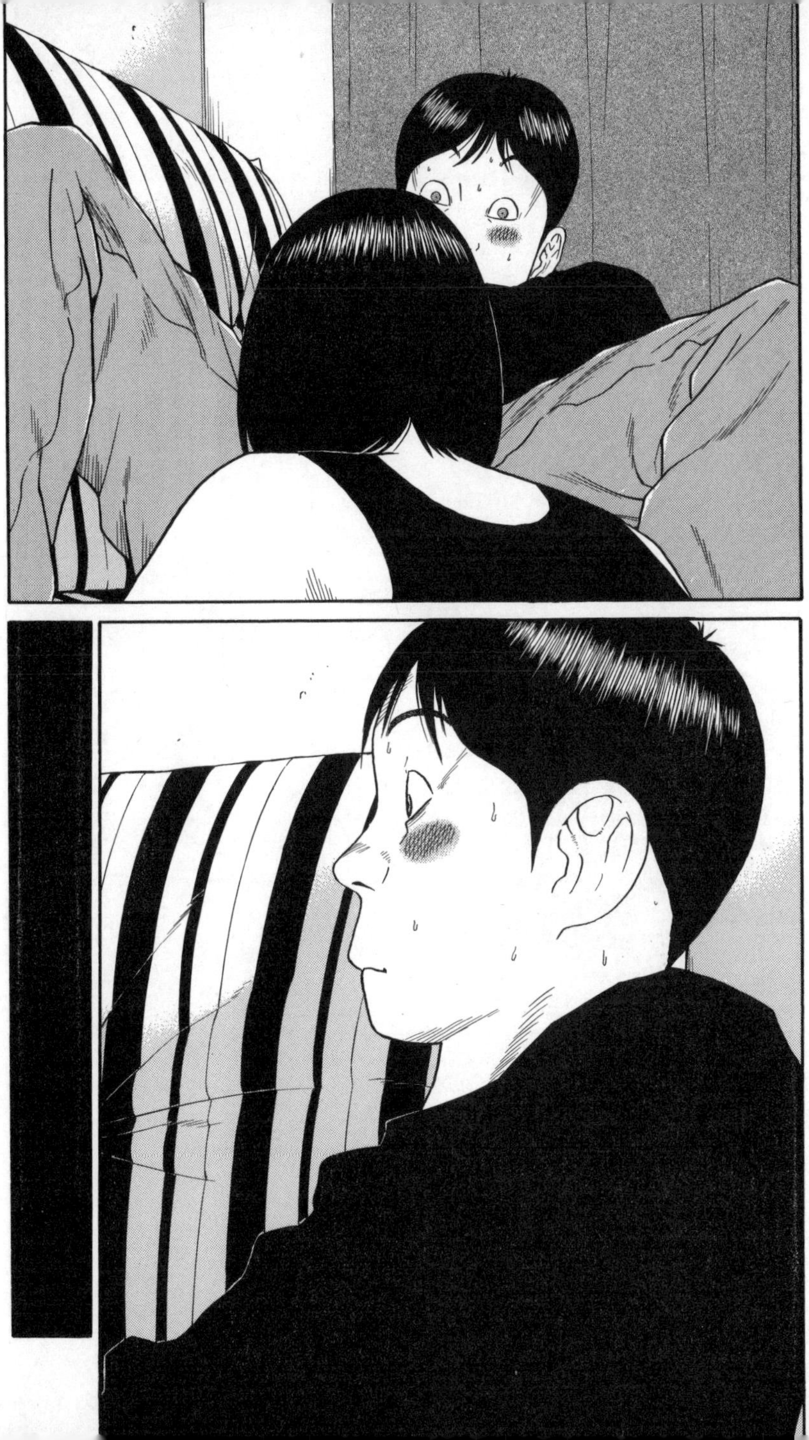

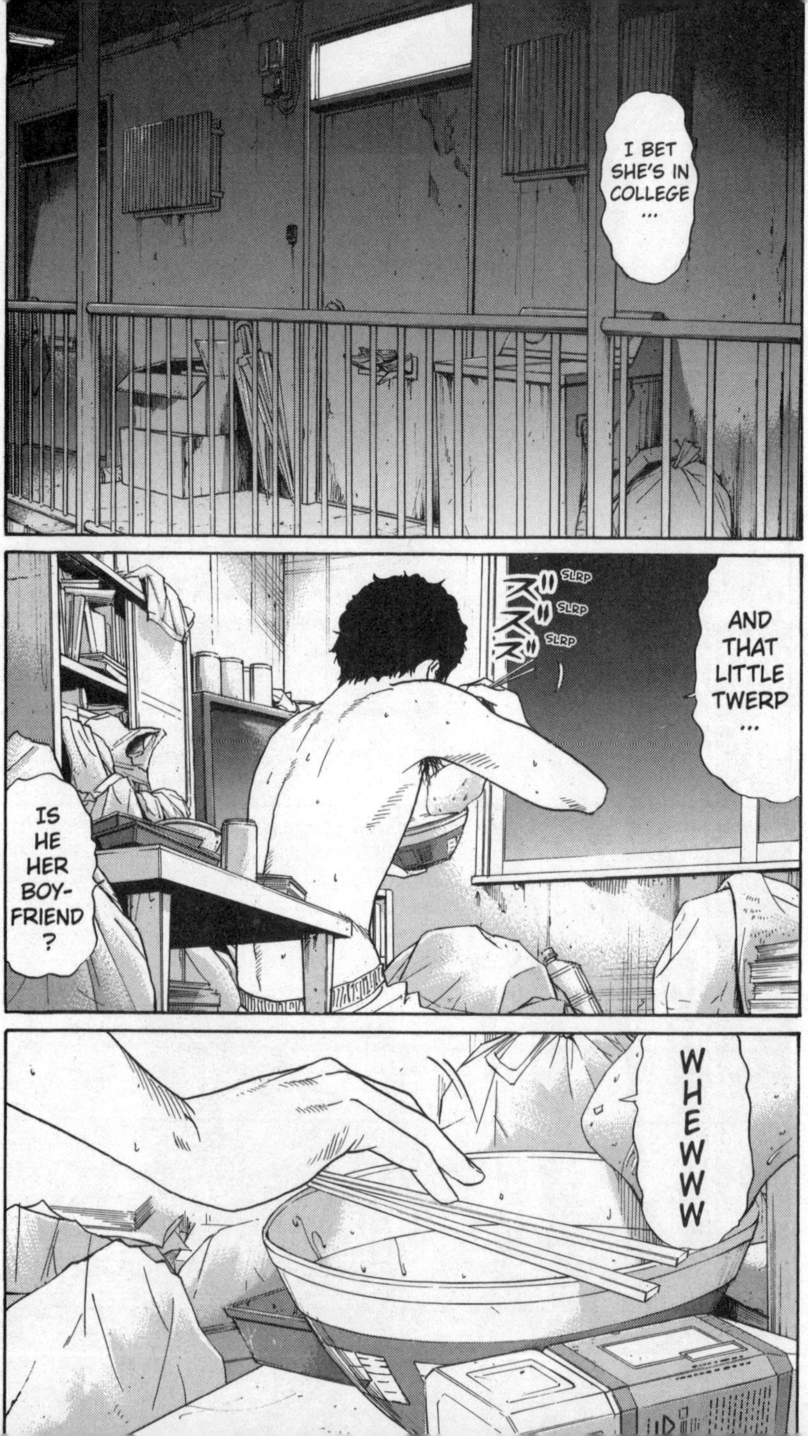
I BET SHE'S IN COLLEGE ...
SLRP SLRP SLRP
AND THAT LITTLE TWERP ...
IS HE HER BOY-FRIEND ?
WHEWWW

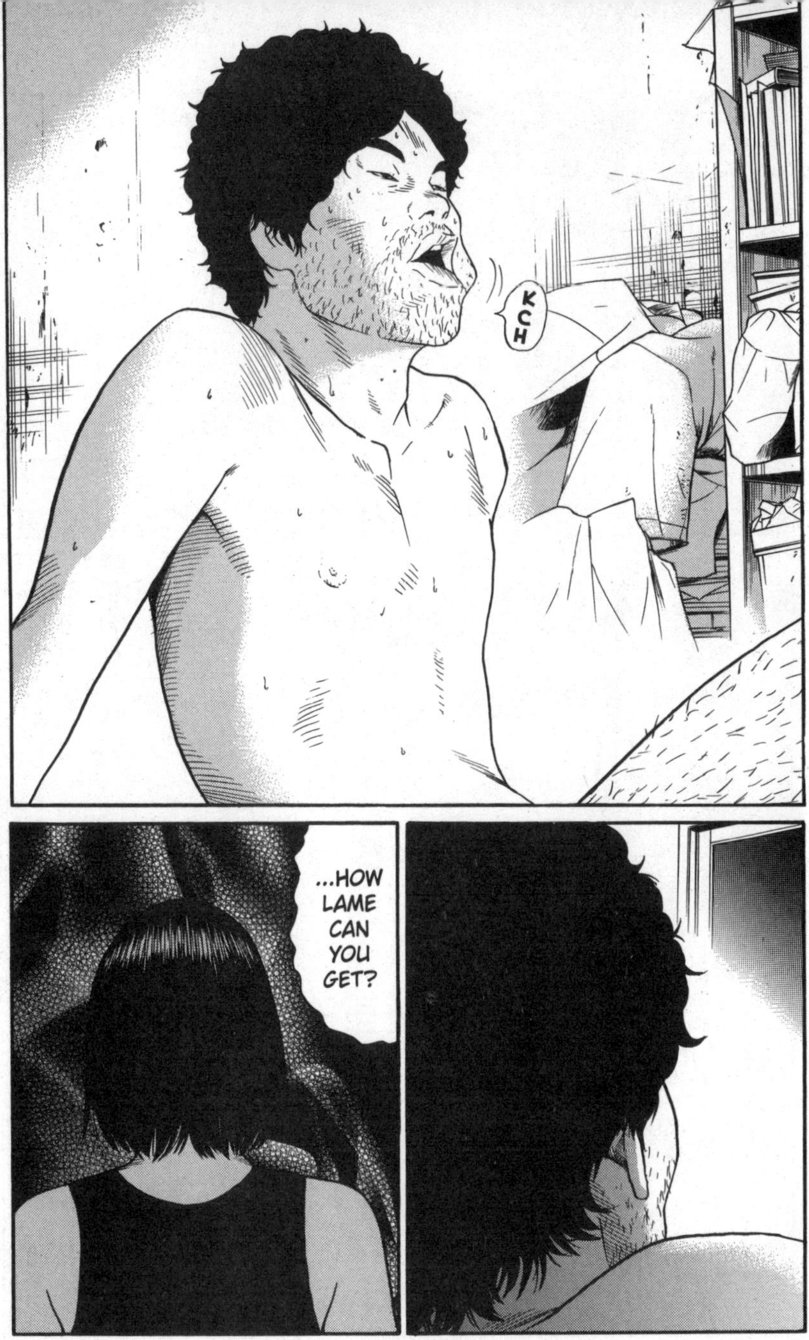
KCH
...HOW LAME CAN YOU GET?

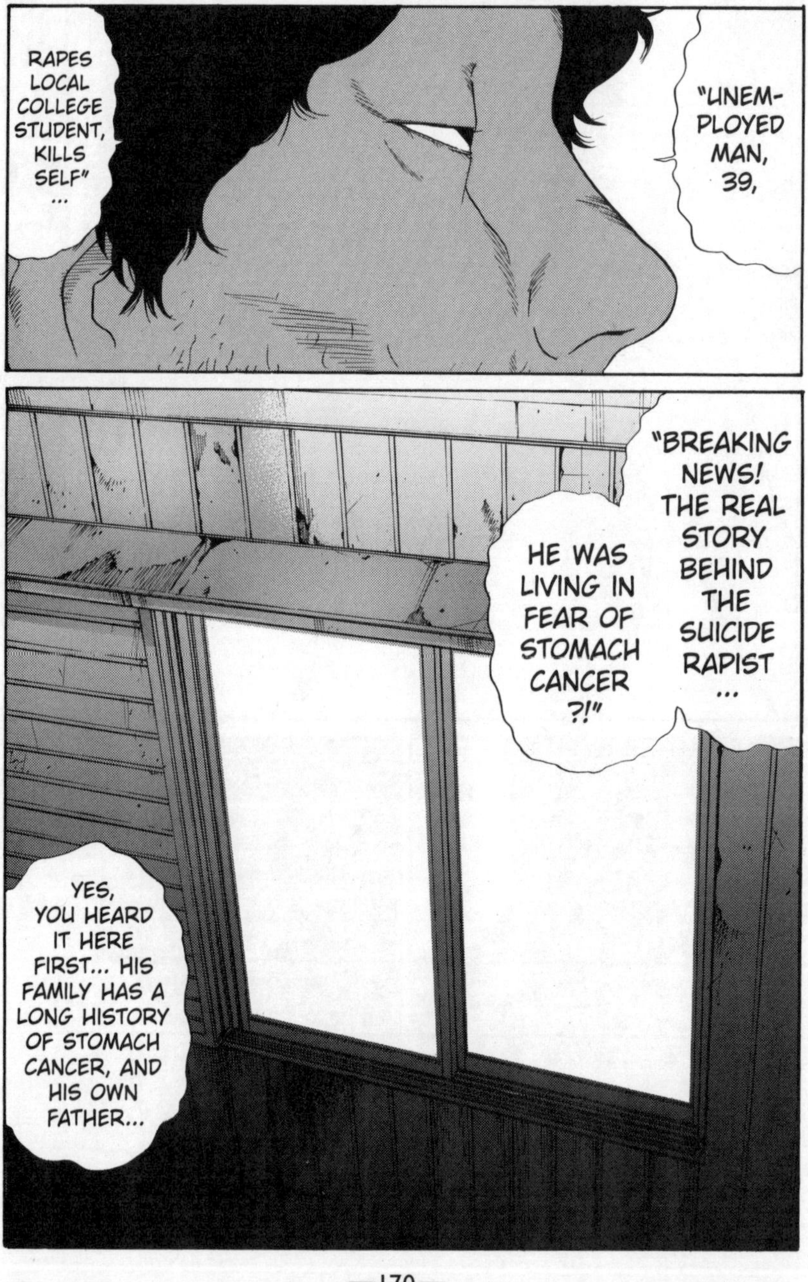
"UNEM-PLOYED MAN, 39,
RAPES LOCAL COLLEGE STUDENT, KILLS SELF" ...
"BREAKING NEWS! THE REAL STORY BEHIND THE SUICIDE RAPIST ...
HE WAS LIVING IN FEAR OF STOMACH CANCER ?!"
YES, YOU HEARD IT HERE FIRST... HIS FAMILY HAS A LONG HISTORY OF STOMACH CANCER, AND HIS OWN FATHER...

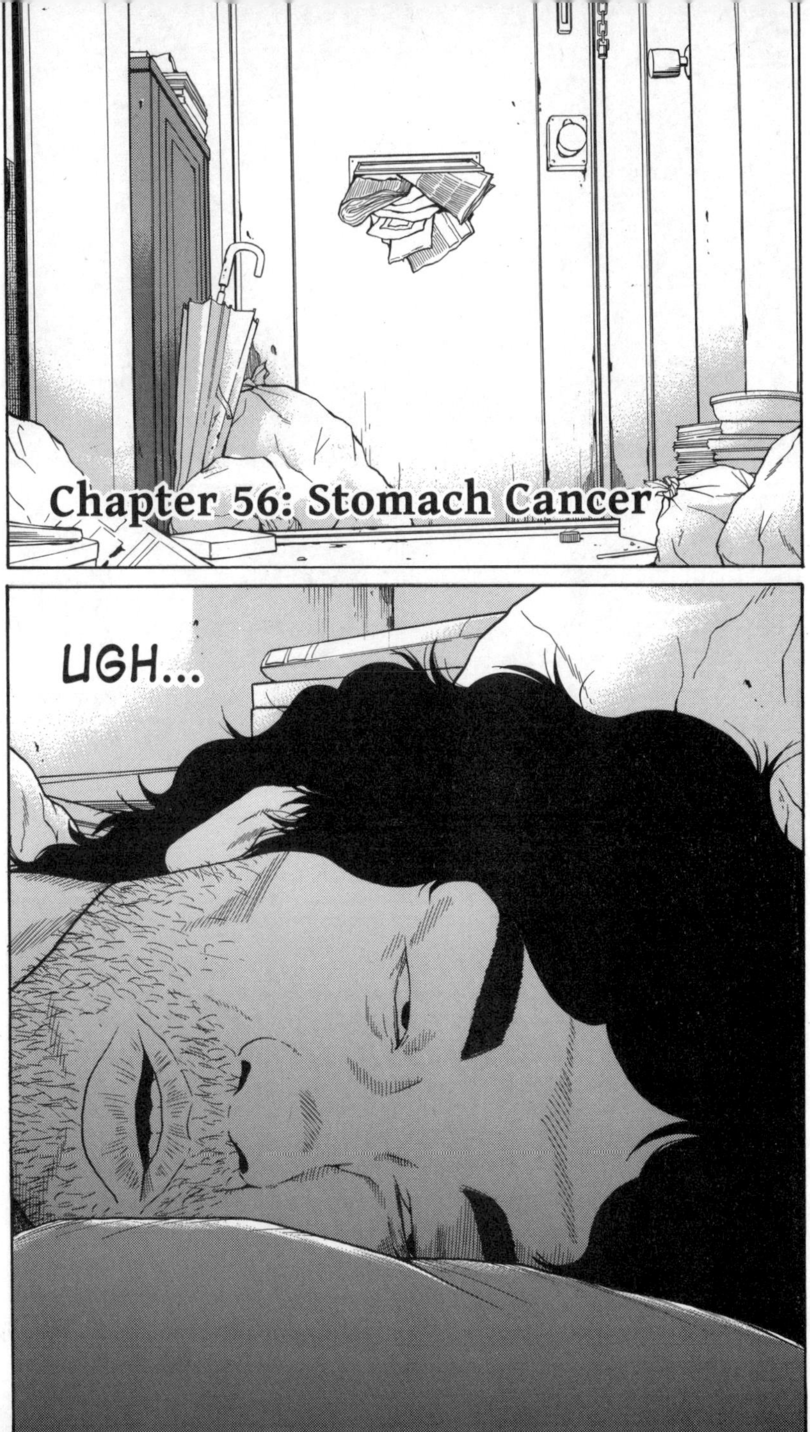
Chapter 56: Stomach Cancer
UGH...

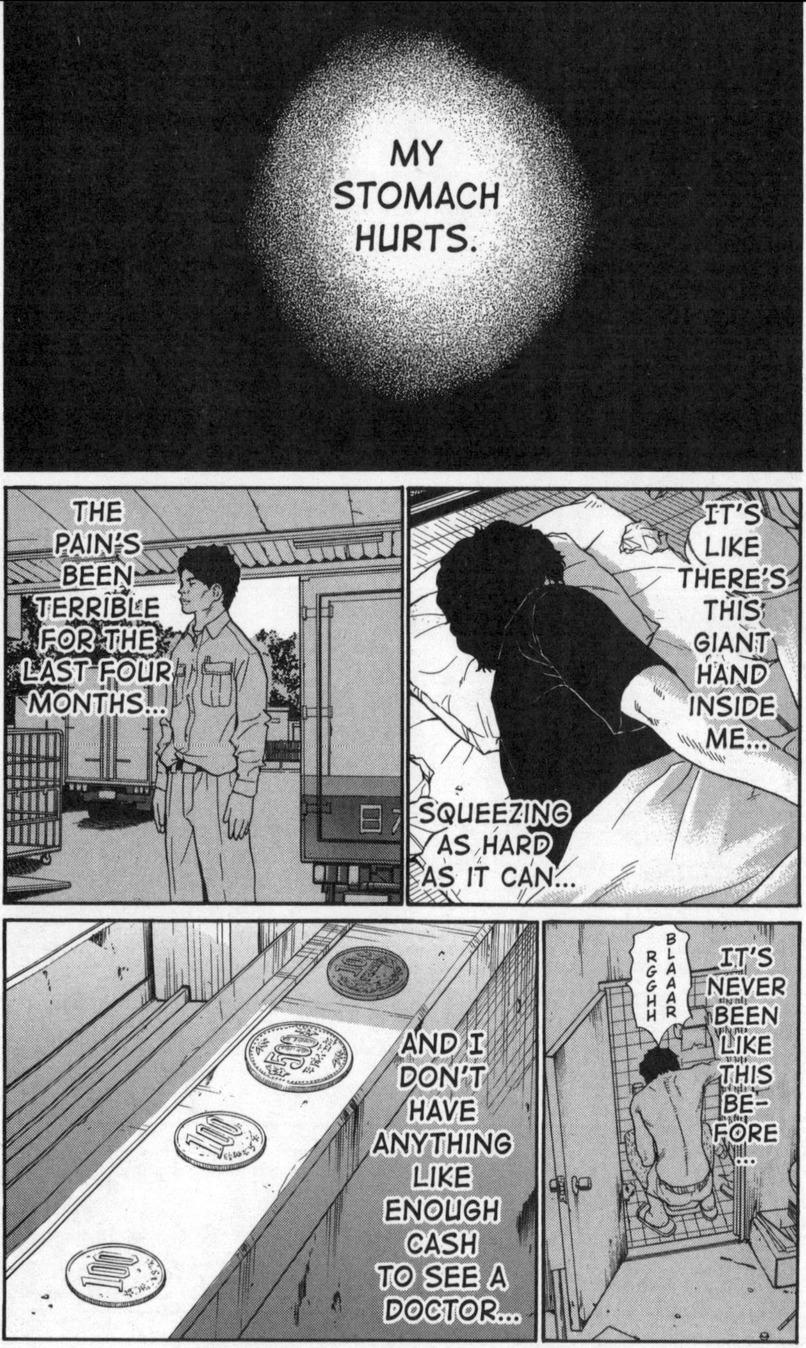
MY STOMACH HURTS.
IT'S LIKE THERE'S THIS GIANT HAND INSIDE ME...
SQUEEZING AS HARD AS IT CAN...
THE PAIN'S BEEN TERRIBLE FOR THE LAST FOUR MONTHS...
BLAAAR
RGGHH
IT'S NEVER BEEN LIKE THIS BEFORE...
AND I DON'T HAVE ANYTHING LIKE ENOUGH CASH TO SEE A DOCTOR...

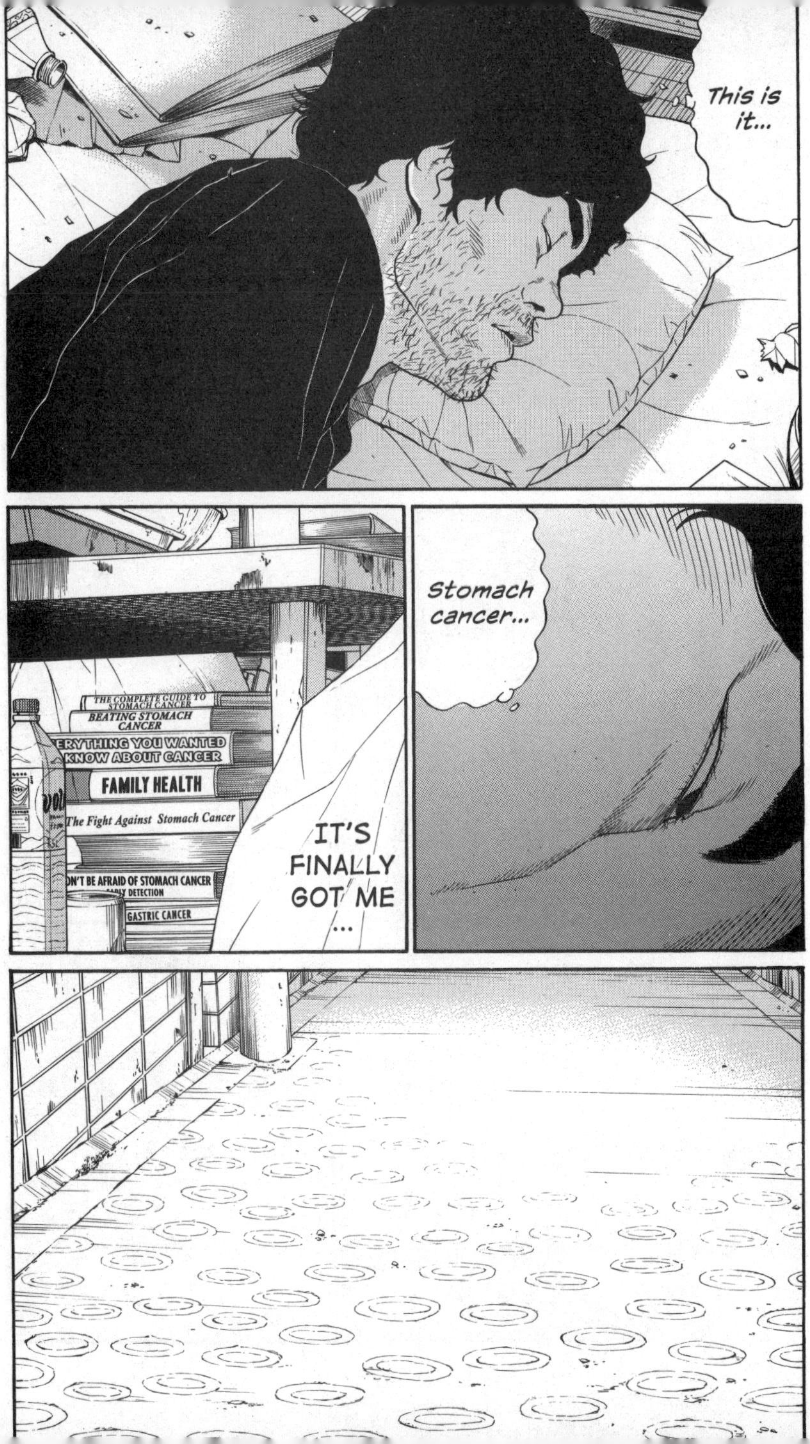
This is it...
Stomach cancer...
IT'S FINALLY GOT ME ...
THE COMPLETE GUIDE TO STOMACH CANCER
BEATING STOMACH CANCER
ERYTHING YOU WANTED
KNOW ABOUT CANCER
FAMILY HEALTH
The Fight Against Stomach Cancer
N'T BE AFRAID OF STOMACH CANCER
GASTRIC CANCER

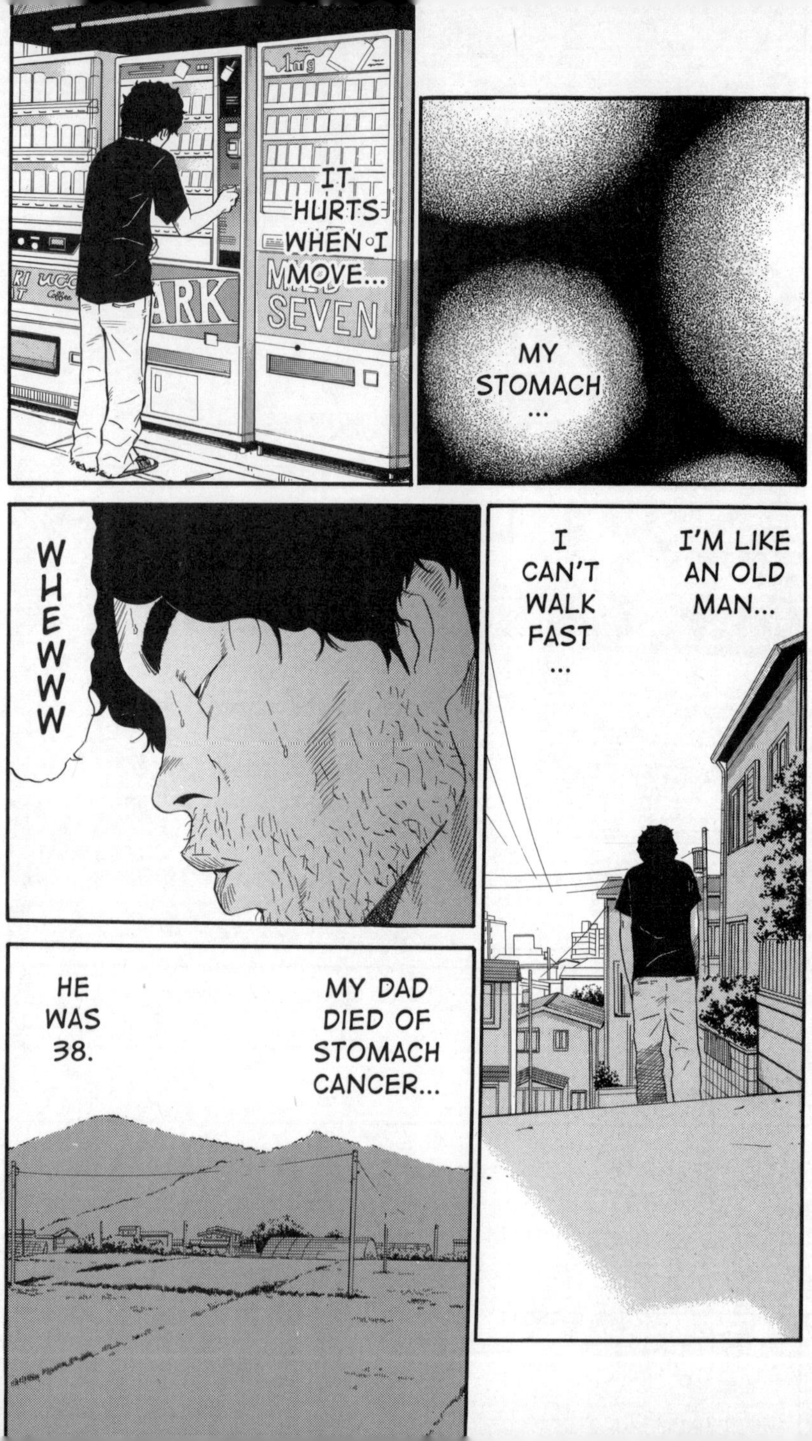
MY STOMACH ...
IT HURTS WHEN I MOVE...
1mg
SEVEN
I'M LIKE AN OLD MAN...
I CAN'T WALK FAST ...
WHEWWW
MY DAD DIED OF STOMACH CANCER...
HE WAS 38.

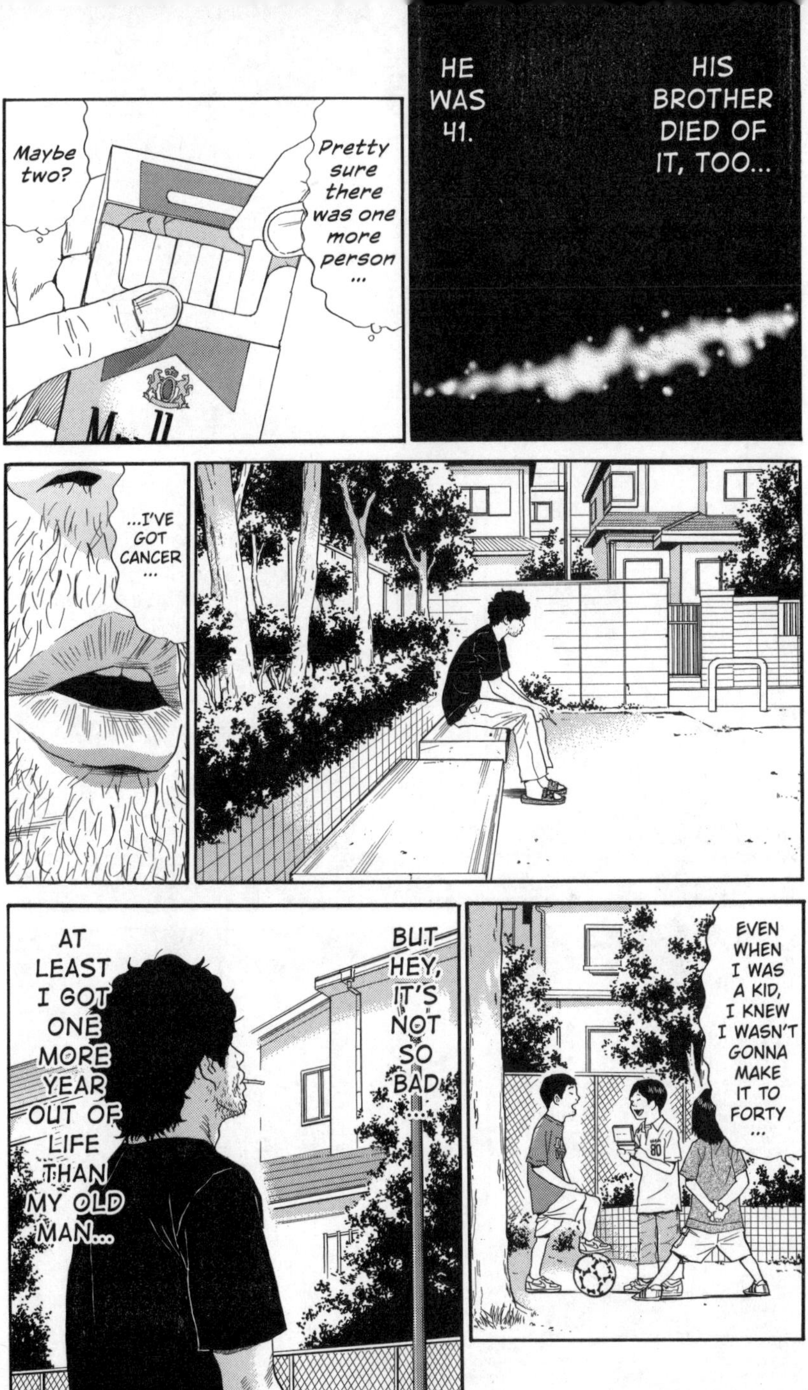
HIS BROTHER DIED OF IT, TOO...
HE WAS 41.
Pretty sure there was one more person...
Maybe two?
...I'VE GOT CANCER...
EVEN WHEN I WAS A KID, I KNEW I WASN'T GONNA MAKE IT TO FORTY...
BUT HEY, IT'S NOT SO BAD...
AT LEAST I GOT ONE MORE YEAR OUT OF LIFE THAN MY OLD MAN...

...
WELL
...

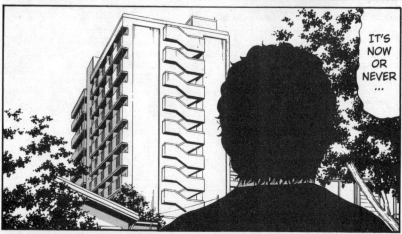

IT'S
NOW
OR
NEVER
...

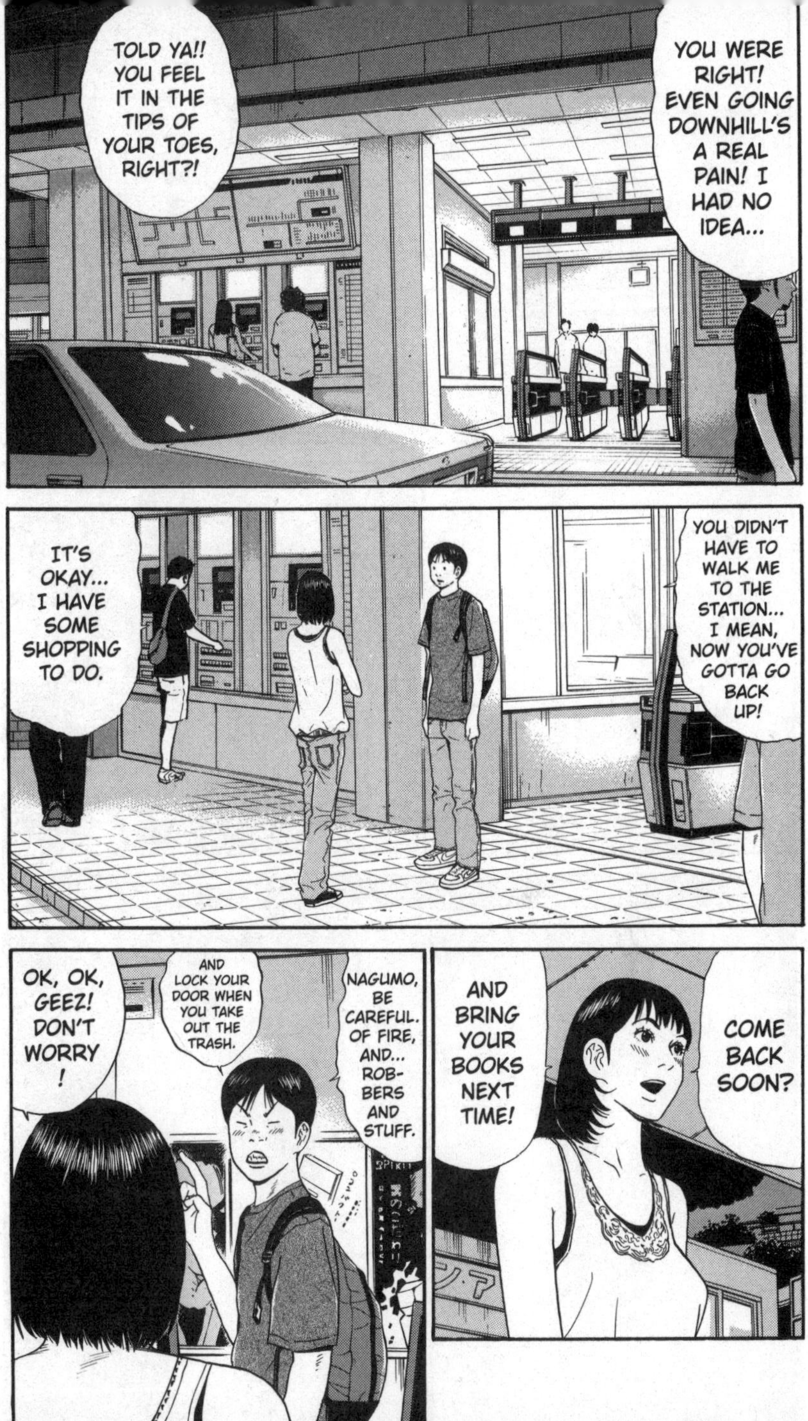
YOU WERE RIGHT! EVEN GOING DOWNHILL'S A REAL PAIN! I HAD NO IDEA...
TOLD YA!! YOU FEEL IT IN THE TIPS OF YOUR TOES, RIGHT?!
YOU DIDN'T HAVE TO WALK ME TO THE STATION... I MEAN, NOW YOU'VE GOTTA GO BACK UP!
IT'S OKAY... I HAVE SOME SHOPPING TO DO.
COME BACK SOON?
AND BRING YOUR BOOKS NEXT TIME!
NAGUMO, BE CAREFUL. OF FIRE, AND... ROB-BERS AND STUFF.
AND LOCK YOUR DOOR WHEN YOU TAKE OUT THE TRASH.
OK, OK, GEEZ! DON'T WORRY!

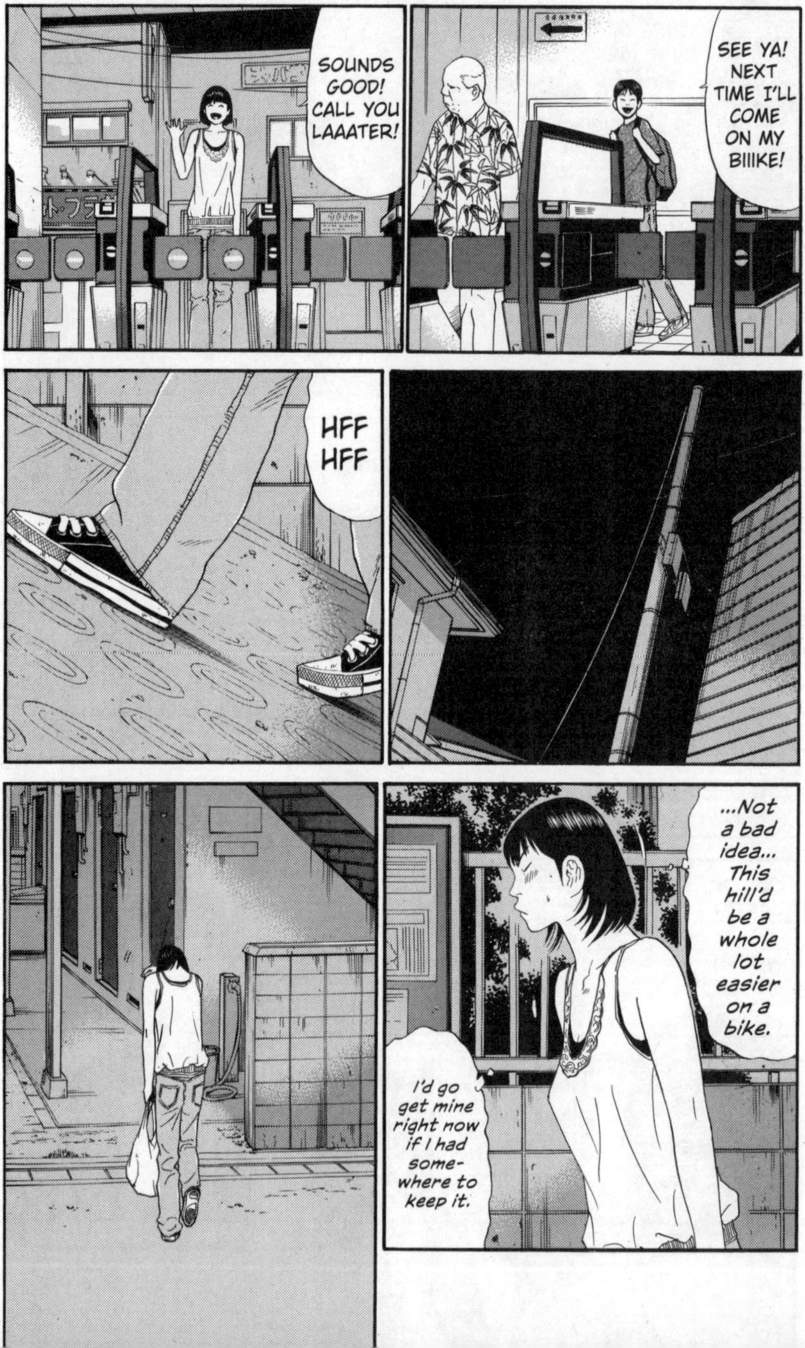
SEE YA! NEXT TIME I'LL COME ON MY BIIIKE!
SOUNDS GOOD! CALL YOU LAAATER!
HFF HFF
...Not a bad idea... This hill'd be a whole lot easier on a bike.
I'd go get mine right now if I had some-where to keep it.

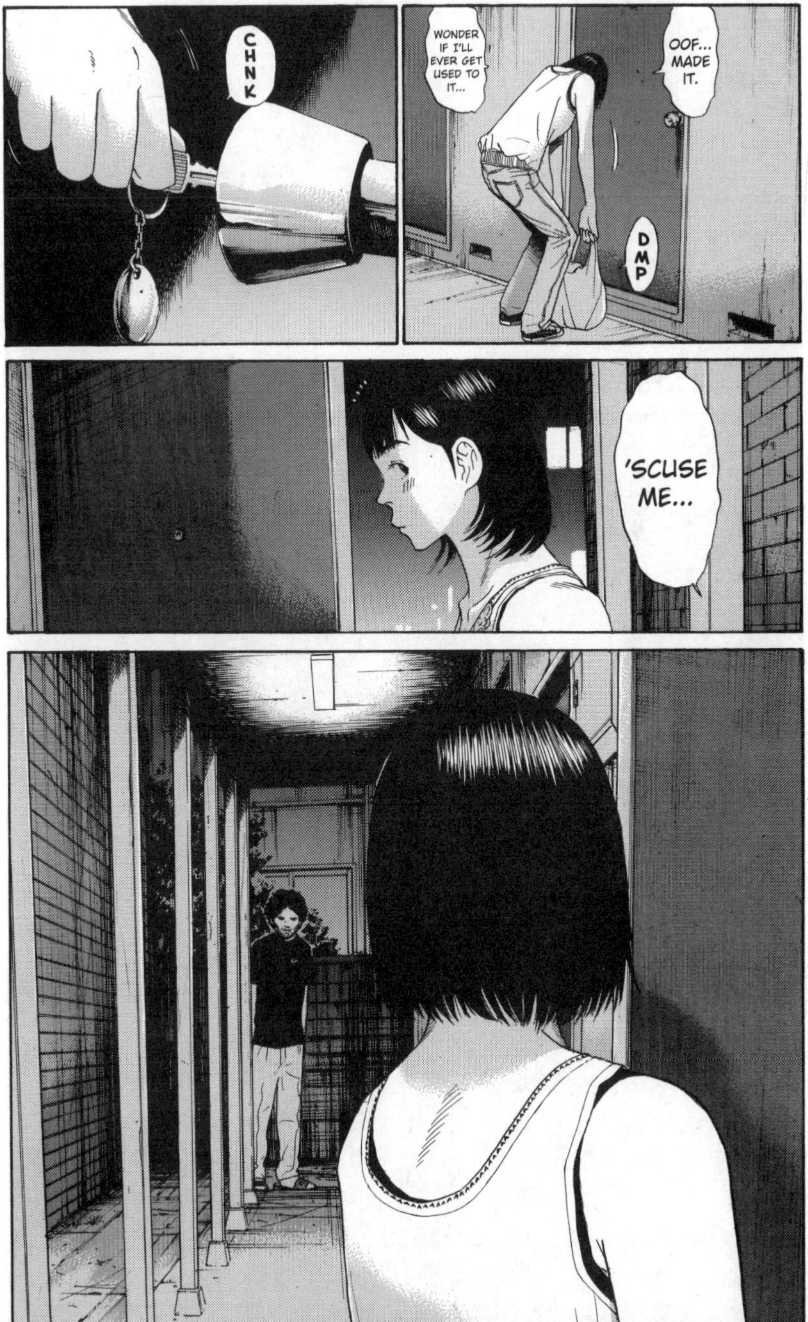
OOF... MADE IT.
DMP
WONDER IF I'LL EVER GET USED TO IT...
CHNK
'SCUSE ME...

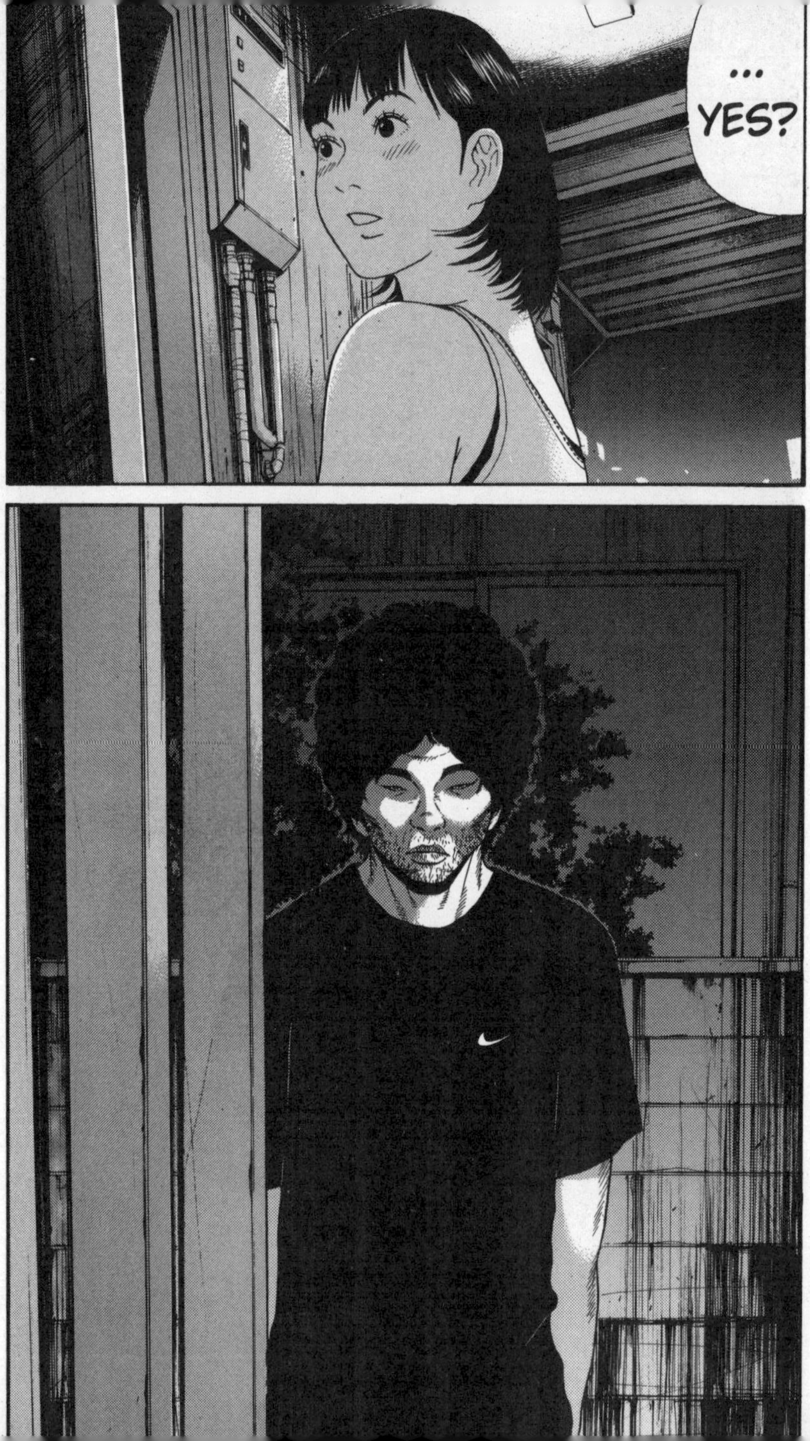
... YES?

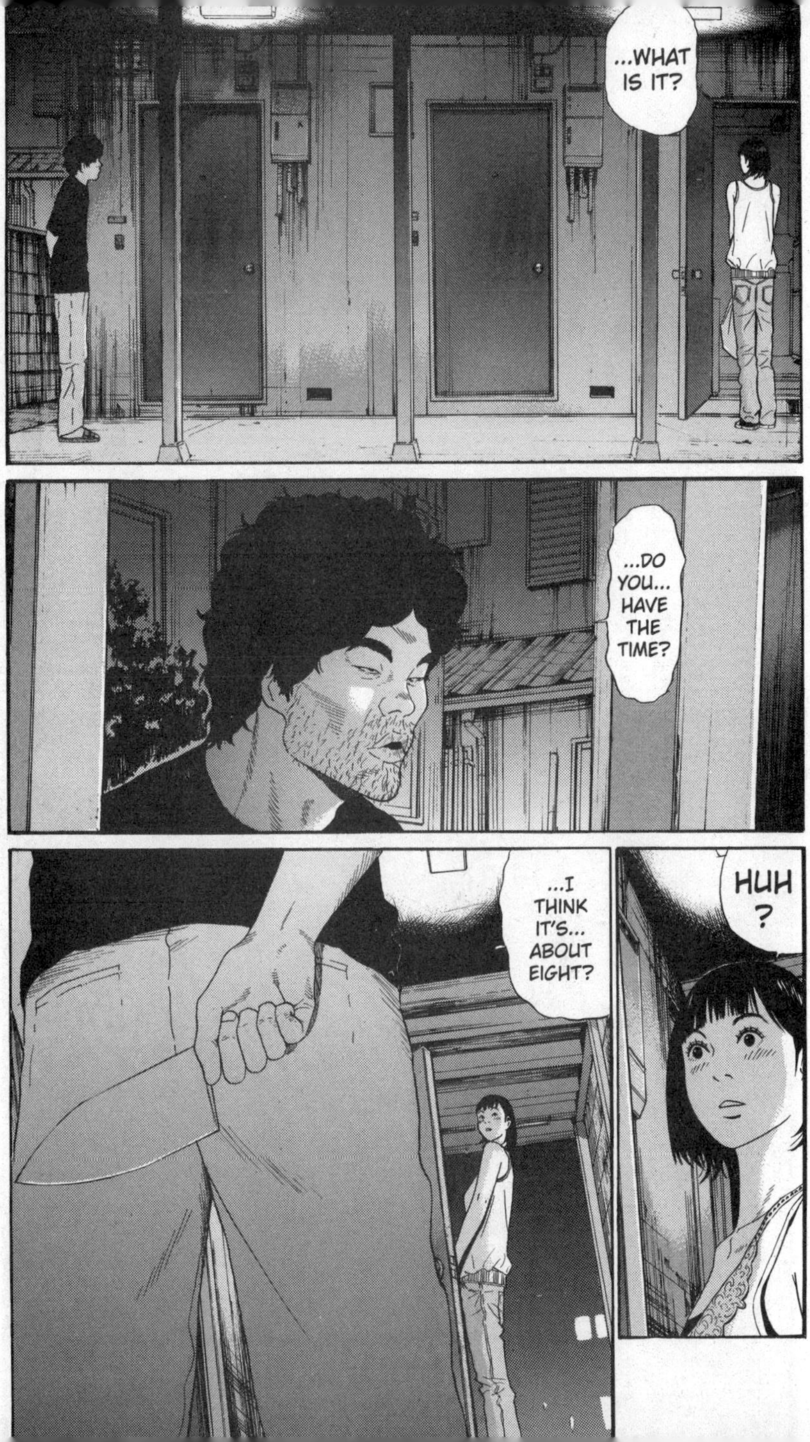
...WHAT IS IT?
...DO YOU... HAVE THE TIME?
HUH?
...I THINK IT'S... ABOUT EIGHT?

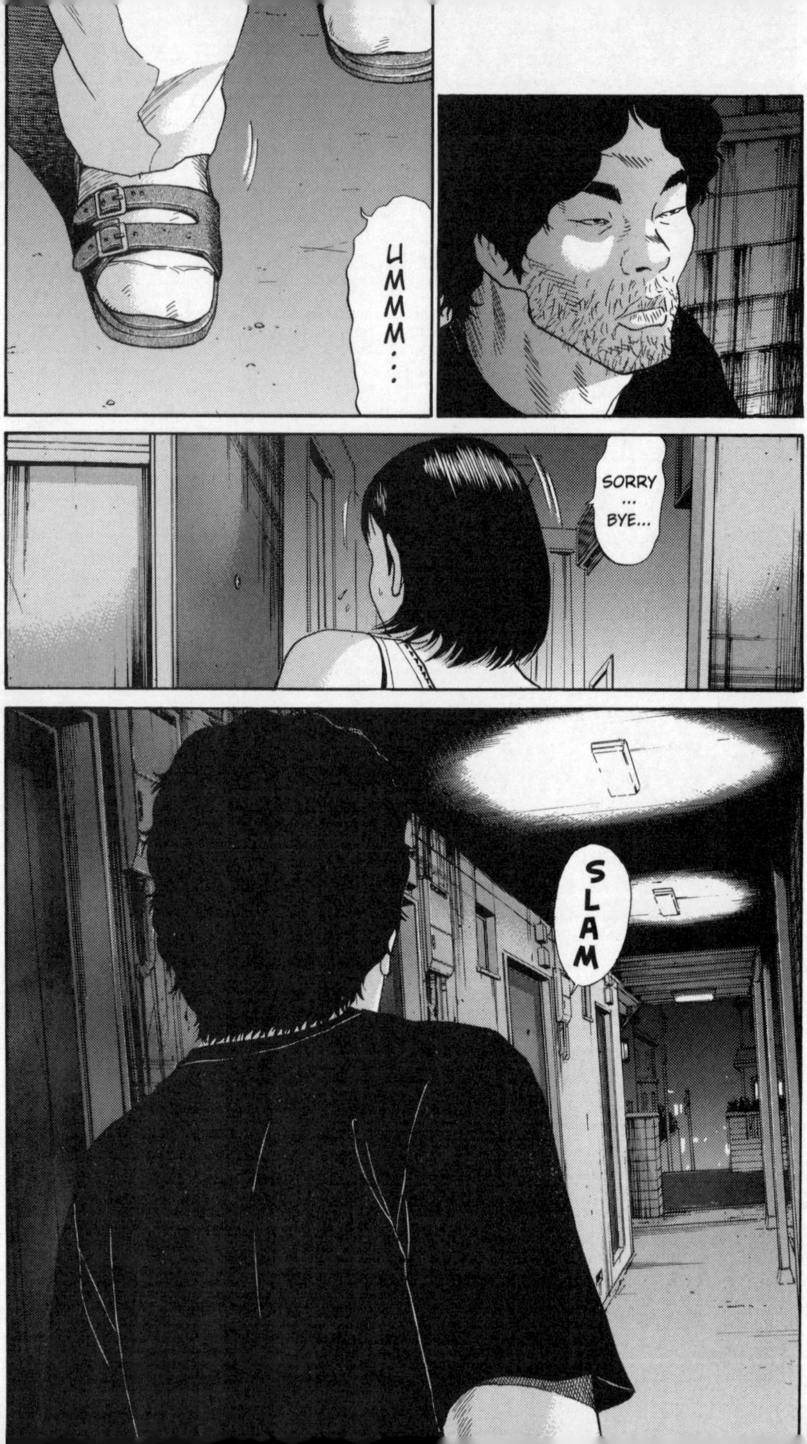
UMMM...
SORRY ... BYE...
SLAM

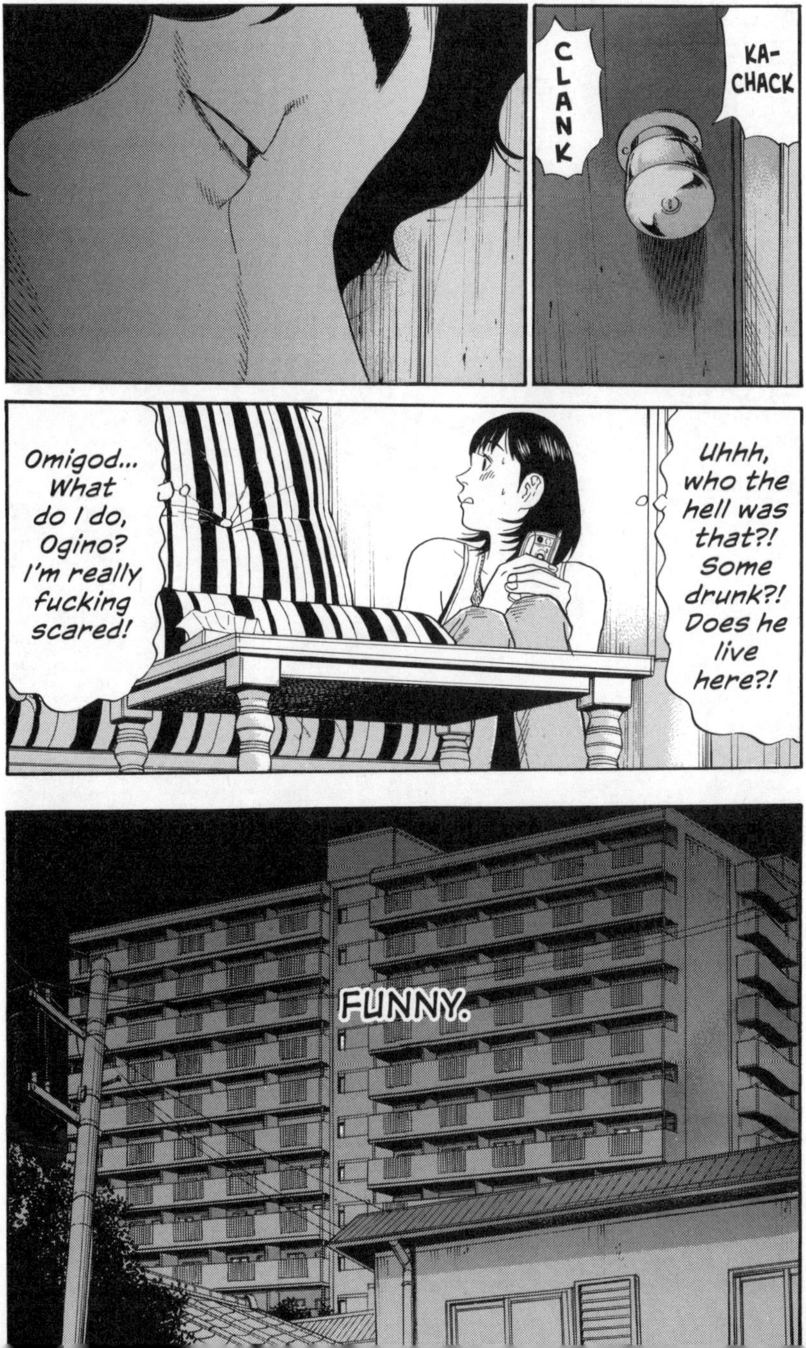
KA-CHACK
CLANK
Uhhh, who the hell was that?! Some drunk?! Does he live here?!
Omigod... What do I do, Ogino? I'm really fucking scared!
FUNNY.

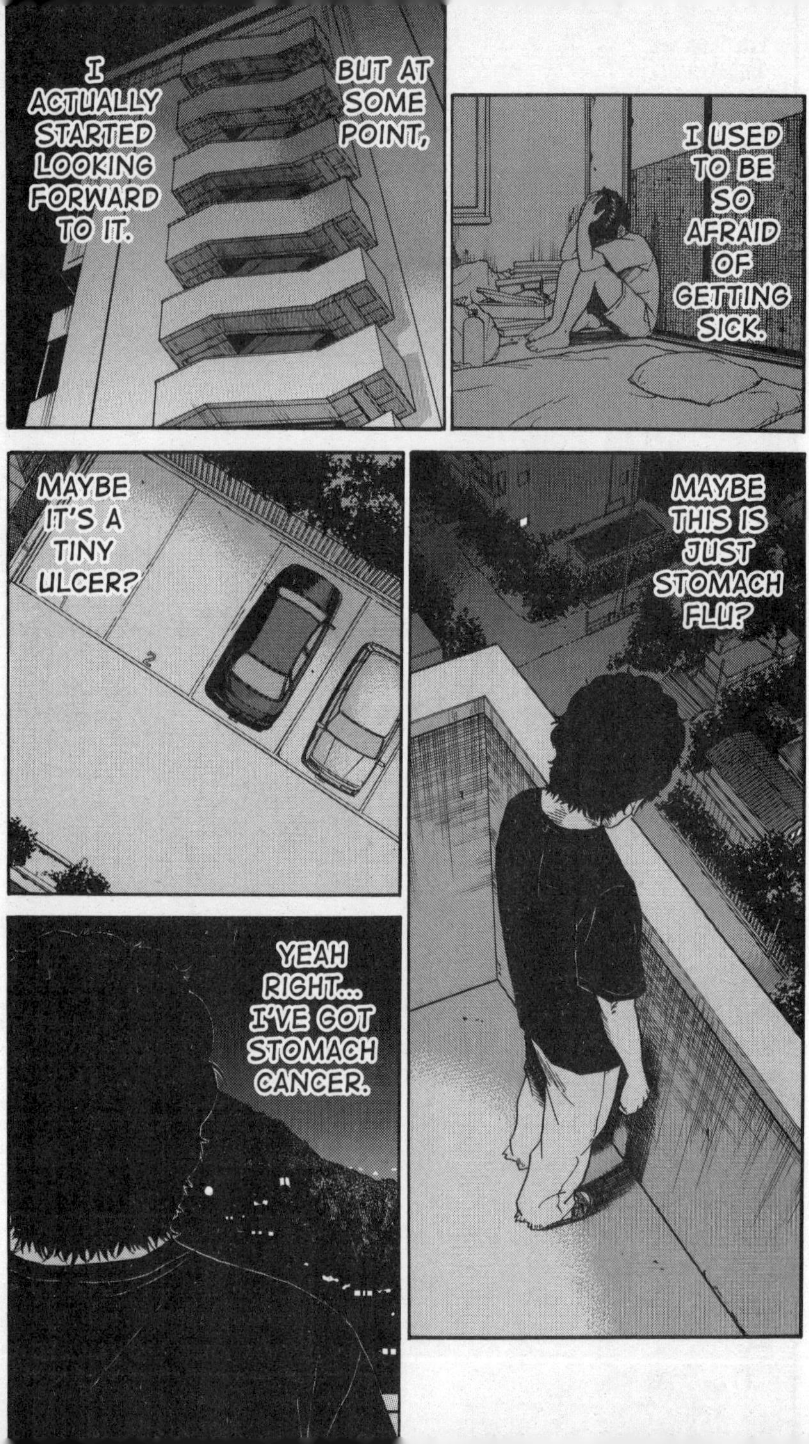
I USED TO BE SO AFRAID OF GETTING SICK.
BUT AT SOME POINT,
I ACTUALLY STARTED LOOKING FORWARD TO IT.
MAYBE THIS IS JUST STOMACH FLU?
MAYBE IT'S A TINY ULCER?
YEAH RIGHT... I'VE GOT STOMACH CANCER.

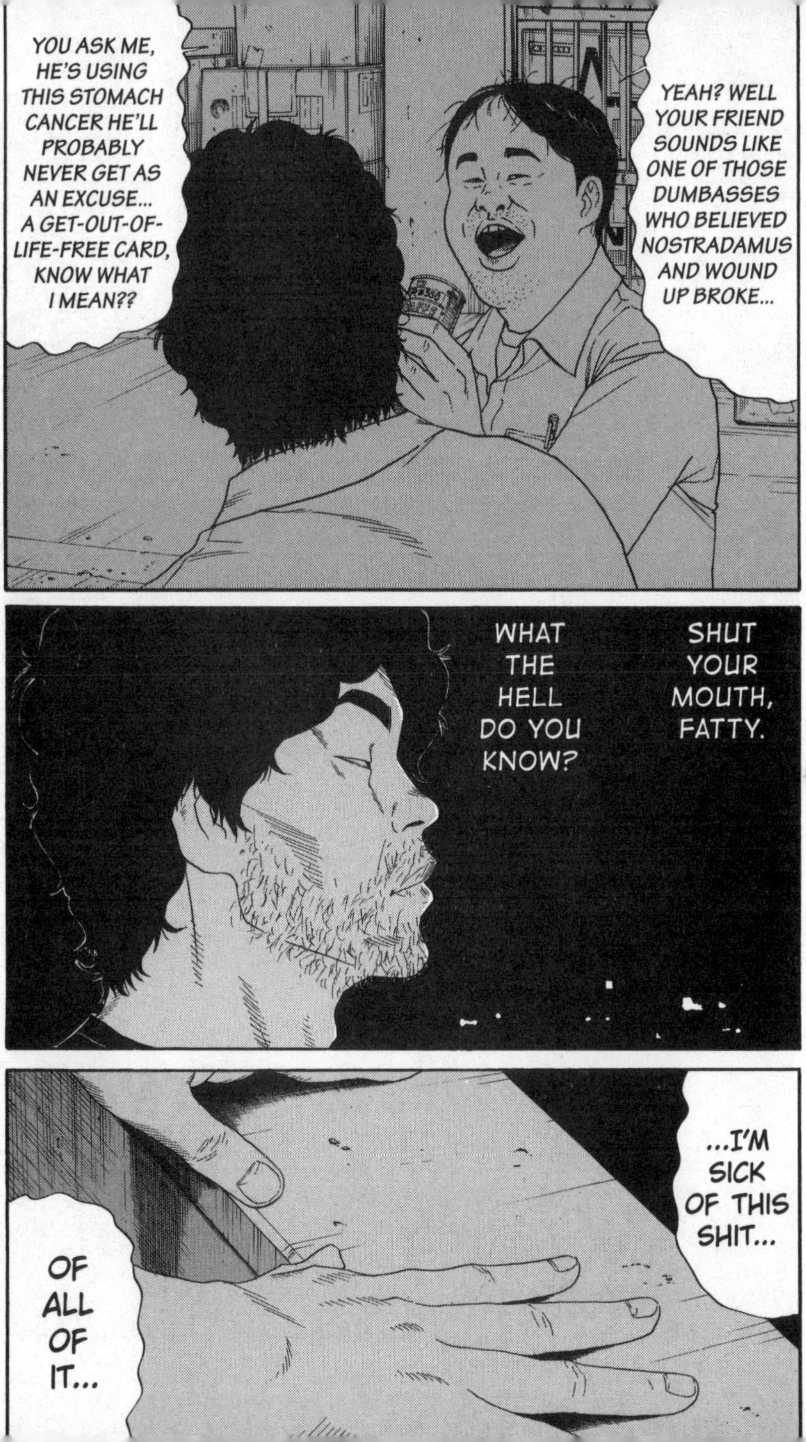
YEAH? WELL YOUR FRIEND SOUNDS LIKE ONE OF THOSE DUMBASSES WHO BELIEVED NOSTRADAMUS AND WOUND UP BROKE...
YOU ASK ME, HE'S USING THIS STOMACH CANCER HE'LL PROBABLY NEVER GET AS AN EXCUSE... A GET-OUT-OF-LIFE-FREE CARD, KNOW WHAT I MEAN??
SHUT YOUR MOUTH, FATTY.
WHAT THE HELL DO YOU KNOW?
...I'M SICK OF THIS SHIT...
OF ALL OF IT...

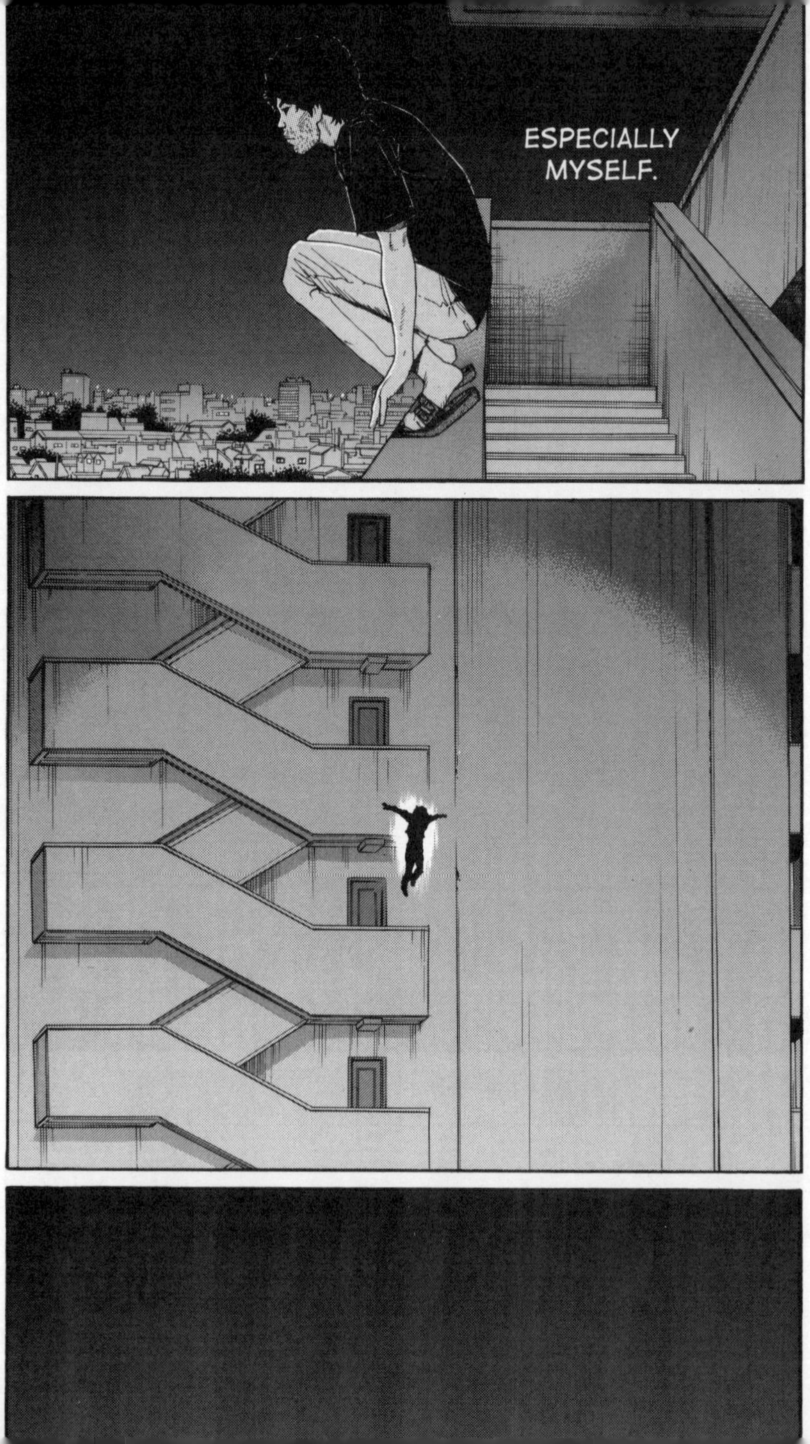
ESPECIALLY
MYSELF.

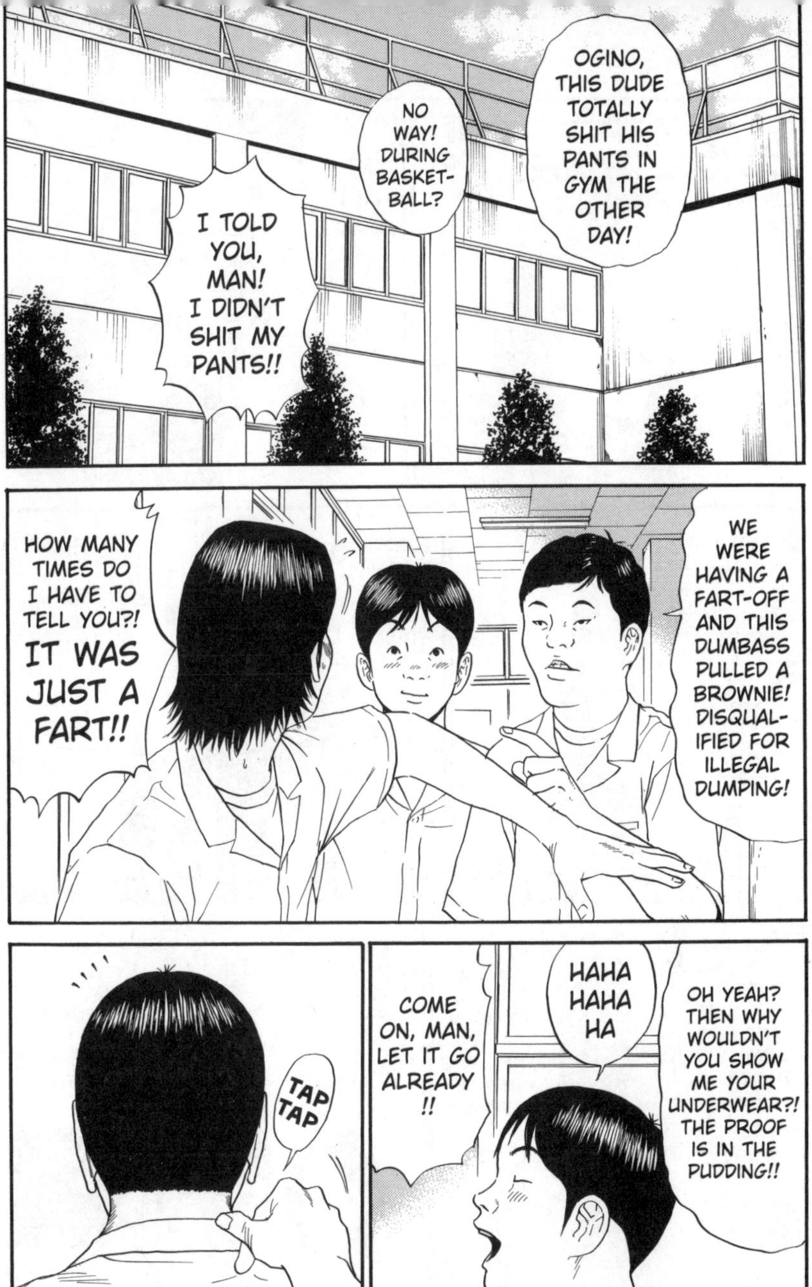
OGINO, THIS DUDE TOTALLY SHIT HIS PANTS IN GYM THE OTHER DAY!
NO WAY! DURING BASKET-BALL?
I TOLD YOU, MAN! I DIDN'T SHIT MY PANTS!!
WE WERE HAVING A FART-OFF AND THIS DUMBASS PULLED A BROWNIE! DISQUAL-IFIED FOR ILLEGAL DUMPING!
HOW MANY TIMES DO I HAVE TO TELL YOU?! IT WAS JUST A FART!!
OH YEAH? THEN WHY WOULDN'T YOU SHOW ME YOUR UNDERWEAR?! THE PROOF IS IN THE PUDDING!!
HAHA HAHA HA
COME ON, MAN, LET IT GO ALREADY !!
TAP TAP

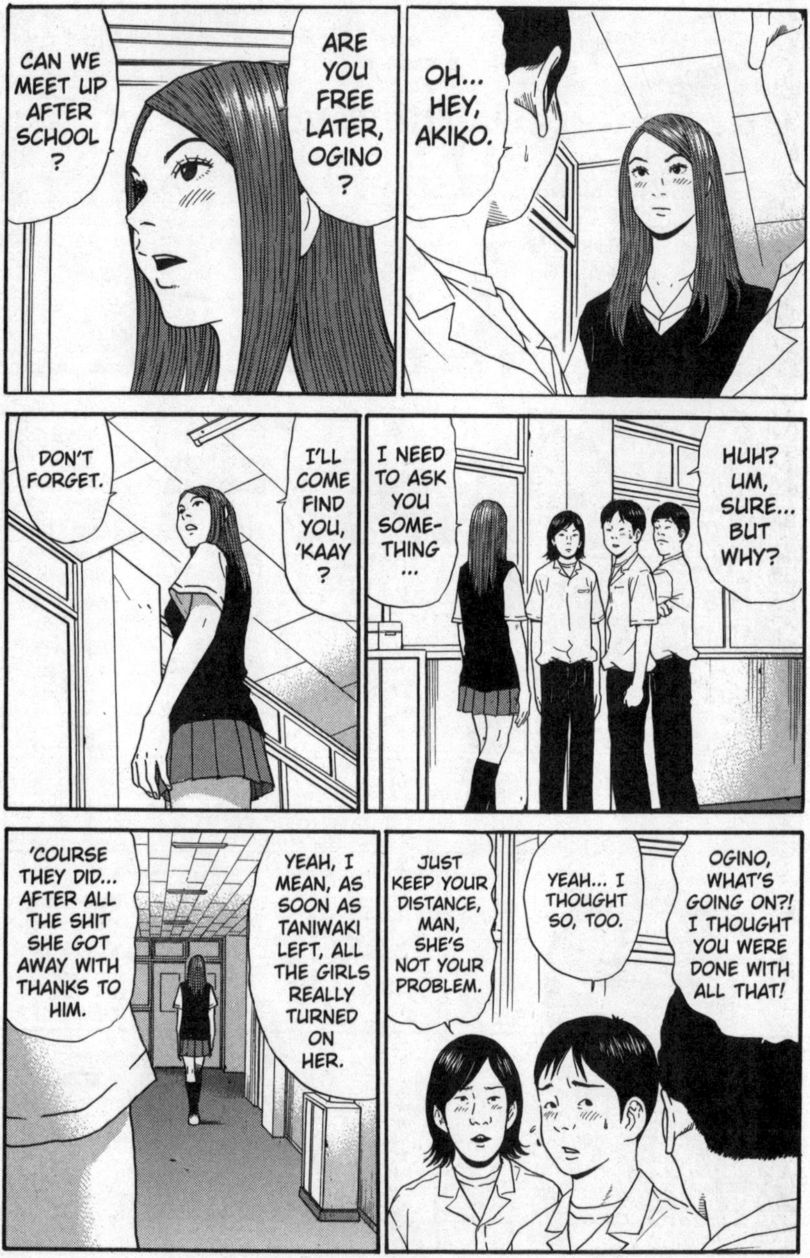
OH... HEY, AKIKO.
ARE YOU FREE LATER, OGINO?
CAN WE MEET UP AFTER SCHOOL?
HUH? UM, SURE... BUT WHY?
I NEED TO ASK YOU SOMETHING...
I'LL COME FIND YOU, 'KAAY?
DON'T FORGET.
OGINO, WHAT'S GOING ON?! I THOUGHT YOU WERE DONE WITH ALL THAT!
YEAH... I THOUGHT SO, TOO.
JUST KEEP YOUR DISTANCE, MAN, SHE'S NOT YOUR PROBLEM.
YEAH, I MEAN, AS SOON AS TANIWAKI LEFT, ALL THE GIRLS REALLY TURNED ON HER.
'COURSE THEY DID... AFTER ALL THE SHIT SHE GOT AWAY WITH THANKS TO HIM.

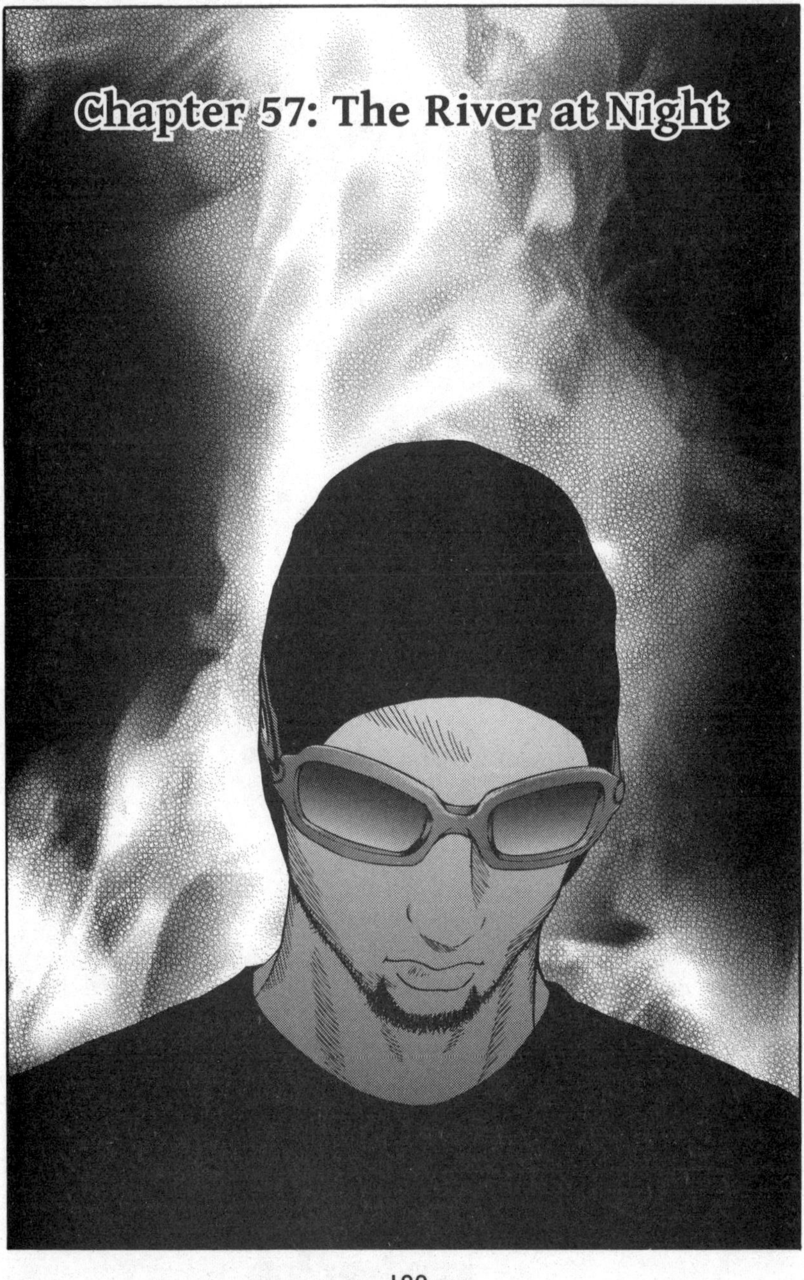
Chapter 57: The River at Night

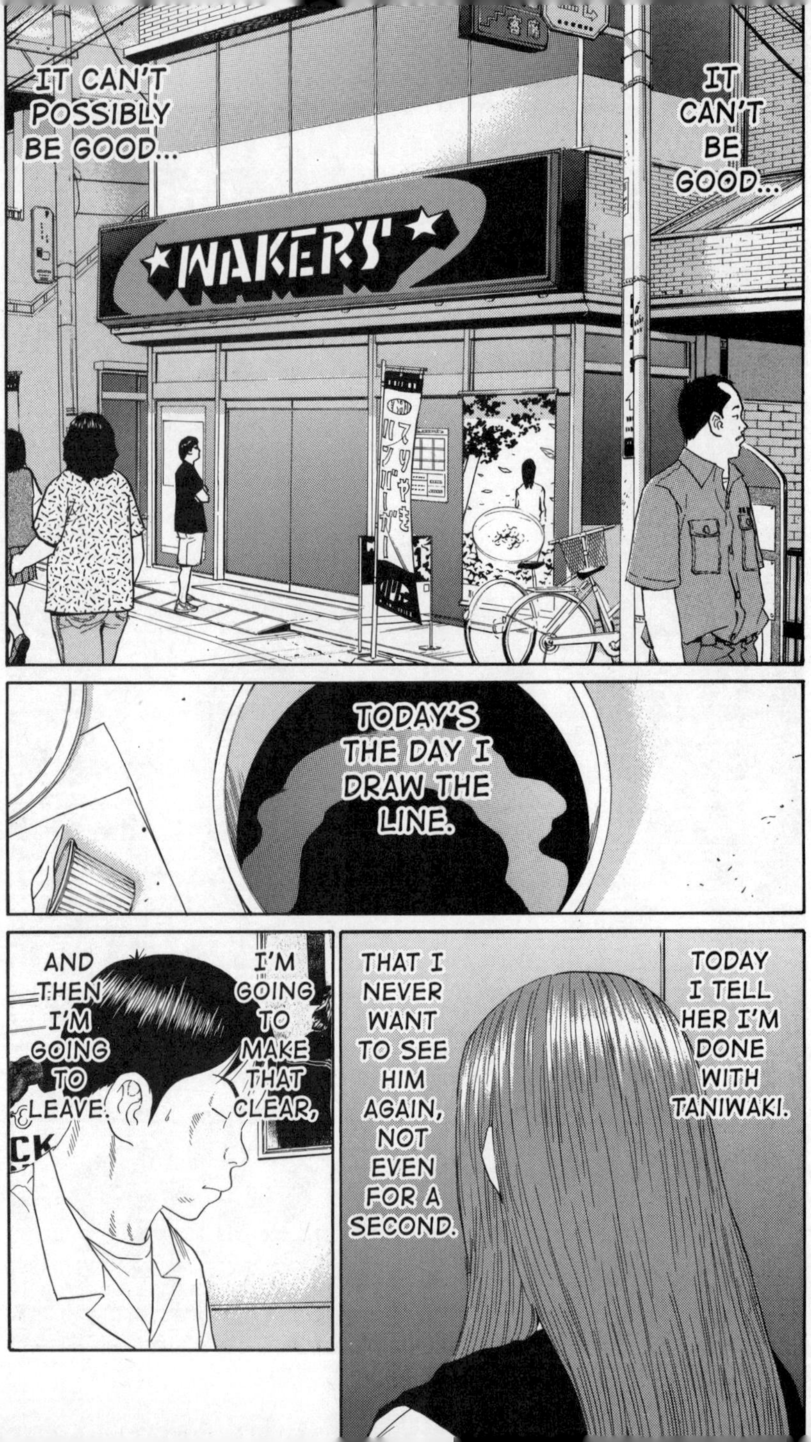
IT CAN'T BE GOOD...
IT CAN'T POSSIBLY BE GOOD...
WAKERS
TODAY'S THE DAY I DRAW THE LINE.
TODAY I TELL HER I'M DONE WITH TANIWAKI.
THAT I NEVER WANT TO SEE HIM AGAIN, NOT EVEN FOR A SECOND.
I'M GOING TO MAKE THAT CLEAR,
AND THEN I'M GOING TO LEAVE.

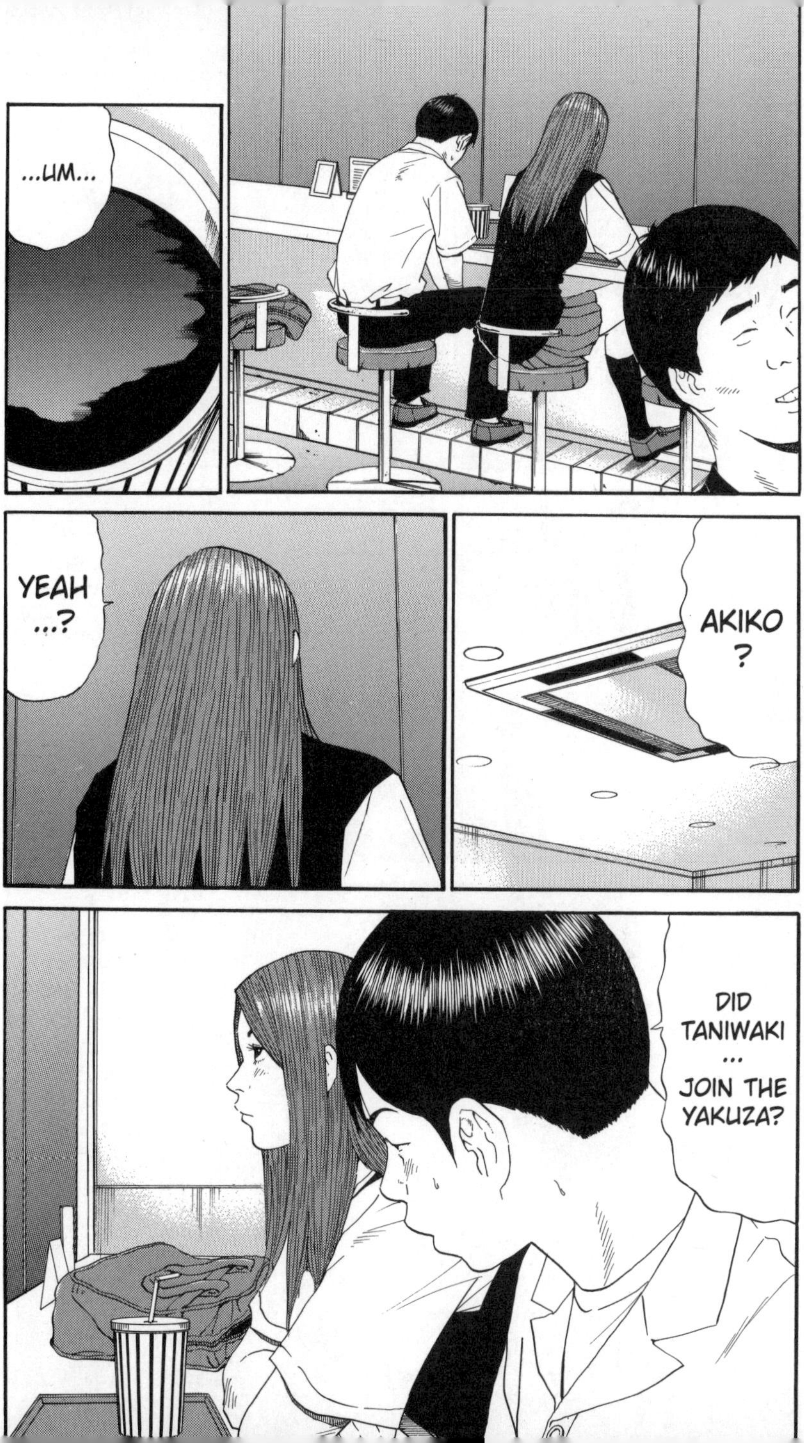
...UM...
AKIKO ?
YEAH ...?
DID TANIWAKI ... JOIN THE YAKUZA?

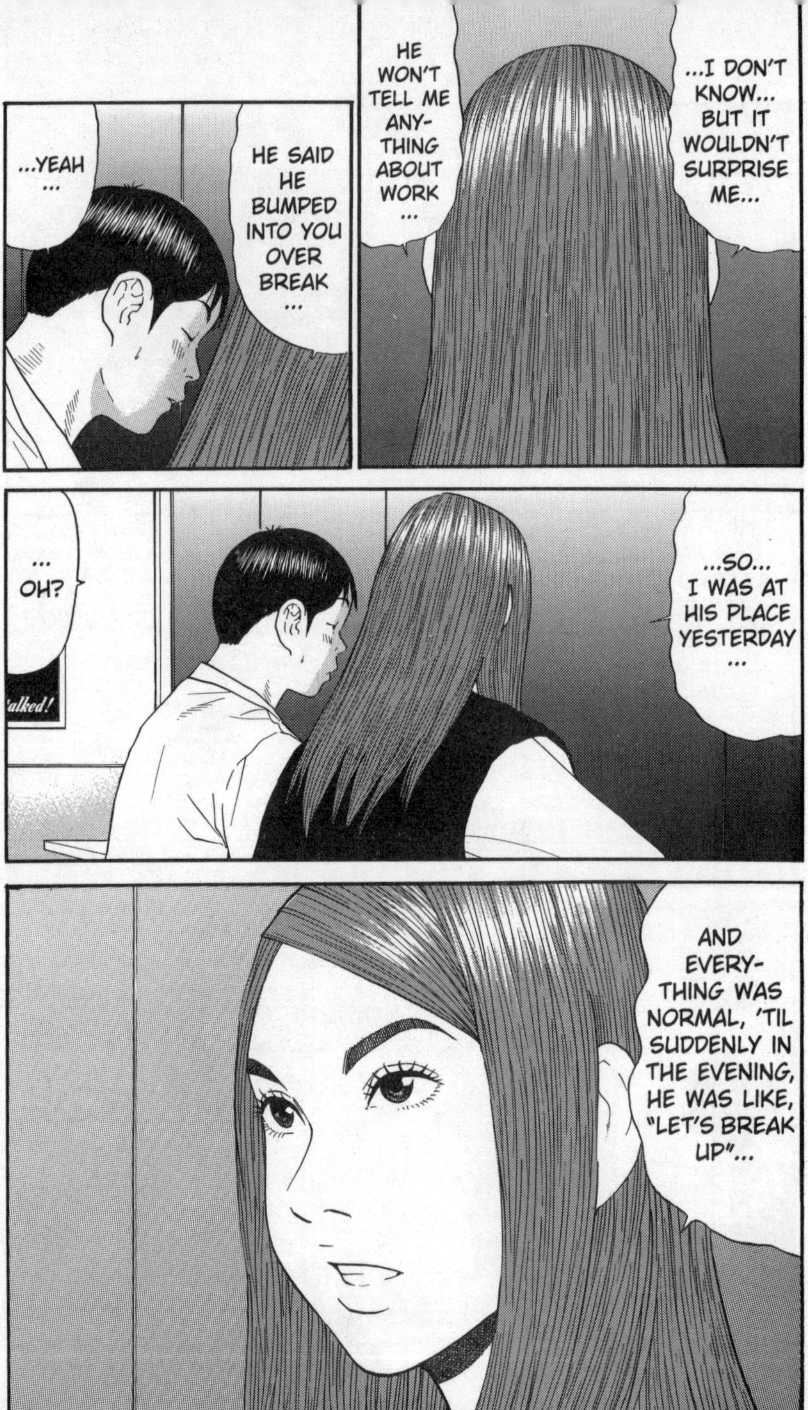
...I DON'T KNOW... BUT IT WOULDN'T SURPRISE ME...
HE WON'T TELL ME ANYTHING ABOUT WORK ...
HE SAID HE BUMPED INTO YOU OVER BREAK ...
...YEAH ...
...SO... I WAS AT HIS PLACE YESTERDAY ...
... OH?
AND EVERYTHING WAS NORMAL, 'TIL SUDDENLY IN THE EVENING, HE WAS LIKE, "LET'S BREAK UP"...

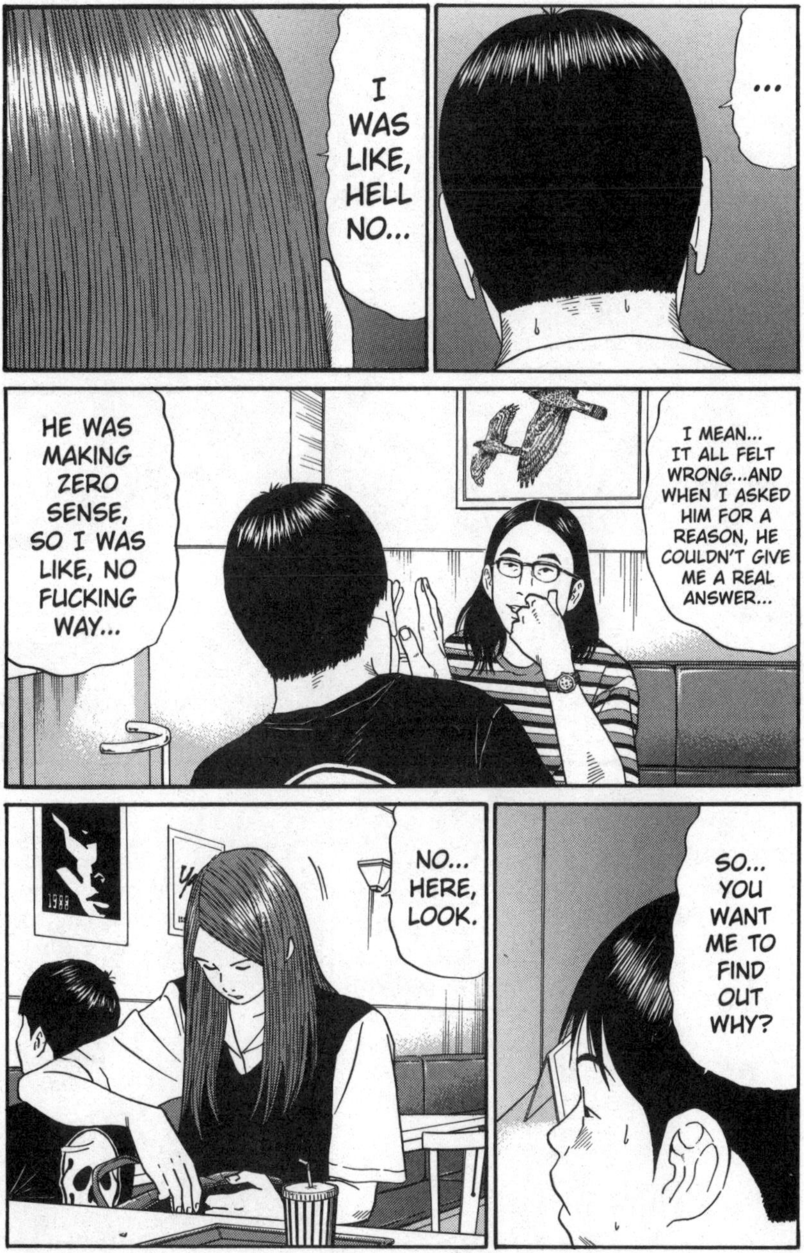
...
I WAS LIKE, HELL NO...
I MEAN... IT ALL FELT WRONG...AND WHEN I ASKED HIM FOR A REASON, HE COULDN'T GIVE ME A REAL ANSWER...
HE WAS MAKING ZERO SENSE, SO I WAS LIKE, NO FUCKING WAY...
SO... YOU WANT ME TO FIND OUT WHY?
NO... HERE, LOOK.

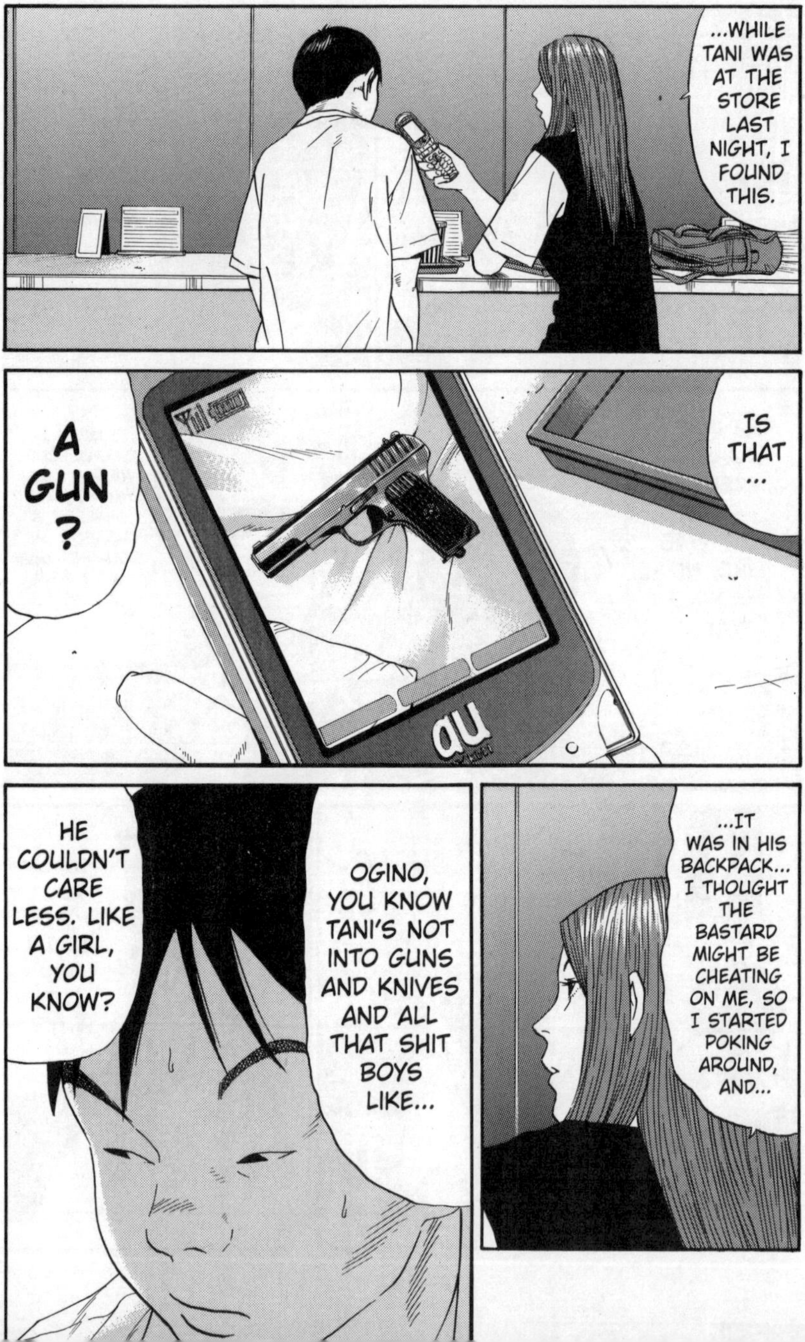
...WHILE TANI WAS AT THE STORE LAST NIGHT, I FOUND THIS.
IS THAT ...
A GUN ?
...IT WAS IN HIS BACKPACK... I THOUGHT THE BASTARD MIGHT BE CHEATING ON ME, SO I STARTED POKING AROUND, AND...
OGINO, YOU KNOW TANI'S NOT INTO GUNS AND KNIVES AND ALL THAT SHIT BOYS LIKE...
HE COULDN'T CARE LESS. LIKE A GIRL, YOU KNOW?

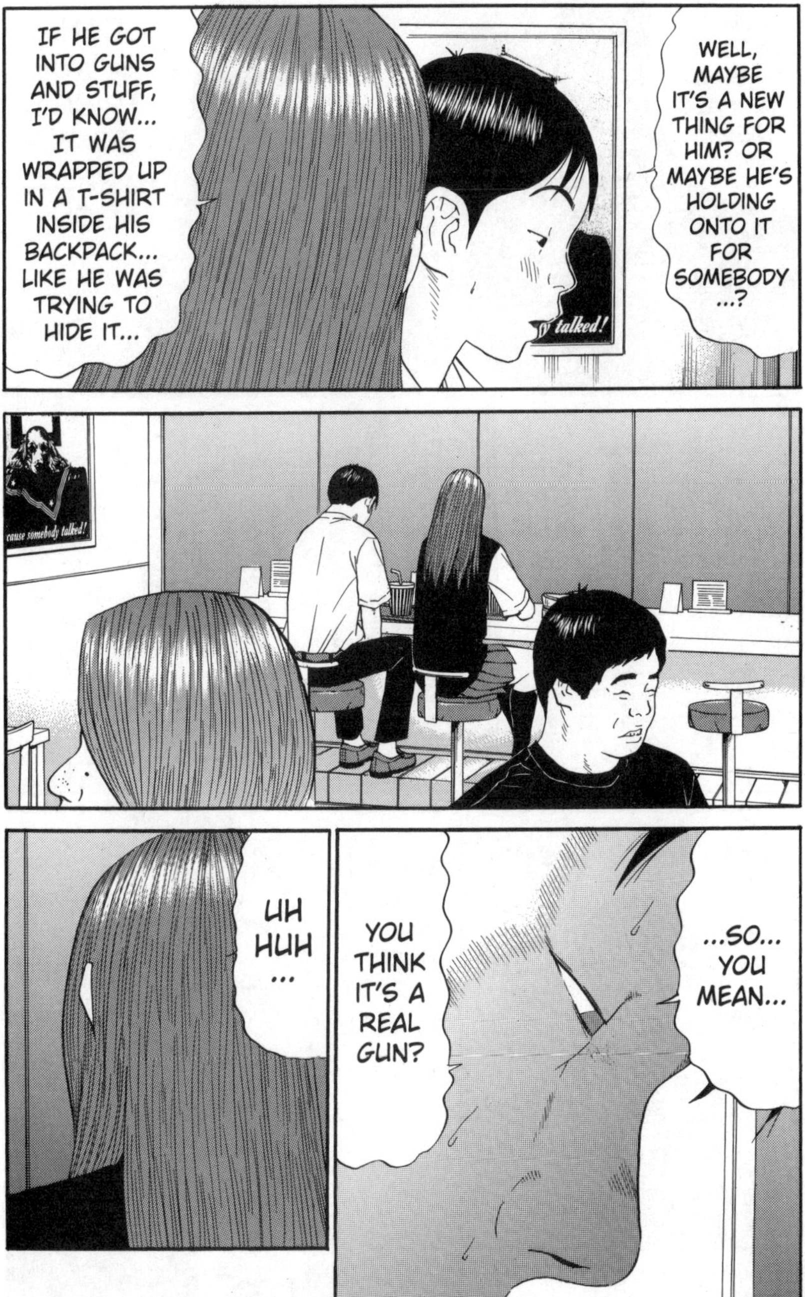
WELL, MAYBE IT'S A NEW THING FOR HIM? OR MAYBE HE'S HOLDING ONTO IT FOR SOMEBODY ...?
IF HE GOT INTO GUNS AND STUFF, I'D KNOW... IT WAS WRAPPED UP IN A T-SHIRT INSIDE HIS BACKPACK... LIKE HE WAS TRYING TO HIDE IT...
cause somebody talked!
...SO... YOU MEAN...
YOU THINK IT'S A REAL GUN?
UH HUH ...

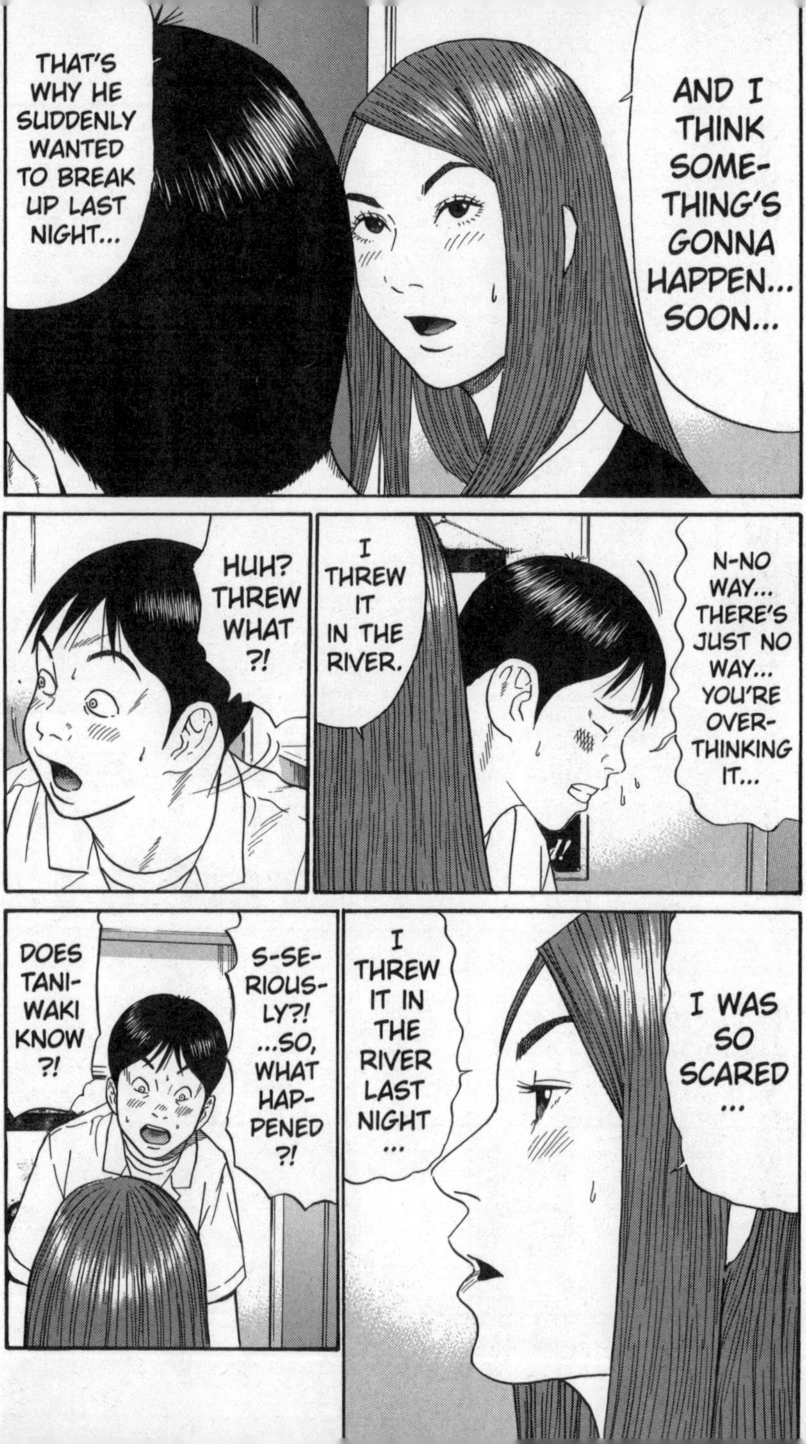
AND I THINK SOME-THING'S GONNA HAPPEN... SOON...
THAT'S WHY HE SUDDENLY WANTED TO BREAK UP LAST NIGHT...
N-NO WAY... THERE'S JUST NO WAY... YOU'RE OVER-THINKING IT...
I THREW IT IN THE RIVER.
HUH? THREW WHAT?!
I WAS SO SCARED...
I THREW IT IN THE RIVER LAST NIGHT...
S-SE-RIOUS-LY?! ...SO, WHAT HAP-PENED?!
DOES TANI-WAKI KNOW?!

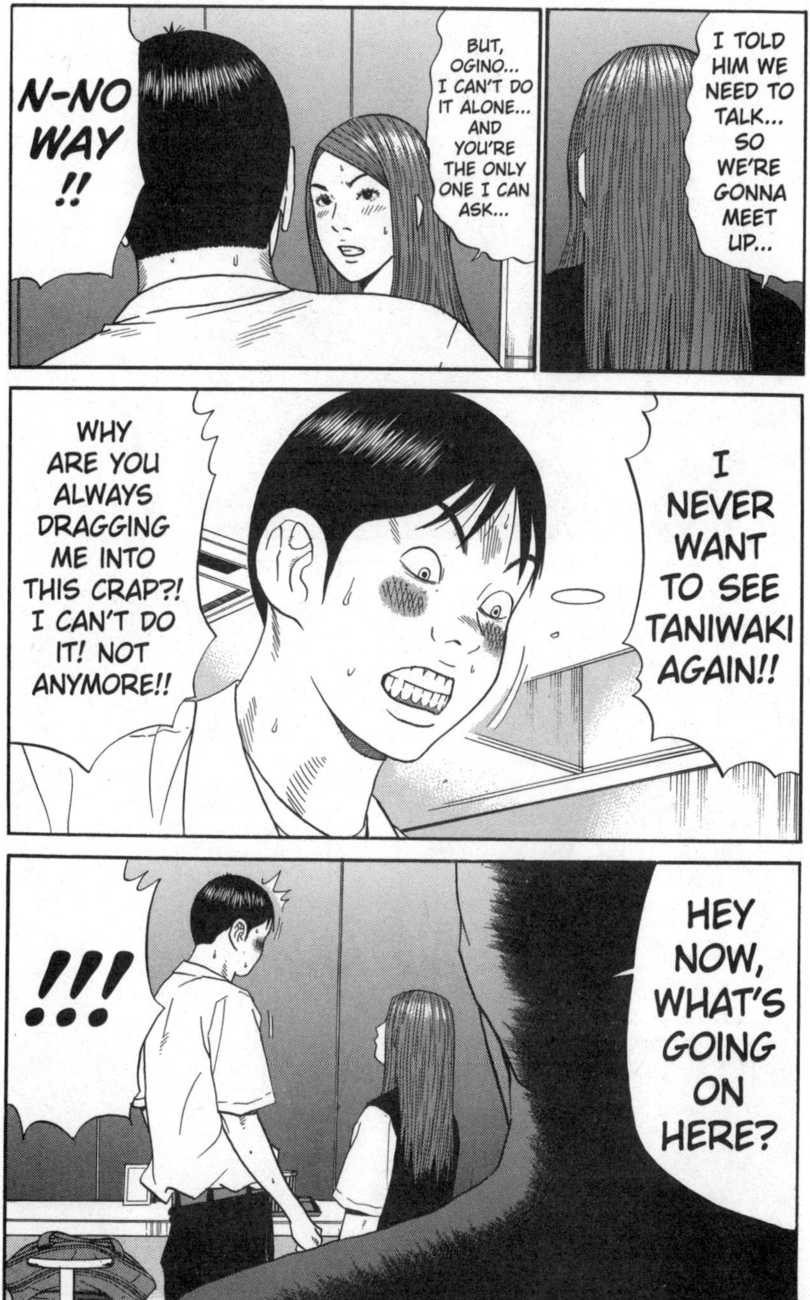
I TOLD HIM WE NEED TO TALK... SO WE'RE GONNA MEET UP...
BUT, OGINO... I CAN'T DO IT ALONE... AND YOU'RE THE ONLY ONE I CAN ASK...
N-NO WAY!!
I NEVER WANT TO SEE TANIWAKI AGAIN!!
WHY ARE YOU ALWAYS DRAGGING ME INTO THIS CRAP?! I CAN'T DO IT! NOT ANYMORE!!
HEY NOW, WHAT'S GOING ON HERE?
!!!

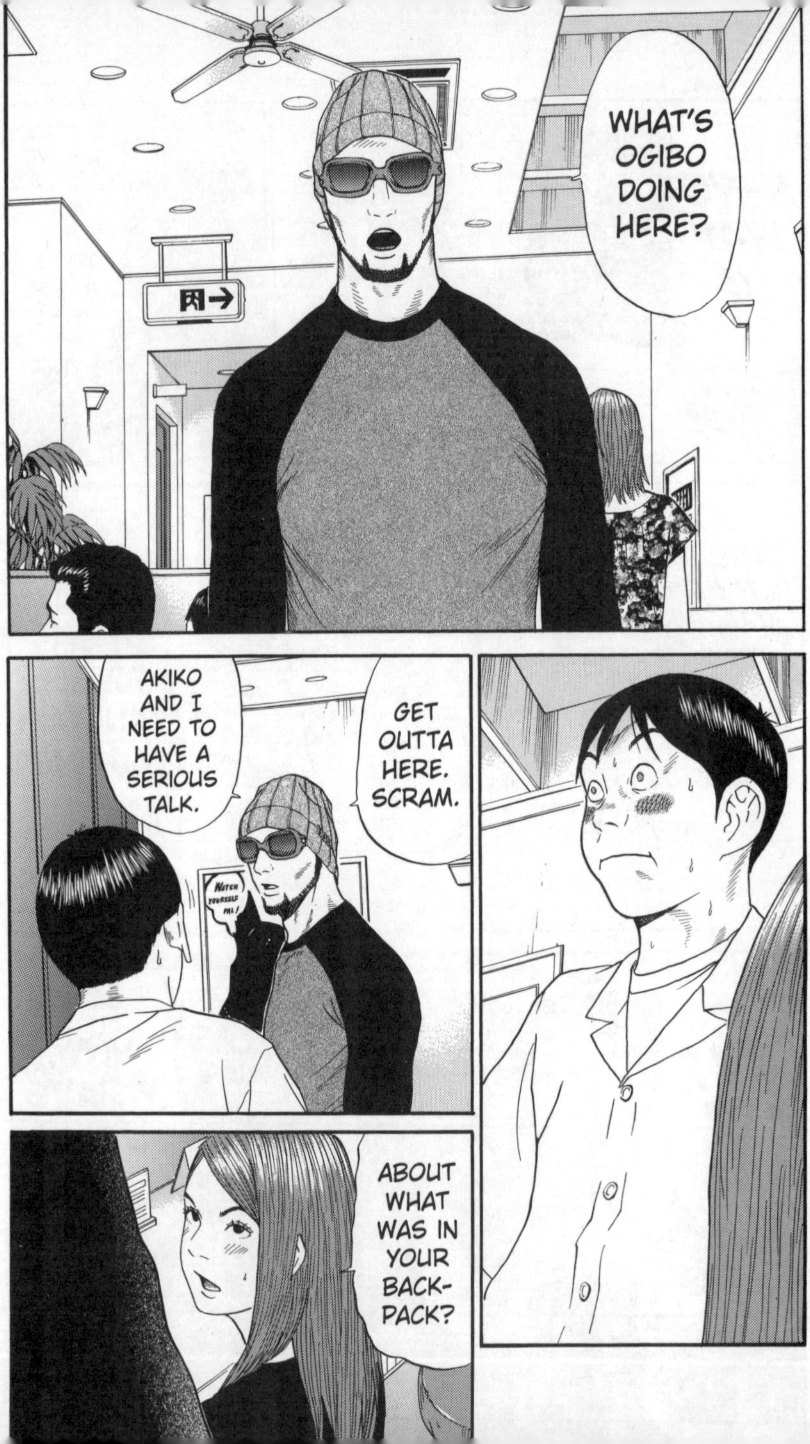
WHAT'S OGIBO DOING HERE?
GET OUTTA HERE. SCRAM.
AKIKO AND I NEED TO HAVE A SERIOUS TALK.
WATCH YOURSELF PAL!
ABOUT WHAT WAS IN YOUR BACKPACK?

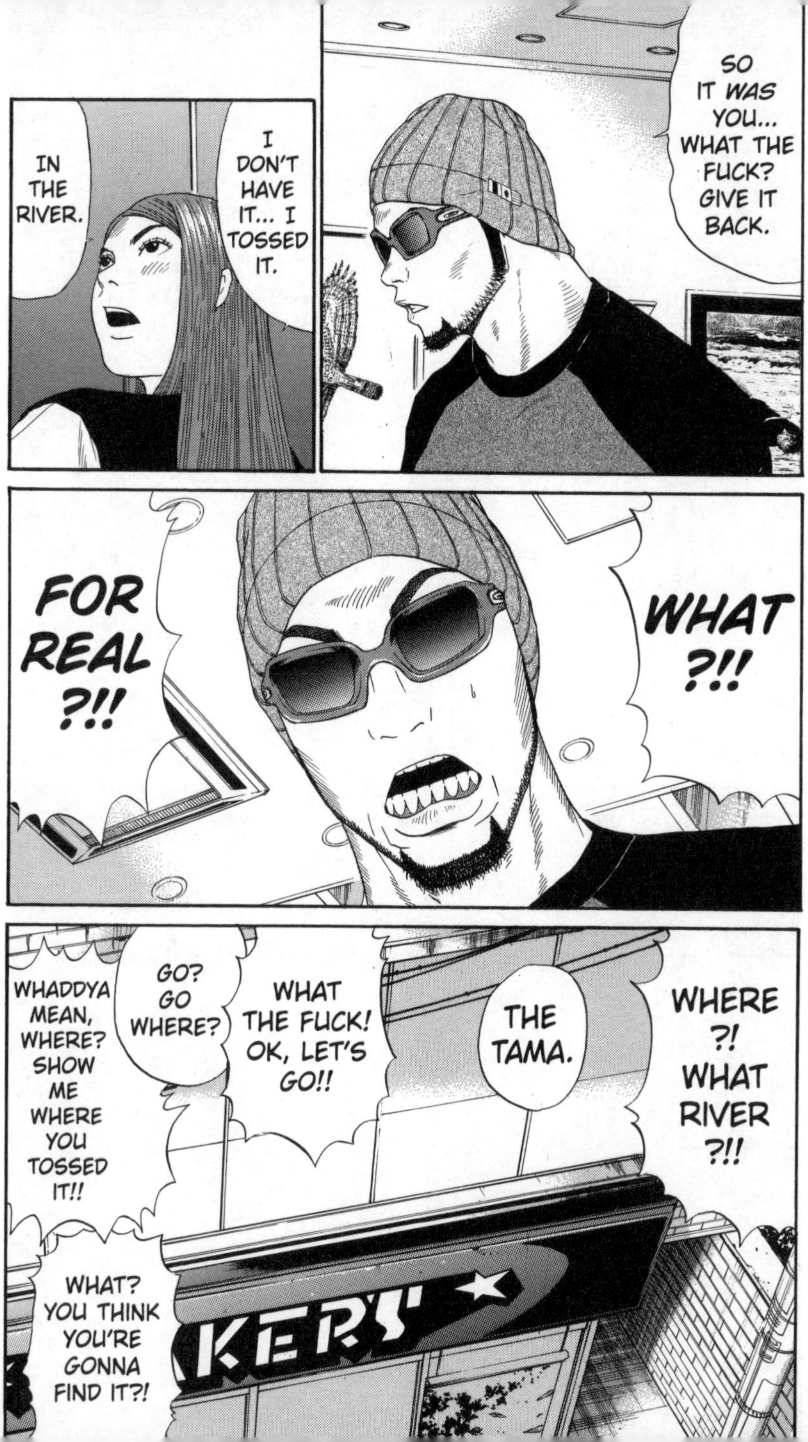
SO IT WAS YOU... WHAT THE FUCK? GIVE IT BACK.
I DON'T HAVE IT... I TOSSED IT.
IN THE RIVER.
WHAT ?!!
FOR REAL ?!!
WHERE ?! WHAT RIVER ?!!
THE TAMA.
WHAT THE FUCK! OK, LET'S GO!!
GO? GO WHERE?
WHADDYA MEAN, WHERE? SHOW ME WHERE YOU TOSSED IT!!
WHAT? YOU THINK YOU'RE GONNA FIND IT?!

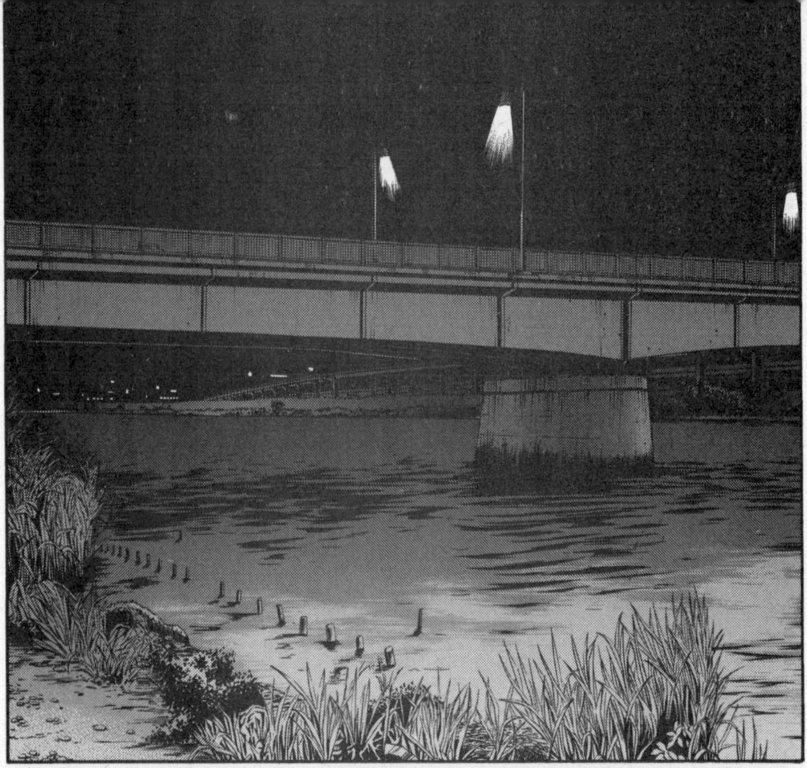
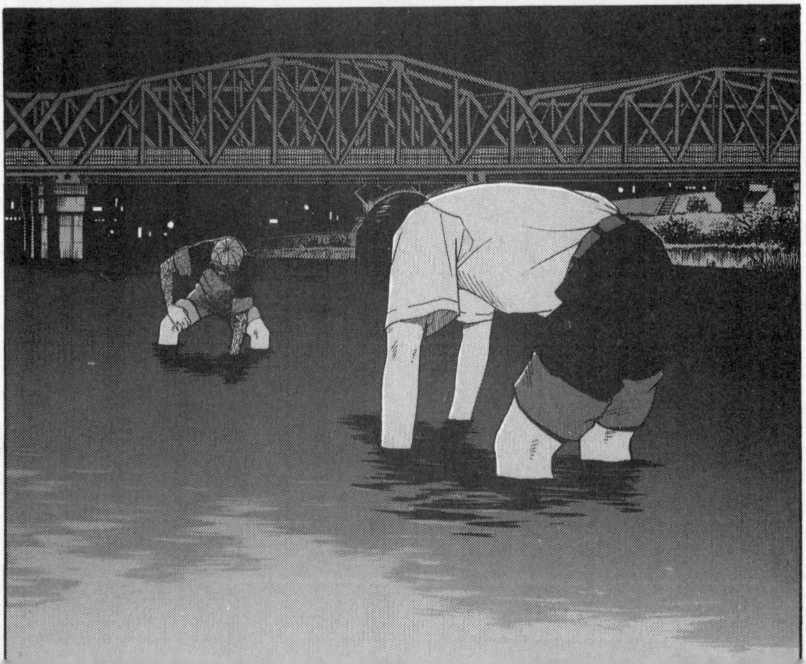

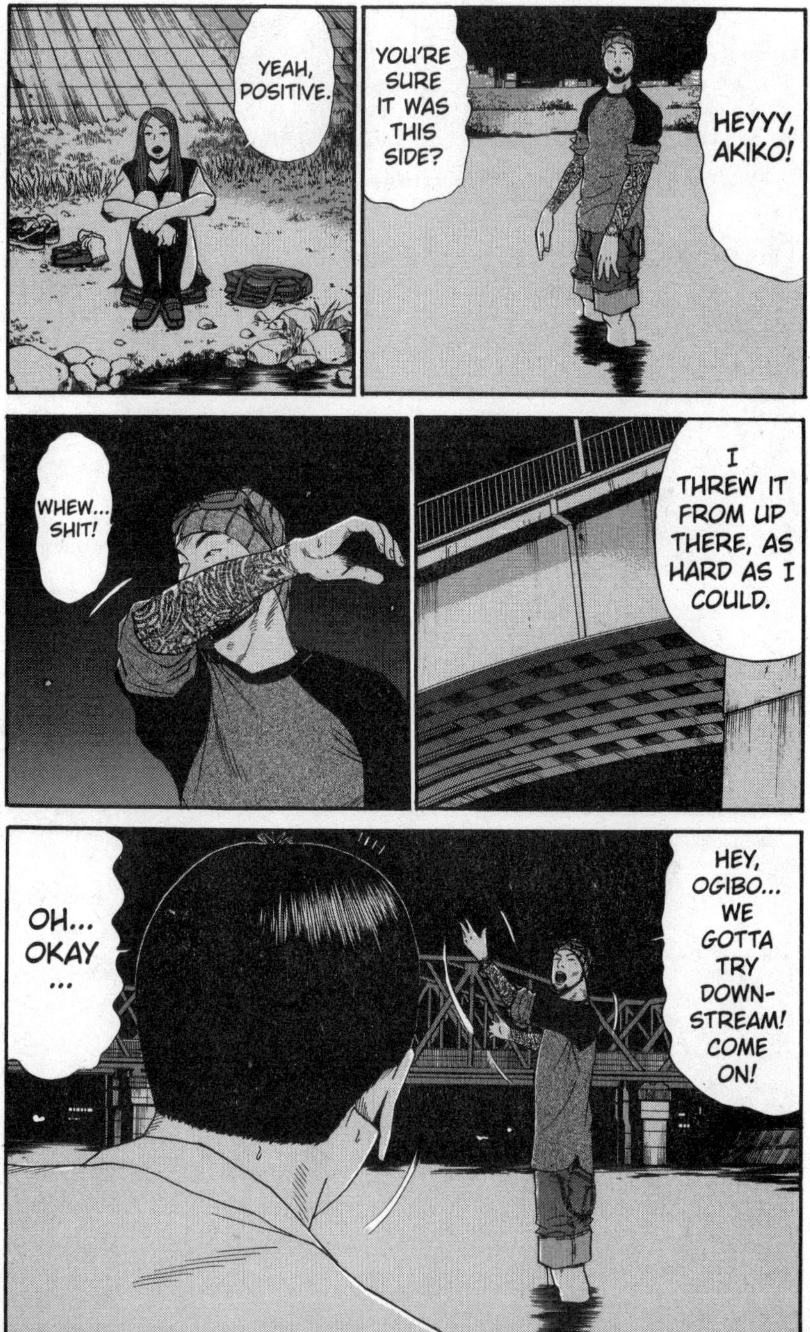
HEYYY, AKIKO!
YOU'RE SURE IT WAS THIS SIDE?
YEAH, POSITIVE.
I THREW IT FROM UP THERE, AS HARD AS I COULD.
WHEW... SHIT!
HEY, OGIBO... WE GOTTA TRY DOWN-STREAM! COME ON!
OH... OKAY...

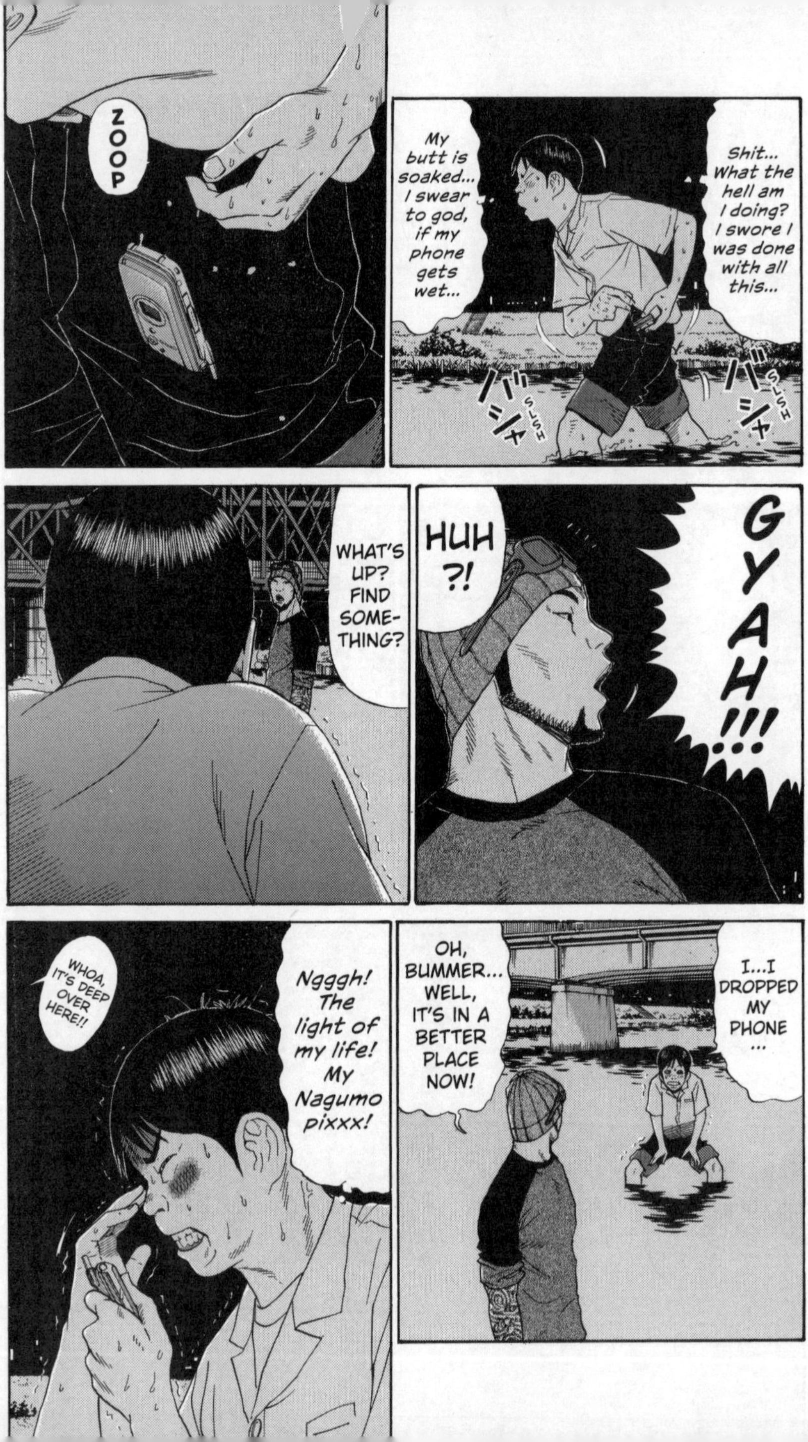
Shit... What the hell am I doing? I swore I was done with all this...
My butt is soaked... I swear to god, if my phone gets wet...
バシャ SLSH
バシャ SLSH
ZOOP
GYAH!!!
HUH ?!
WHAT'S UP? FIND SOME-THING?
I...I DROPPED MY PHONE ...
OH, BUMMER... WELL, IT'S IN A BETTER PLACE NOW!
Ngggh! The light of my life! My Nagumo pixxx!
WHOA, IT'S DEEP OVER HERE!!

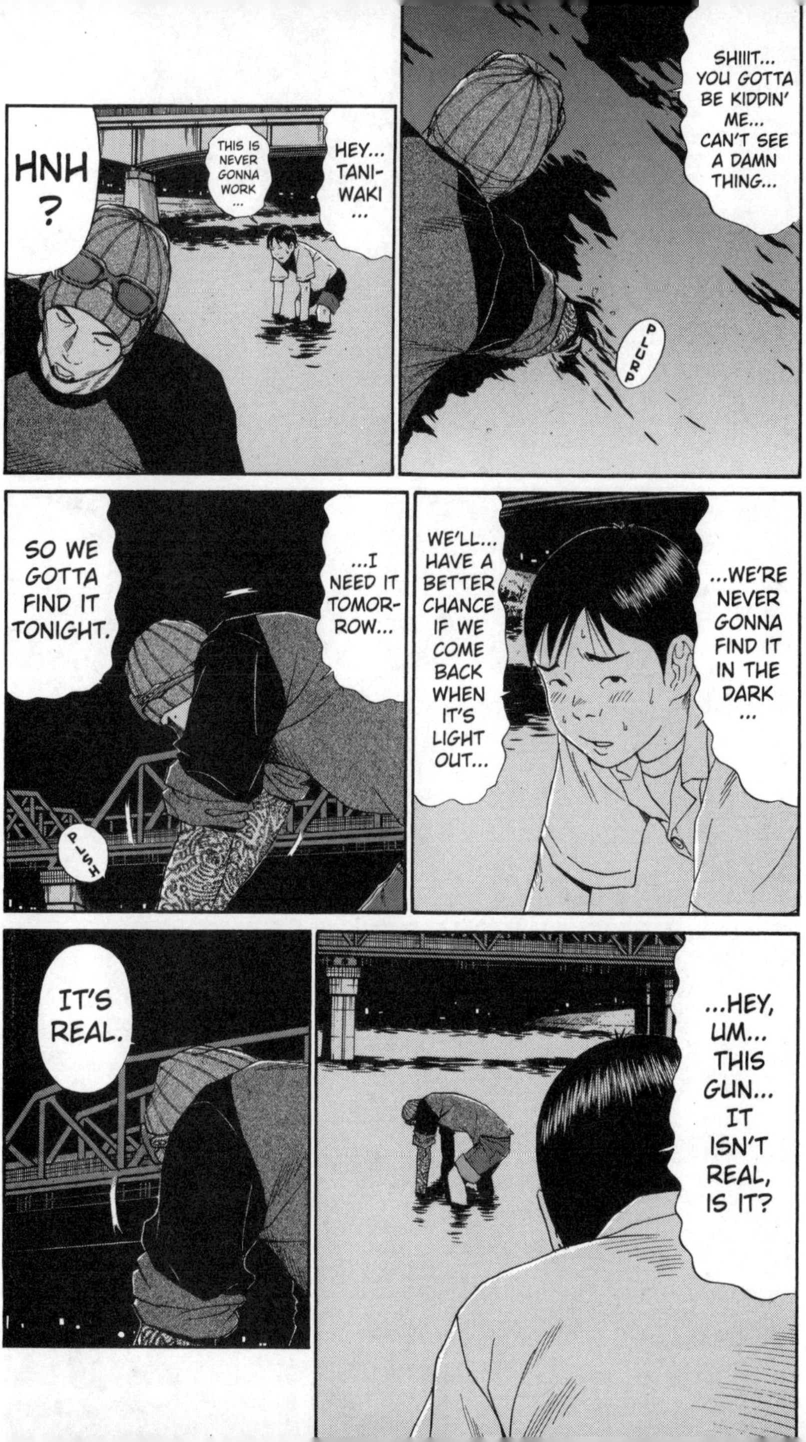
SHIIIT... YOU GOTTA BE KIDDIN' ME... CAN'T SEE A DAMN THING...
PLURP
HEY... TANI-WAKI ...
THIS IS NEVER GONNA WORK ...
HNH ?
...WE'RE NEVER GONNA FIND IT IN THE DARK ...
WE'LL... HAVE A BETTER CHANCE IF WE COME BACK WHEN IT'S LIGHT OUT...
...I NEED IT TOMOR-ROW...
SO WE GOTTA FIND IT TONIGHT.
PLSH
...HEY, UM... THIS GUN... IT ISN'T REAL, IS IT?
IT'S REAL.

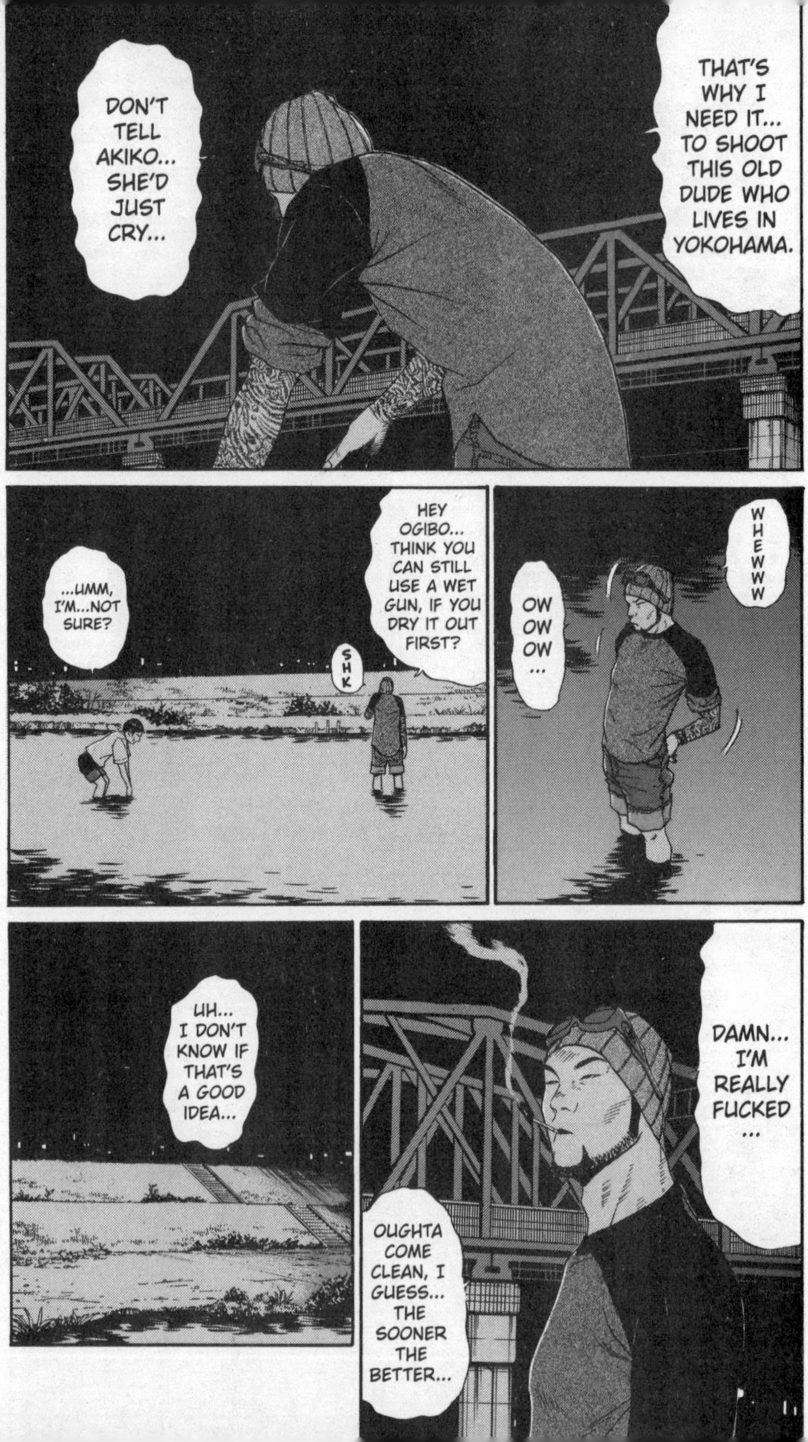
THAT'S WHY I NEED IT... TO SHOOT THIS OLD DUDE WHO LIVES IN YOKOHAMA.
DON'T TELL AKIKO... SHE'D JUST CRY...
WHEWWW
OW OW OW...
HEY OGIBO... THINK YOU CAN STILL USE A WET GUN, IF YOU DRY IT OUT FIRST?
SHK
...UMM, I'M...NOT SURE?
DAMN... I'M REALLY FUCKED...
OUGHTA COME CLEAN, I GUESS... THE SOONER THE BETTER...
UH... I DON'T KNOW IF THAT'S A GOOD IDEA...

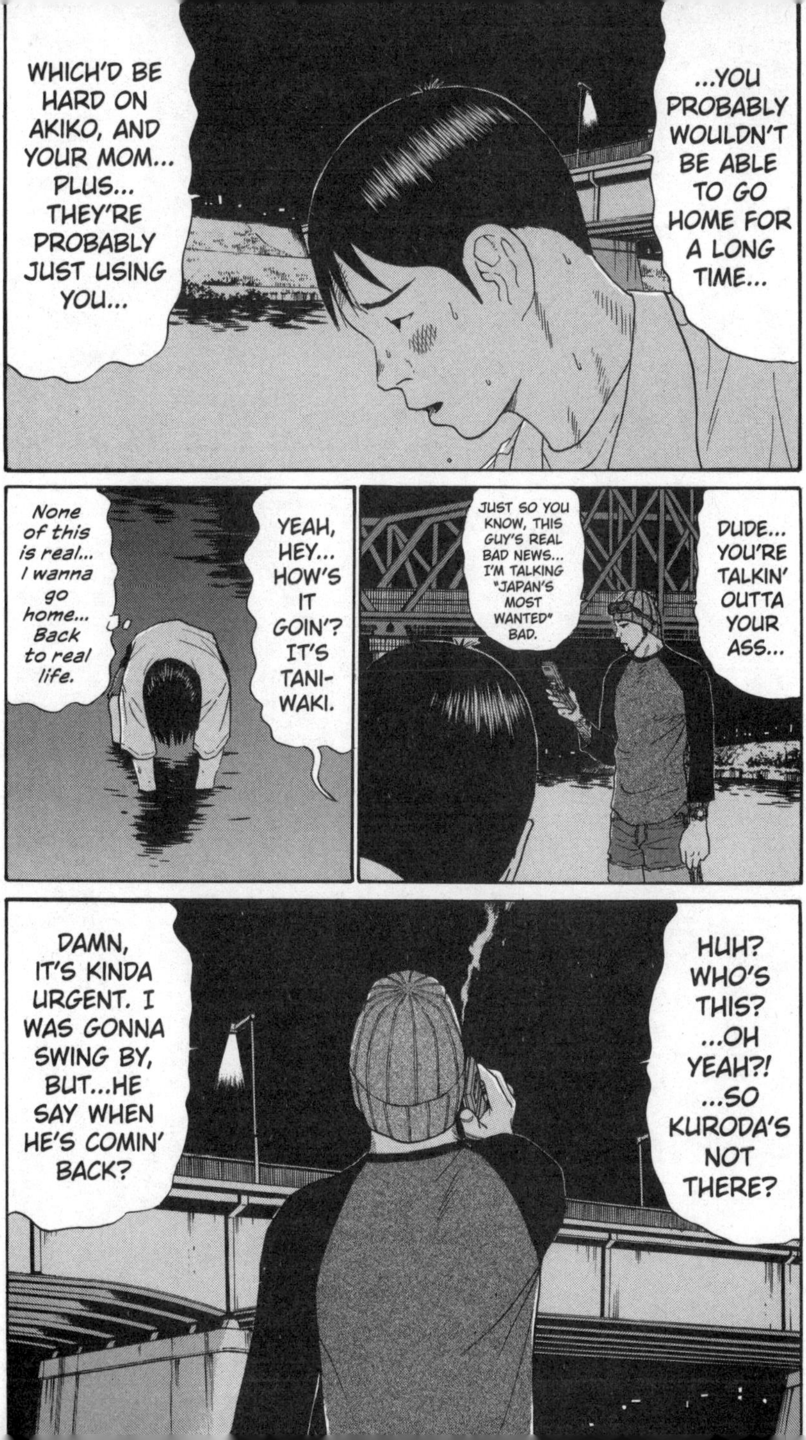
...YOU PROBABLY WOULDN'T BE ABLE TO GO HOME FOR A LONG TIME...
WHICH'D BE HARD ON AKIKO, AND YOUR MOM... PLUS... THEY'RE PROBABLY JUST USING YOU...
DUDE... YOU'RE TALKIN' OUTTA YOUR ASS...
JUST SO YOU KNOW, THIS GUY'S REAL BAD NEWS... I'M TALKING "JAPAN'S MOST WANTED" BAD.
YEAH, HEY... HOW'S IT GOIN'? IT'S TANI-WAKI.
*None of this is real... I wanna go home... Back to real life.*
HUH? WHO'S THIS? ...OH YEAH?! ...SO KURODA'S NOT THERE?
DAMN, IT'S KINDA URGENT. I WAS GONNA SWING BY, BUT...HE SAY WHEN HE'S COMIN' BACK?

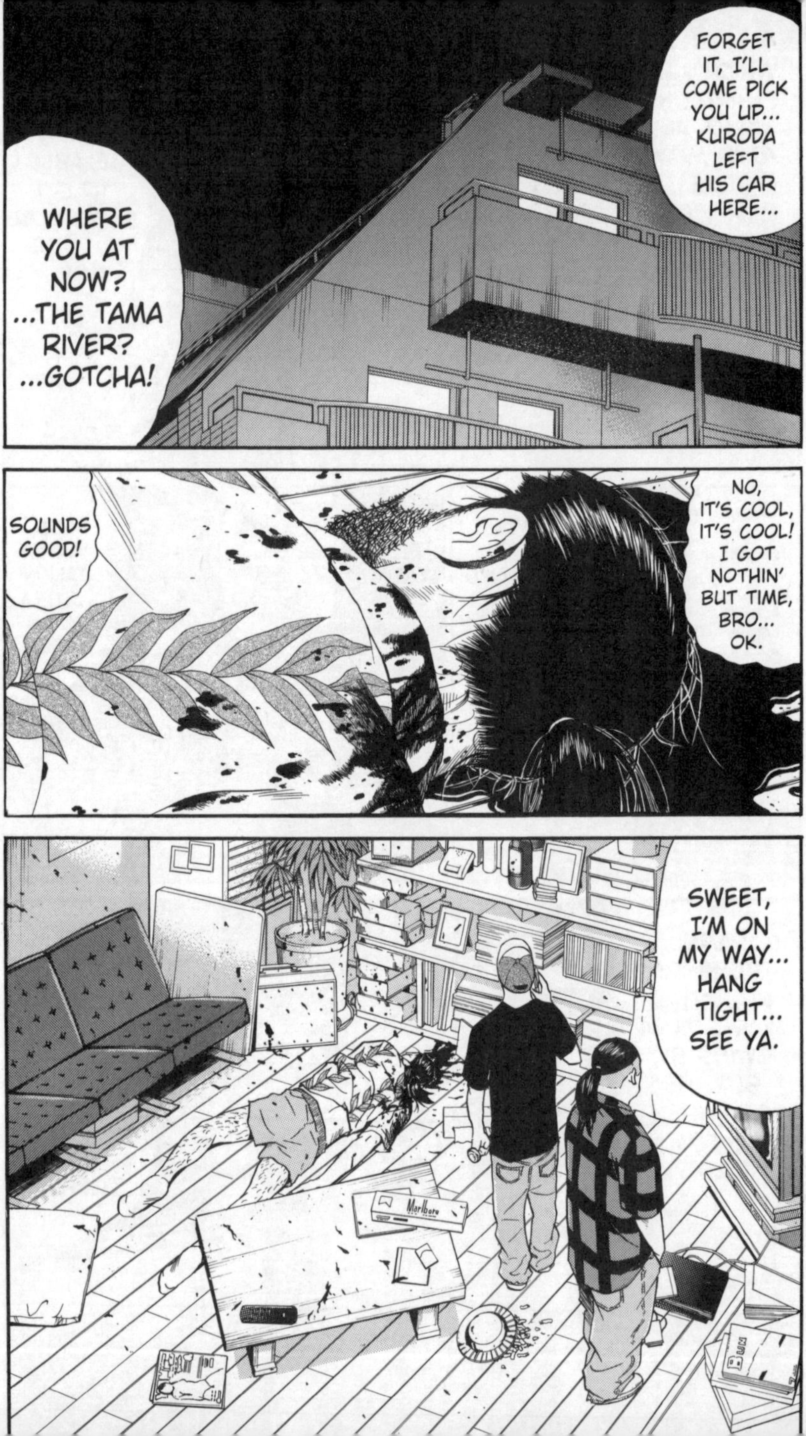
FORGET IT, I'LL COME PICK YOU UP... KURODA LEFT HIS CAR HERE...
WHERE YOU AT NOW? ...THE TAMA RIVER? ...GOTCHA!
NO, IT'S COOL, IT'S COOL! I GOT NOTHIN' BUT TIME, BRO... OK.
SOUNDS GOOD!
SWEET, I'M ON MY WAY... HANG TIGHT... SEE YA.
Marlboro

# CIGUATERA

## 17 fuga of youth

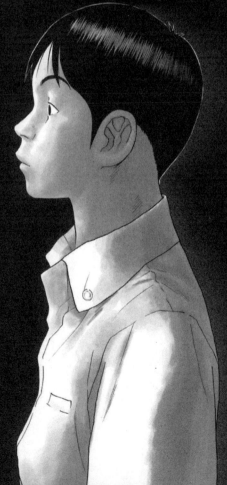

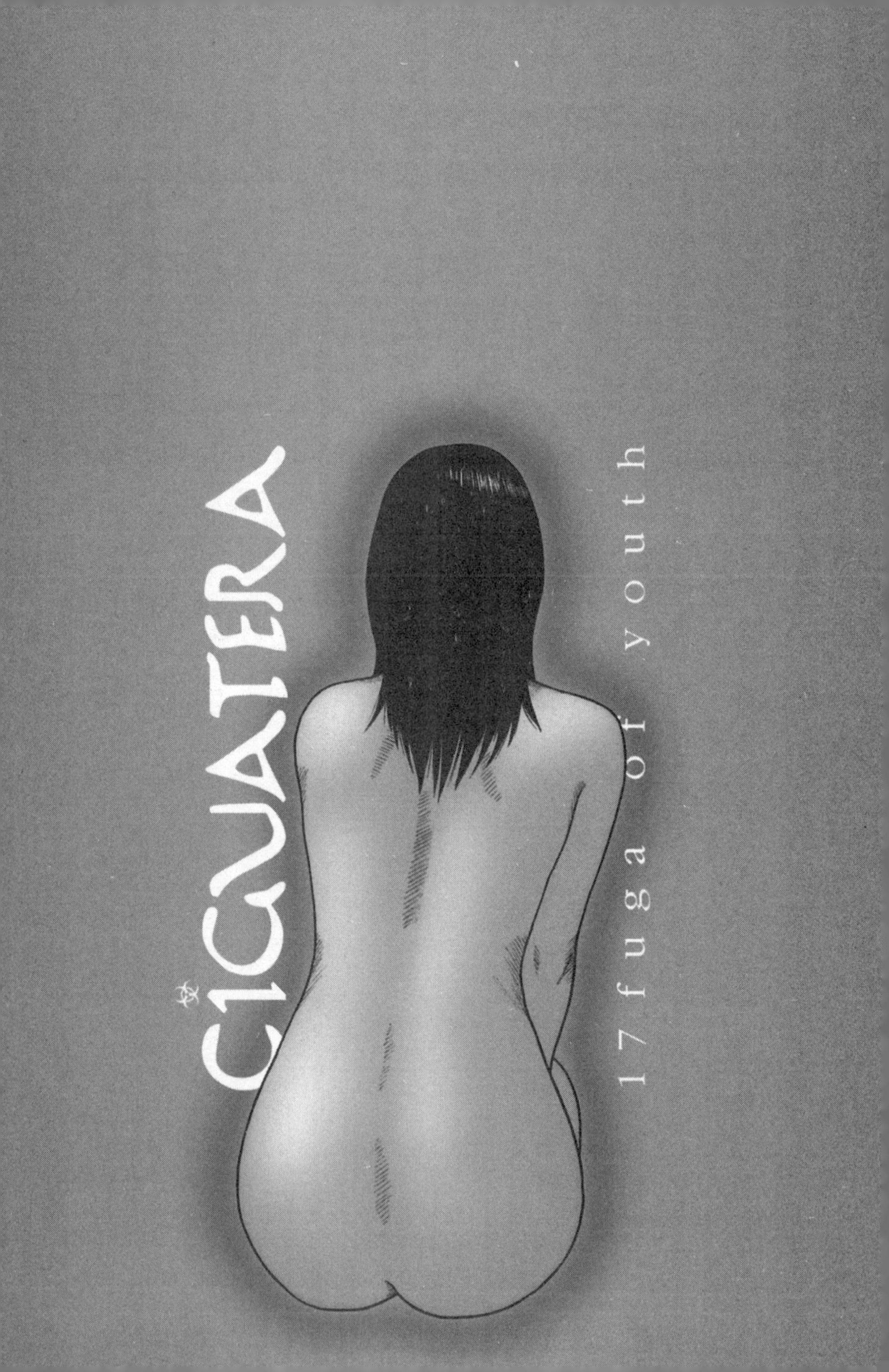
CIGUATERA
17 fuga of youth

# Chapter 58: Out of the Ordinary

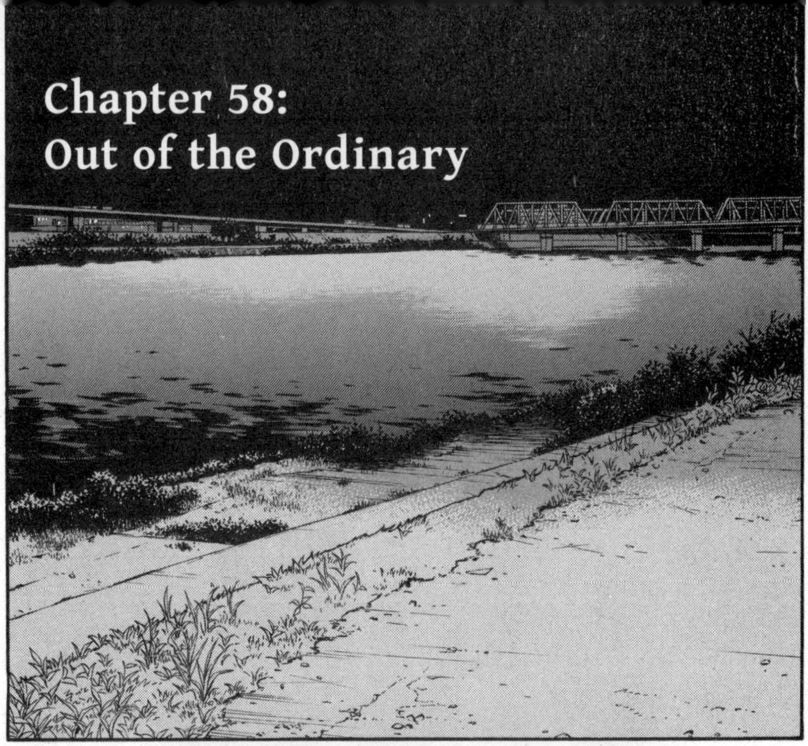

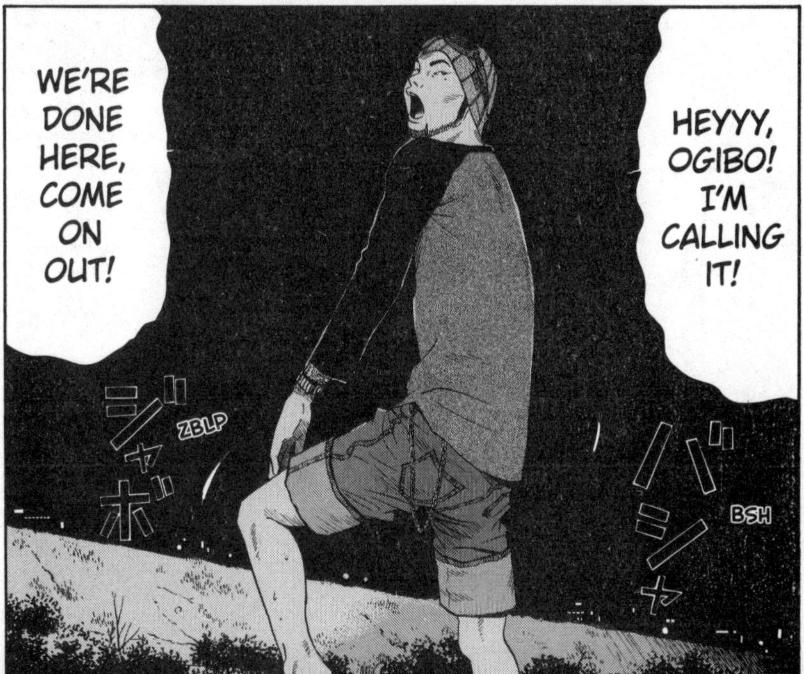
HEYYY, OGIBO! I'M CALLING IT!
WE'RE DONE HERE, COME ON OUT!
BSH
ZBLP

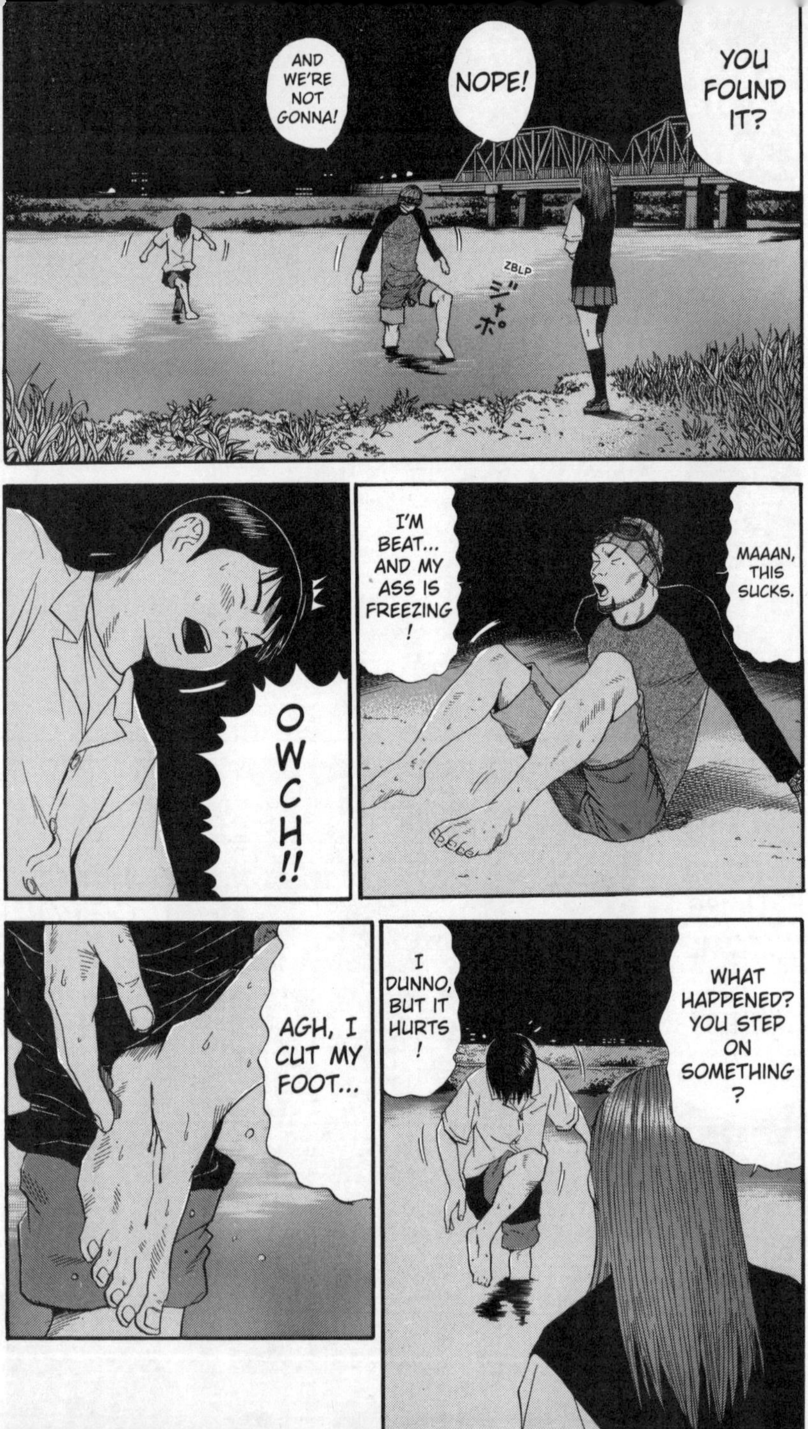
YOU FOUND IT?
NOPE!
AND WE'RE NOT GONNA!
ZBLP
ジャポ
MAAAN, THIS SUCKS.
I'M BEAT... AND MY ASS IS FREEZING!
OWCH!!
WHAT HAPPENED? YOU STEP ON SOMETHING?
I DUNNO, BUT IT HURTS!
AGH, I CUT MY FOOT...

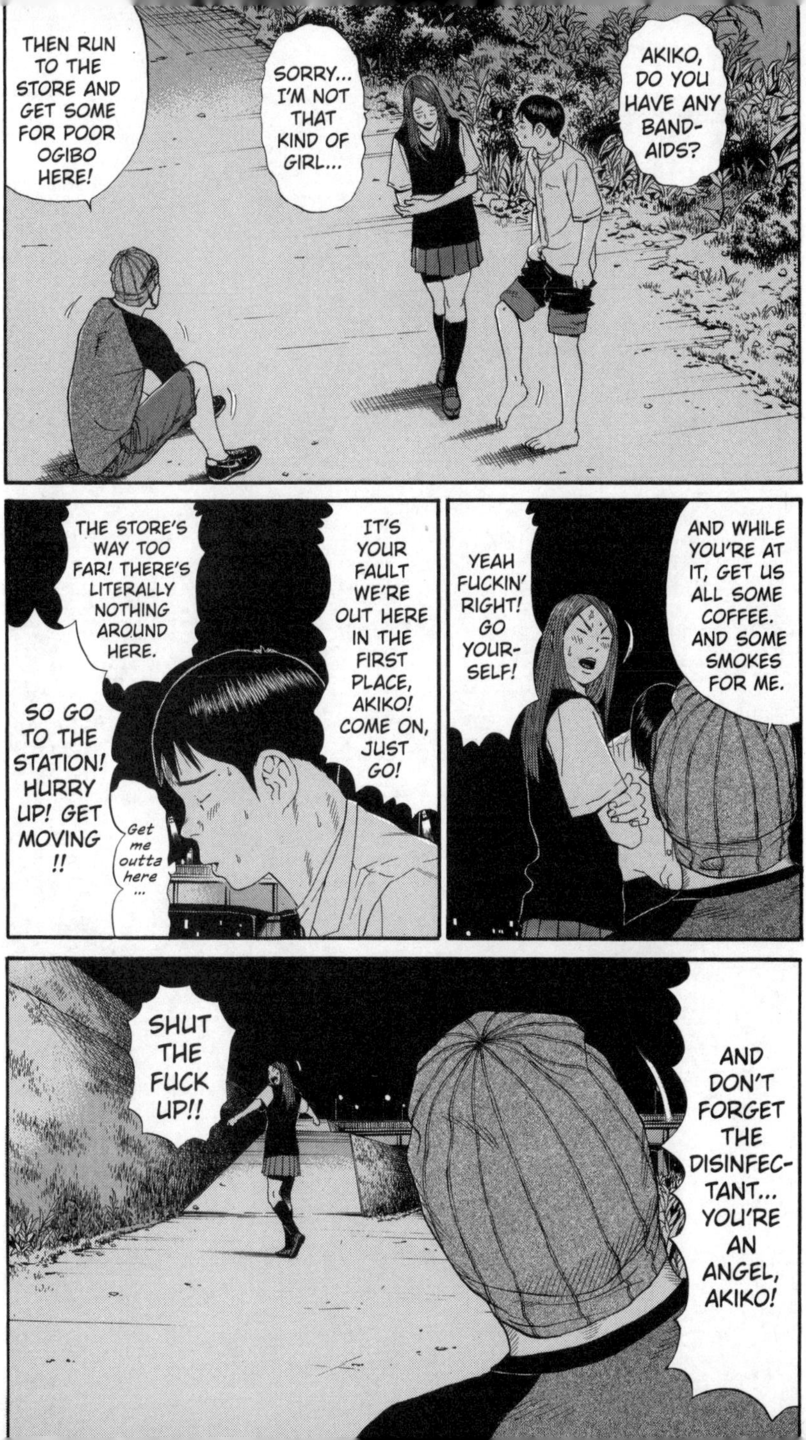
AKIKO, DO YOU HAVE ANY BAND-AIDS?
SORRY... I'M NOT THAT KIND OF GIRL...
THEN RUN TO THE STORE AND GET SOME FOR POOR OGIBO HERE!
AND WHILE YOU'RE AT IT, GET US ALL SOME COFFEE. AND SOME SMOKES FOR ME.
YEAH FUCKIN' RIGHT! GO YOURSELF!
IT'S YOUR FAULT WE'RE OUT HERE IN THE FIRST PLACE, AKIKO! COME ON, JUST GO!
THE STORE'S WAY TOO FAR! THERE'S LITERALLY NOTHING AROUND HERE.
Get me outta here ...
SO GO TO THE STATION! HURRY UP! GET MOVING !!
AND DON'T FORGET THE DISINFECTANT... YOU'RE AN ANGEL, AKIKO!
SHUT THE FUCK UP!!

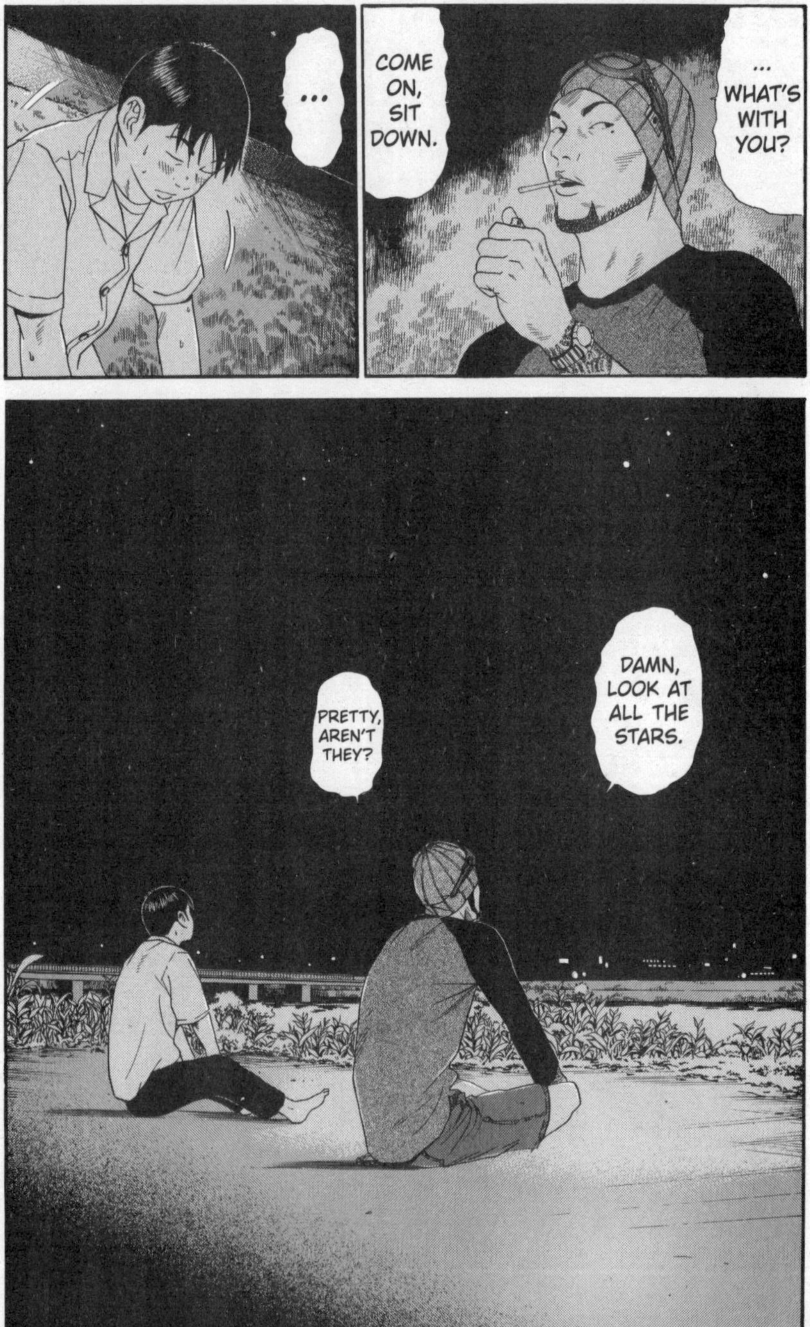
... WHAT'S WITH YOU?
COME ON, SIT DOWN.
...
DAMN, LOOK AT ALL THE STARS.
PRETTY, AREN'T THEY?

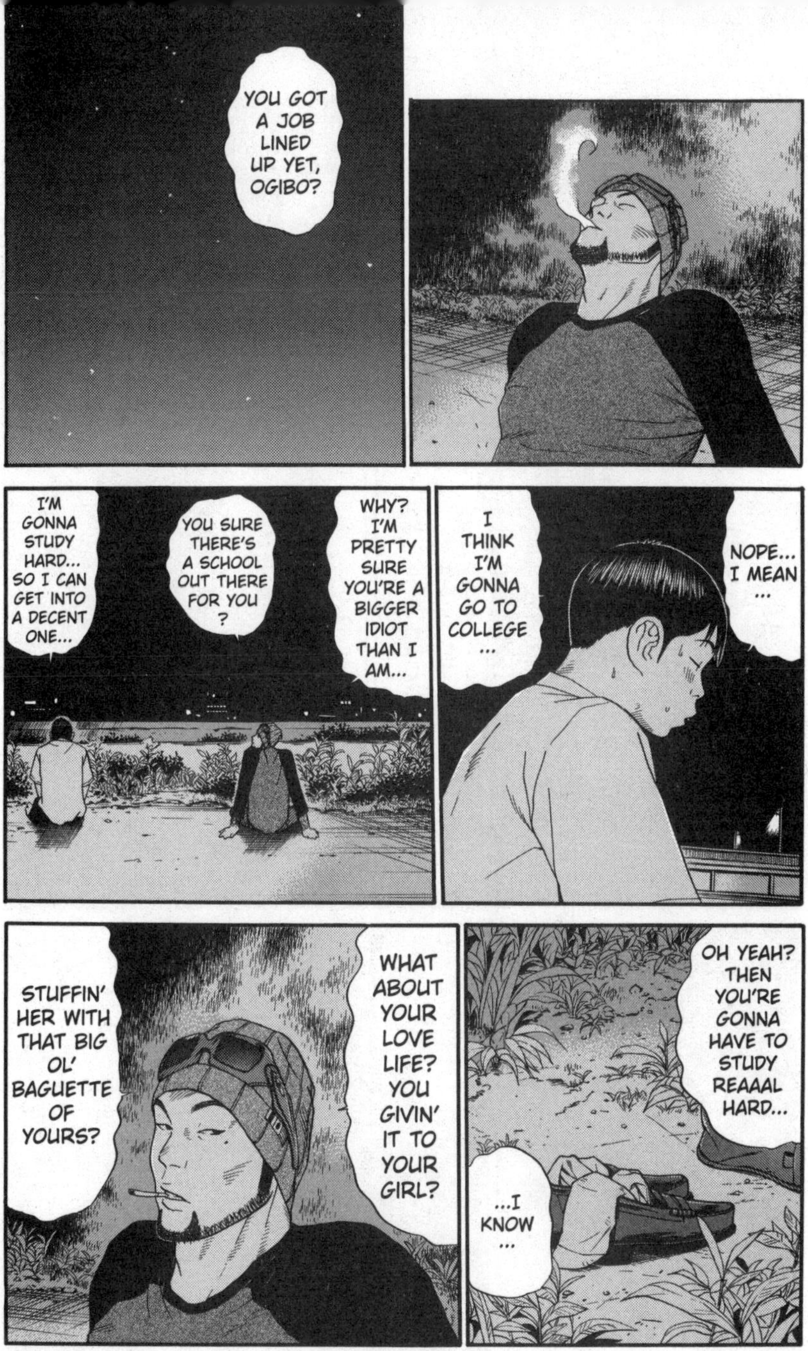
YOU GOT A JOB LINED UP YET, OGIBO?
NOPE... I MEAN ...
I THINK I'M GONNA GO TO COLLEGE ...
WHY? I'M PRETTY SURE YOU'RE A BIGGER IDIOT THAN I AM...
YOU SURE THERE'S A SCHOOL OUT THERE FOR YOU ?
I'M GONNA STUDY HARD... SO I CAN GET INTO A DECENT ONE...
OH YEAH? THEN YOU'RE GONNA HAVE TO STUDY REAAAL HARD...
...I KNOW ...
WHAT ABOUT YOUR LOVE LIFE? YOU GIVIN' IT TO YOUR GIRL?
STUFFIN' HER WITH THAT BIG OL' BAGUETTE OF YOURS?

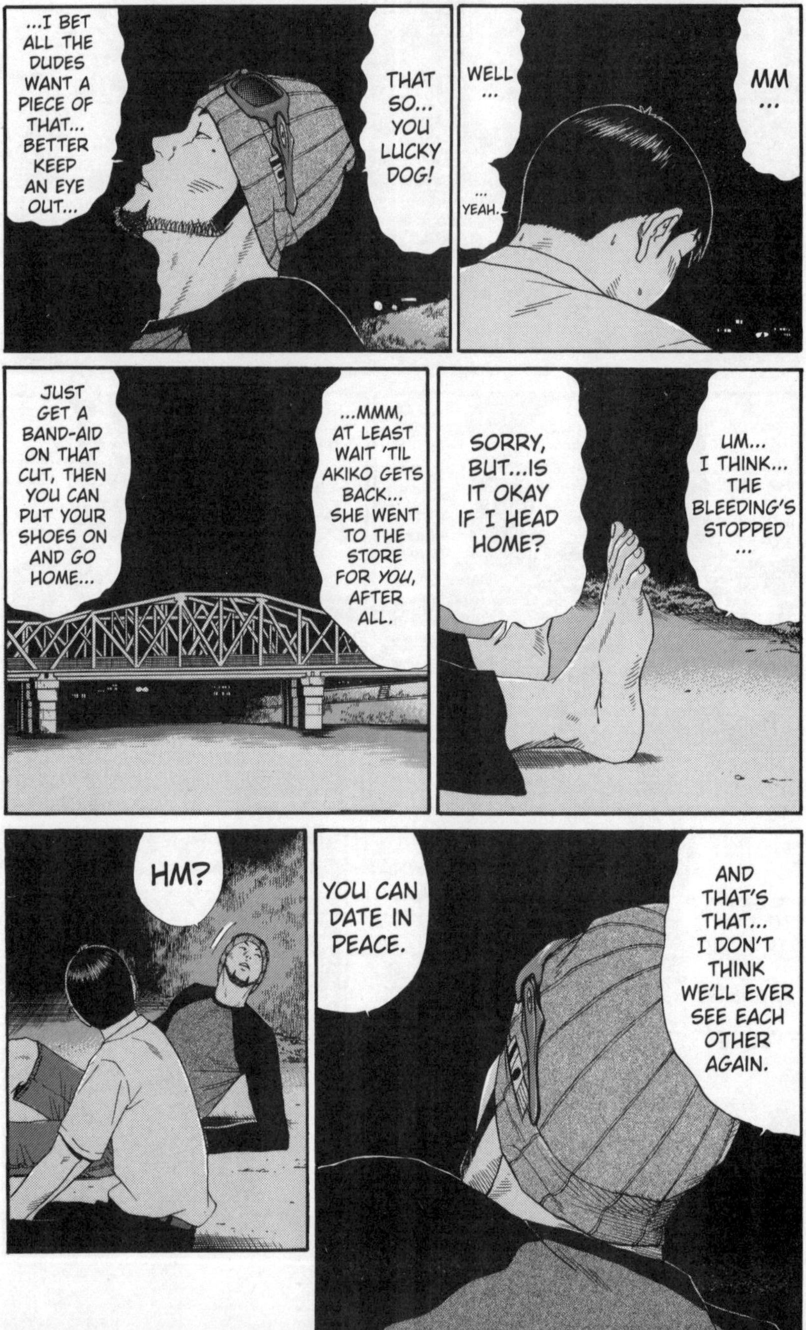
MM ...
WELL ...
... YEAH.
THAT SO... YOU LUCKY DOG!
...I BET ALL THE DUDES WANT A PIECE OF THAT... BETTER KEEP AN EYE OUT...
UM... I THINK... THE BLEEDING'S STOPPED ...
SORRY, BUT...IS IT OKAY IF I HEAD HOME?
...MMM, AT LEAST WAIT 'TIL AKIKO GETS BACK... SHE WENT TO THE STORE FOR *YOU*, AFTER ALL.
JUST GET A BAND-AID ON THAT CUT, THEN YOU CAN PUT YOUR SHOES ON AND GO HOME...
AND THAT'S THAT... I DON'T THINK WE'LL EVER SEE EACH OTHER AGAIN.
YOU CAN DATE IN PEACE.
HM?

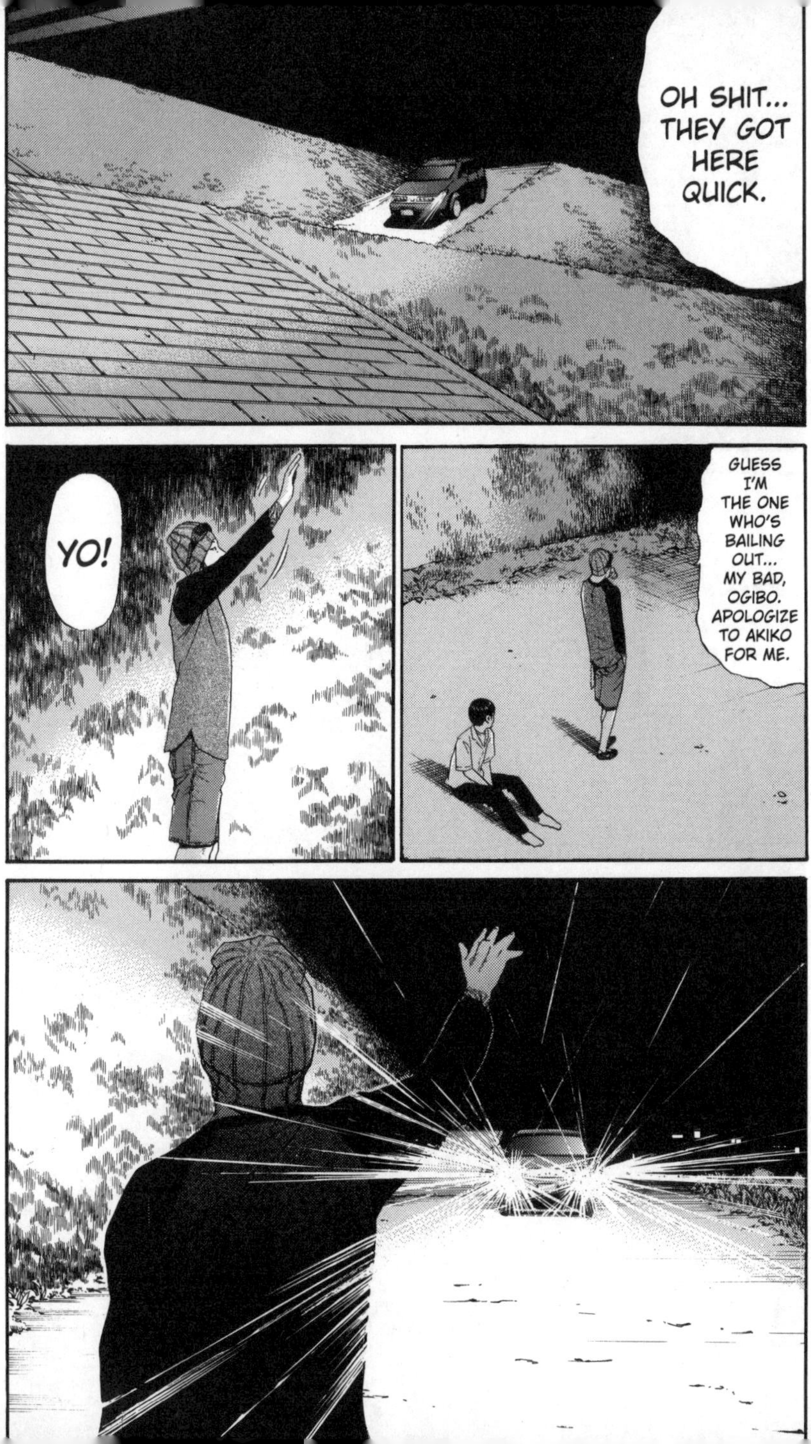
OH SHIT... THEY GOT HERE QUICK.
GUESS I'M THE ONE WHO'S BAILING OUT... MY BAD, OGIBO. APOLOGIZE TO AKIKO FOR ME.
YO!

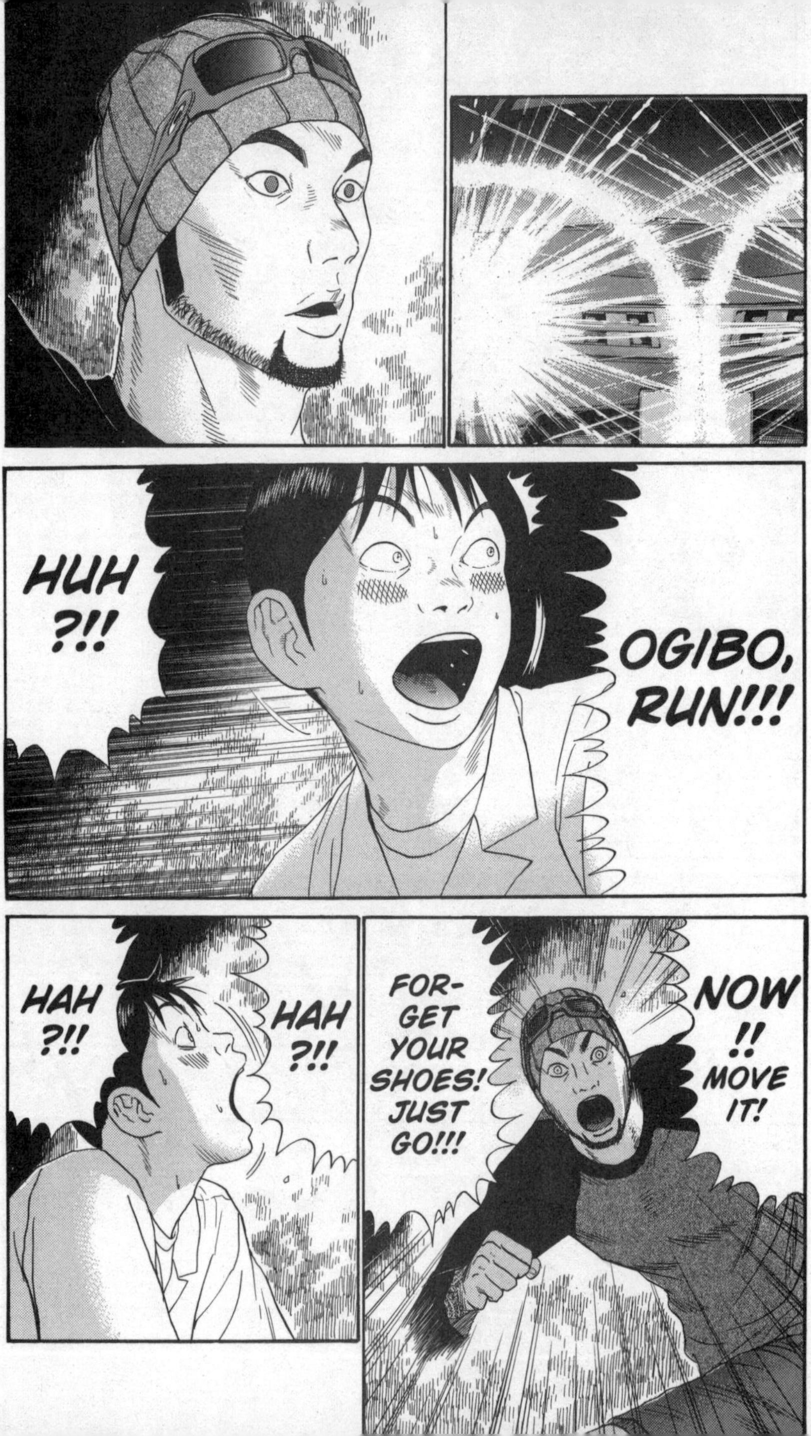
OGIBO, RUN!!!
HUH ?!!
NOW !! MOVE IT!
FOR-GET YOUR SHOES! JUST GO!!!
HAH ?!!
HAH ?!!

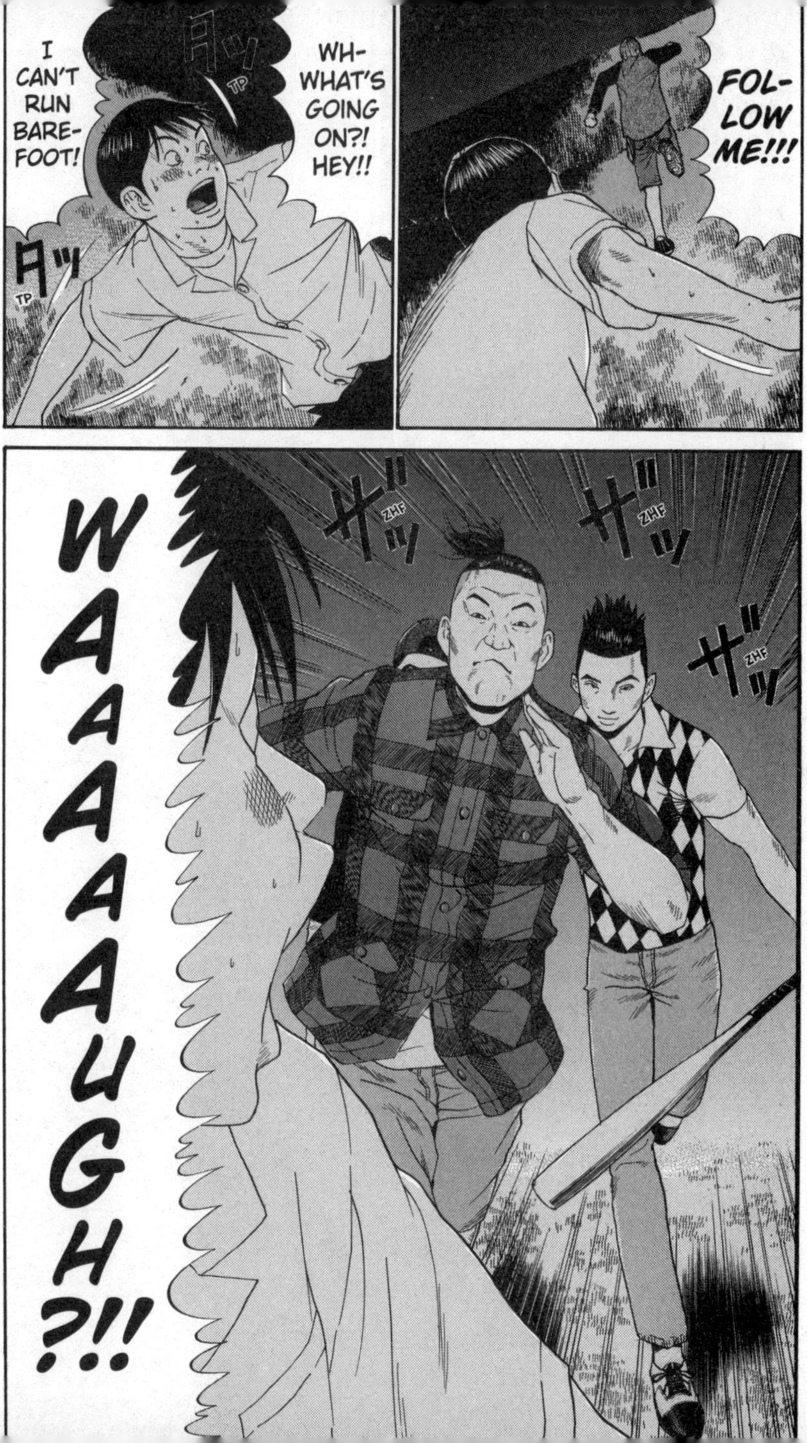
FOL-
LOW
ME!!!
WH-
WHAT'S
GOING
ON?!
HEY!!
TP
I
CAN'T
RUN
BARE-
FOOT!
TP
ZHF
ZHF
ZHF
WAAAAAAUGH?!!

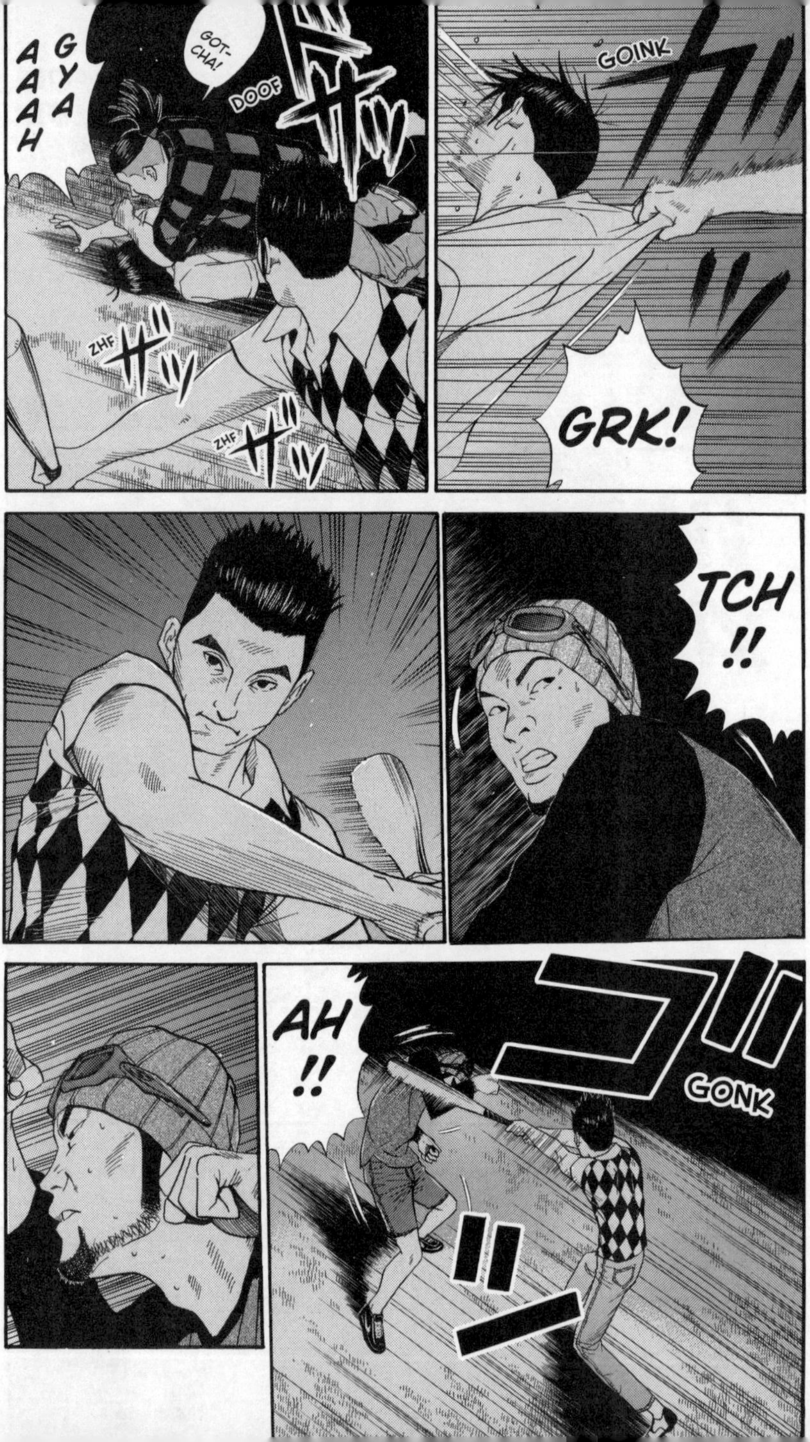
GOINK
GRK!
GOT-CHA!
DOOF
GYAAAAH
ZHF
ZHF
TCH!!
AH!!
GONK

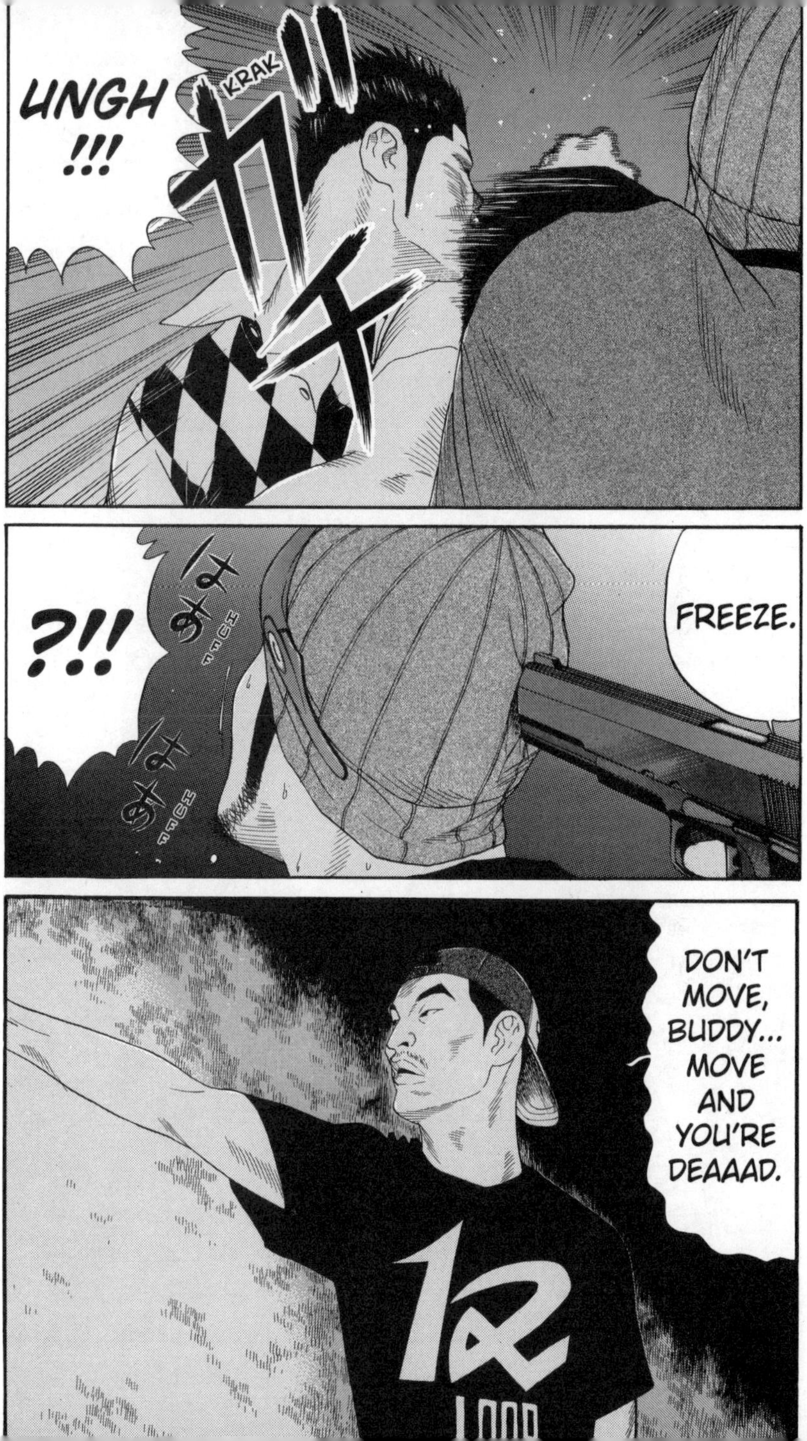
KRAK
UNGH!!!
FREEZE.
?!!
DON'T MOVE, BUDDY... MOVE AND YOU'RE DEAAAD.

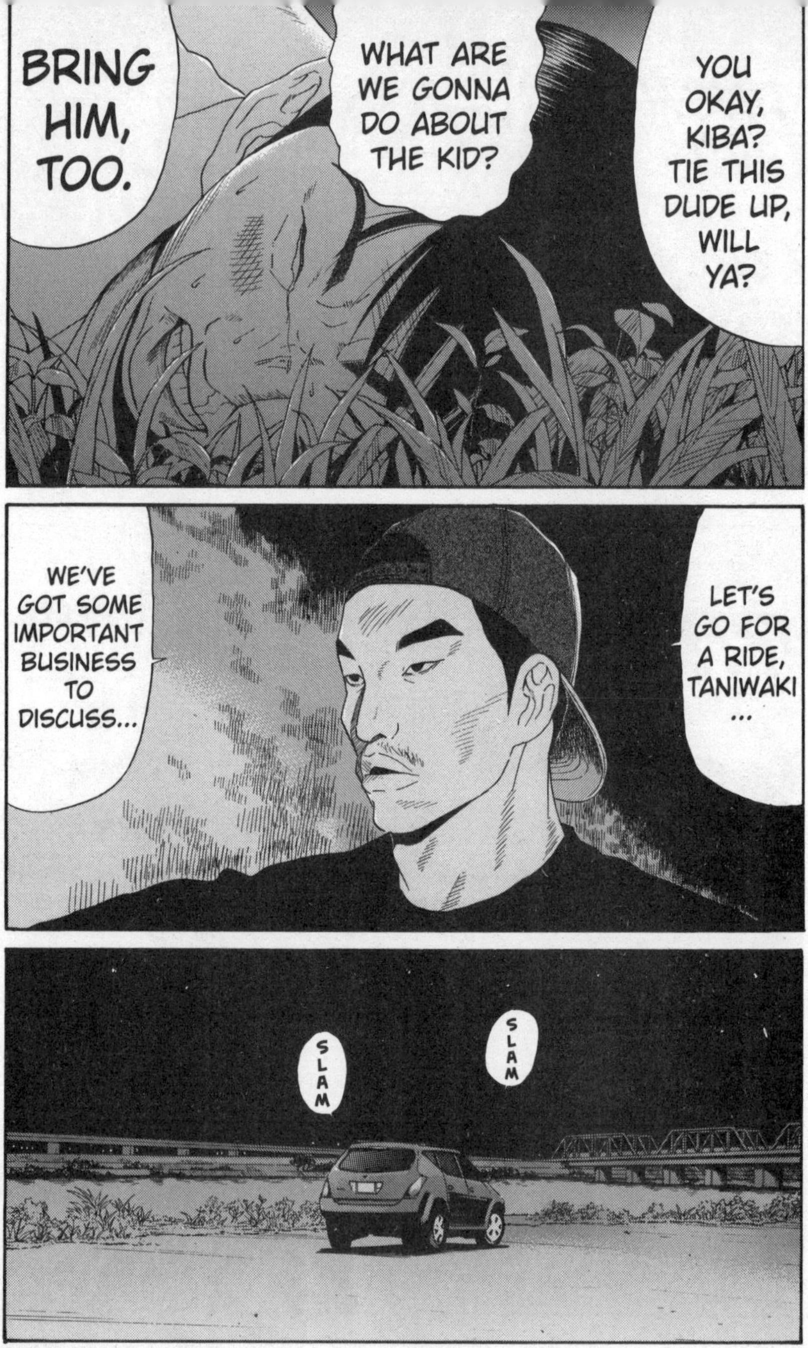
YOU OKAY, KIBA? TIE THIS DUDE UP, WILL YA?
WHAT ARE WE GONNA DO ABOUT THE KID?
BRING HIM, TOO.
LET'S GO FOR A RIDE, TANIWAKI ...
WE'VE GOT SOME IMPORTANT BUSINESS TO DISCUSS...
SLAM
SLAM

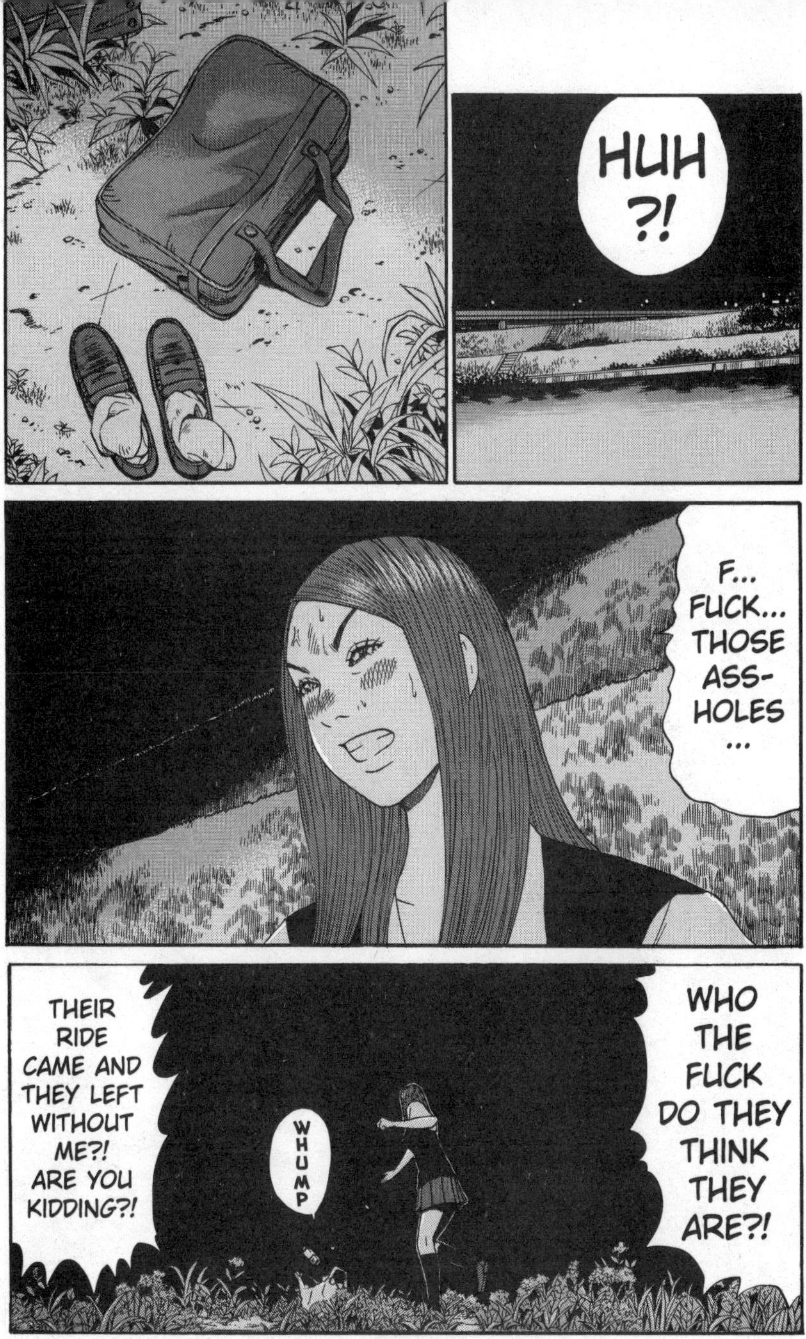
HUH ?!
F... FUCK... THOSE ASS-HOLES ...
WHO THE FUCK DO THEY THINK THEY ARE?!
WHUMP
THEIR RIDE CAME AND THEY LEFT WITHOUT ME?! ARE YOU KIDDING?!

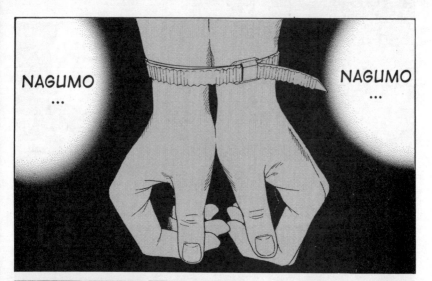

NAGUMO...

NAGUMO...

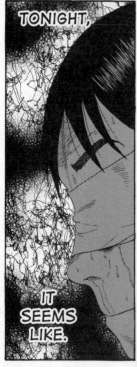

TONIGHT,

IT SEEMS LIKE.

THEY'RE GOING TO KILL ME...

I'M GOING TO DIE...

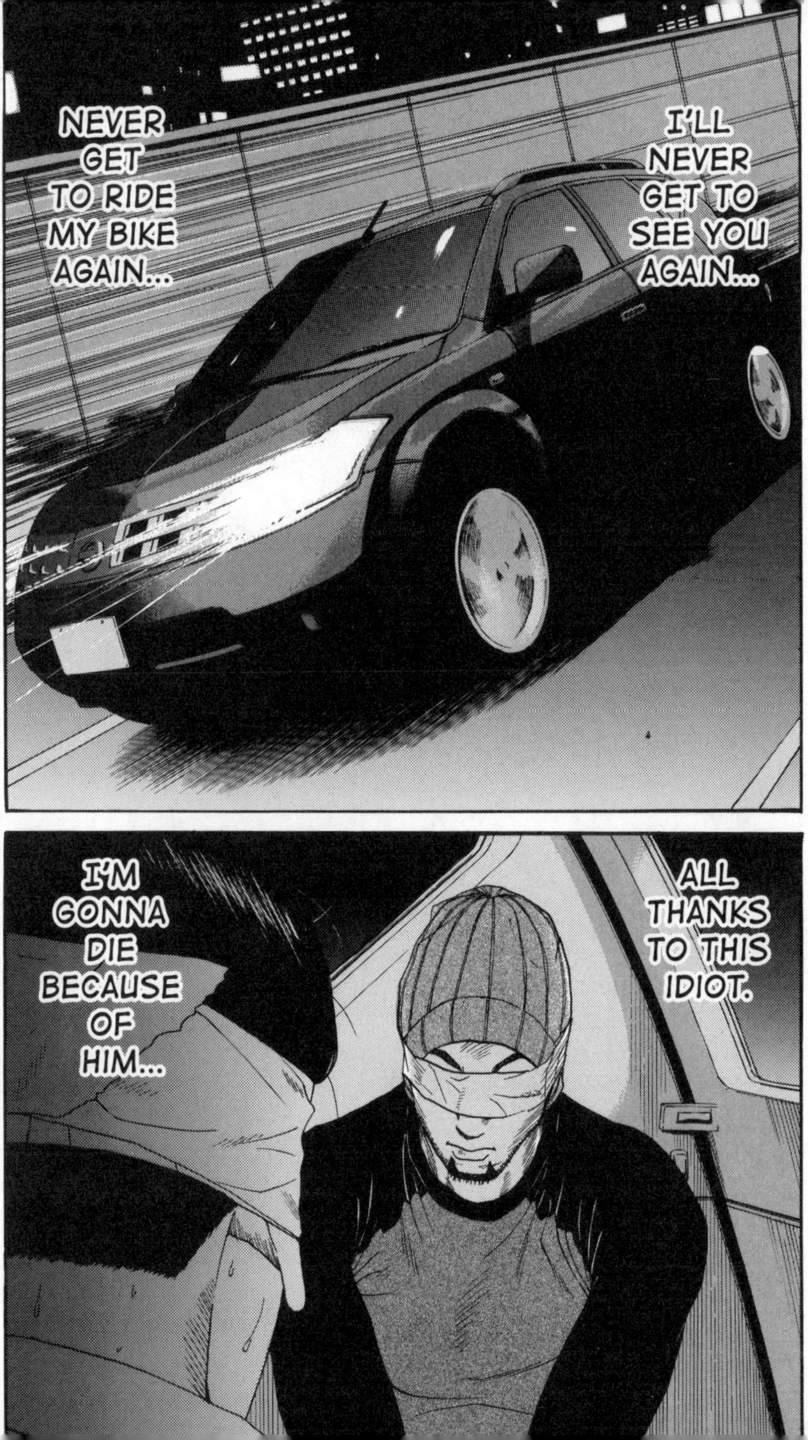
I'LL NEVER GET TO SEE YOU AGAIN...
NEVER GET TO RIDE MY BIKE AGAIN...
ALL THANKS TO THIS IDIOT.
I'M GONNA DIE BECAUSE OF HIM...

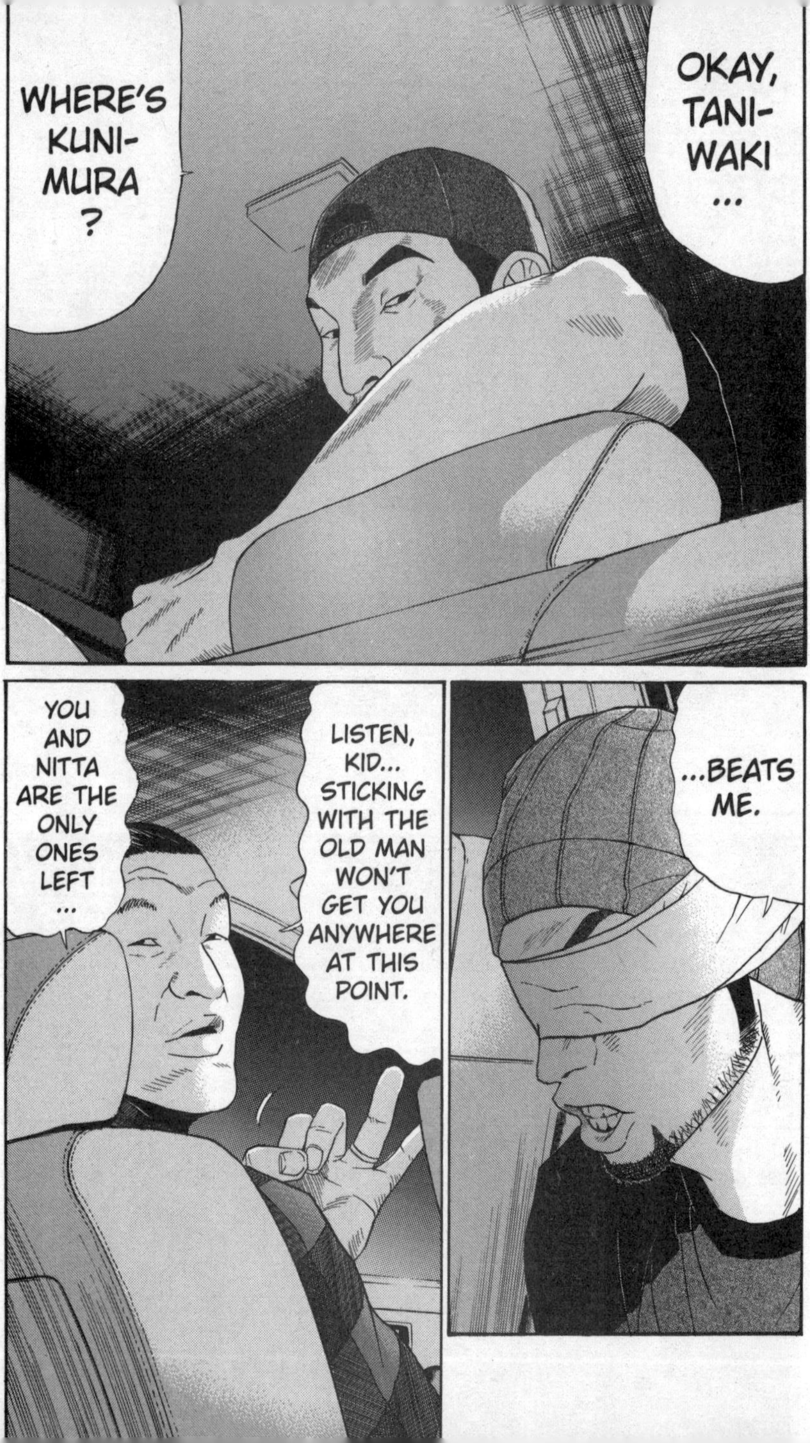
OKAY, TANI-WAKI ...
WHERE'S KUNI-MURA ?
...BEATS ME.
LISTEN, KID... STICKING WITH THE OLD MAN WON'T GET YOU ANYWHERE AT THIS POINT.
YOU AND NITTA ARE THE ONLY ONES LEFT ...

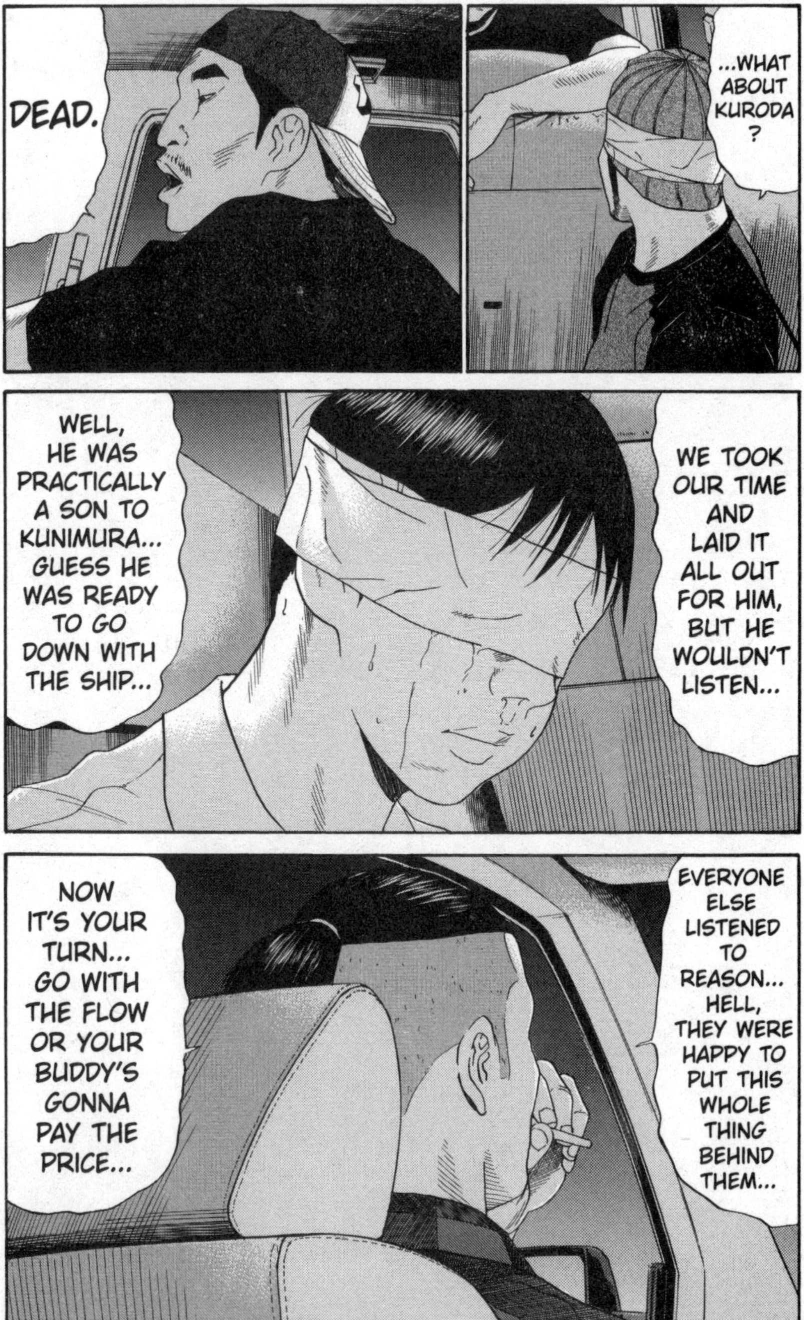
...WHAT ABOUT KURODA?
DEAD.
WE TOOK OUR TIME AND LAID IT ALL OUT FOR HIM, BUT HE WOULDN'T LISTEN...
WELL, HE WAS PRACTICALLY A SON TO KUNIMURA... GUESS HE WAS READY TO GO DOWN WITH THE SHIP...
EVERYONE ELSE LISTENED TO REASON... HELL, THEY WERE HAPPY TO PUT THIS WHOLE THING BEHIND THEM...
NOW IT'S YOUR TURN... GO WITH THE FLOW OR YOUR BUDDY'S GONNA PAY THE PRICE...

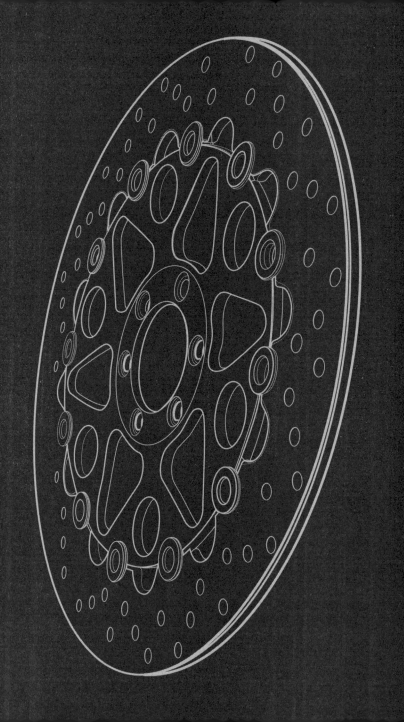

# Chapter 59: Reason

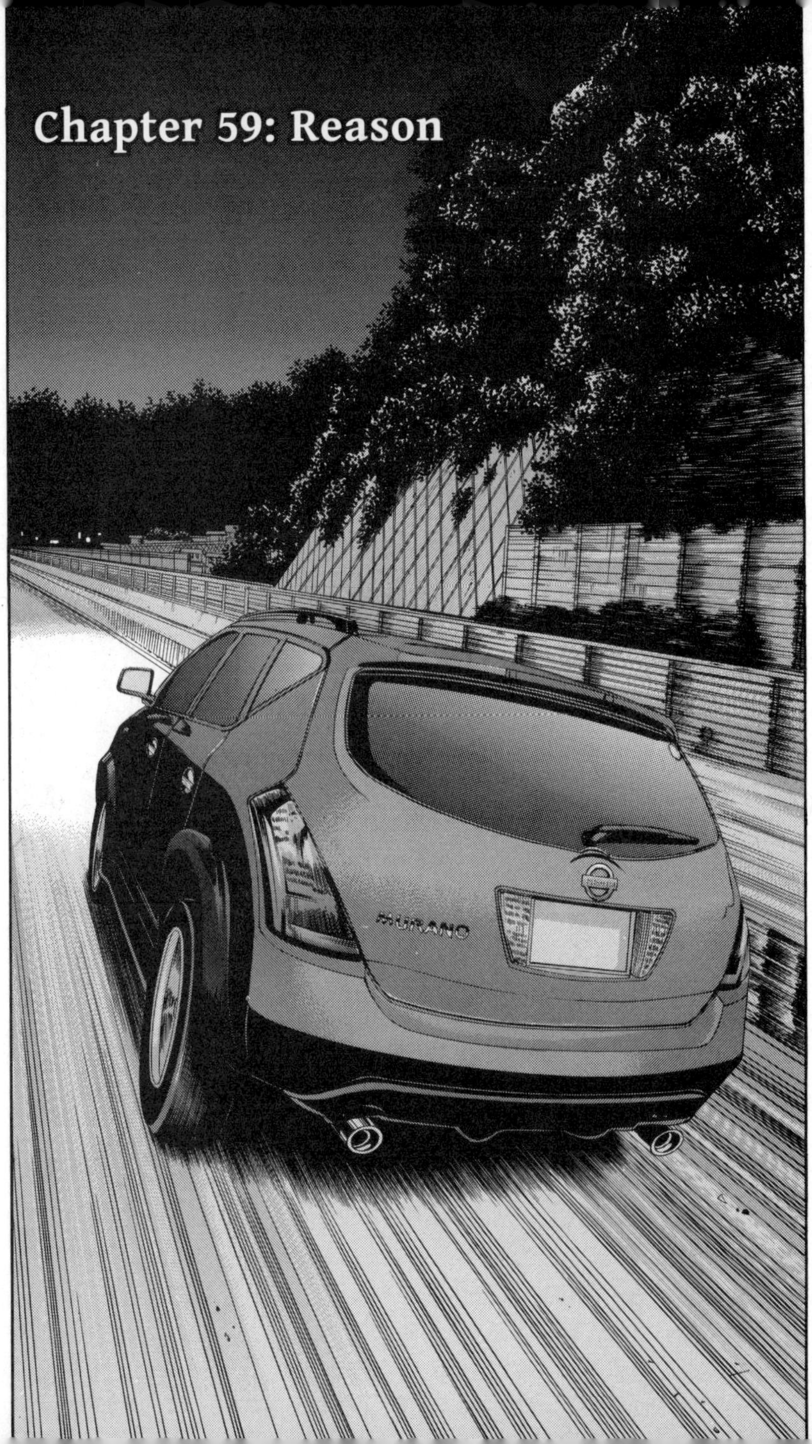
MURANO

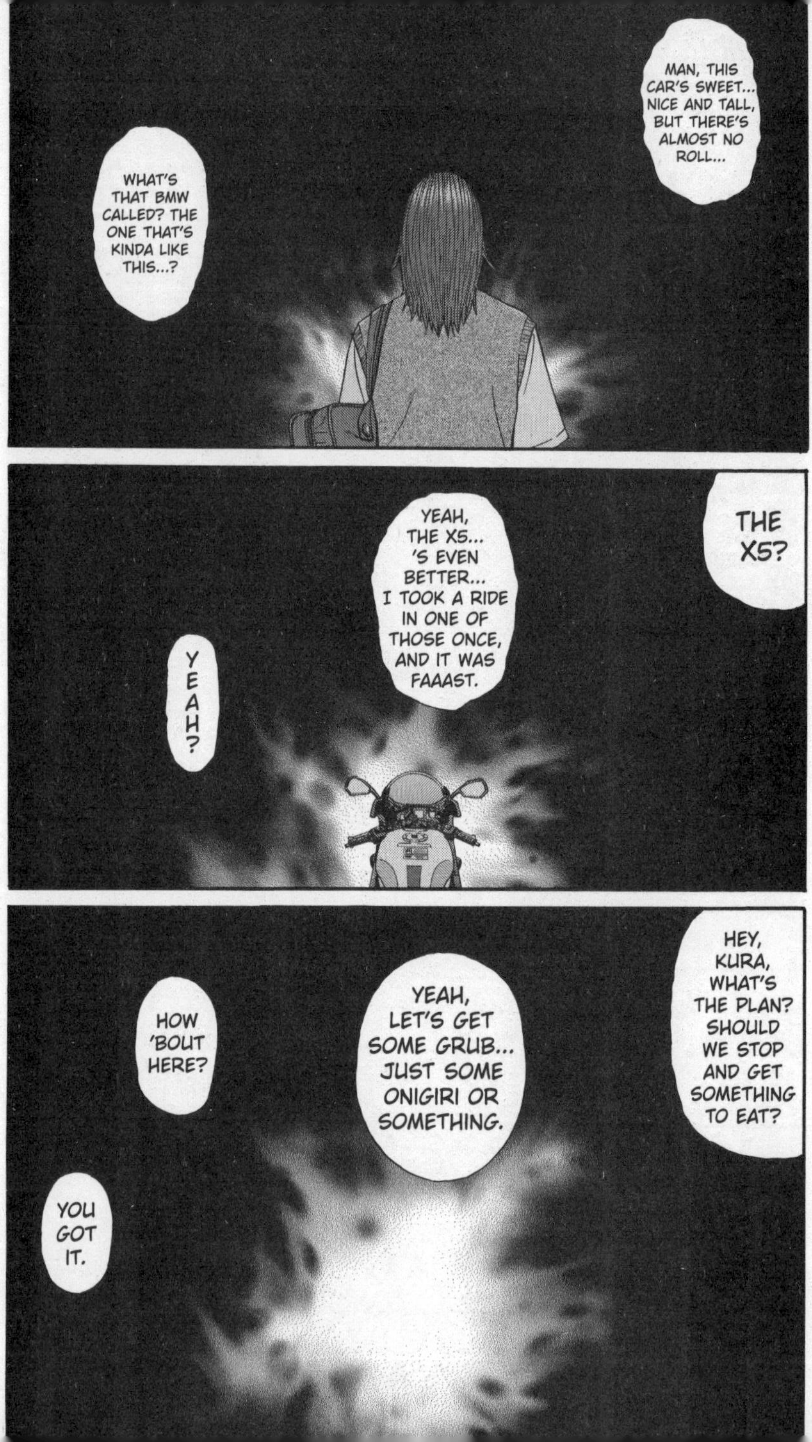
MAN, THIS CAR'S SWEET... NICE AND TALL, BUT THERE'S ALMOST NO ROLL...
WHAT'S THAT BMW CALLED? THE ONE THAT'S KINDA LIKE THIS...?
THE X5?
YEAH, THE X5... 'S EVEN BETTER... I TOOK A RIDE IN ONE OF THOSE ONCE, AND IT WAS FAAAST.
YEAH?
HEY, KURA, WHAT'S THE PLAN? SHOULD WE STOP AND GET SOMETHING TO EAT?
YEAH, LET'S GET SOME GRUB... JUST SOME ONIGIRI OR SOMETHING.
HOW 'BOUT HERE?
YOU GOT IT.

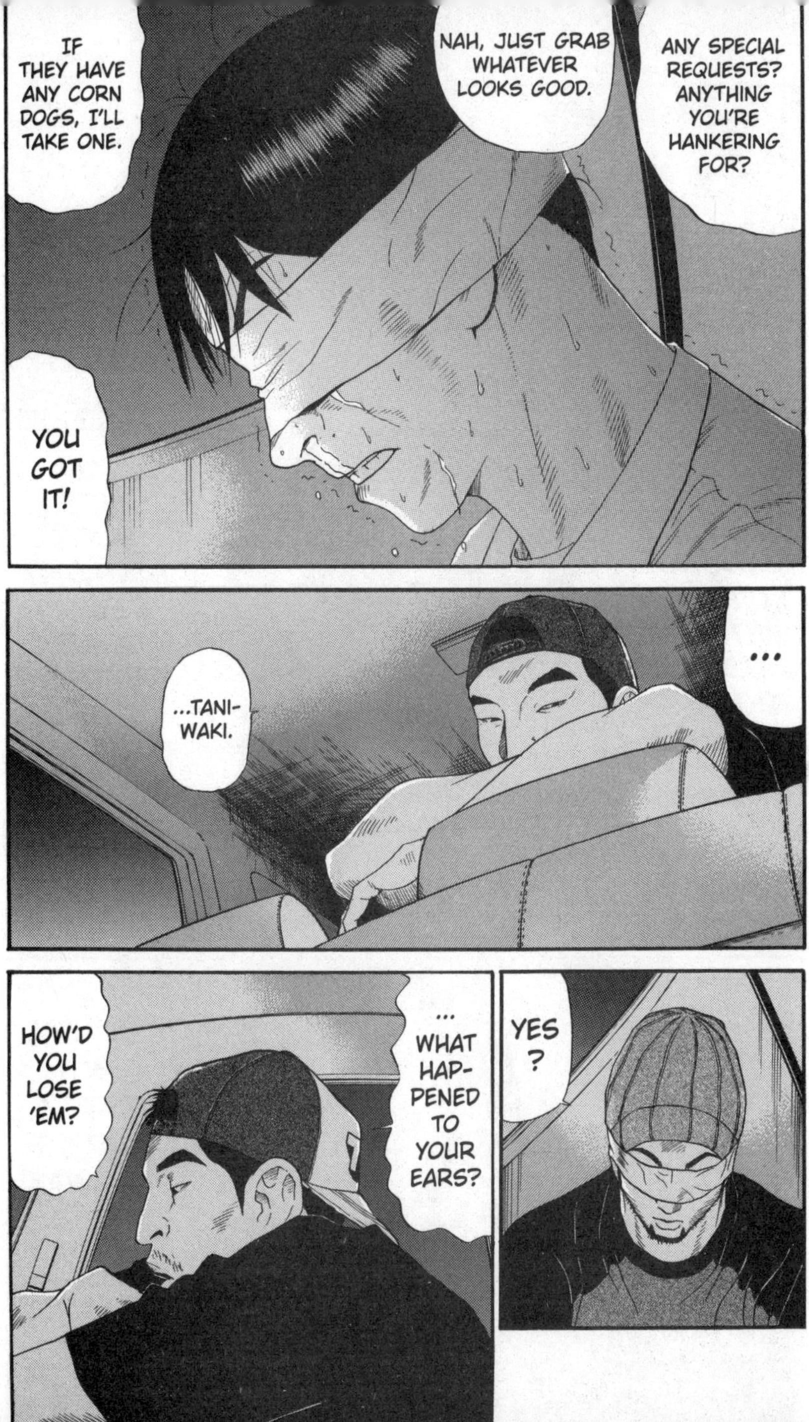
ANY SPECIAL REQUESTS? ANYTHING YOU'RE HANKERING FOR?
NAH, JUST GRAB WHATEVER LOOKS GOOD.
IF THEY HAVE ANY CORN DOGS, I'LL TAKE ONE.
YOU GOT IT!
...
...TANI-WAKI.
YES?
... WHAT HAP-PENED TO YOUR EARS?
HOW'D YOU LOSE 'EM?

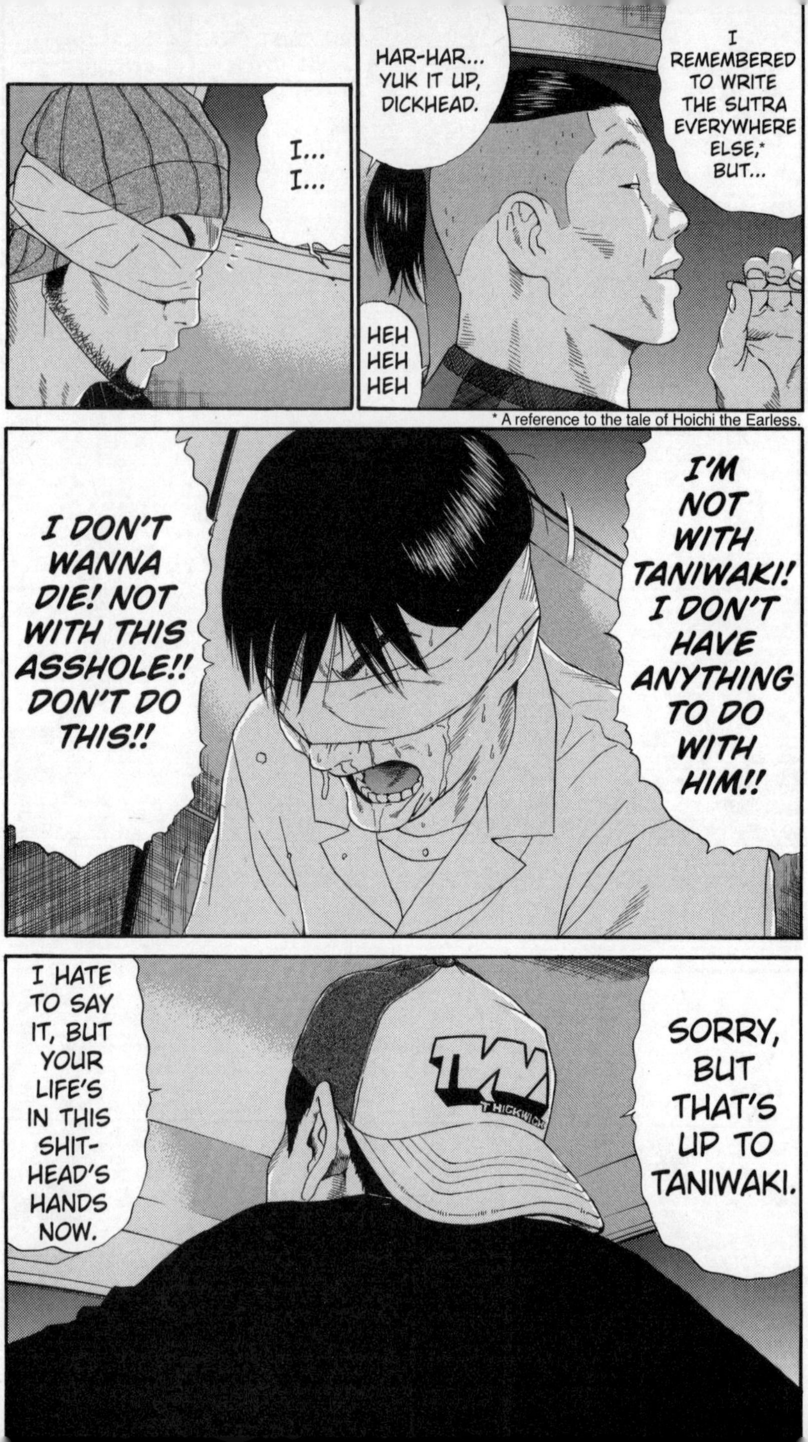
I REMEMBERED TO WRITE THE SUTRA EVERYWHERE ELSE,* BUT...
HAR-HAR... YUK IT UP, DICKHEAD.
HEH HEH HEH
I... I...
I'M NOT WITH TANIWAKI! I DON'T HAVE ANYTHING TO DO WITH HIM!!
I DON'T WANNA DIE! NOT WITH THIS ASSHOLE!! DON'T DO THIS!!
SORRY, BUT THAT'S UP TO TANIWAKI.
I HATE TO SAY IT, BUT YOUR LIFE'S IN THIS SHIT-HEAD'S HANDS NOW.

* A reference to the tale of Hoichi the Earless.

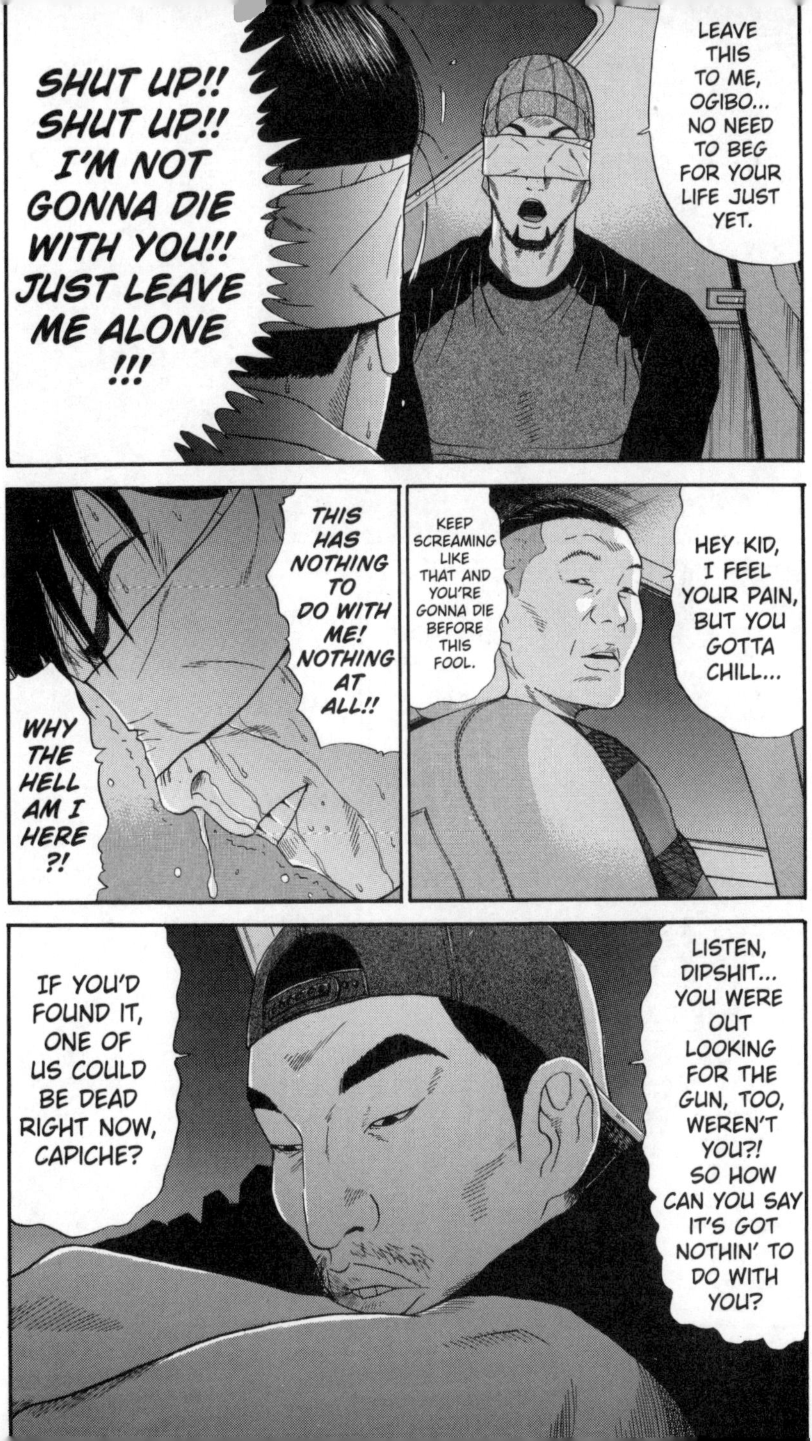
LEAVE THIS TO ME, OGIBO... NO NEED TO BEG FOR YOUR LIFE JUST YET.
SHUT UP!! SHUT UP!! I'M NOT GONNA DIE WITH YOU!! JUST LEAVE ME ALONE !!!
HEY KID, I FEEL YOUR PAIN, BUT YOU GOTTA CHILL...
KEEP SCREAMING LIKE THAT AND YOU'RE GONNA DIE BEFORE THIS FOOL.
THIS HAS NOTHING TO DO WITH ME! NOTHING AT ALL!!
WHY THE HELL AM I HERE ?!
LISTEN, DIPSHIT... YOU WERE OUT LOOKING FOR THE GUN, TOO, WEREN'T YOU?! SO HOW CAN YOU SAY IT'S GOT NOTHIN' TO DO WITH YOU?
IF YOU'D FOUND IT, ONE OF US COULD BE DEAD RIGHT NOW, CAPICHE?

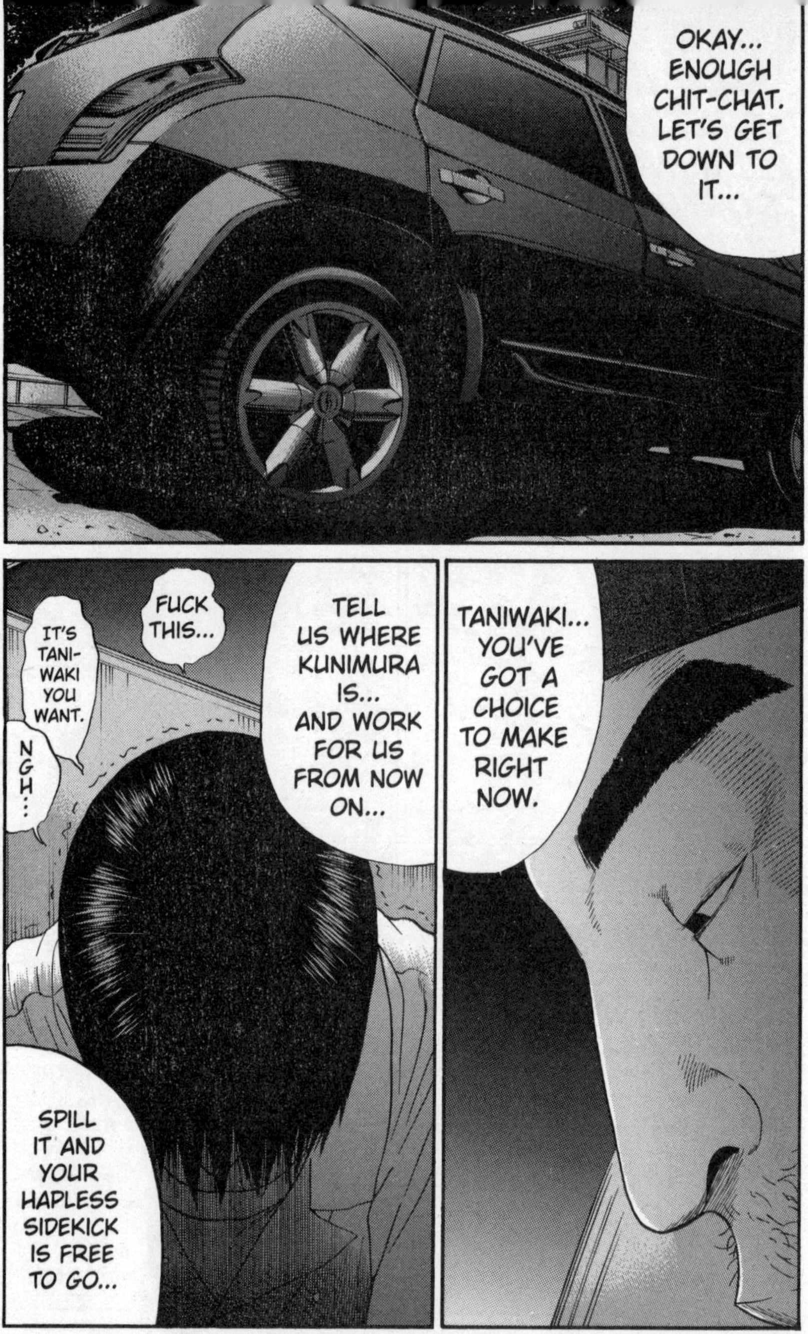
OKAY... ENOUGH CHIT-CHAT. LET'S GET DOWN TO IT...
TANIWAKI... YOU'VE GOT A CHOICE TO MAKE RIGHT NOW.
TELL US WHERE KUNIMURA IS... AND WORK FOR US FROM NOW ON...
FUCK THIS...
IT'S TANI-WAKI YOU WANT.
NGH...
SPILL IT AND YOUR HAPLESS SIDEKICK IS FREE TO GO...

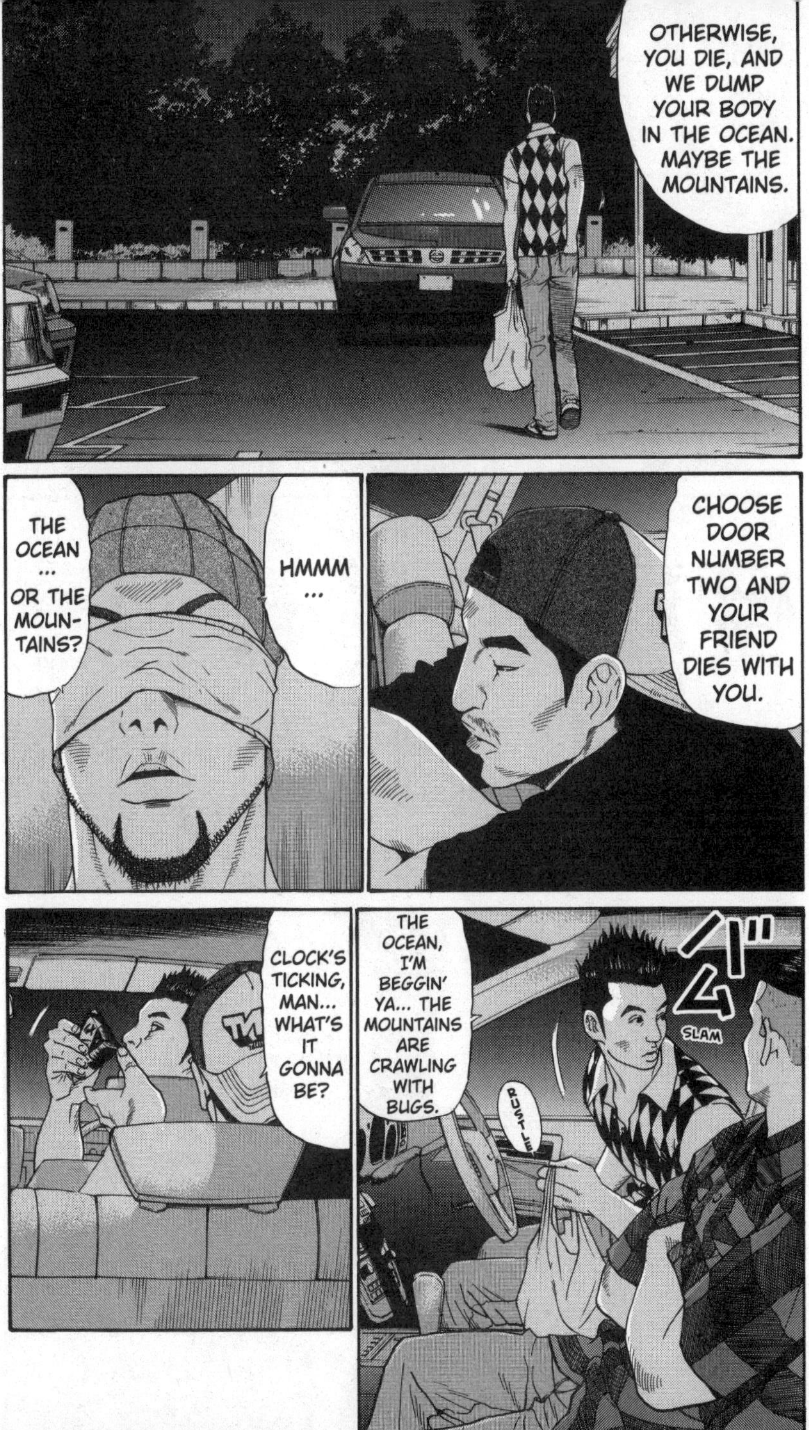
OTHERWISE, YOU DIE, AND WE DUMP YOUR BODY IN THE OCEAN. MAYBE THE MOUNTAINS.
CHOOSE DOOR NUMBER TWO AND YOUR FRIEND DIES WITH YOU.
HMMM ...
THE OCEAN ... OR THE MOUN-TAINS?
SLAM
THE OCEAN, I'M BEGGIN' YA... THE MOUNTAINS ARE CRAWLING WITH BUGS.
RUSTLE
CLOCK'S TICKING, MAN... WHAT'S IT GONNA BE?

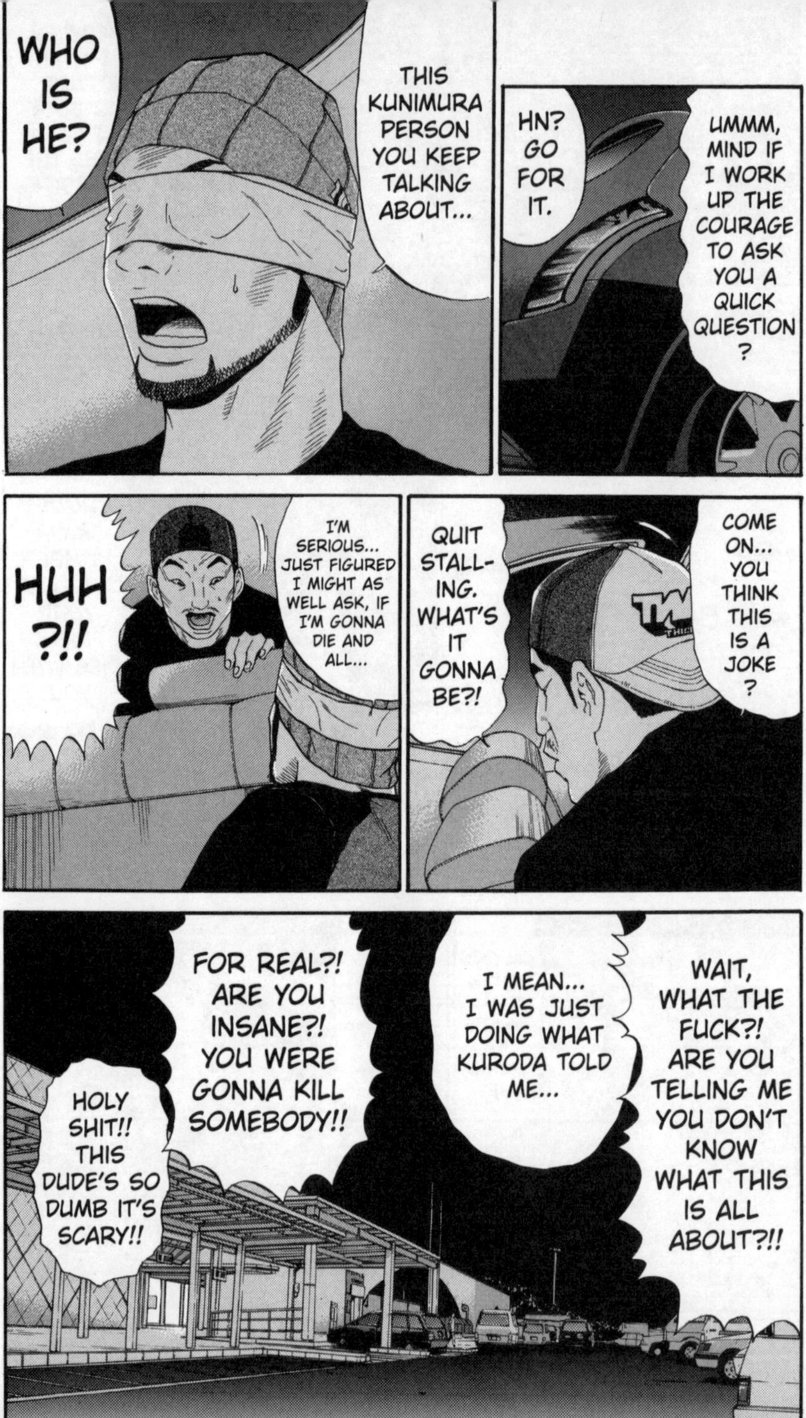
UMMM, MIND IF I WORK UP THE COURAGE TO ASK YOU A QUICK QUESTION?
HN? GO FOR IT.
THIS KUNIMURA PERSON YOU KEEP TALKING ABOUT...
WHO IS HE?
COME ON... YOU THINK THIS IS A JOKE?
QUIT STALL-ING. WHAT'S IT GONNA BE?!
I'M SERIOUS... JUST FIGURED I MIGHT AS WELL ASK, IF I'M GONNA DIE AND ALL...
HUH?!!
WAIT, WHAT THE FUCK?! ARE YOU TELLING ME YOU DON'T KNOW WHAT THIS IS ALL ABOUT?!!
I MEAN... I WAS JUST DOING WHAT KURODA TOLD ME...
FOR REAL?! ARE YOU INSANE?! YOU WERE GONNA KILL SOMEBODY!!
HOLY SHIT!! THIS DUDE'S SO DUMB IT'S SCARY!!

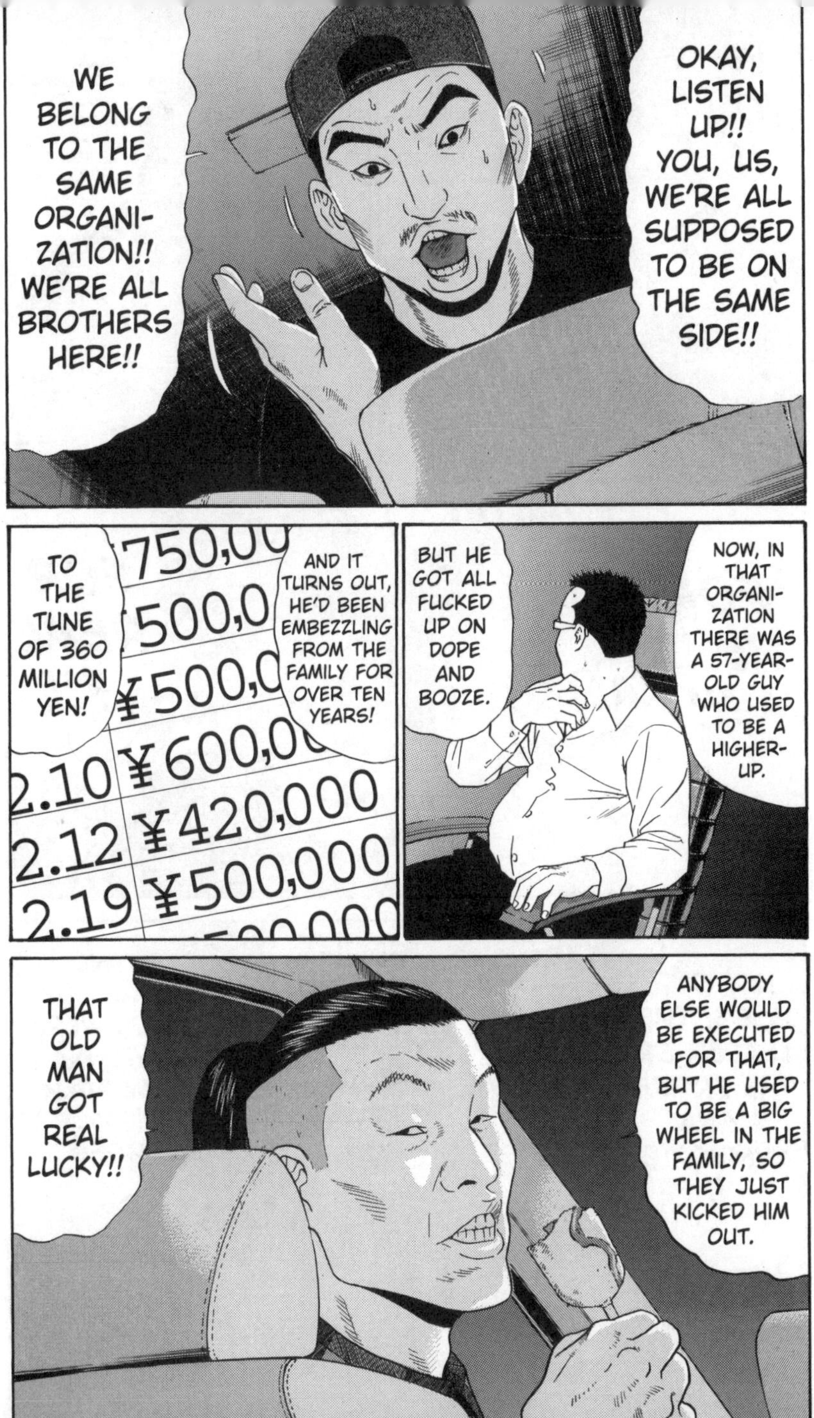
OKAY, LISTEN UP!! YOU, US, WE'RE ALL SUPPOSED TO BE ON THE SAME SIDE!!
WE BELONG TO THE SAME ORGANIZATION!! WE'RE ALL BROTHERS HERE!!
NOW, IN THAT ORGANIZATION THERE WAS A 57-YEAR-OLD GUY WHO USED TO BE A HIGHER-UP.
BUT HE GOT ALL FUCKED UP ON DOPE AND BOOZE.
AND IT TURNS OUT, HE'D BEEN EMBEZZLING FROM THE FAMILY FOR OVER TEN YEARS!
TO THE TUNE OF 360 MILLION YEN!
2.10 ¥600,00
2.12 ¥420,000
2.19 ¥500,000
ANYBODY ELSE WOULD BE EXECUTED FOR THAT, BUT HE USED TO BE A BIG WHEEL IN THE FAMILY, SO THEY JUST KICKED HIM OUT.
THAT OLD MAN GOT REAL LUCKY!!

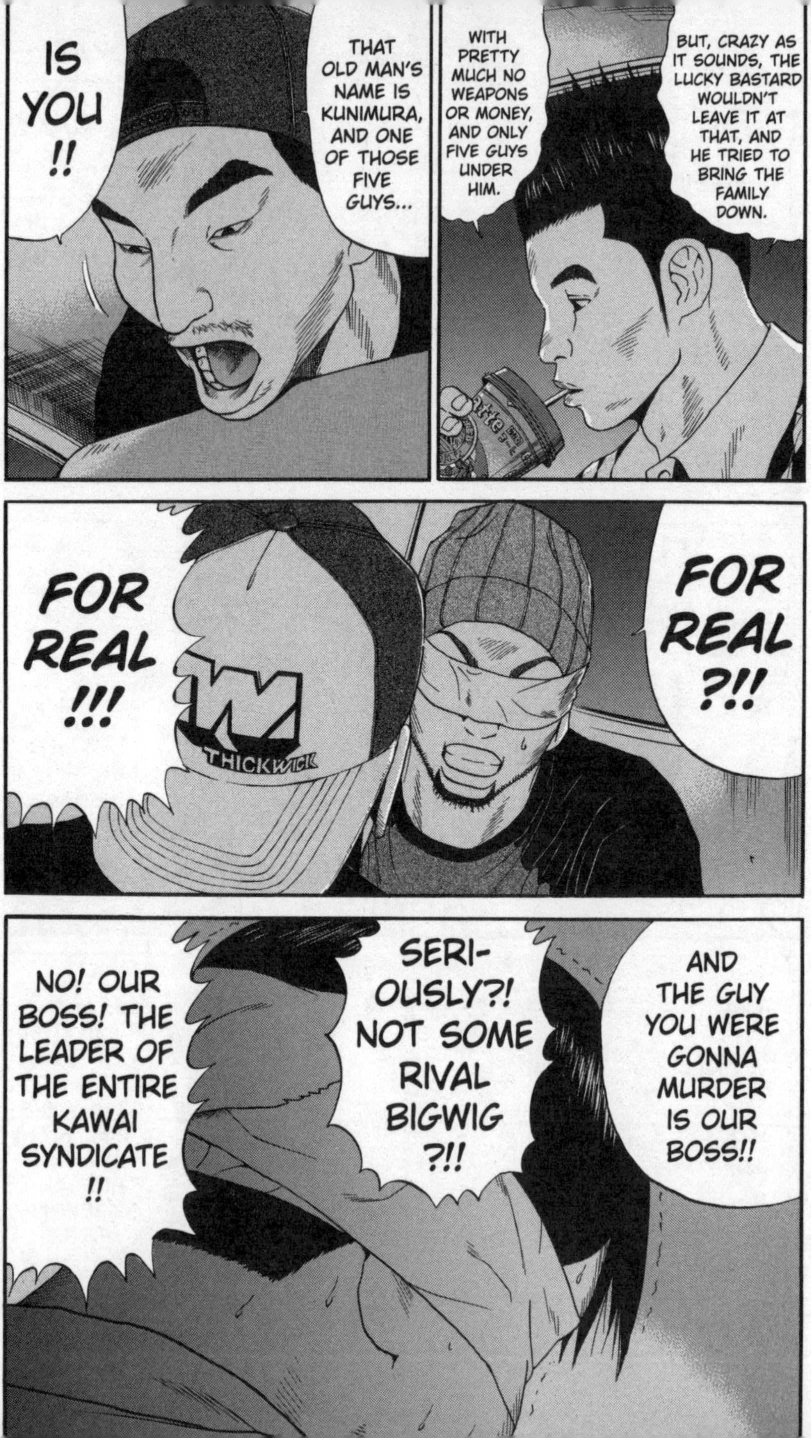
BUT, CRAZY AS IT SOUNDS, THE LUCKY BASTARD WOULDN'T LEAVE IT AT THAT, AND HE TRIED TO BRING THE FAMILY DOWN.
WITH PRETTY MUCH NO WEAPONS OR MONEY, AND ONLY FIVE GUYS UNDER HIM.
THAT OLD MAN'S NAME IS KUNIMURA, AND ONE OF THOSE FIVE GUYS...
IS YOU !!
FOR REAL ?!!
FOR REAL !!!
THICKWICK
AND THE GUY YOU WERE GONNA MURDER IS OUR BOSS!!
SERI-OUSLY?! NOT SOME RIVAL BIGWIG ?!!
NO! OUR BOSS! THE LEADER OF THE ENTIRE KAWAI SYNDICATE !!

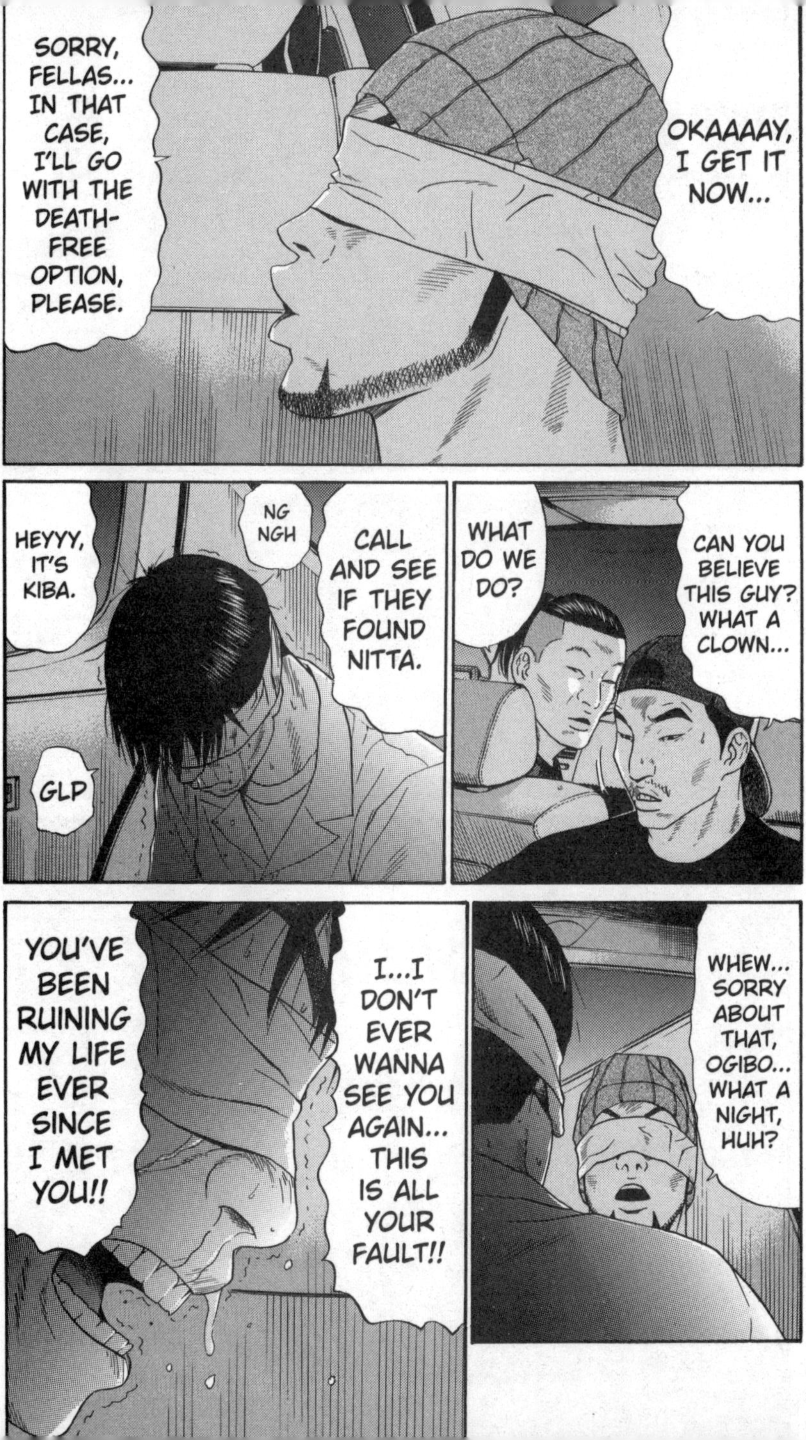
OKAAAAY, I GET IT NOW...
SORRY, FELLAS... IN THAT CASE, I'LL GO WITH THE DEATH-FREE OPTION, PLEASE.
CAN YOU BELIEVE THIS GUY? WHAT A CLOWN...
WHAT DO WE DO?
CALL AND SEE IF THEY FOUND NITTA.
NG NGH
HEYYY, IT'S KIBA.
GLP
WHEW... SORRY ABOUT THAT, OGIBO... WHAT A NIGHT, HUH?
I...I DON'T EVER WANNA SEE YOU AGAIN... THIS IS ALL YOUR FAULT!!
YOU'VE BEEN RUINING MY LIFE EVER SINCE I MET YOU!!

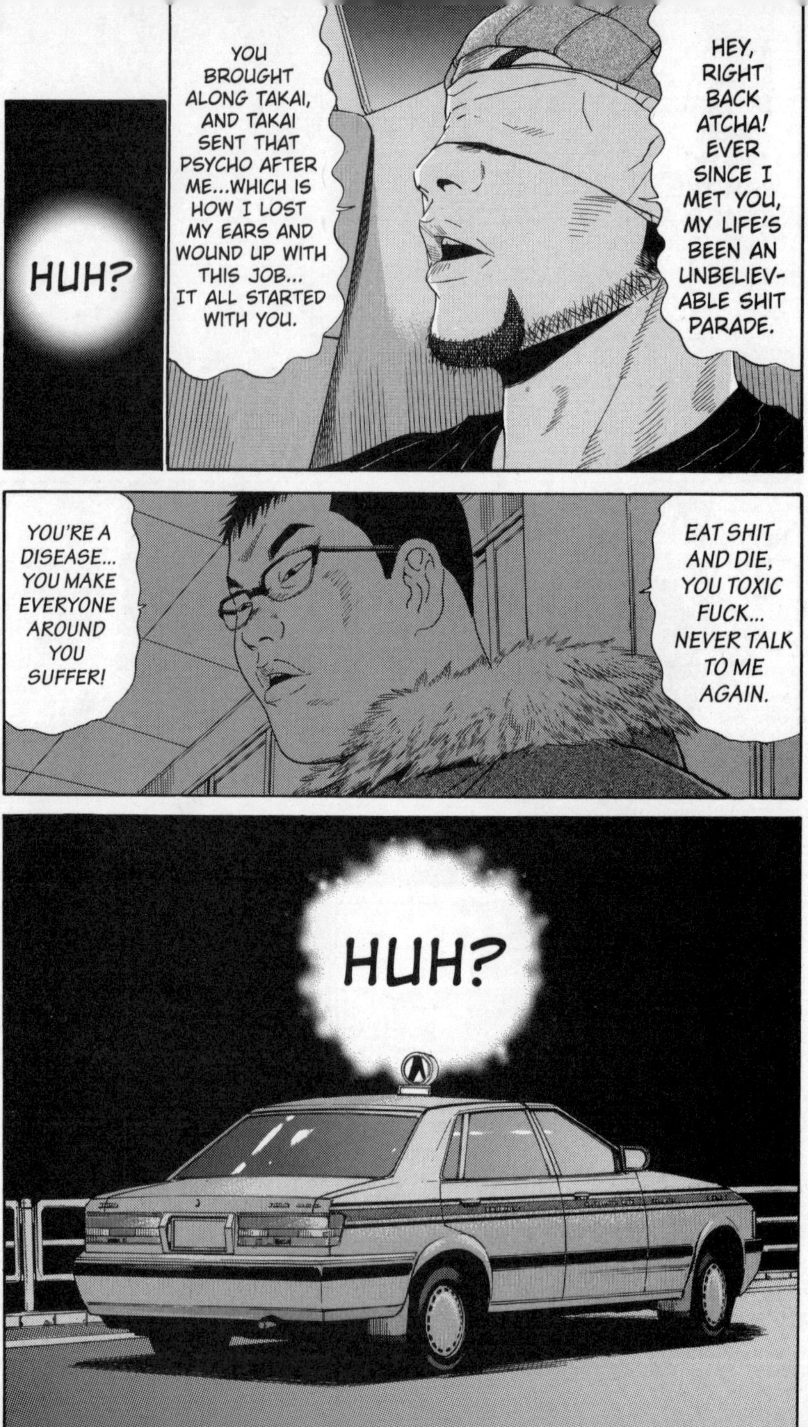
HEY, RIGHT BACK ATCHA! EVER SINCE I MET YOU, MY LIFE'S BEEN AN UNBELIEV-ABLE SHIT PARADE.
YOU BROUGHT ALONG TAKAI, AND TAKAI SENT THAT PSYCHO AFTER ME...WHICH IS HOW I LOST MY EARS AND WOUND UP WITH THIS JOB... IT ALL STARTED WITH YOU.
HUH?
EAT SHIT AND DIE, YOU TOXIC FUCK... NEVER TALK TO ME AGAIN.
YOU'RE A DISEASE... YOU MAKE EVERYONE AROUND YOU SUFFER!
HUH?

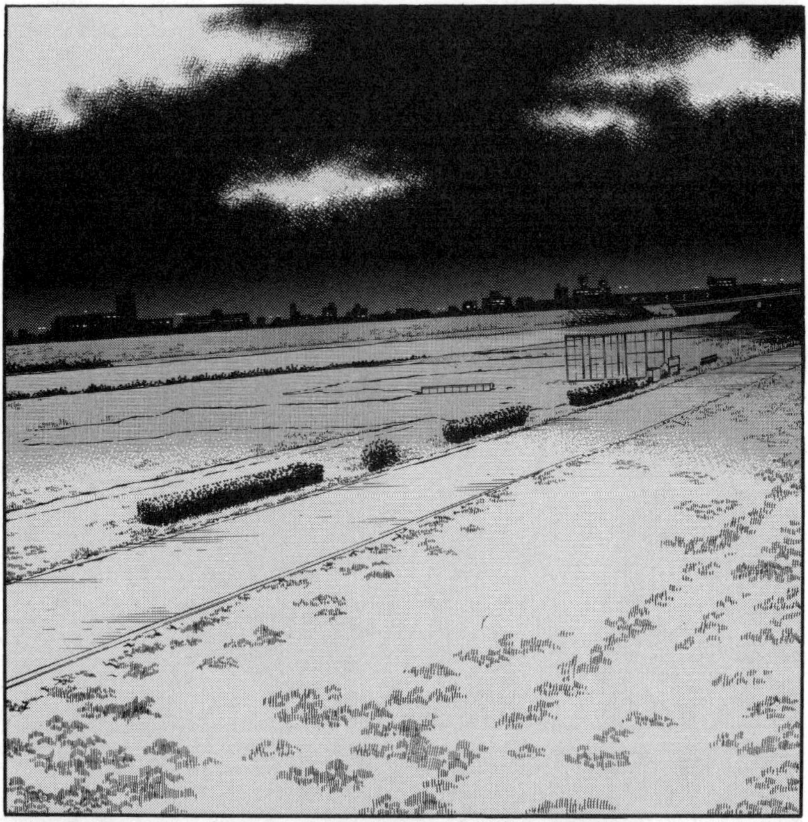

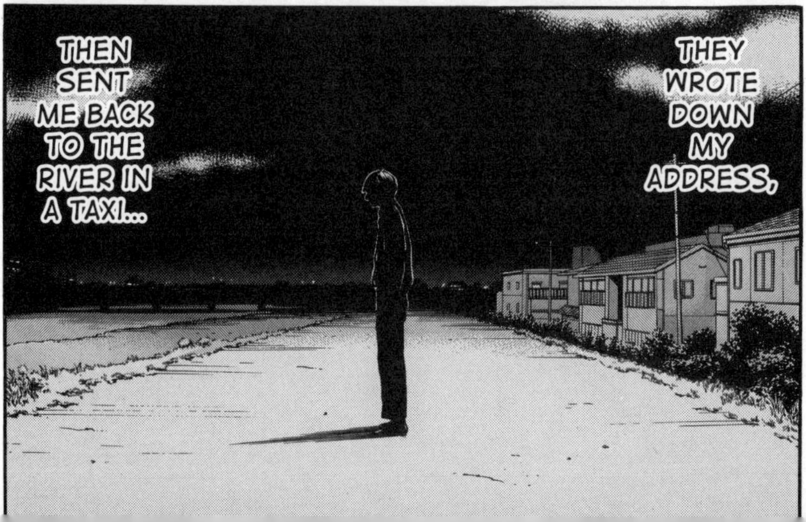
THEY WROTE DOWN MY ADDRESS,
THEN SENT ME BACK TO THE RIVER IN A TAXI...

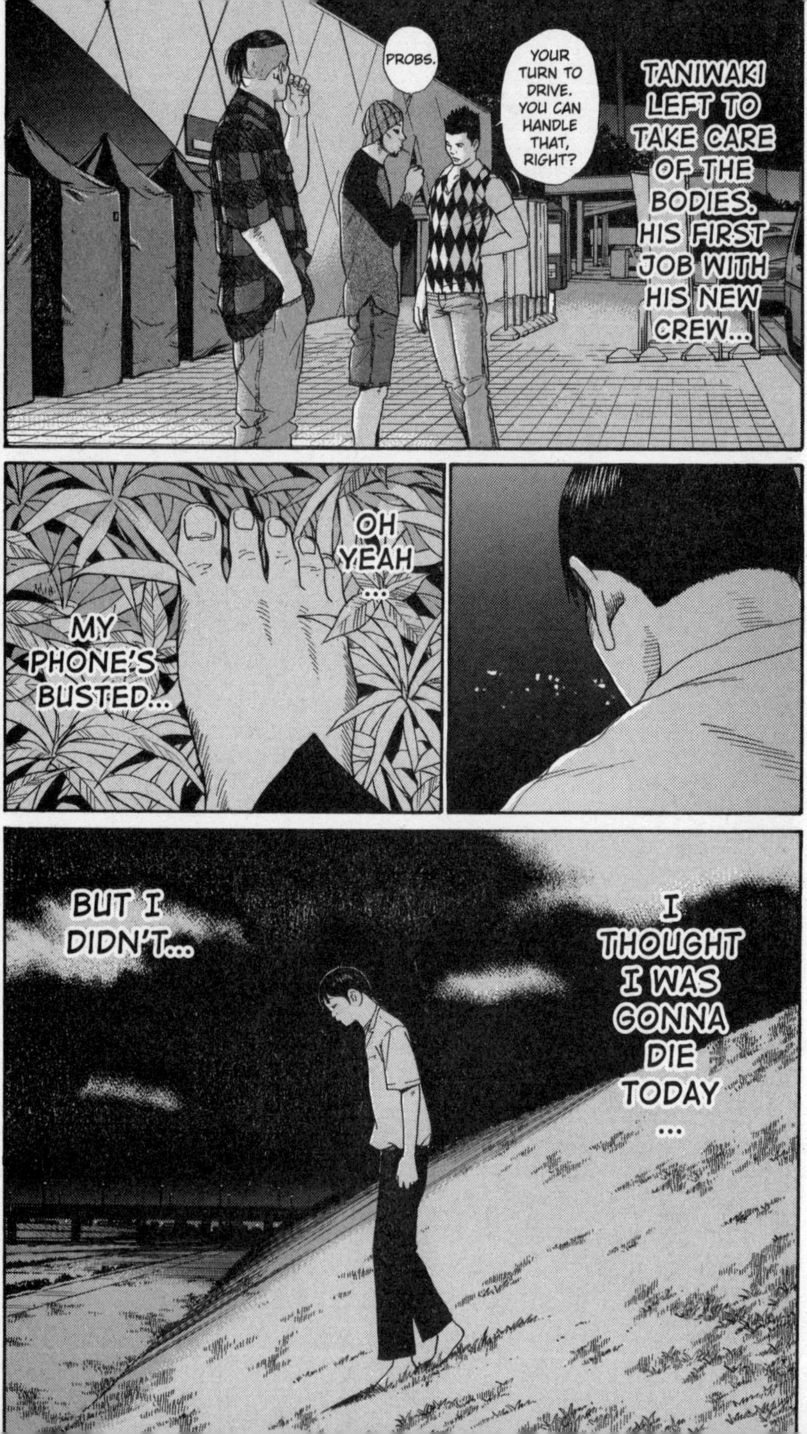
TANIWAKI LEFT TO TAKE CARE OF THE BODIES. HIS FIRST JOB WITH HIS NEW CREW...
YOUR TURN TO DRIVE. YOU CAN HANDLE THAT, RIGHT?
PROBS.
OH YEAH ...
MY PHONE'S BUSTED...
I THOUGHT I WAS GONNA DIE TODAY ...
BUT I DIDN'T...

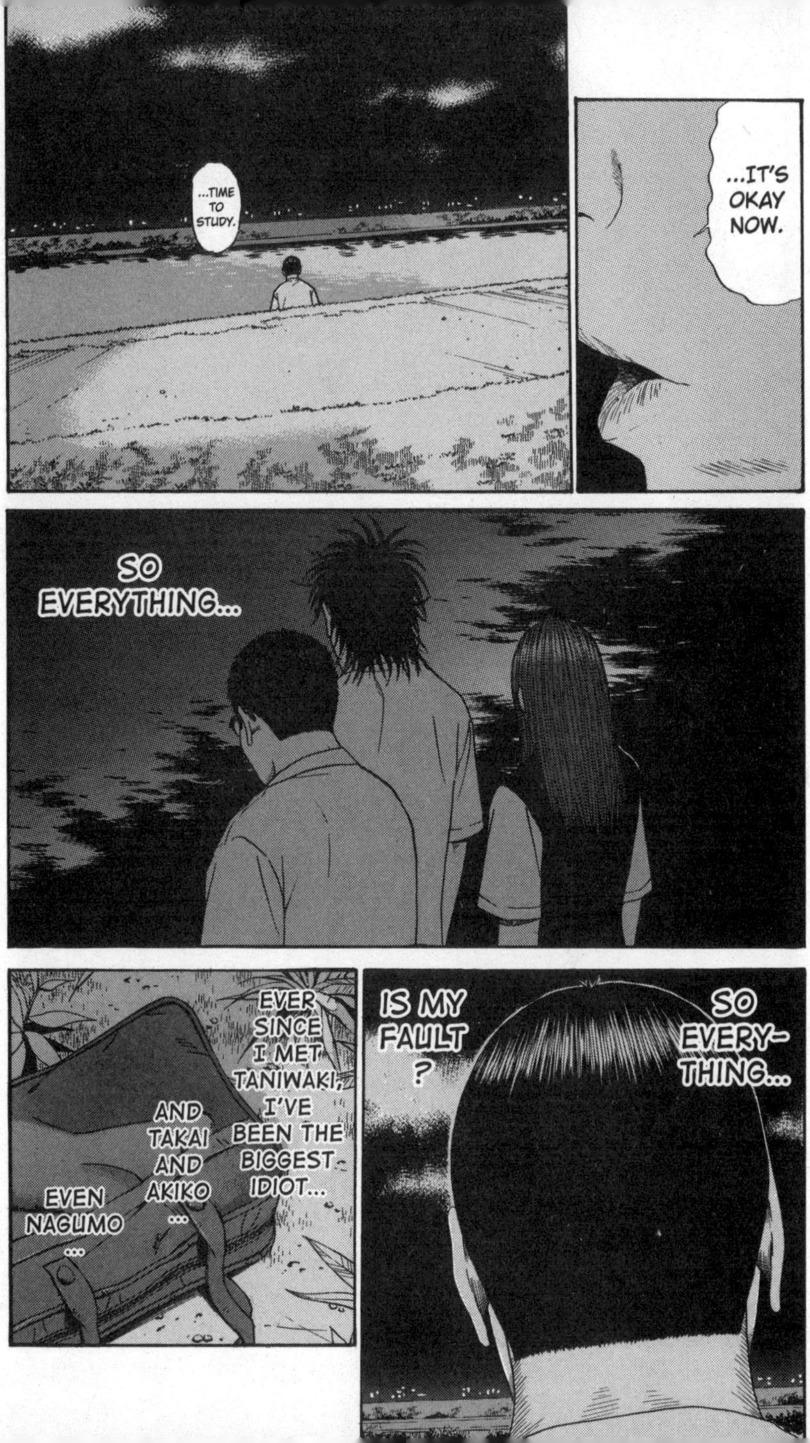
...IT'S OKAY NOW.
...TIME TO STUDY.
SO EVERYTHING...
SO EVERY-THING...
IS MY FAULT ?
EVER SINCE I MET TANIWAKI, I'VE BEEN THE BIGGEST IDIOT...
AND TAKAI AND AKIKO ...
EVEN NAGUMO ...

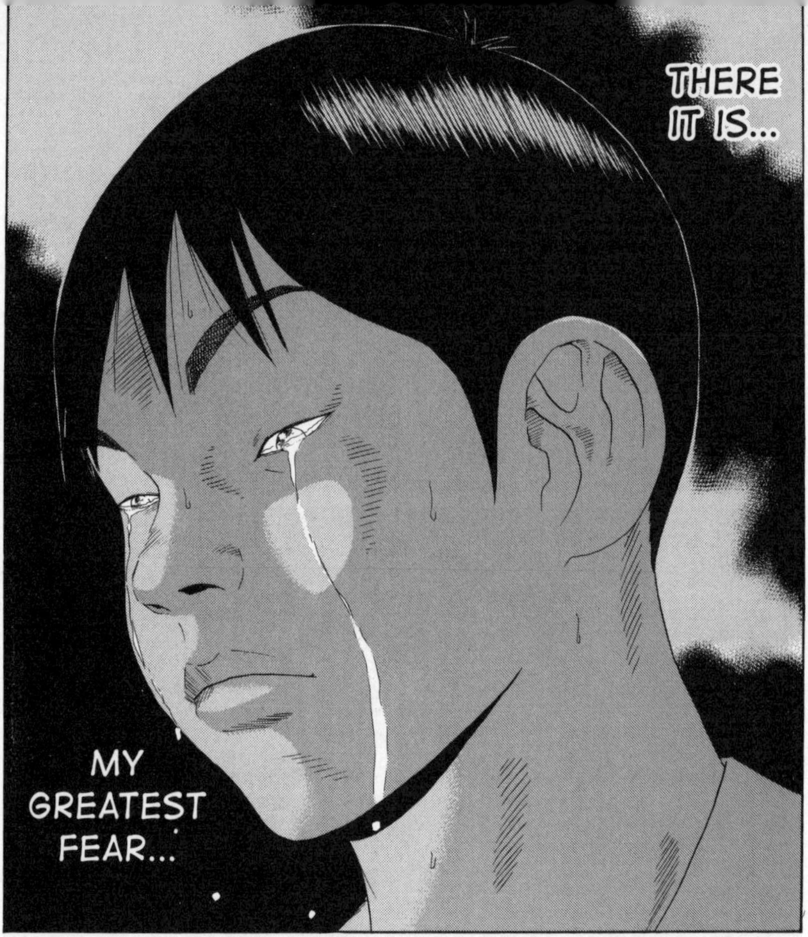
THERE IT IS...
MY GREATEST FEAR...

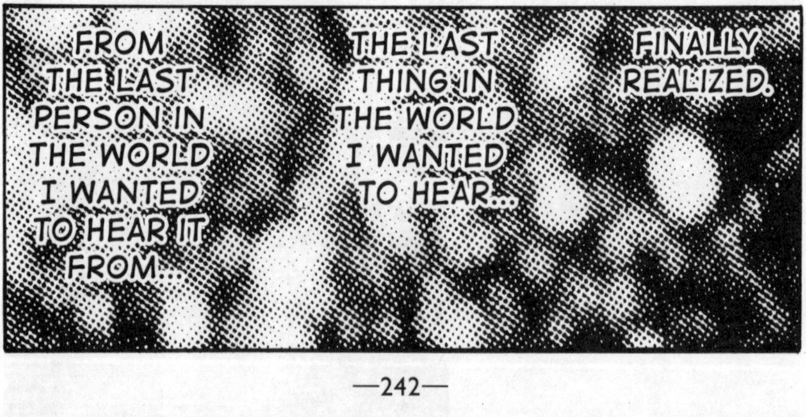
FINALLY REALIZED.
THE LAST THING IN THE WORLD I WANTED TO HEAR...
FROM THE LAST PERSON IN THE WORLD I WANTED TO HEAR IT FROM...

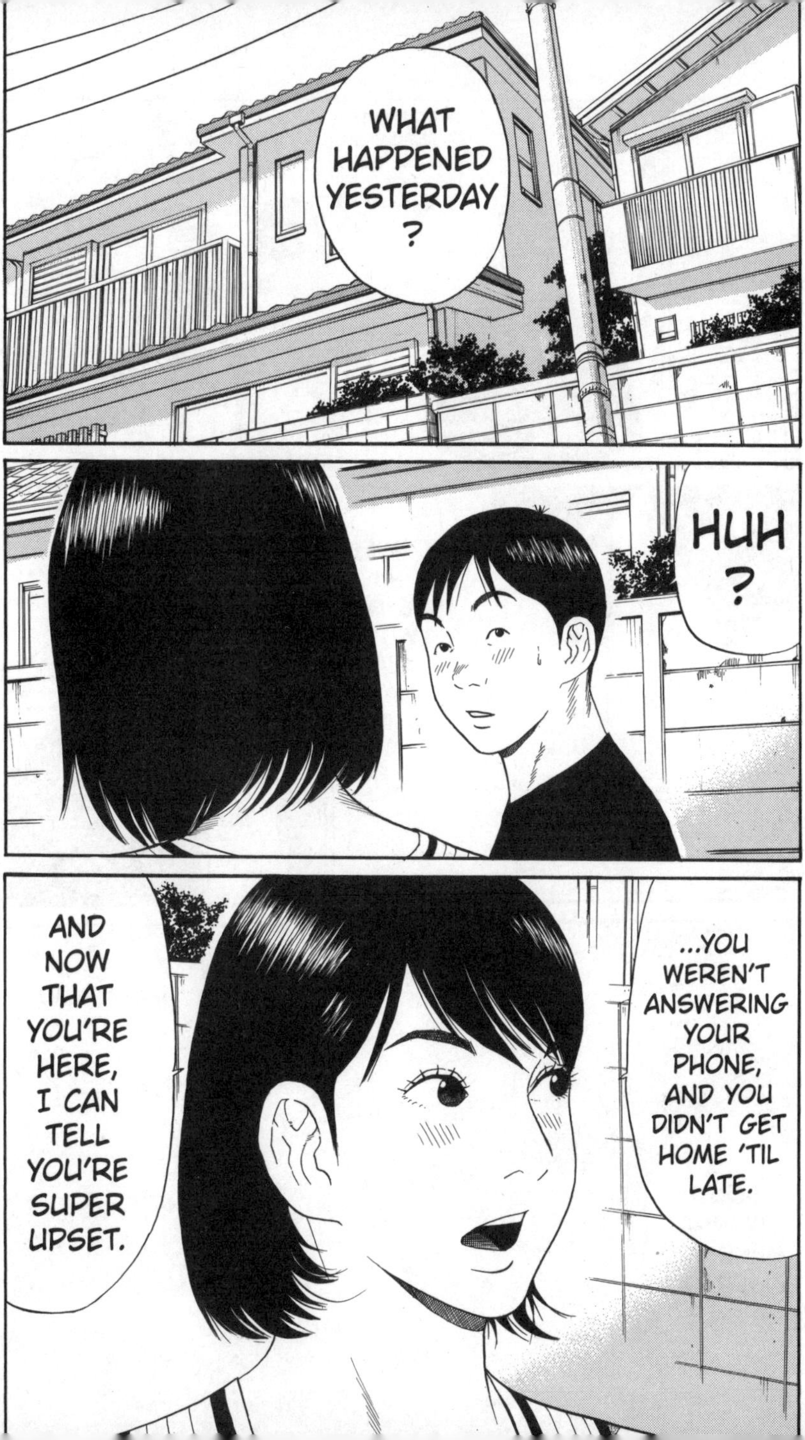
WHAT HAPPENED YESTERDAY ?
HUH ?
...YOU WEREN'T ANSWERING YOUR PHONE, AND YOU DIDN'T GET HOME 'TIL LATE.
AND NOW THAT YOU'RE HERE, I CAN TELL YOU'RE SUPER UPSET.

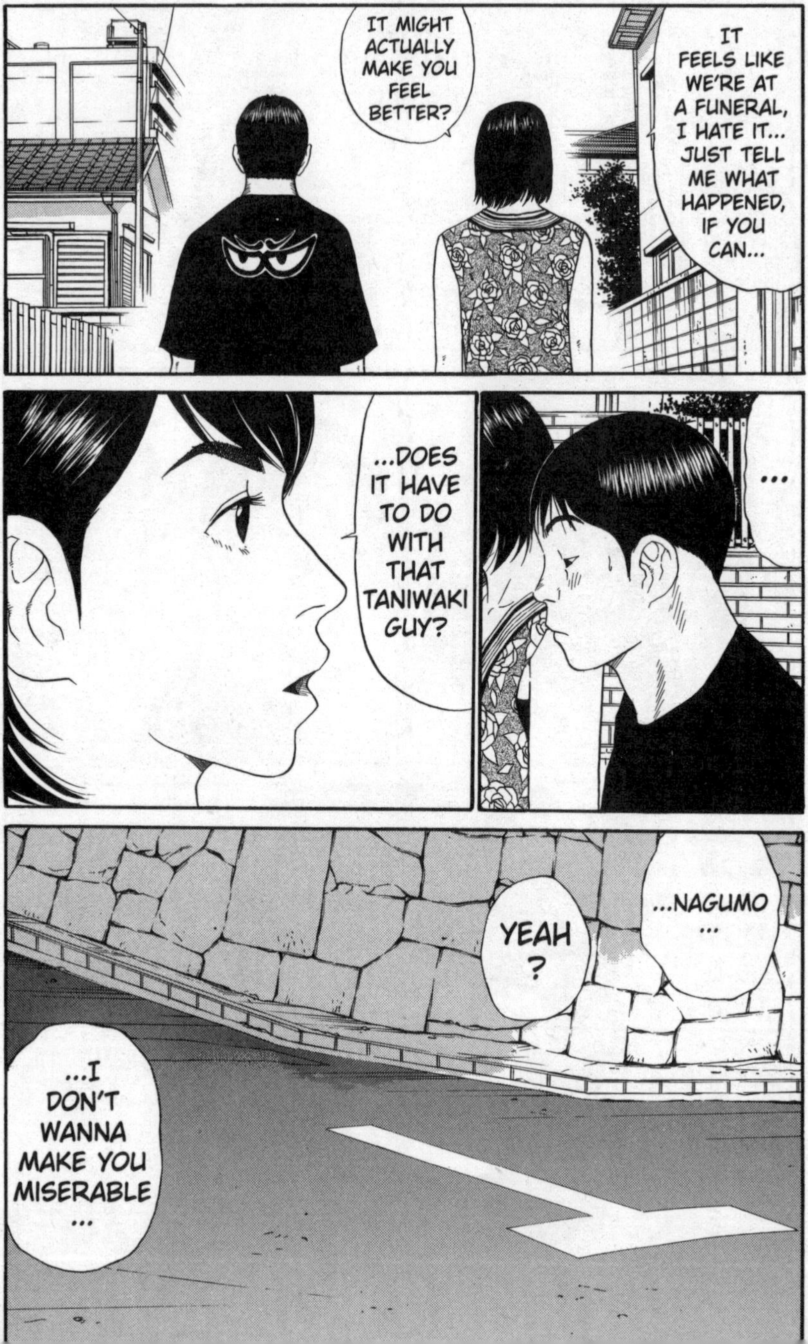
IT FEELS LIKE WE'RE AT A FUNERAL, I HATE IT... JUST TELL ME WHAT HAPPENED, IF YOU CAN...
IT MIGHT ACTUALLY MAKE YOU FEEL BETTER?
...
...DOES IT HAVE TO DO WITH THAT TANIWAKI GUY?
...NAGUMO ...
YEAH ?
...I DON'T WANNA MAKE YOU MISERABLE ...

# Chapter 60: Pass/Fail

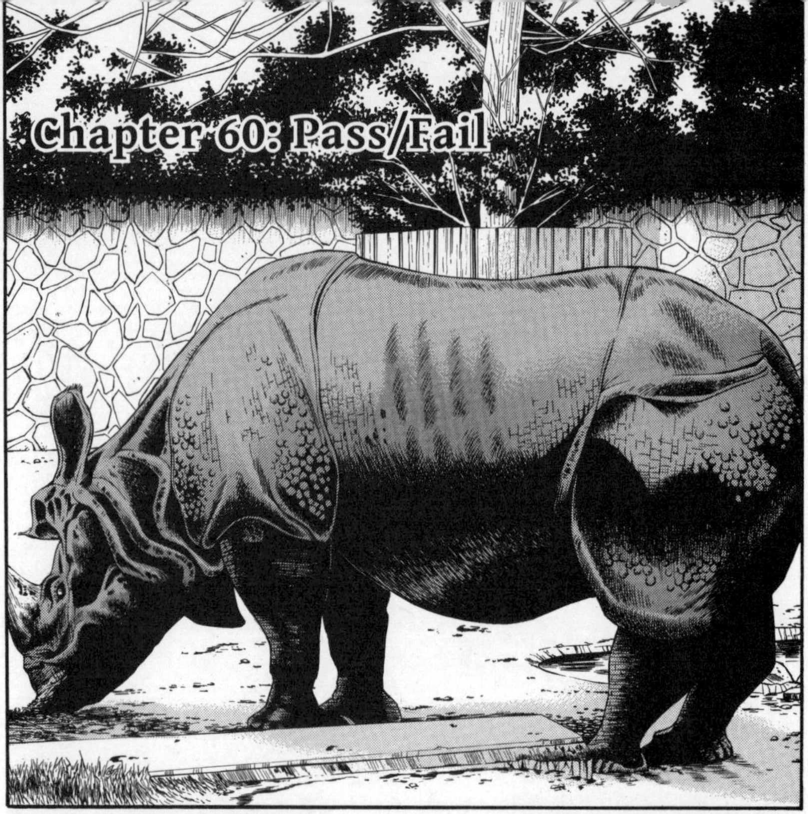

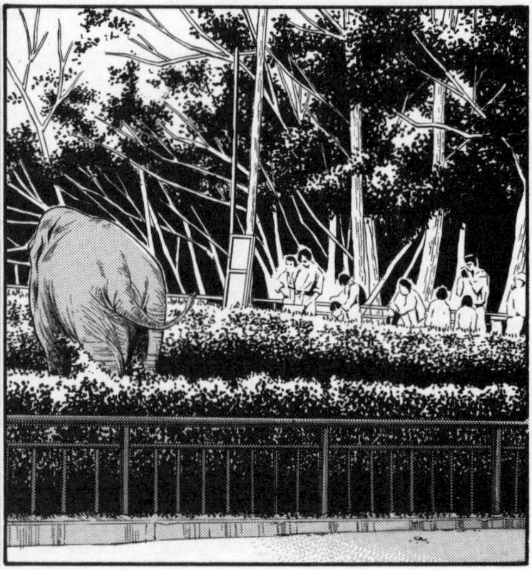

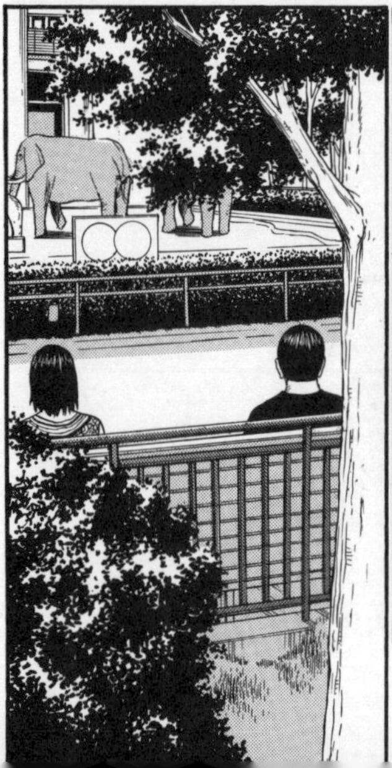

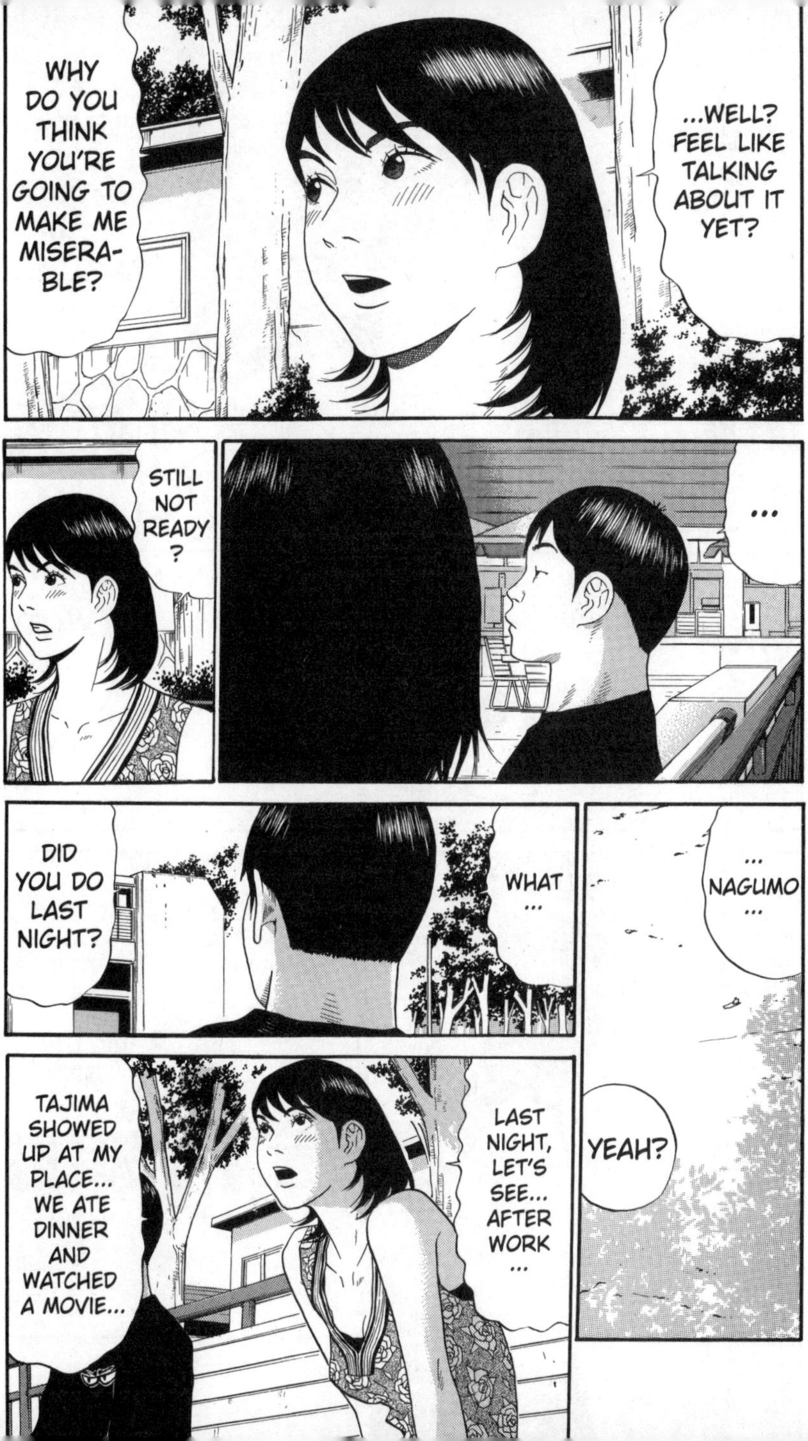

...WELL? FEEL LIKE TALKING ABOUT IT YET?
WHY DO YOU THINK YOU'RE GOING TO MAKE ME MISERA-BLE?
...
STILL NOT READY ?
... NAGUMO ...
YEAH?
WHAT ...
DID YOU DO LAST NIGHT?
LAST NIGHT, LET'S SEE... AFTER WORK ...
TAJIMA SHOWED UP AT MY PLACE... WE ATE DINNER AND WATCHED A MOVIE...

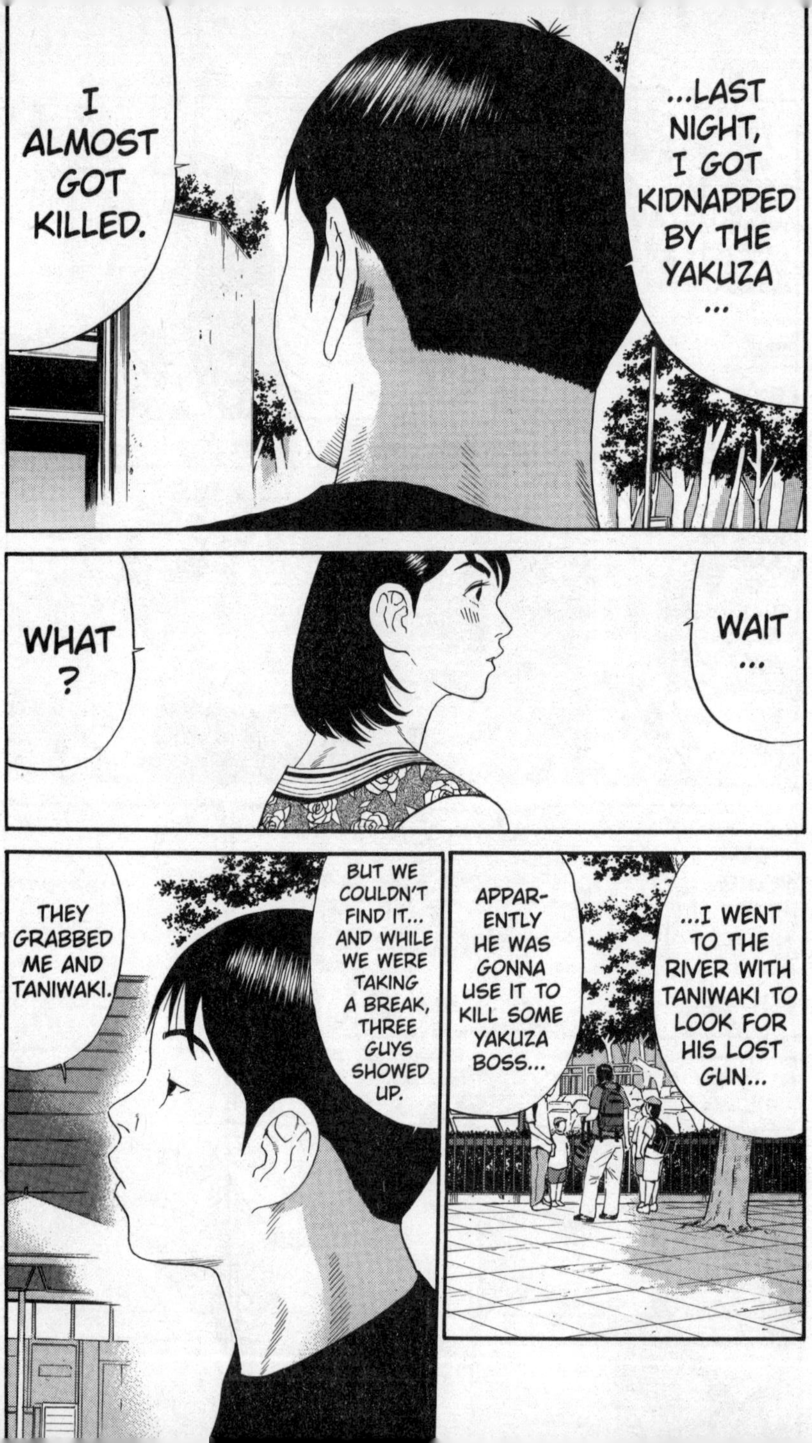
...LAST NIGHT, I GOT KIDNAPPED BY THE YAKUZA ...
I ALMOST GOT KILLED.
WAIT ...
WHAT ?
...I WENT TO THE RIVER WITH TANIWAKI TO LOOK FOR HIS LOST GUN...
APPAR-ENTLY HE WAS GONNA USE IT TO KILL SOME YAKUZA BOSS...
BUT WE COULDN'T FIND IT... AND WHILE WE WERE TAKING A BREAK, THREE GUYS SHOWED UP.
THEY GRABBED ME AND TANIWAKI.

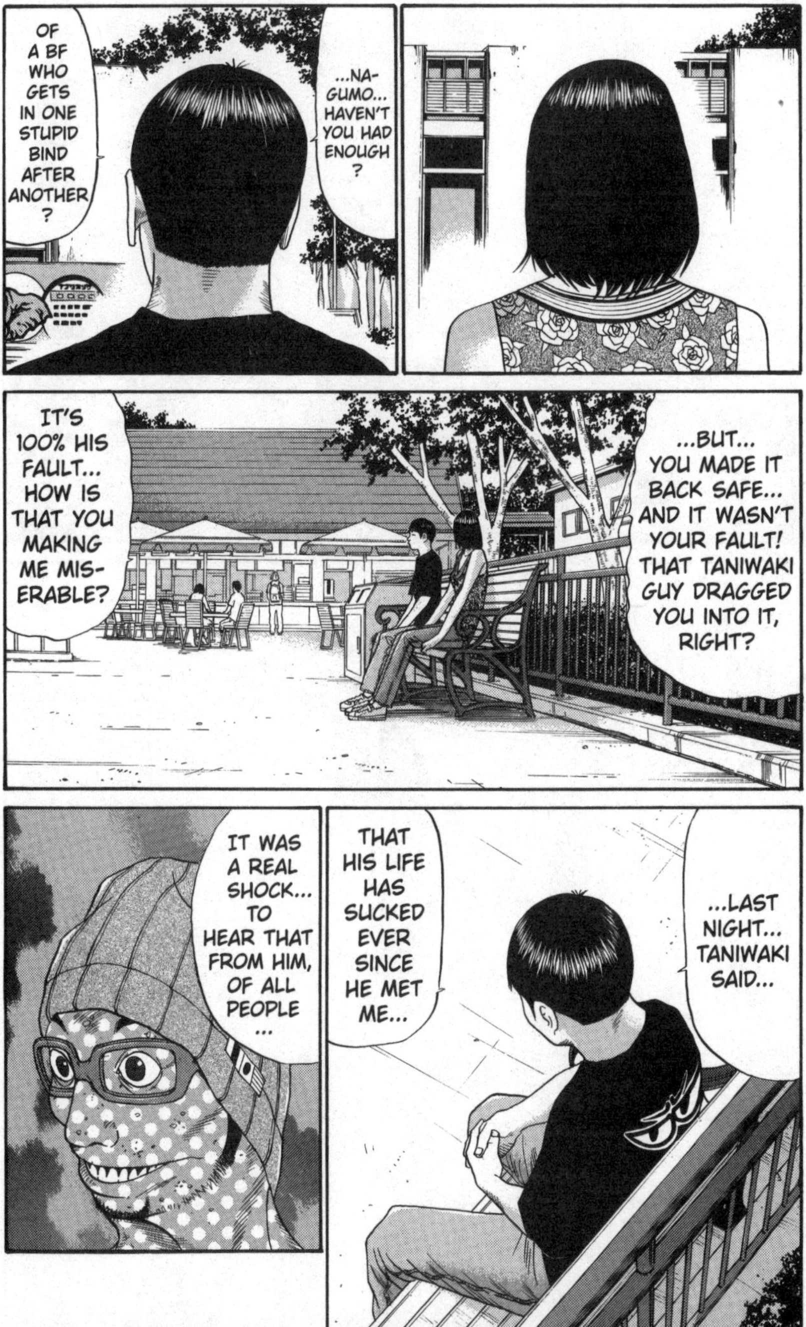
...NA-GUMO... HAVEN'T YOU HAD ENOUGH?
OF A BF WHO GETS IN ONE STUPID BIND AFTER ANOTHER?
...BUT... YOU MADE IT BACK SAFE... AND IT WASN'T YOUR FAULT! THAT TANIWAKI GUY DRAGGED YOU INTO IT, RIGHT?
IT'S 100% HIS FAULT... HOW IS THAT YOU MAKING ME MIS-ERABLE?
...LAST NIGHT... TANIWAKI SAID...
THAT HIS LIFE HAS SUCKED EVER SINCE HE MET ME...
IT WAS A REAL SHOCK... TO HEAR THAT FROM HIM, OF ALL PEOPLE...

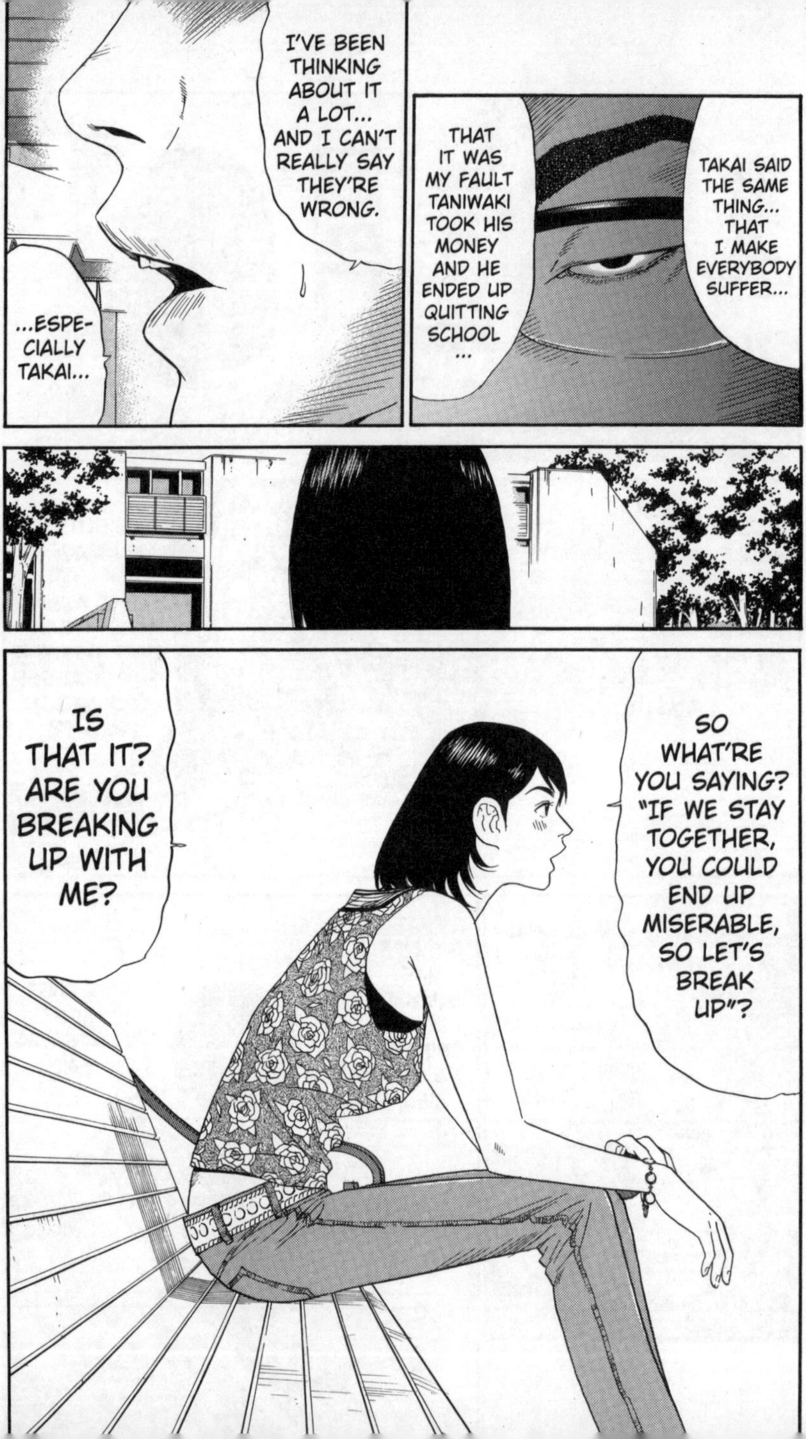
TAKAI SAID THE SAME THING... THAT I MAKE EVERYBODY SUFFER...
THAT IT WAS MY FAULT TANIWAKI TOOK HIS MONEY AND HE ENDED UP QUITTING SCHOOL...
I'VE BEEN THINKING ABOUT IT A LOT... AND I CAN'T REALLY SAY THEY'RE WRONG.
...ESPE-CIALLY TAKAI...
SO WHAT'RE YOU SAYING? "IF WE STAY TOGETHER, YOU COULD END UP MISERABLE, SO LET'S BREAK UP"?
IS THAT IT? ARE YOU BREAKING UP WITH ME?

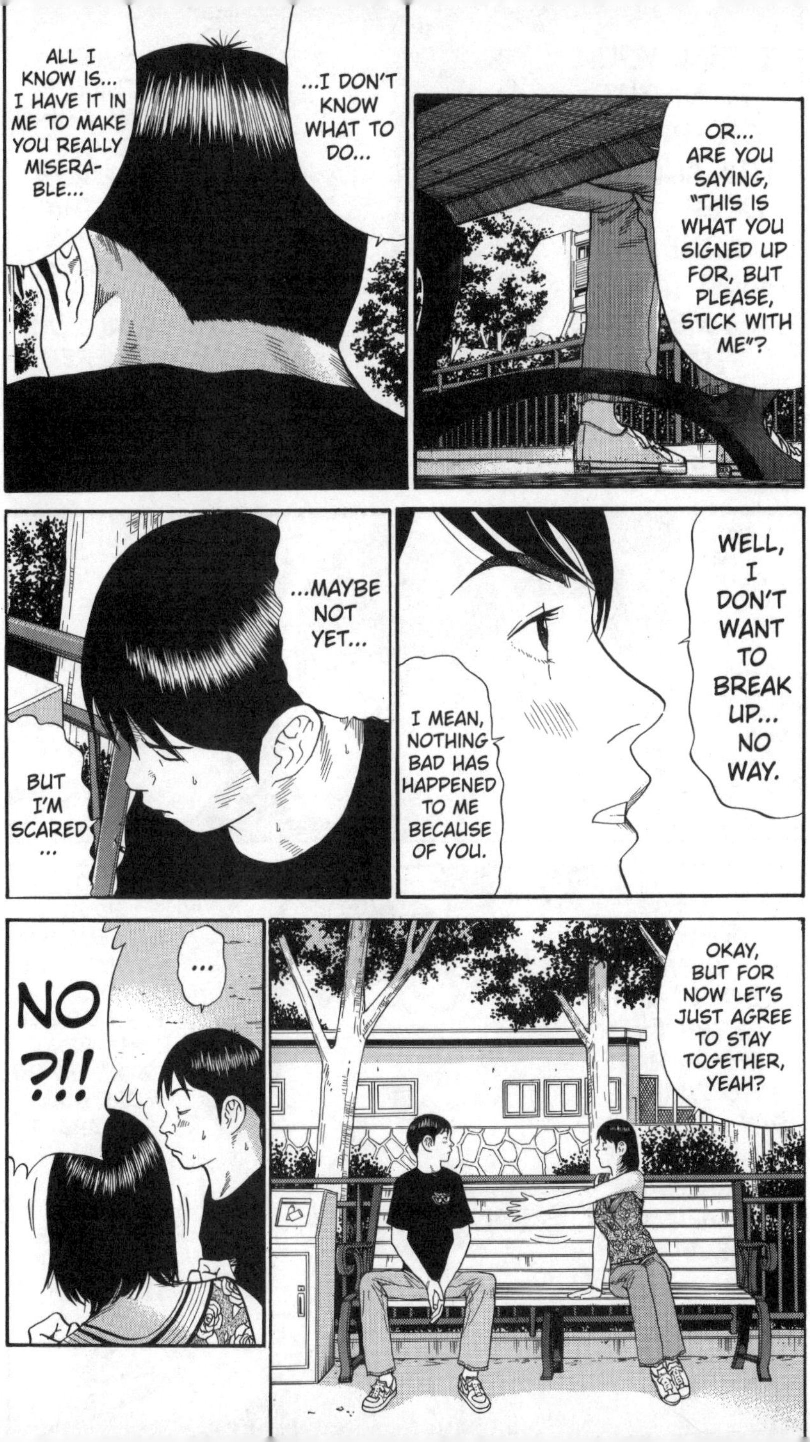
OR... ARE YOU SAYING, "THIS IS WHAT YOU SIGNED UP FOR, BUT PLEASE, STICK WITH ME"?
...I DON'T KNOW WHAT TO DO...
ALL I KNOW IS... I HAVE IT IN ME TO MAKE YOU REALLY MISERA-BLE...
WELL, I DON'T WANT TO BREAK UP... NO WAY.
I MEAN, NOTHING BAD HAS HAPPENED TO ME BECAUSE OF YOU.
...MAYBE NOT YET...
BUT I'M SCARED...
OKAY, BUT FOR NOW LET'S JUST AGREE TO STAY TOGETHER, YEAH?
...
NO ?!!

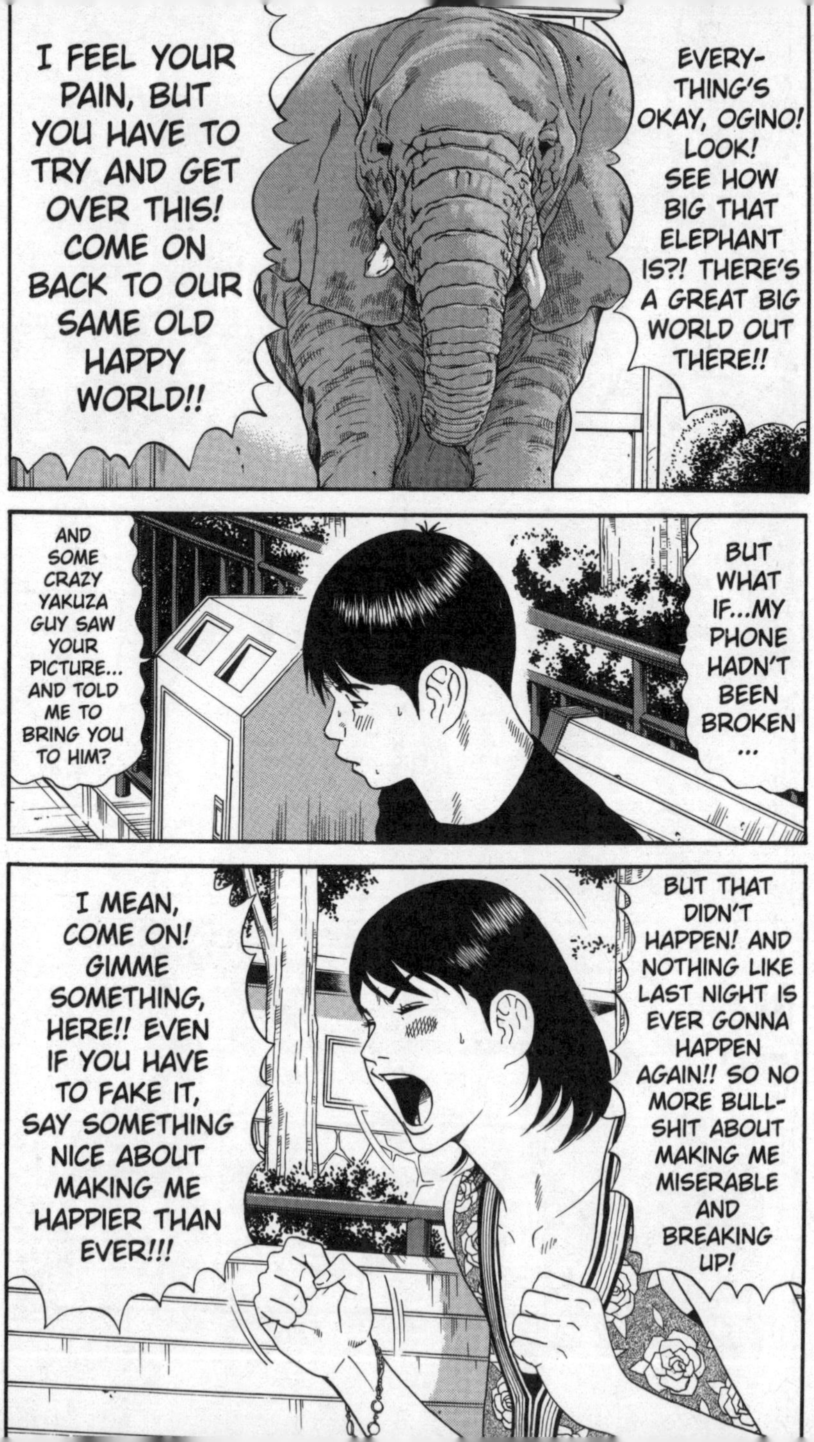
EVERY-THING'S OKAY, OGINO! LOOK! SEE HOW BIG THAT ELEPHANT IS?! THERE'S A GREAT BIG WORLD OUT THERE!!
I FEEL YOUR PAIN, BUT YOU HAVE TO TRY AND GET OVER THIS! COME ON BACK TO OUR SAME OLD HAPPY WORLD!!
BUT WHAT IF...MY PHONE HADN'T BEEN BROKEN...
AND SOME CRAZY YAKUZA GUY SAW YOUR PICTURE... AND TOLD ME TO BRING YOU TO HIM?
BUT THAT DIDN'T HAPPEN! AND NOTHING LIKE LAST NIGHT IS EVER GONNA HAPPEN AGAIN!! SO NO MORE BULL-SHIT ABOUT MAKING ME MISERABLE AND BREAKING UP!
I MEAN, COME ON! GIMME SOMETHING, HERE!! EVEN IF YOU HAVE TO FAKE IT, SAY SOMETHING NICE ABOUT MAKING ME HAPPIER THAN EVER!!!

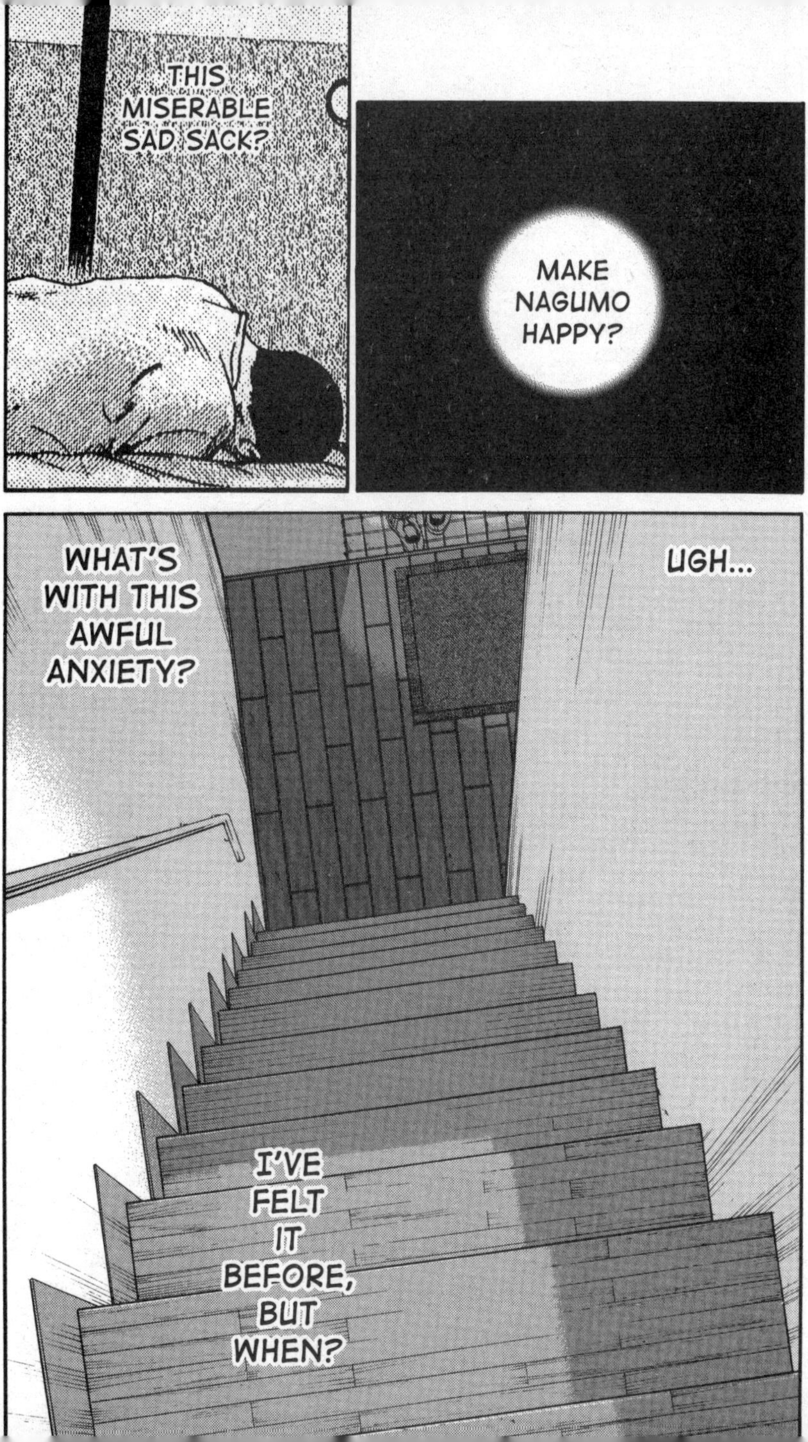
MAKE NAGUMO HAPPY?
THIS MISERABLE SAD SACK?
UGH...
WHAT'S WITH THIS AWFUL ANXIETY?
I'VE FELT IT BEFORE, BUT WHEN?

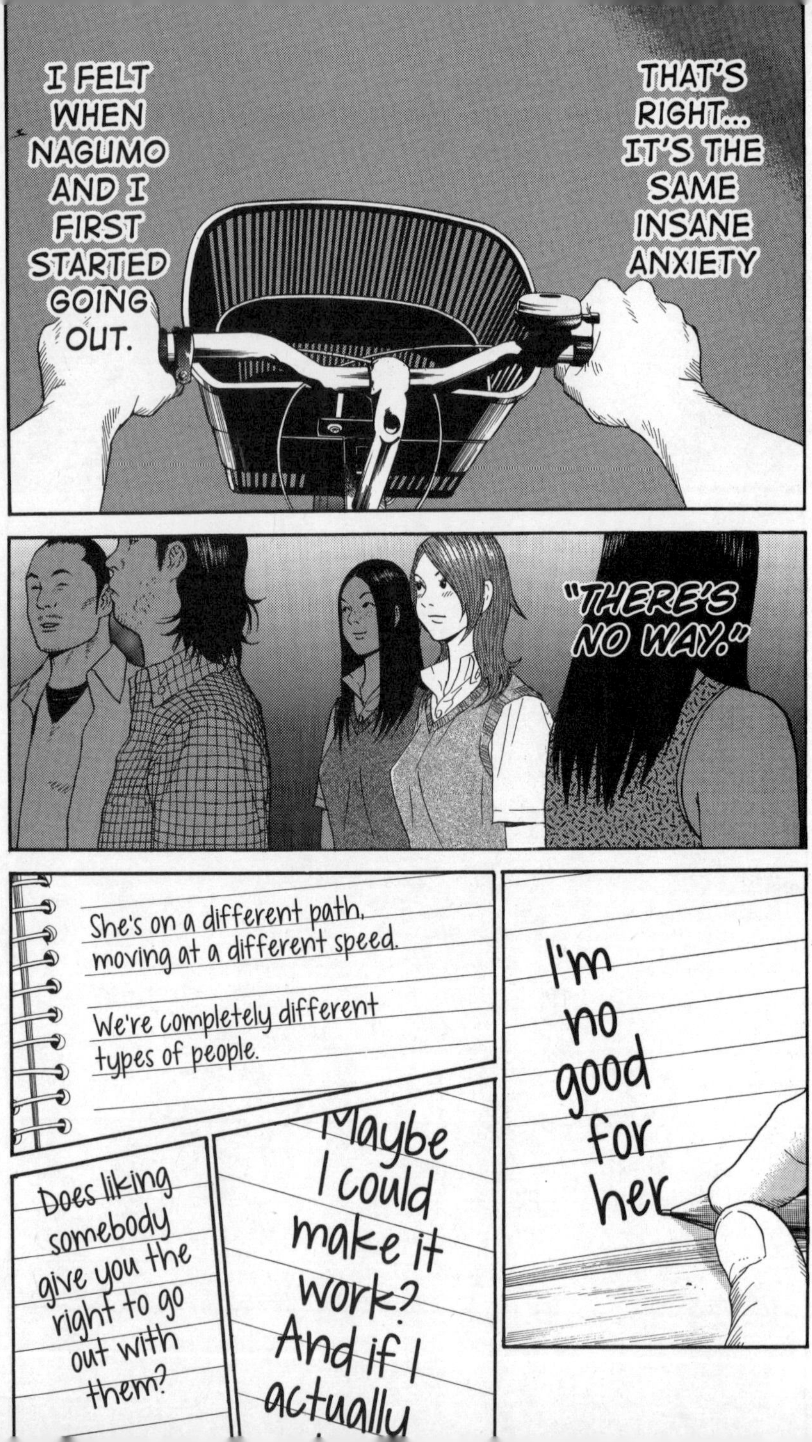
THAT'S RIGHT... IT'S THE SAME INSANE ANXIETY
I FELT WHEN NAGUMO AND I FIRST STARTED GOING OUT.
"THERE'S NO WAY."
I'm no good for her
She's on a different path, moving at a different speed.
We're completely different types of people.
Maybe I could make it work? And if I actually
Does liking somebody give you the right to go out with them?

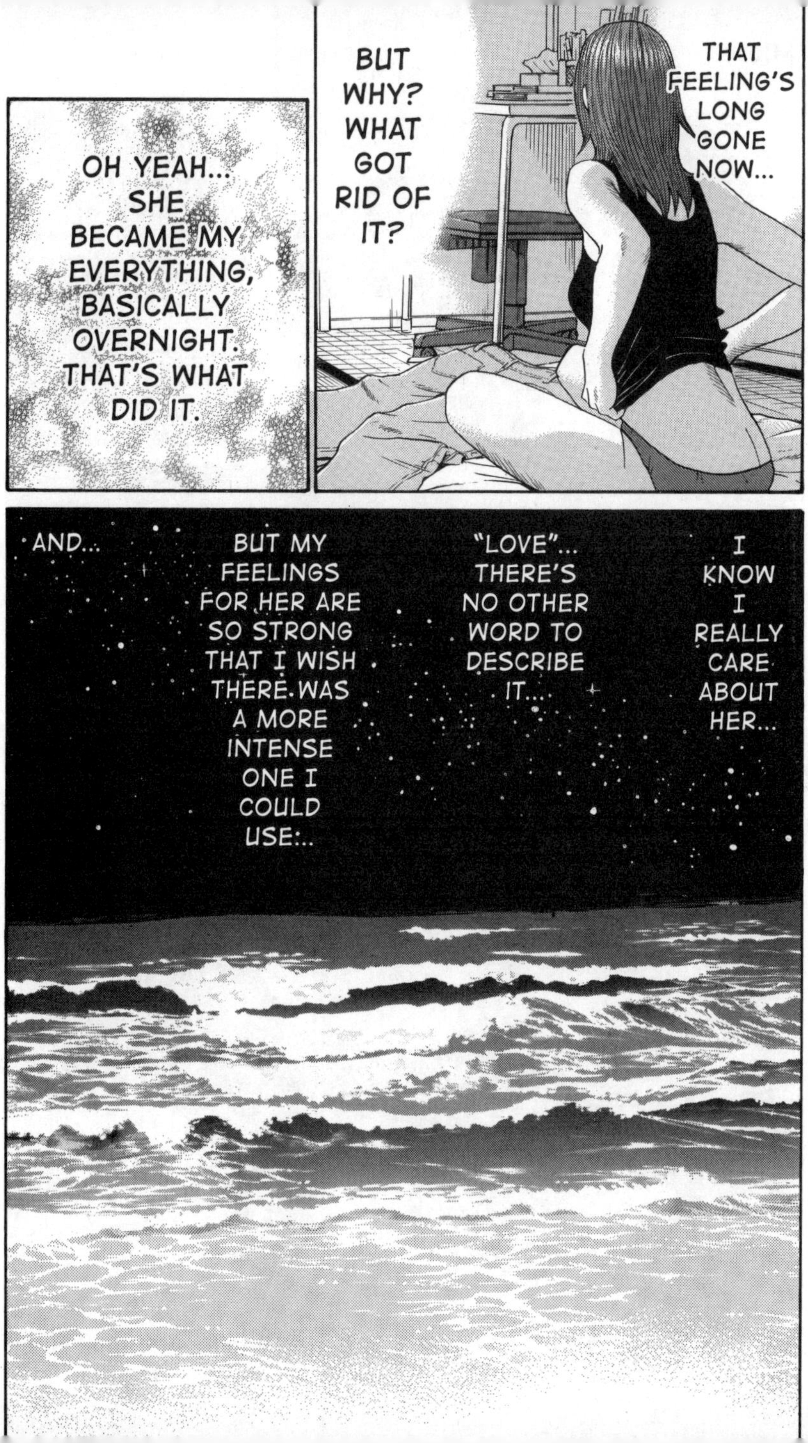
THAT FEELING'S LONG GONE NOW...
BUT WHY? WHAT GOT RID OF IT?
OH YEAH... SHE BECAME MY EVERYTHING, BASICALLY OVERNIGHT. THAT'S WHAT DID IT.
I KNOW I REALLY CARE ABOUT HER...
"LOVE"... THERE'S NO OTHER WORD TO DESCRIBE IT...
BUT MY FEELINGS FOR HER ARE SO STRONG THAT I WISH THERE WAS A MORE INTENSE ONE I COULD USE...
AND...

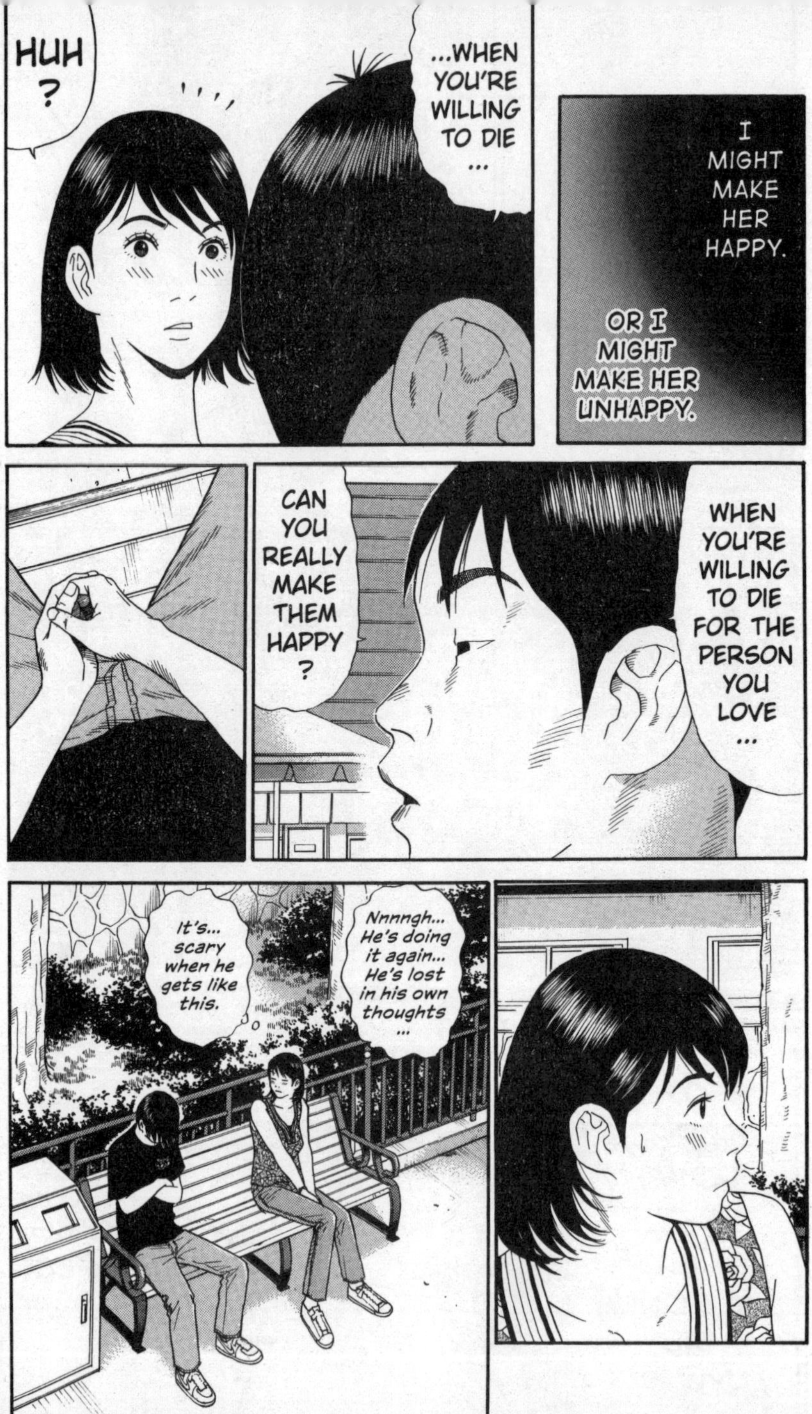
I MIGHT MAKE HER HAPPY.
OR I MIGHT MAKE HER UNHAPPY.
...WHEN YOU'RE WILLING TO DIE ...
HUH ?
WHEN YOU'RE WILLING TO DIE FOR THE PERSON YOU LOVE ...
CAN YOU REALLY MAKE THEM HAPPY ?
Nnnngh... He's doing it again... He's lost in his own thoughts ...
It's... scary when he gets like this.

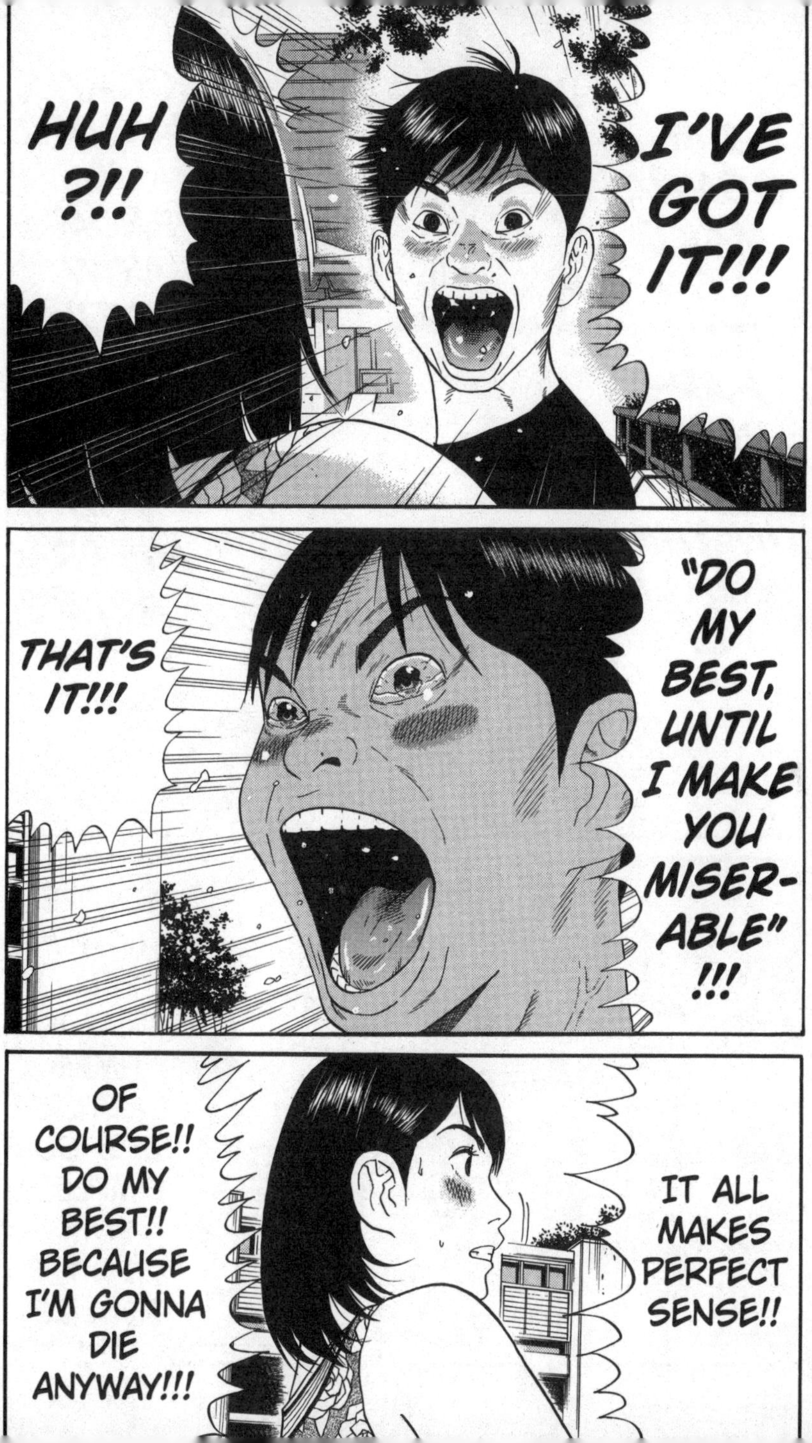
I'VE GOT IT!!!
HUH ?!!
"DO MY BEST, UNTIL I MAKE YOU MISER-ABLE" !!!
THAT'S IT!!!
IT ALL MAKES PERFECT SENSE!!
OF COURSE!! DO MY BEST!! BECAUSE I'M GONNA DIE ANYWAY!!!

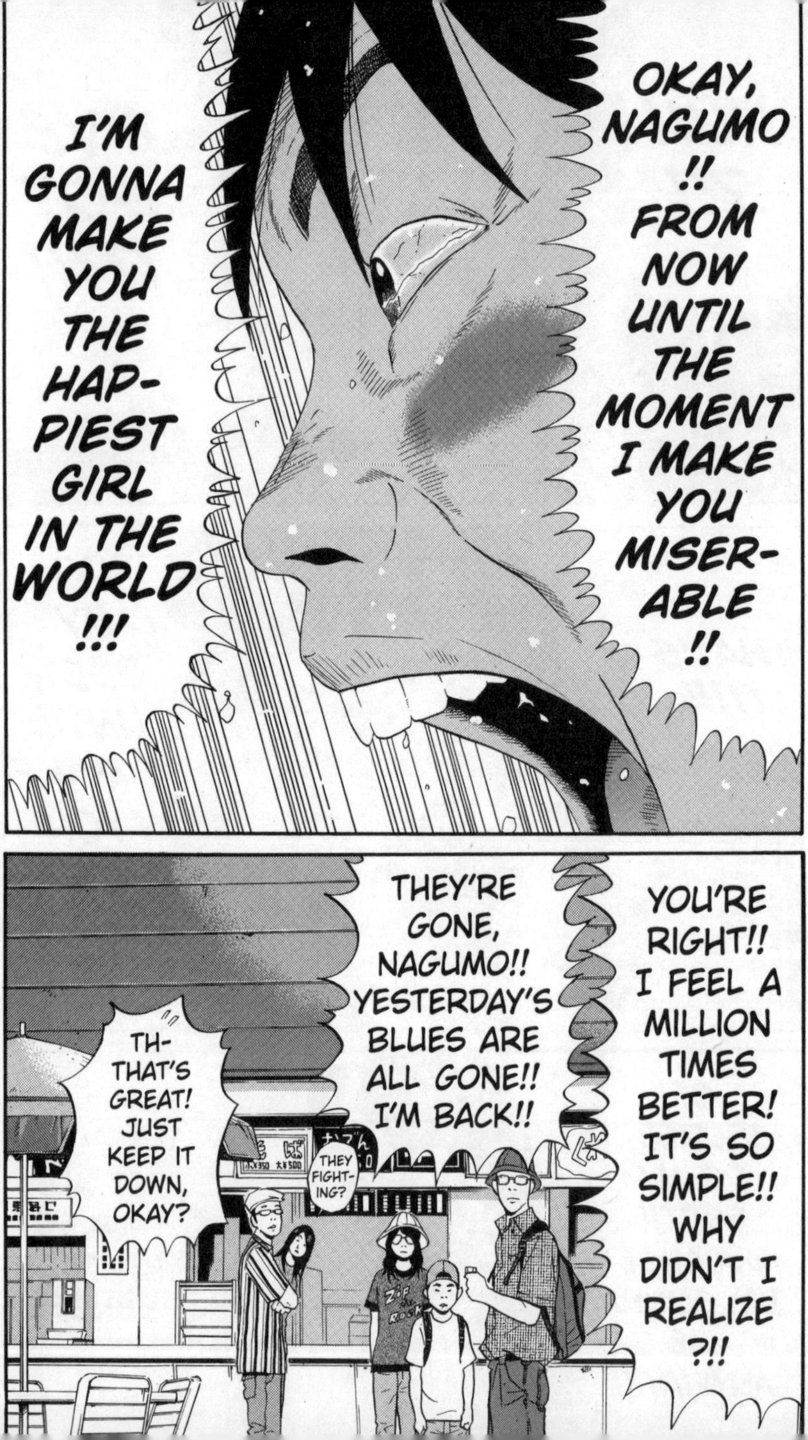
OKAY, NAGUMO!! FROM NOW UNTIL THE MOMENT I MAKE YOU MISERABLE!!
I'M GONNA MAKE YOU THE HAPPIEST GIRL IN THE WORLD!!!
YOU'RE RIGHT!! I FEEL A MILLION TIMES BETTER! IT'S SO SIMPLE!! WHY DIDN'T I REALIZE?!!
THEY'RE GONE, NAGUMO!! YESTERDAY'S BLUES ARE ALL GONE!! I'M BACK!!
THEY FIGHTING?
TH-THAT'S GREAT! JUST KEEP IT DOWN, OKAY?

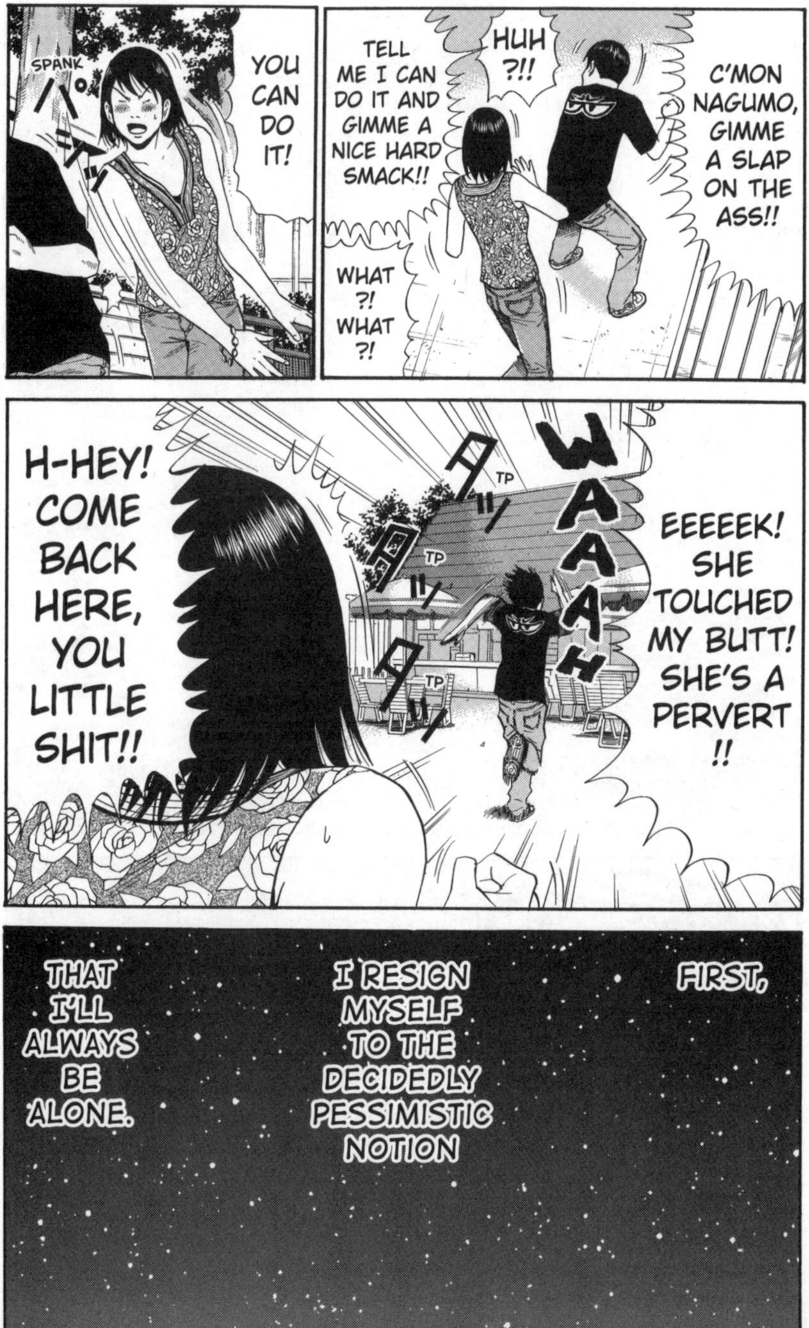
C'MON NAGUMO, GIMME A SLAP ON THE ASS!!
HUH ?!!
TELL ME I CAN DO IT AND GIMME A NICE HARD SMACK!!
WHAT ?! WHAT ?!
YOU CAN DO IT!
SPANK
EEEEEK! SHE TOUCHED MY BUTT! SHE'S A PERVERT !!
WAAAH
TP
TP
TP
H-HEY! COME BACK HERE, YOU LITTLE SHIT!!
FIRST,
I RESIGN MYSELF TO THE DECIDEDLY PESSIMISTIC NOTION
THAT I'LL ALWAYS BE ALONE.

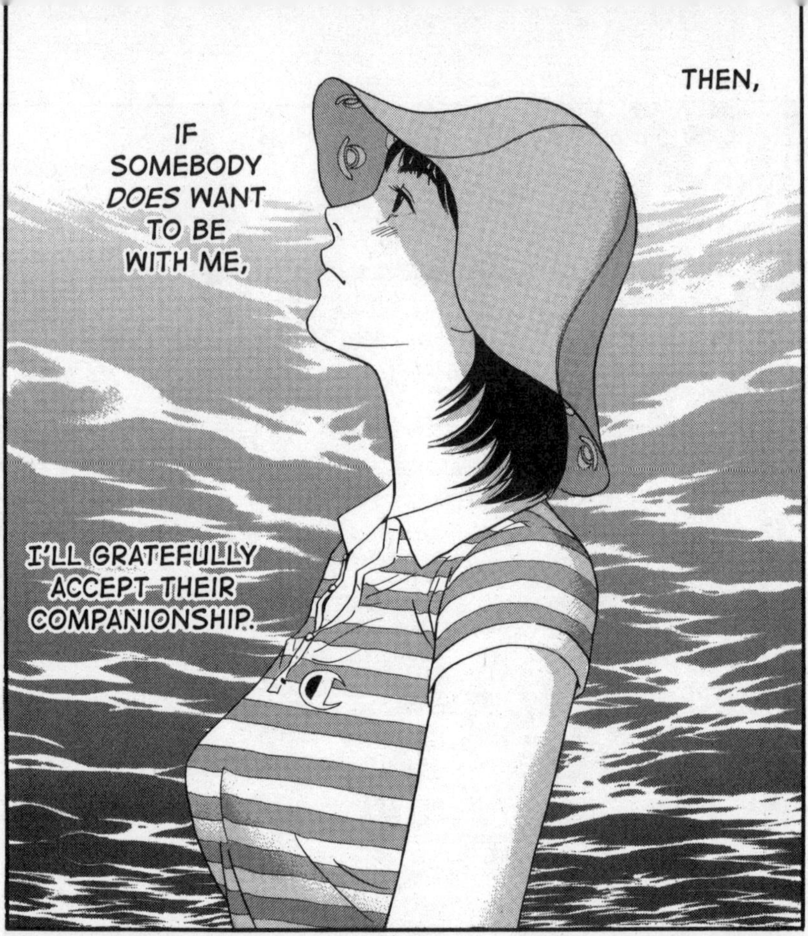
THEN,
IF SOMEBODY *DOES* WANT TO BE WITH ME,
I'LL GRATEFULLY ACCEPT THEIR COMPANIONSHIP.
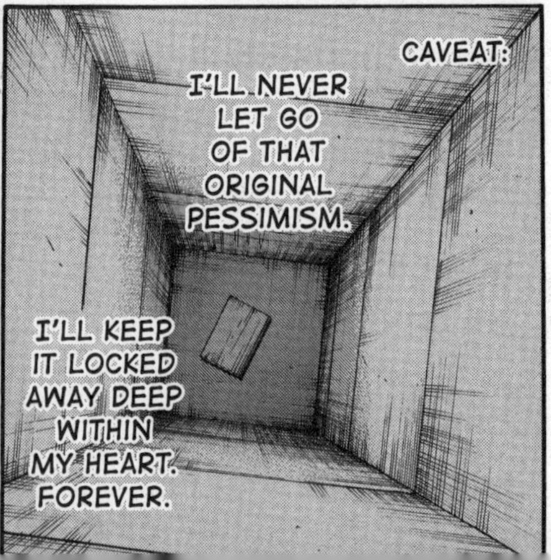
CAVEAT:
I'LL NEVER LET GO OF THAT ORIGINAL PESSIMISM.
I'LL KEEP IT LOCKED AWAY DEEP WITHIN MY HEART. FOREVER.
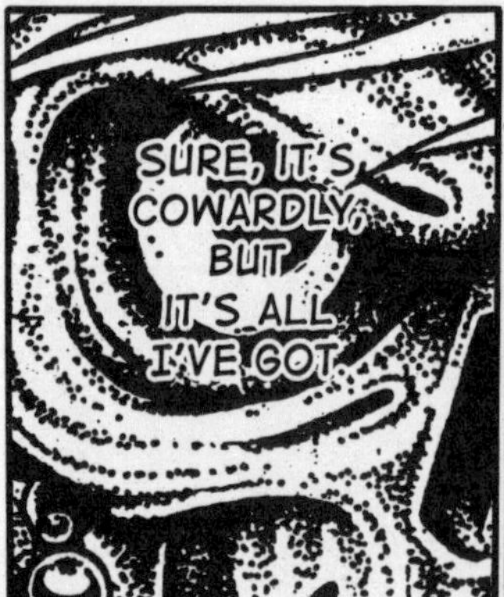
SURE, IT'S COWARDLY, BUT IT'S ALL I'VE GOT.

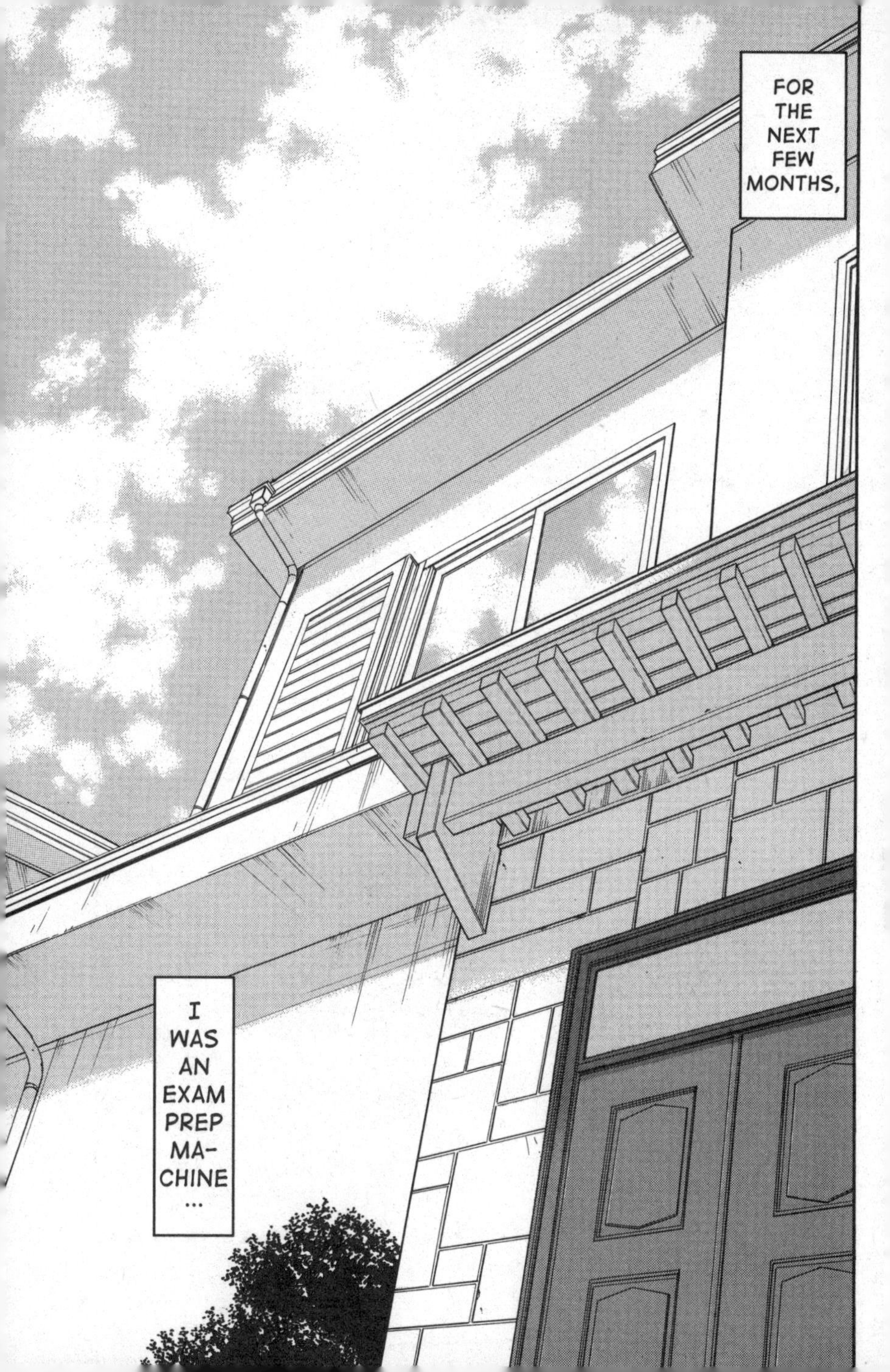
FOR THE NEXT FEW MONTHS,
I WAS AN EXAM PREP MA-CHINE...

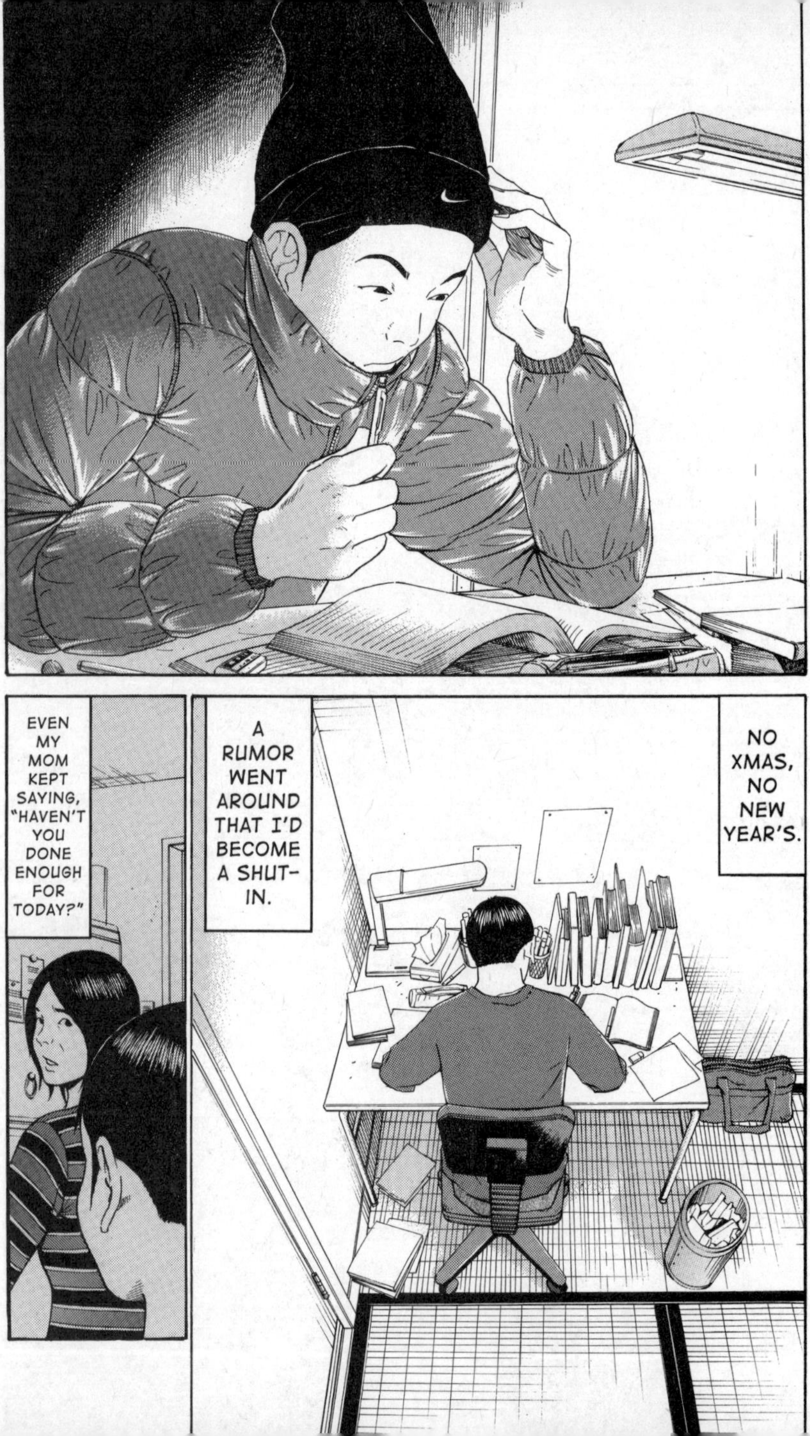
NO XMAS, NO NEW YEAR'S.
A RUMOR WENT AROUND THAT I'D BECOME A SHUT-IN.
EVEN MY MOM KEPT SAYING, "HAVEN'T YOU DONE ENOUGH FOR TODAY?"

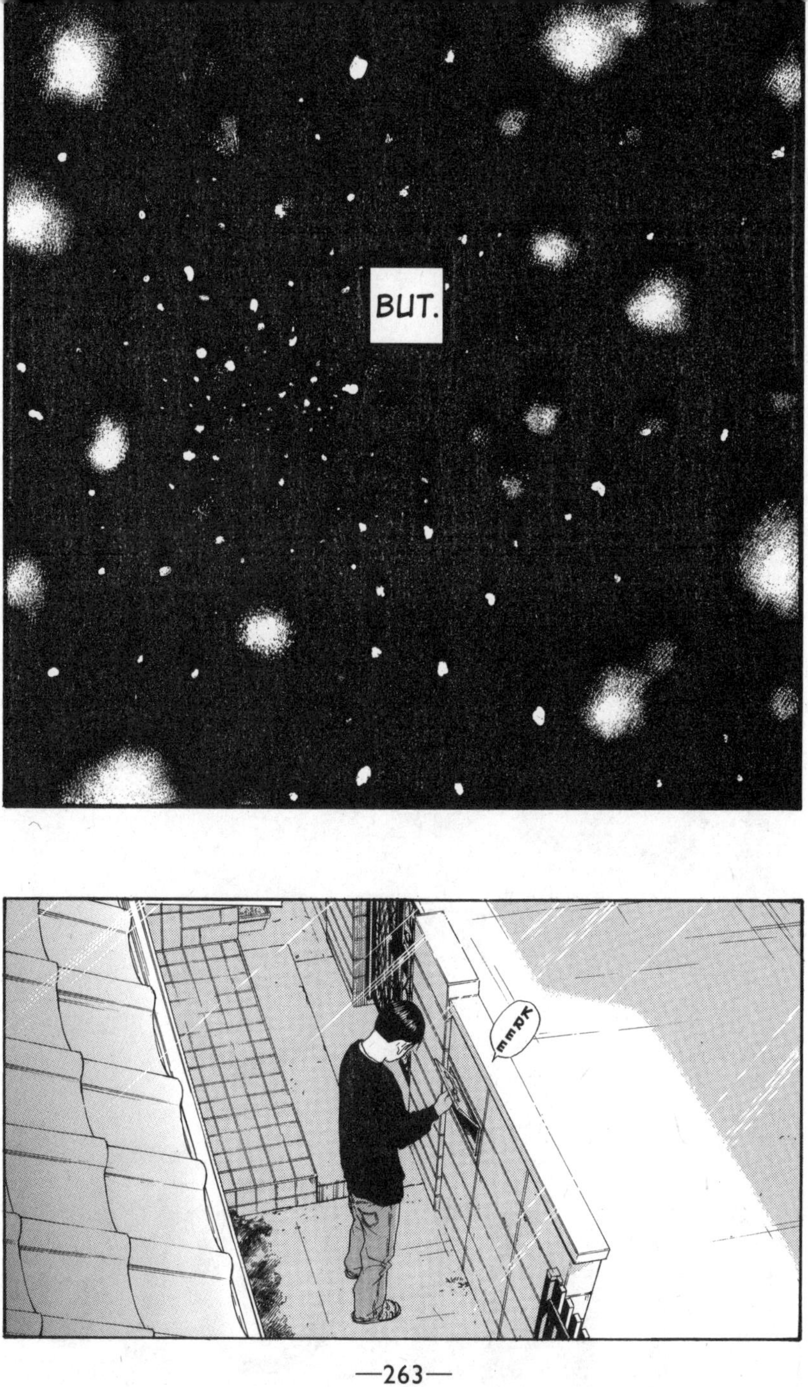
BUT.
EERK

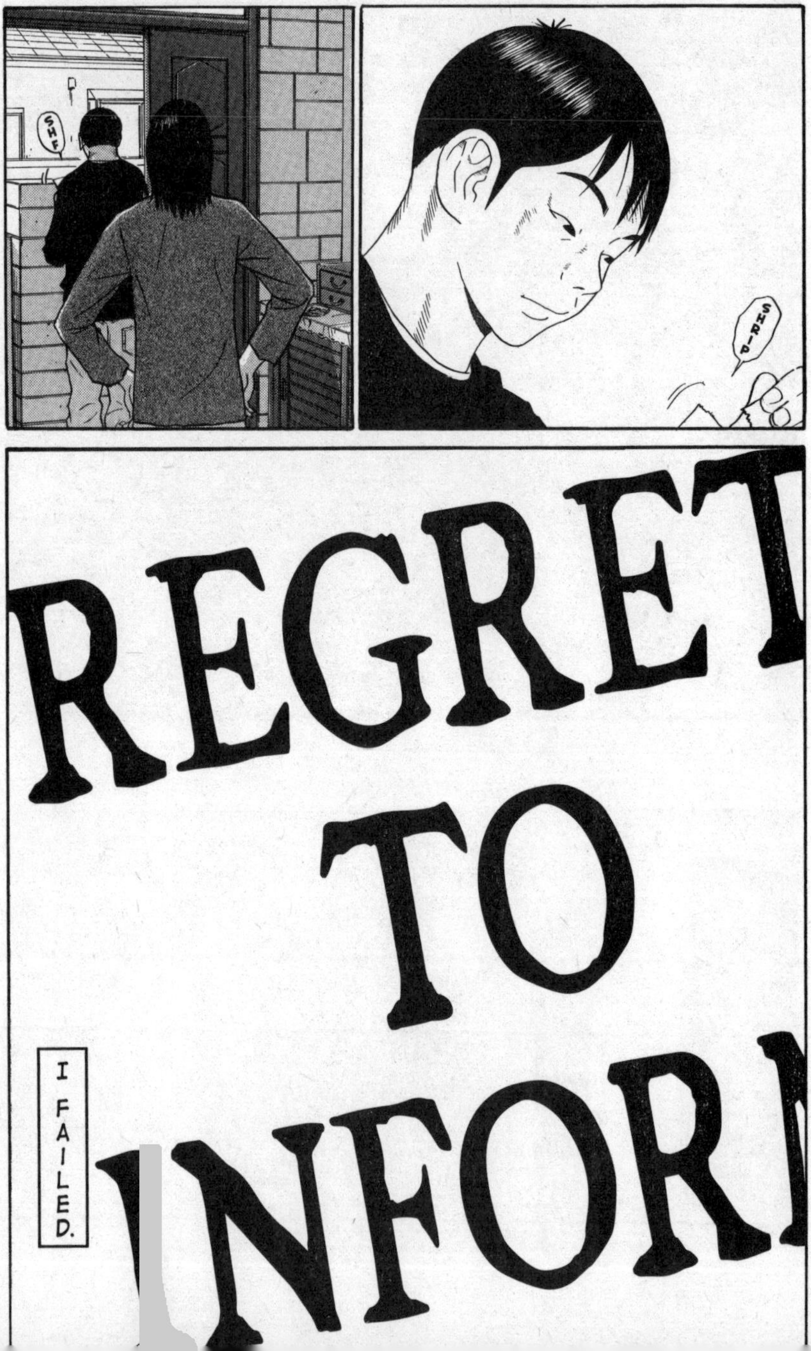
SHRIP
SHF
REGRET
TO
INFOR
I FAILED.

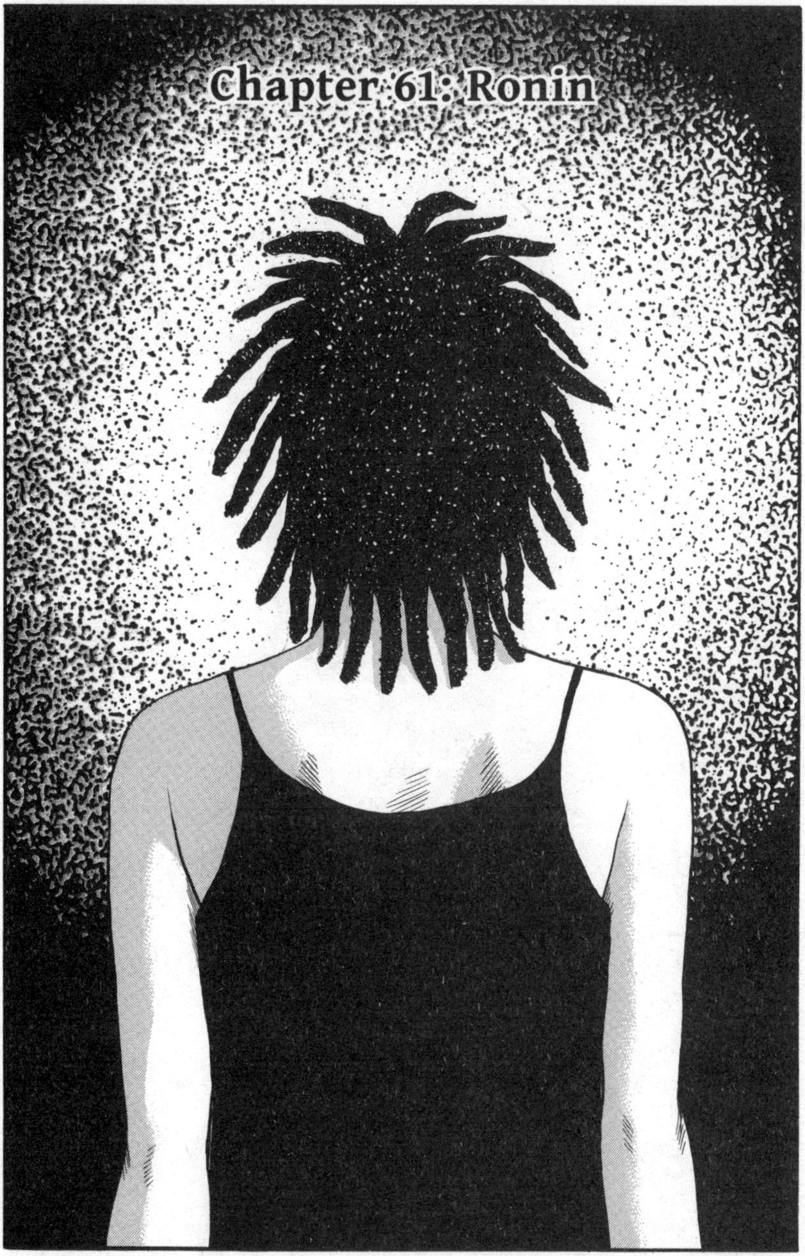
Chapter 61: Ronin

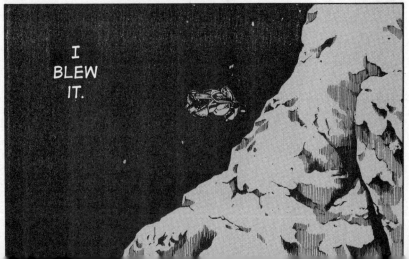

I
BLEW
IT.

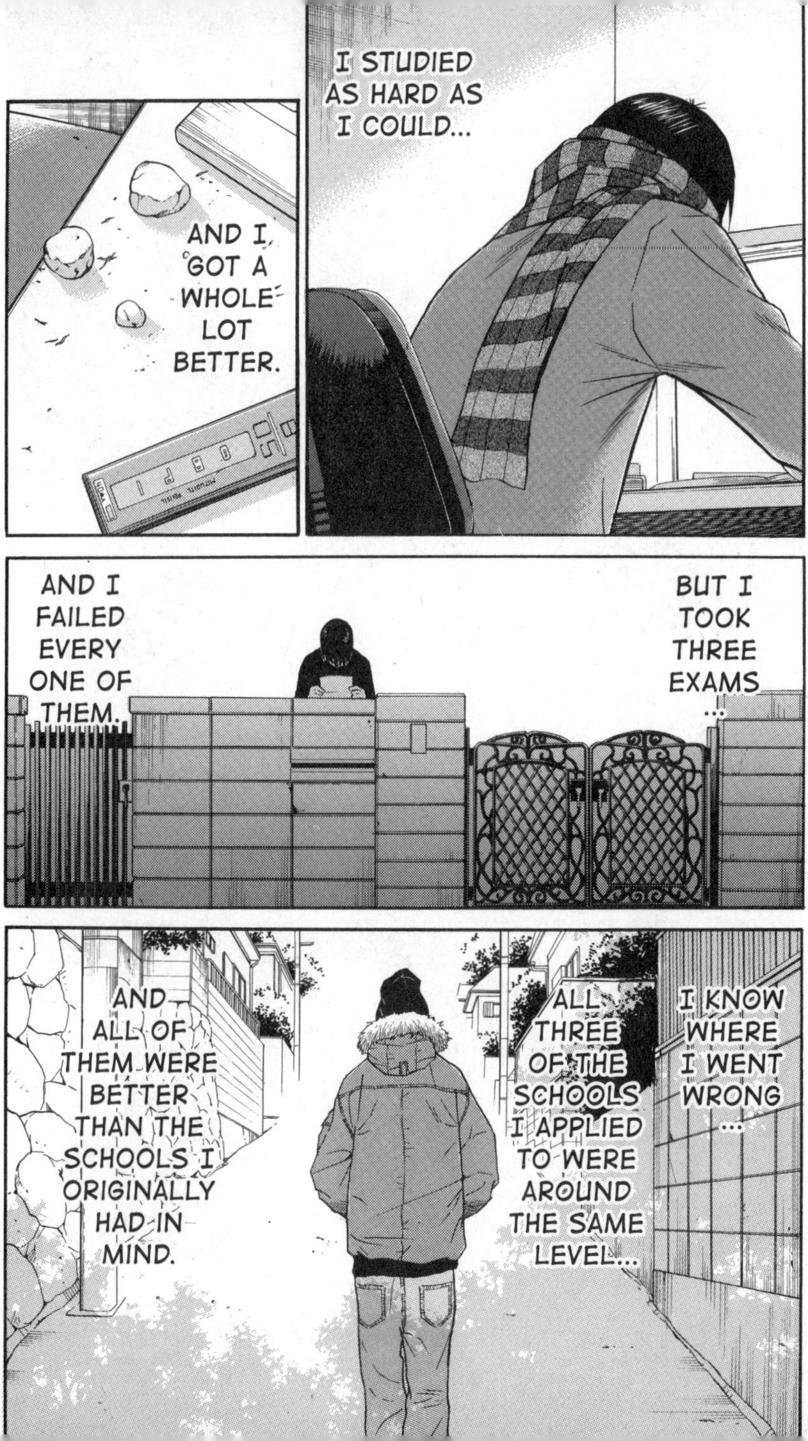
I STUDIED AS HARD AS I COULD...
AND I GOT A WHOLE LOT BETTER.
BUT I TOOK THREE EXAMS...
AND I FAILED EVERY ONE OF THEM.
I KNOW WHERE I WENT WRONG...
ALL THREE OF THE SCHOOLS I APPLIED TO WERE AROUND THE SAME LEVEL...
AND ALL OF THEM WERE BETTER THAN THE SCHOOLS I ORIGINALLY HAD IN MIND.

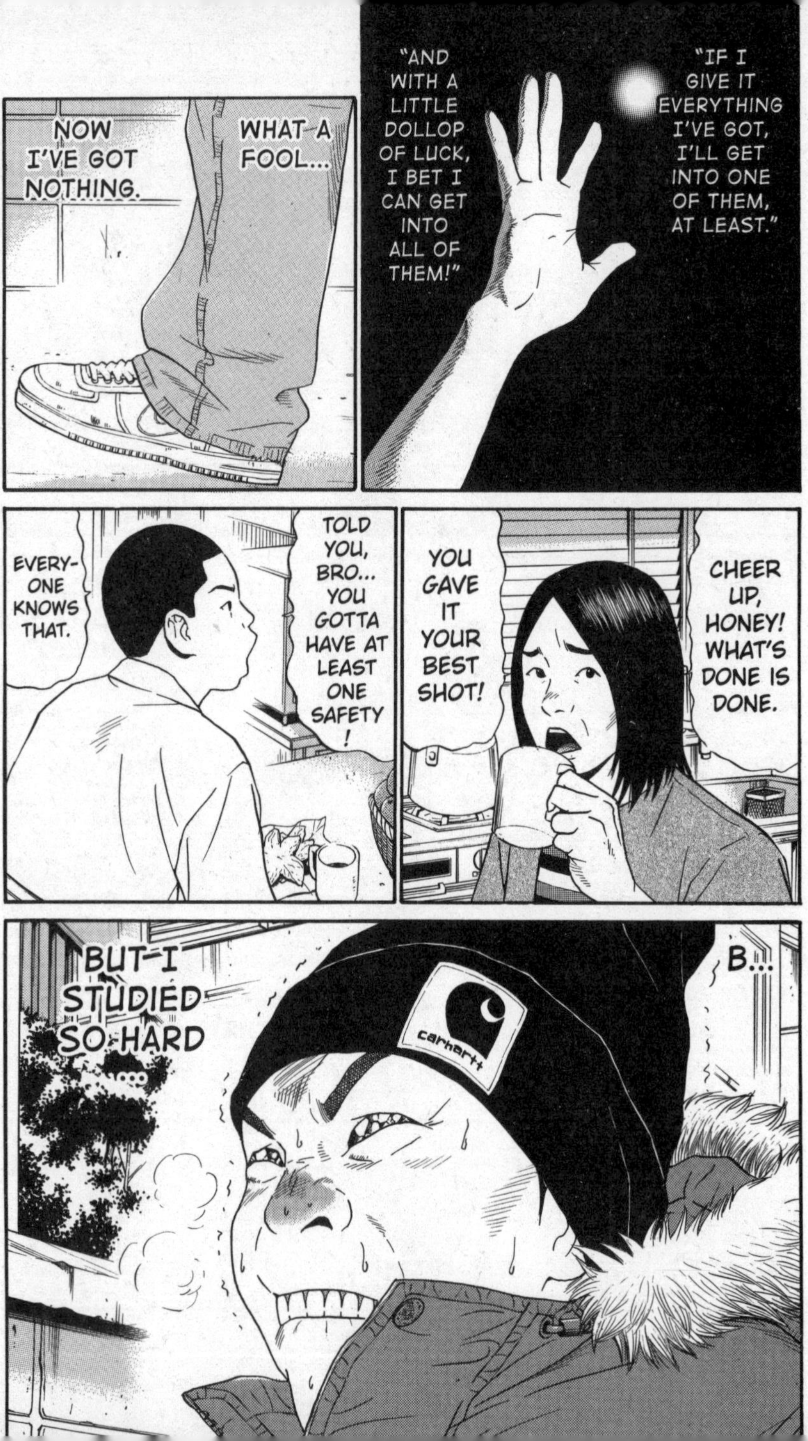
"IF I GIVE IT EVERYTHING I'VE GOT, I'LL GET INTO ONE OF THEM, AT LEAST."
"AND WITH A LITTLE DOLLOP OF LUCK, I BET I CAN GET INTO ALL OF THEM!"
WHAT A FOOL...
NOW I'VE GOT NOTHING.
CHEER UP, HONEY! WHAT'S DONE IS DONE.
YOU GAVE IT YOUR BEST SHOT!
TOLD YOU, BRO... YOU GOTTA HAVE AT LEAST ONE SAFETY!
EVERY-ONE KNOWS THAT.
B...
BUT I STUDIED SO HARD...

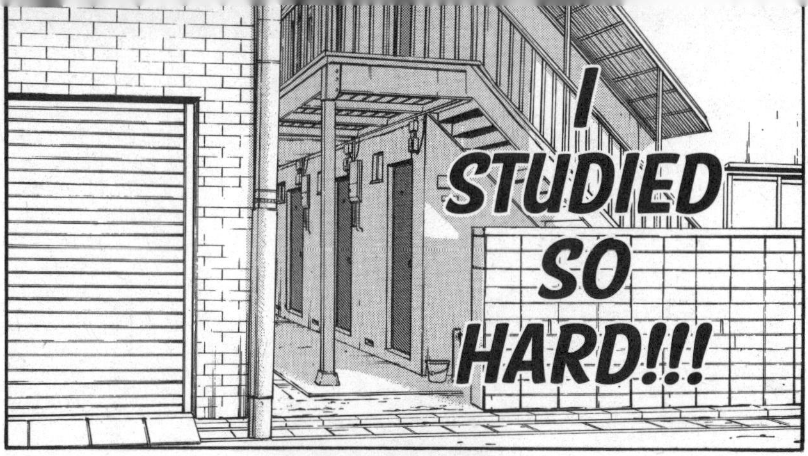
I STUDIED SO HARD!!!

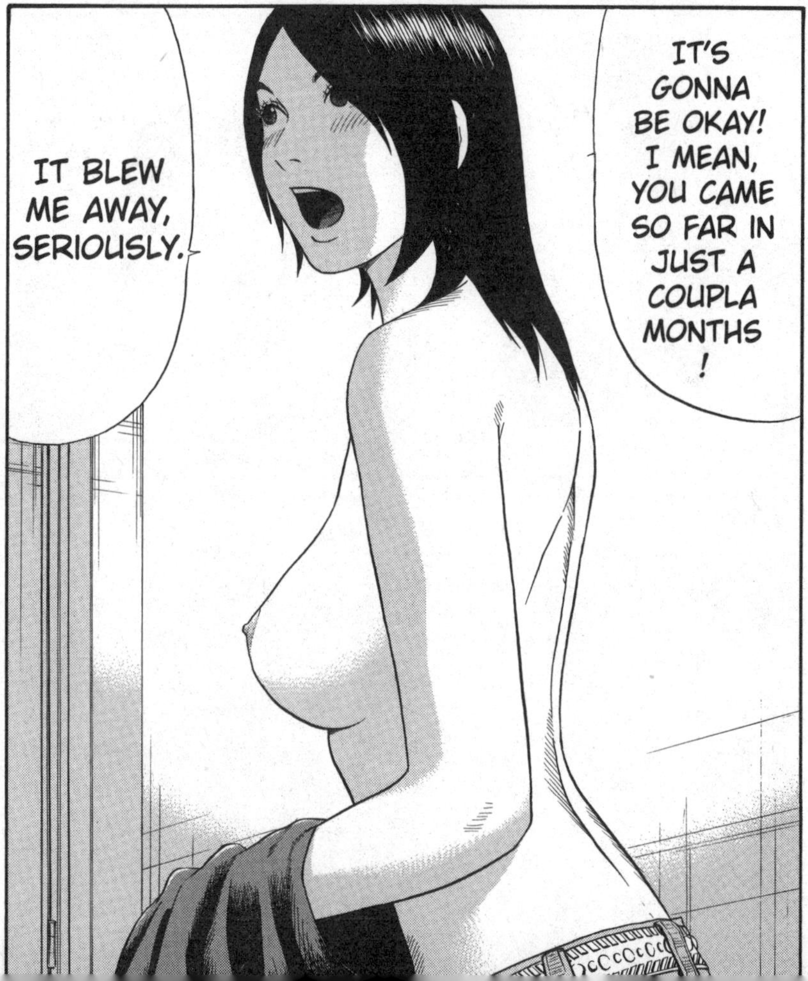
IT'S GONNA BE OKAY! I MEAN, YOU CAME SO FAR IN JUST A COUPLA MONTHS!
IT BLEW ME AWAY, SERIOUSLY.

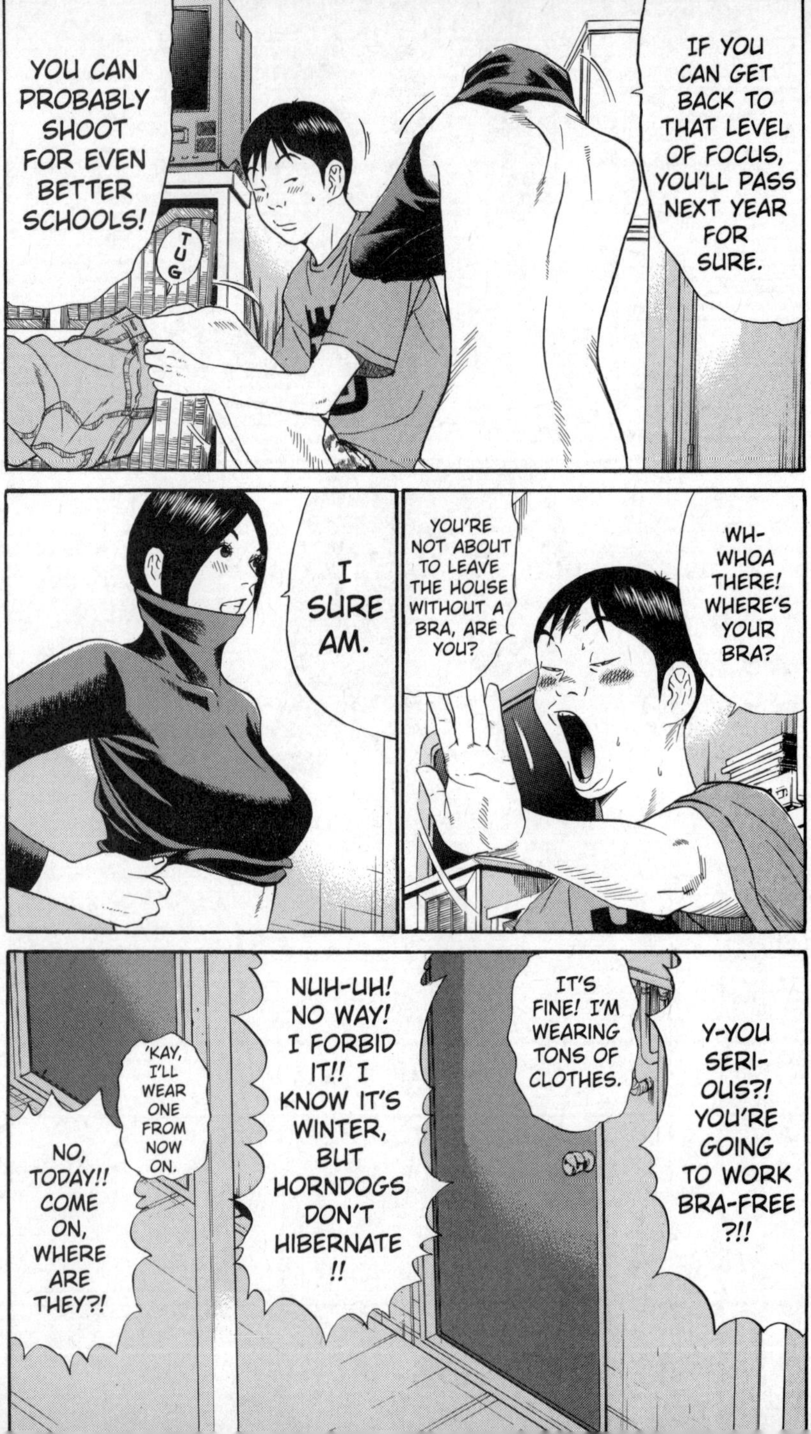
IF YOU CAN GET BACK TO THAT LEVEL OF FOCUS, YOU'LL PASS NEXT YEAR FOR SURE.
YOU CAN PROBABLY SHOOT FOR EVEN BETTER SCHOOLS!
TUG
WH-WHOA THERE! WHERE'S YOUR BRA?
YOU'RE NOT ABOUT TO LEAVE THE HOUSE WITHOUT A BRA, ARE YOU?
I SURE AM.
Y-YOU SERI-OUS?! YOU'RE GOING TO WORK BRA-FREE?!!
IT'S FINE! I'M WEARING TONS OF CLOTHES.
NUH-UH! NO WAY! I FORBID IT!! I KNOW IT'S WINTER, BUT HORNDOGS DON'T HIBERNATE!!
'KAY, I'LL WEAR ONE FROM NOW ON.
NO, TODAY!! COME ON, WHERE ARE THEY?!

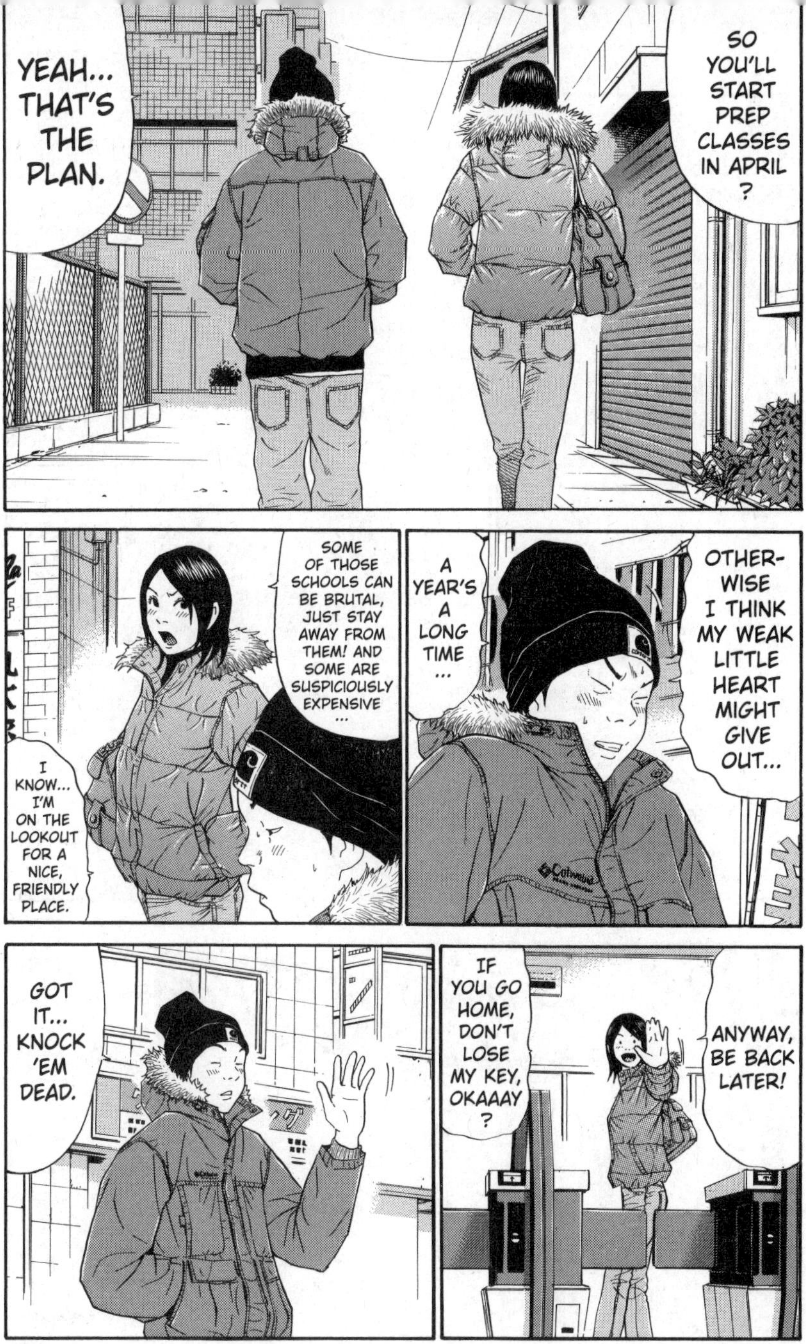
SO YOU'LL START PREP CLASSES IN APRIL?
YEAH... THAT'S THE PLAN.
OTHER-WISE I THINK MY WEAK LITTLE HEART MIGHT GIVE OUT...
A YEAR'S A LONG TIME...
SOME OF THOSE SCHOOLS CAN BE BRUTAL, JUST STAY AWAY FROM THEM! AND SOME ARE SUSPICIOUSLY EXPENSIVE...
I KNOW... I'M ON THE LOOKOUT FOR A NICE, FRIENDLY PLACE.
ANYWAY, BE BACK LATER!
IF YOU GO HOME, DON'T LOSE MY KEY, OKAAAY?
GOT IT... KNOCK 'EM DEAD.

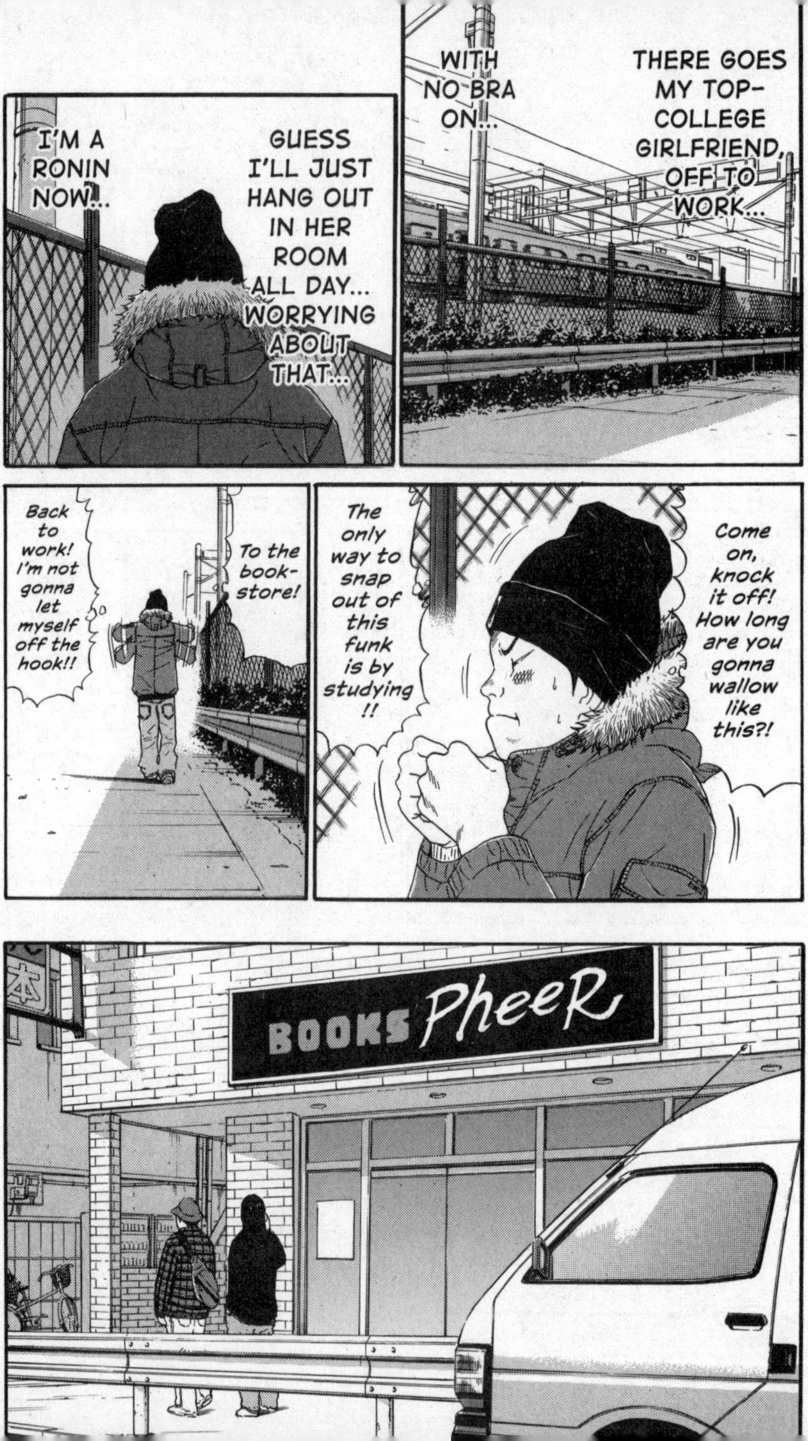
THERE GOES MY TOP-COLLEGE GIRLFRIEND, OFF TO WORK...
WITH NO BRA ON...
GUESS I'LL JUST HANG OUT IN HER ROOM ALL DAY... WORRYING ABOUT THAT...
I'M A RONIN NOW...
Come on, knock it off! How long are you gonna wallow like this?!
The only way to snap out of this funk is by studying!!
To the book-store!
Back to work! I'm not gonna let myself off the hook!!
BOOKS PheeR
本

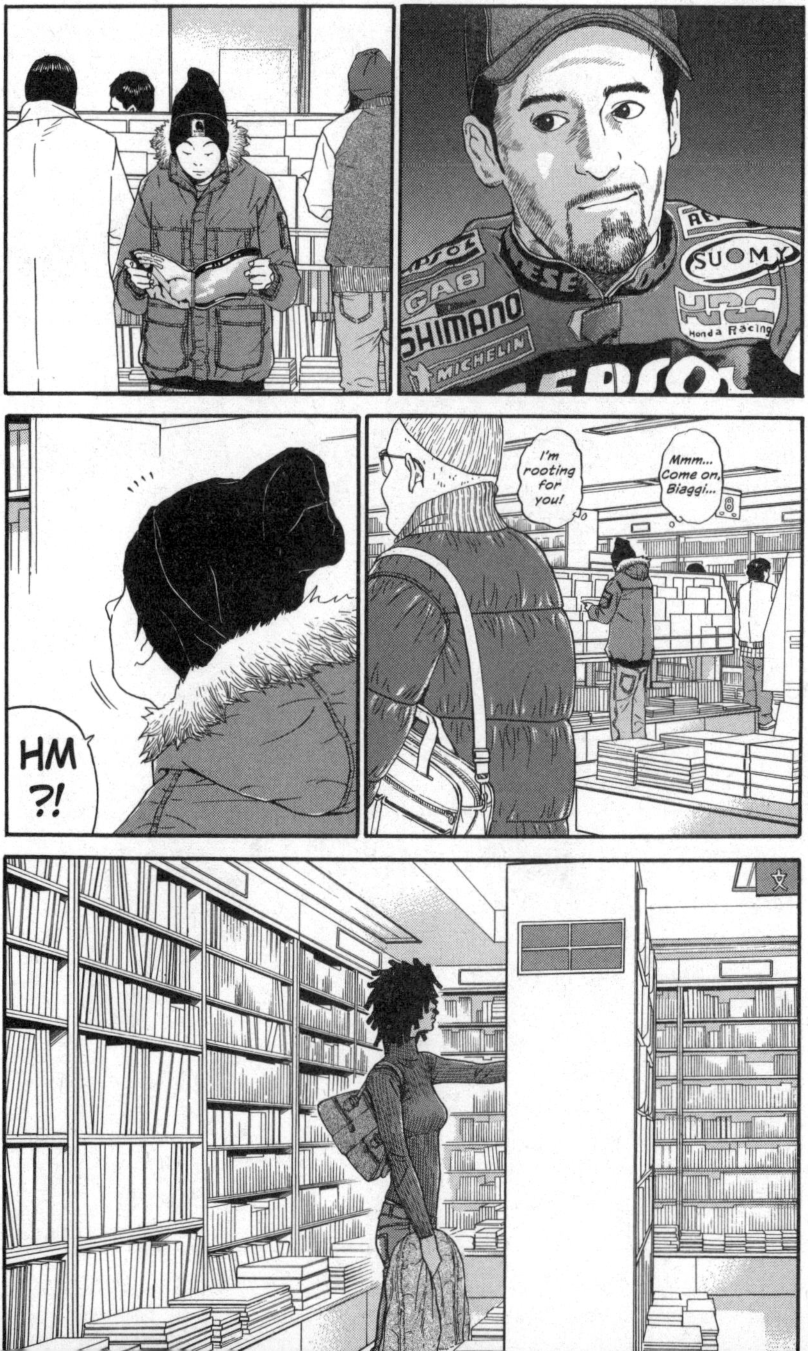
SUOMY
HRC
Honda Racing
SHIMANO
MICHELIN
Mmm... Come on, Biaggi...
I'm rooting for you!
HM ?!
文

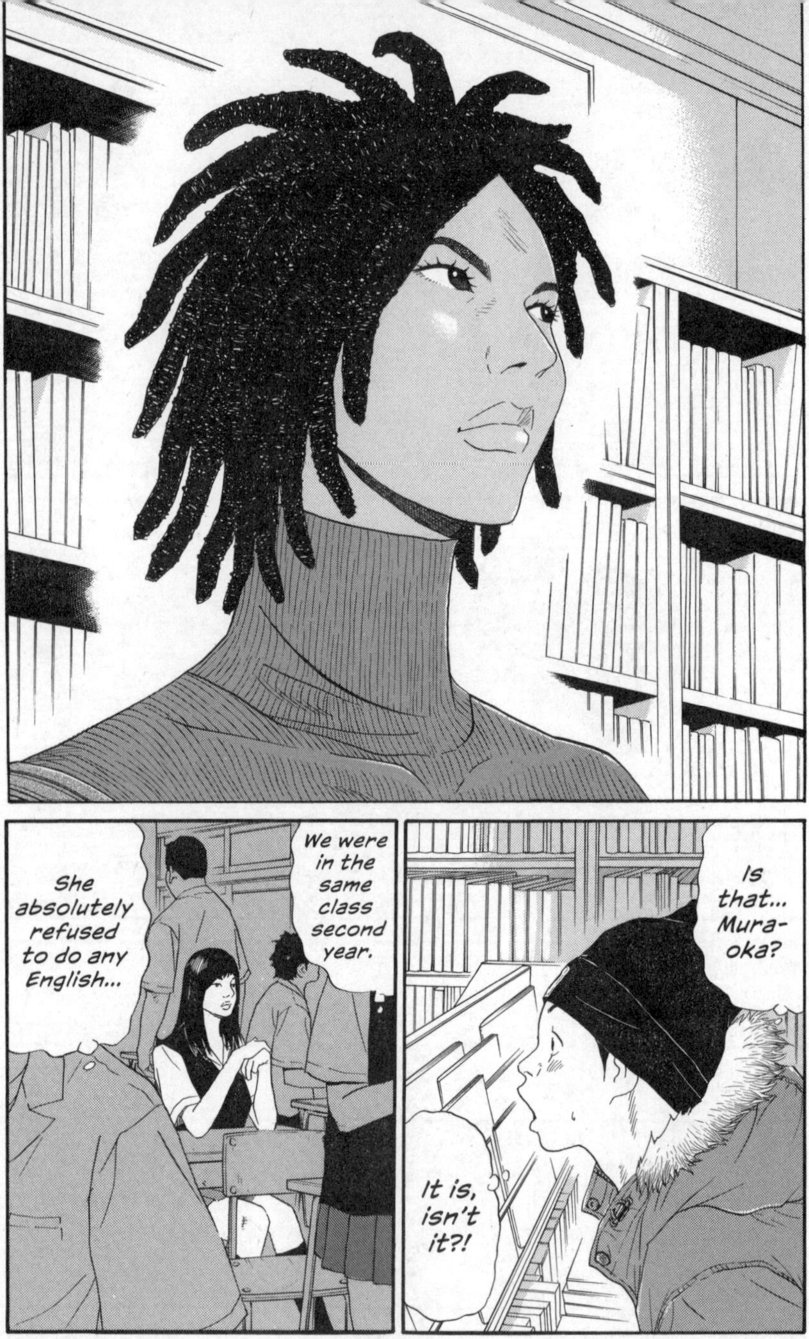
Is that... Mura-oka?
It is, isn't it?!
We were in the same class second year.
She absolutely refused to do any English...

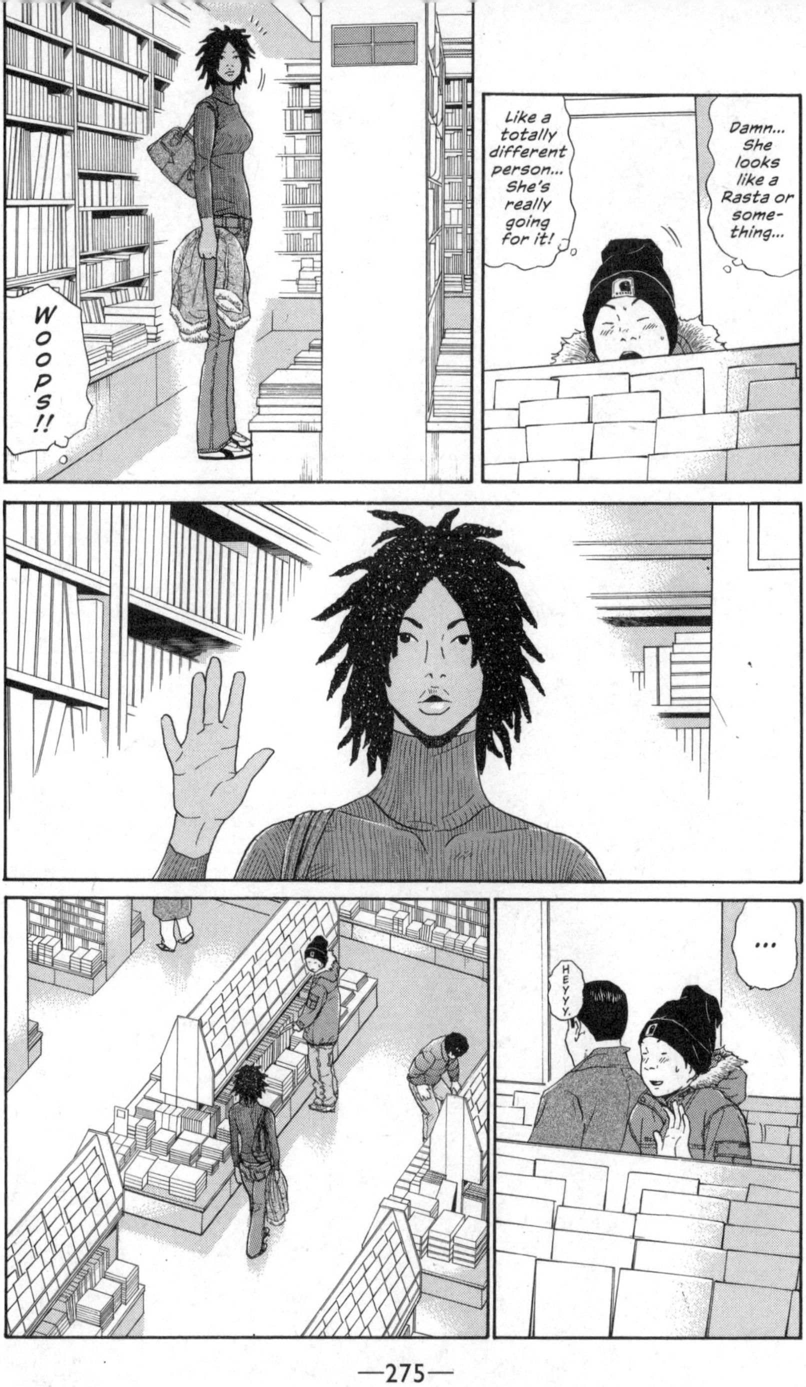
Damn... She looks like a Rasta or some-thing...
Like a totally different person... She's really going for it!
WOOPS!!
...
HEYYY.

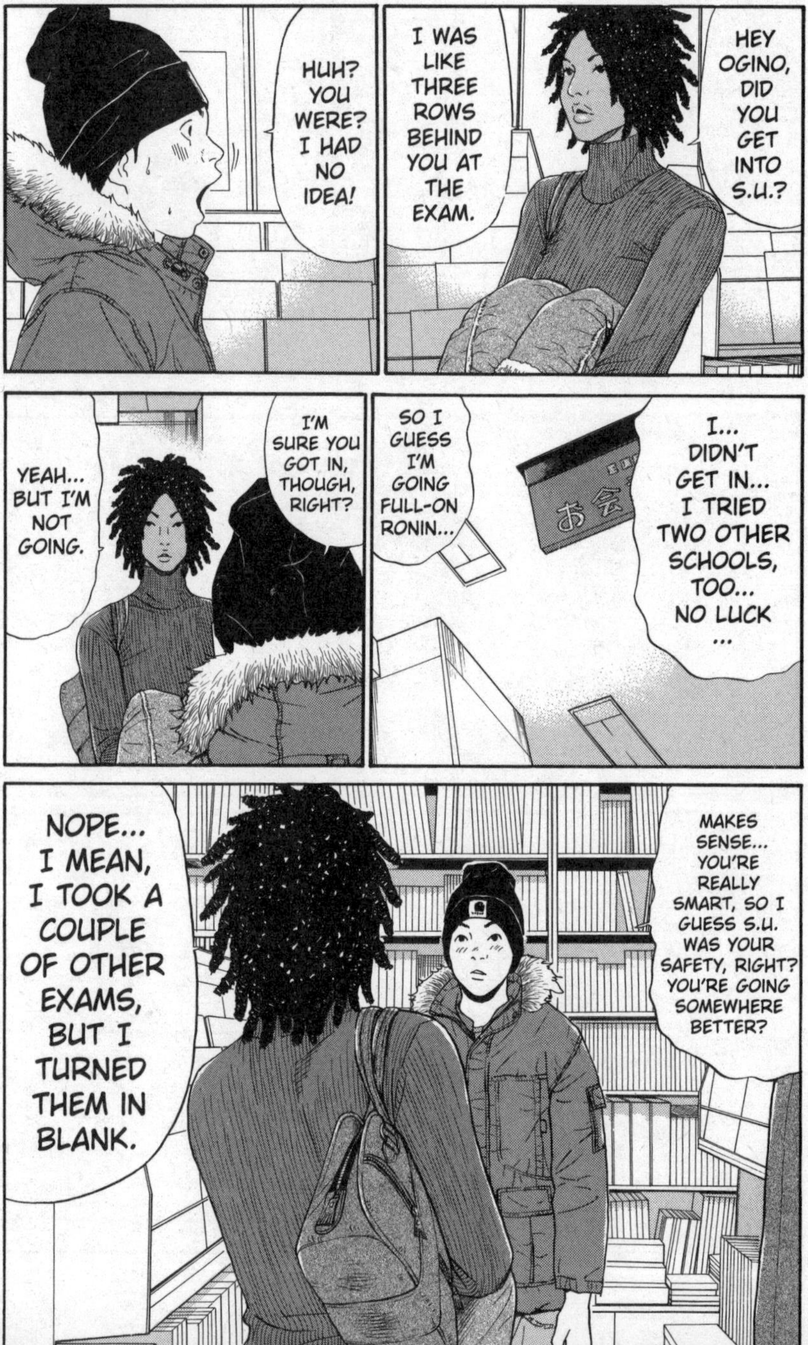
HEY OGINO, DID YOU GET INTO S.U.?
I WAS LIKE THREE ROWS BEHIND YOU AT THE EXAM.
HUH? YOU WERE? I HAD NO IDEA!
I... DIDN'T GET IN... I TRIED TWO OTHER SCHOOLS, TOO... NO LUCK ...
SO I GUESS I'M GOING FULL-ON RONIN...
I'M SURE YOU GOT IN, THOUGH, RIGHT?
YEAH... BUT I'M NOT GOING.
MAKES SENSE... YOU'RE REALLY SMART, SO I GUESS S.U. WAS YOUR SAFETY, RIGHT? YOU'RE GOING SOMEWHERE BETTER?
NOPE... I MEAN, I TOOK A COUPLE OF OTHER EXAMS, BUT I TURNED THEM IN BLANK.

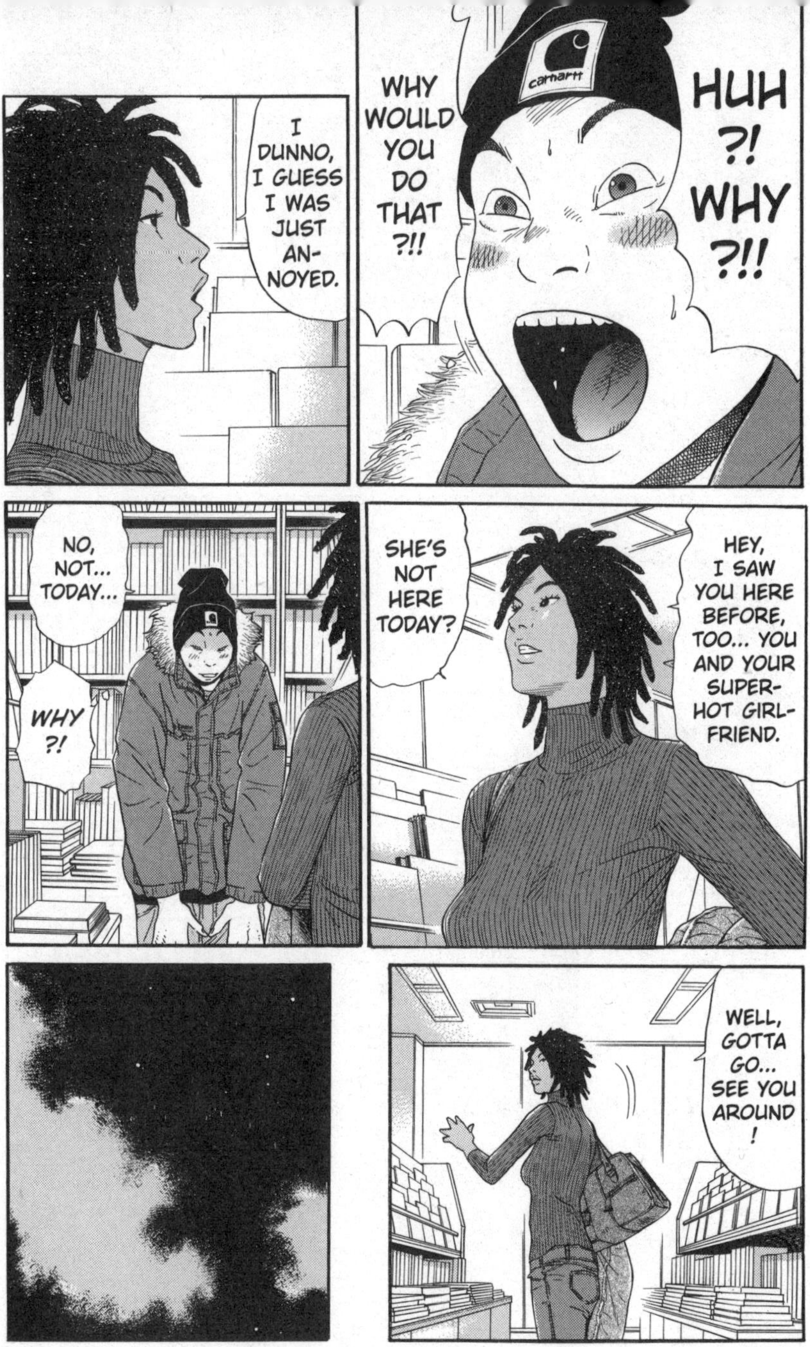
HUH?! WHY WHY?!!
WHY WOULD YOU DO THAT?!!
I DUNNO, I GUESS I WAS JUST ANNOYED.
HEY, I SAW YOU HERE BEFORE, TOO... YOU AND YOUR SUPER-HOT GIRLFRIEND.
SHE'S NOT HERE TODAY?
NO, NOT... TODAY...
WHY?!
WELL, GOTTA GO... SEE YOU AROUND!

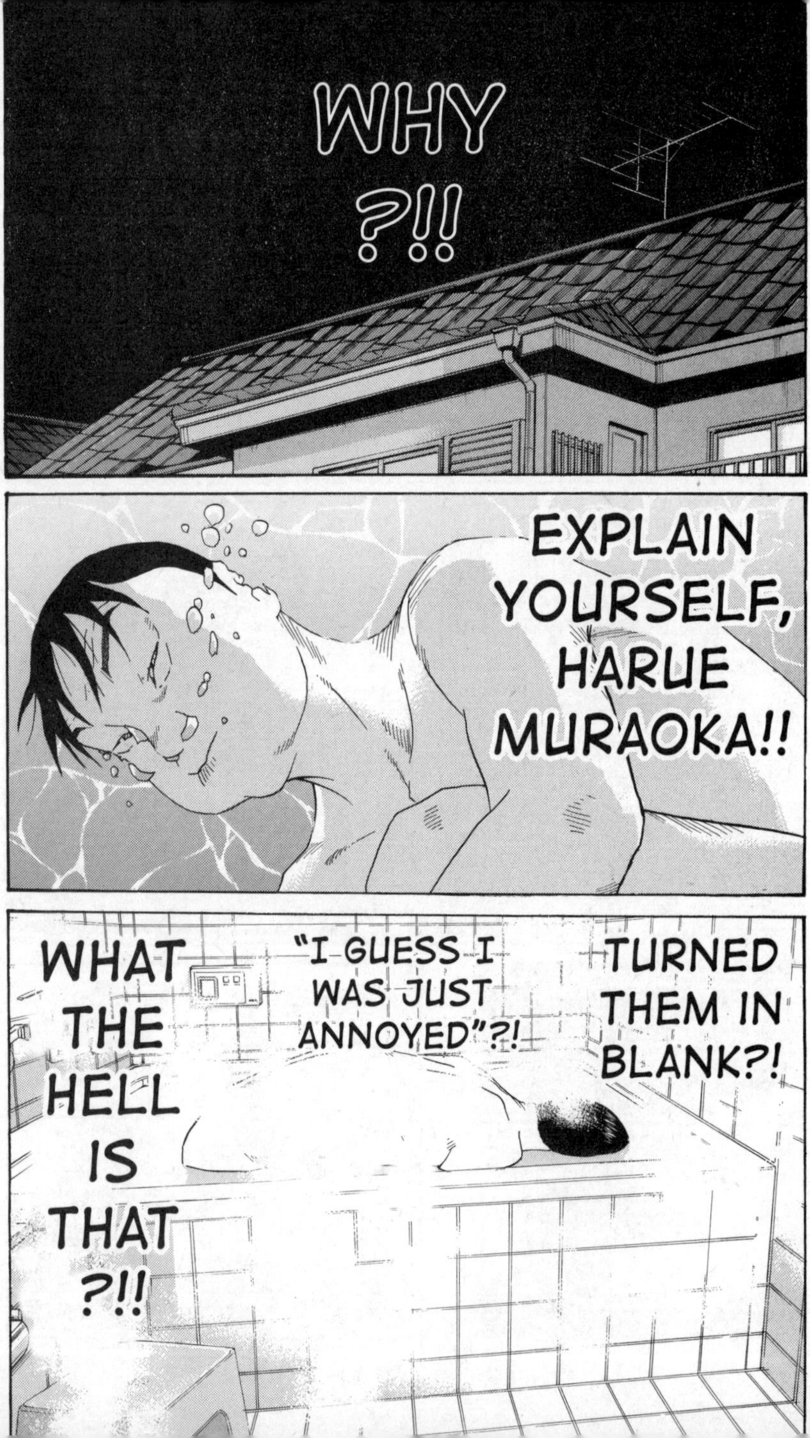
WHY ?!!
EXPLAIN YOURSELF, HARUE MURAOKA!!
TURNED THEM IN BLANK?!
"I GUESS I WAS JUST ANNOYED"?!
WHAT THE HELL IS THAT ?!!

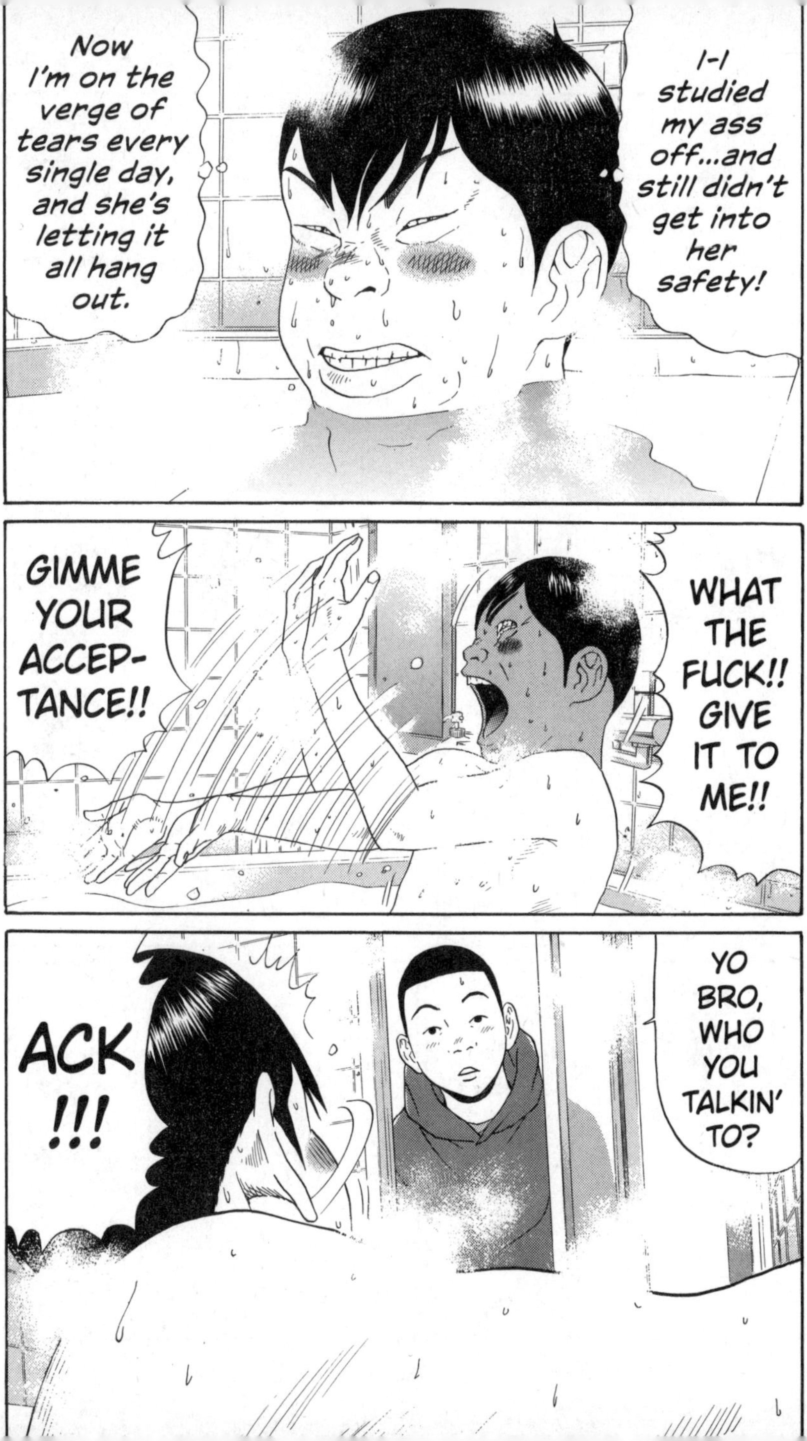
I-I studied my ass off...and still didn't get into her safety!
Now I'm on the verge of tears every single day, and she's letting it all hang out.
WHAT THE FUCK!! GIVE IT TO ME!!
GIMME YOUR ACCEPTANCE!!
YO BRO, WHO YOU TALKIN' TO?
ACK!!!

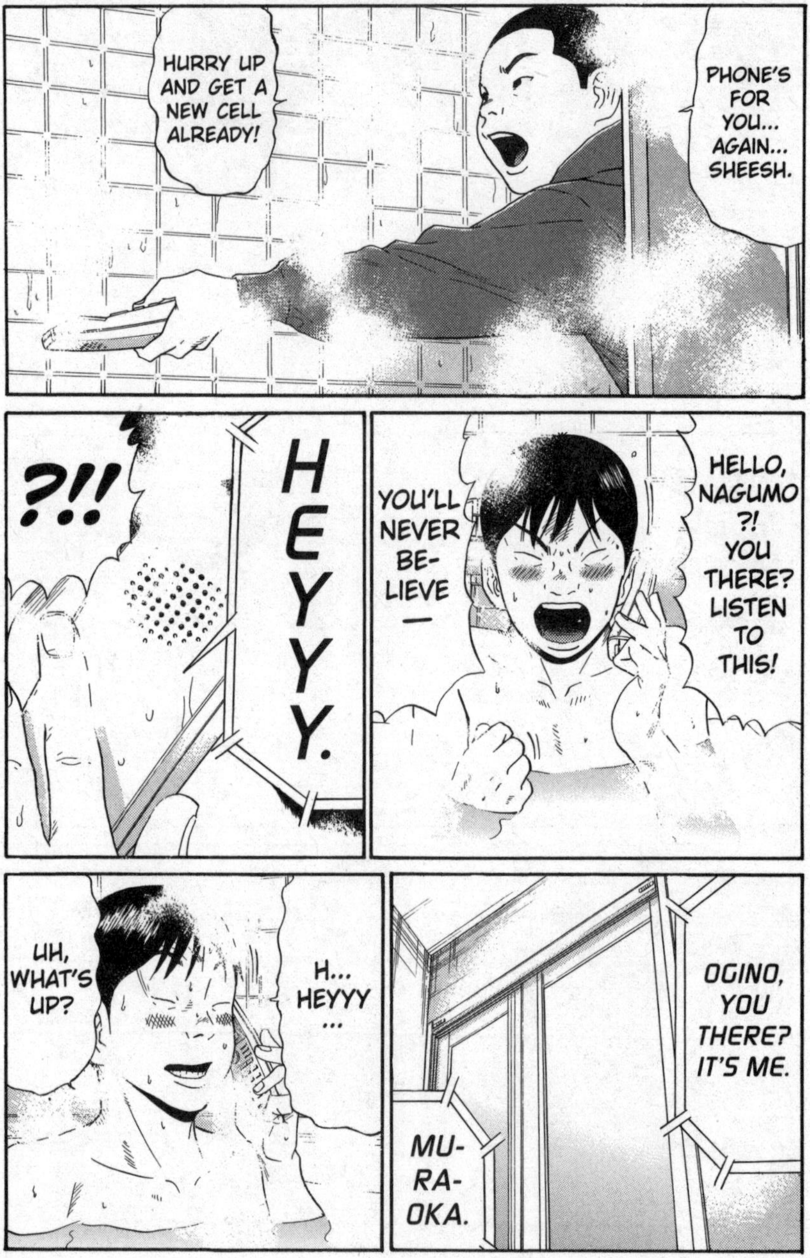
PHONE'S FOR YOU... AGAIN... SHEESH.
HURRY UP AND GET A NEW CELL ALREADY!
HELLO, NAGUMO ?! YOU THERE? LISTEN TO THIS!
YOU'LL NEVER BE- LIEVE —
HEYY.
?!!
OGINO, YOU THERE? IT'S ME.
MU- RA- OKA.
H... HEYYY ...
UH, WHAT'S UP?

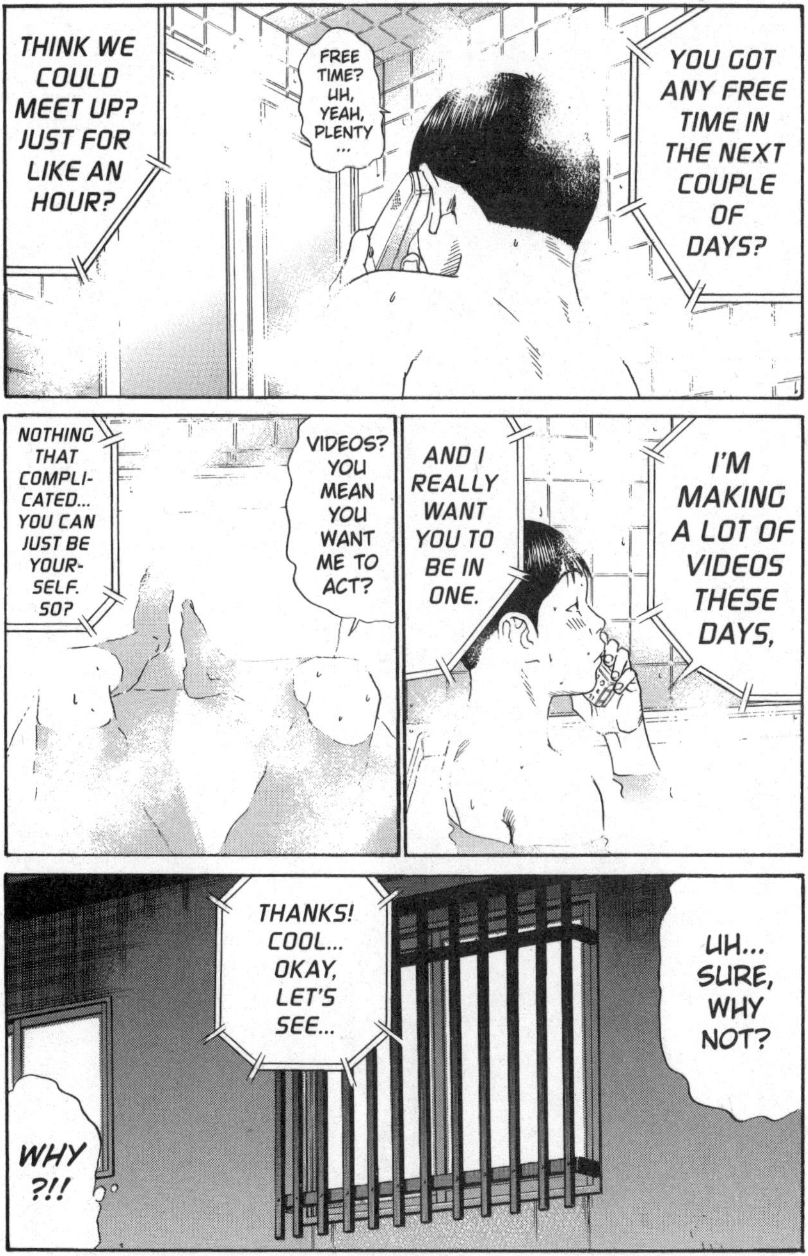
YOU GOT ANY FREE TIME IN THE NEXT COUPLE OF DAYS?
FREE TIME? UH, YEAH, PLENTY...
THINK WE COULD MEET UP? JUST FOR LIKE AN HOUR?
I'M MAKING A LOT OF VIDEOS THESE DAYS,
AND I REALLY WANT YOU TO BE IN ONE.
VIDEOS? YOU MEAN YOU WANT ME TO ACT?
NOTHING THAT COMPLICATED... YOU CAN JUST BE YOURSELF. SO?
UH... SURE, WHY NOT?
THANKS! COOL... OKAY, LET'S SEE...
WHY ?!!

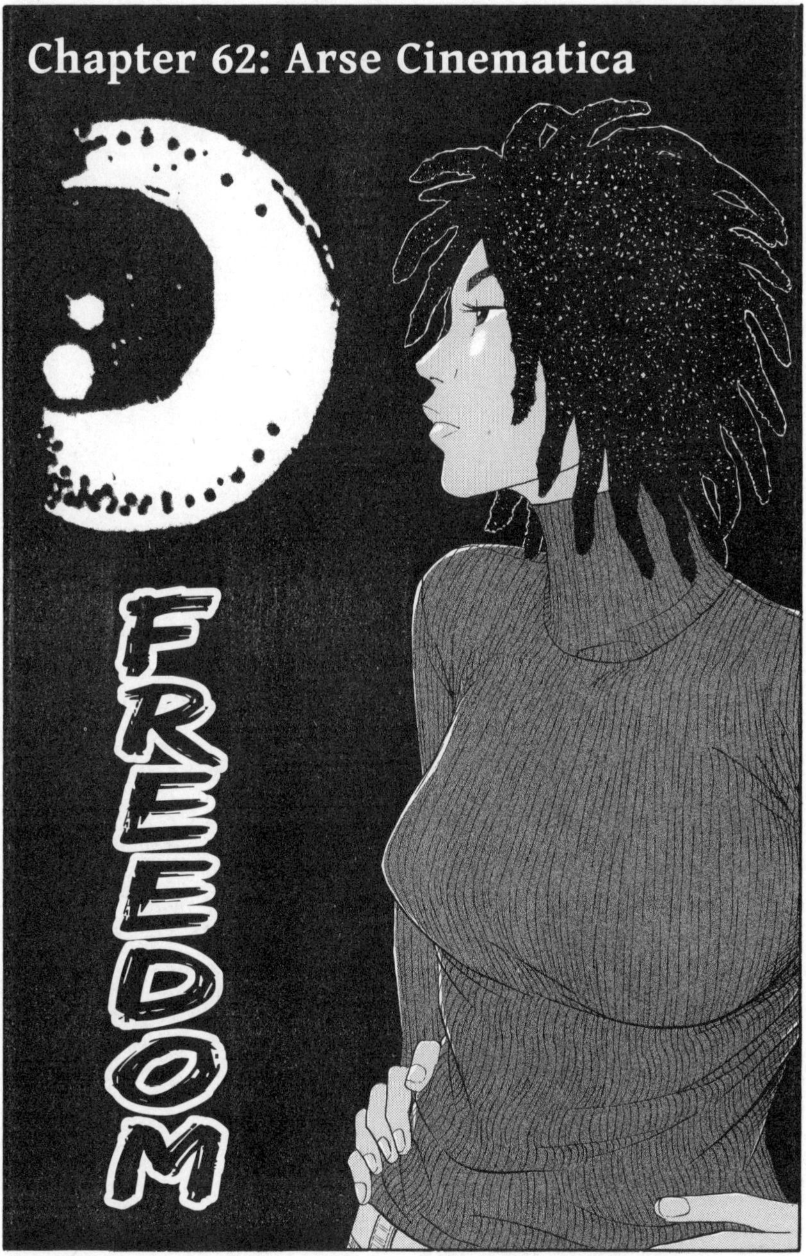
Chapter 62: Arse Cinematica
FREEDOM

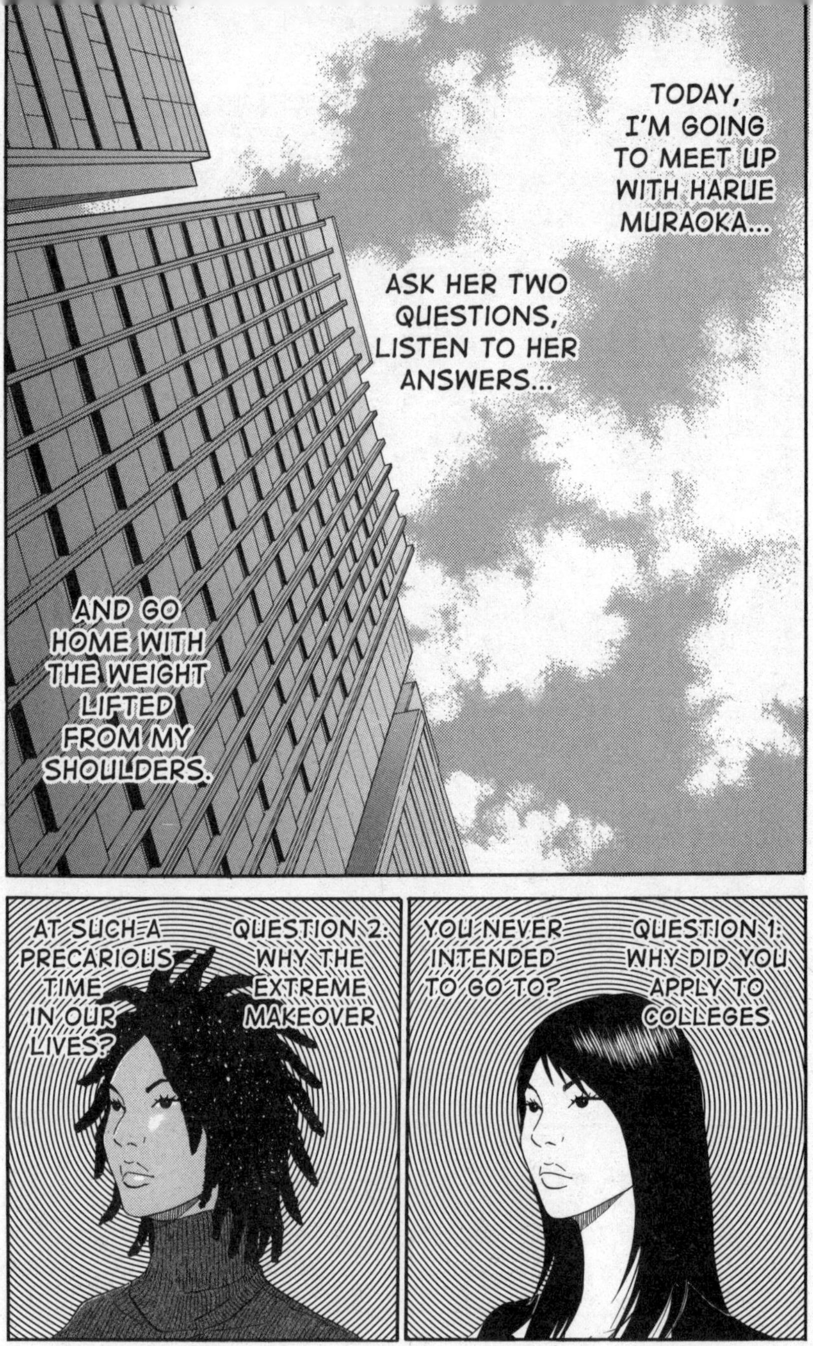
TODAY, I'M GOING TO MEET UP WITH HARUE MURAOKA...
ASK HER TWO QUESTIONS, LISTEN TO HER ANSWERS...
AND GO HOME WITH THE WEIGHT LIFTED FROM MY SHOULDERS.
QUESTION 1: WHY DID YOU APPLY TO COLLEGES
YOU NEVER INTENDED TO GO TO?
QUESTION 2: WHY THE EXTREME MAKEOVER
AT SUCH A PRECARIOUS TIME IN OUR LIVES?

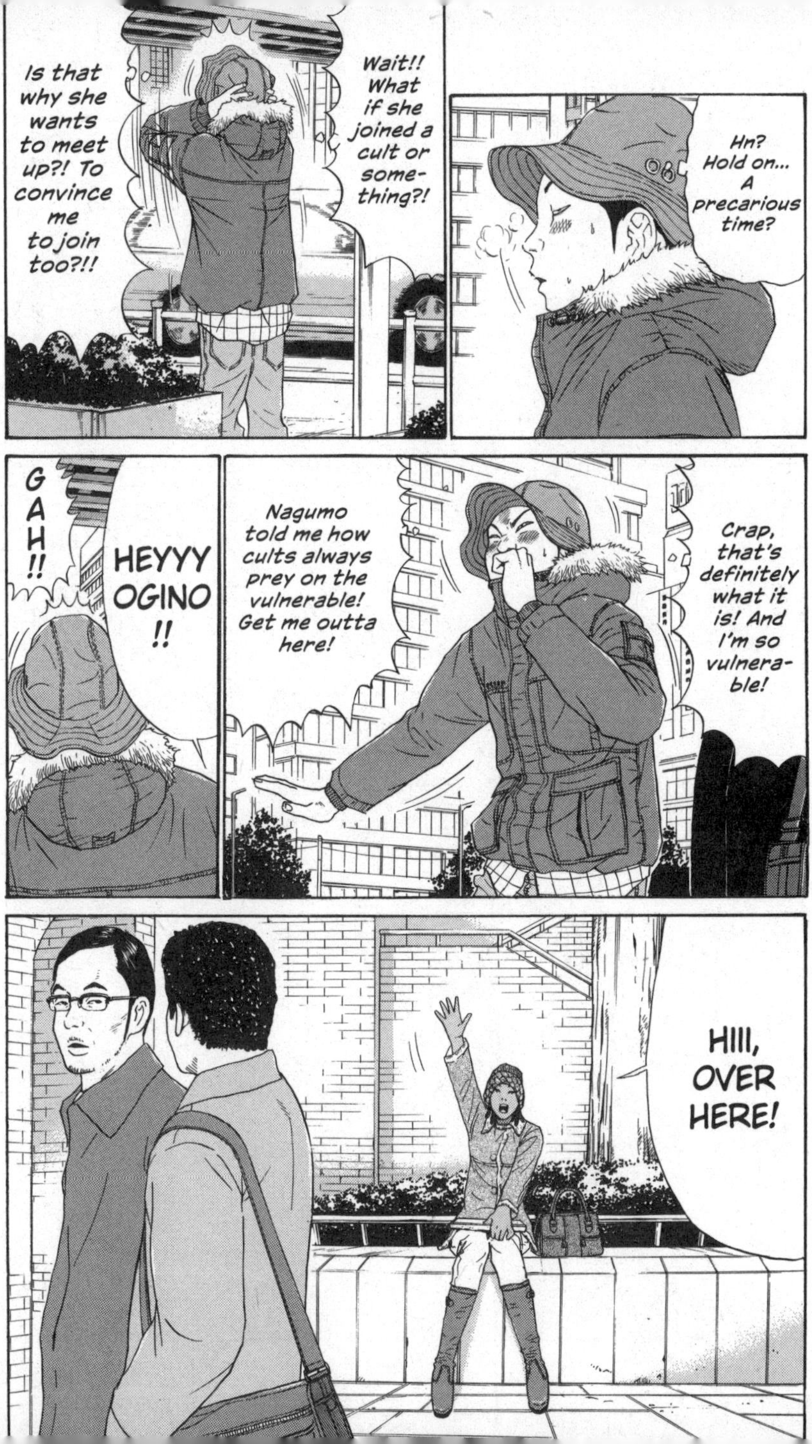
Hn? Hold on... A precarious time?
Wait!! What if she joined a cult or some-thing?!
Is that why she wants to meet up?! To convince me to join too?!!
Crap, that's definitely what it is! And I'm so vulnera-ble!
Nagumo told me how cults always prey on the vulnerable! Get me outta here!
HEYYY OGINO !!
GAH!!
HIII, OVER HERE!

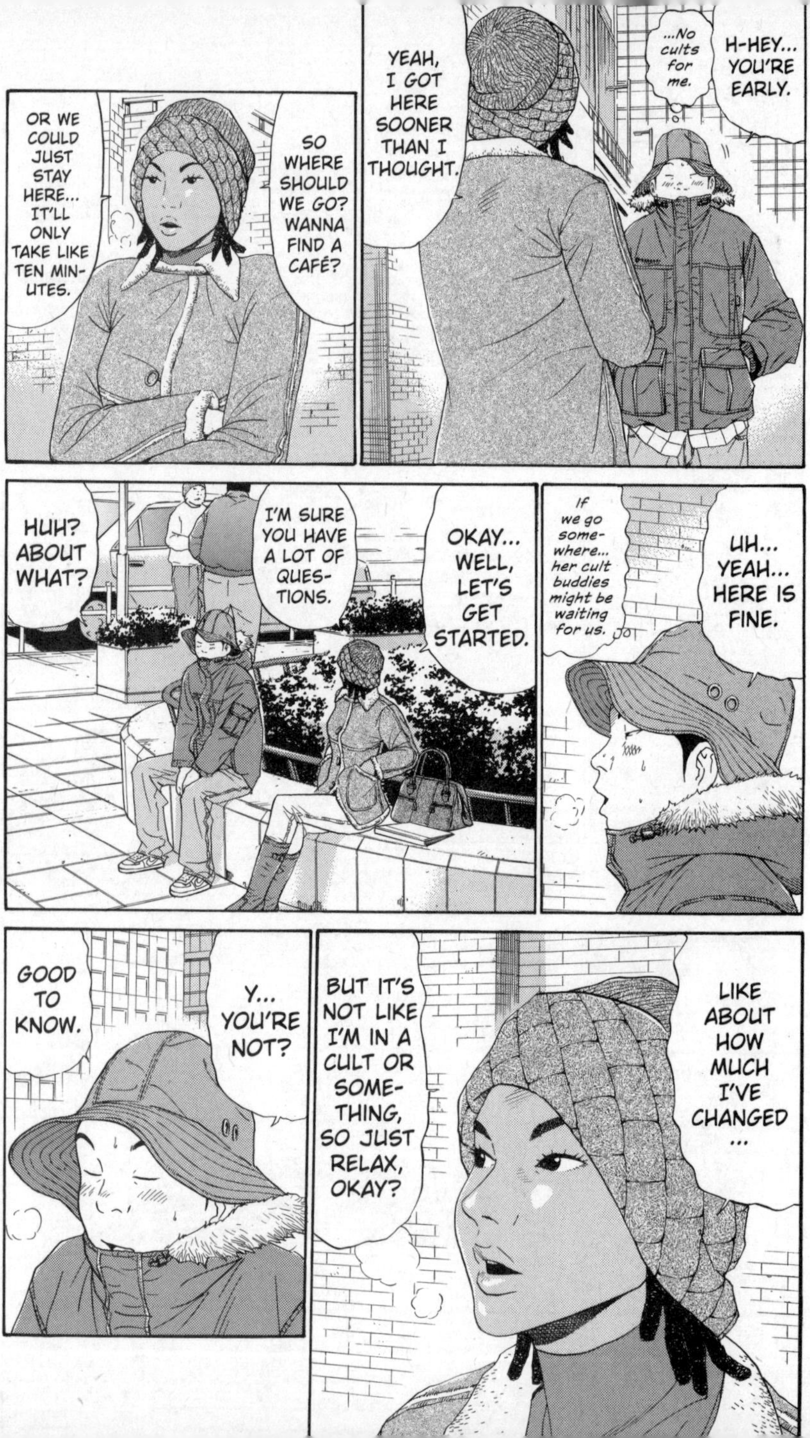
H-HEY... YOU'RE EARLY.
...No cults for me.
YEAH, I GOT HERE SOONER THAN I THOUGHT.
SO WHERE SHOULD WE GO? WANNA FIND A CAFÉ?
OR WE COULD JUST STAY HERE... IT'LL ONLY TAKE LIKE TEN MINUTES.
UH... YEAH... HERE IS FINE.
If we go somewhere... her cult buddies might be waiting for us.
OKAY... WELL, LET'S GET STARTED.
I'M SURE YOU HAVE A LOT OF QUESTIONS.
HUH? ABOUT WHAT?
LIKE ABOUT HOW MUCH I'VE CHANGED...
BUT IT'S NOT LIKE I'M IN A CULT OR SOMETHING, SO JUST RELAX, OKAY?
Y... YOU'RE NOT?
GOOD TO KNOW.

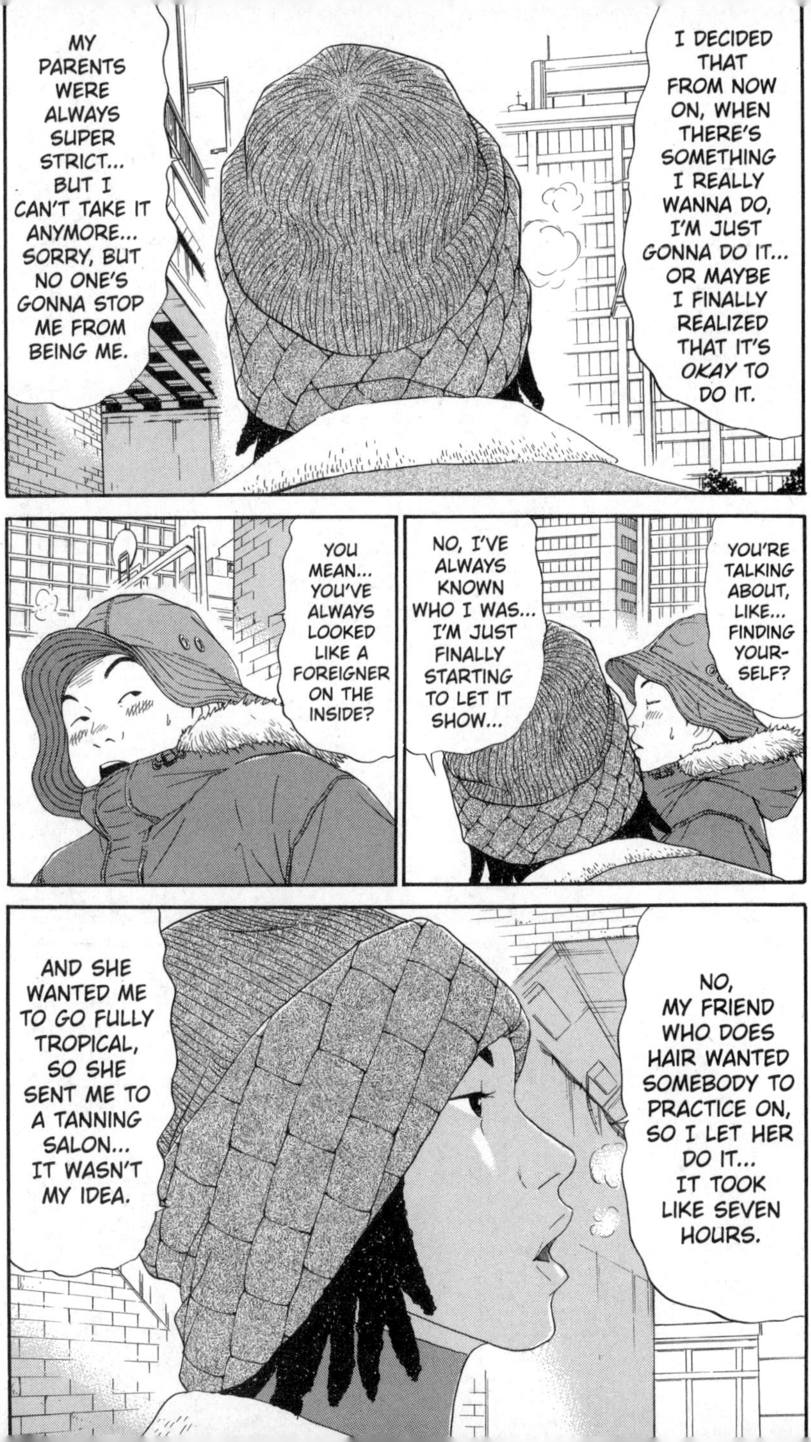
I DECIDED THAT FROM NOW ON, WHEN THERE'S SOMETHING I REALLY WANNA DO, I'M JUST GONNA DO IT... OR MAYBE I FINALLY REALIZED THAT IT'S *OKAY* TO DO IT.
MY PARENTS WERE ALWAYS SUPER STRICT... BUT I CAN'T TAKE IT ANYMORE... SORRY, BUT NO ONE'S GONNA STOP ME FROM BEING ME.
YOU'RE TALKING ABOUT, LIKE... FINDING YOUR-SELF?
NO, I'VE ALWAYS KNOWN WHO I WAS... I'M JUST FINALLY STARTING TO LET IT SHOW...
YOU MEAN... YOU'VE ALWAYS LOOKED LIKE A FOREIGNER ON THE INSIDE?
NO, MY FRIEND WHO DOES HAIR WANTED SOMEBODY TO PRACTICE ON, SO I LET HER DO IT... IT TOOK LIKE SEVEN HOURS.
AND SHE WANTED ME TO GO FULLY TROPICAL, SO SHE SENT ME TO A TANNING SALON... IT WASN'T MY IDEA.

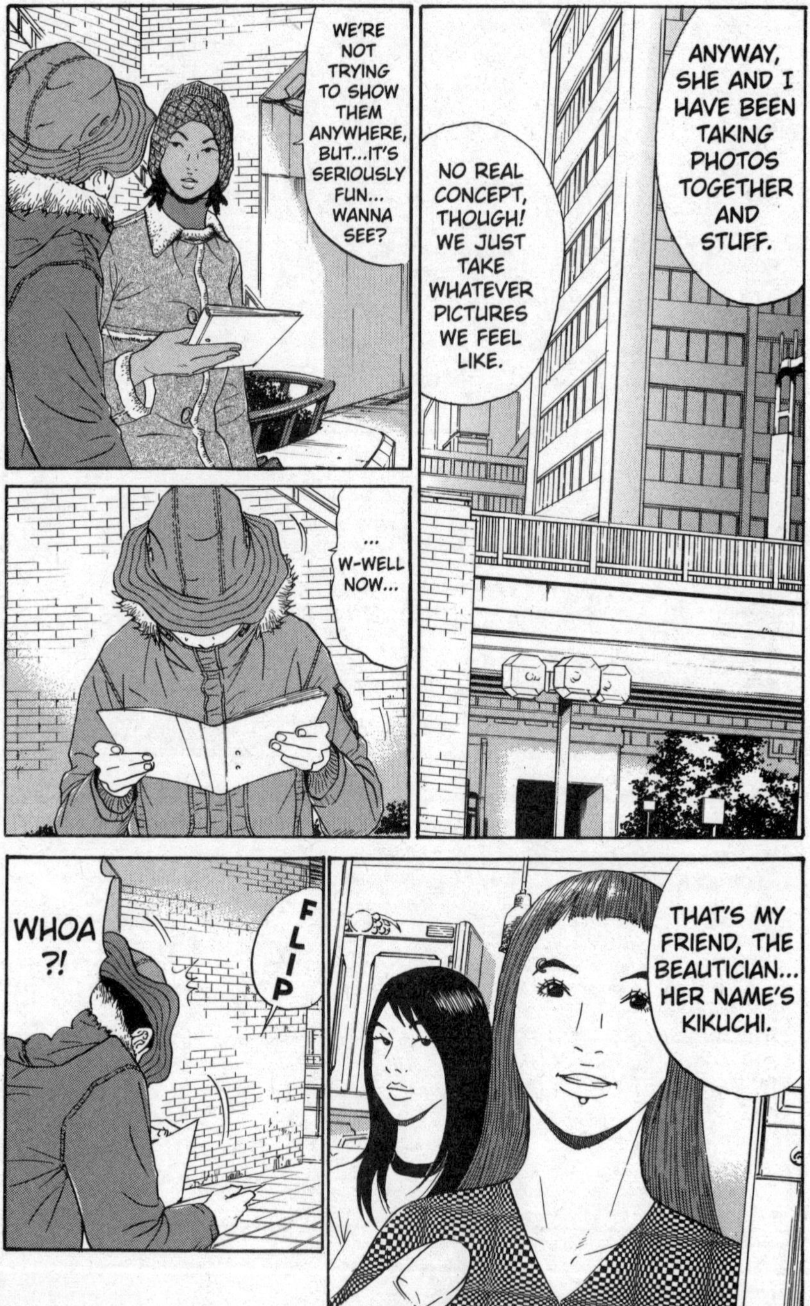
ANYWAY, SHE AND I HAVE BEEN TAKING PHOTOS TOGETHER AND STUFF.
NO REAL CONCEPT, THOUGH! WE JUST TAKE WHATEVER PICTURES WE FEEL LIKE.
WE'RE NOT TRYING TO SHOW THEM ANYWHERE, BUT...IT'S SERIOUSLY FUN... WANNA SEE?
... W-WELL NOW...
THAT'S MY FRIEND, THE BEAUTICIAN... HER NAME'S KIKUCHI.
FLIP
WHOA ?!

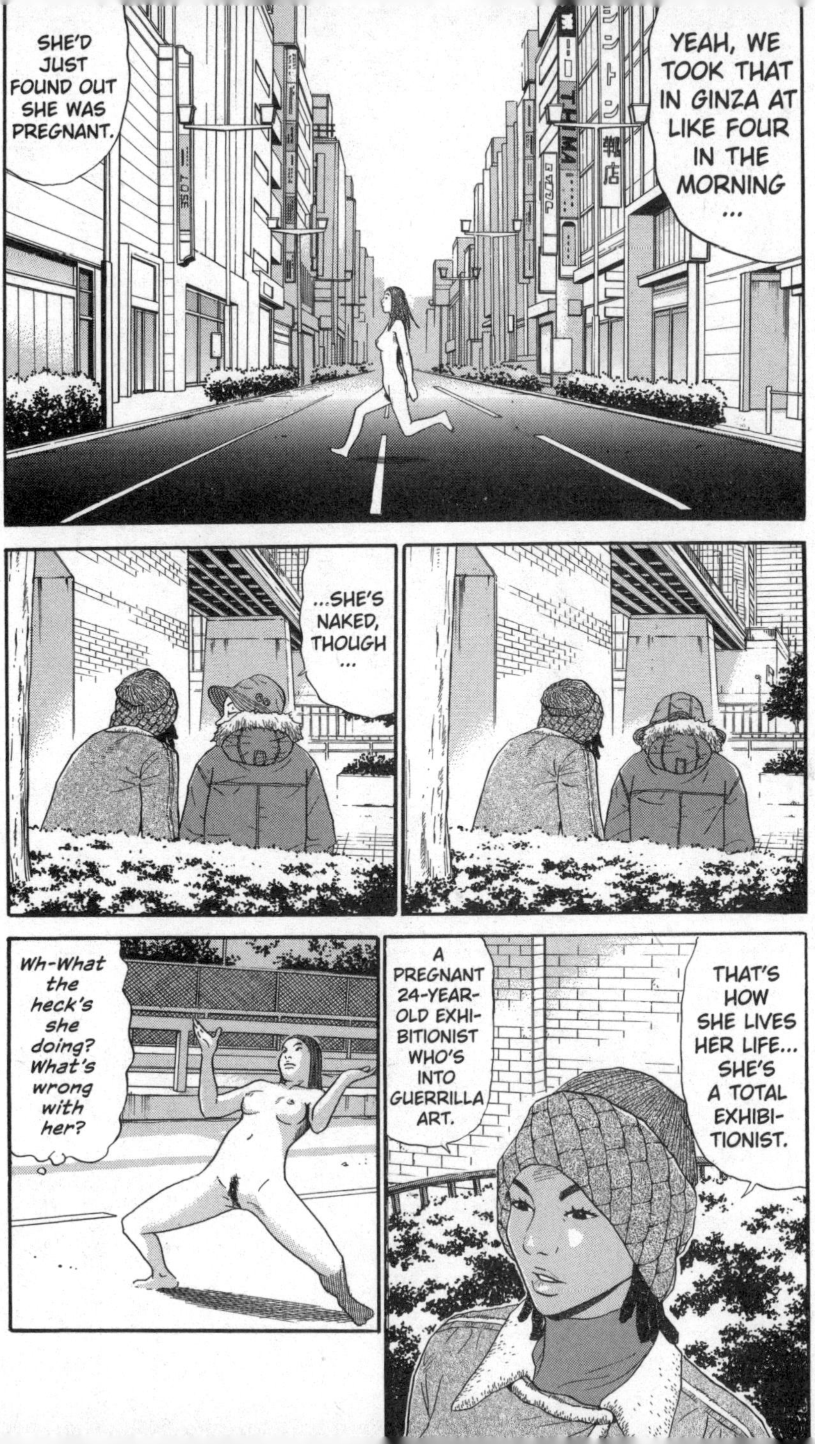
YEAH, WE TOOK THAT IN GINZA AT LIKE FOUR IN THE MORNING ...
SHE'D JUST FOUND OUT SHE WAS PREGNANT.
...SHE'S NAKED, THOUGH ...
THAT'S HOW SHE LIVES HER LIFE... SHE'S A TOTAL EXHIBITIONIST.
A PREGNANT 24-YEAR-OLD EXHIBITIONIST WHO'S INTO GUERRILLA ART.
Wh-What the heck's she doing? What's wrong with her?

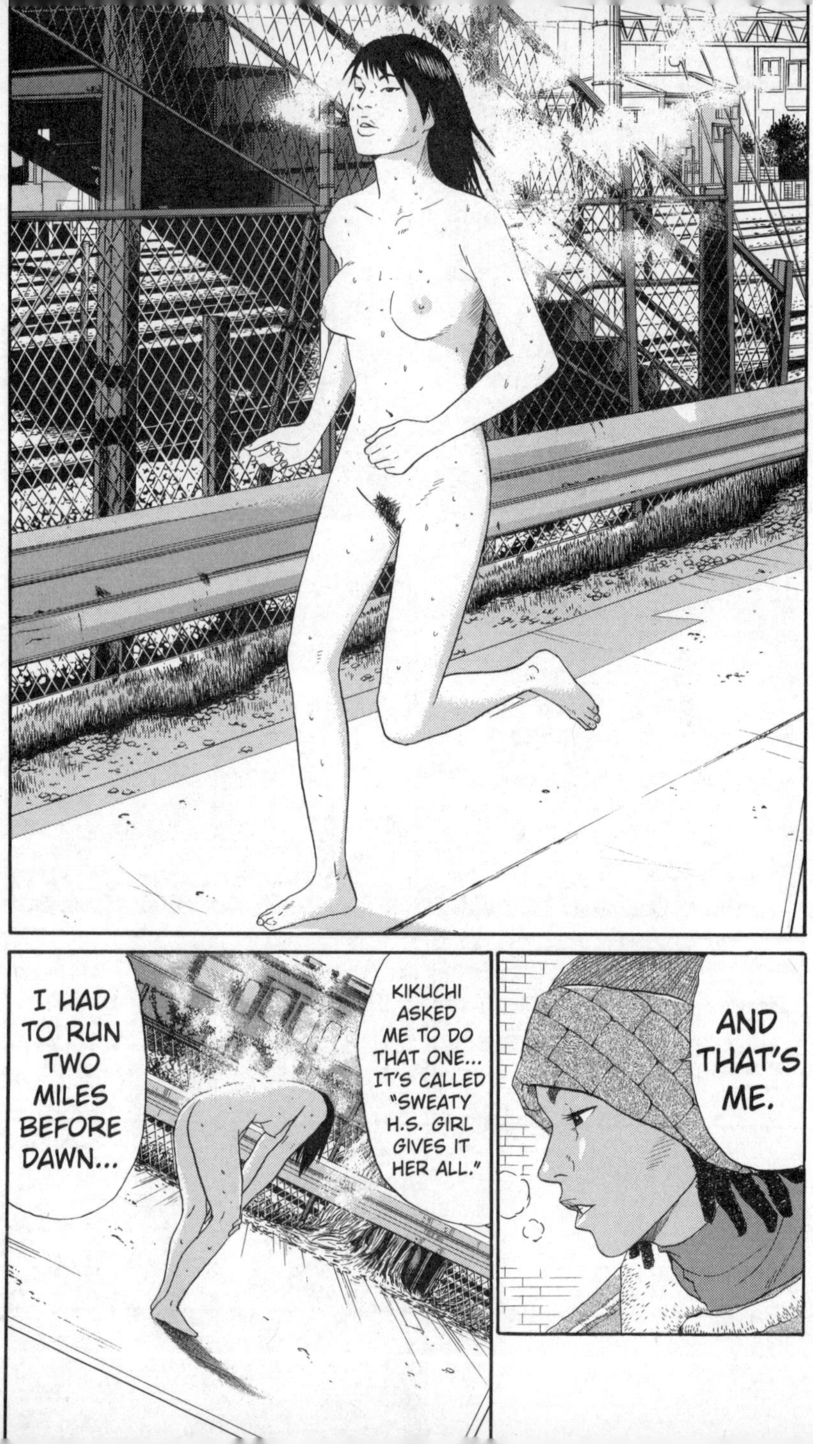
AND THAT'S ME.
KIKUCHI ASKED ME TO DO THAT ONE... IT'S CALLED "SWEATY H.S. GIRL GIVES IT HER ALL."
I HAD TO RUN TWO MILES BEFORE DAWN...

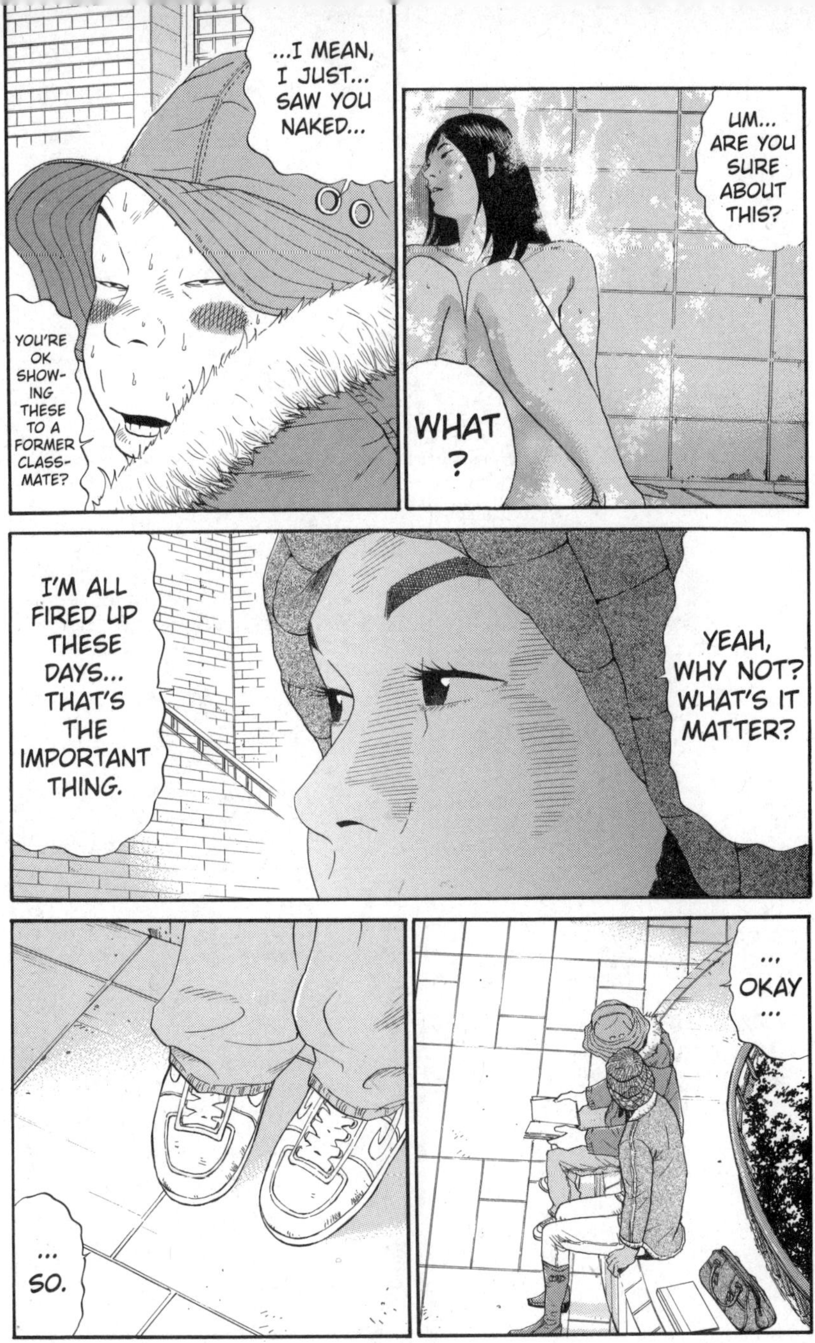
UM... ARE YOU SURE ABOUT THIS?
WHAT?
...I MEAN, I JUST... SAW YOU NAKED...
YOU'RE OK SHOWING THESE TO A FORMER CLASSMATE?
YEAH, WHY NOT? WHAT'S IT MATTER?
I'M ALL FIRED UP THESE DAYS... THAT'S THE IMPORTANT THING.
...OKAY...
...SO.

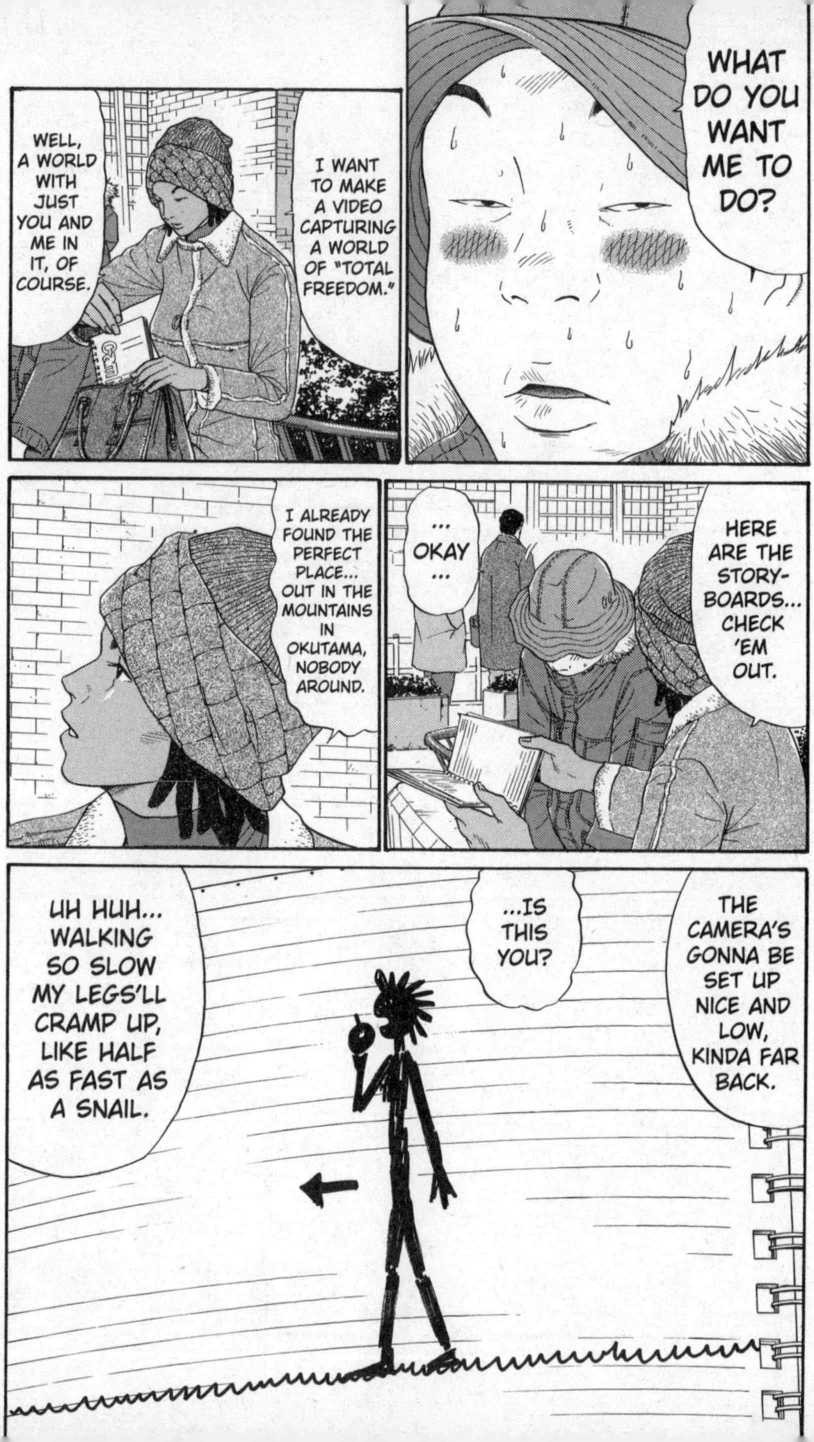
WHAT DO YOU WANT ME TO DO?
I WANT TO MAKE A VIDEO CAPTURING A WORLD OF "TOTAL FREEDOM."
WELL, A WORLD WITH JUST YOU AND ME IN IT, OF COURSE.
HERE ARE THE STORY-BOARDS... CHECK 'EM OUT.
... OKAY ...
I ALREADY FOUND THE PERFECT PLACE... OUT IN THE MOUNTAINS IN OKUTAMA, NOBODY AROUND.
THE CAMERA'S GONNA BE SET UP NICE AND LOW, KINDA FAR BACK.
...IS THIS YOU?
UH HUH... WALKING SO SLOW MY LEGS'LL CRAMP UP, LIKE HALF AS FAST AS A SNAIL.

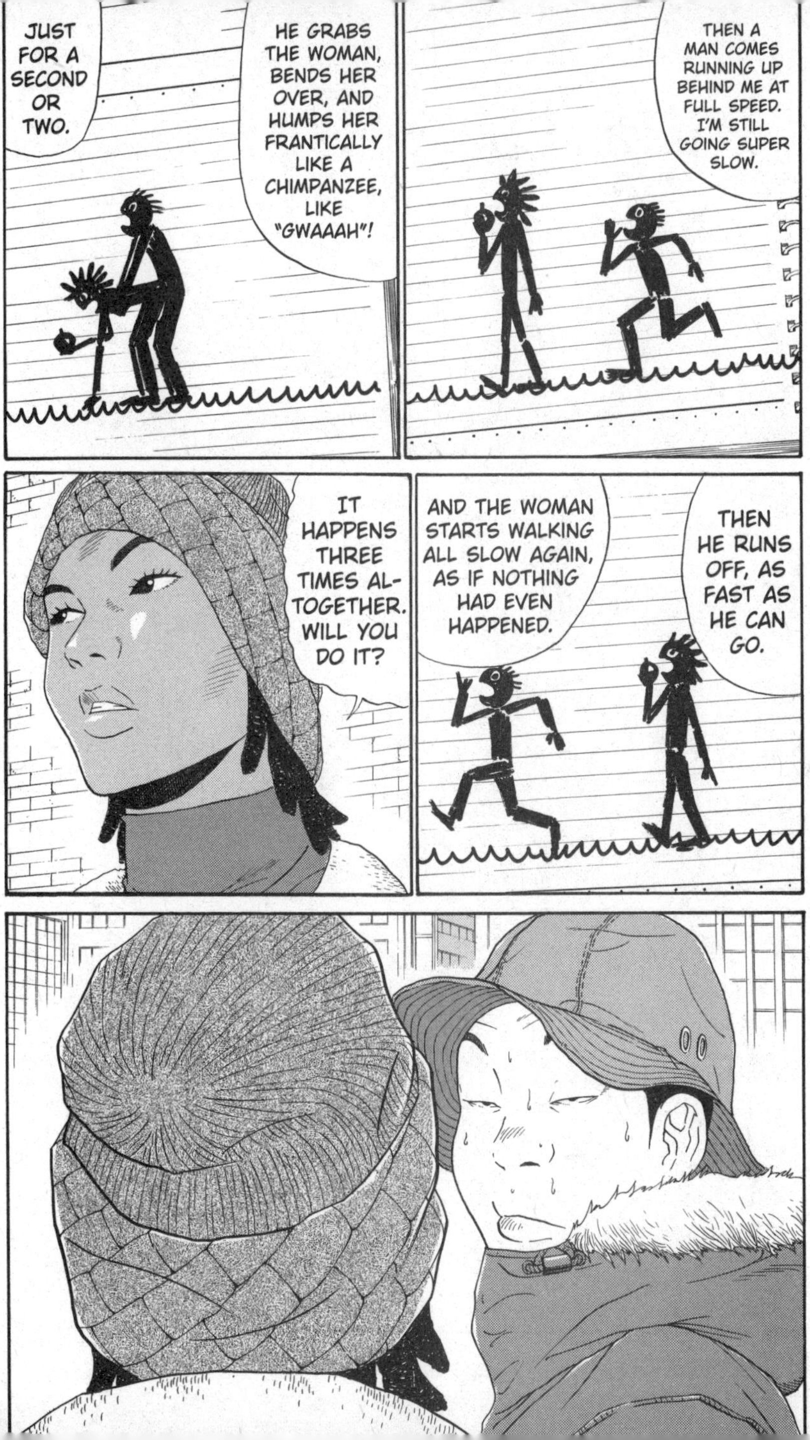
THEN A MAN COMES RUNNING UP BEHIND ME AT FULL SPEED. I'M STILL GOING SUPER SLOW.
HE GRABS THE WOMAN, BENDS HER OVER, AND HUMPS HER FRANTICALLY LIKE A CHIMPANZEE, LIKE "GWAAAH"!
JUST FOR A SECOND OR TWO.
THEN HE RUNS OFF, AS FAST AS HE CAN GO.
AND THE WOMAN STARTS WALKING ALL SLOW AGAIN, AS IF NOTHING HAD EVEN HAPPENED.
IT HAPPENS THREE TIMES AL-TOGETHER. WILL YOU DO IT?

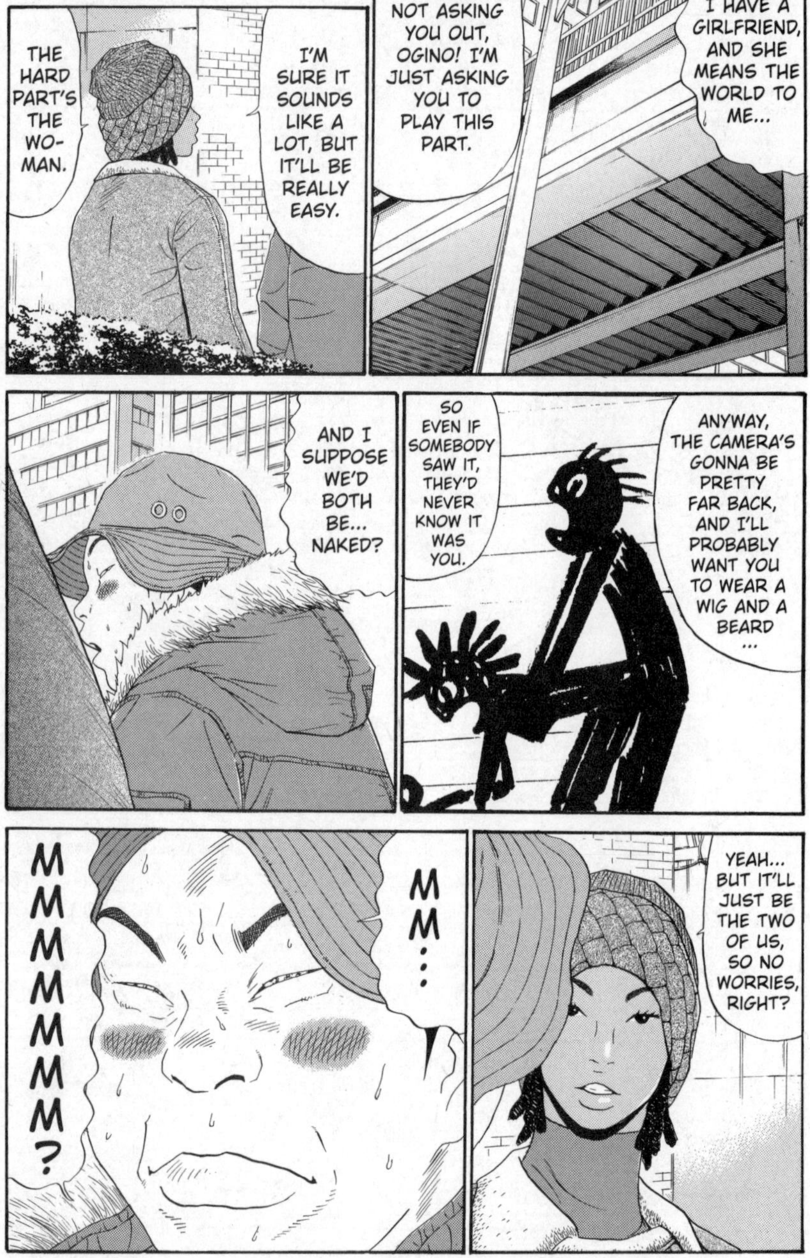
...UHHH... B-BUT, I HAVE A GIRLFRIEND, AND SHE MEANS THE WORLD TO ME...
I KNOW THAT. I'M NOT ASKING YOU OUT, OGINO! I'M JUST ASKING YOU TO PLAY THIS PART.
I'M SURE IT SOUNDS LIKE A LOT, BUT IT'LL BE REALLY EASY.
THE HARD PART'S THE WO-MAN.
ANYWAY, THE CAMERA'S GONNA BE PRETTY FAR BACK, AND I'LL PROBABLY WANT YOU TO WEAR A WIG AND A BEARD ...
SO EVEN IF SOMEBODY SAW IT, THEY'D NEVER KNOW IT WAS YOU.
AND I SUPPOSE WE'D BOTH BE... NAKED?
YEAH... BUT IT'LL JUST BE THE TWO OF US, SO NO WORRIES, RIGHT?
MM...
MMMMMMM?

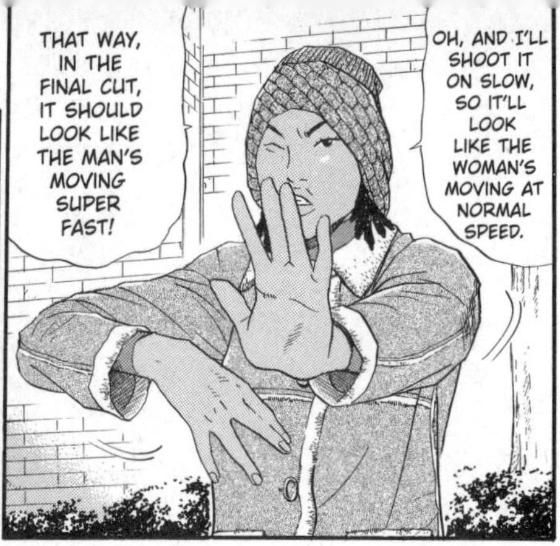
THAT WAY, IN THE FINAL CUT, IT SHOULD LOOK LIKE THE MAN'S MOVING SUPER FAST!
OH, AND I'LL SHOOT IT ON SLOW, SO IT'LL LOOK LIKE THE WOMAN'S MOVING AT NORMAL SPEED.
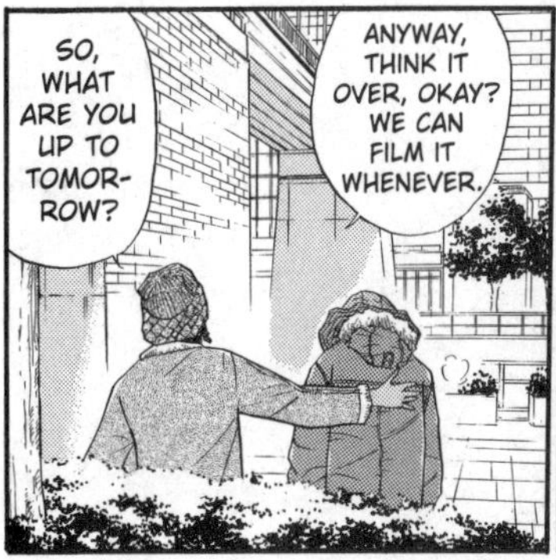
ANYWAY, THINK IT OVER, OKAY? WE CAN FILM IT WHENEVER.
SO, WHAT ARE YOU UP TO TOMOR-ROW?

THE NEXT DAY

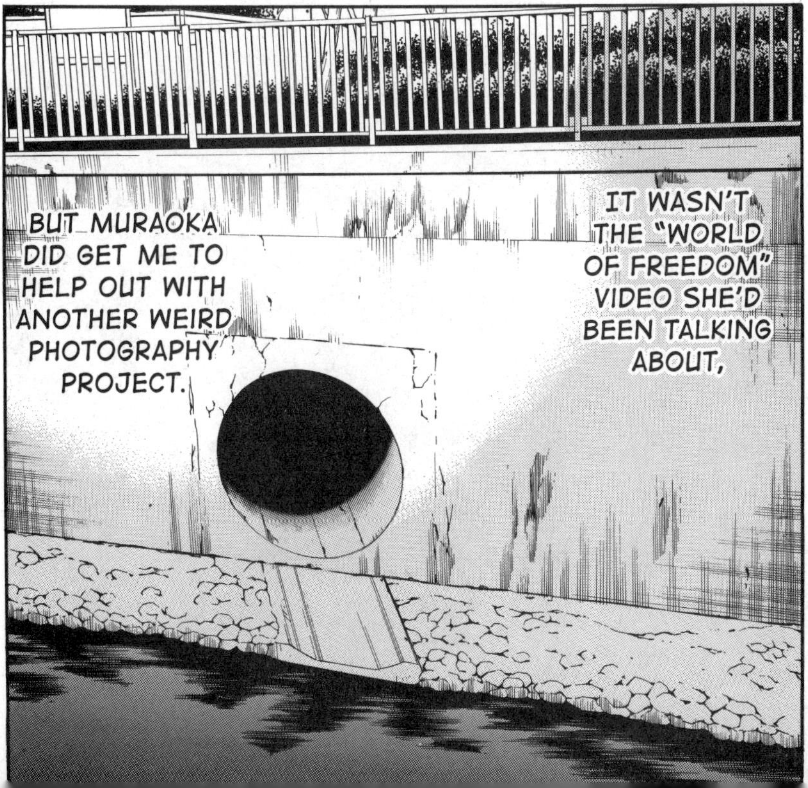
IT WASN'T THE "WORLD OF FREEDOM" VIDEO SHE'D BEEN TALKING ABOUT,
BUT MURAOKA DID GET ME TO HELP OUT WITH ANOTHER WEIRD PHOTOGRAPHY PROJECT.

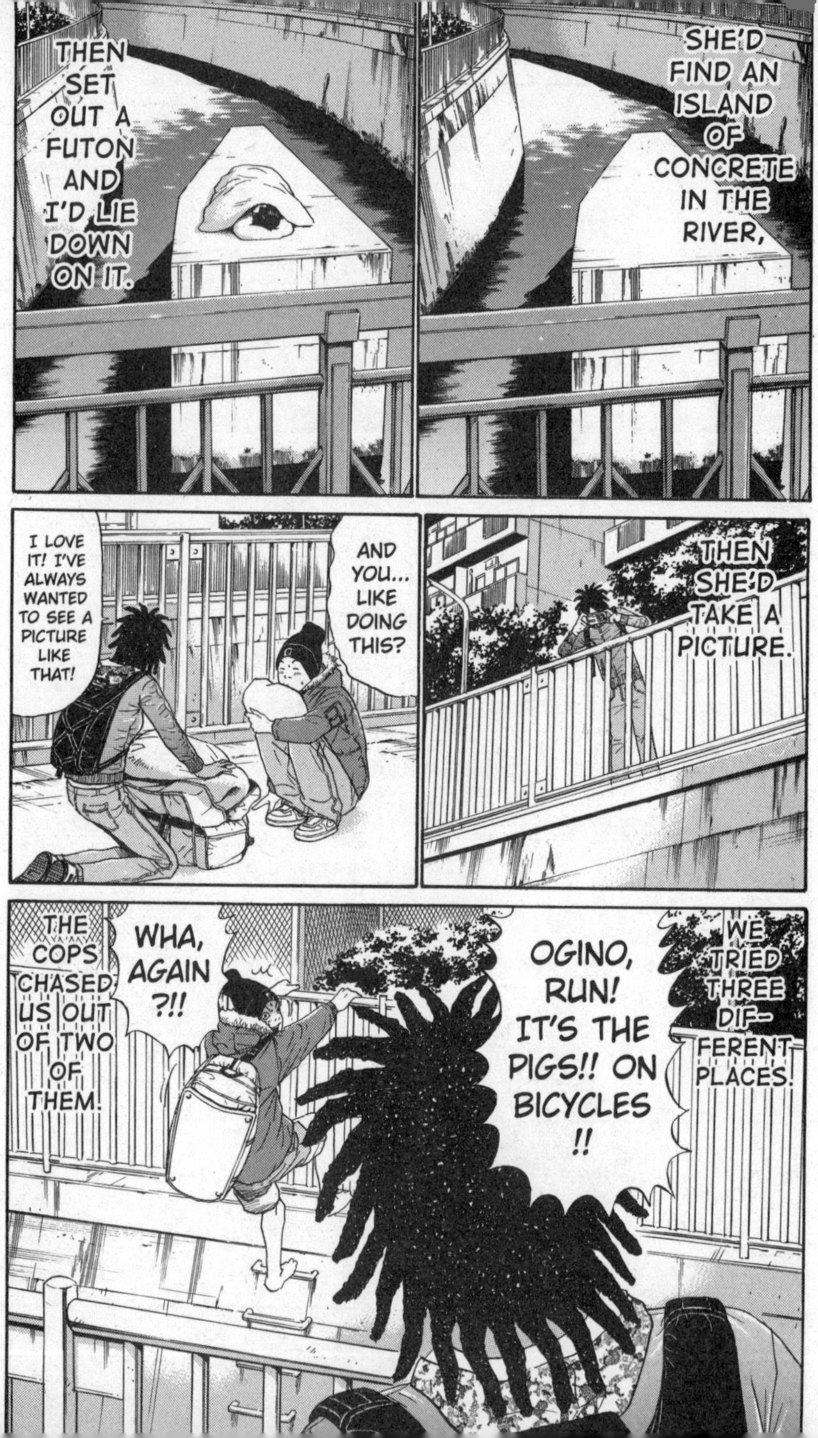
SHE'D FIND AN ISLAND OF CONCRETE IN THE RIVER,
THEN SET OUT A FUTON AND I'D LIE DOWN ON IT.
THEN SHE'D TAKE A PICTURE.
AND YOU... LIKE DOING THIS?
I LOVE IT! I'VE ALWAYS WANTED TO SEE A PICTURE LIKE THAT!
WE TRIED THREE DIF-FERENT PLACES.
OGINO, RUN! IT'S THE PIGS!! ON BICYCLES !!
WHA, AGAIN ?!!
THE COPS CHASED US OUT OF TWO OF THEM.

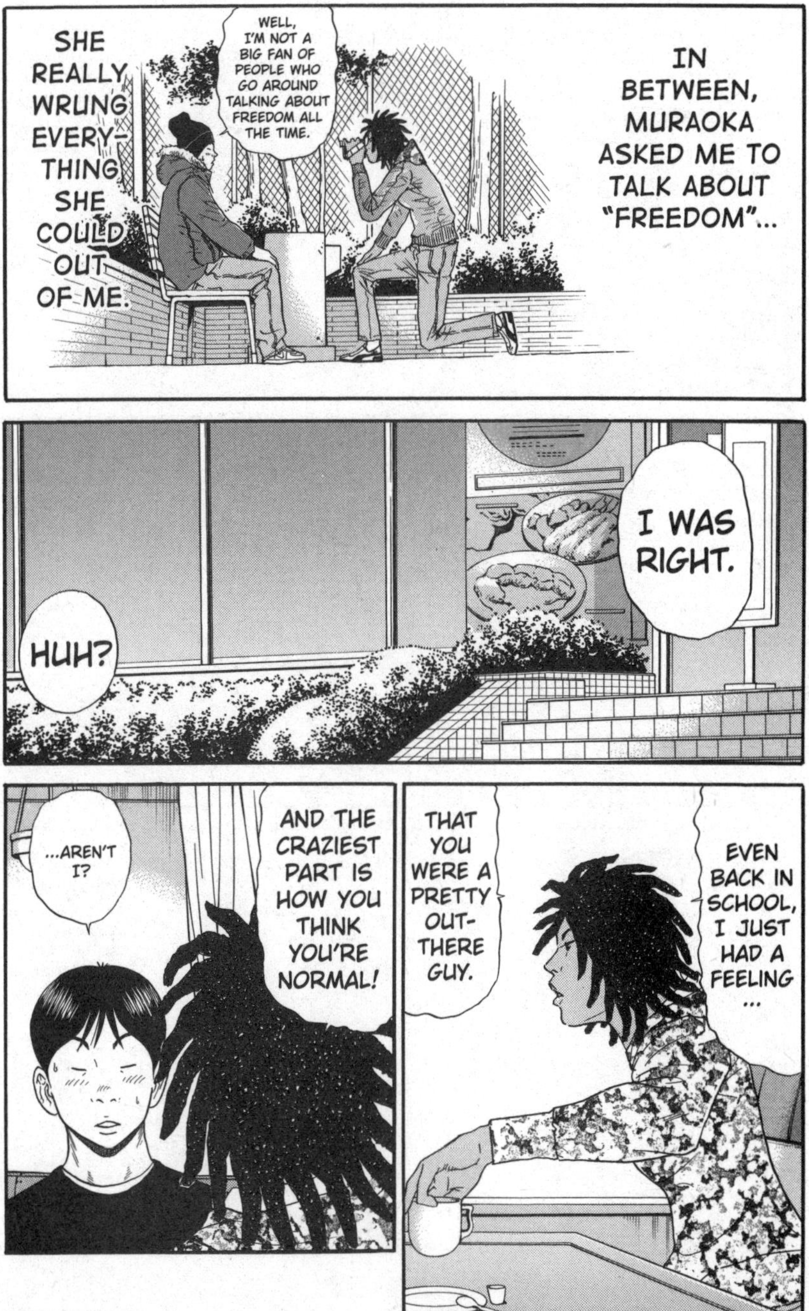
IN BETWEEN, MURAOKA ASKED ME TO TALK ABOUT "FREEDOM"...
WELL, I'M NOT A BIG FAN OF PEOPLE WHO GO AROUND TALKING ABOUT FREEDOM ALL THE TIME.
SHE REALLY WRUNG EVERY-THING SHE COULD OUT OF ME.
I WAS RIGHT.
HUH?
EVEN BACK IN SCHOOL, I JUST HAD A FEELING...
THAT YOU WERE A PRETTY OUT-THERE GUY.
AND THE CRAZIEST PART IS HOW YOU THINK YOU'RE NORMAL!
...AREN'T I?

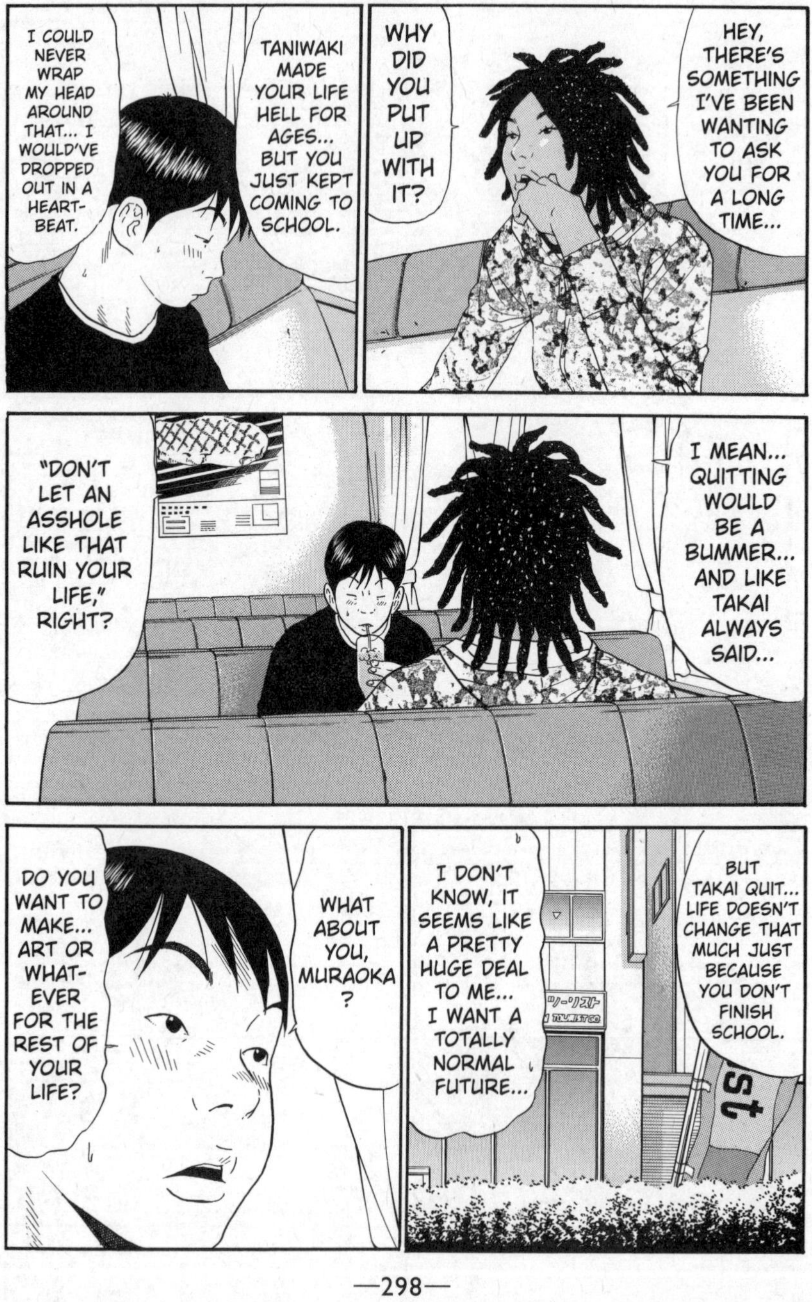
HEY, THERE'S SOMETHING I'VE BEEN WANTING TO ASK YOU FOR A LONG TIME...
WHY DID YOU PUT UP WITH IT?
TANIWAKI MADE YOUR LIFE HELL FOR AGES... BUT YOU JUST KEPT COMING TO SCHOOL.
I COULD NEVER WRAP MY HEAD AROUND THAT... I WOULD'VE DROPPED OUT IN A HEART-BEAT.
I MEAN... QUITTING WOULD BE A BUMMER... AND LIKE TAKAI ALWAYS SAID...
"DON'T LET AN ASSHOLE LIKE THAT RUIN YOUR LIFE," RIGHT?
BUT TAKAI QUIT... LIFE DOESN'T CHANGE THAT MUCH JUST BECAUSE YOU DON'T FINISH SCHOOL.
I DON'T KNOW, IT SEEMS LIKE A PRETTY HUGE DEAL TO ME... I WANT A TOTALLY NORMAL FUTURE...
WHAT ABOUT YOU, MURAOKA?
DO YOU WANT TO MAKE... ART OR WHAT-EVER FOR THE REST OF YOUR LIFE?

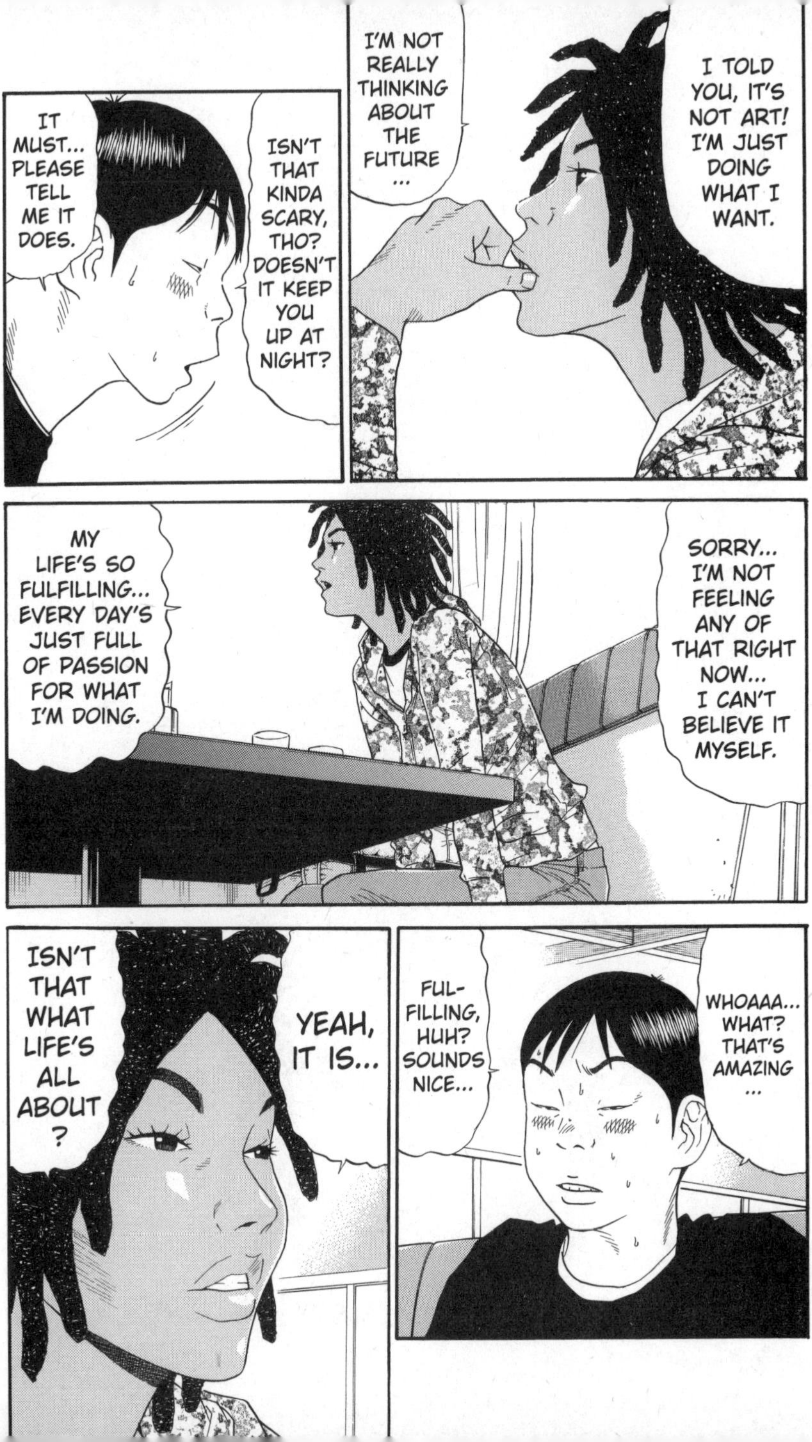
I TOLD YOU, IT'S NOT ART! I'M JUST DOING WHAT I WANT.
I'M NOT REALLY THINKING ABOUT THE FUTURE ...
ISN'T THAT KINDA SCARY, THO? DOESN'T IT KEEP YOU UP AT NIGHT?
IT MUST... PLEASE TELL ME IT DOES.
SORRY... I'M NOT FEELING ANY OF THAT RIGHT NOW... I CAN'T BELIEVE IT MYSELF.
MY LIFE'S SO FULFILLING... EVERY DAY'S JUST FULL OF PASSION FOR WHAT I'M DOING.
WHOAAA... WHAT? THAT'S AMAZING ...
FUL-FILLING, HUH? SOUNDS NICE...
YEAH, IT IS...
ISN'T THAT WHAT LIFE'S ALL ABOUT ?

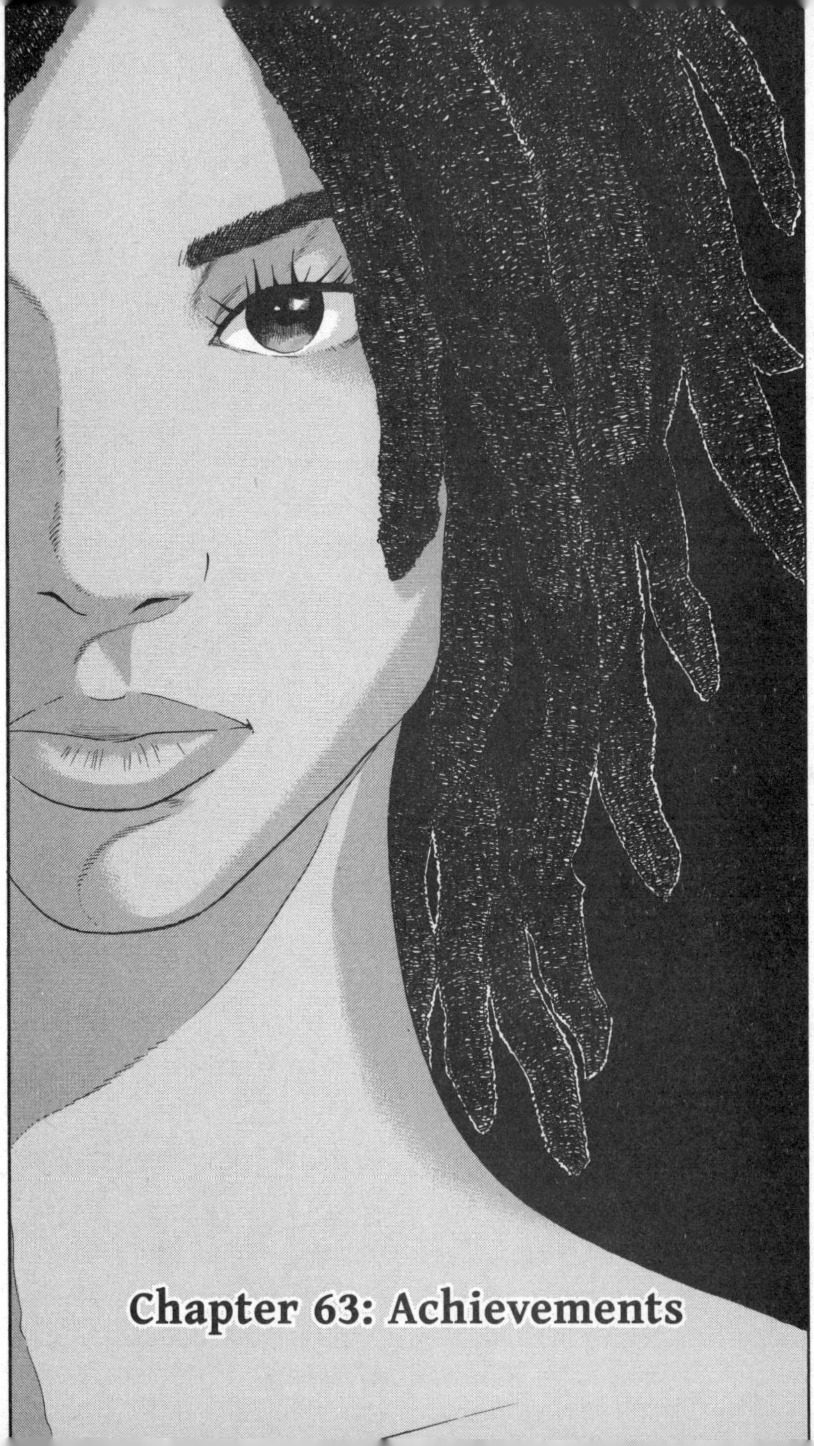

# Chapter 63: Achievements

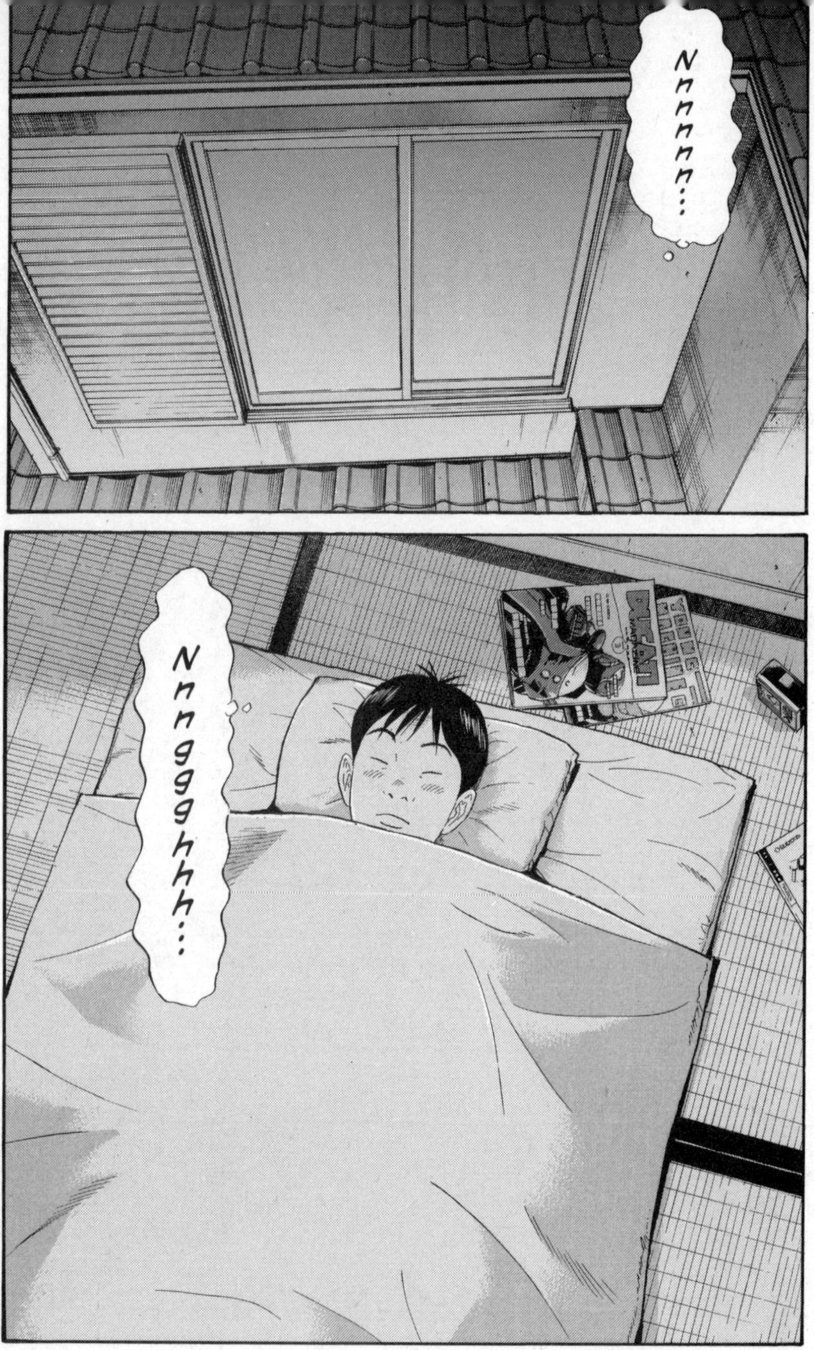
Nnnnnn...
Nnngghhh...

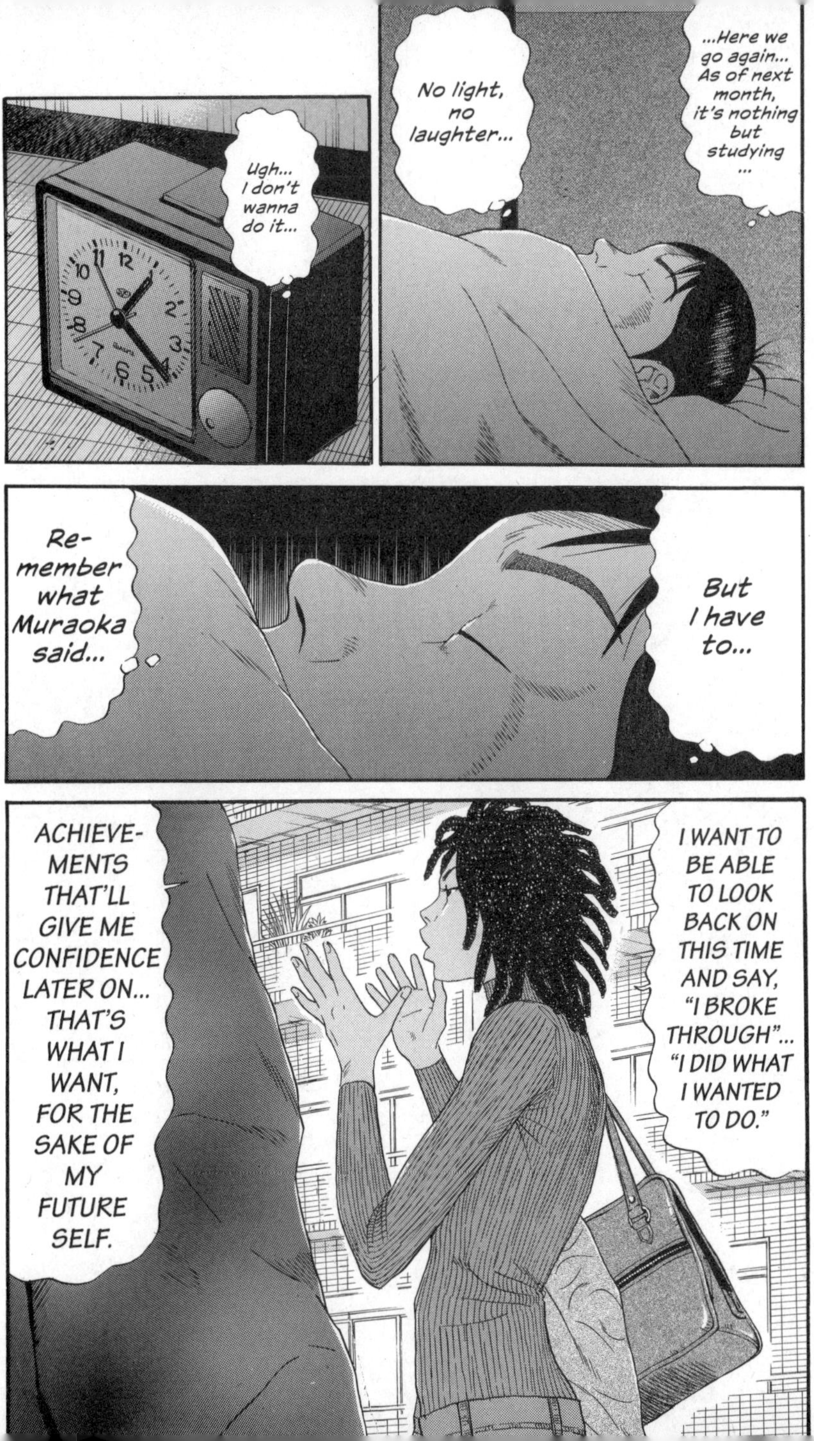
...Here we go again... As of next month, it's nothing but studying ...
No light, no laughter...
Ugh... I don't wanna do it...
But I have to...
Re-member what Muraoka said...
I WANT TO BE ABLE TO LOOK BACK ON THIS TIME AND SAY, "I BROKE THROUGH"... "I DID WHAT I WANTED TO DO."
ACHIEVE-MENTS THAT'LL GIVE ME CONFIDENCE LATER ON... THAT'S WHAT I WANT, FOR THE SAKE OF MY FUTURE SELF.

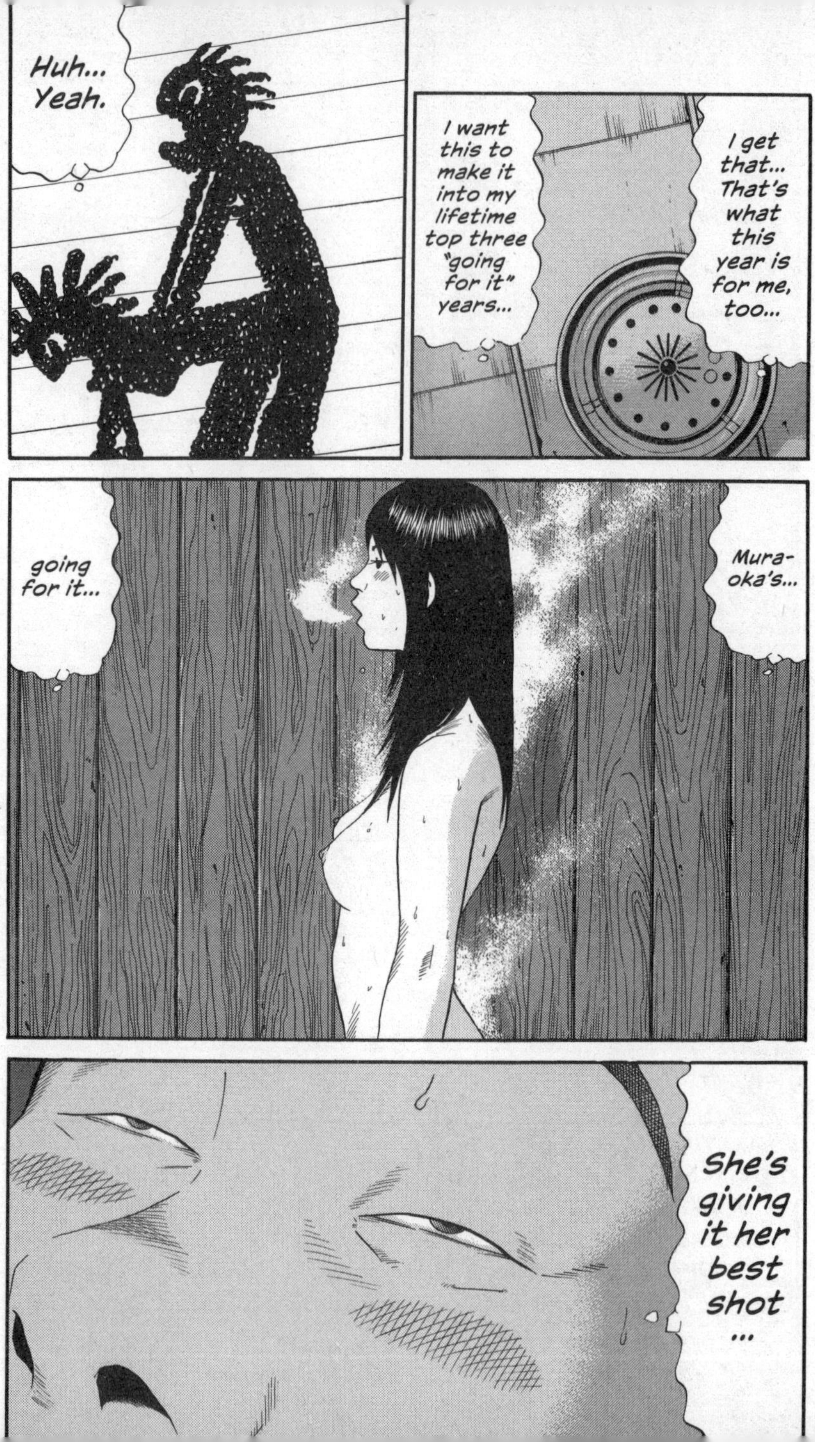
I get that... That's what this year is for me, too...
I want this to make it into my lifetime top three "going for it" years...
Huh... Yeah.
Mura-oka's...
going for it...
She's giving it her best shot ...

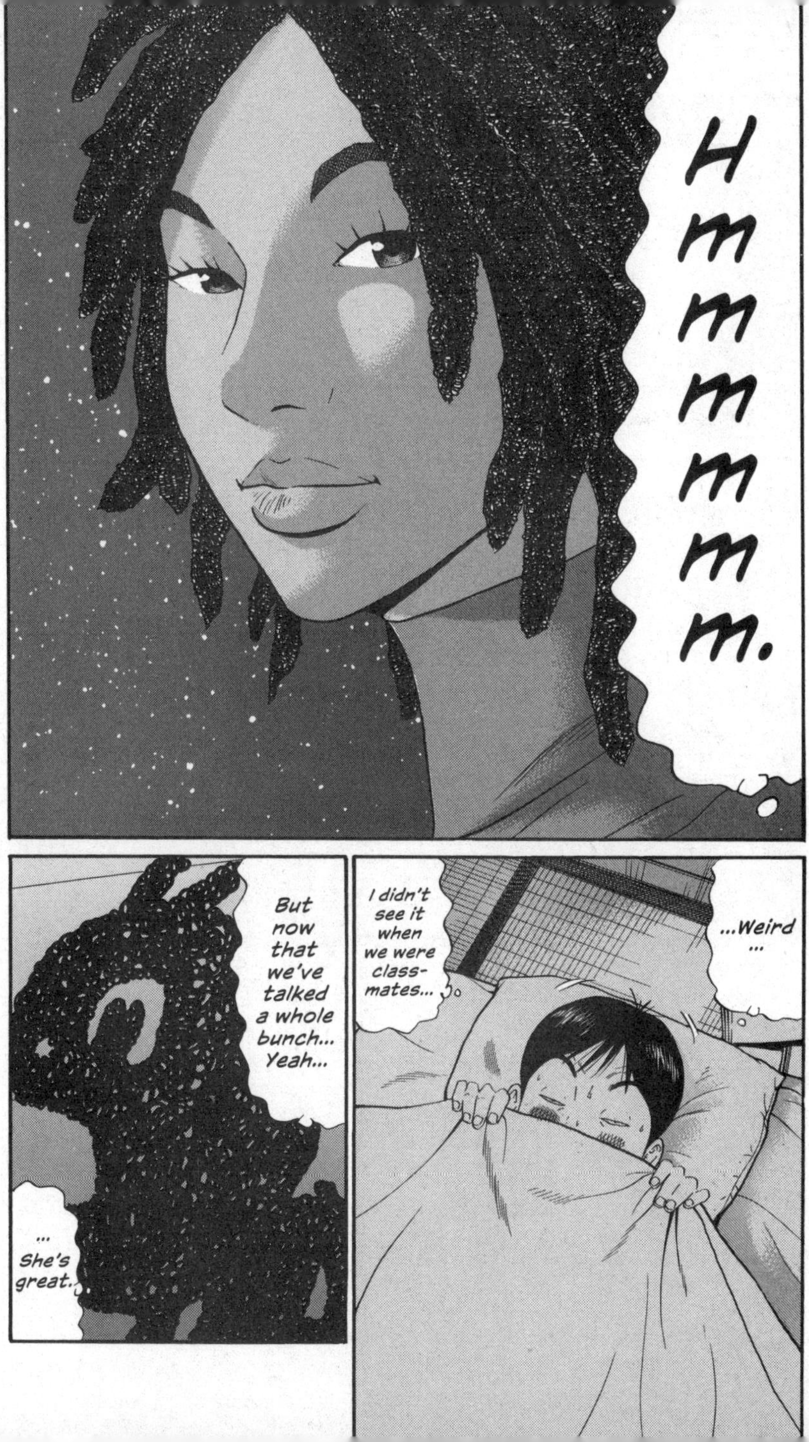
Hmmmmmm.
...Weird ...
I didn't see it when we were class-mates...
But now that we've talked a whole bunch... Yeah...
... She's great.

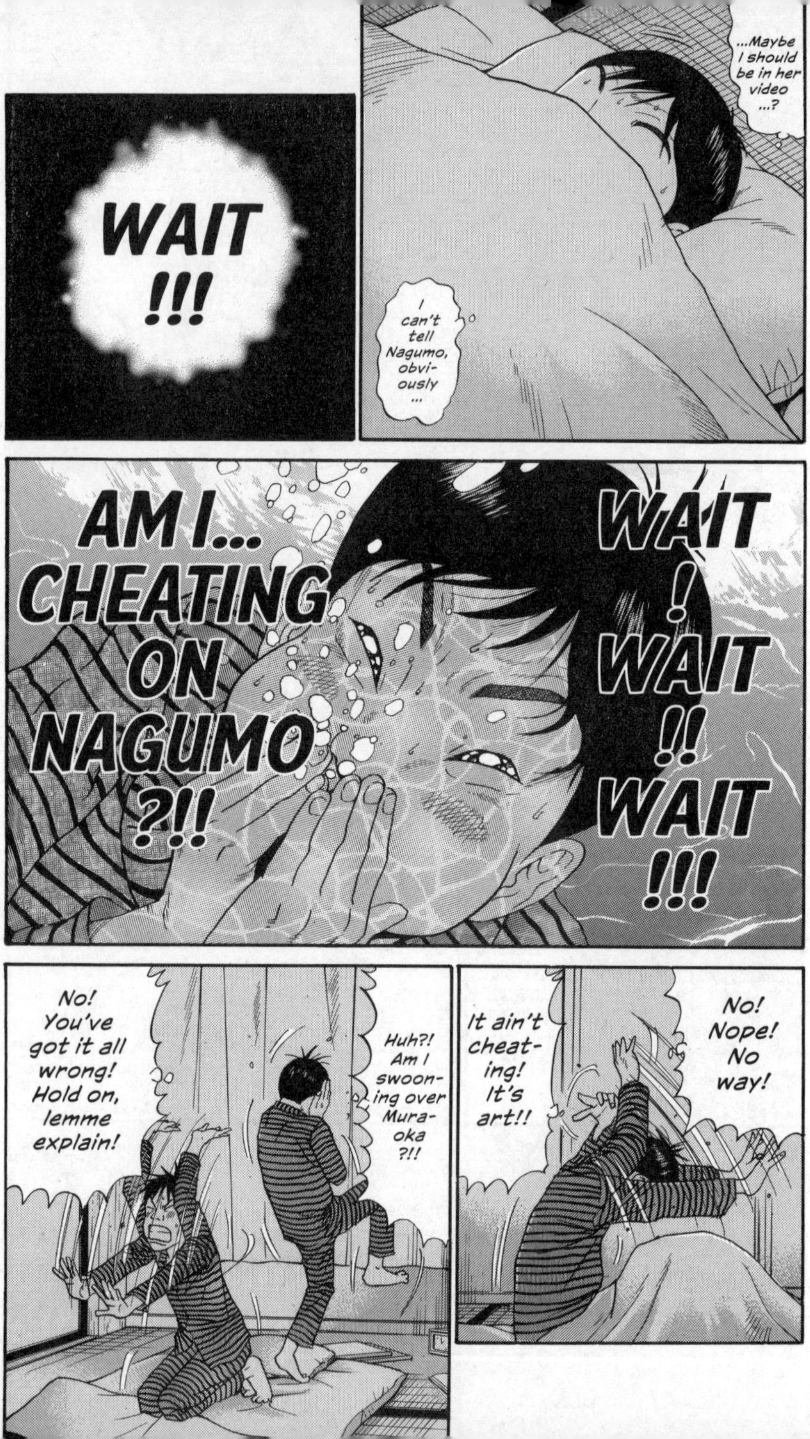
...Maybe I should be in her video ...?
I can't tell Nagumo, obviously ...
WAIT !!!
WAIT ! WAIT !! WAIT !!!
AM I... CHEATING ON NAGUMO ?!!
No! Nope! No way!
It ain't cheating! It's art!!
Huh?! Am I swooning over Muraoka ?!!
No! You've got it all wrong! Hold on, lemme explain!

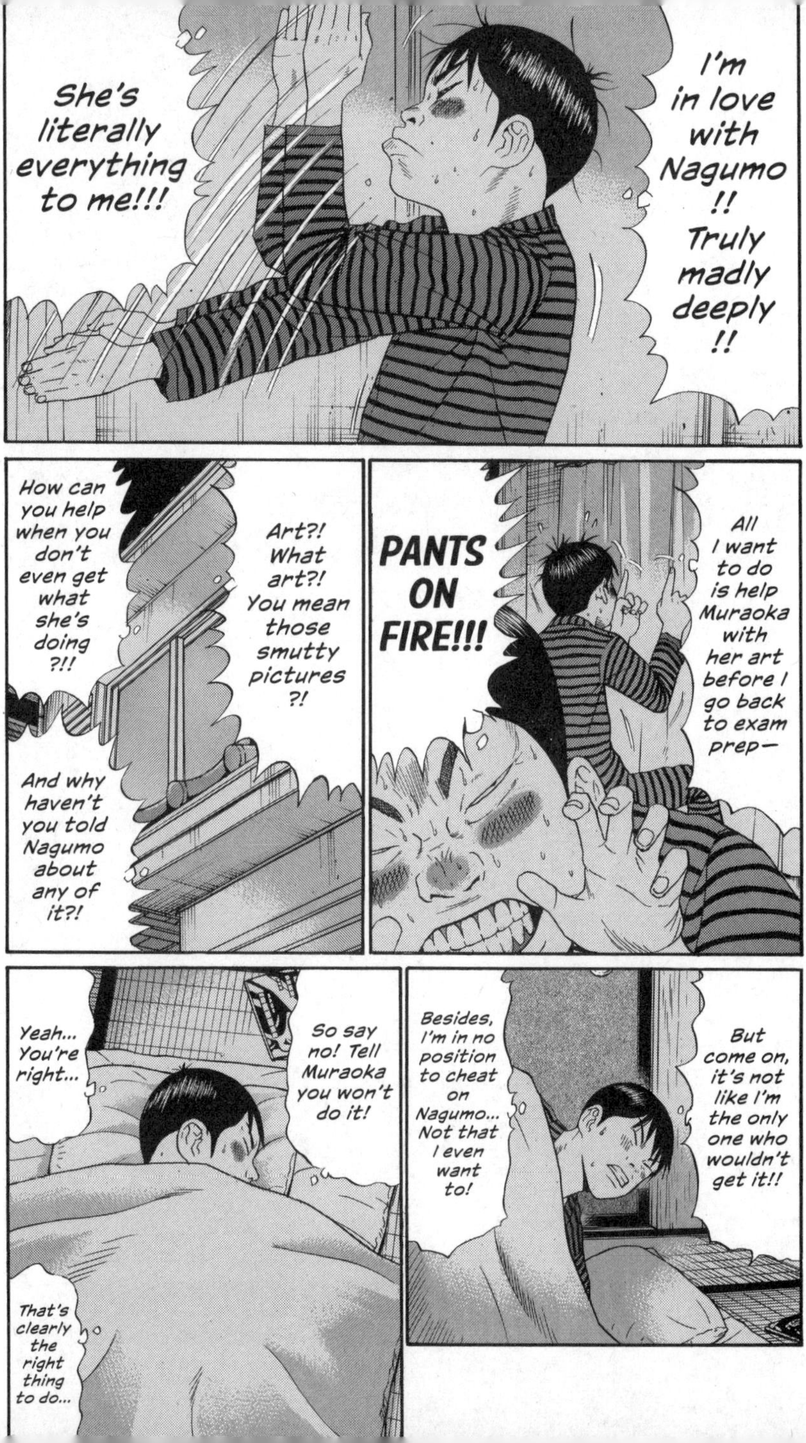
I'm in love with Nagumo!! Truly madly deeply!!
She's literally everything to me!!!
All I want to do is help Muraoka with her art before I go back to exam prep—
PANTS ON FIRE!!!
Art?! What art?! You mean those smutty pictures?!
How can you help when you don't even get what she's doing?!!
And why haven't you told Nagumo about any of it?!
But come on, it's not like I'm the only one who wouldn't get it!!
Besides, I'm in no position to cheat on Nagumo... Not that I even want to!
So say no! Tell Muraoka you won't do it!
Yeah... You're right...
That's clearly the right thing to do...

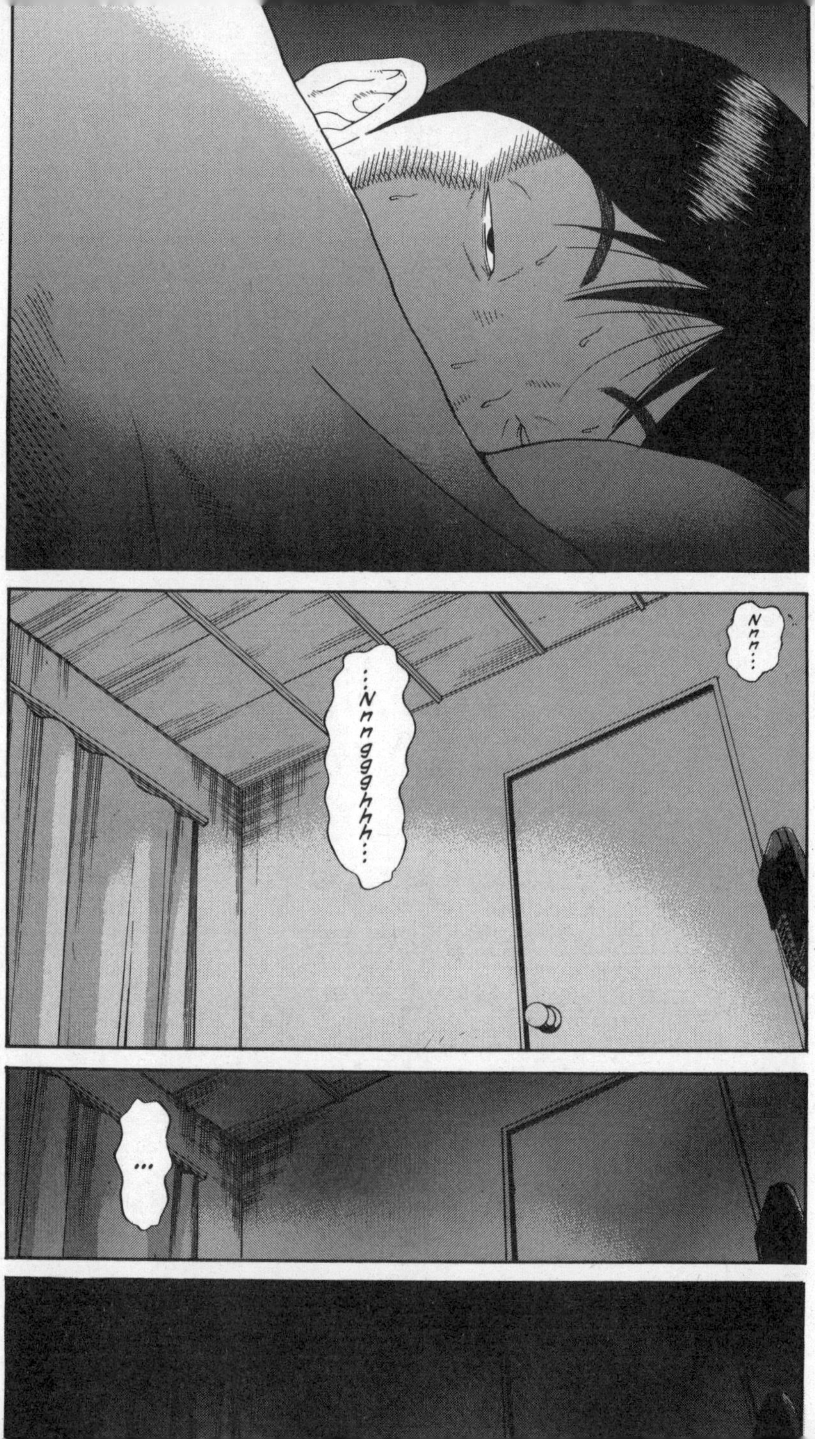
Nnn...
...Nnngggghhh...
...

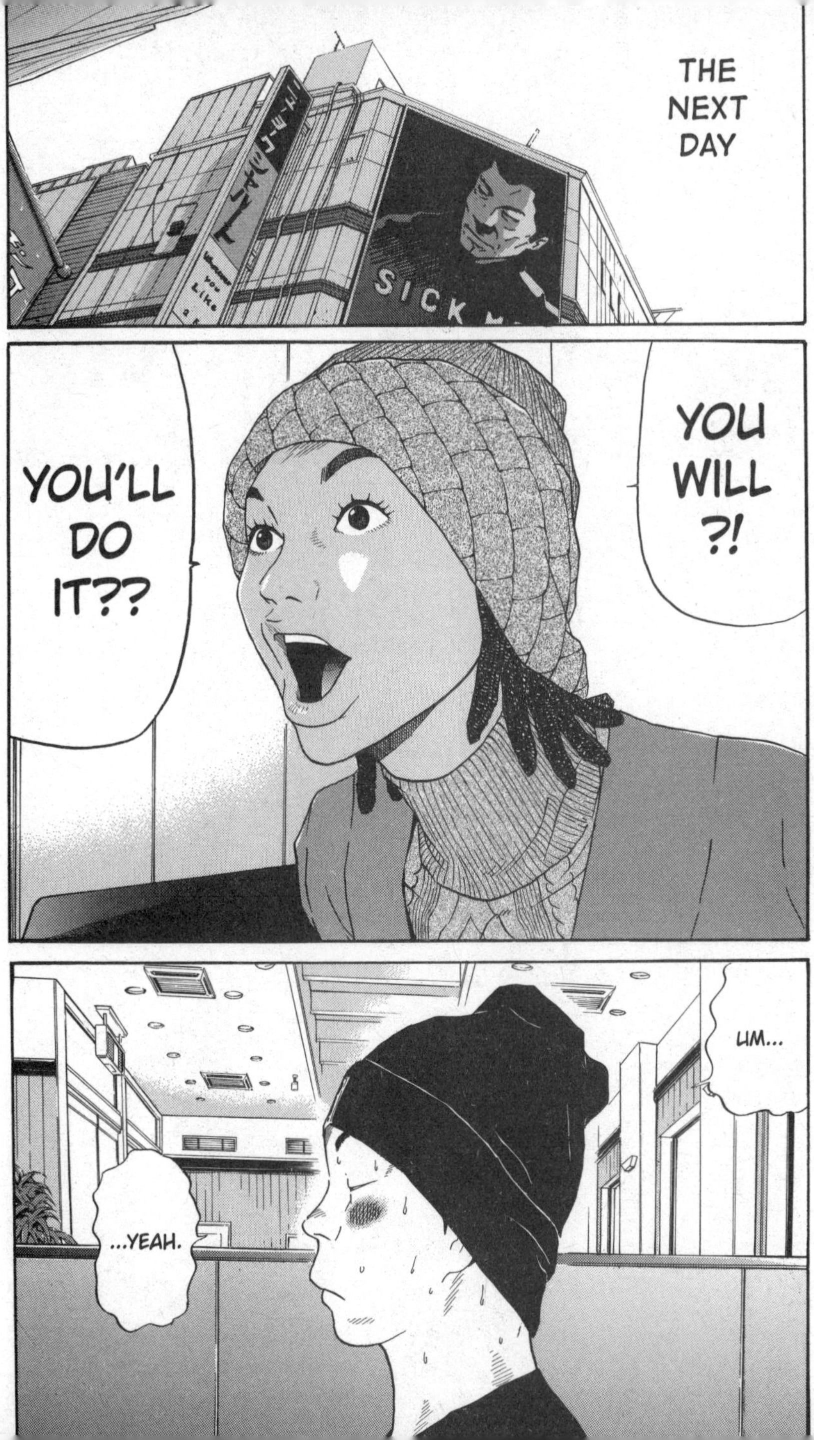
THE NEXT DAY
YOU WILL ?!
YOU'LL DO IT??
UM...
...YEAH.

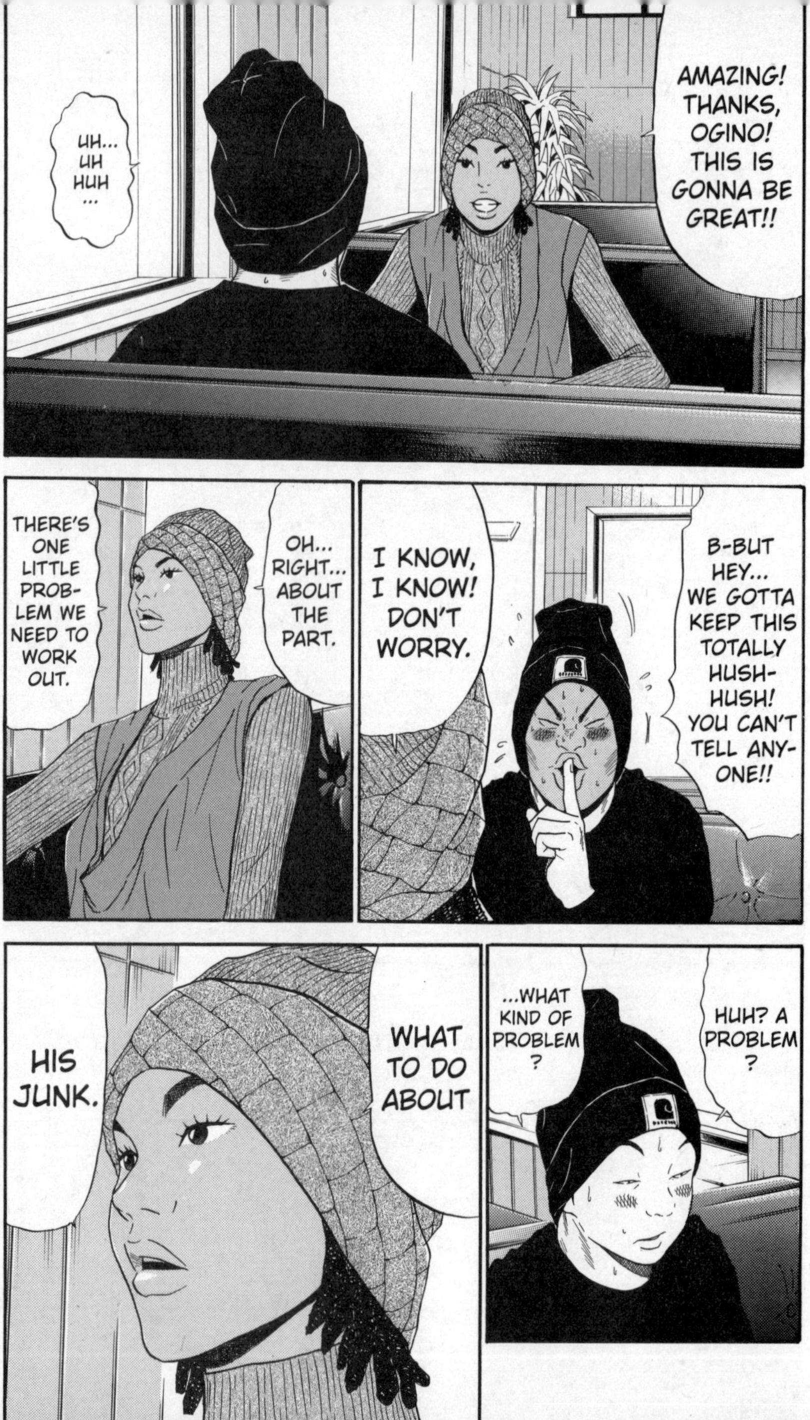
AMAZING! THANKS, OGINO! THIS IS GONNA BE GREAT!!
UH... UH HUH...
B-BUT HEY... WE GOTTA KEEP THIS TOTALLY HUSH-HUSH! YOU CAN'T TELL ANY-ONE!!
I KNOW, I KNOW! DON'T WORRY.
OH... RIGHT... ABOUT THE PART.
THERE'S ONE LITTLE PROB-LEM WE NEED TO WORK OUT.
HUH? A PROBLEM?
...WHAT KIND OF PROBLEM?
WHAT TO DO ABOUT
HIS JUNK.

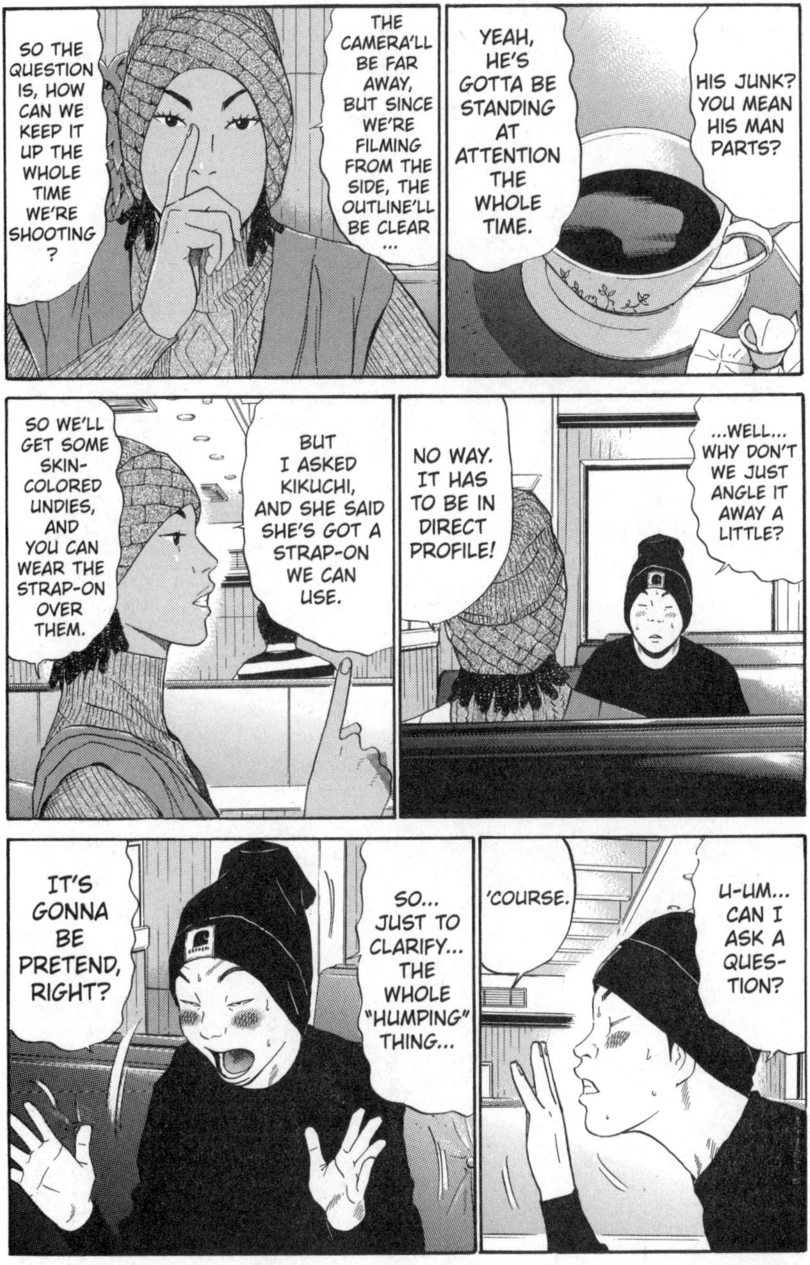
HIS JUNK? YOU MEAN HIS MAN PARTS?
YEAH, HE'S GOTTA BE STANDING AT ATTENTION THE WHOLE TIME.
THE CAMERA'LL BE FAR AWAY, BUT SINCE WE'RE FILMING FROM THE SIDE, THE OUTLINE'LL BE CLEAR ...
SO THE QUESTION IS, HOW CAN WE KEEP IT UP THE WHOLE TIME WE'RE SHOOTING ?
...WELL... WHY DON'T WE JUST ANGLE IT AWAY A LITTLE?
NO WAY. IT HAS TO BE IN DIRECT PROFILE!
BUT I ASKED KIKUCHI, AND SHE SAID SHE'S GOT A STRAP-ON WE CAN USE.
SO WE'LL GET SOME SKIN-COLORED UNDIES, AND YOU CAN WEAR THE STRAP-ON OVER THEM.
U-UM... CAN I ASK A QUES-TION?
'COURSE.
SO... JUST TO CLARIFY... THE WHOLE "HUMPING" THING...
IT'S GONNA BE PRETEND, RIGHT?

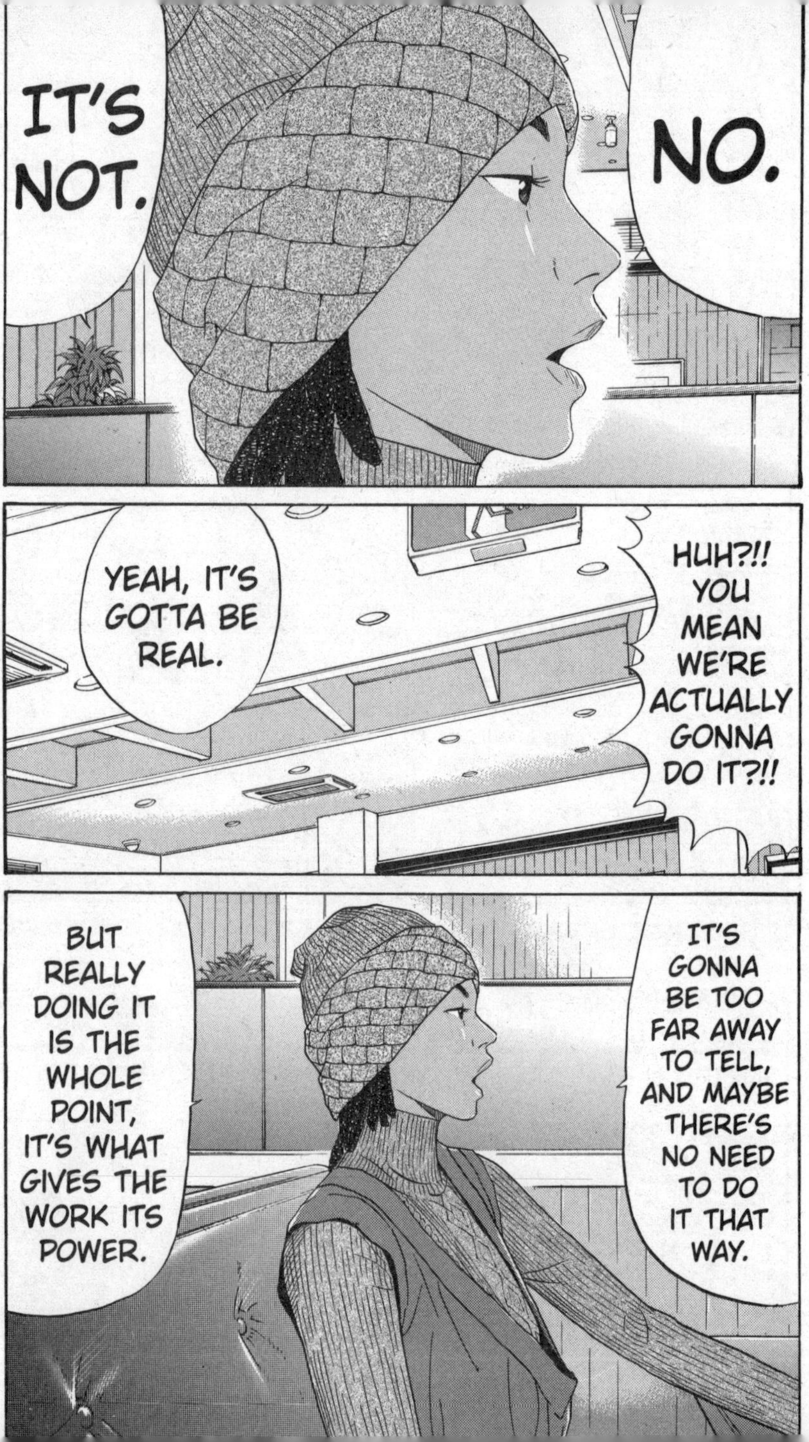
NO.
IT'S NOT.
HUH?!! YOU MEAN WE'RE ACTUALLY GONNA DO IT?!!
YEAH, IT'S GOTTA BE REAL.
IT'S GONNA BE TOO FAR AWAY TO TELL, AND MAYBE THERE'S NO NEED TO DO IT THAT WAY.
BUT REALLY DOING IT IS THE WHOLE POINT, IT'S WHAT GIVES THE WORK ITS POWER.

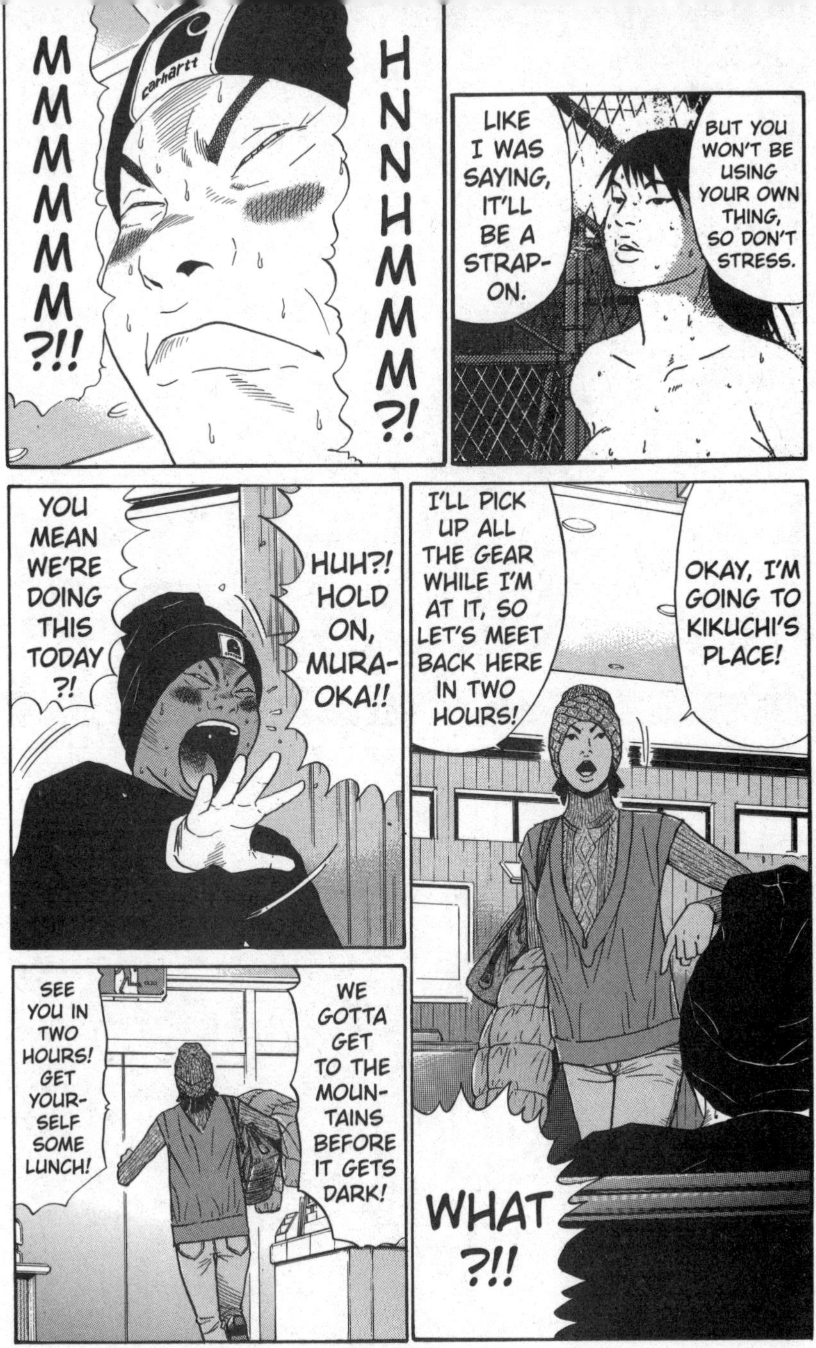
BUT YOU WON'T BE USING YOUR OWN THING, SO DON'T STRESS.
LIKE I WAS SAYING, IT'LL BE A STRAP-ON.
HNNHMMMMM?!
MMMMMMM?!!
OKAY, I'M GOING TO KIKUCHI'S PLACE!
I'LL PICK UP ALL THE GEAR WHILE I'M AT IT, SO LET'S MEET BACK HERE IN TWO HOURS!
WHAT?!!
HUH?! HOLD ON, MURA-OKA!!
YOU MEAN WE'RE DOING THIS TODAY?!
WE GOTTA GET TO THE MOUN-TAINS BEFORE IT GETS DARK!
SEE YOU IN TWO HOURS! GET YOUR-SELF SOME LUNCH!

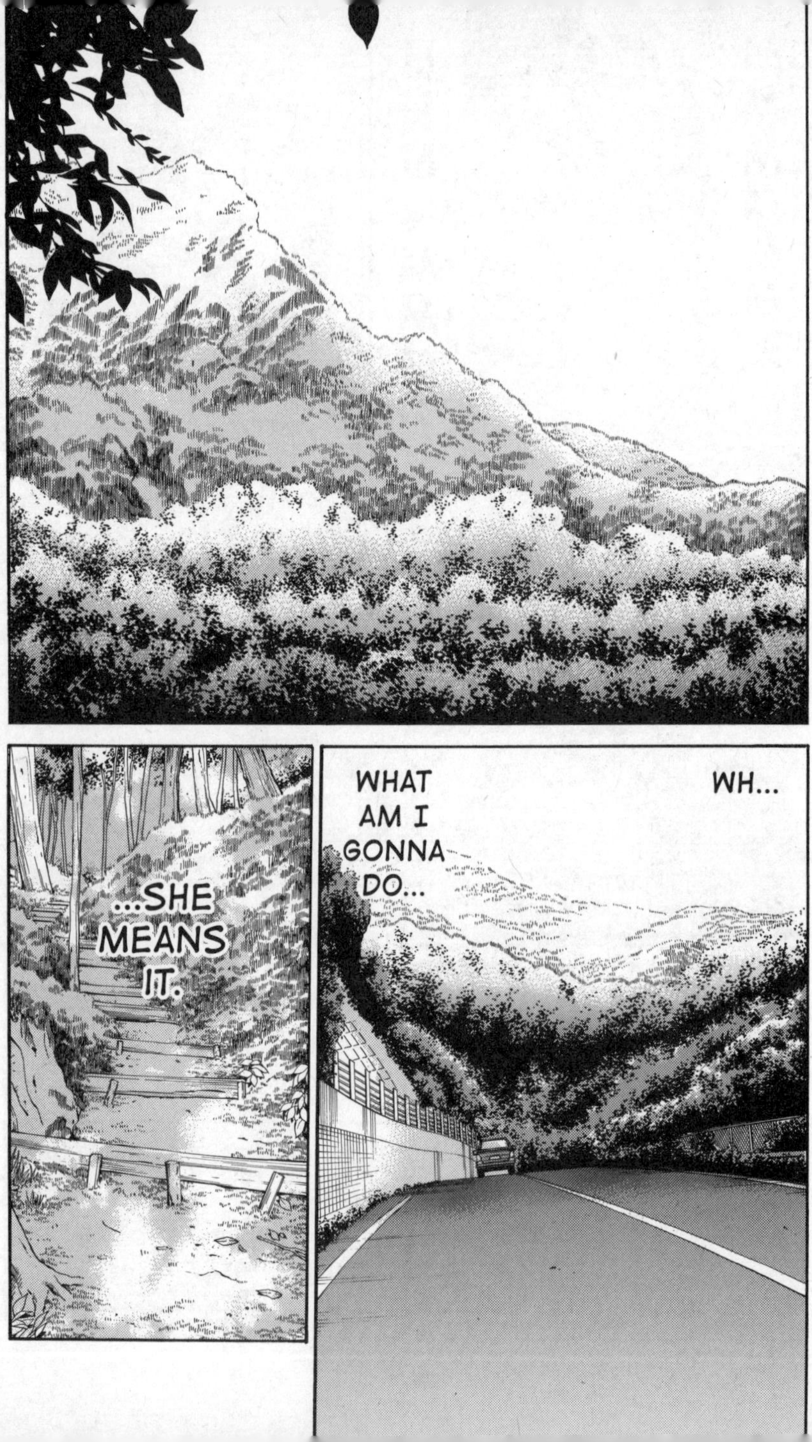
WH...
WHAT AM I GONNA DO...
...SHE MEANS IT.

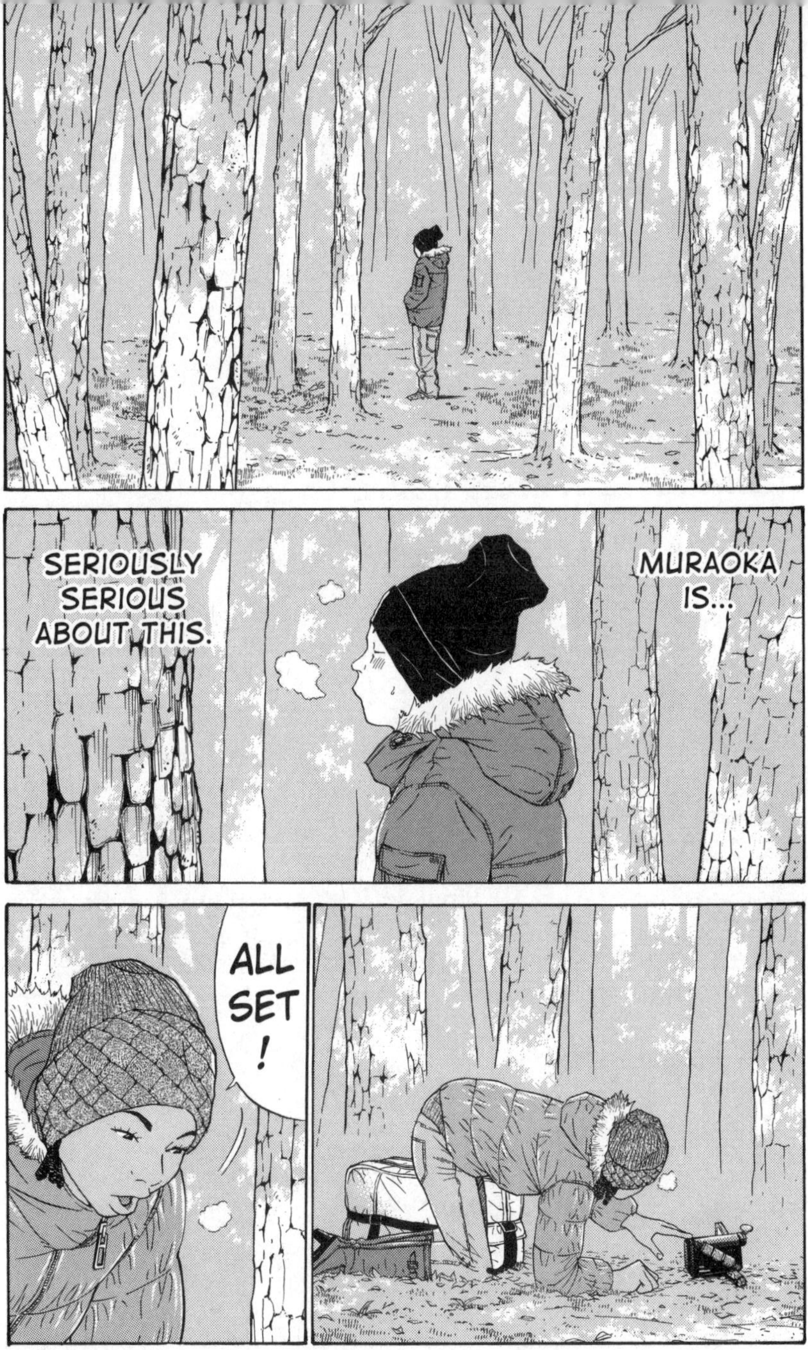
MURAOKA IS...
SERIOUSLY SERIOUS ABOUT THIS.
ALL SET!

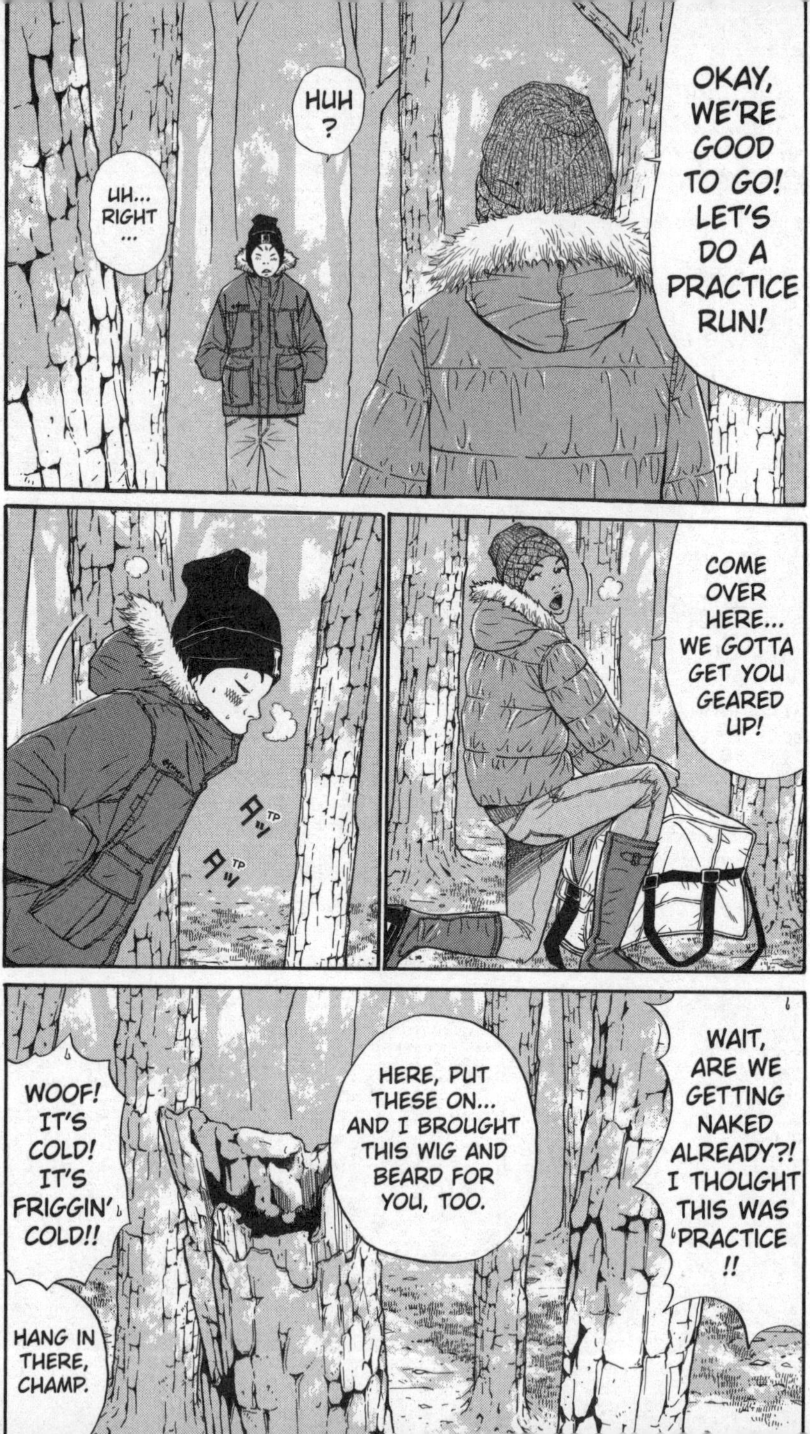
OKAY, WE'RE GOOD TO GO! LET'S DO A PRACTICE RUN!
HUH?
UH... RIGHT ...
COME OVER HERE... WE GOTTA GET YOU GEARED UP!
TP
TP
WAIT, ARE WE GETTING NAKED ALREADY?! I THOUGHT THIS WAS PRACTICE!!
HERE, PUT THESE ON... AND I BROUGHT THIS WIG AND BEARD FOR YOU, TOO.
WOOF! IT'S COLD! IT'S FRIGGIN' COLD!!
HANG IN THERE, CHAMP.

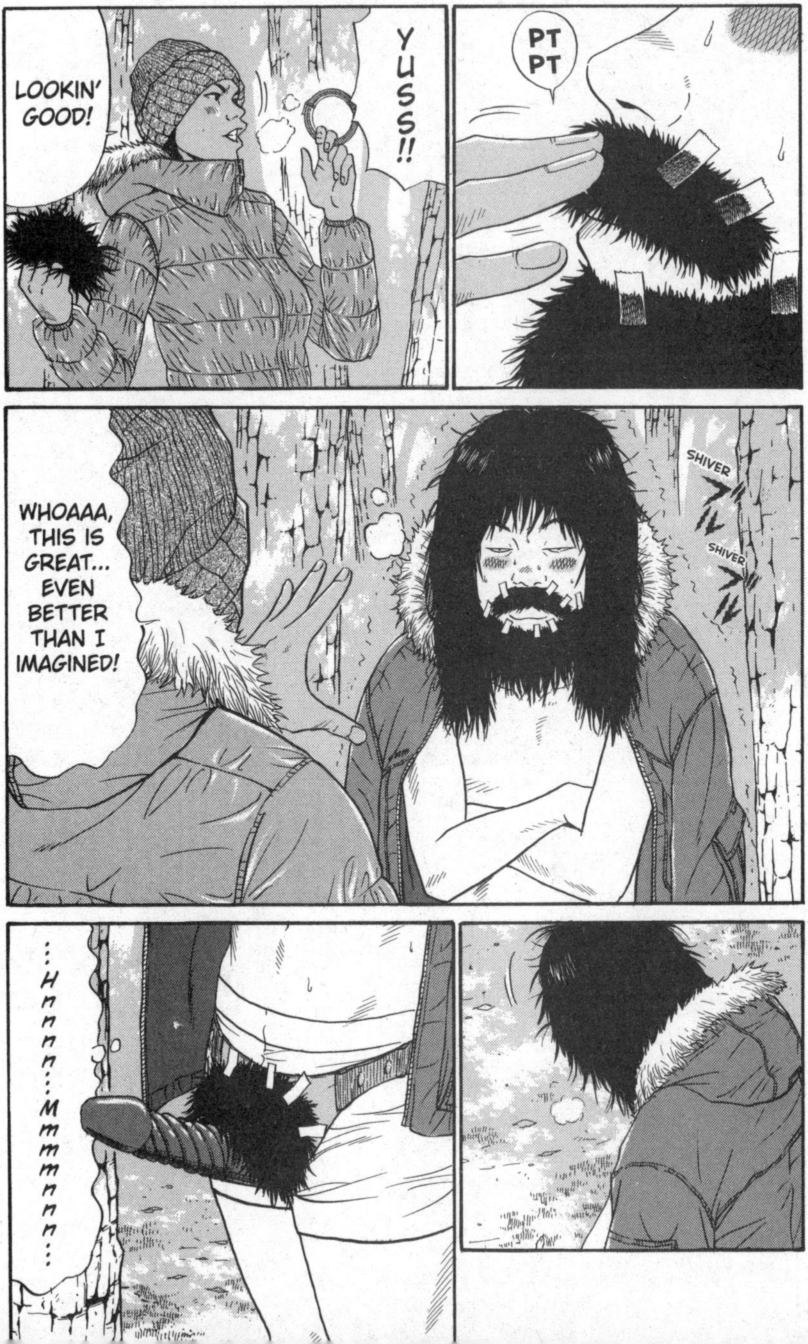
PT PT
LOOKIN' GOOD!
YUSS!!
WHOAAA, THIS IS GREAT... EVEN BETTER THAN I IMAGINED!
SHIVER
SHIVER
...Hnnnn...Mmmmmnnn...

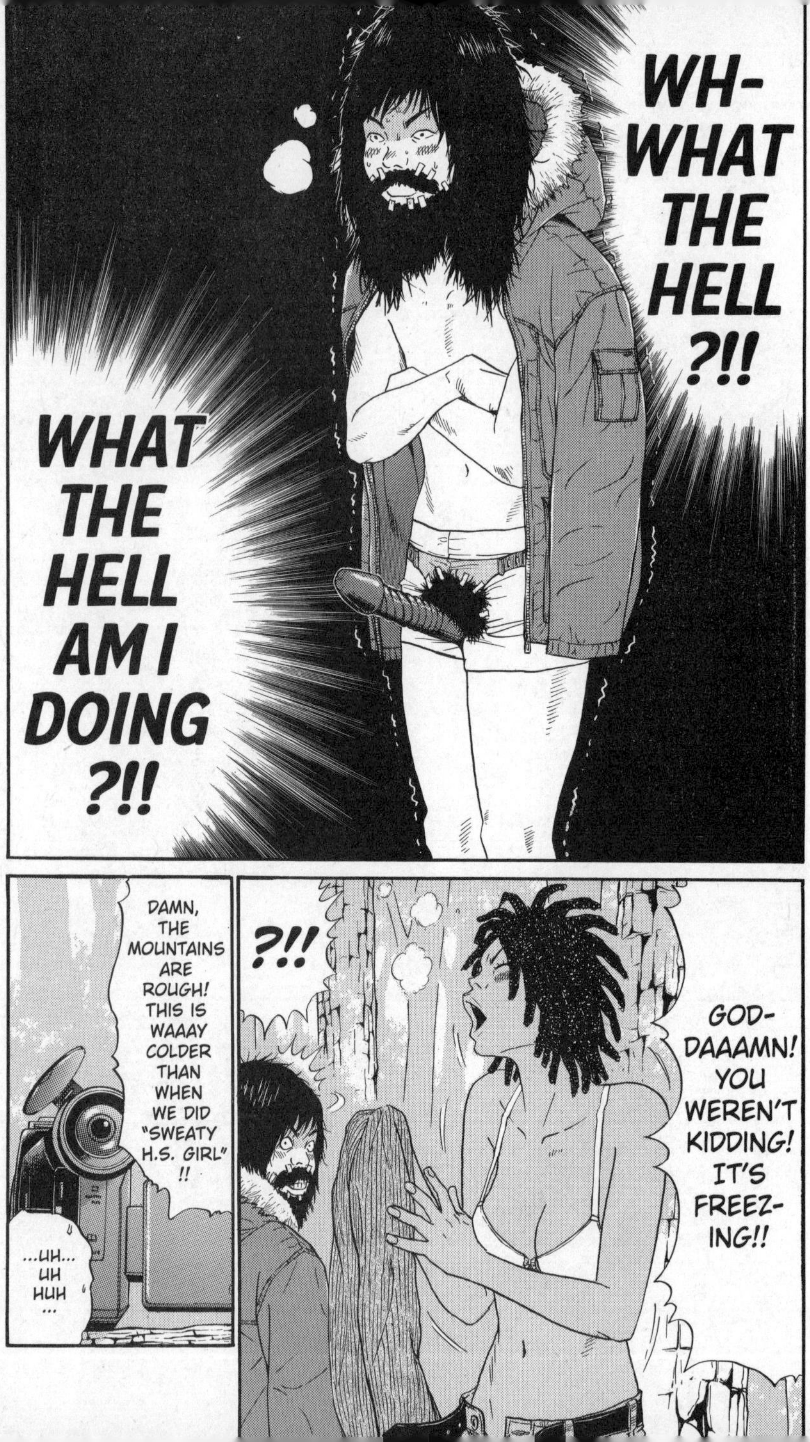
WH-WHAT THE HELL ?!!
WHAT THE HELL AM I DOING ?!!
GOD-DAAAMN! YOU WEREN'T KIDDING! IT'S FREEZ-ING!!
?!!
DAMN, THE MOUNTAINS ARE ROUGH! THIS IS WAAAY COLDER THAN WHEN WE DID "SWEATY H.S. GIRL" !!
...UH... UH HUH ...

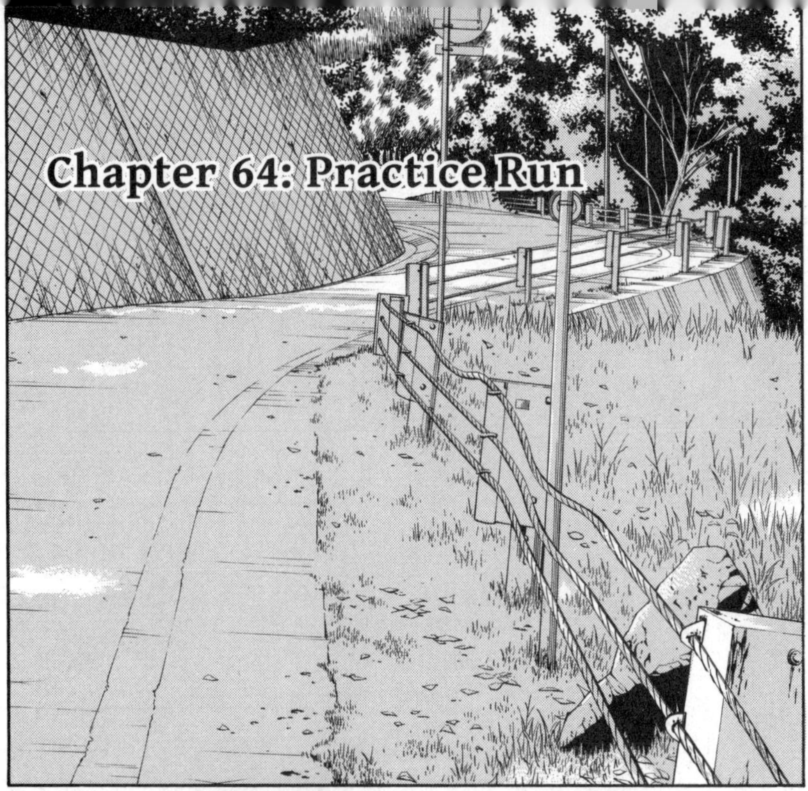
Chapter 64: Practice Run

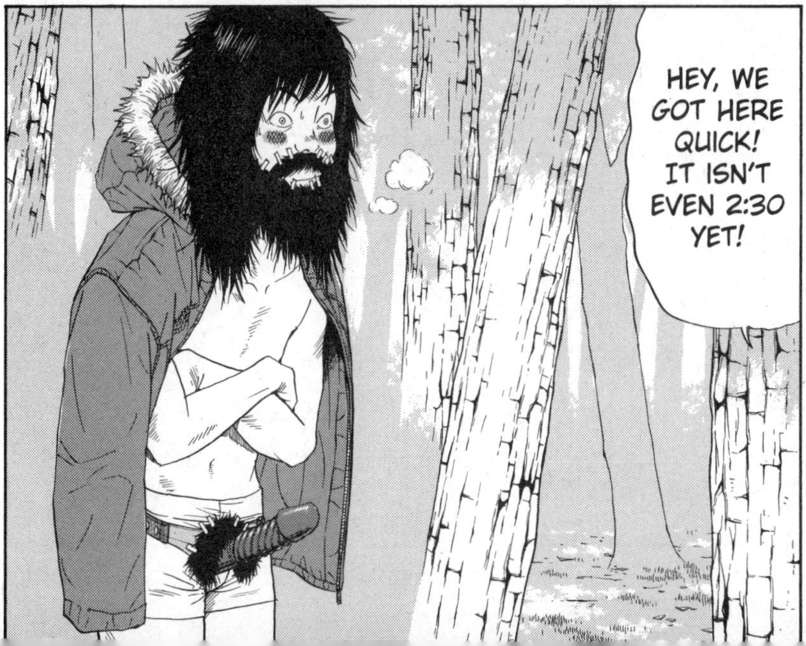
HEY, WE GOT HERE QUICK! IT ISN'T EVEN 2:30 YET!

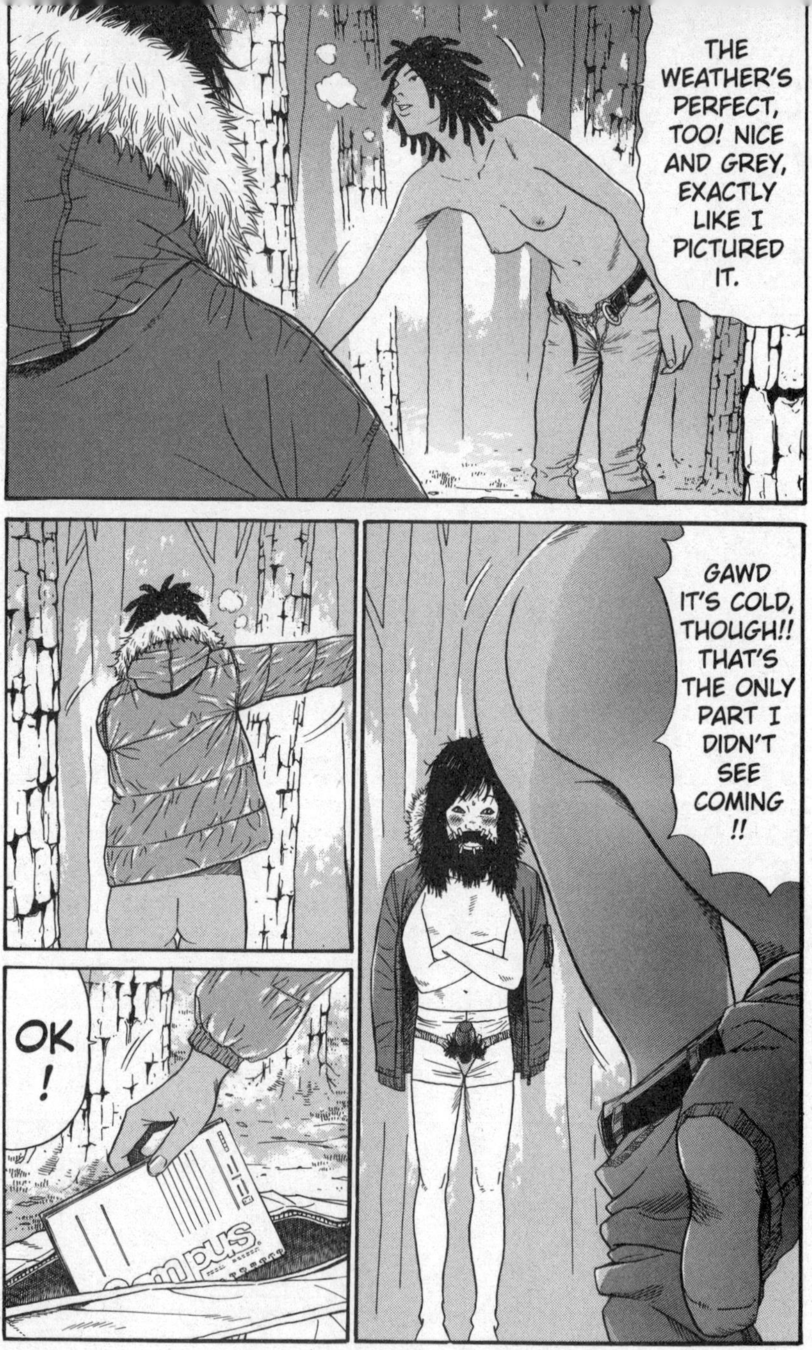
THE WEATHER'S PERFECT, TOO! NICE AND GREY, EXACTLY LIKE I PICTURED IT.
GAWD IT'S COLD, THOUGH!! THAT'S THE ONLY PART I DIDN'T SEE COMING !!
OK !

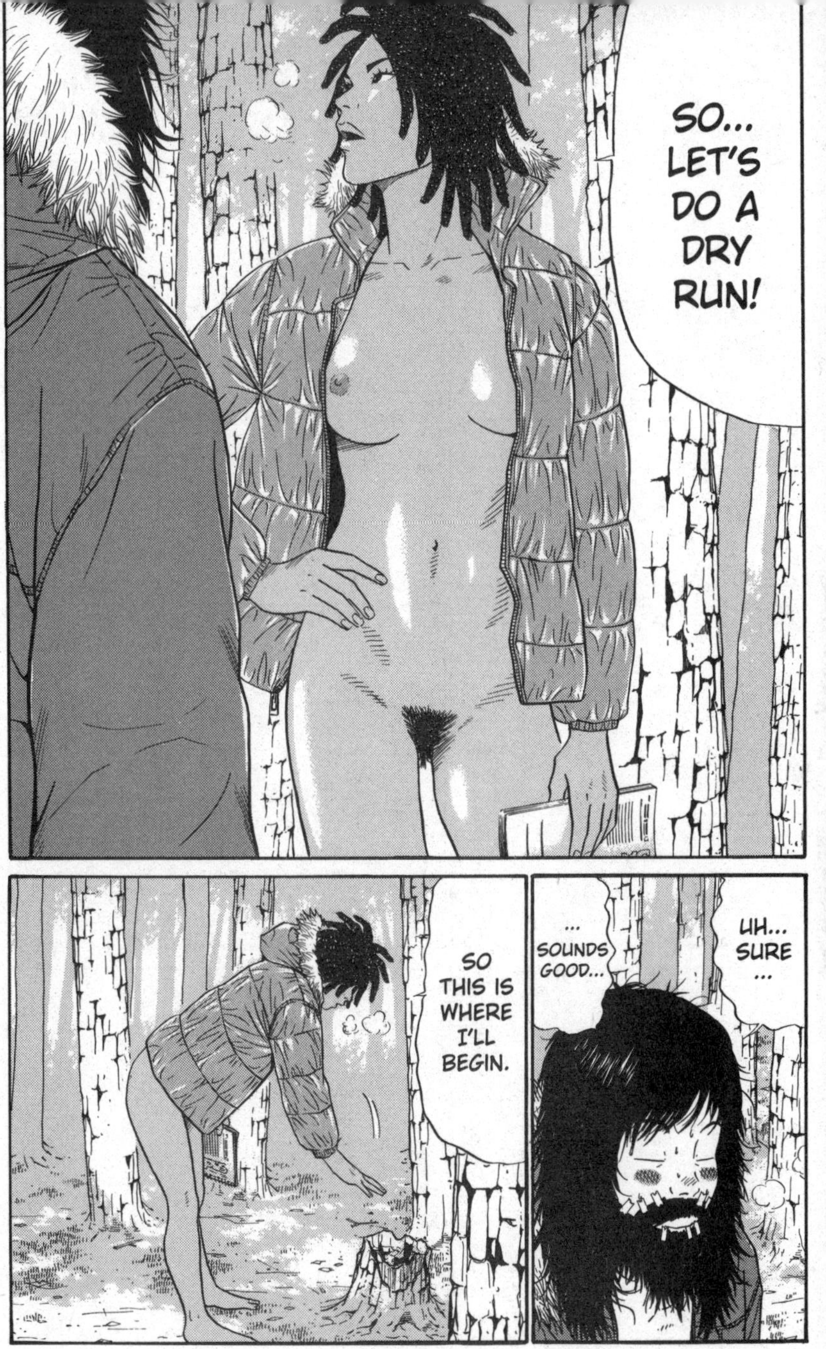
SO... LET'S DO A DRY RUN!
UH... SURE ...
... SOUNDS GOOD...
SO THIS IS WHERE I'LL BEGIN.

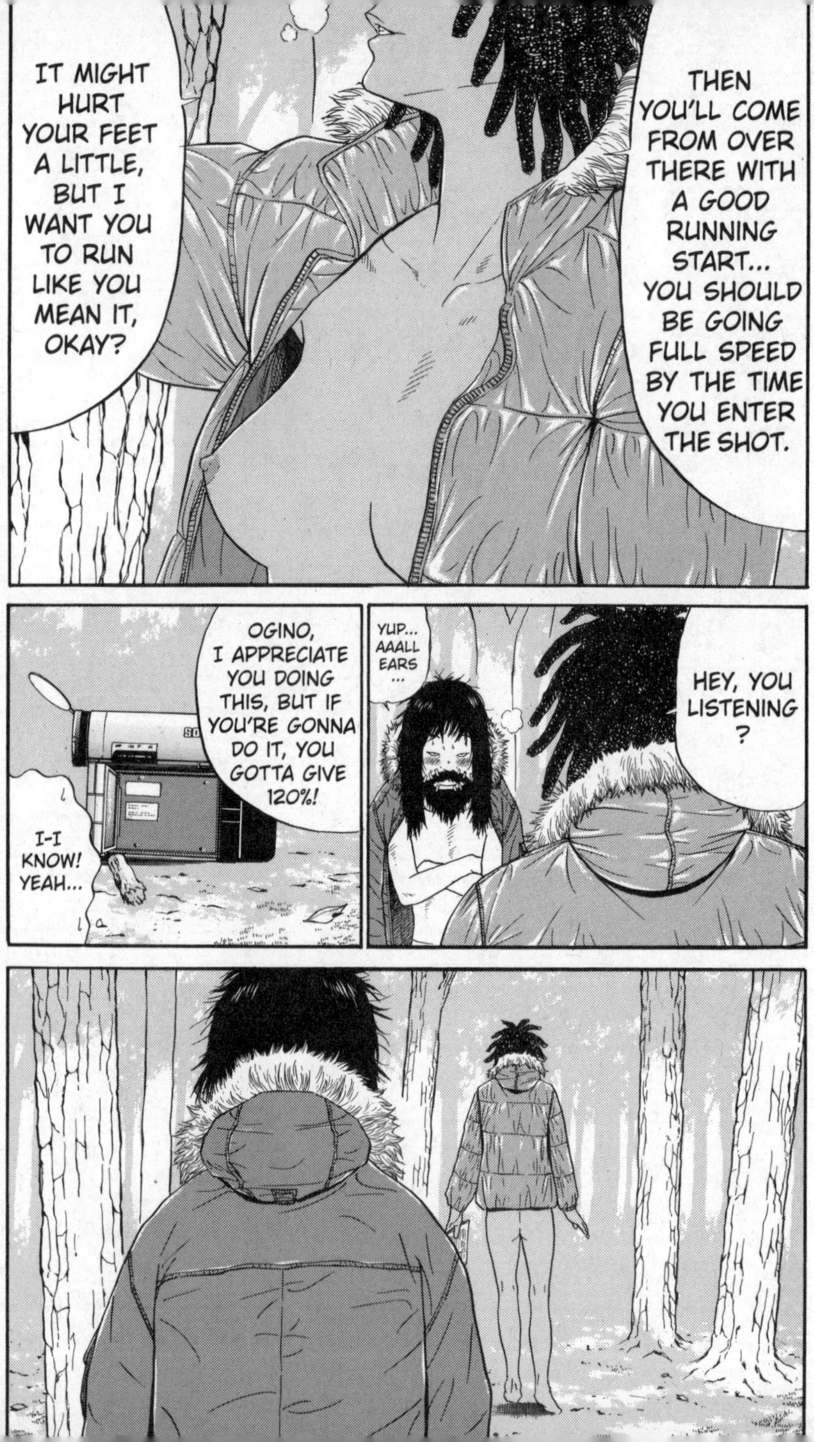
THEN YOU'LL COME FROM OVER THERE WITH A GOOD RUNNING START... YOU SHOULD BE GOING FULL SPEED BY THE TIME YOU ENTER THE SHOT.
IT MIGHT HURT YOUR FEET A LITTLE, BUT I WANT YOU TO RUN LIKE YOU MEAN IT, OKAY?
HEY, YOU LISTENING ?
YUP... AAALL EARS ...
OGINO, I APPRECIATE YOU DOING THIS, BUT IF YOU'RE GONNA DO IT, YOU GOTTA GIVE 120%!
I-I KNOW! YEAH...

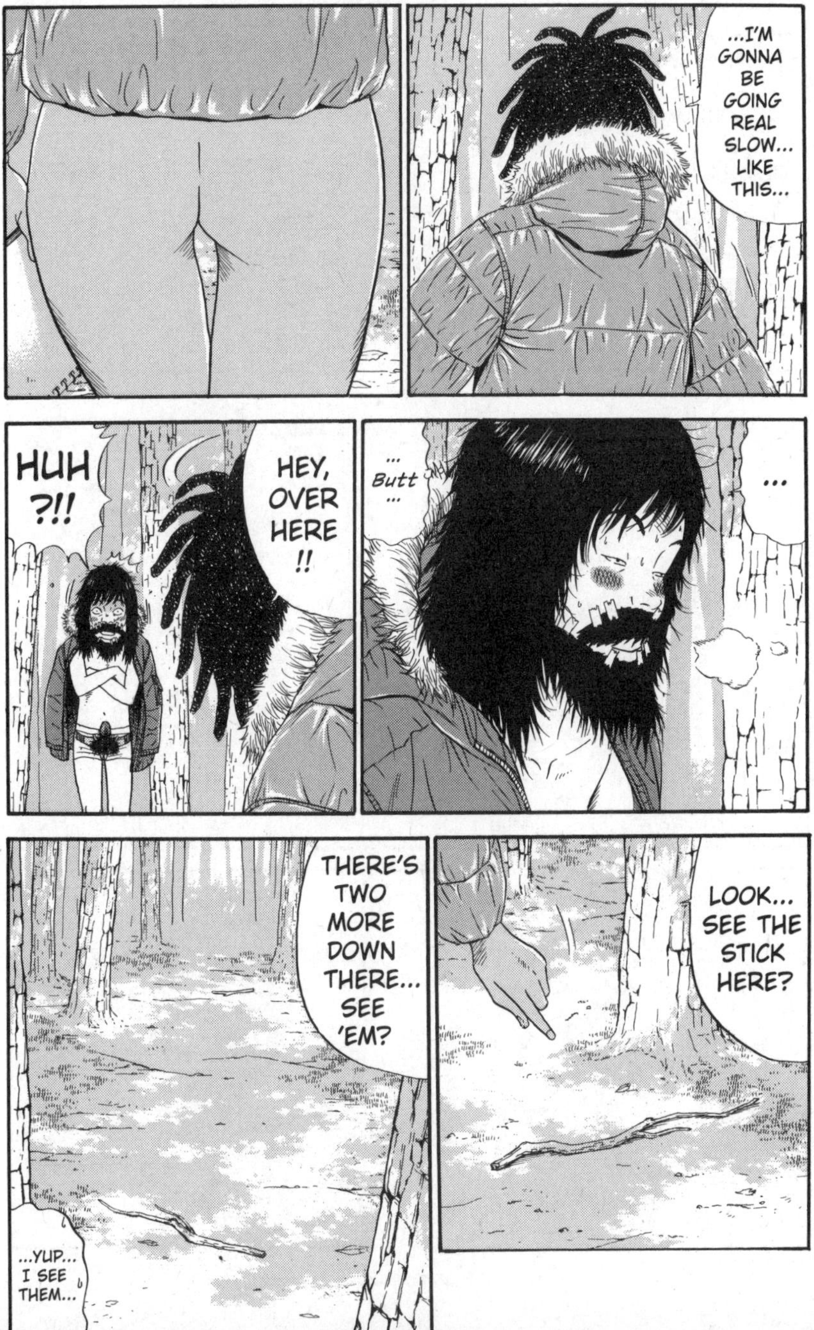
...I'M GONNA BE GOING REAL SLOW... LIKE THIS...
...
... Butt ...
HEY, OVER HERE !!
HUH ?!!
LOOK... SEE THE STICK HERE?
THERE'S TWO MORE DOWN THERE... SEE 'EM?
...YUP... I SEE THEM...

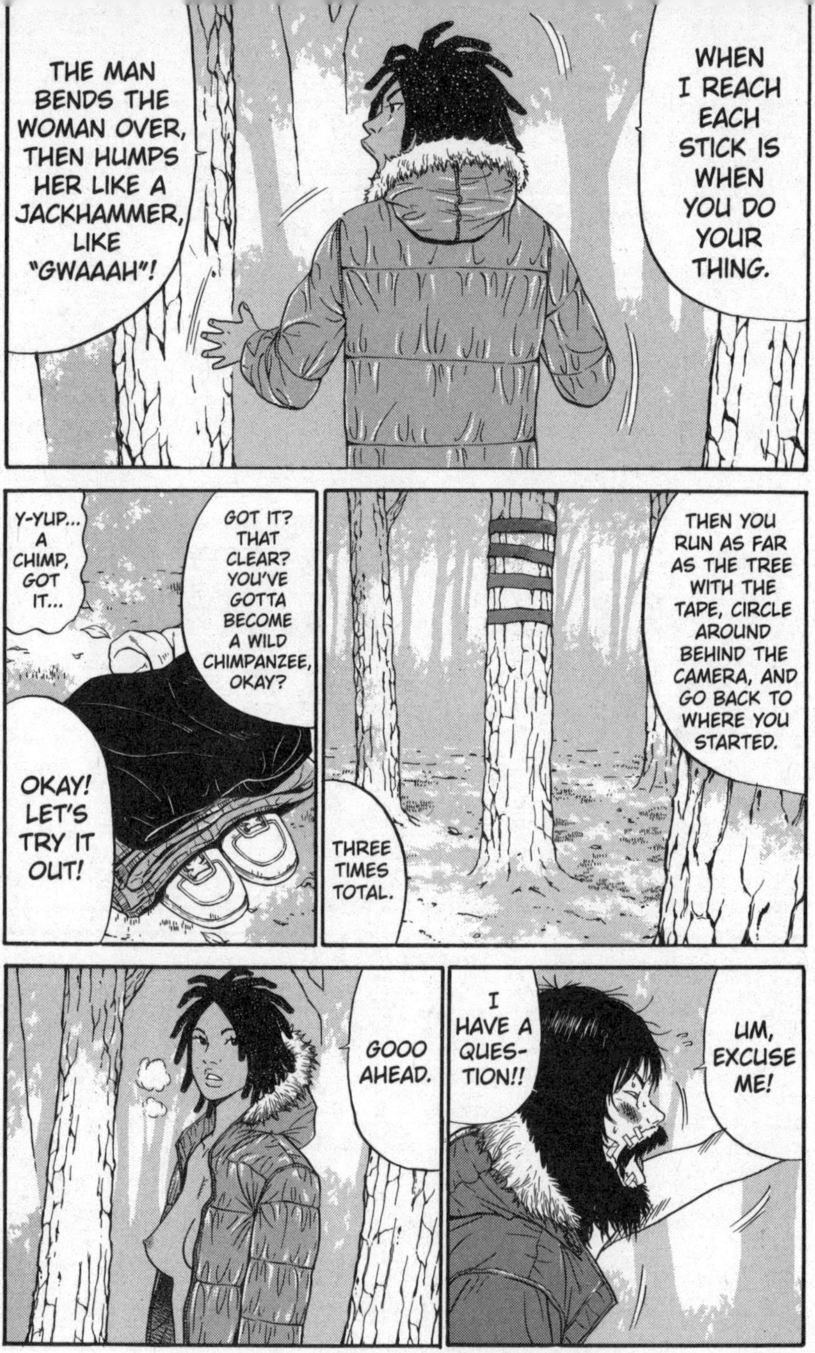
WHEN I REACH EACH STICK IS WHEN YOU DO YOUR THING.
THE MAN BENDS THE WOMAN OVER, THEN HUMPS HER LIKE A JACKHAMMER, LIKE "GWAAAH"!
THEN YOU RUN AS FAR AS THE TREE WITH THE TAPE, CIRCLE AROUND BEHIND THE CAMERA, AND GO BACK TO WHERE YOU STARTED.
THREE TIMES TOTAL.
GOT IT? THAT CLEAR? YOU'VE GOTTA BECOME A WILD CHIMPANZEE, OKAY?
Y-YUP... A CHIMP, GOT IT...
OKAY! LET'S TRY IT OUT!
UM, EXCUSE ME!
I HAVE A QUES-TION!!
GOOO AHEAD.

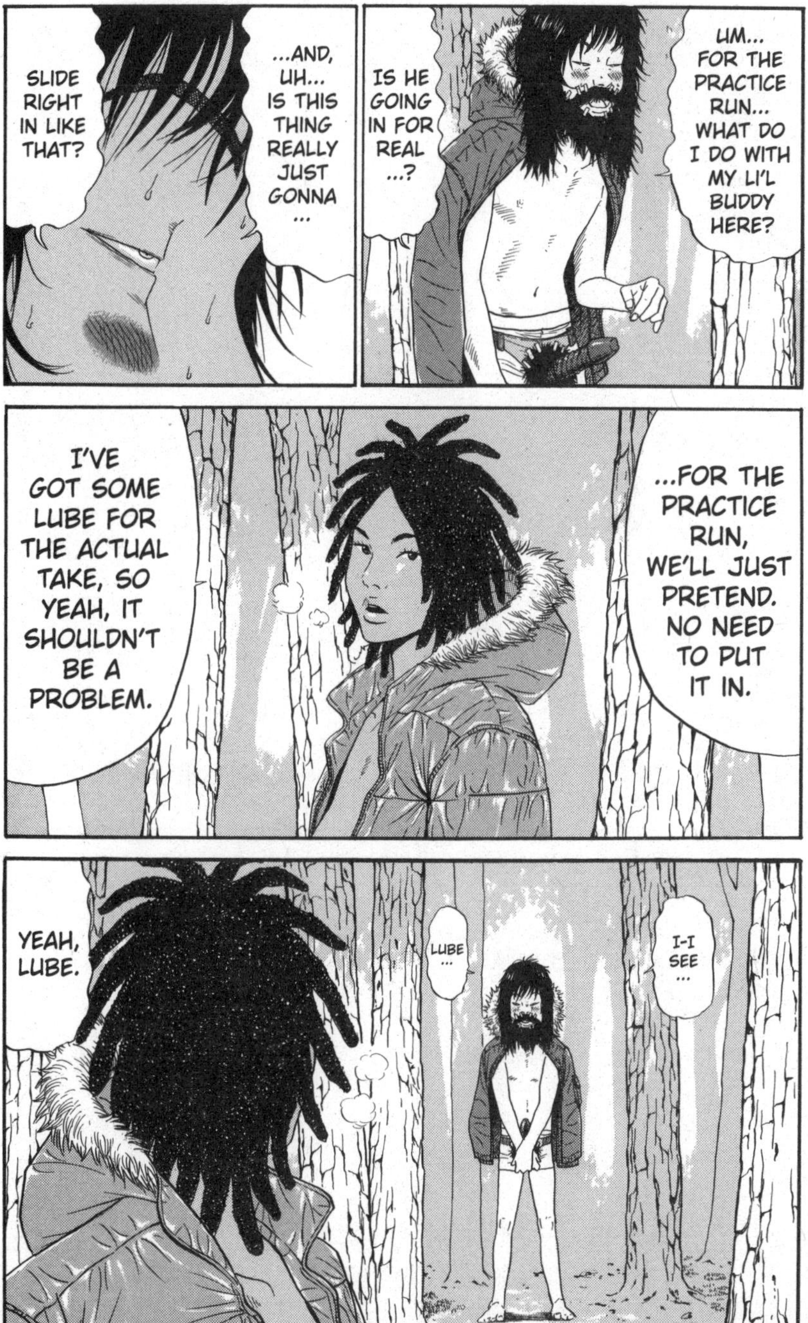
UM... FOR THE PRACTICE RUN... WHAT DO I DO WITH MY LI'L BUDDY HERE?
IS HE GOING IN FOR REAL ...?
...AND, UH... IS THIS THING REALLY JUST GONNA ...
SLIDE RIGHT IN LIKE THAT?
...FOR THE PRACTICE RUN, WE'LL JUST PRETEND. NO NEED TO PUT IT IN.
I'VE GOT SOME LUBE FOR THE ACTUAL TAKE, SO YEAH, IT SHOULDN'T BE A PROBLEM.
I-I SEE ...
LUBE ...
YEAH, LUBE.

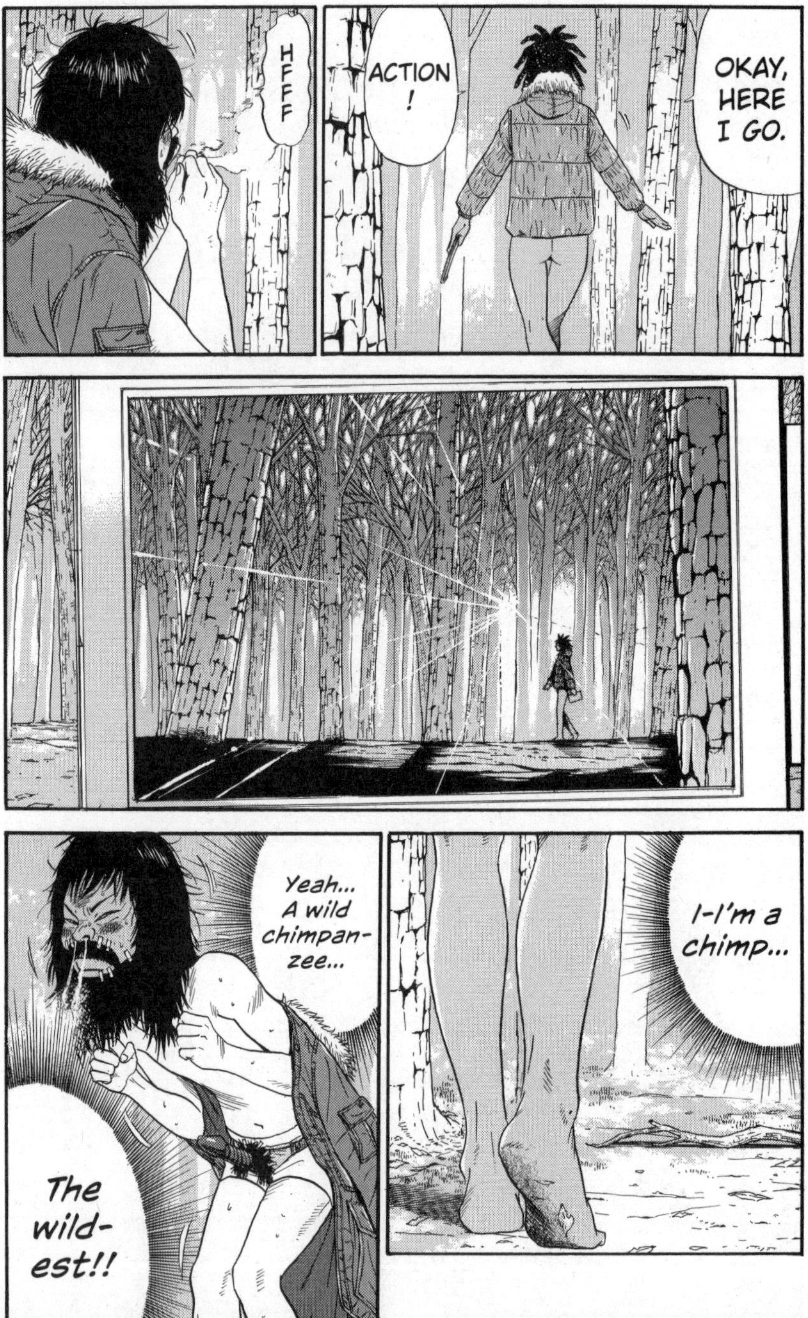
OKAY, HERE I GO.
ACTION!
HFFF
I-I'm a chimp...
Yeah... A wild chimpanzee...
The wildest!!

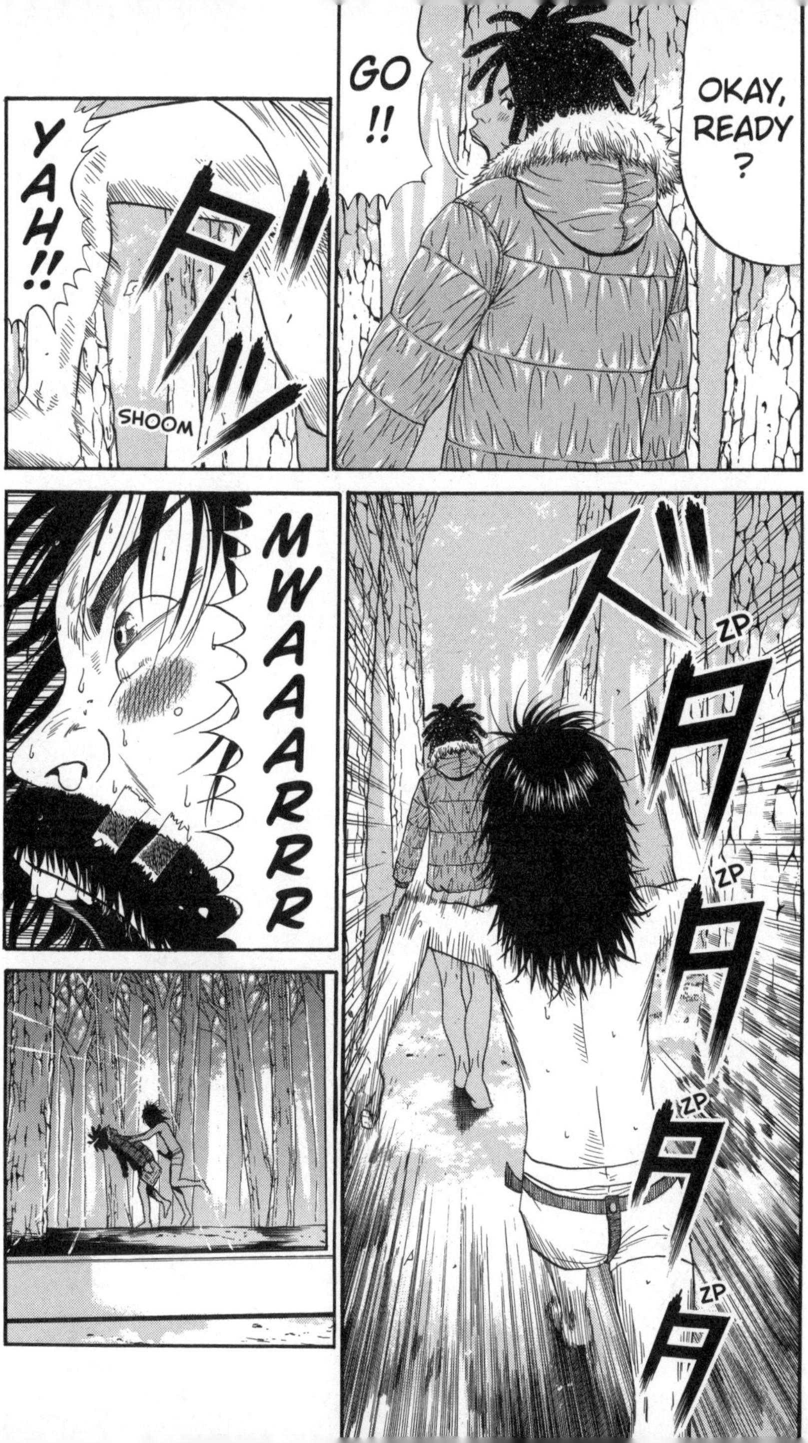
OKAY, READY?
GO!!
YAH!!
ダッ
SHOOM
ズダダダダ
ZP
ZP
ZP
ZP
MWAAAARRR

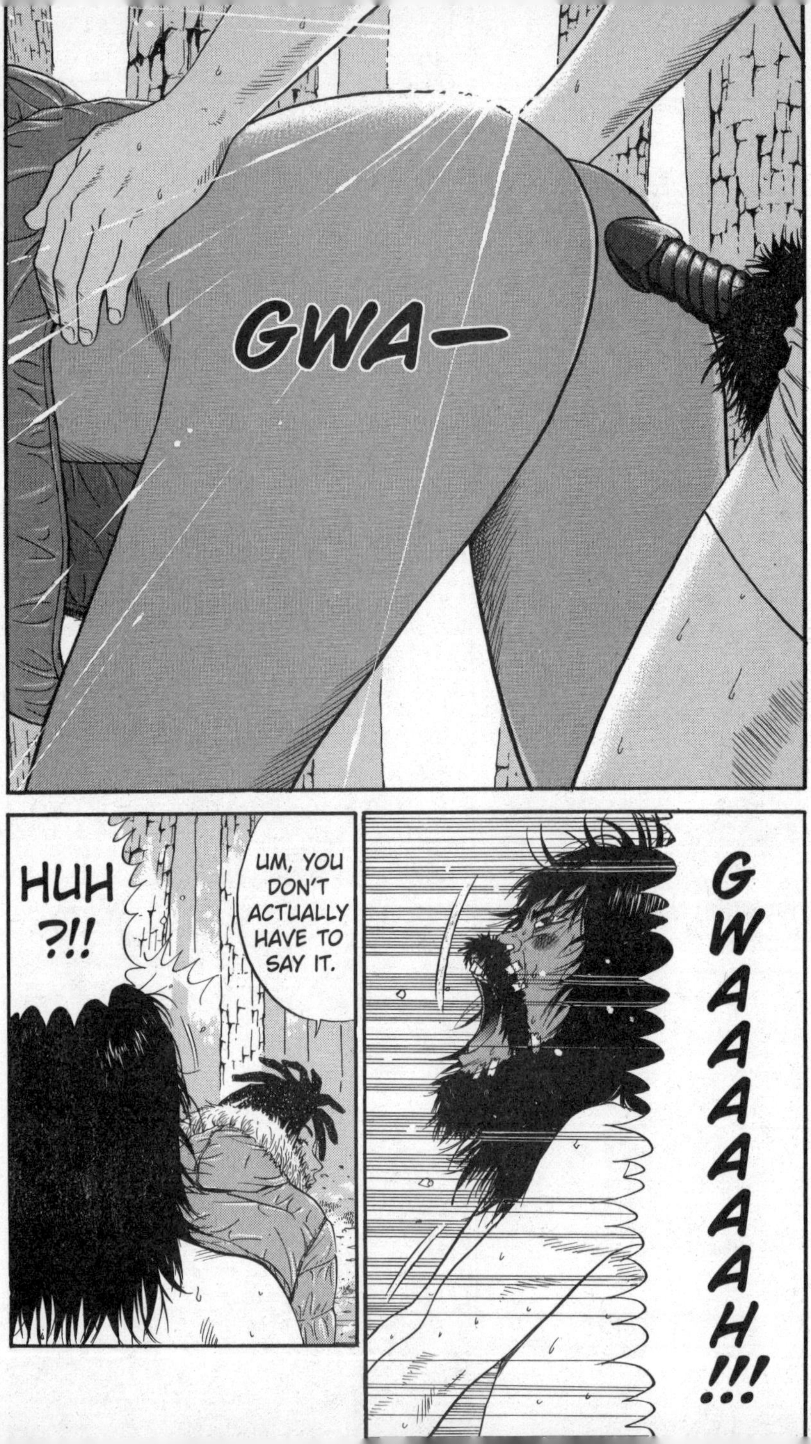
GWA—
GWAAAAAAAH!!!
UM, YOU DON'T ACTUALLY HAVE TO SAY IT.
HUH ?!!

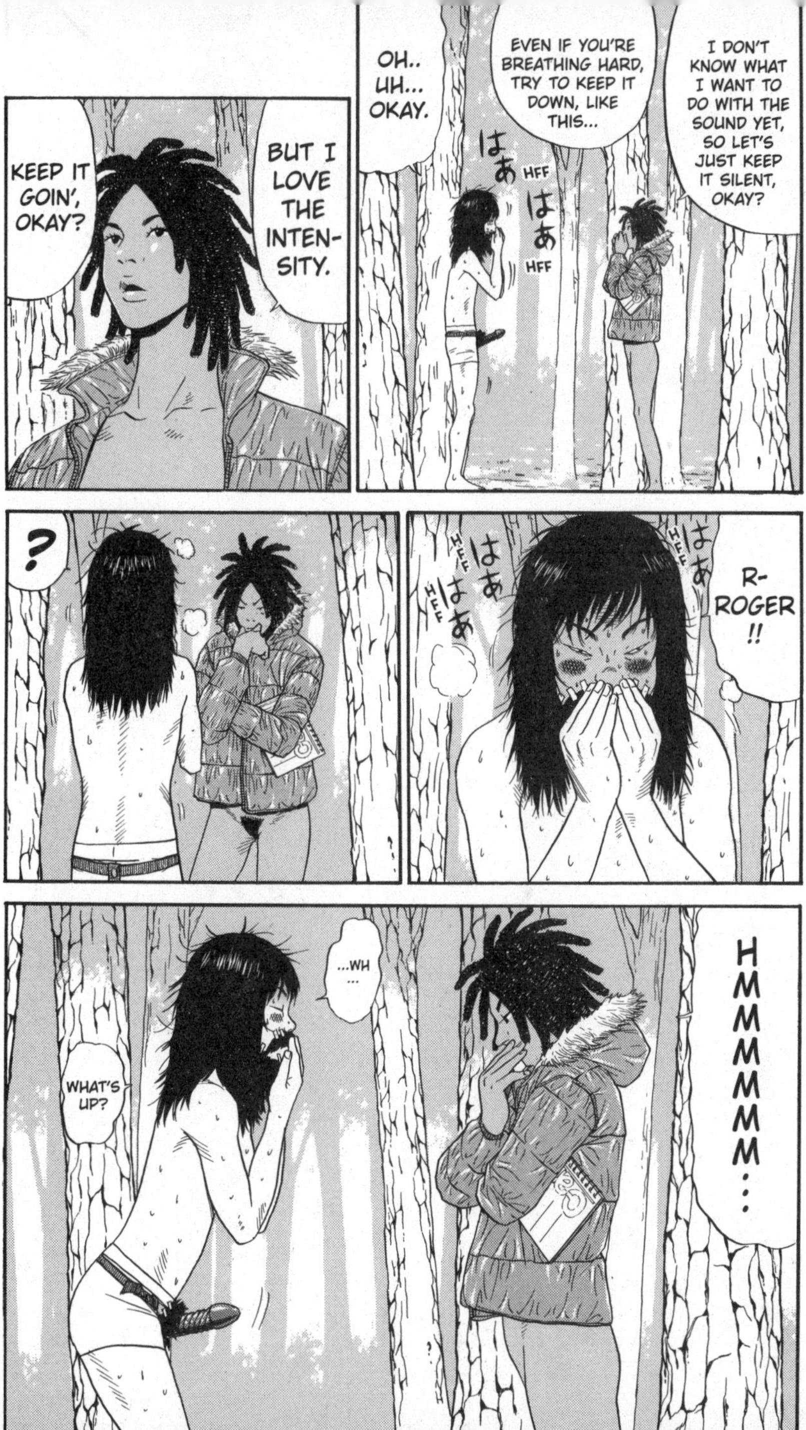
I DON'T KNOW WHAT I WANT TO DO WITH THE SOUND YET, SO LET'S JUST KEEP IT SILENT, OKAY?
EVEN IF YOU'RE BREATHING HARD, TRY TO KEEP IT DOWN, LIKE THIS...
OH.. UH... OKAY.
はあ HFF
はあ HFF
BUT I LOVE THE INTEN-SITY.
KEEP IT GOIN', OKAY?
R-ROGER!!
はあ HFF
はあ HFF
はあ HFF
?
HMMMMMM...
...WH...
WHAT'S UP?

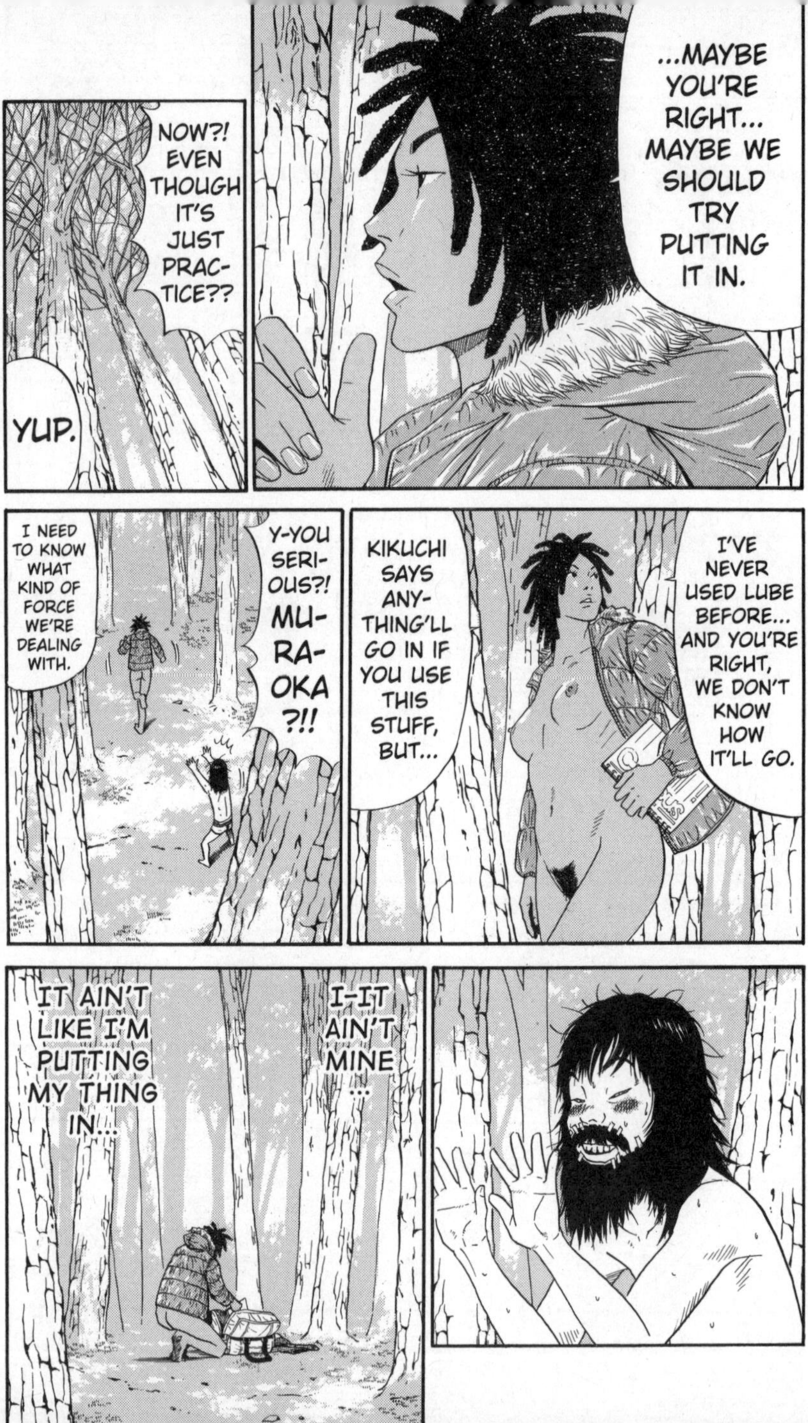
...MAYBE YOU'RE RIGHT... MAYBE WE SHOULD TRY PUTTING IT IN.
NOW?! EVEN THOUGH IT'S JUST PRACTICE??
YUP.
I'VE NEVER USED LUBE BEFORE... AND YOU'RE RIGHT, WE DON'T KNOW HOW IT'LL GO.
KIKUCHI SAYS ANYTHING'LL GO IN IF YOU USE THIS STUFF, BUT...
Y-YOU SERIOUS?! MURAOKA?!!
I NEED TO KNOW WHAT KIND OF FORCE WE'RE DEALING WITH.
I-IT AIN'T MINE...
IT AIN'T LIKE I'M PUTTING MY THING IN...

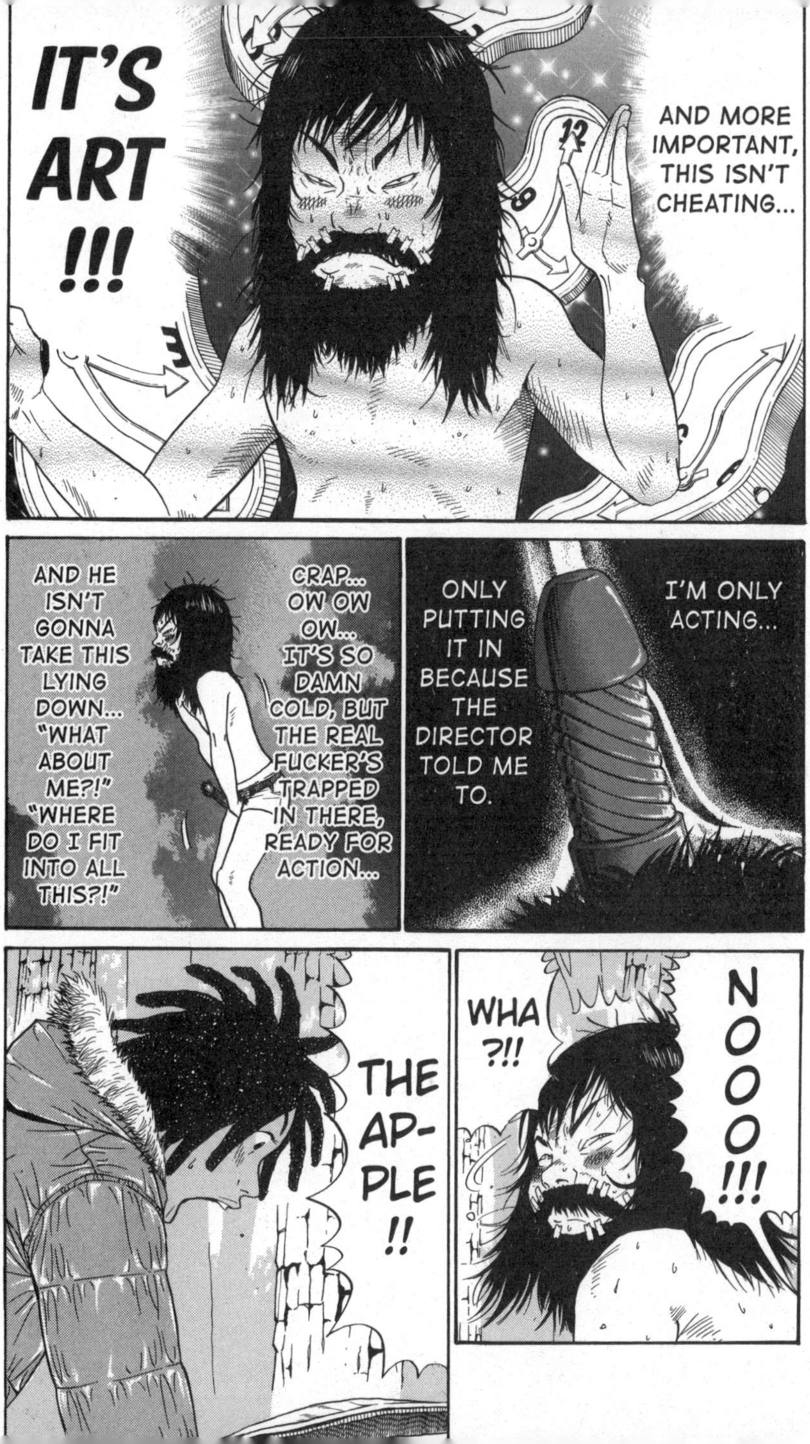
AND MORE IMPORTANT, THIS ISN'T CHEATING...
IT'S ART!!!
I'M ONLY ACTING...
ONLY PUTTING IT IN BECAUSE THE DIRECTOR TOLD ME TO.
CRAP... OW OW OW... IT'S SO DAMN COLD, BUT THE REAL FUCKER'S TRAPPED IN THERE, READY FOR ACTION...
AND HE ISN'T GONNA TAKE THIS LYING DOWN... "WHAT ABOUT ME?!" "WHERE DO I FIT INTO ALL THIS?!"
NOOOO!!!
WHA?!!
THE AP-PLE!!

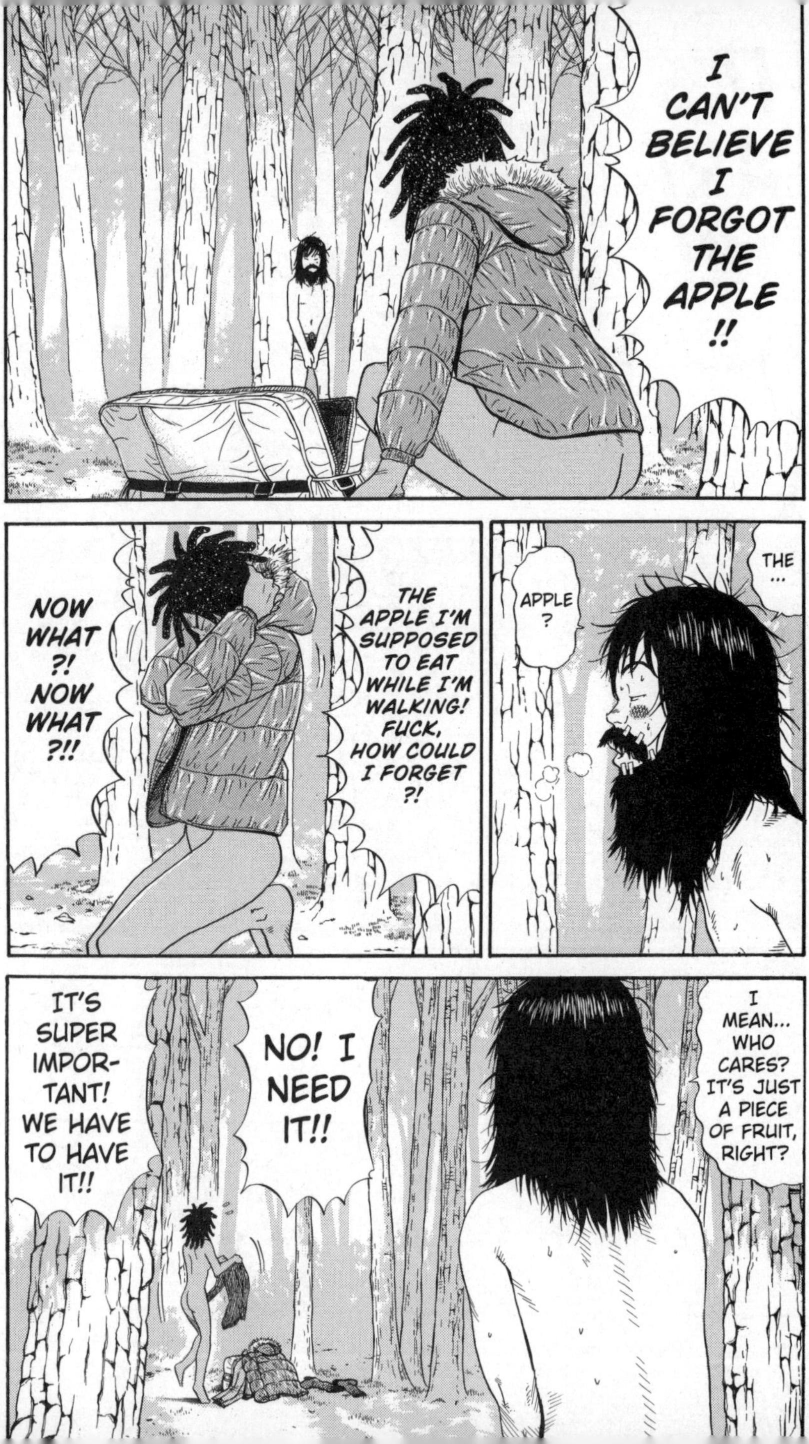

I CAN'T BELIEVE I FORGOT THE APPLE !!
THE...
APPLE ?
THE APPLE I'M SUPPOSED TO EAT WHILE I'M WALKING! FUCK, HOW COULD I FORGET ?!
NOW WHAT ?! NOW WHAT ?!!
I MEAN... WHO CARES? IT'S JUST A PIECE OF FRUIT, RIGHT?
NO! I NEED IT!!
IT'S SUPER IMPOR-TANT! WE HAVE TO HAVE IT!!

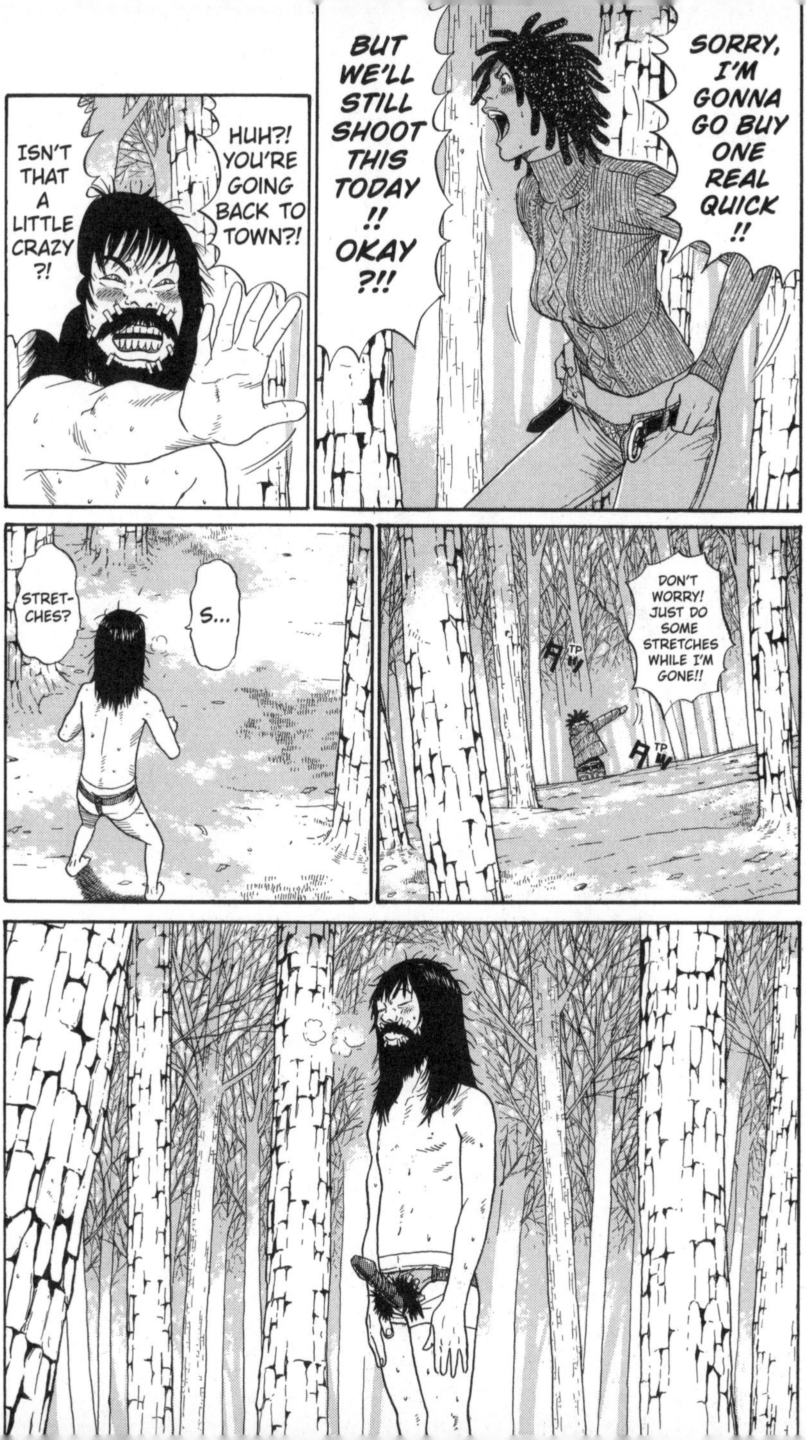
SORRY, I'M GONNA GO BUY ONE REAL QUICK!!
BUT WE'LL STILL SHOOT THIS TODAY!! OKAY?!!
HUH?! YOU'RE GOING BACK TO TOWN?!
ISN'T THAT A LITTLE CRAZY?!
DON'T WORRY! JUST DO SOME STRETCHES WHILE I'M GONE!!
TP
TP
S...
STRET-CHES?

HNG く"っ

HNG く"っ

HNG く"っ

HNG く"っ

...I saw it...

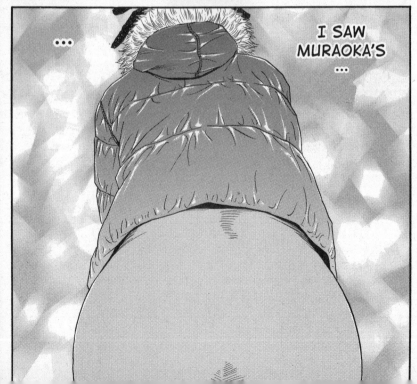

...

I SAW MURAOKA'S

...

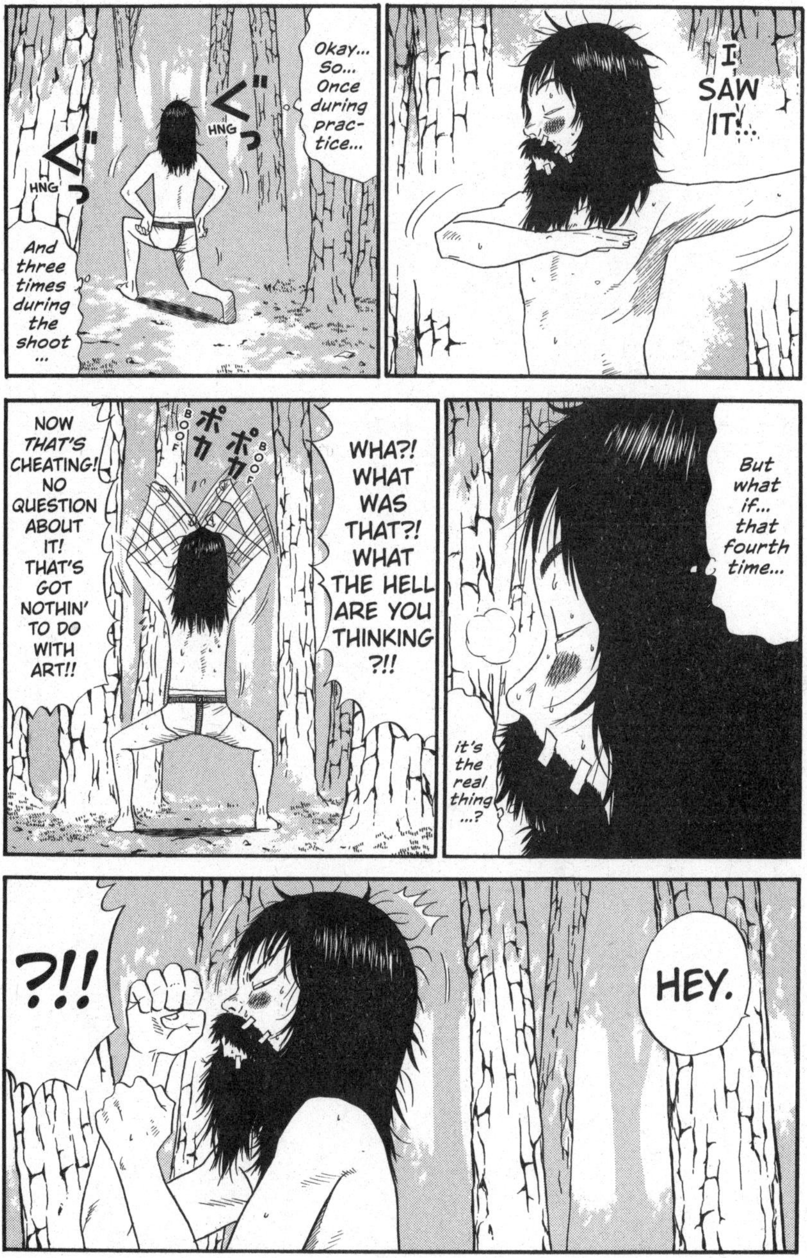
I SAW IT!...
Okay... So... Once during prac-tice...
ぐっ
HNG
ぐっ
HNG
And three times during the shoot...
But what if... that fourth time...
it's the real thing...?
WHA?! WHAT WAS THAT?! WHAT THE HELL ARE YOU THINKING?!!
ポカ
BOOF
ポカ
BOOF
NOW THAT'S CHEATING! NO QUESTION ABOUT IT! THAT'S GOT NOTHIN' TO DO WITH ART!!
HEY.
?!!

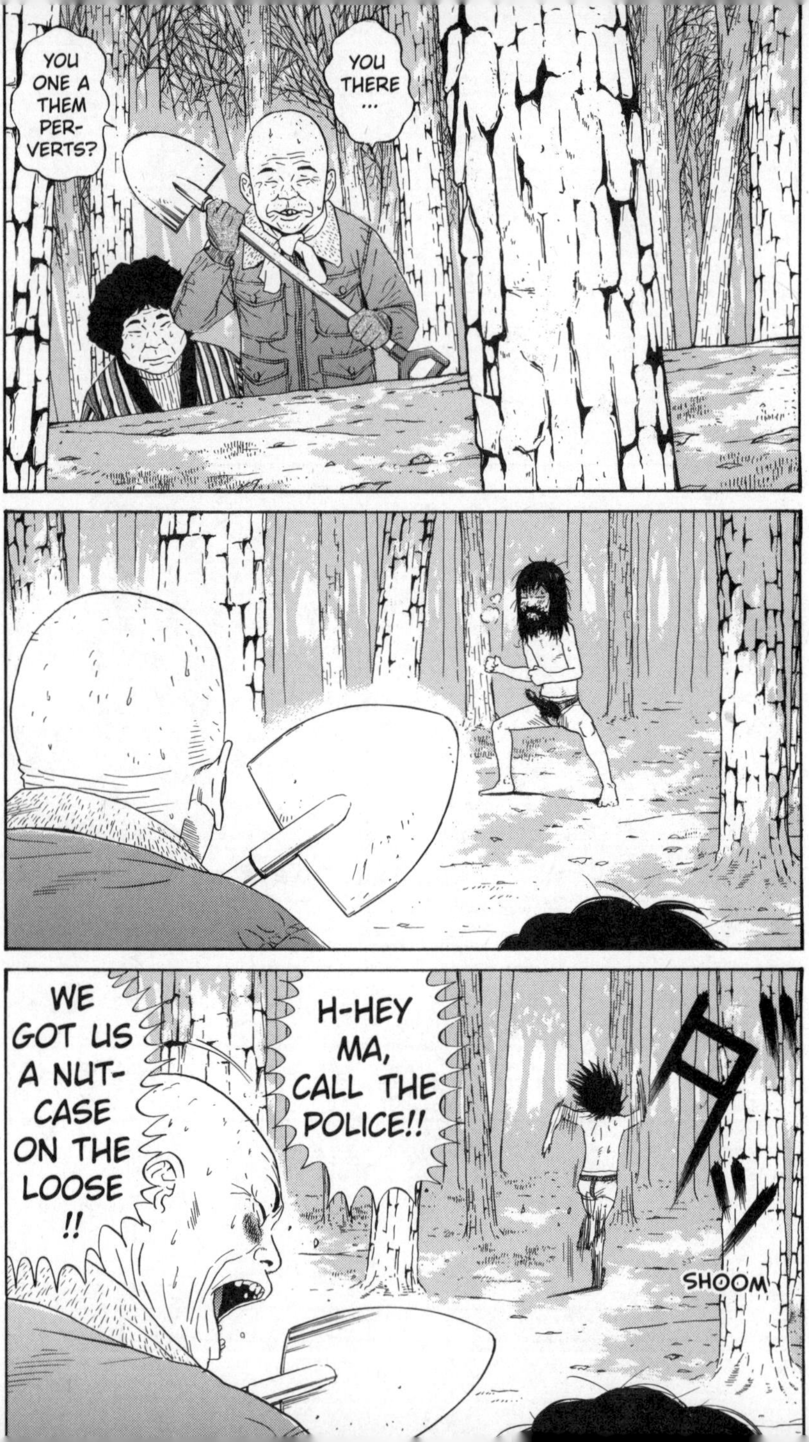
YOU THERE ...
YOU ONE A THEM PER-VERTS?
H-HEY MA, CALL THE POLICE!!
WE GOT US A NUT-CASE ON THE LOOSE !!
SHOOM

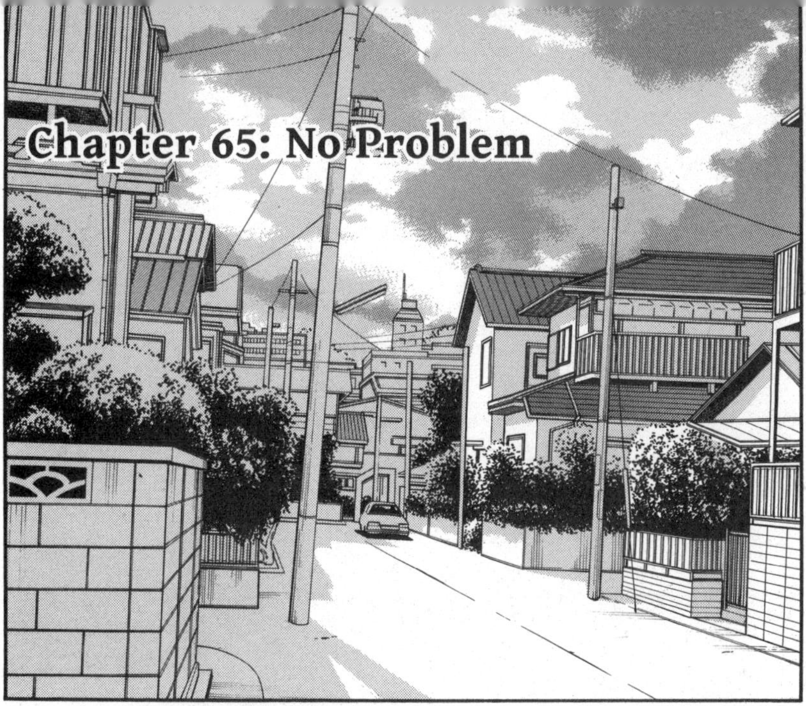
Chapter 65: No Problem
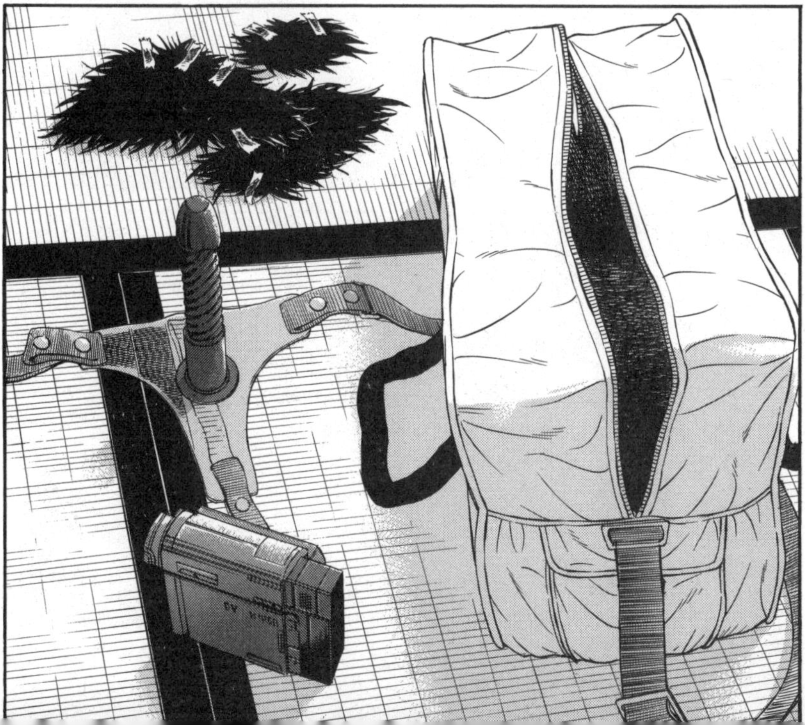

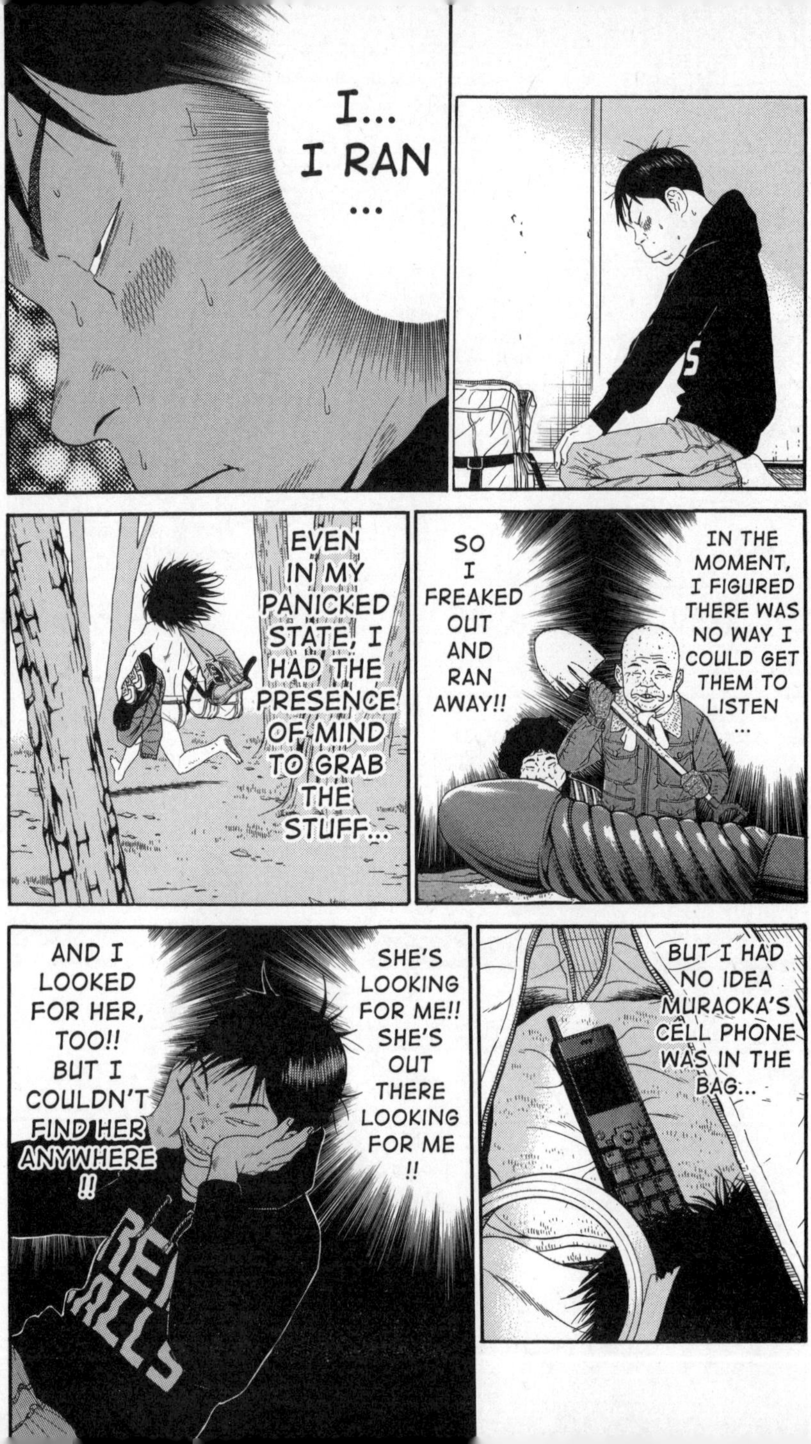
I... I RAN ...
IN THE MOMENT, I FIGURED THERE WAS NO WAY I COULD GET THEM TO LISTEN ...
SO I FREAKED OUT AND RAN AWAY!!
EVEN IN MY PANICKED STATE, I HAD THE PRESENCE OF MIND TO GRAB THE STUFF...
BUT I HAD NO IDEA MURAOKA'S CELL PHONE WAS IN THE BAG...
SHE'S LOOKING FOR ME!! SHE'S OUT THERE LOOKING FOR ME !!
AND I LOOKED FOR HER, TOO!! BUT I COULDN'T FIND HER ANYWHERE !!

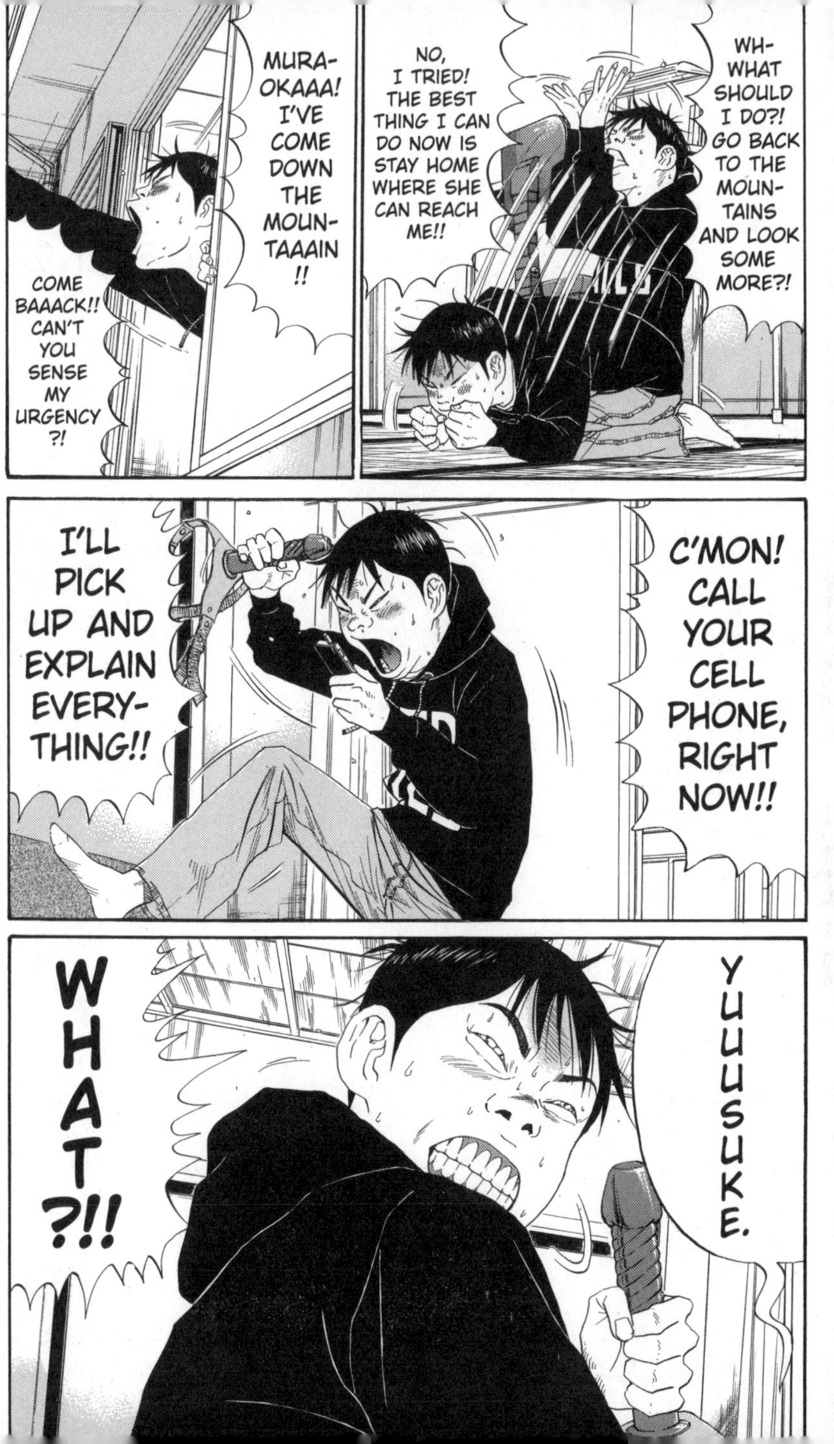
WH-WHAT SHOULD I DO?! GO BACK TO THE MOUNTAINS AND LOOK SOME MORE?!
NO, I TRIED! THE BEST THING I CAN DO NOW IS STAY HOME WHERE SHE CAN REACH ME!!
MURA-OKAAA! I'VE COME DOWN THE MOUN-TAAAIN!!
COME BAAACK!! CAN'T YOU SENSE MY URGENCY?!
C'MON! CALL YOUR CELL PHONE, RIGHT NOW!!
I'LL PICK UP AND EXPLAIN EVERY-THING!!
YUUUSUKE.
WHAT?!!

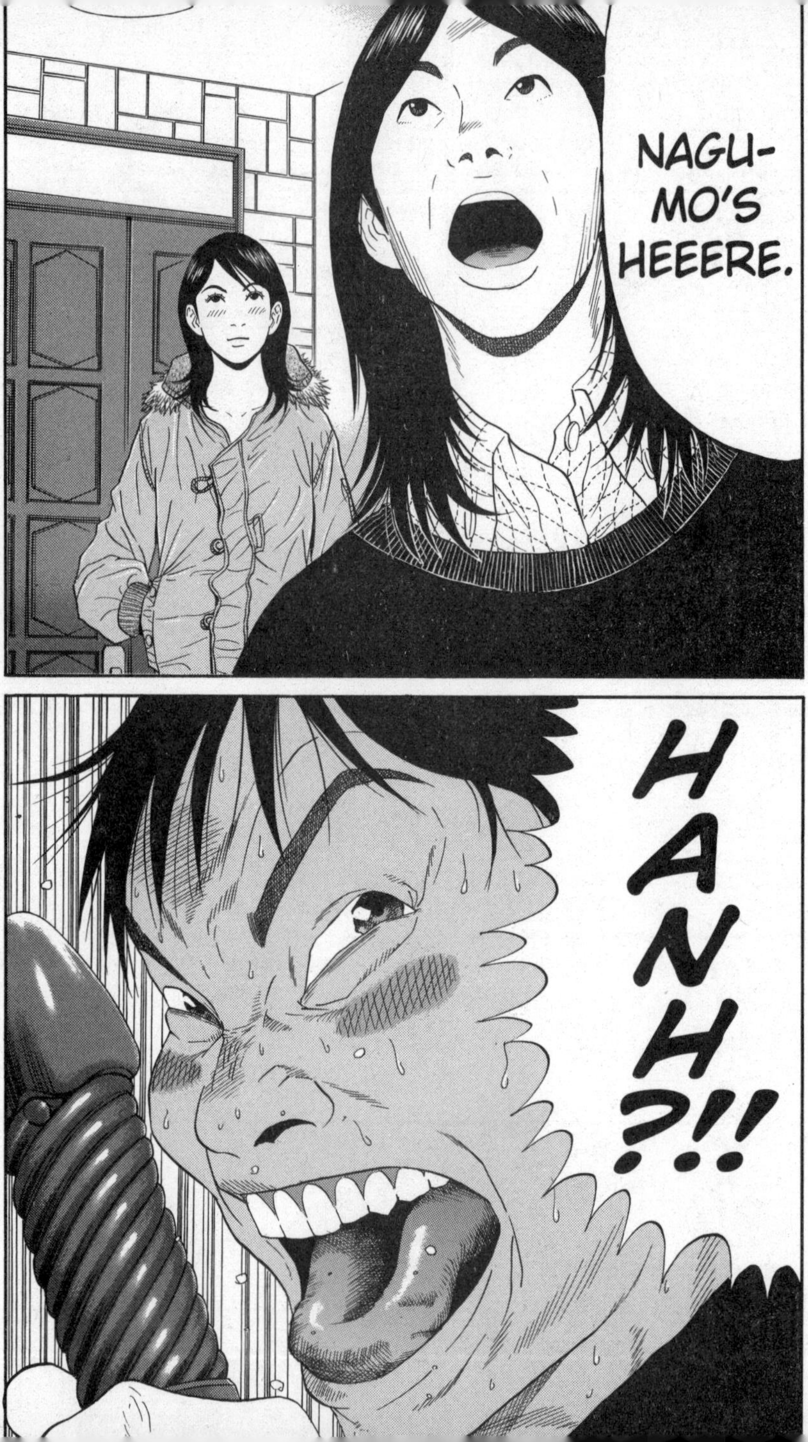
NAGU-
MO'S
HEEERE.
HANH?!!

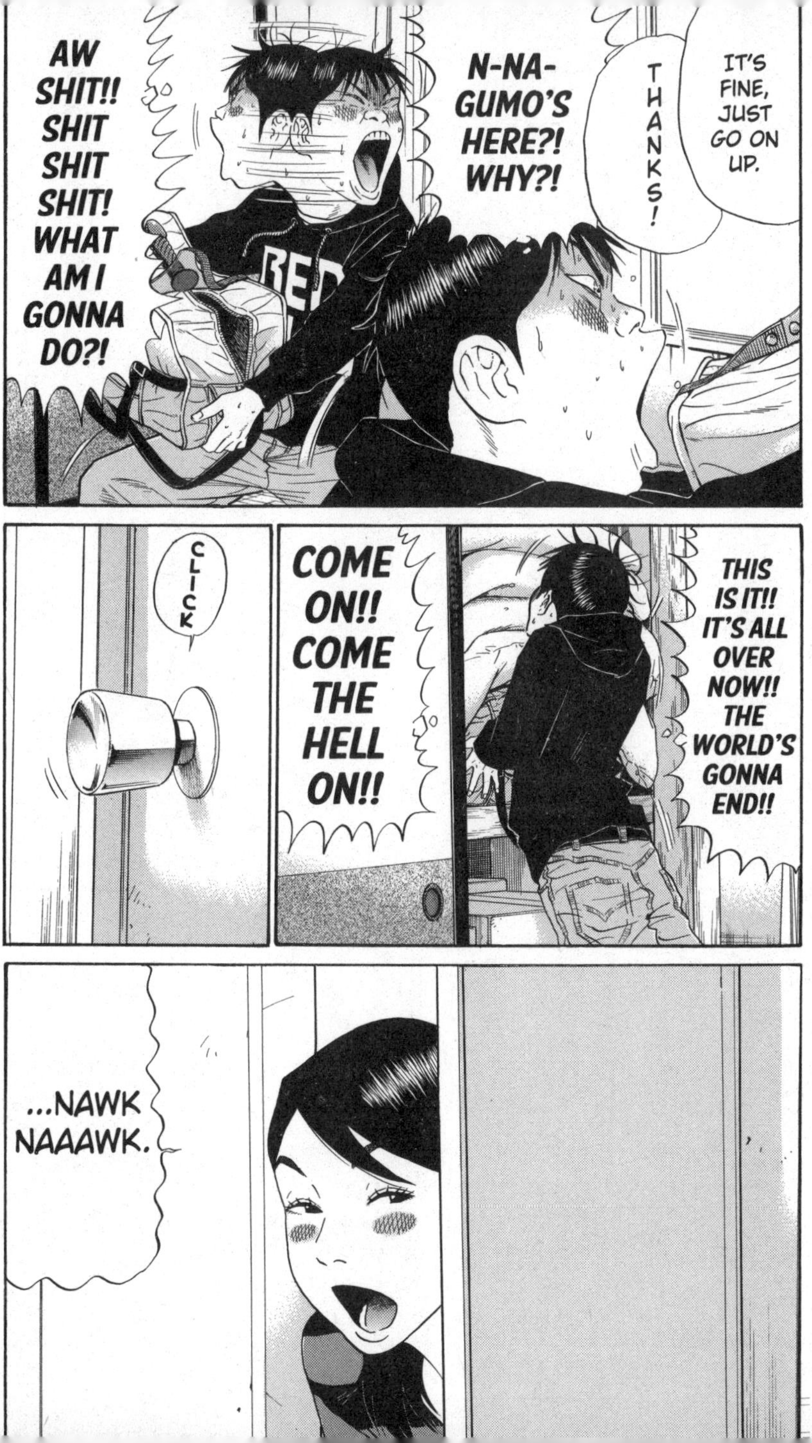
IT'S FINE, JUST GO ON UP.
THANKS!
N-NAGUMO'S HERE?! WHY?!
AW SHIT!! SHIT SHIT SHIT! WHAT AM I GONNA DO?!
THIS IS IT!! IT'S ALL OVER NOW!! THE WORLD'S GONNA END!!
COME ON!! COME THE HELL ON!!
CLICK
...NAWK NAAAWK.

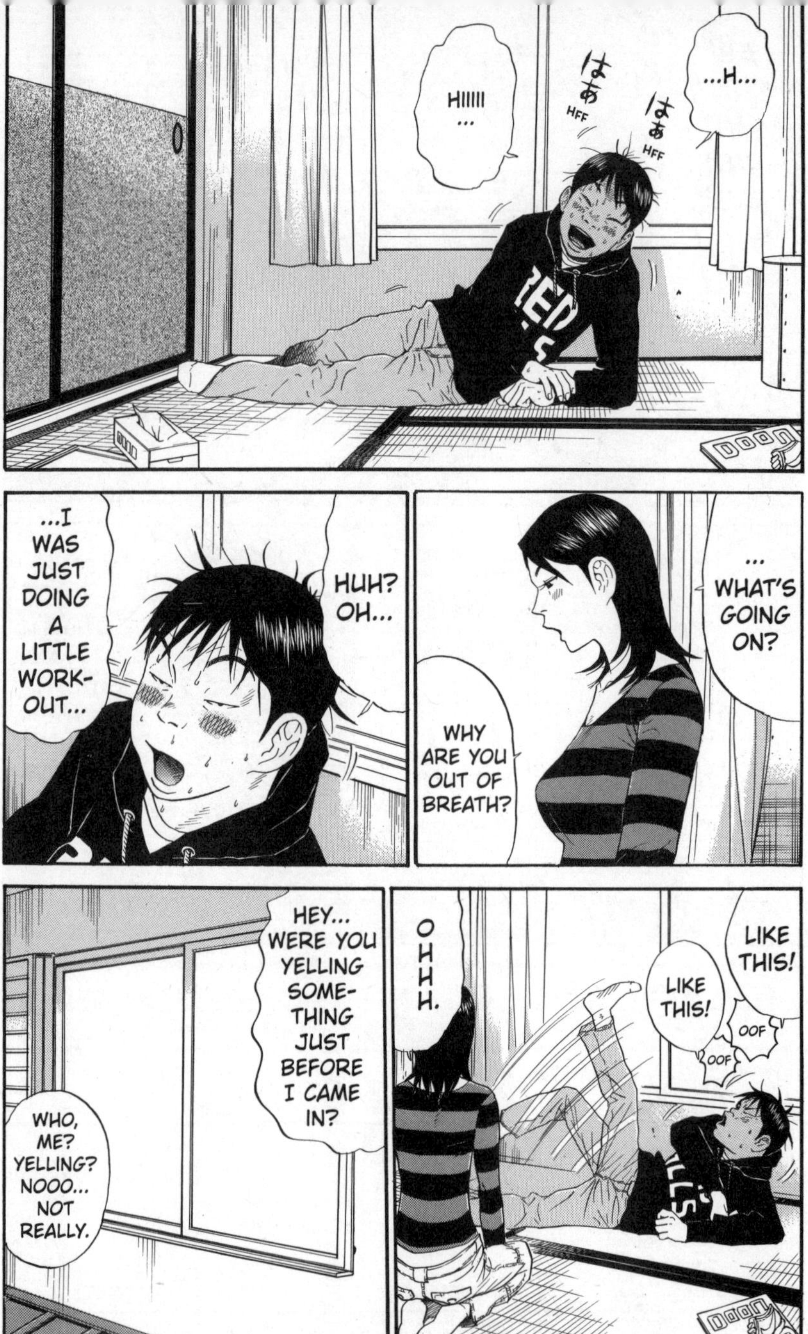
...H...
はぁ HFF
はぁ HFF
HIIIII ...
... WHAT'S GOING ON?
WHY ARE YOU OUT OF BREATH?
HUH? OH...
...I WAS JUST DOING A LITTLE WORK-OUT...
LIKE THIS!
LIKE THIS!
OOF
OOF
OHHH.
HEY... WERE YOU YELLING SOME-THING JUST BEFORE I CAME IN?
WHO, ME? YELLING? NOOO... NOT REALLY.

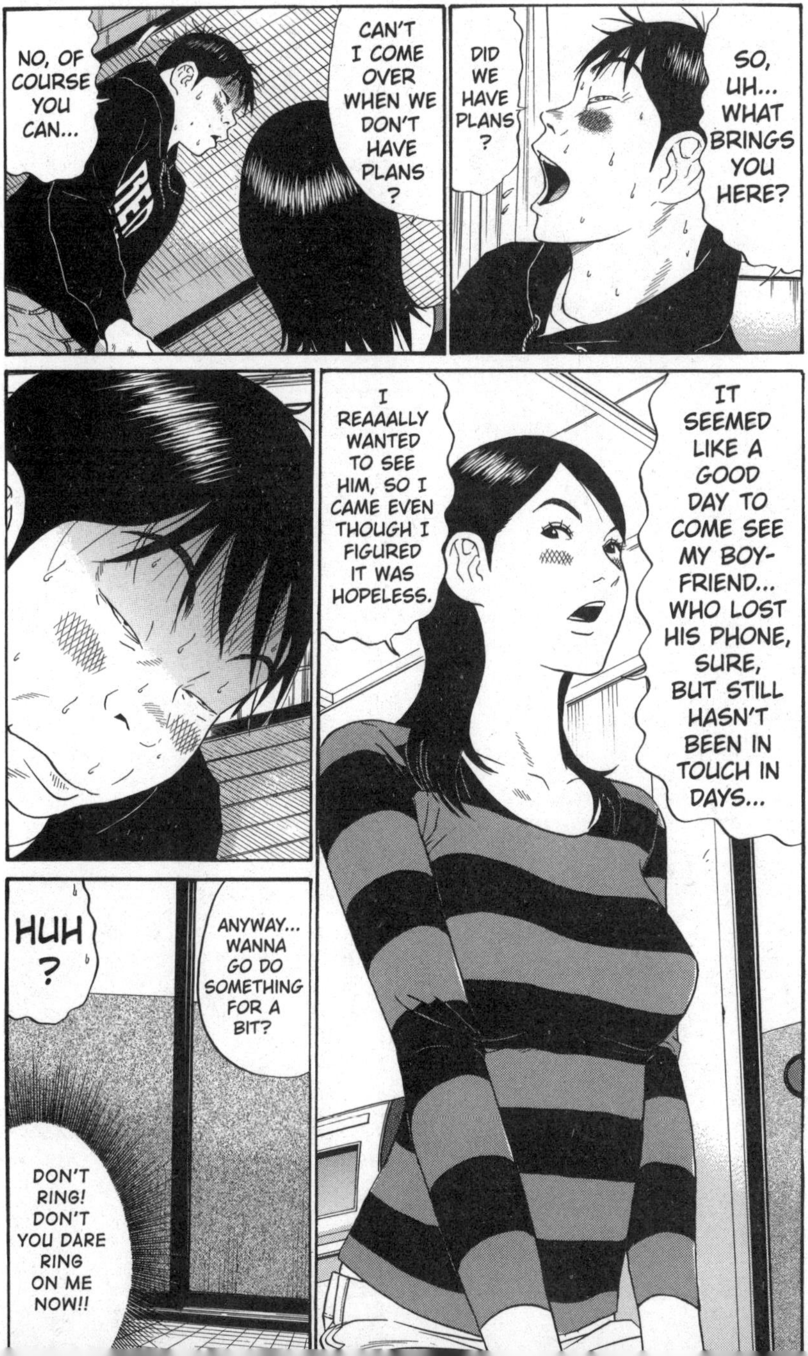
SO, UH... WHAT BRINGS YOU HERE?
DID WE HAVE PLANS?
CAN'T I COME OVER WHEN WE DON'T HAVE PLANS?
NO, OF COURSE YOU CAN...
IT SEEMED LIKE A GOOD DAY TO COME SEE MY BOY-FRIEND... WHO LOST HIS PHONE, SURE, BUT STILL HASN'T BEEN IN TOUCH IN DAYS...
I REAAALLY WANTED TO SEE HIM, SO I CAME EVEN THOUGH I FIGURED IT WAS HOPELESS.
ANYWAY... WANNA GO DO SOMETHING FOR A BIT?
HUH?
DON'T RING! DON'T YOU DARE RING ON ME NOW!!

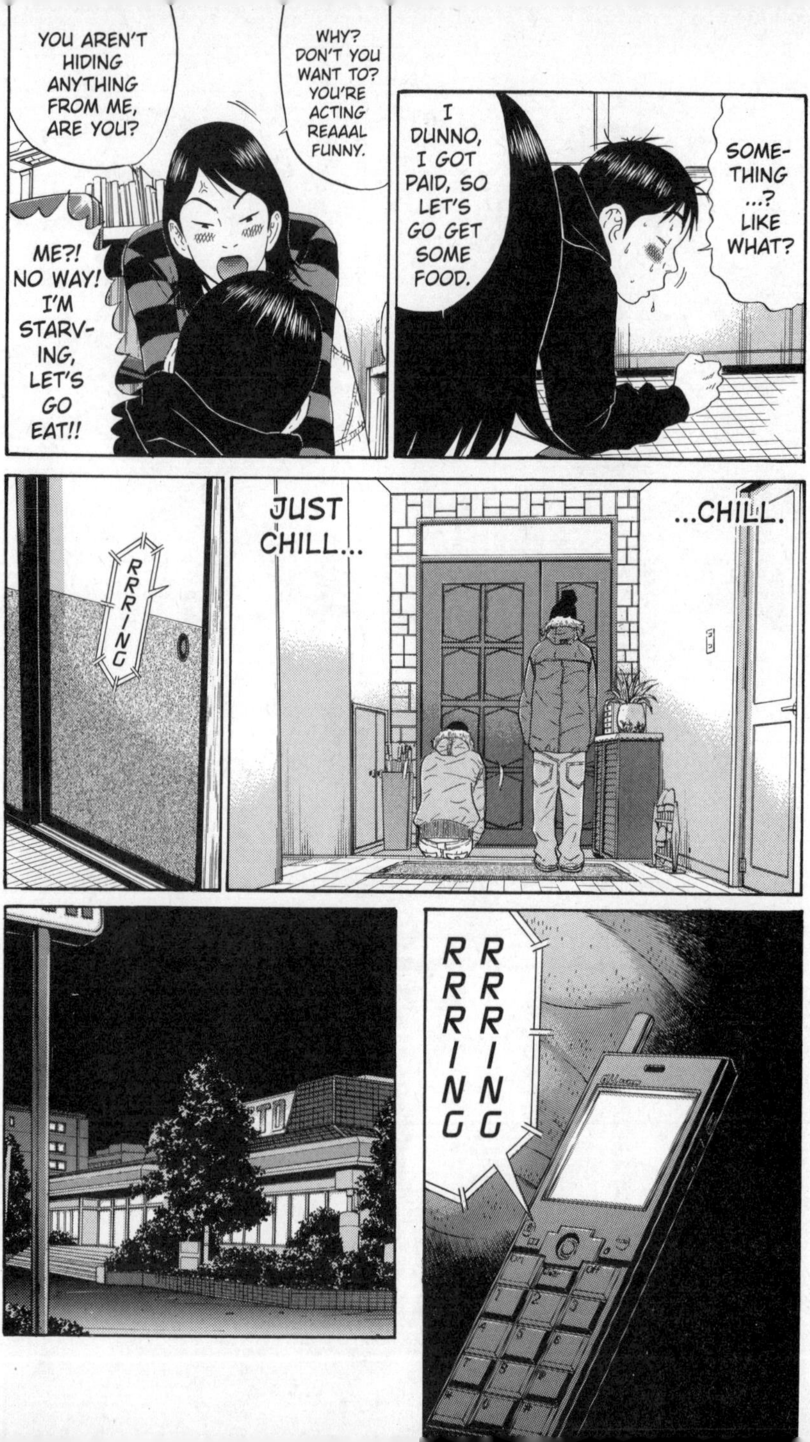
SOMETHING...? LIKE WHAT?
I DUNNO, I GOT PAID, SO LET'S GO GET SOME FOOD.
WHY? DON'T YOU WANT TO? YOU'RE ACTING REAAAL FUNNY.
YOU AREN'T HIDING ANYTHING FROM ME, ARE YOU?
ME?! NO WAY! I'M STARVING, LET'S GO EAT!!
...CHILL.
JUST CHILL...
RRRING
RRRING
RRRING

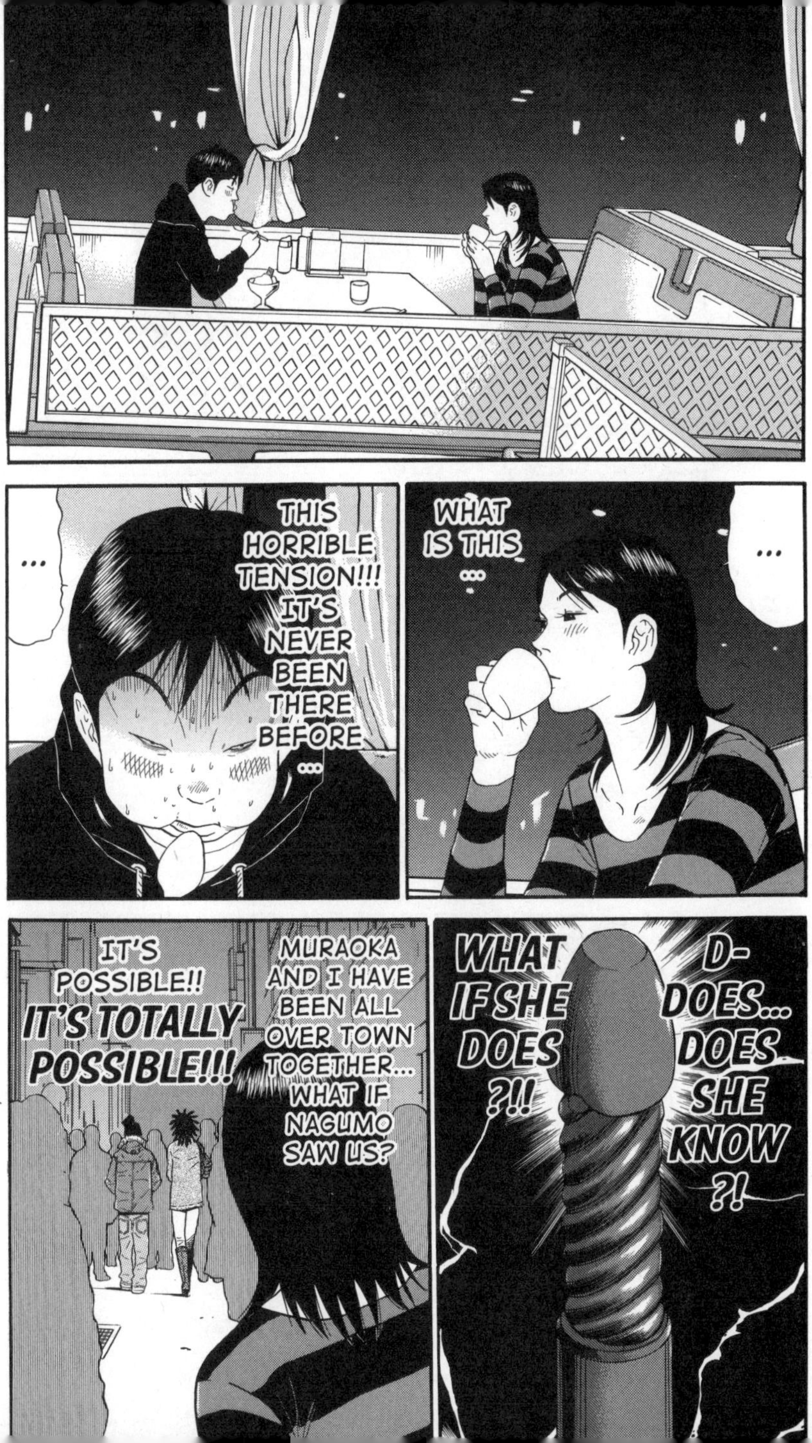
...
WHAT IS THIS ...
THIS HORRIBLE TENSION!!! IT'S NEVER BEEN THERE BEFORE ...
...
D-DOES... DOES SHE KNOW?!
WHAT IF SHE DOES?!!
MURAOKA AND I HAVE BEEN ALL OVER TOWN TOGETHER... WHAT IF NAGUMO SAW US?
IT'S POSSIBLE!! IT'S TOTALLY POSSIBLE!!!

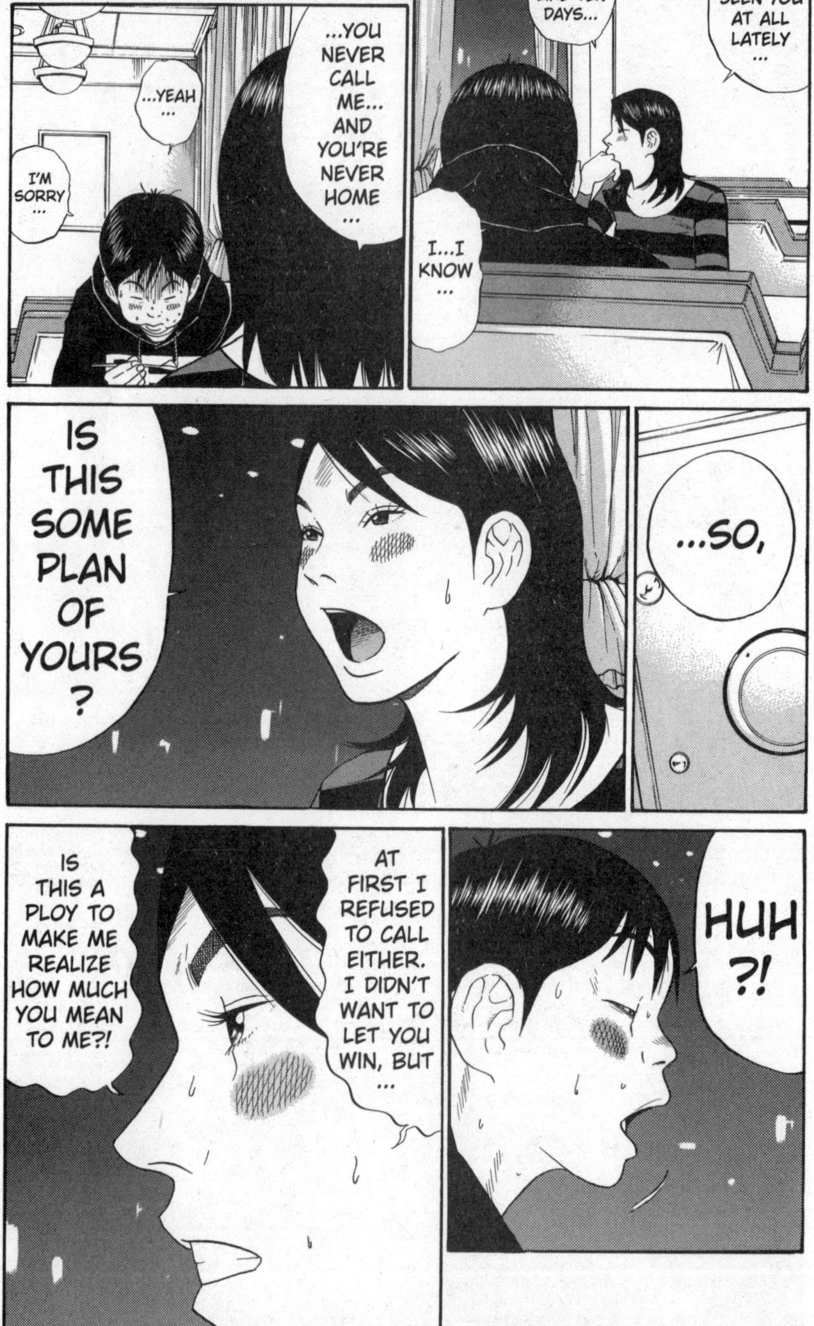
...I HAVEN'T SEEN YOU AT ALL LATELY...
IT'S BEEN LIKE TEN DAYS...
I...I KNOW...
...YOU NEVER CALL ME... AND YOU'RE NEVER HOME...
...YEAH...
I'M SORRY...
...SO,
IS THIS SOME PLAN OF YOURS?
HUH?!
AT FIRST I REFUSED TO CALL EITHER. I DIDN'T WANT TO LET YOU WIN, BUT...
IS THIS A PLOY TO MAKE ME REALIZE HOW MUCH YOU MEAN TO ME?!

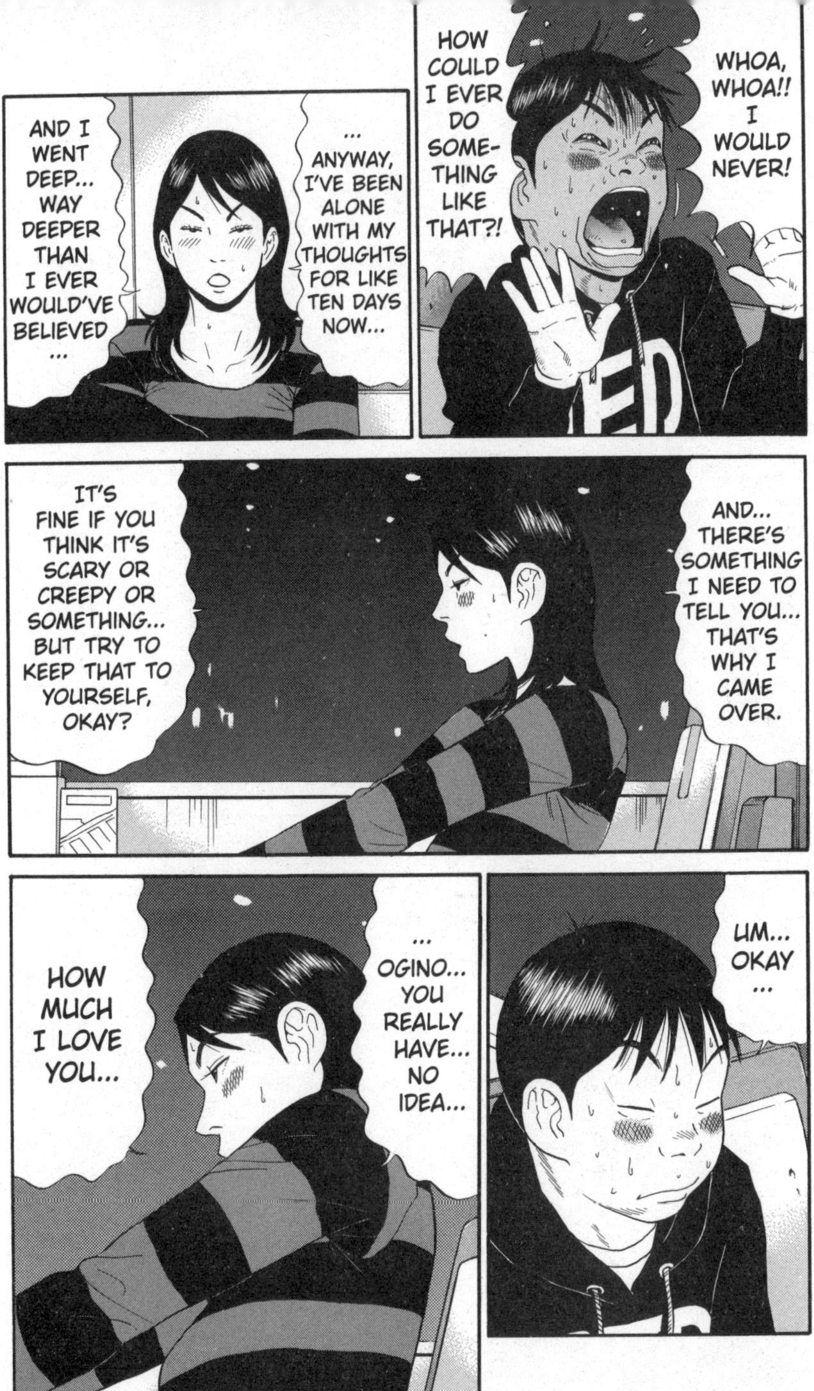
WHOA, WHOA!! I WOULD NEVER!
HOW COULD I EVER DO SOMETHING LIKE THAT?!
... ANYWAY, I'VE BEEN ALONE WITH MY THOUGHTS FOR LIKE TEN DAYS NOW...
AND I WENT DEEP... WAY DEEPER THAN I EVER WOULD'VE BELIEVED...
AND... THERE'S SOMETHING I NEED TO TELL YOU... THAT'S WHY I CAME OVER.
IT'S FINE IF YOU THINK IT'S SCARY OR CREEPY OR SOMETHING... BUT TRY TO KEEP THAT TO YOURSELF, OKAY?
UM... OKAY...
... OGINO... YOU REALLY HAVE... NO IDEA...
HOW MUCH I LOVE YOU...

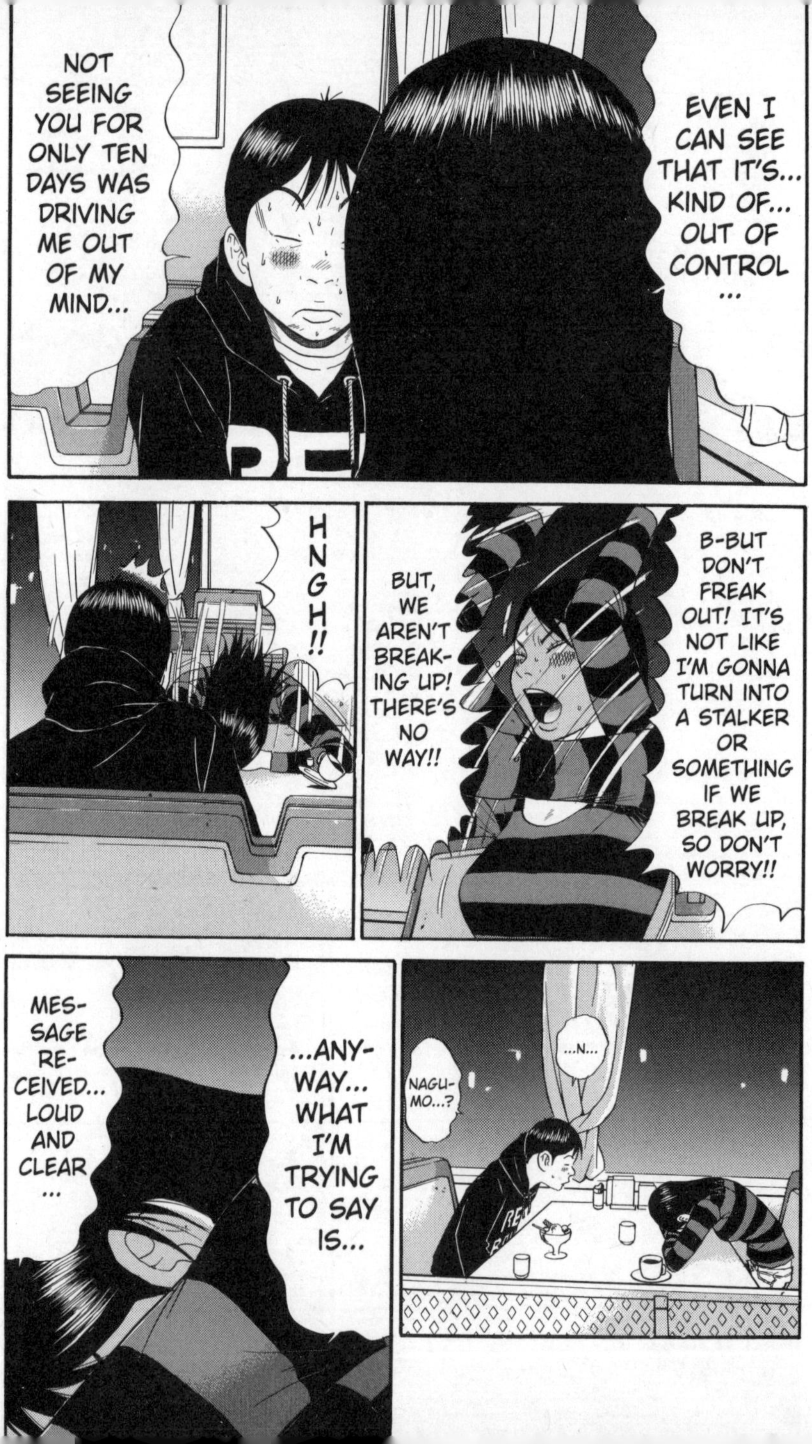
NOT SEEING YOU FOR ONLY TEN DAYS WAS DRIVING ME OUT OF MY MIND...
EVEN I CAN SEE THAT IT'S... KIND OF... OUT OF CONTROL...
B-BUT DON'T FREAK OUT! IT'S NOT LIKE I'M GONNA TURN INTO A STALKER OR SOMETHING IF WE BREAK UP, SO DON'T WORRY!!
BUT, WE AREN'T BREAK-ING UP! THERE'S NO WAY!!
HNGH!!
...N...
NAGU-MO...?
...ANY-WAY... WHAT I'M TRYING TO SAY IS...
MES-SAGE RE-CEIVED... LOUD AND CLEAR...

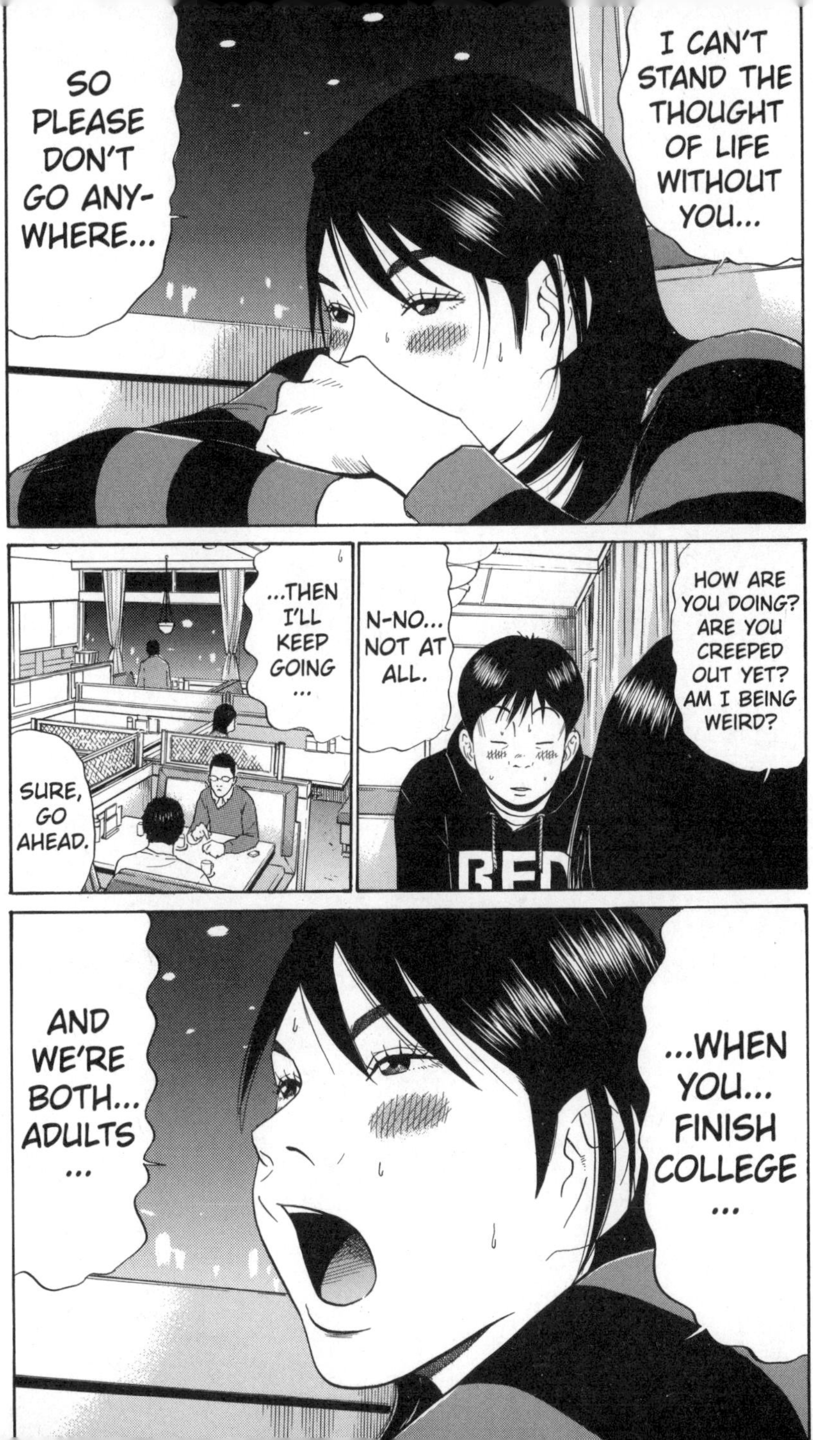
I CAN'T STAND THE THOUGHT OF LIFE WITHOUT YOU...
SO PLEASE DON'T GO ANY-WHERE...
HOW ARE YOU DOING? ARE YOU CREEPED OUT YET? AM I BEING WEIRD?
N-NO... NOT AT ALL.
...THEN I'LL KEEP GOING...
SURE, GO AHEAD.
...WHEN YOU... FINISH COLLEGE...
AND WE'RE BOTH... ADULTS...

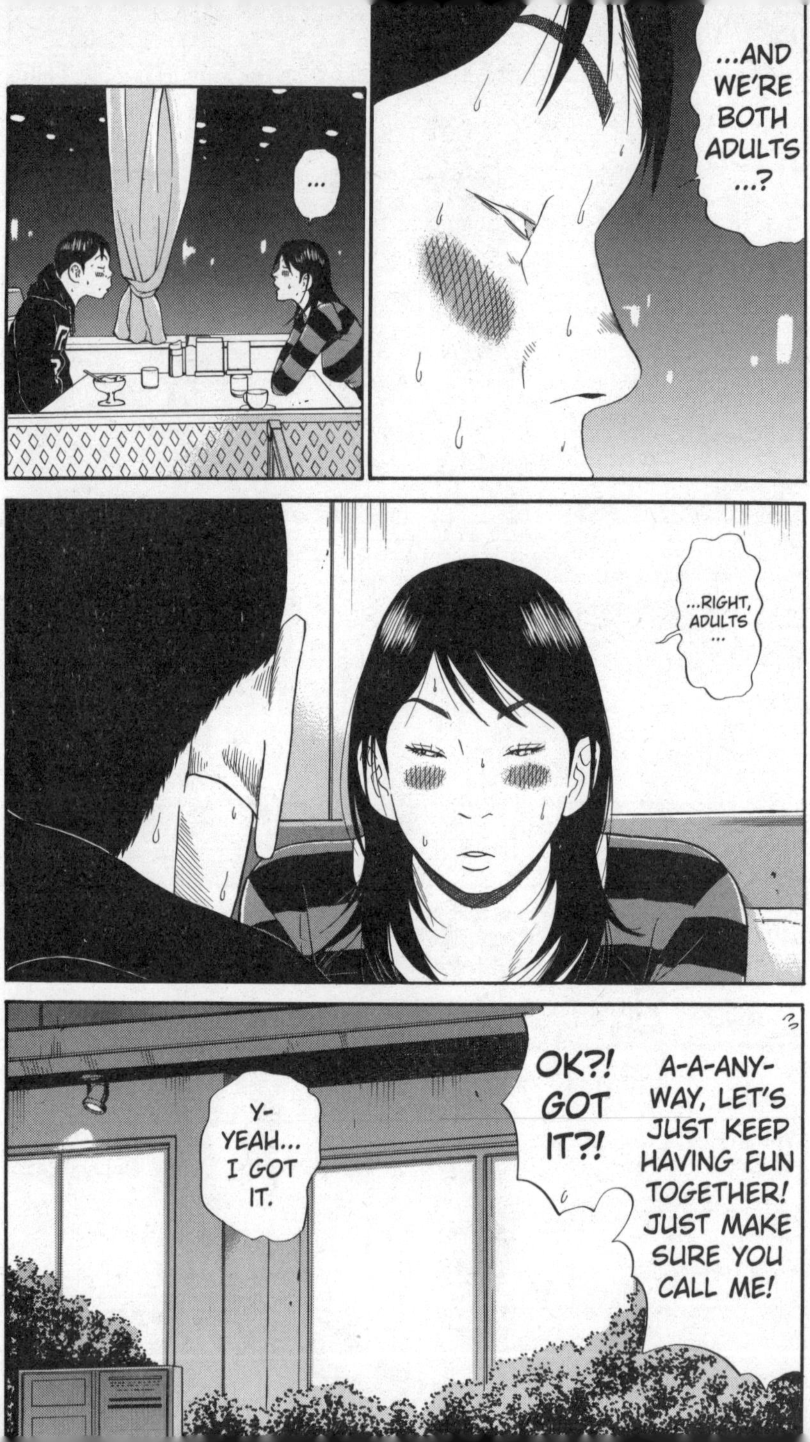
...AND WE'RE BOTH ADULTS ...?
...
...RIGHT, ADULTS ...
A-A-ANY-WAY, LET'S JUST KEEP HAVING FUN TOGETHER! JUST MAKE SURE YOU CALL ME!
OK?! GOT IT?!
Y-YEAH... I GOT IT.

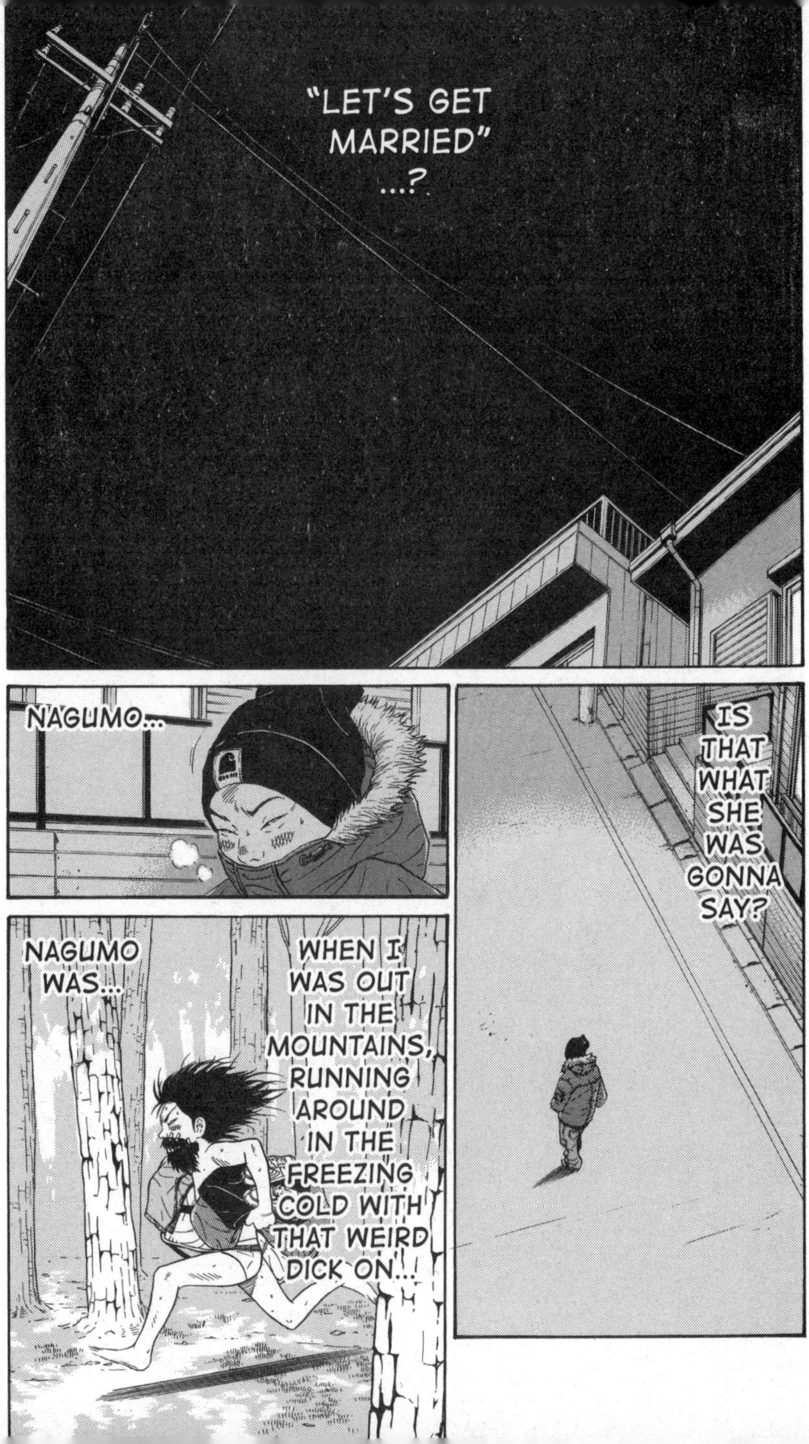
"LET'S GET MARRIED" ...?
IS THAT WHAT SHE WAS GONNA SAY?
NAGUMO...
WHEN I WAS OUT IN THE MOUNTAINS, RUNNING AROUND IN THE FREEZING COLD WITH THAT WEIRD DICK ON...
NAGUMO WAS...

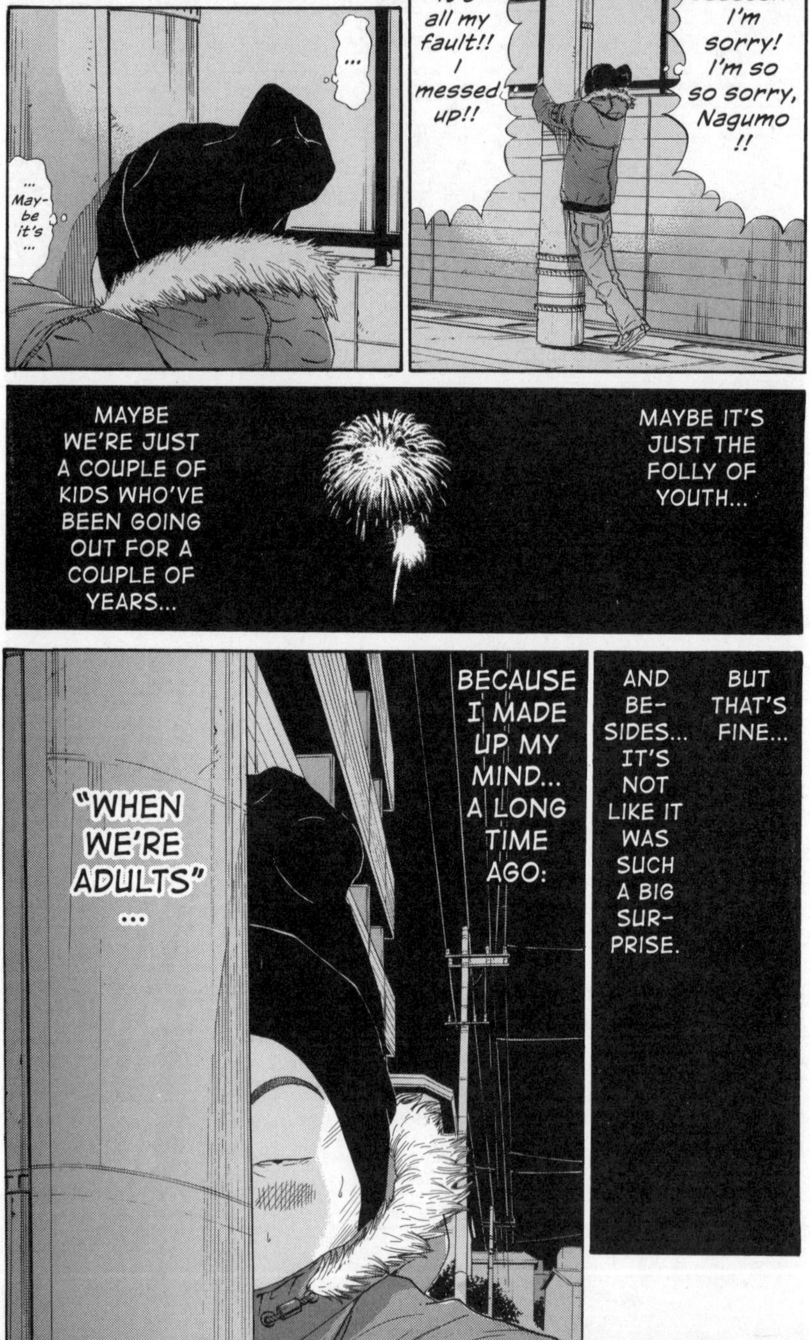
Gaaaaah! I'm sorry! I'm so so sorry, Nagumo!!
It's all my fault!! I messed up!!
...
... Maybe it's ...
MAYBE IT'S JUST THE FOLLY OF YOUTH...
MAYBE WE'RE JUST A COUPLE OF KIDS WHO'VE BEEN GOING OUT FOR A COUPLE OF YEARS...
BUT THAT'S FINE...
AND BESIDES... IT'S NOT LIKE IT WAS SUCH A BIG SURPRISE.
BECAUSE I MADE UP MY MIND... A LONG TIME AGO:
"WHEN WE'RE ADULTS" ...

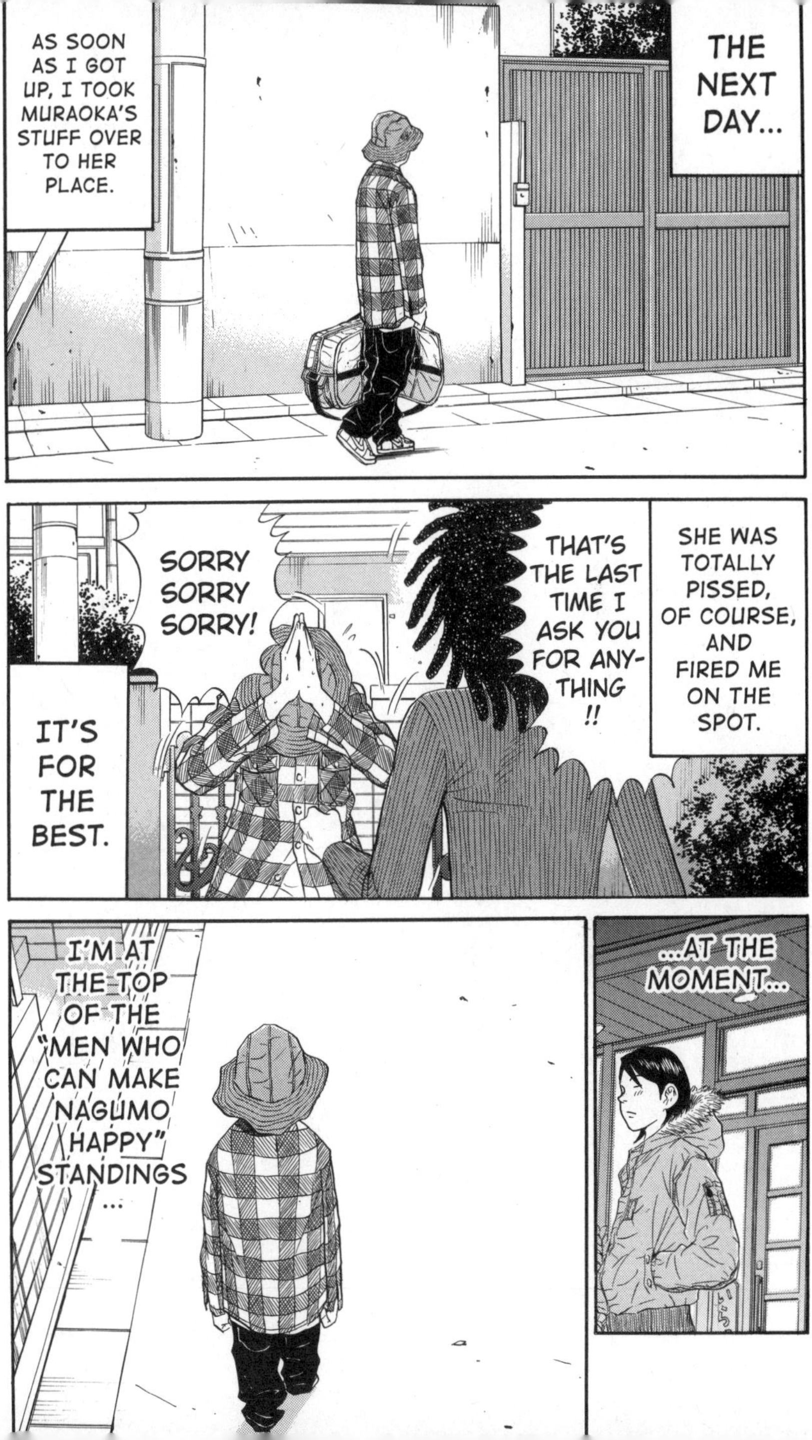
THE NEXT DAY...
AS SOON AS I GOT UP, I TOOK MURAOKA'S STUFF OVER TO HER PLACE.
SHE WAS TOTALLY PISSED, OF COURSE, AND FIRED ME ON THE SPOT.
THAT'S THE LAST TIME I ASK YOU FOR ANYTHING!!
SORRY SORRY SORRY!
IT'S FOR THE BEST.
...AT THE MOMENT...
I'M AT THE TOP OF THE "MEN WHO CAN MAKE NAGUMO HAPPY" STANDINGS...

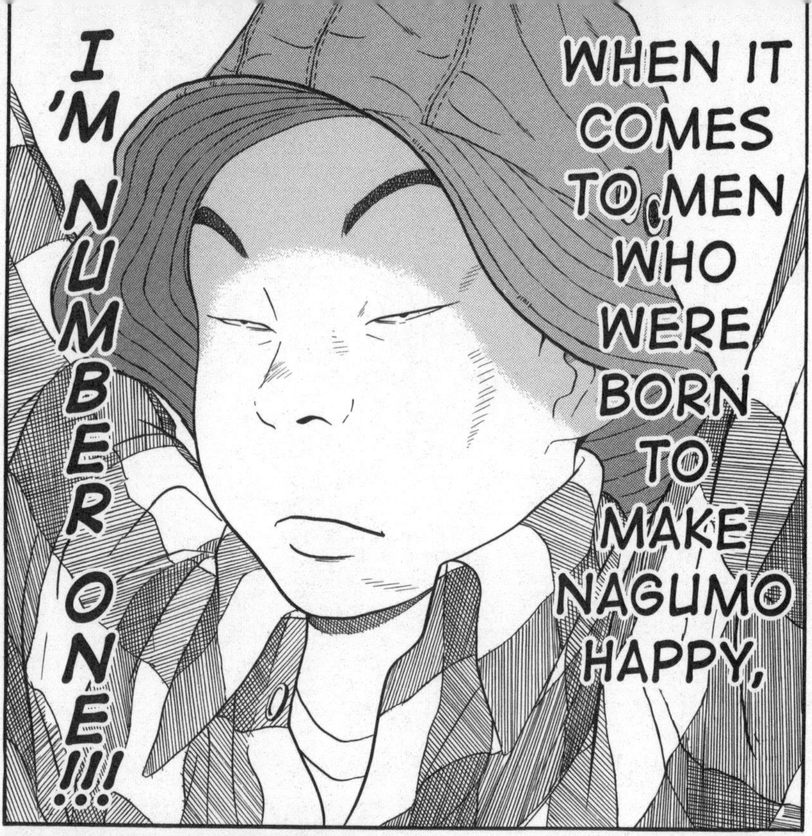
WHEN IT COMES TO MEN WHO WERE BORN TO MAKE NAGUMO HAPPY,
I'M NUMBER ONE!!!

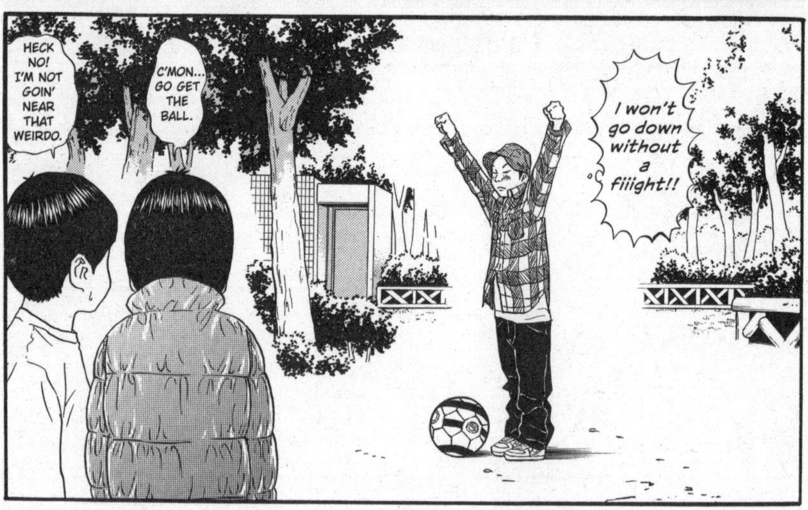
I won't go down without a fiiight!!
C'MON... GO GET THE BALL.
HECK NO! I'M NOT GOIN' NEAR THAT WEIRDO.

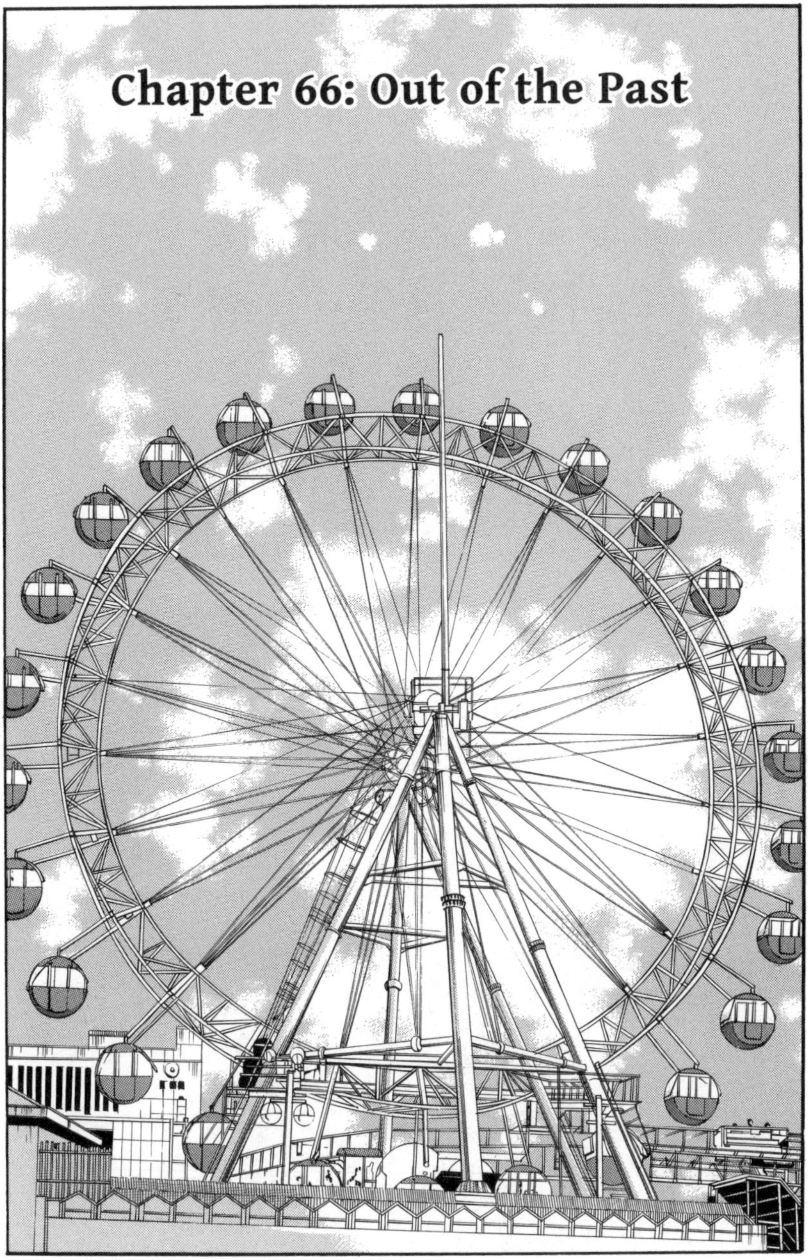
Chapter 66: Out of the Past

The first time we had sex...

"This is what we're all living for?!" It kinda blew my mind.

The first time we had sex... I had this flash of insight...

...

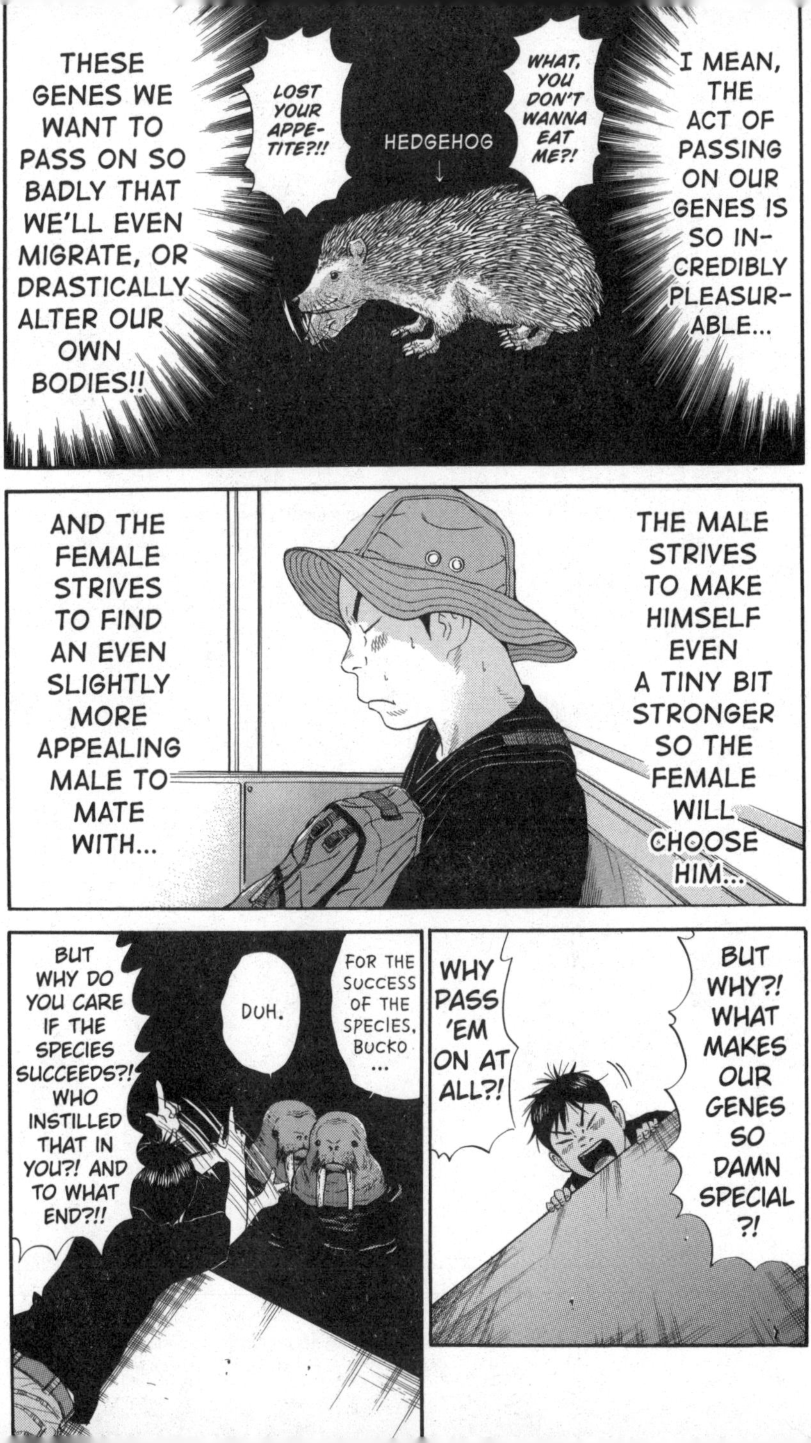
I MEAN, THE ACT OF PASSING ON OUR GENES IS SO IN-CREDIBLY PLEASUR-ABLE...
WHAT, YOU DON'T WANNA EAT ME?!
HEDGEHOG ↓
LOST YOUR APPE-TITE?!!
THESE GENES WE WANT TO PASS ON SO BADLY THAT WE'LL EVEN MIGRATE, OR DRASTICALLY ALTER OUR OWN BODIES!!
THE MALE STRIVES TO MAKE HIMSELF EVEN A TINY BIT STRONGER SO THE FEMALE WILL CHOOSE HIM...
AND THE FEMALE STRIVES TO FIND AN EVEN SLIGHTLY MORE APPEALING MALE TO MATE WITH...
BUT WHY?! WHAT MAKES OUR GENES SO DAMN SPECIAL?!
WHY PASS 'EM ON AT ALL?!
FOR THE SUCCESS OF THE SPECIES, BUCKO...
DUH.
BUT WHY DO YOU CARE IF THE SPECIES SUCCEEDS?! WHO INSTILLED THAT IN YOU?! AND TO WHAT END?!!

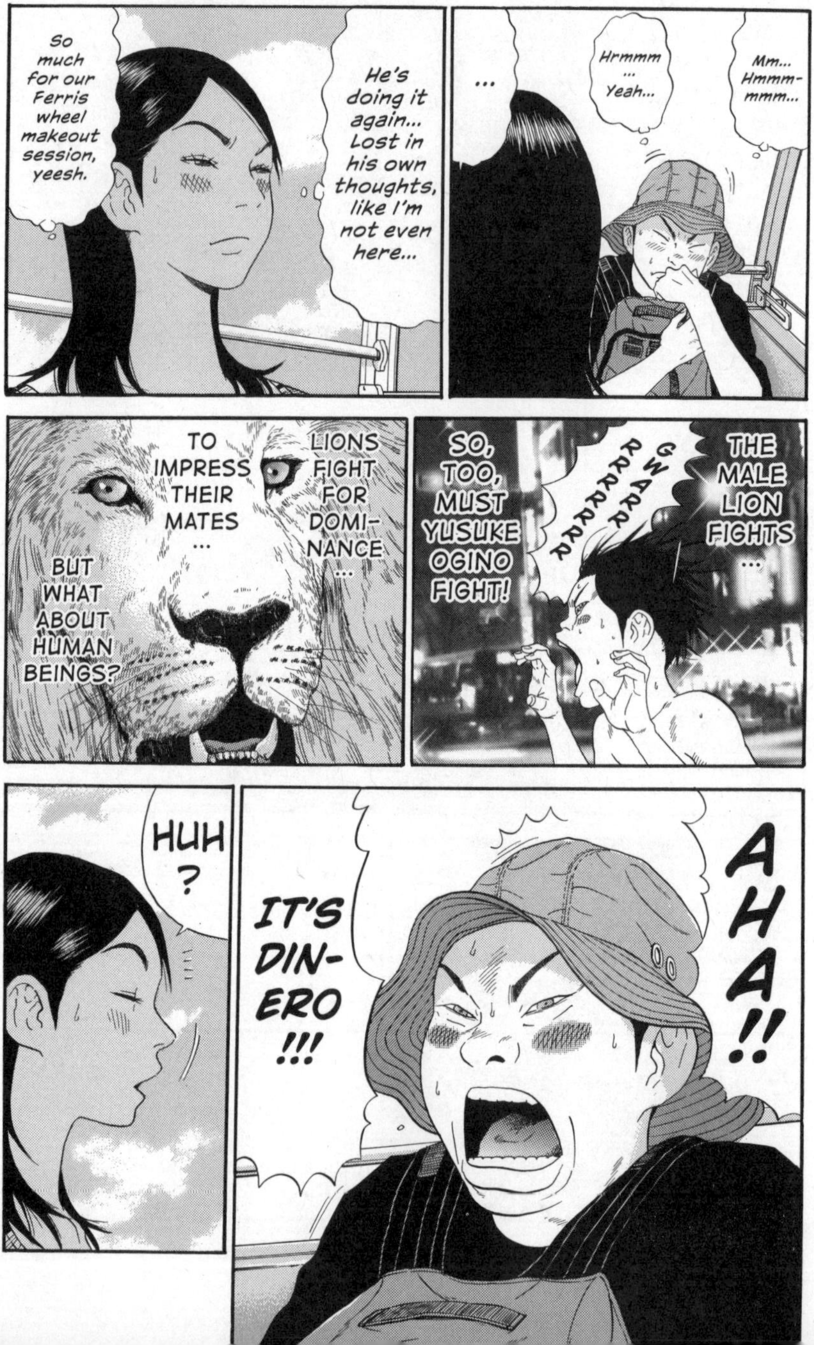
Mm... Hmmm-mmm...
Hrmmm ... Yeah...
...
He's doing it again... Lost in his own thoughts, like I'm not even here...
So much for our Ferris wheel makeout session, yeesh.
THE MALE LION FIGHTS ...
GWARRR RRRRRR
SO, TOO, MUST YUSUKE OGINO FIGHT!
LIONS FIGHT FOR DOMI-NANCE ...
TO IMPRESS THEIR MATES ...
BUT WHAT ABOUT HUMAN BEINGS?
AHA!!
IT'S DIN-ERO !!!
HUH ?

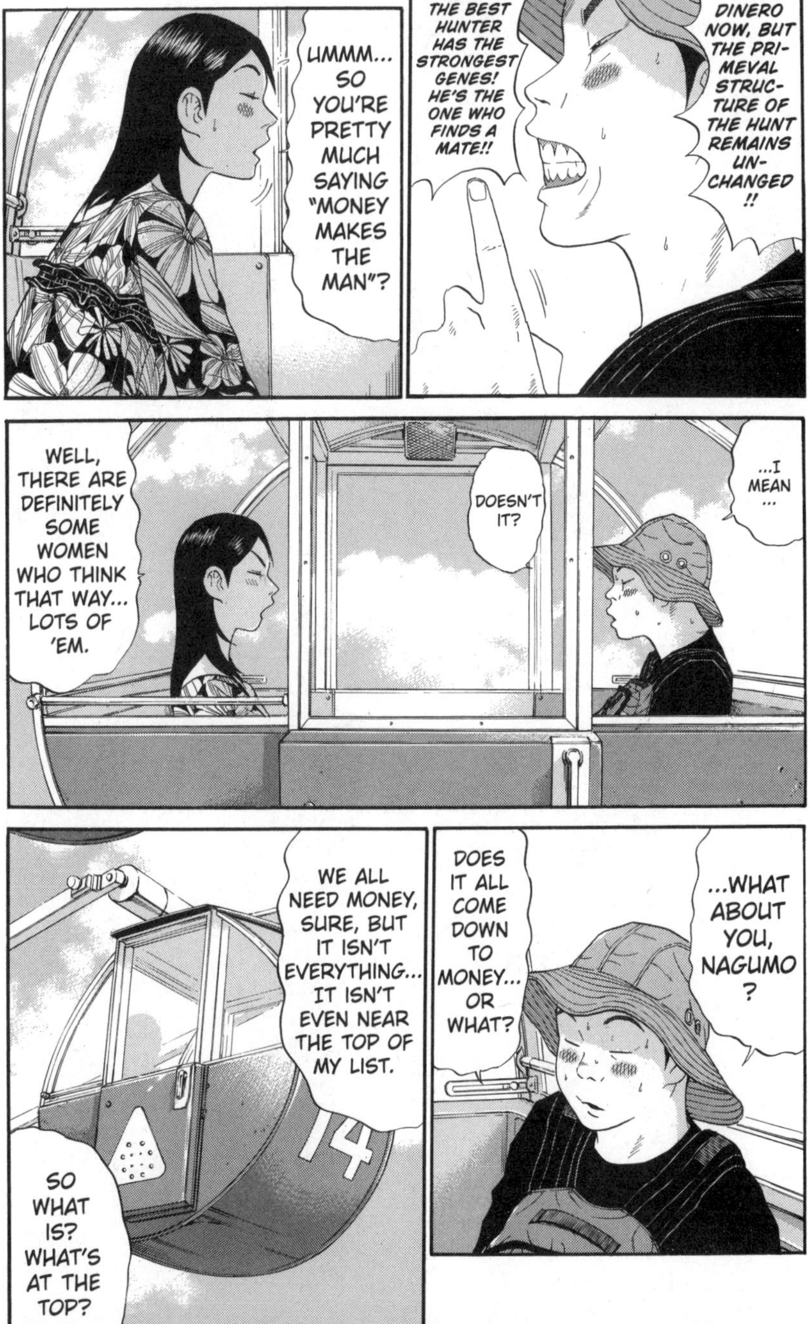
THE PREY MAY BE DINERO NOW, BUT THE PRI-MEVAL STRUC-TURE OF THE HUNT REMAINS UN-CHANGED!!
WORK IS HOW WE HUNT, AND THE BEST HUNTER HAS THE STRONGEST GENES! HE'S THE ONE WHO FINDS A MATE!!
UMMM... SO YOU'RE PRETTY MUCH SAYING "MONEY MAKES THE MAN"?
...I MEAN ...
DOESN'T IT?
WELL, THERE ARE DEFINITELY SOME WOMEN WHO THINK THAT WAY... LOTS OF 'EM.
...WHAT ABOUT YOU, NAGUMO?
DOES IT ALL COME DOWN TO MONEY... OR WHAT?
WE ALL NEED MONEY, SURE, BUT IT ISN'T EVERYTHING... IT ISN'T EVEN NEAR THE TOP OF MY LIST.
14
SO WHAT IS? WHAT'S AT THE TOP?

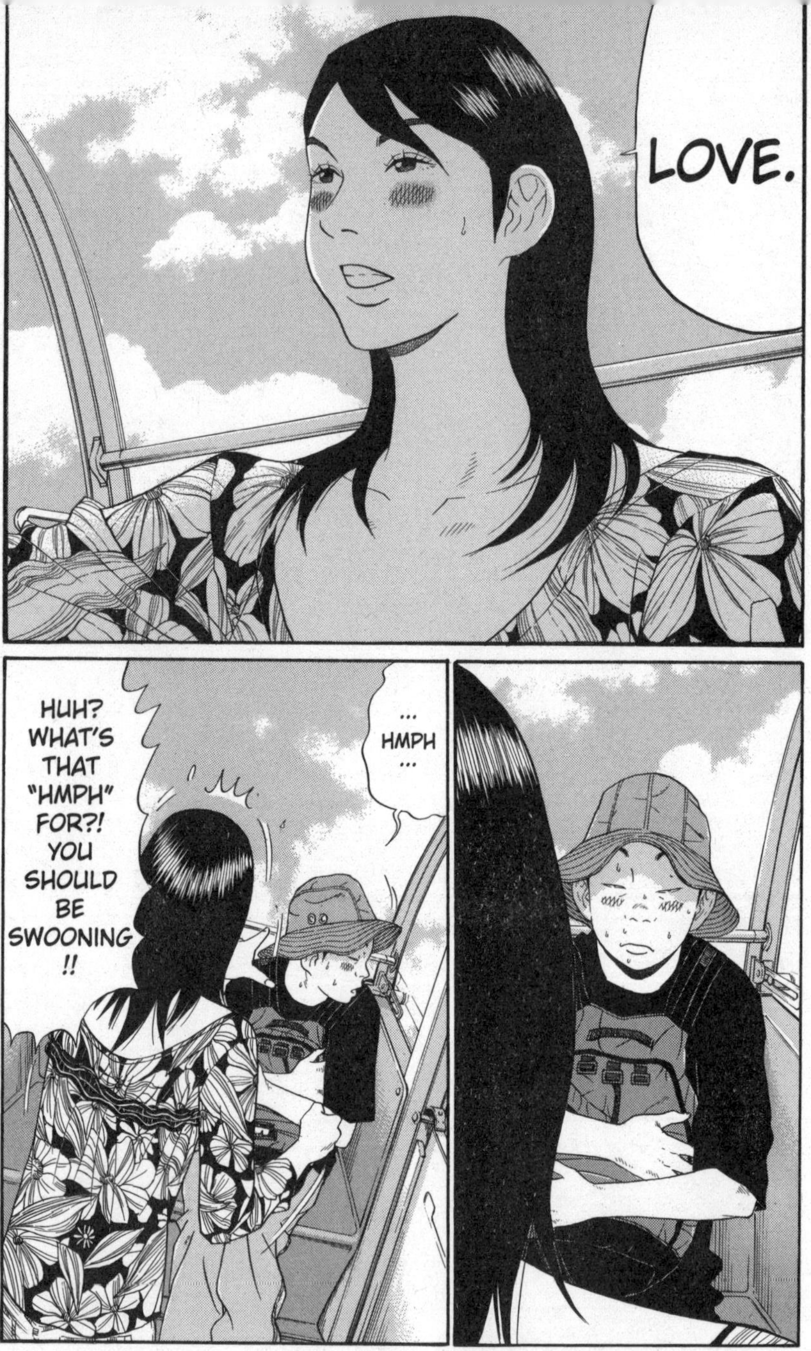
LOVE.
... HMPH ...
HUH? WHAT'S THAT "HMPH" FOR?! YOU SHOULD BE SWOONING !!

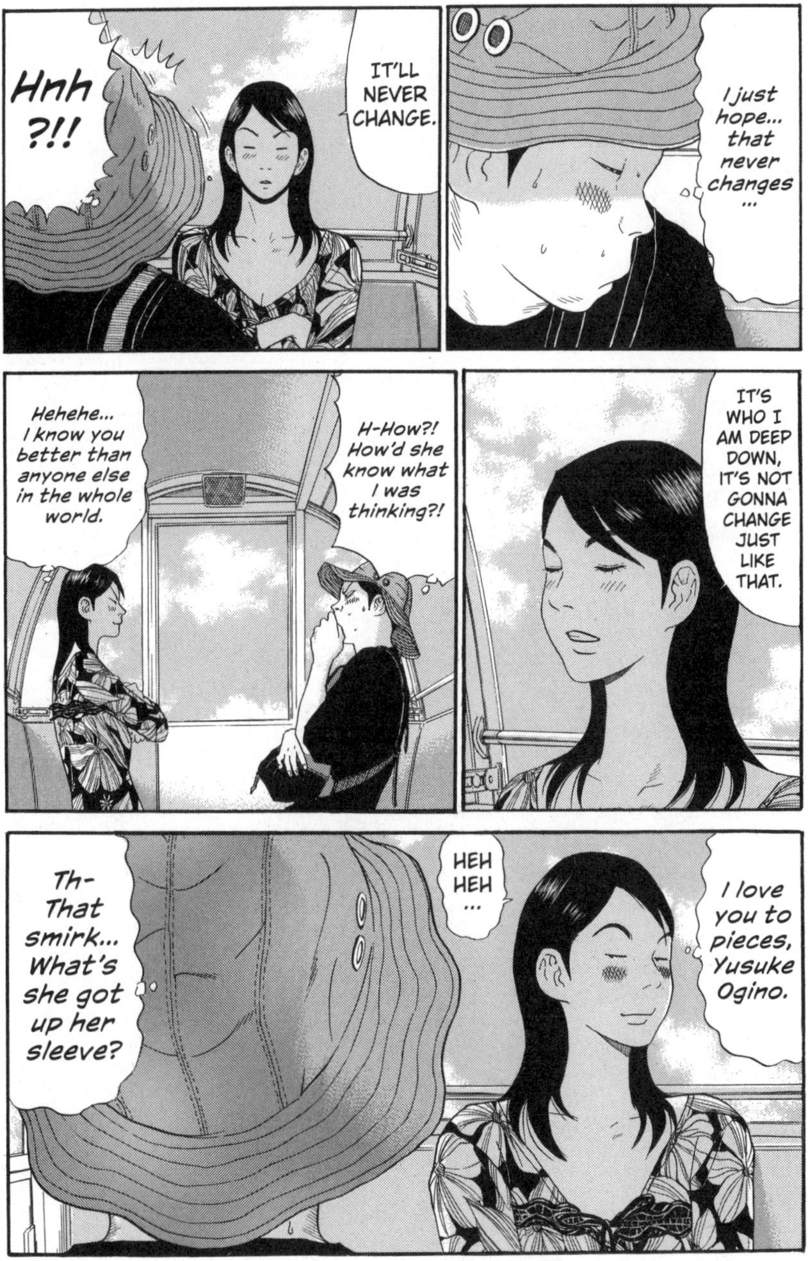
I just hope... that never changes ...
IT'LL NEVER CHANGE.
Hnh ?!!
IT'S WHO I AM DEEP DOWN, IT'S NOT GONNA CHANGE JUST LIKE THAT.
H-How?! How'd she know what I was thinking?!
Hehehe... I know you better than anyone else in the whole world.
I love you to pieces, Yusuke Ogino.
HEH HEH ...
Th-That smirk... What's she got up her sleeve?

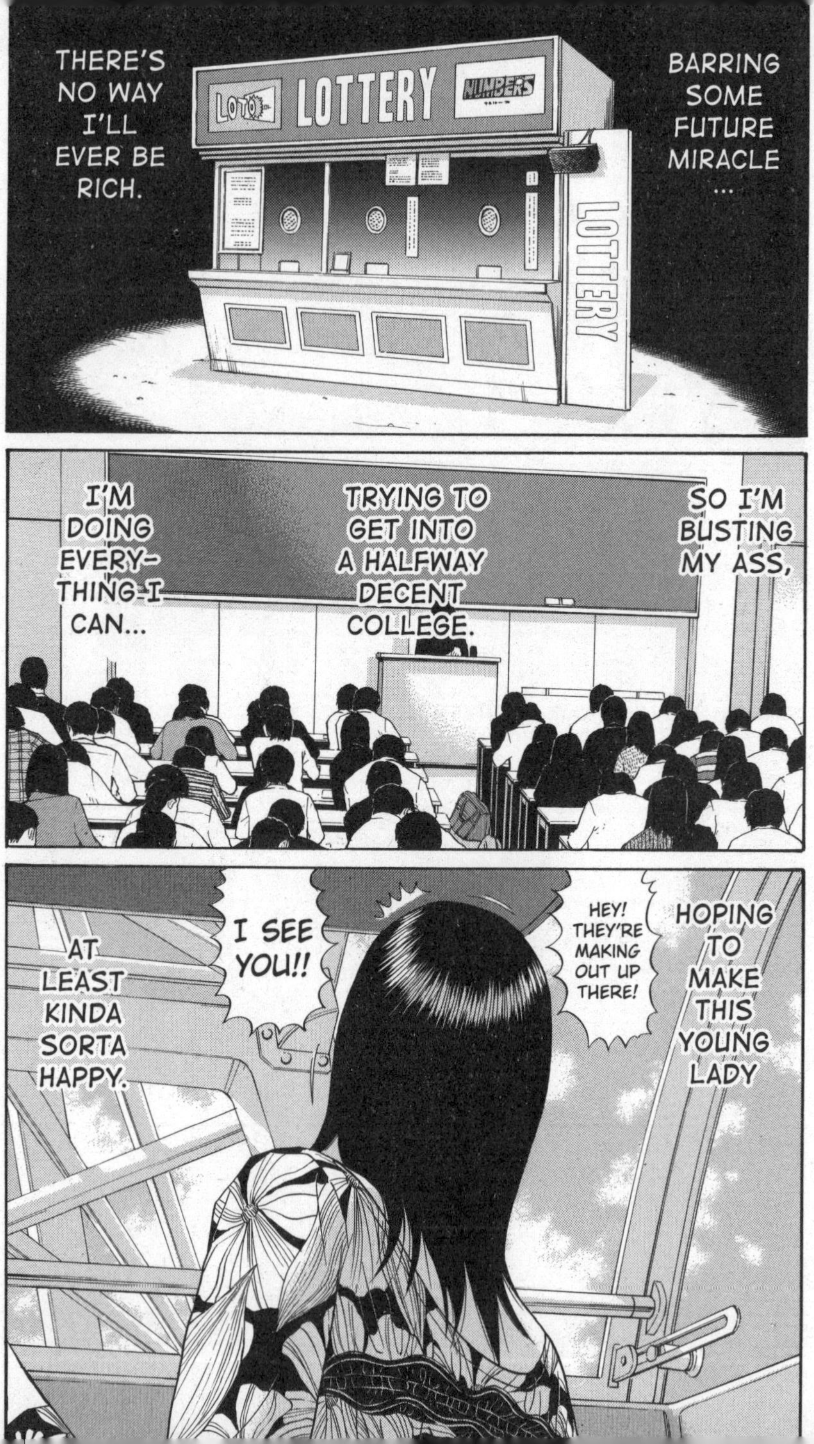
BARRING SOME FUTURE MIRACLE ...
LOTTERY
LOTO
NUMBERS
LOTTERY
THERE'S NO WAY I'LL EVER BE RICH.
SO I'M BUSTING MY ASS,
TRYING TO GET INTO A HALFWAY DECENT COLLEGE.
I'M DOING EVERY-THING I CAN...
HOPING TO MAKE THIS YOUNG LADY
HEY! THEY'RE MAKING OUT UP THERE!
I SEE YOU!!
AT LEAST KINDA SORTA HAPPY.

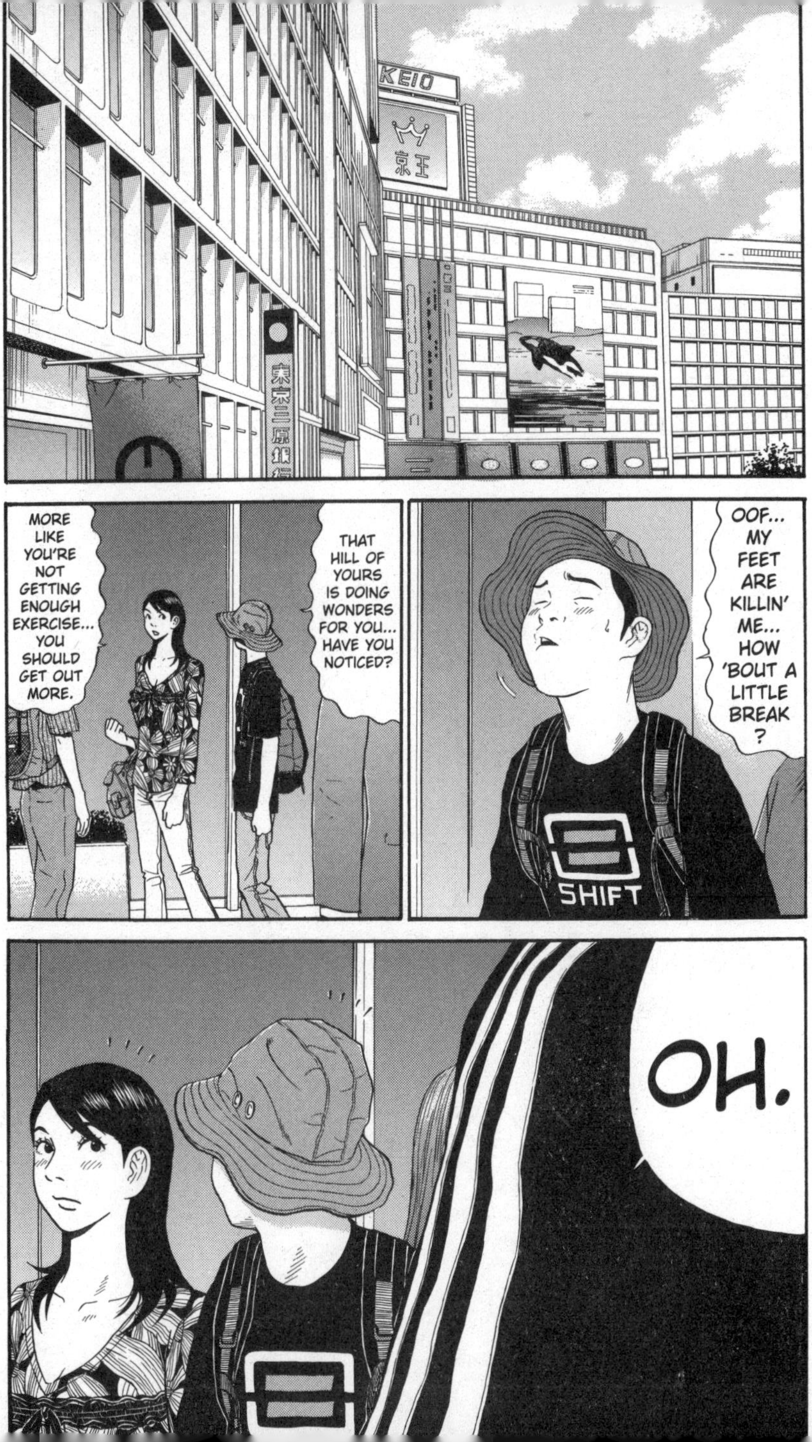
KEIO
京王
OOF... MY FEET ARE KILLIN' ME... HOW 'BOUT A LITTLE BREAK?
SHIFT
THAT HILL OF YOURS IS DOING WONDERS FOR YOU... HAVE YOU NOTICED?
MORE LIKE YOU'RE NOT GETTING ENOUGH EXERCISE... YOU SHOULD GET OUT MORE.
OH.

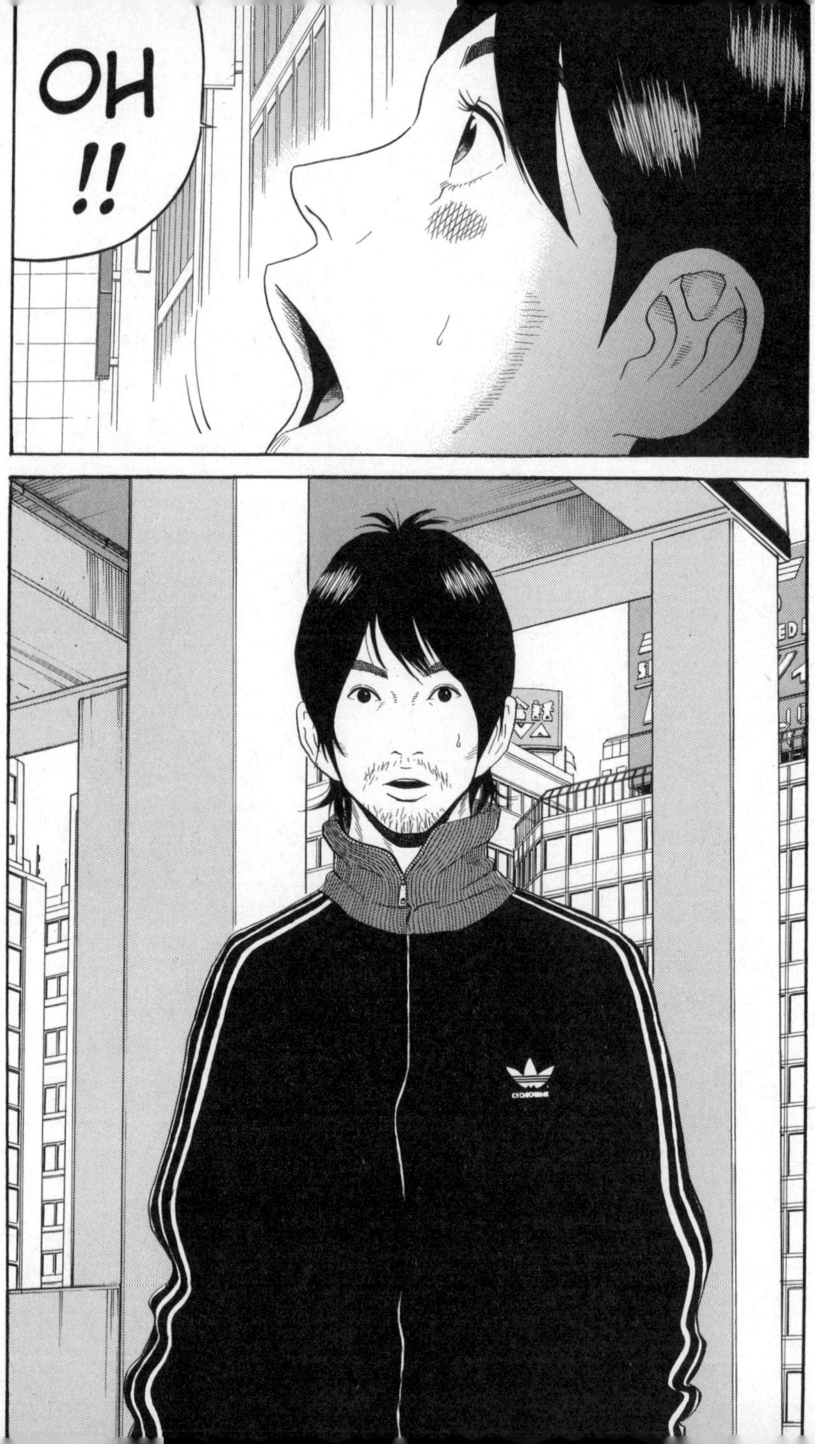
OH !!

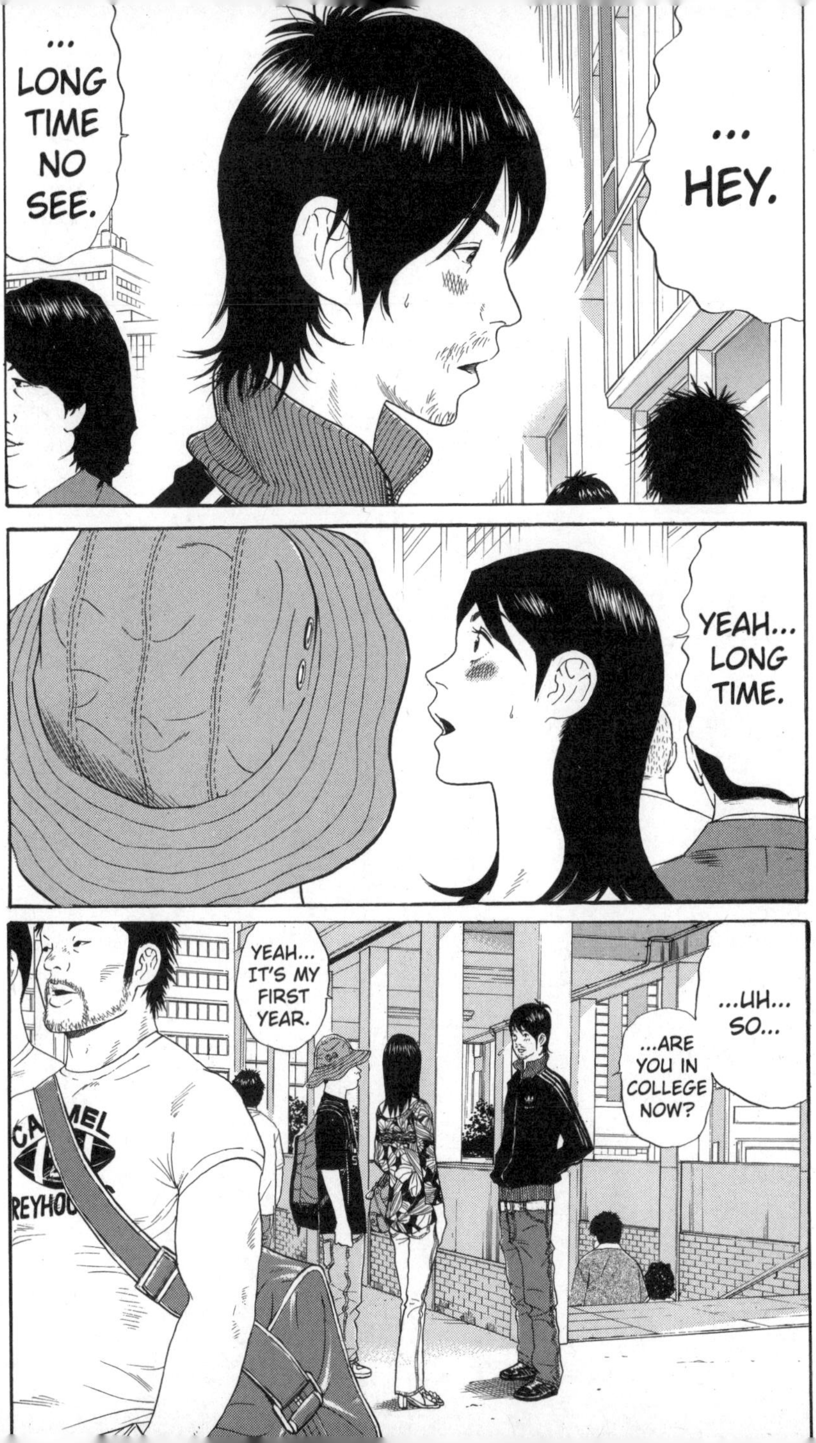
... HEY.
... LONG TIME NO SEE.
YEAH... LONG TIME.
...UH... SO...
...ARE YOU IN COLLEGE NOW?
YEAH... IT'S MY FIRST YEAR.

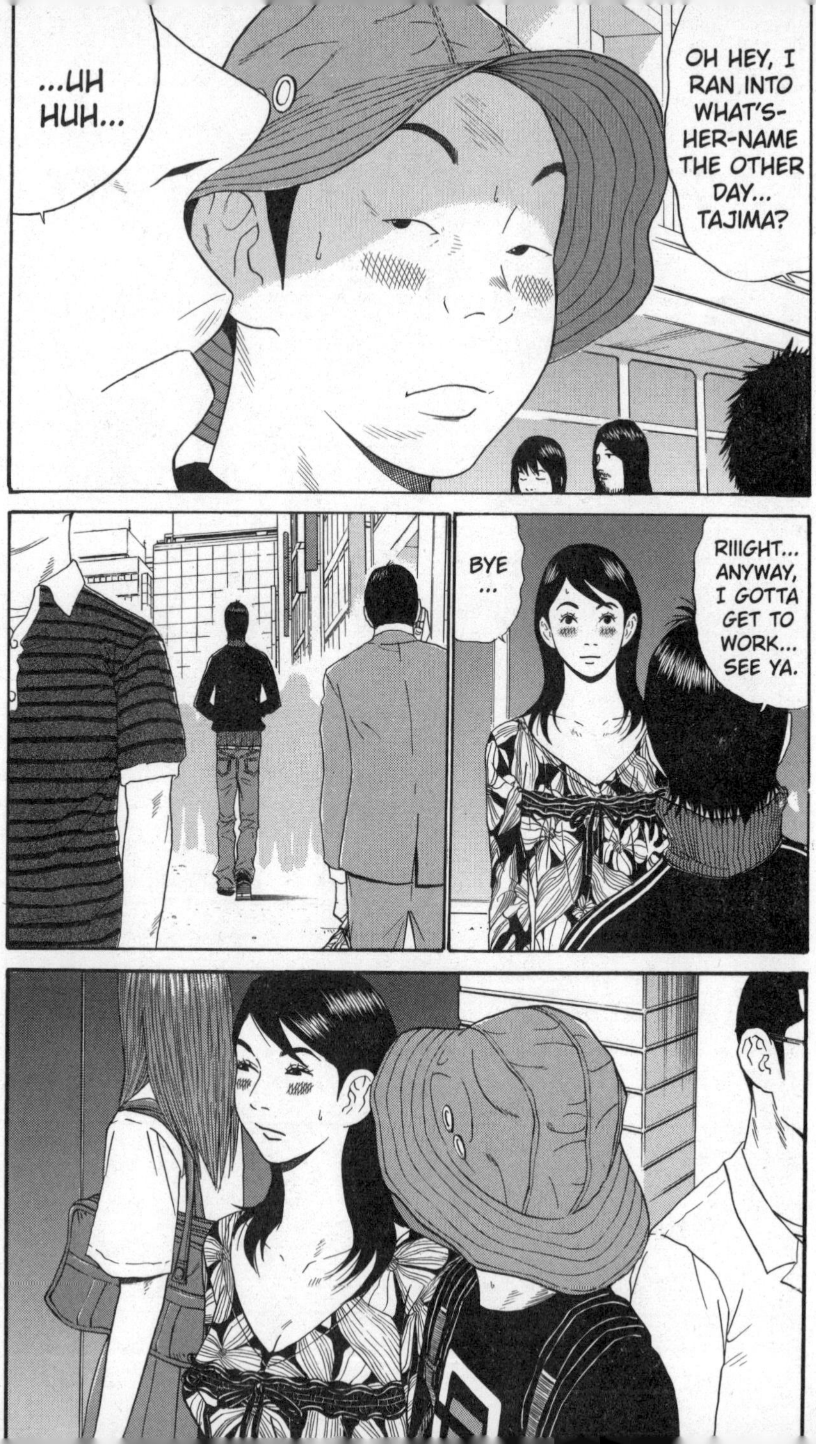
OH HEY, I RAN INTO WHAT'S-HER-NAME THE OTHER DAY... TAJIMA?
...UH HUH...
RIIIGHT... ANYWAY, I GOTTA GET TO WORK... SEE YA.
BYE ...

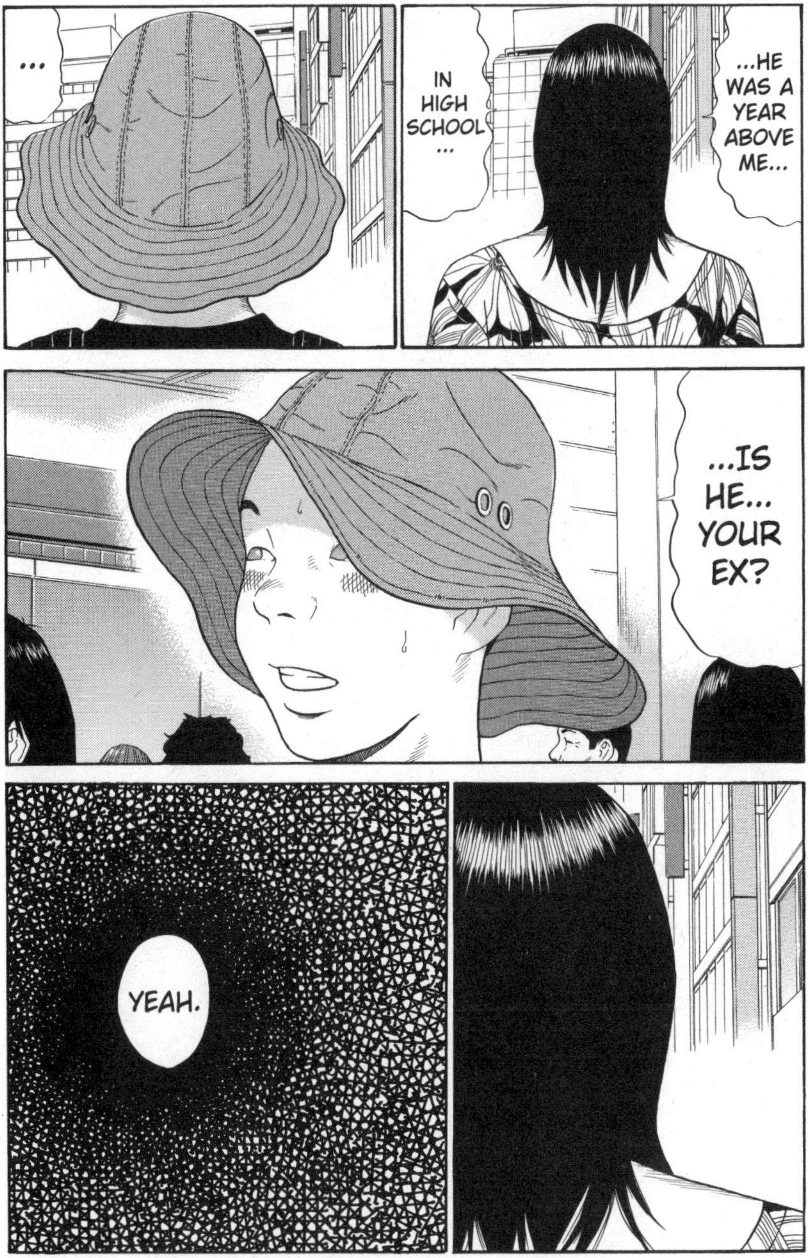
IN HIGH SCHOOL...
...HE WAS A YEAR ABOVE ME...
...
...IS HE... YOUR EX?
YEAH.

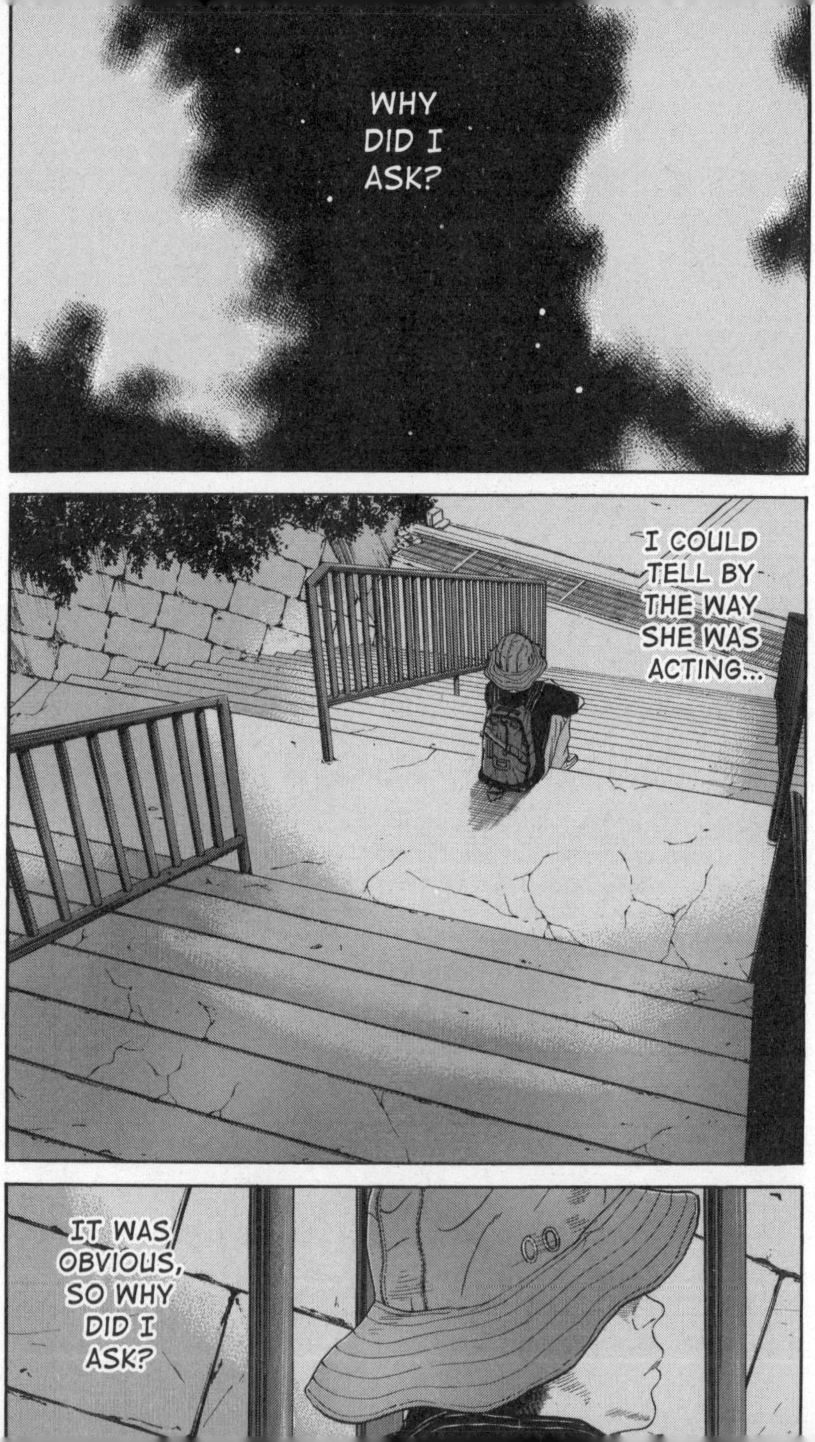
WHY DID I ASK?
I COULD TELL BY THE WAY SHE WAS ACTING...
IT WAS OBVIOUS, SO WHY DID I ASK?

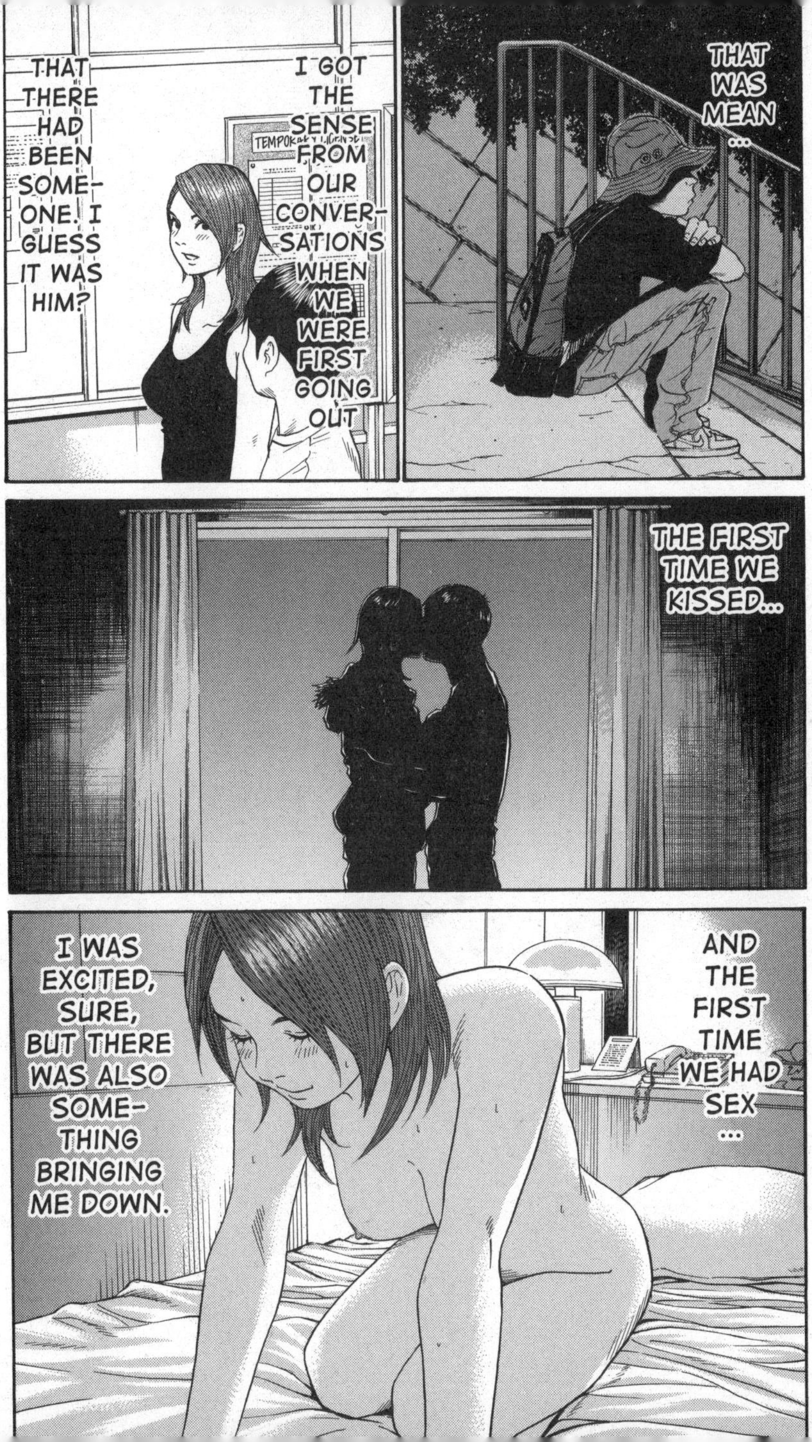
THAT WAS MEAN ...
I GOT THE SENSE FROM OUR CONVERSATIONS WHEN WE WERE FIRST GOING OUT
THAT THERE HAD BEEN SOMEONE. I GUESS IT WAS HIM?
THE FIRST TIME WE KISSED...
AND THE FIRST TIME WE HAD SEX ...
I WAS EXCITED, SURE, BUT THERE WAS ALSO SOMETHING BRINGING ME DOWN.

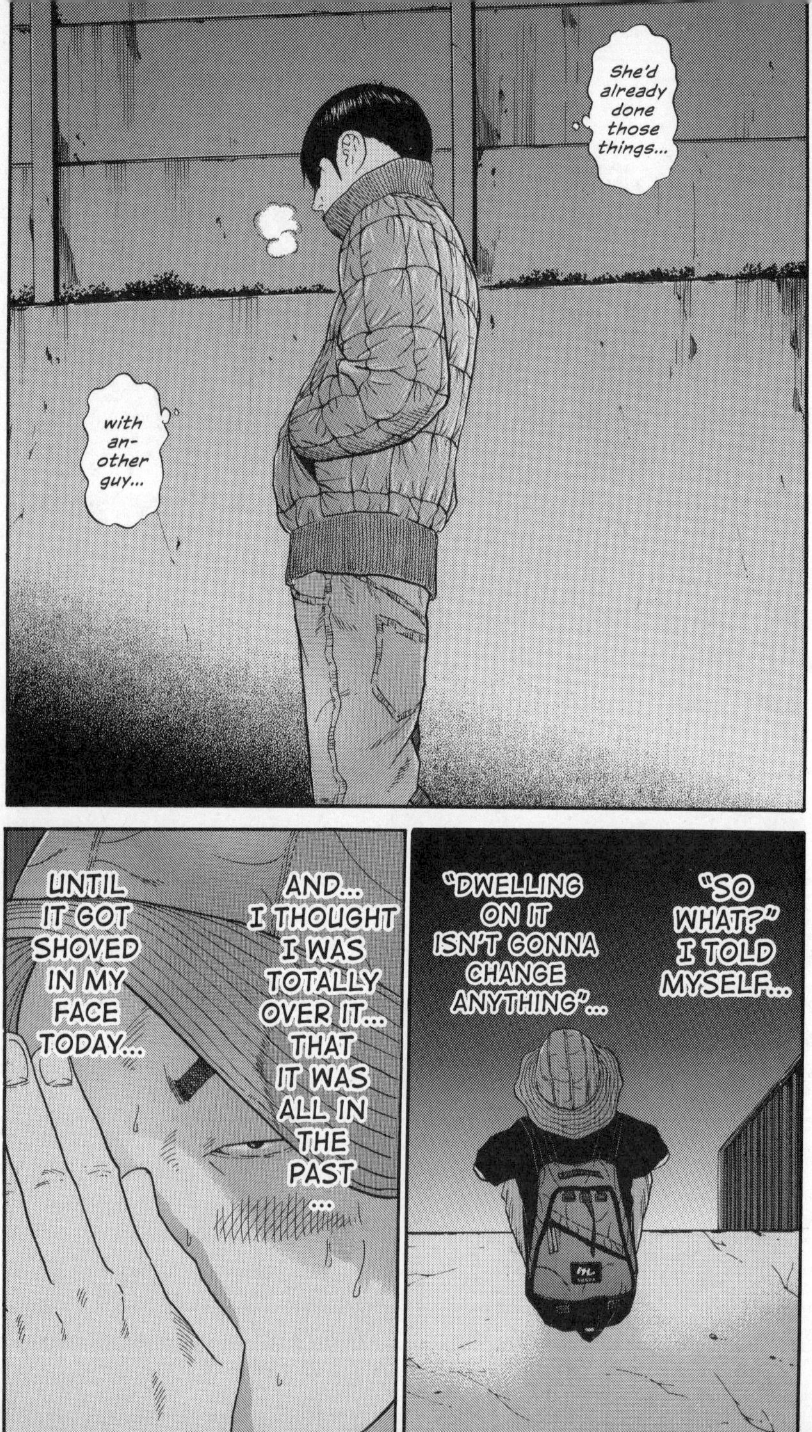
She'd already done those things...
with an-other guy...
"SO WHAT?" I TOLD MYSELF...
"DWELLING ON IT ISN'T GONNA CHANGE ANYTHING"...
AND... I THOUGHT I WAS TOTALLY OVER IT... THAT IT WAS ALL IN THE PAST...
UNTIL IT GOT SHOVED IN MY FACE TODAY...

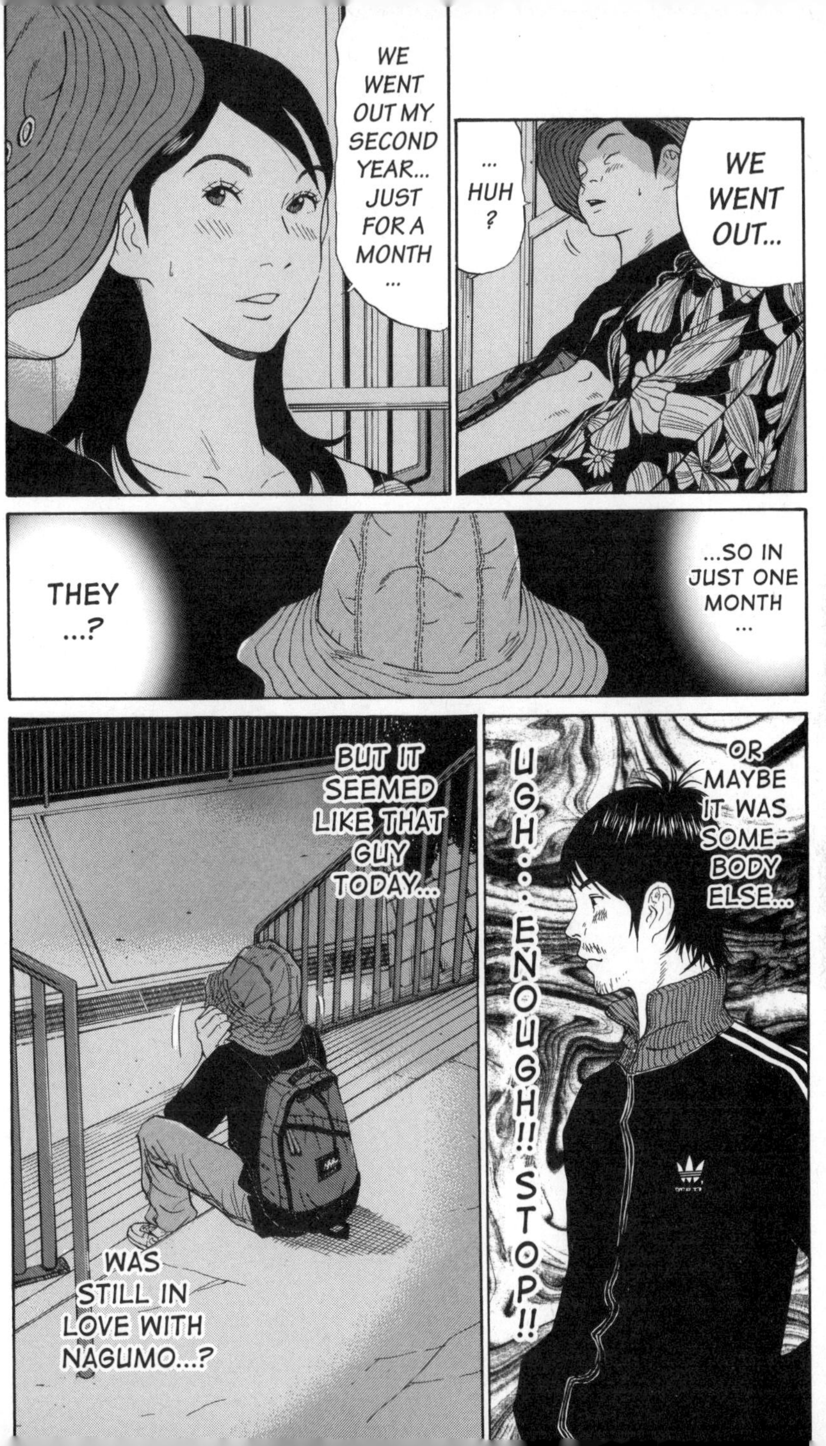
WE WENT OUT...
... HUH ?
WE WENT OUT MY SECOND YEAR... JUST FOR A MONTH ...
...SO IN JUST ONE MONTH ...
THEY ...?
OR MAYBE IT WAS SOME-BODY ELSE...
UGH... ENOUGH!! STOP!!
BUT IT SEEMED LIKE THAT GUY TODAY...
WAS STILL IN LOVE WITH NAGUMO...?

# Chapter 67: Unchewable

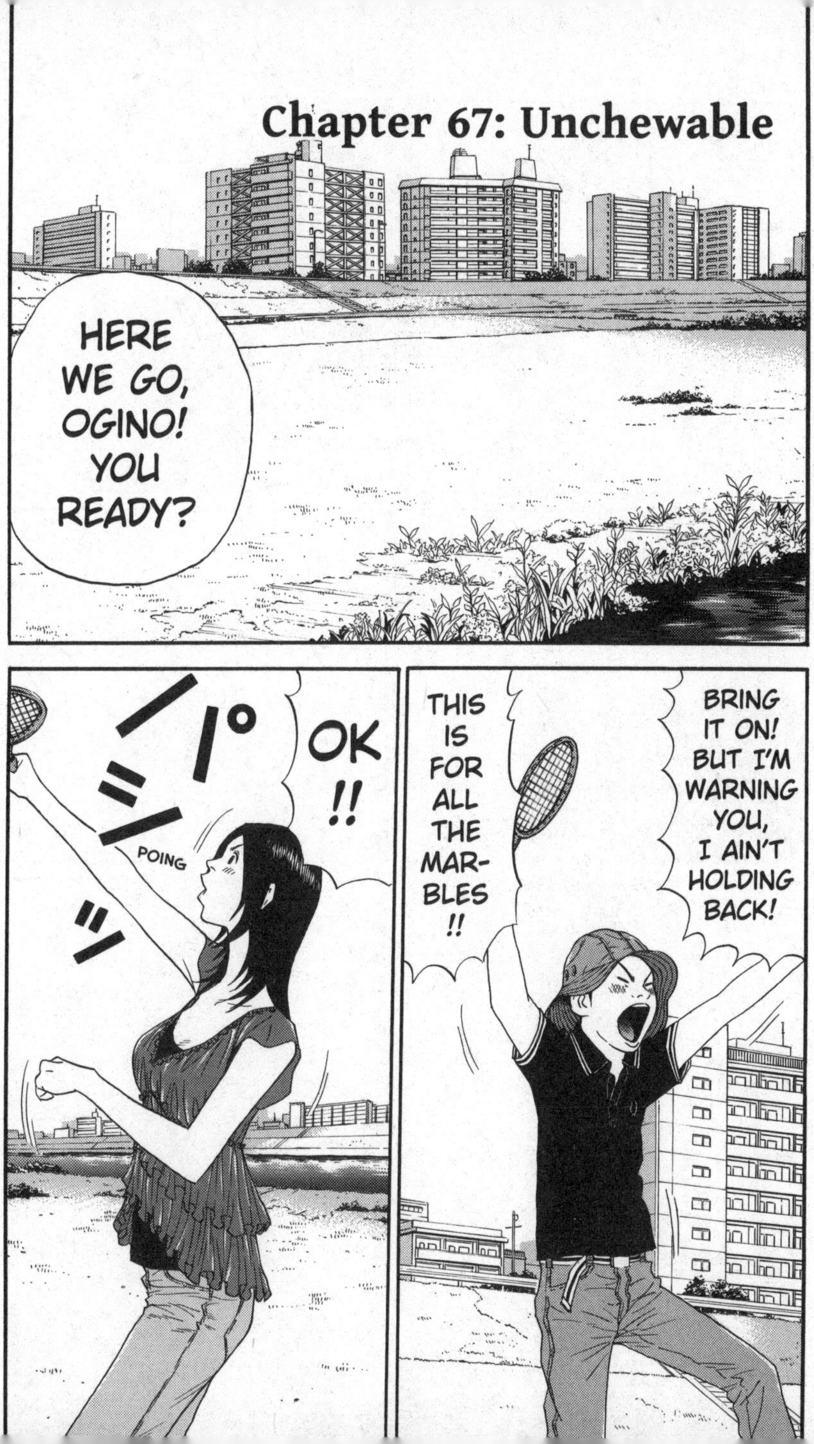
HERE WE GO, OGINO! YOU READY?
BRING IT ON! BUT I'M WARNING YOU, I AIN'T HOLDING BACK!
THIS IS FOR ALL THE MAR-BLES!!
OK!!
POING

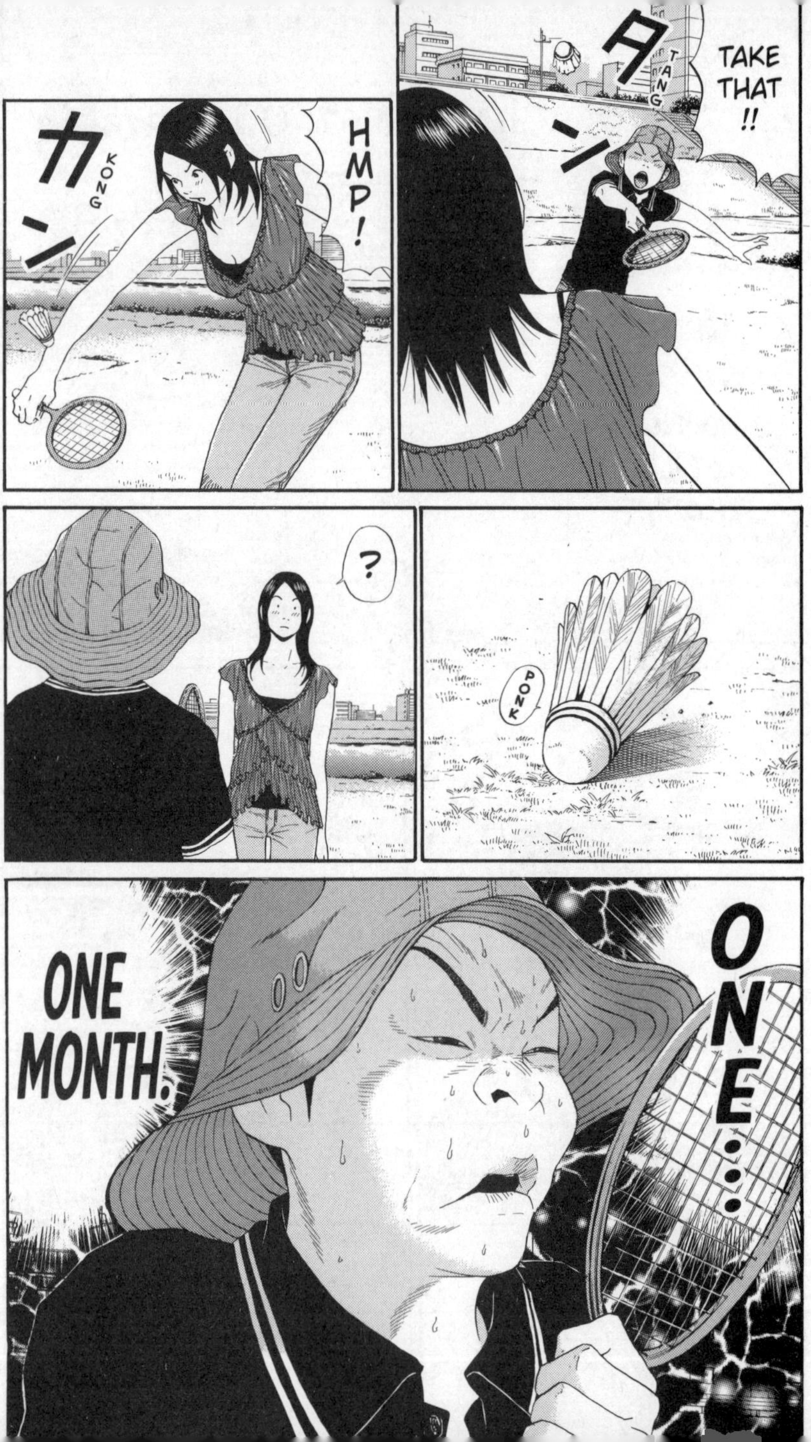
タン
TANG
TAKE THAT !!
カン
KONG
HMP!
PONK
?
ONE...
ONE MONTH.

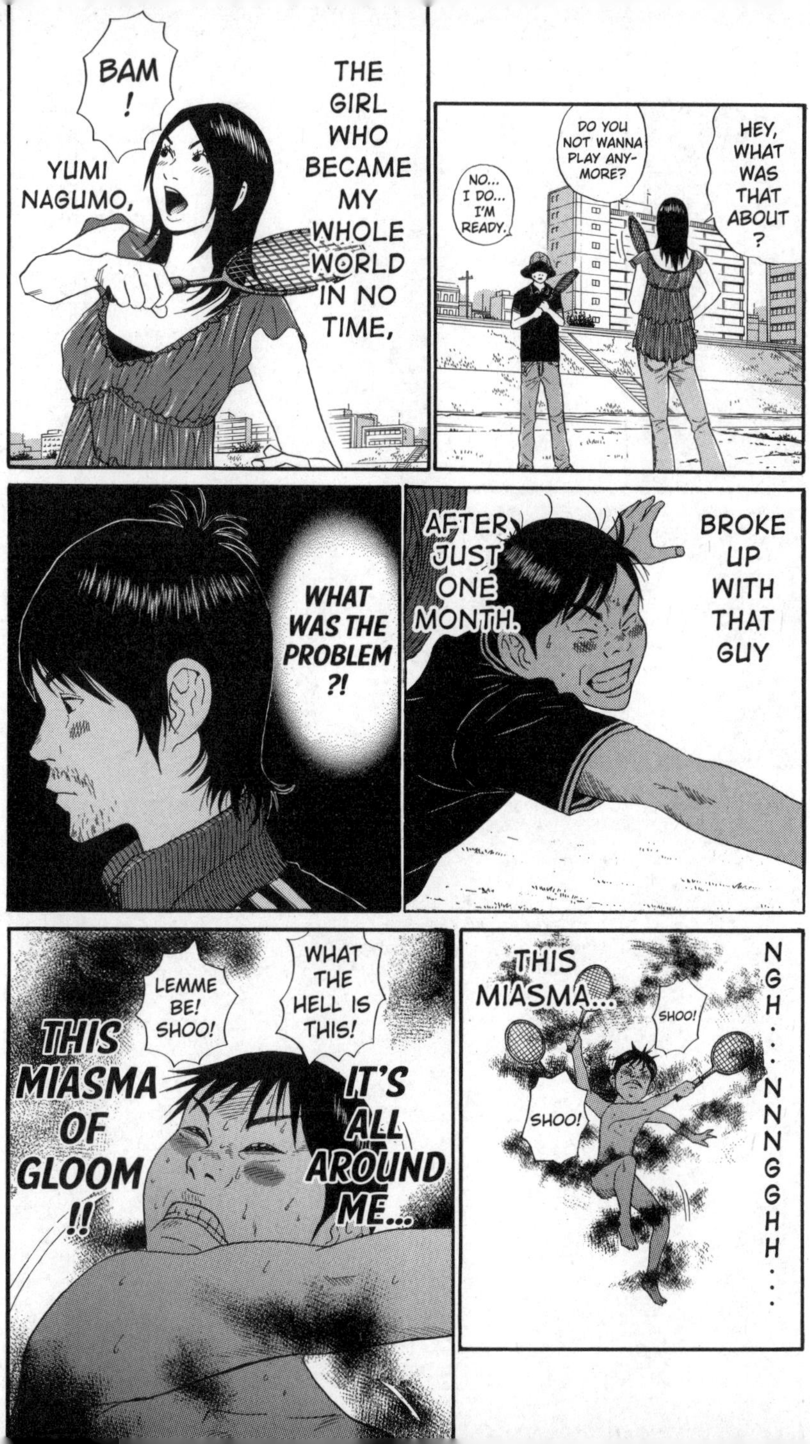
HEY, WHAT WAS THAT ABOUT?
DO YOU NOT WANNA PLAY ANY-MORE?
NO... I DO... I'M READY.
THE GIRL WHO BECAME MY WHOLE WORLD IN NO TIME,
BAM!
YUMI NAGUMO,
BROKE UP WITH THAT GUY
AFTER JUST ONE MONTH.
WHAT WAS THE PROBLEM?!
NGH...NNNGGH...
THIS MIASMA...
SHOO!
SHOO!
WHAT THE HELL IS THIS!
LEMME BE! SHOO!
IT'S ALL AROUND ME...
THIS MIASMA OF GLOOM!!

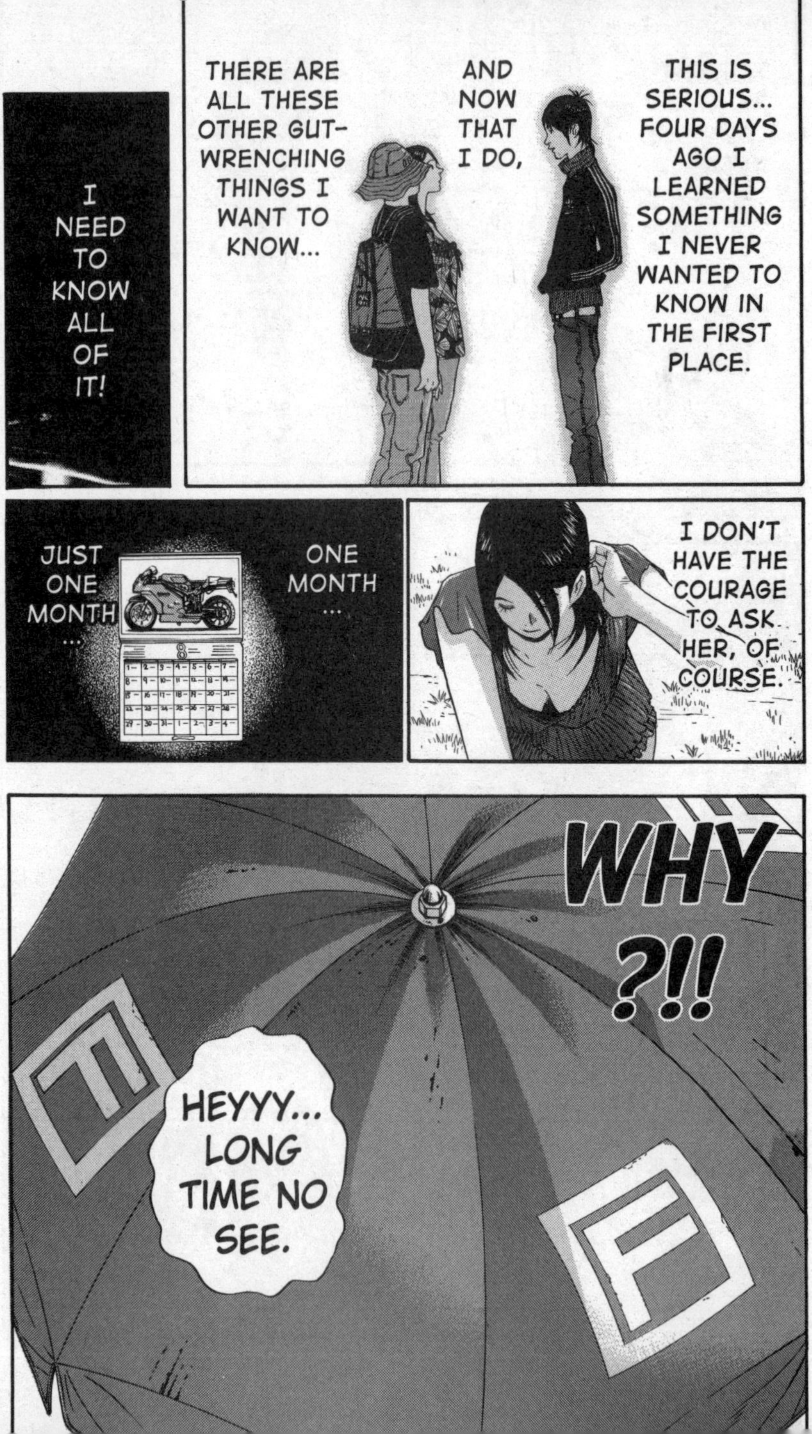
THIS IS SERIOUS... FOUR DAYS AGO I LEARNED SOMETHING I NEVER WANTED TO KNOW IN THE FIRST PLACE.
AND NOW THAT I DO,
THERE ARE ALL THESE OTHER GUT-WRENCHING THINGS I WANT TO KNOW...
I NEED TO KNOW ALL OF IT!
I DON'T HAVE THE COURAGE TO ASK HER, OF COURSE.
ONE MONTH ...
JUST ONE MONTH ...
WHY ?!!
HEYYY... LONG TIME NO SEE.

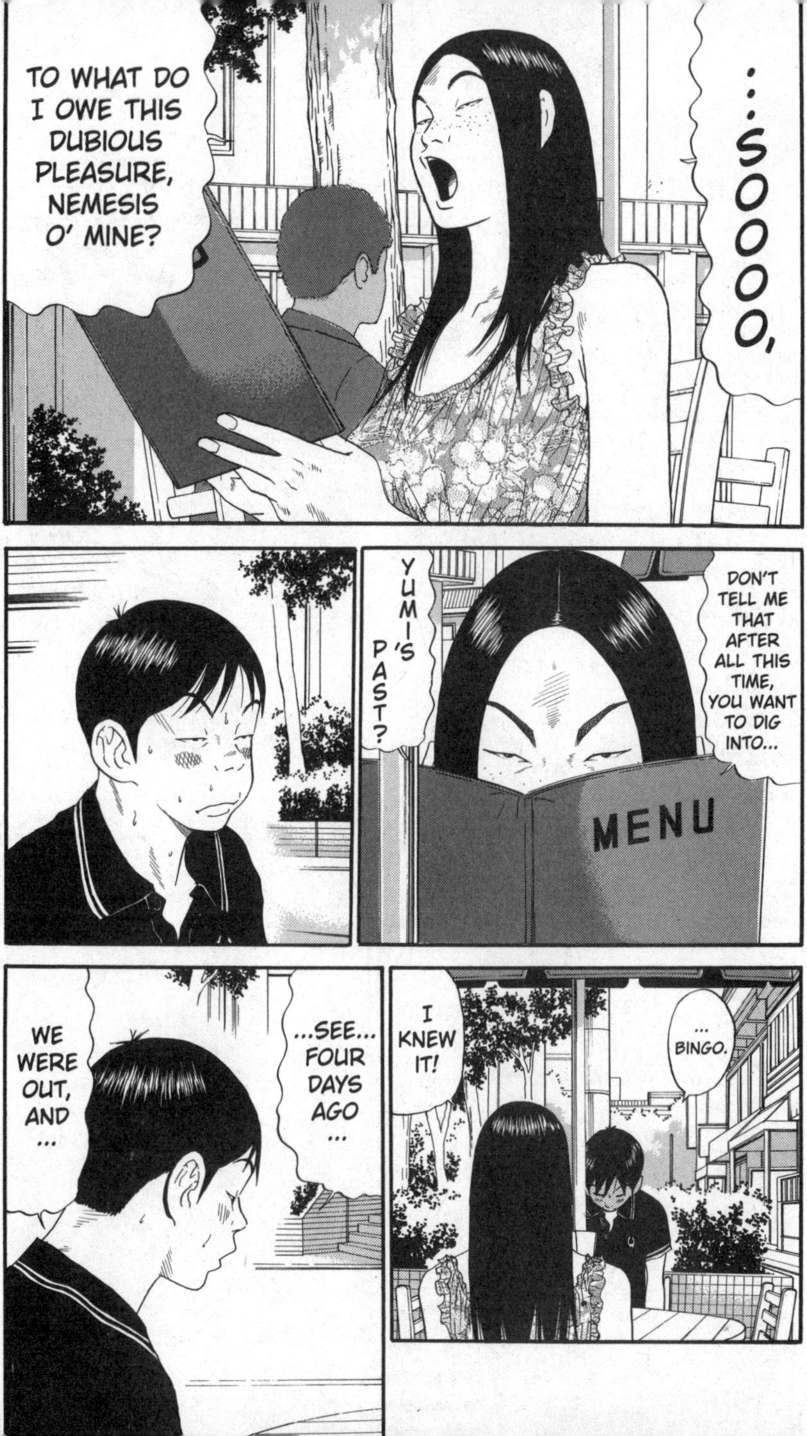
...SOOOO,
TO WHAT DO I OWE THIS DUBIOUS PLEASURE, NEMESIS O' MINE?
DON'T TELL ME THAT AFTER ALL THIS TIME, YOU WANT TO DIG INTO...
YUMI'S PAST?
MENU
... BINGO.
I KNEW IT!
...SEE... FOUR DAYS AGO ...
WE WERE OUT, AND ...

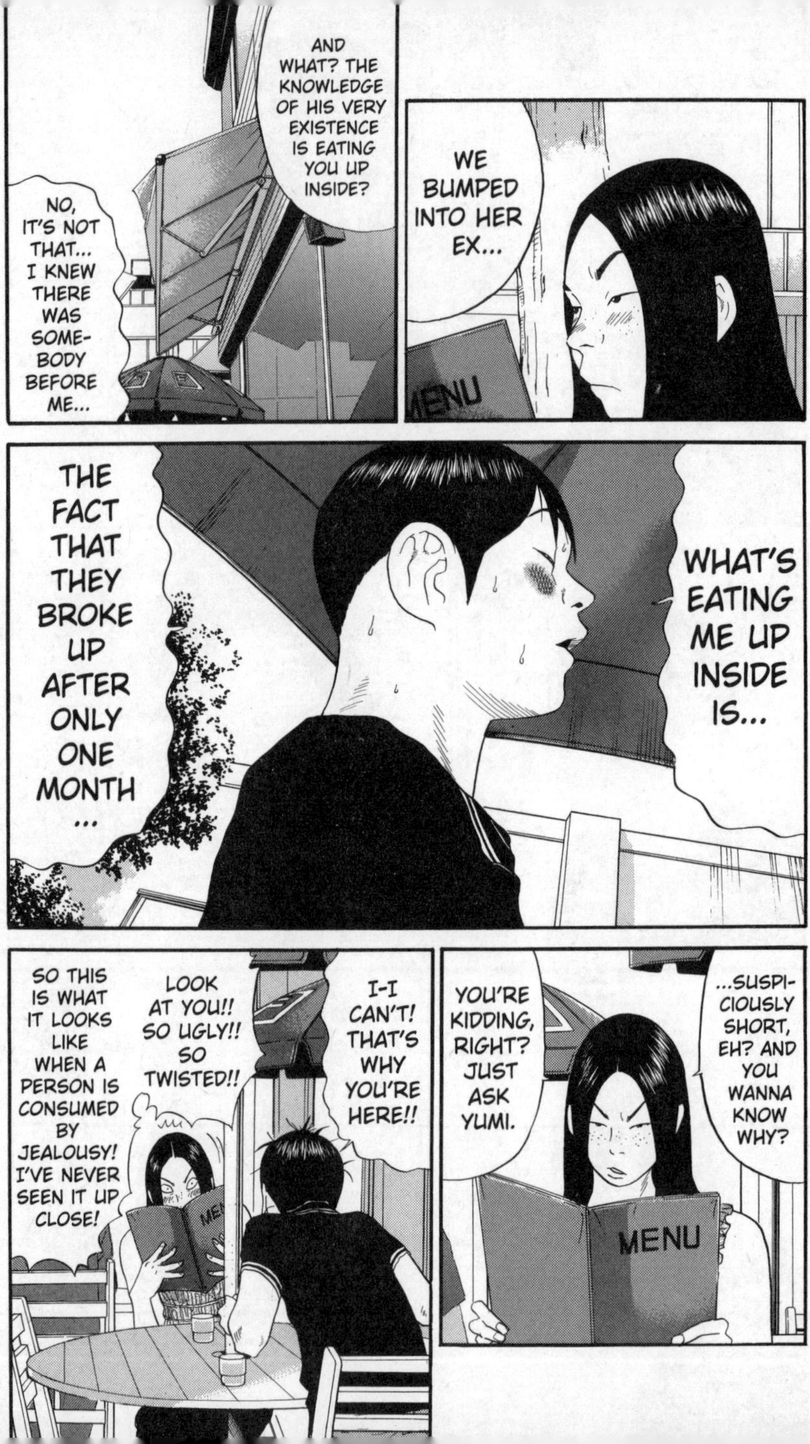
WE BUMPED INTO HER EX...
AND WHAT? THE KNOWLEDGE OF HIS VERY EXISTENCE IS EATING YOU UP INSIDE?
NO, IT'S NOT THAT... I KNEW THERE WAS SOMEBODY BEFORE ME...
WHAT'S EATING ME UP INSIDE IS...
THE FACT THAT THEY BROKE UP AFTER ONLY ONE MONTH...
...SUSPICIOUSLY SHORT, EH? AND YOU WANNA KNOW WHY?
YOU'RE KIDDING, RIGHT? JUST ASK YUMI.
MENU
I-I CAN'T! THAT'S WHY YOU'RE HERE!!
LOOK AT YOU!! SO UGLY!! SO TWISTED!!
SO THIS IS WHAT IT LOOKS LIKE WHEN A PERSON IS CONSUMED BY JEALOUSY! I'VE NEVER SEEN IT UP CLOSE!

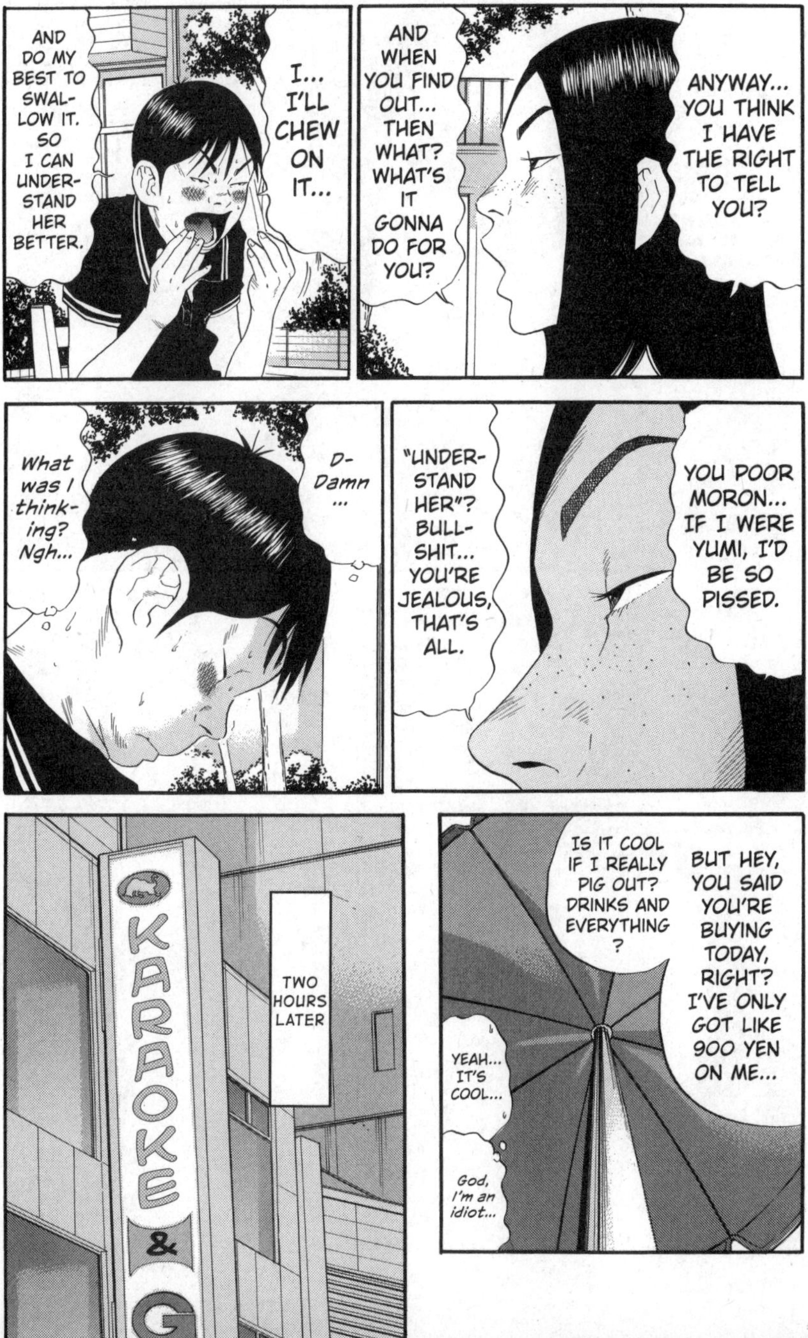
ANYWAY... YOU THINK I HAVE THE RIGHT TO TELL YOU?
AND WHEN YOU FIND OUT... THEN WHAT? WHAT'S IT GONNA DO FOR YOU?
I... I'LL CHEW ON IT...
AND DO MY BEST TO SWAL-LOW IT. SO I CAN UNDER-STAND HER BETTER.
YOU POOR MORON... IF I WERE YUMI, I'D BE SO PISSED.
"UNDER-STAND HER"? BULL-SHIT... YOU'RE JEALOUS, THAT'S ALL.
D-Damn...
What was I think-ing? Ngh...
BUT HEY, YOU SAID YOU'RE BUYING TODAY, RIGHT? I'VE ONLY GOT LIKE 900 YEN ON ME...
IS IT COOL IF I REALLY PIG OUT? DRINKS AND EVERYTHING?
YEAH... IT'S COOL...
God, I'm an idiot...
TWO HOURS LATER
KARAOKE & G

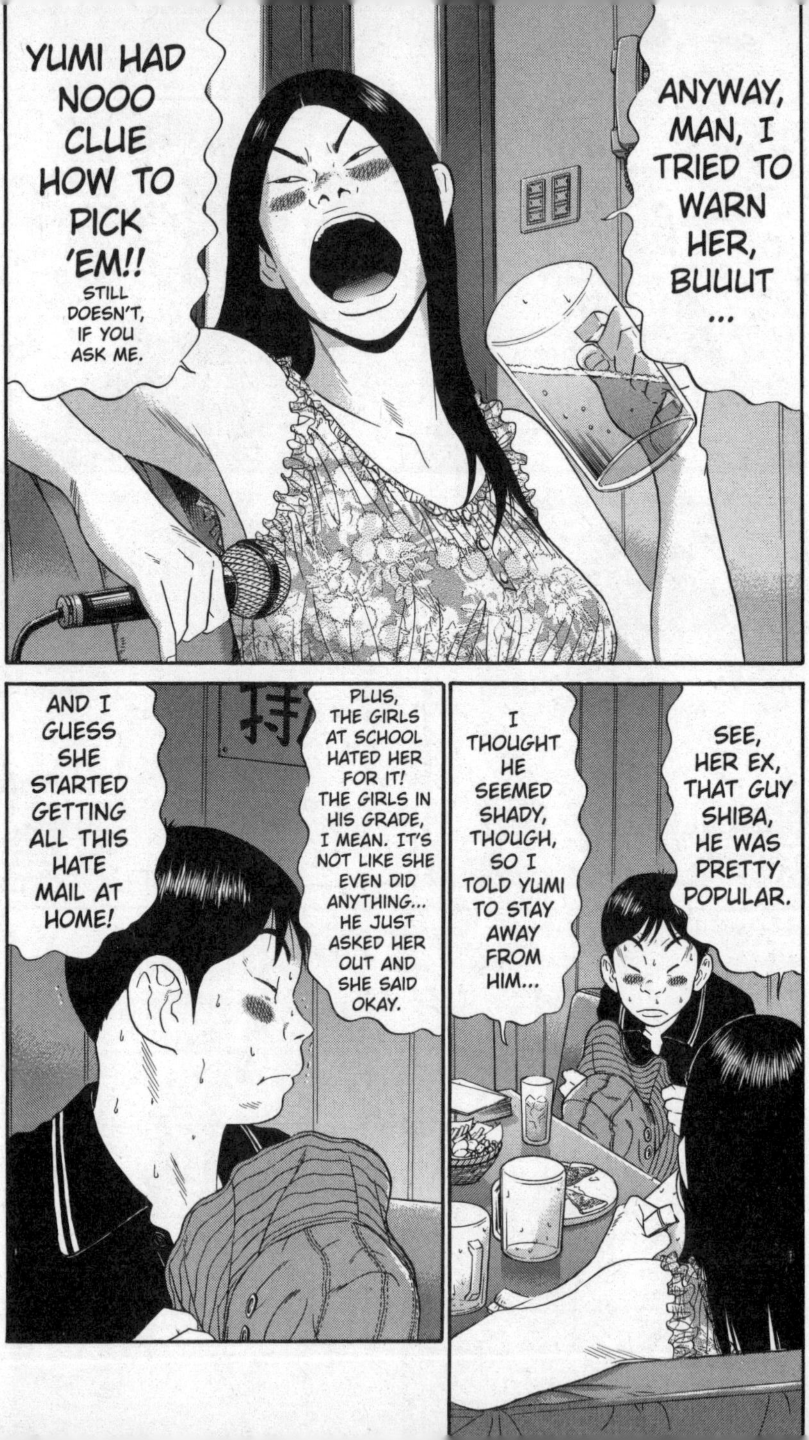
ANYWAY, MAN, I TRIED TO WARN HER, BUUUT ...
YUMI HAD NOOO CLUE HOW TO PICK 'EM!!
STILL DOESN'T, IF YOU ASK ME.
SEE, HER EX, THAT GUY SHIBA, HE WAS PRETTY POPULAR.
I THOUGHT HE SEEMED SHADY, THOUGH, SO I TOLD YUMI TO STAY AWAY FROM HIM...
PLUS, THE GIRLS AT SCHOOL HATED HER FOR IT! THE GIRLS IN HIS GRADE, I MEAN. IT'S NOT LIKE SHE EVEN DID ANYTHING... HE JUST ASKED HER OUT AND SHE SAID OKAY.
AND I GUESS SHE STARTED GETTING ALL THIS HATE MAIL AT HOME!

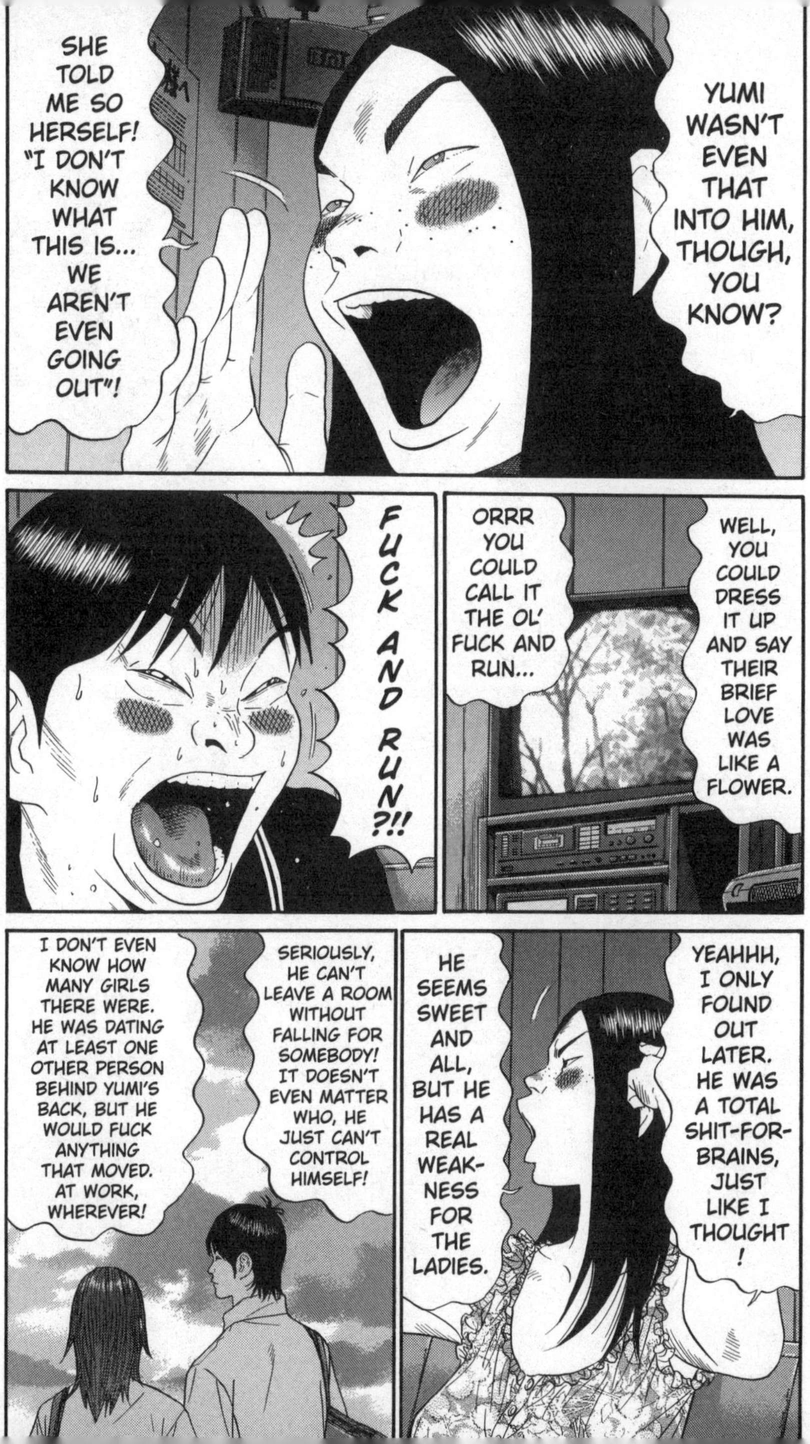
YUMI WASN'T EVEN THAT INTO HIM, THOUGH, YOU KNOW?
SHE TOLD ME SO HERSELF! "I DON'T KNOW WHAT THIS IS... WE AREN'T EVEN GOING OUT"!
WELL, YOU COULD DRESS IT UP AND SAY THEIR BRIEF LOVE WAS LIKE A FLOWER.
ORRR YOU COULD CALL IT THE OL' FUCK AND RUN...
FUCK AND RUN?!!
YEAHHH, I ONLY FOUND OUT LATER. HE WAS A TOTAL SHIT-FOR-BRAINS, JUST LIKE I THOUGHT!
HE SEEMS SWEET AND ALL, BUT HE HAS A REAL WEAK-NESS FOR THE LADIES.
SERIOUSLY, HE CAN'T LEAVE A ROOM WITHOUT FALLING FOR SOMEBODY! IT DOESN'T EVEN MATTER WHO, HE JUST CAN'T CONTROL HIMSELF!
I DON'T EVEN KNOW HOW MANY GIRLS THERE WERE. HE WAS DATING AT LEAST ONE OTHER PERSON BEHIND YUMI'S BACK, BUT HE WOULD FUCK ANYTHING THAT MOVED. AT WORK, WHEREVER!

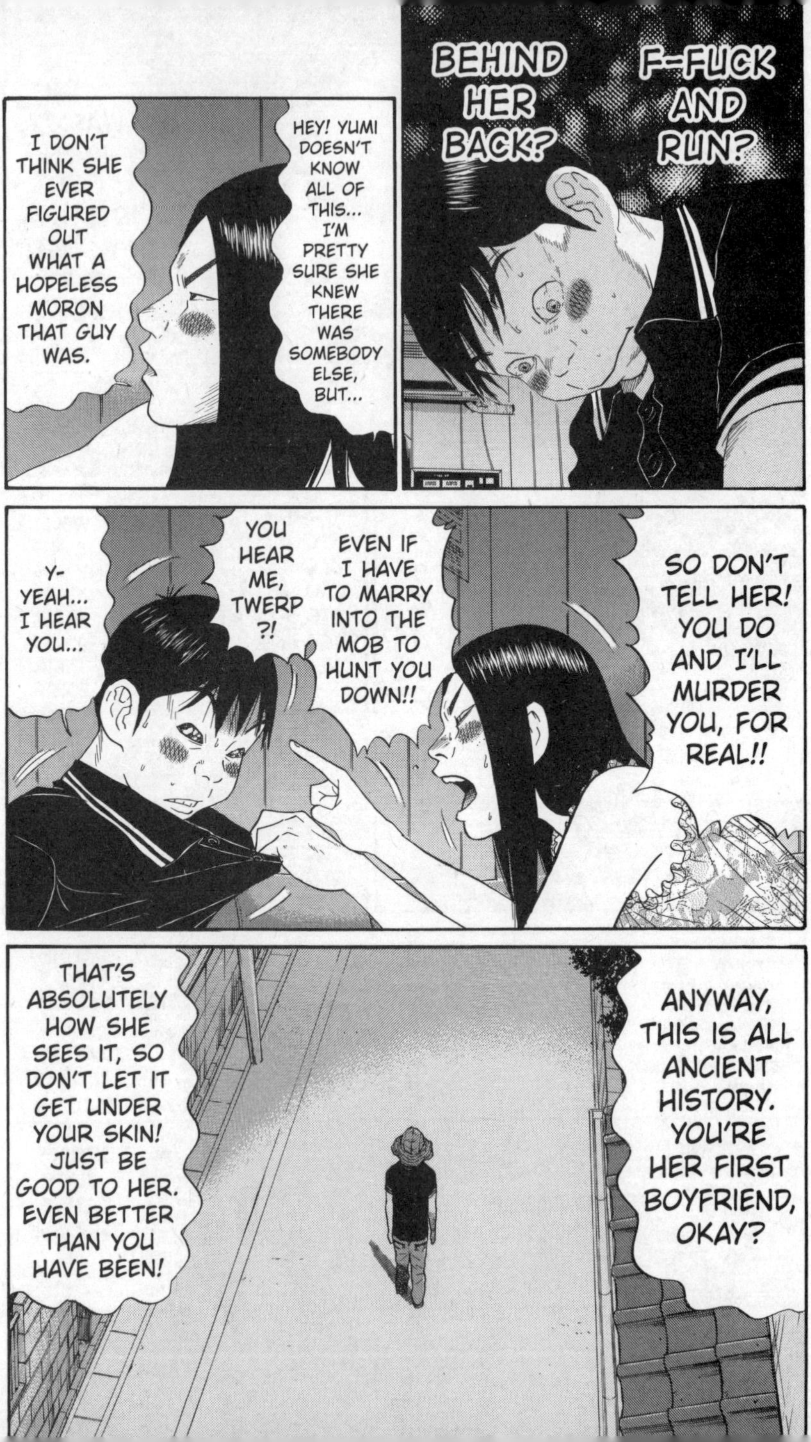
F-FUCK AND RUN?
BEHIND HER BACK?
HEY! YUMI DOESN'T KNOW ALL OF THIS... I'M PRETTY SURE SHE KNEW THERE WAS SOMEBODY ELSE, BUT...
I DON'T THINK SHE EVER FIGURED OUT WHAT A HOPELESS MORON THAT GUY WAS.
SO DON'T TELL HER! YOU DO AND I'LL MURDER YOU, FOR REAL!!
EVEN IF I HAVE TO MARRY INTO THE MOB TO HUNT YOU DOWN!!
YOU HEAR ME, TWERP?!
Y-YEAH... I HEAR YOU...
ANYWAY, THIS IS ALL ANCIENT HISTORY. YOU'RE HER FIRST BOYFRIEND, OKAY?
THAT'S ABSOLUTELY HOW SHE SEES IT, SO DON'T LET IT GET UNDER YOUR SKIN! JUST BE GOOD TO HER. EVEN BETTER THAN YOU HAVE BEEN!

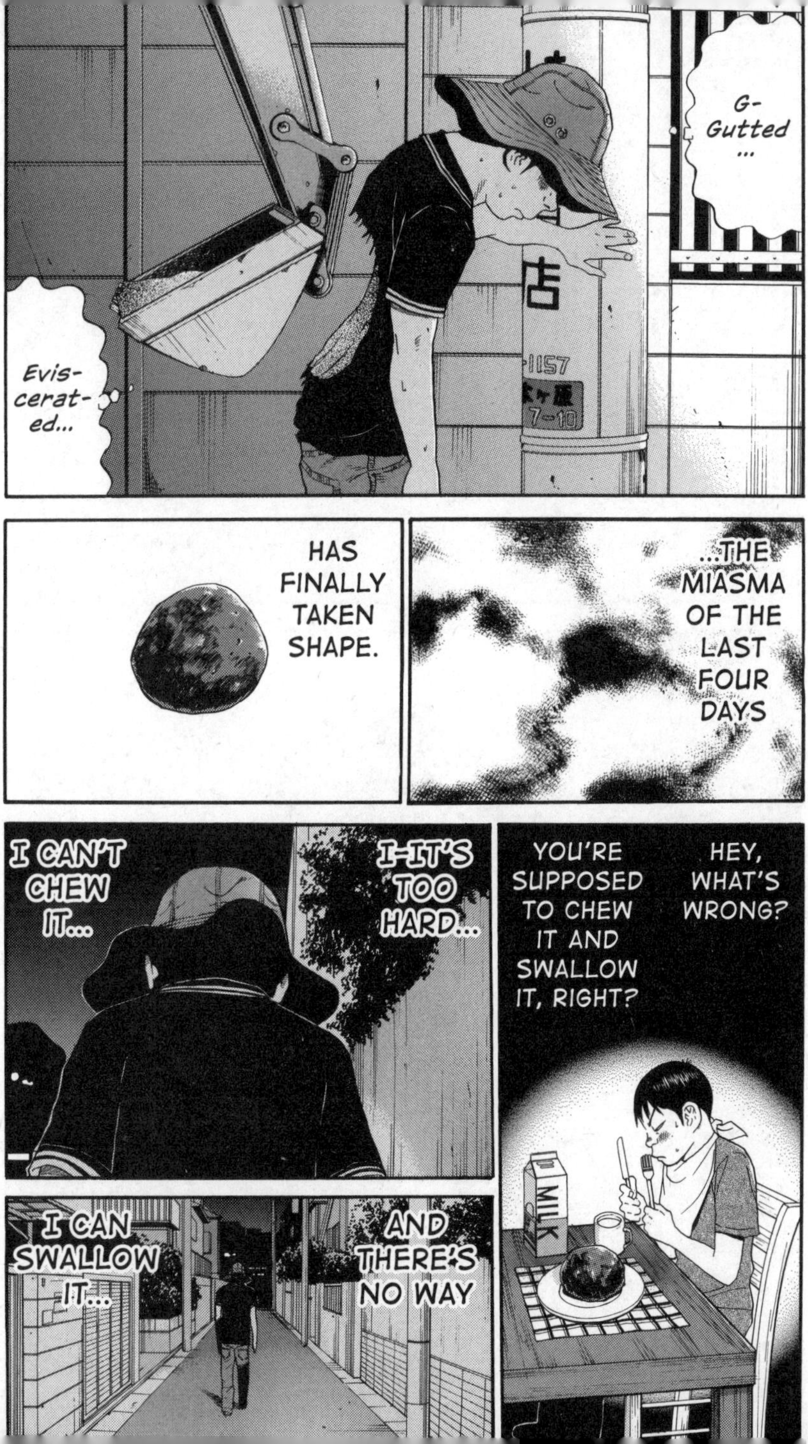
G-Gutted...
Evis-cerat-ed...
...THE MIASMA OF THE LAST FOUR DAYS
HAS FINALLY TAKEN SHAPE.
HEY, WHAT'S WRONG?
YOU'RE SUPPOSED TO CHEW IT AND SWALLOW IT, RIGHT?
MILK
I-IT'S TOO HARD...
I CAN'T CHEW IT...
AND THERE'S NO WAY
I CAN SWALLOW IT...

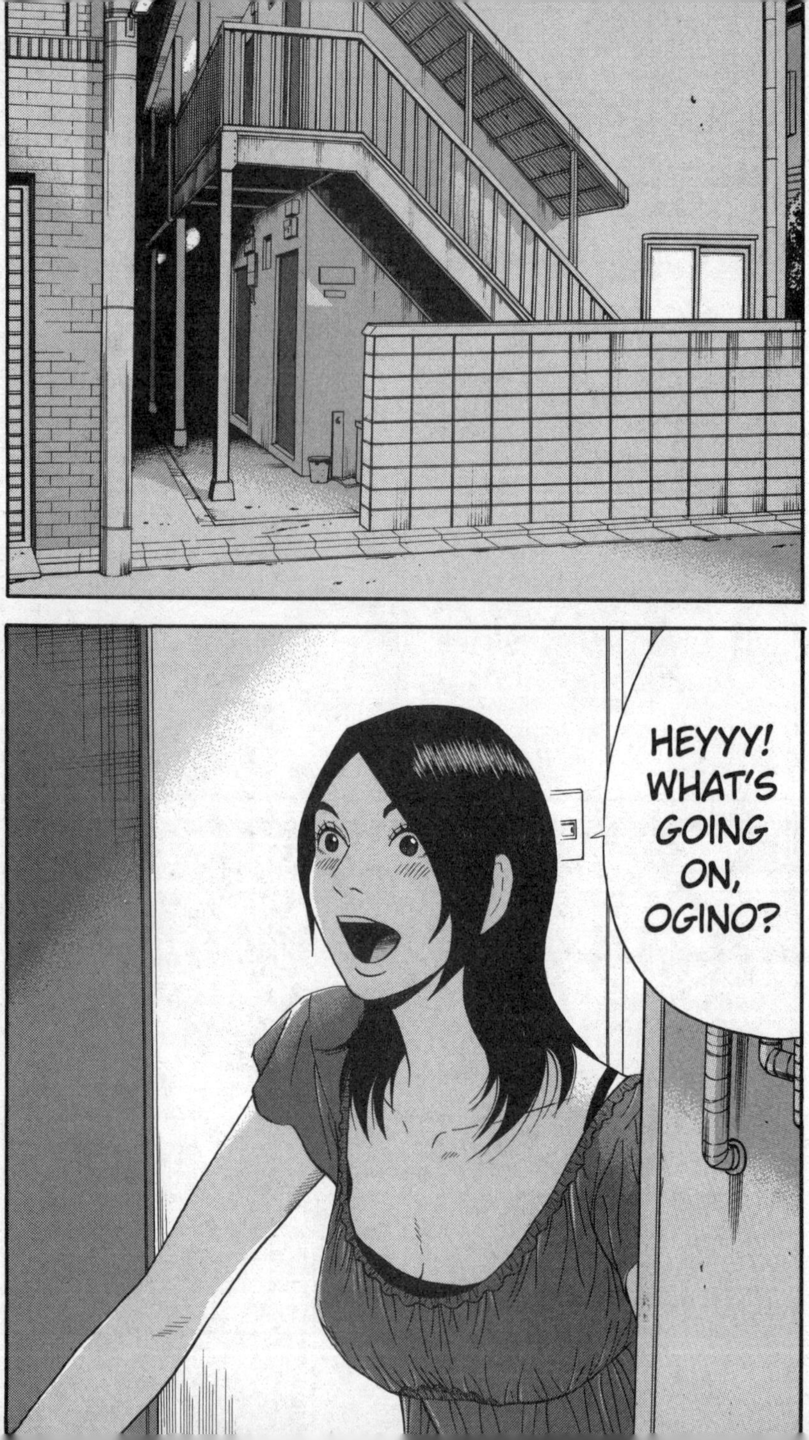
HEYYY! WHAT'S GOING ON, OGINO?

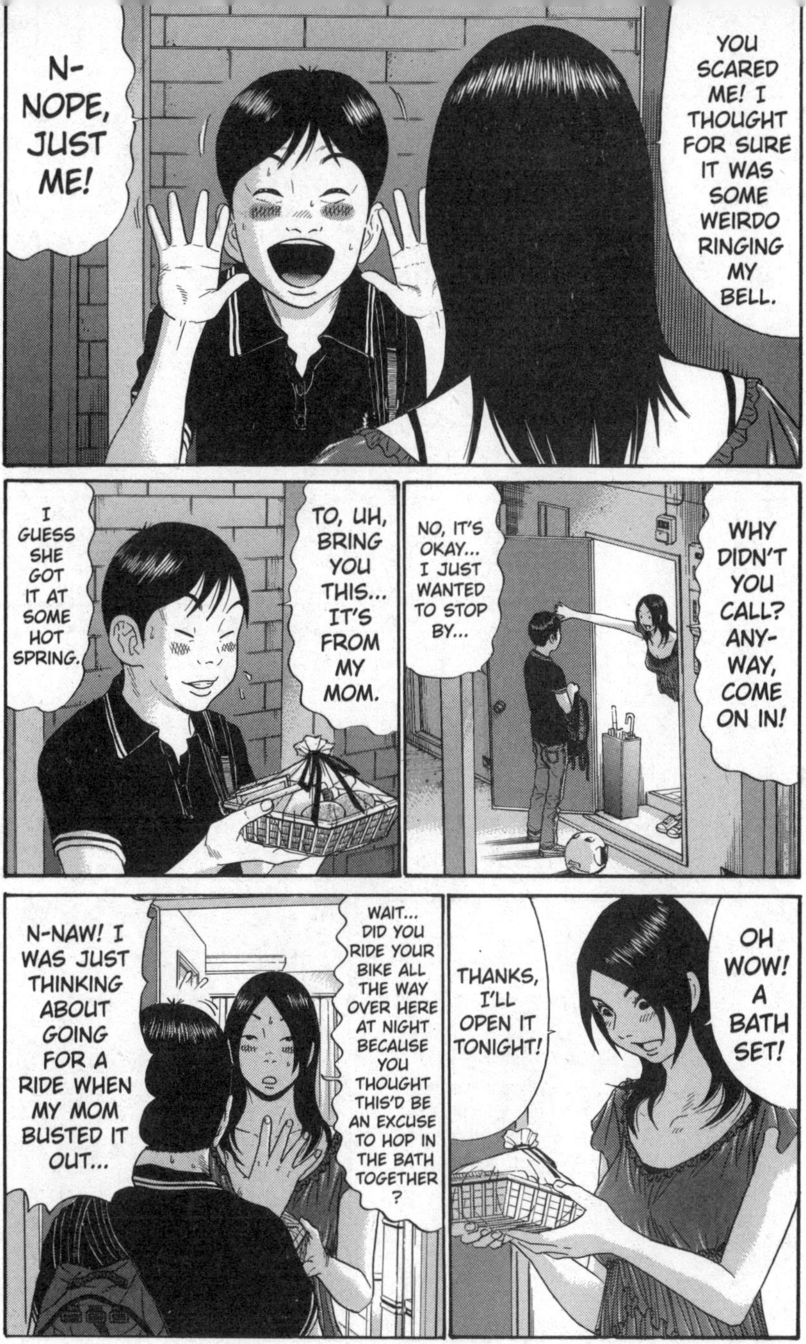
YOU SCARED ME! I THOUGHT FOR SURE IT WAS SOME WEIRDO RINGING MY BELL.
N-NOPE, JUST ME!
WHY DIDN'T YOU CALL? ANY-WAY, COME ON IN!
NO, IT'S OKAY... I JUST WANTED TO STOP BY...
TO, UH, BRING YOU THIS... IT'S FROM MY MOM.
I GUESS SHE GOT IT AT SOME HOT SPRING.
OH WOW! A BATH SET!
THANKS, I'LL OPEN IT TONIGHT!
WAIT... DID YOU RIDE YOUR BIKE ALL THE WAY OVER HERE AT NIGHT BECAUSE YOU THOUGHT THIS'D BE AN EXCUSE TO HOP IN THE BATH TOGETHER?
N-NAW! I WAS JUST THINKING ABOUT GOING FOR A RIDE WHEN MY MOM BUSTED IT OUT...

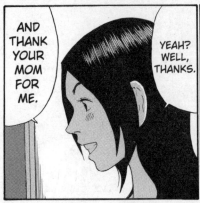

UM... ANYWAY, THAT'S WHY I CAME BY...
I'D BETTER GET GOING... GOT AN EARLY MORNING.
YEAH? WELL, THANKS.
AND THANK YOUR MOM FOR ME.
...BUT YOU WERE HOPING WE'D GET IN THE TUB TOGETHER, RIGHT?
NOT TONIGHT... MAYBE NEXT TIME? DON'T YOU HAVE WORK IN THE MORNING?
DON'T WORRY ABOUT SEEING ME OFF... LATER.
SWEET DREAMS.
KLIK

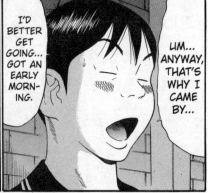

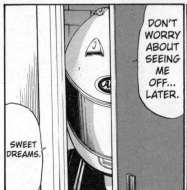

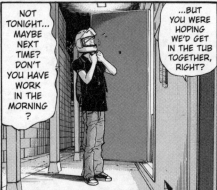

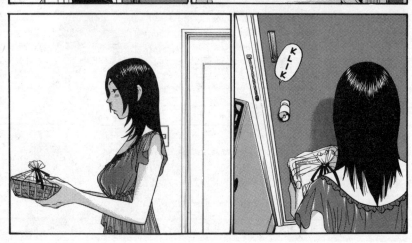

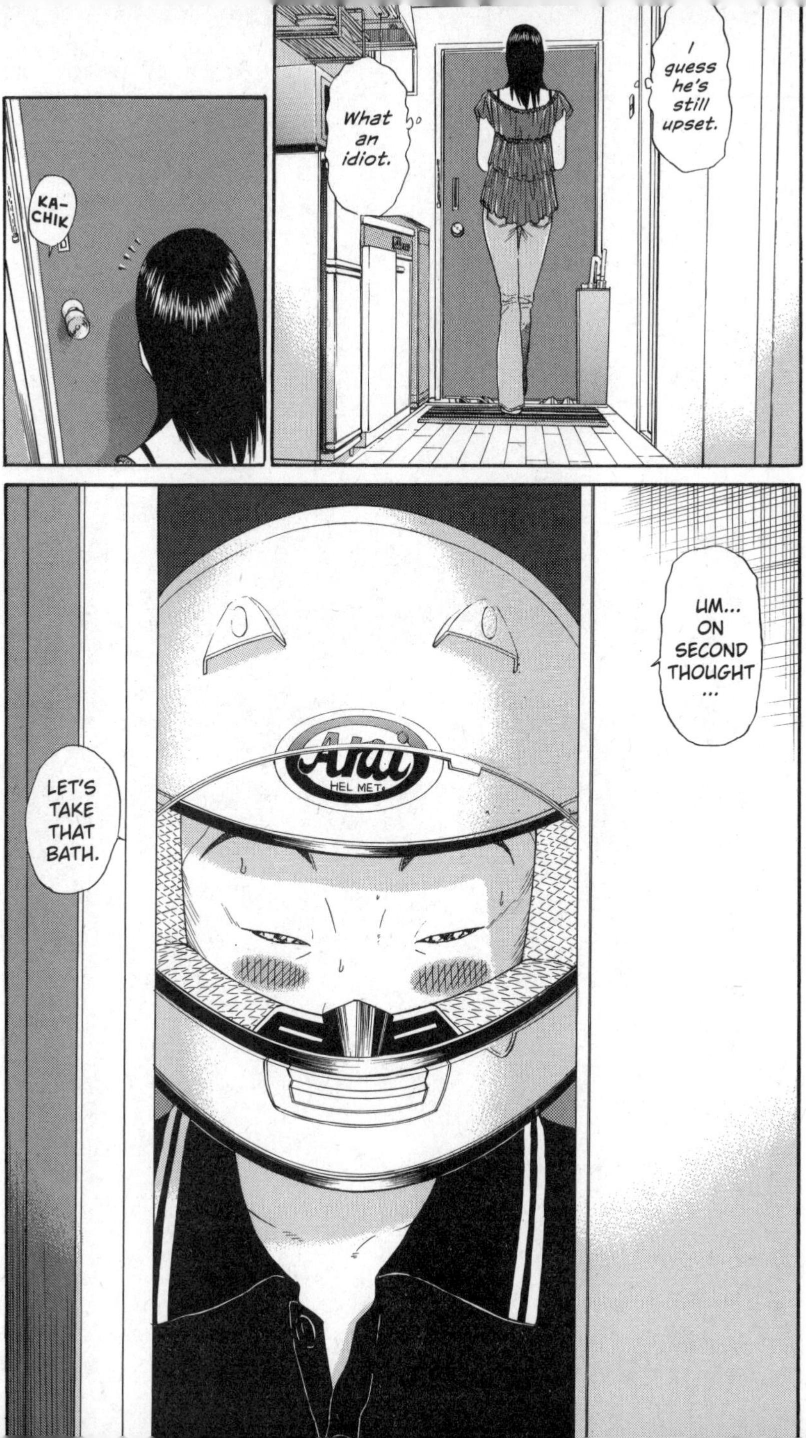

I guess he's still upset.
What an idiot.
KA-CHIK
UM... ON SECOND THOUGHT...
LET'S TAKE THAT BATH.

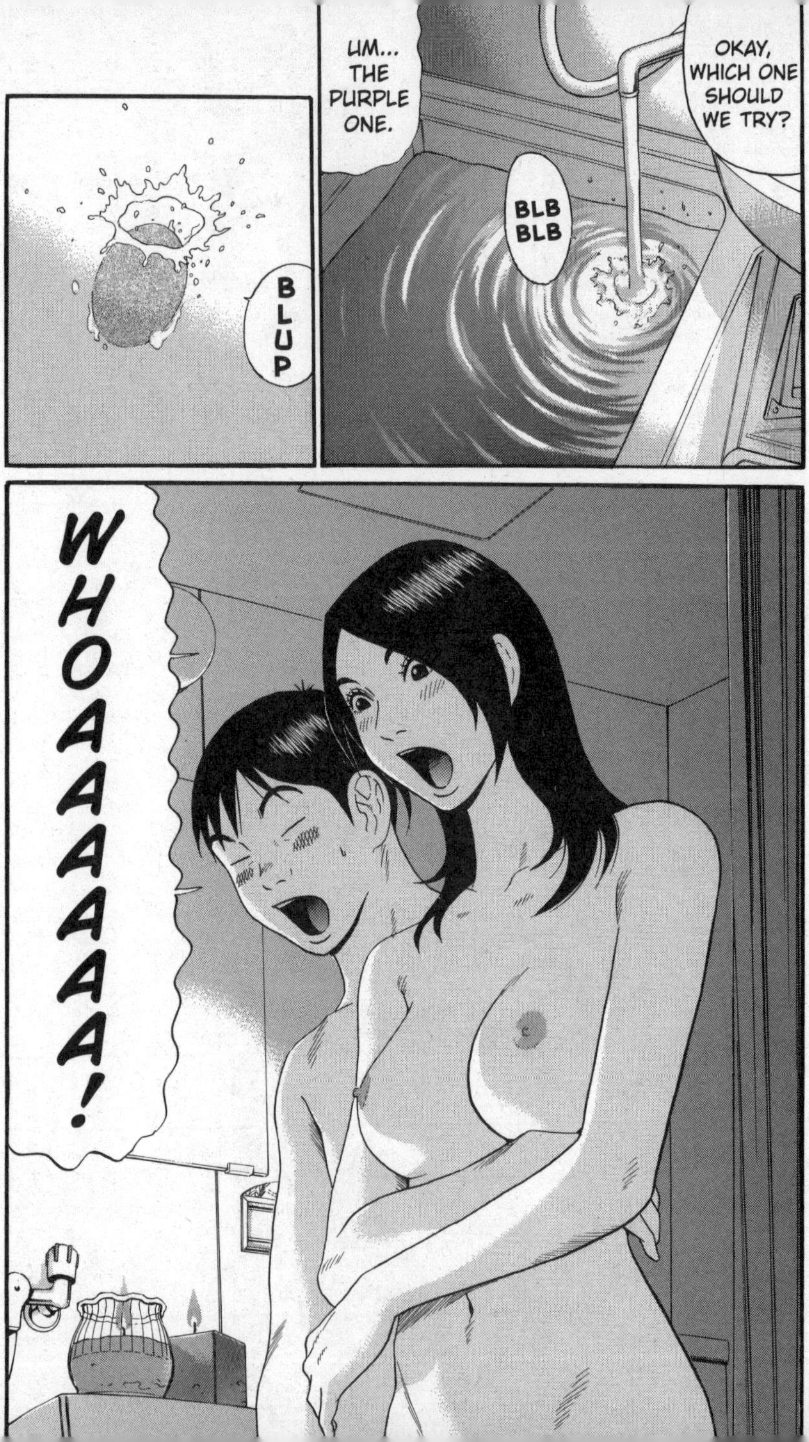
OKAY, WHICH ONE SHOULD WE TRY?
UM... THE PURPLE ONE.
BLB BLB
BLUP
WHOAAAAAAA!

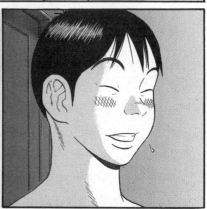

HUH?

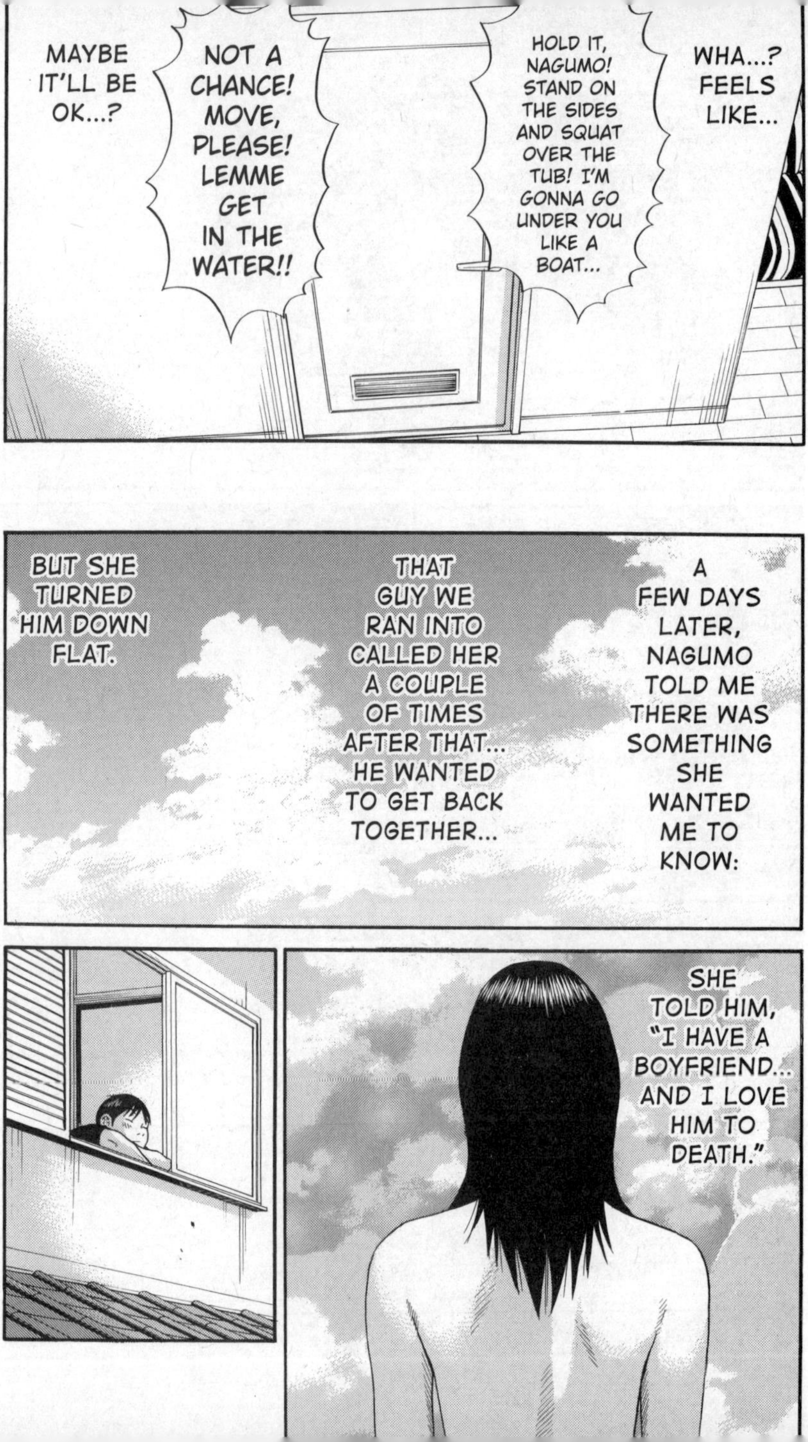
WHA...? FEELS LIKE...
HOLD IT, NAGUMO! STAND ON THE SIDES AND SQUAT OVER THE TUB! I'M GONNA GO UNDER YOU LIKE A BOAT...
NOT A CHANCE! MOVE, PLEASE! LEMME GET IN THE WATER!!
MAYBE IT'LL BE OK...?
A FEW DAYS LATER, NAGUMO TOLD ME THERE WAS SOMETHING SHE WANTED ME TO KNOW:
THAT GUY WE RAN INTO CALLED HER A COUPLE OF TIMES AFTER THAT... HE WANTED TO GET BACK TOGETHER...
BUT SHE TURNED HIM DOWN FLAT.
SHE TOLD HIM, "I HAVE A BOYFRIEND... AND I LOVE HIM TO DEATH."

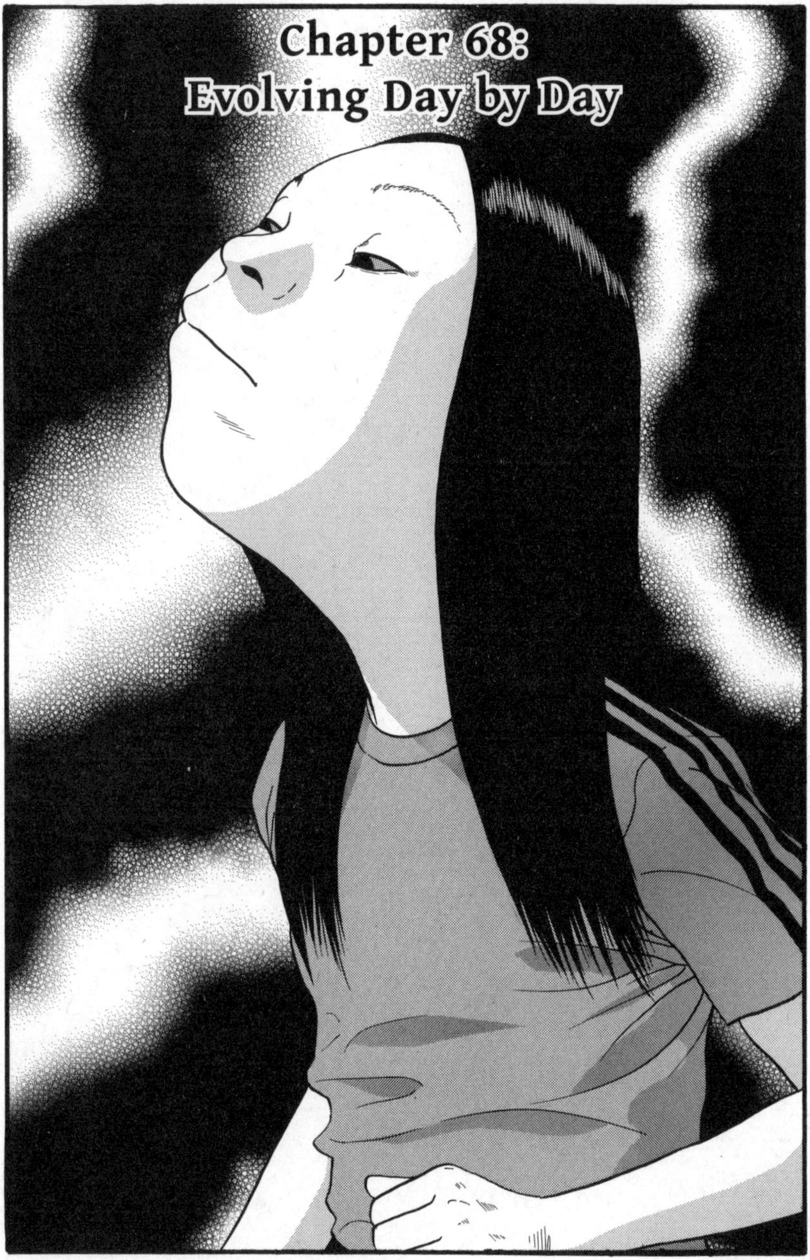
Chapter 68:
Evolving Day by Day

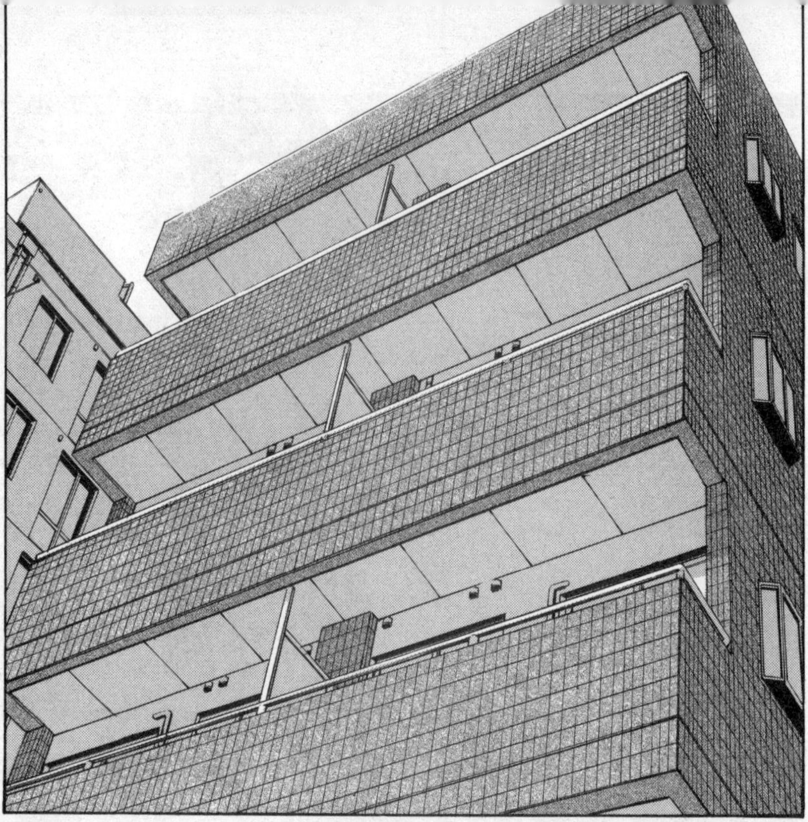

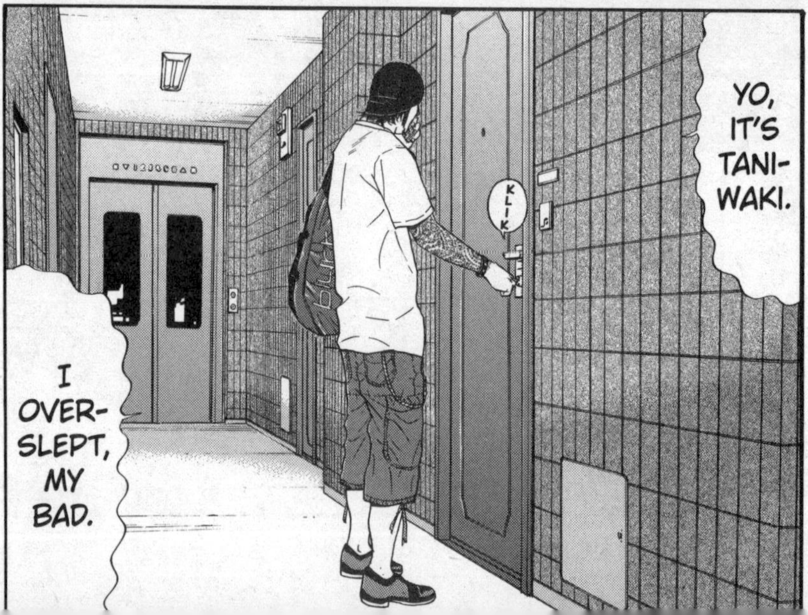
YO, IT'S TANI-WAKI.
KLIK
I OVER-SLEPT, MY BAD.

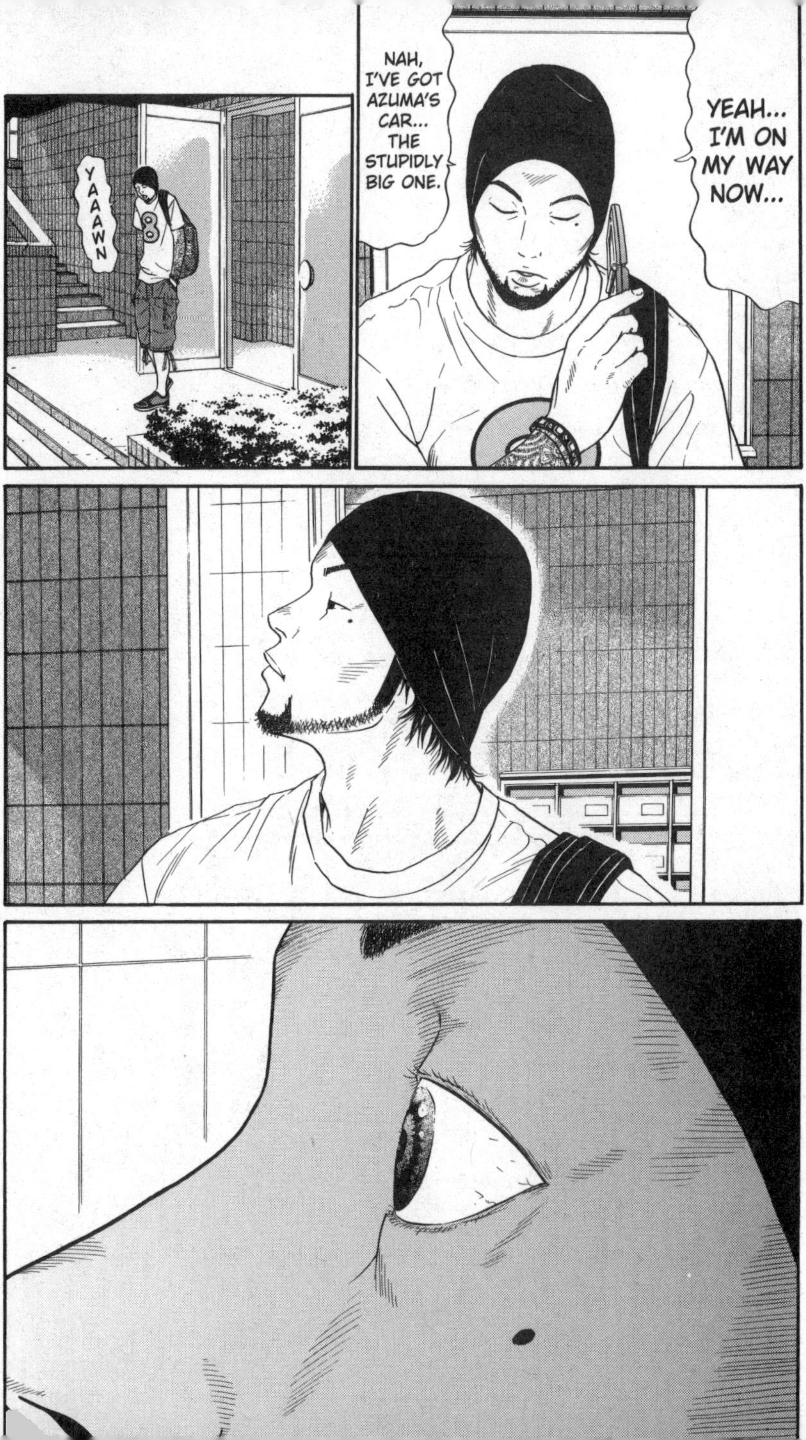
YEAH... I'M ON MY WAY NOW...
NAH, I'VE GOT AZUMA'S CAR... THE STUPIDLY BIG ONE.
YAAAWN

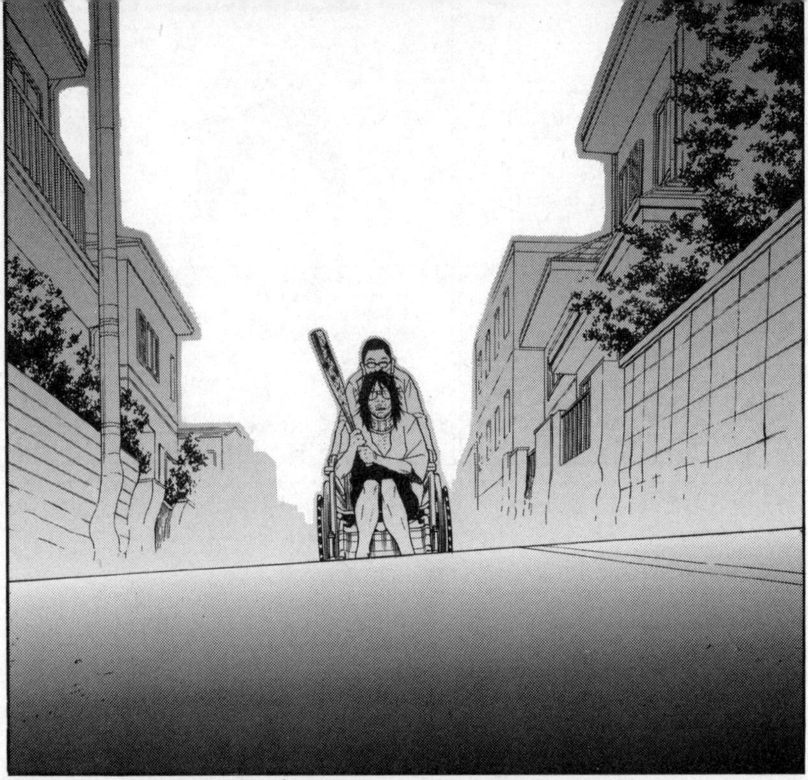
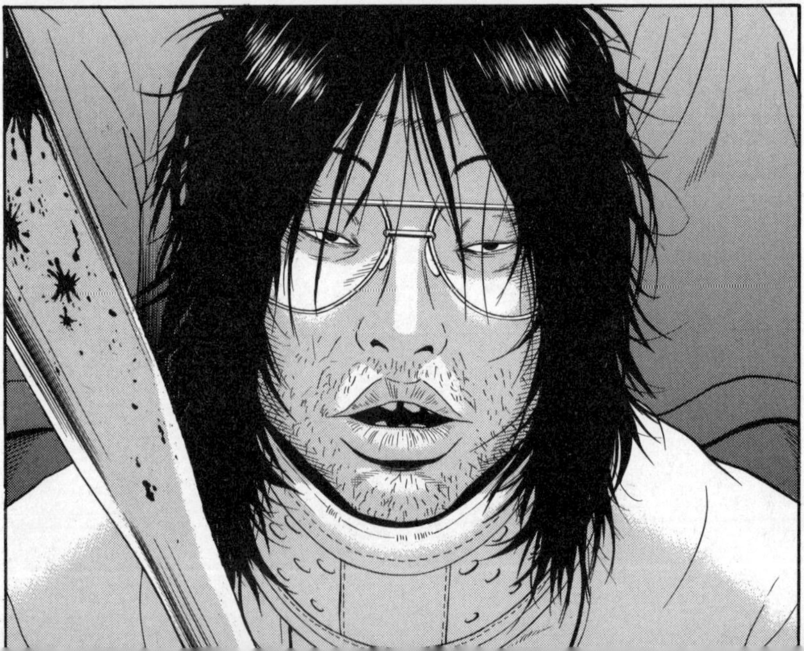

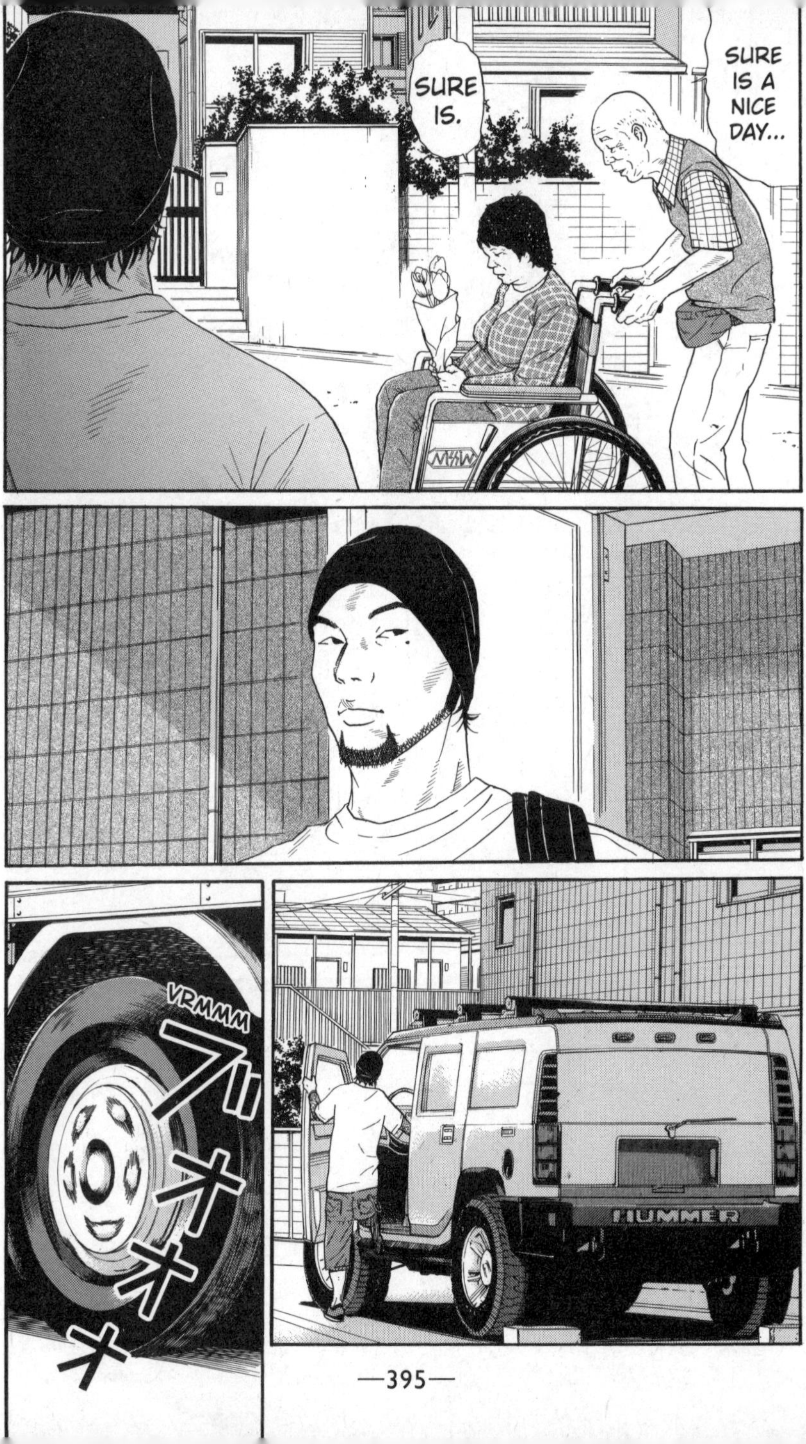
SURE IS A NICE DAY...
SURE IS.
HUMMER
VRMMM
ブオオオオ

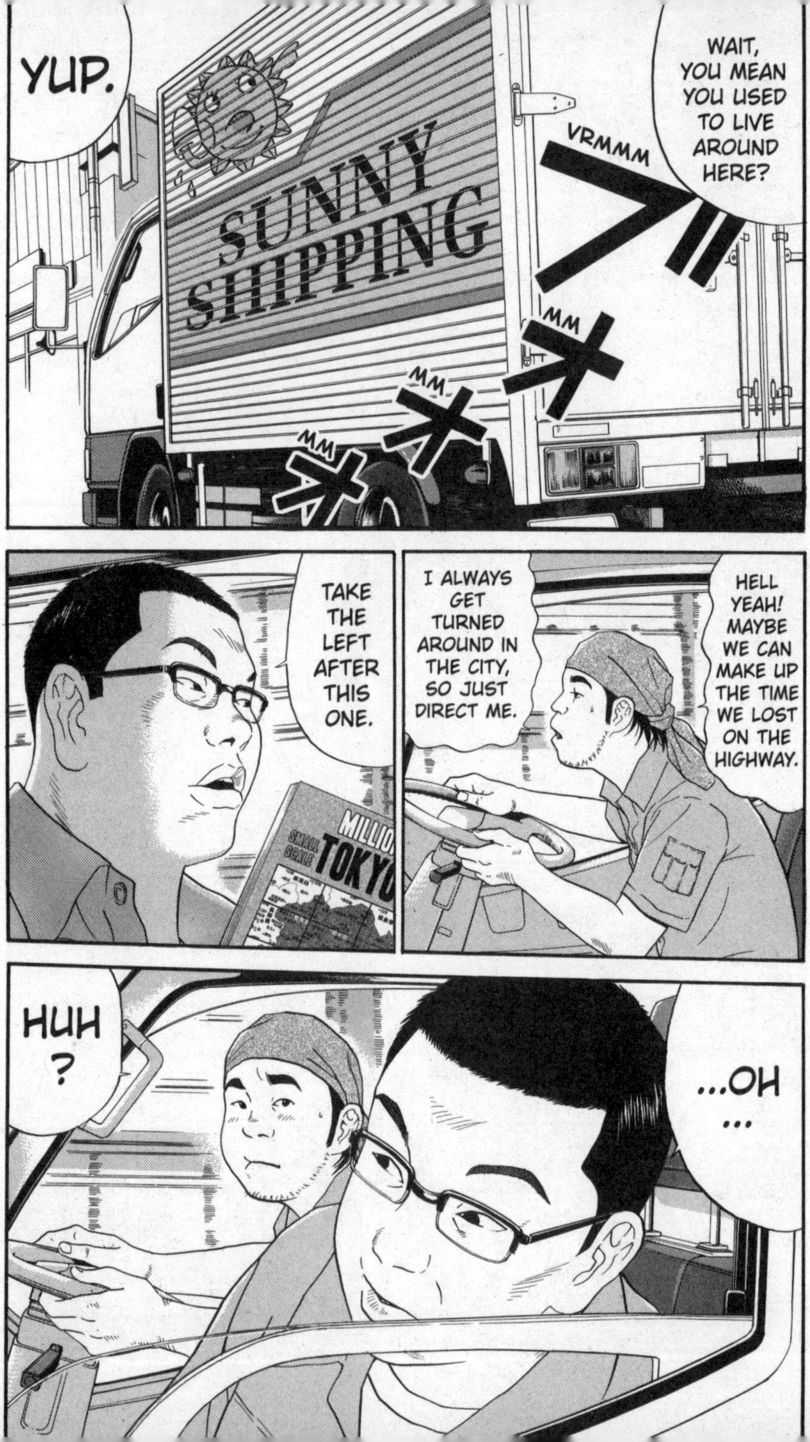
WAIT, YOU MEAN YOU USED TO LIVE AROUND HERE?
VRMMM
SUNNY SHIPPING
MM
MM
MM
YUP.
HELL YEAH! MAYBE WE CAN MAKE UP THE TIME WE LOST ON THE HIGHWAY.
I ALWAYS GET TURNED AROUND IN THE CITY, SO JUST DIRECT ME.
TAKE THE LEFT AFTER THIS ONE.
SMALL SCALE
...OH ...
HUH ?

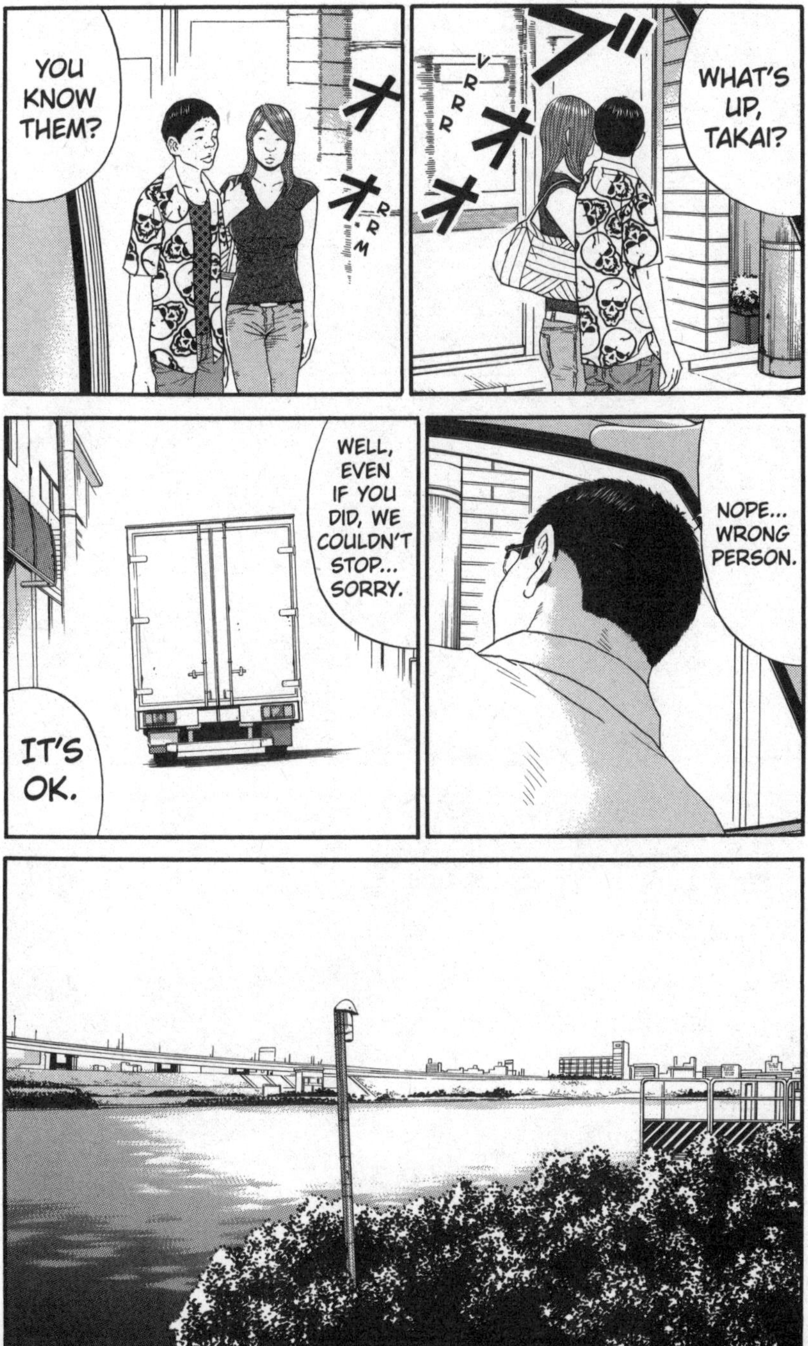
WHAT'S UP, TAKAI?
ヴォォォ
VRRR
YOU KNOW THEM?
ォォ
RRRM
NOPE... WRONG PERSON.
WELL, EVEN IF YOU DID, WE COULDN'T STOP... SORRY.
IT'S OK.

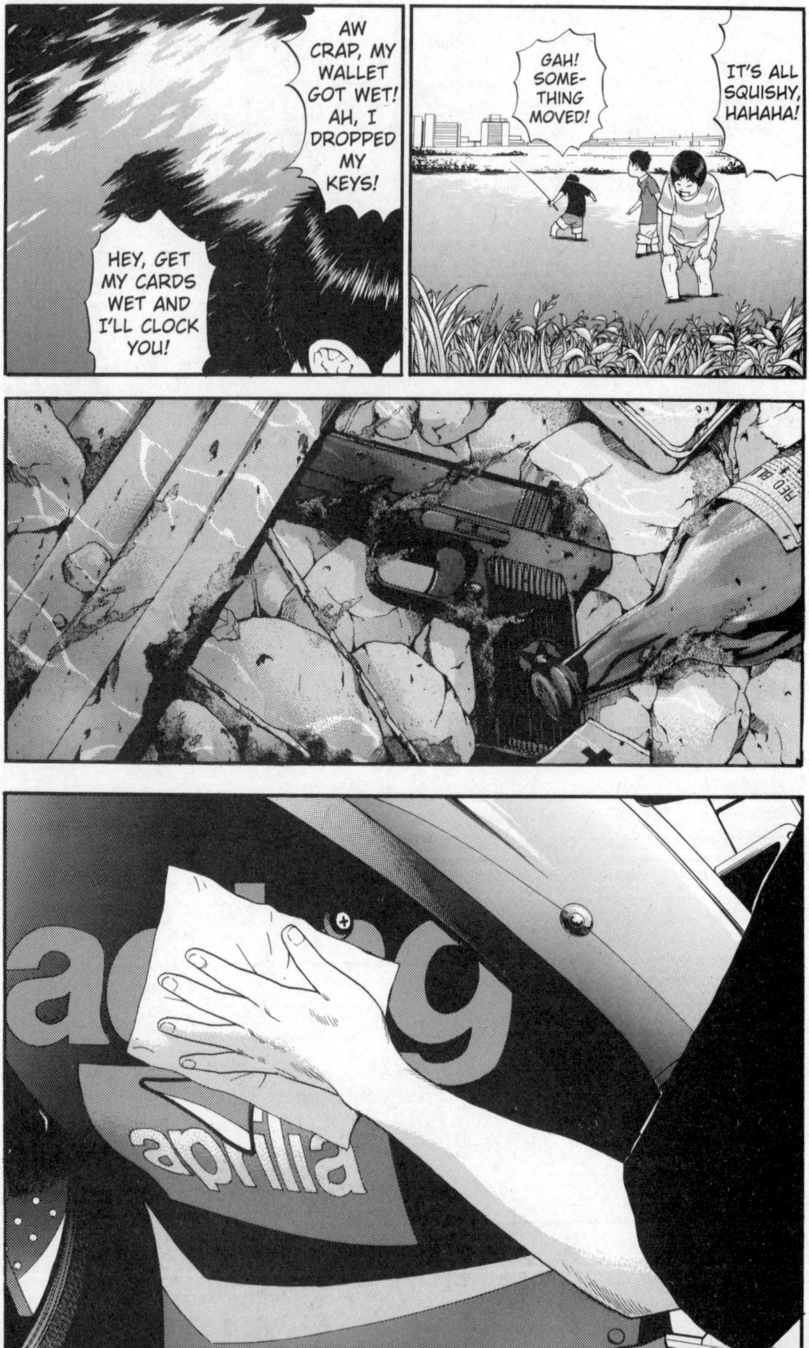
IT'S ALL SQUISHY, HAHAHA!
GAH! SOME-THING MOVED!
AW CRAP, MY WALLET GOT WET! AH, I DROPPED MY KEYS!
HEY, GET MY CARDS WET AND I'LL CLOCK YOU!
aprilia

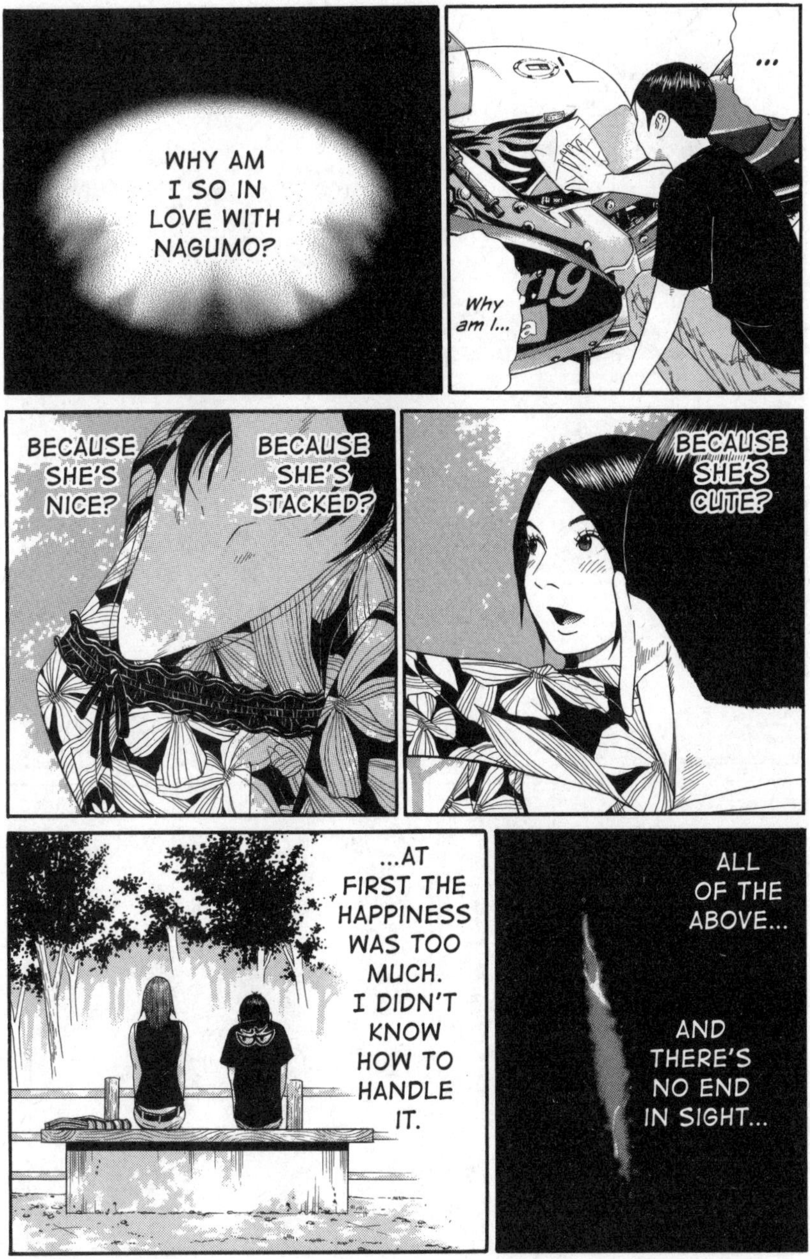
...
Why am I...
WHY AM I SO IN LOVE WITH NAGUMO?
BECAUSE SHE'S CUTE?
BECAUSE SHE'S STACKED?
BECAUSE SHE'S NICE?
ALL OF THE ABOVE...
AND THERE'S NO END IN SIGHT...
...AT FIRST THE HAPPINESS WAS TOO MUCH. I DIDN'T KNOW HOW TO HANDLE IT.

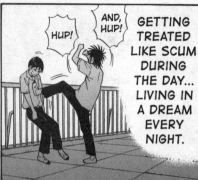

GETTING TREATED LIKE SCUM DURING THE DAY... LIVING IN A DREAM EVERY NIGHT.
AND, HUP!
HUP!
...And now the dream never ends ...
Crap ...
I don't know if I can cope ...
HEY YUSUKE, HAVE YOU SEEN MY WATCH?
THE GOLD ONE WITH THE BROWN STRAP ?
...MOM.
YEAH ?

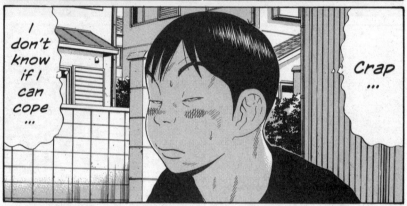

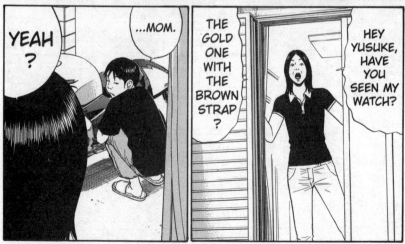

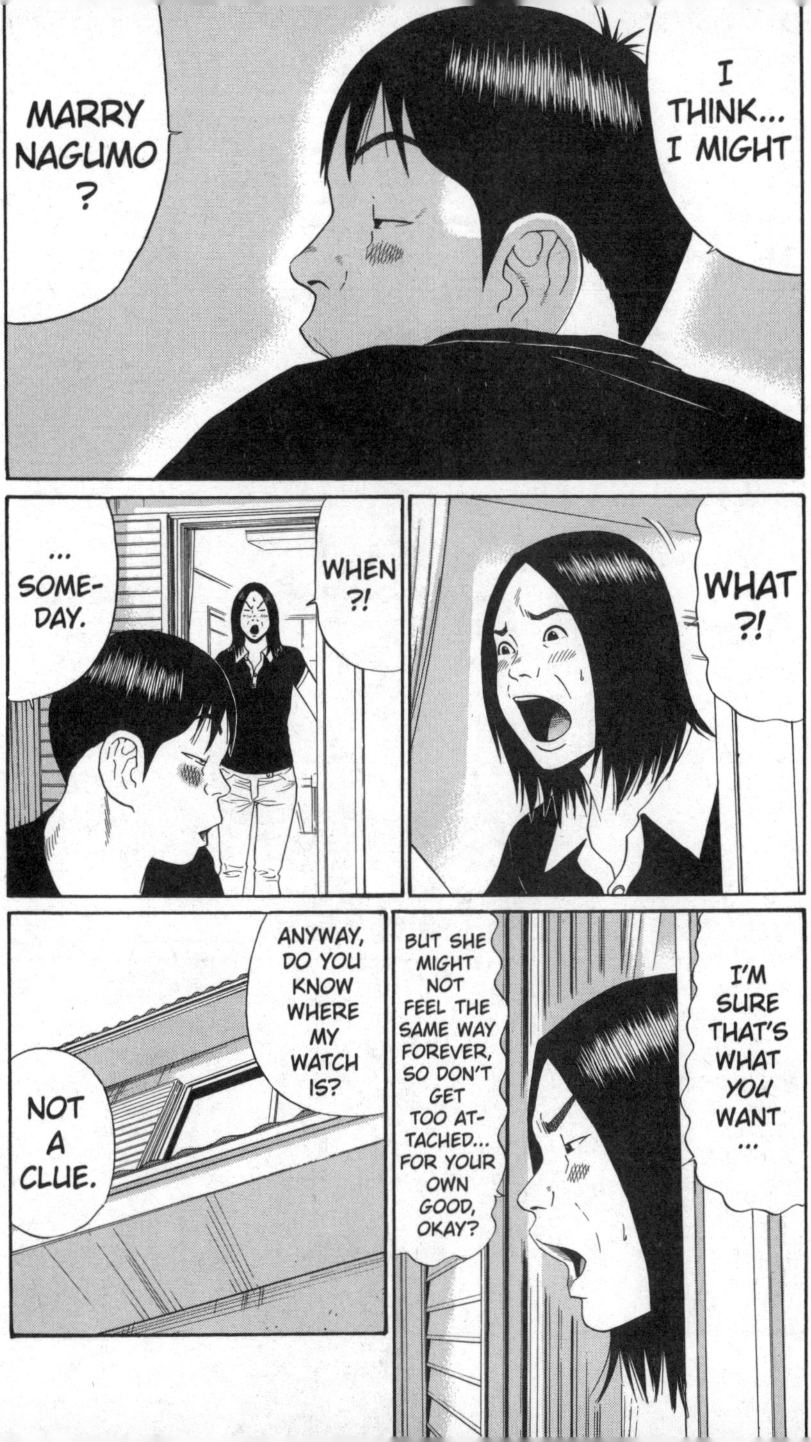
I THINK... I MIGHT
MARRY NAGUMO ?
WHAT ?!
WHEN ?!
... SOME-DAY.
I'M SURE THAT'S WHAT YOU WANT ...
BUT SHE MIGHT NOT FEEL THE SAME WAY FOREVER, SO DON'T GET TOO AT-TACHED... FOR YOUR OWN GOOD, OKAY?
ANYWAY, DO YOU KNOW WHERE MY WATCH IS?
NOT A CLUE.

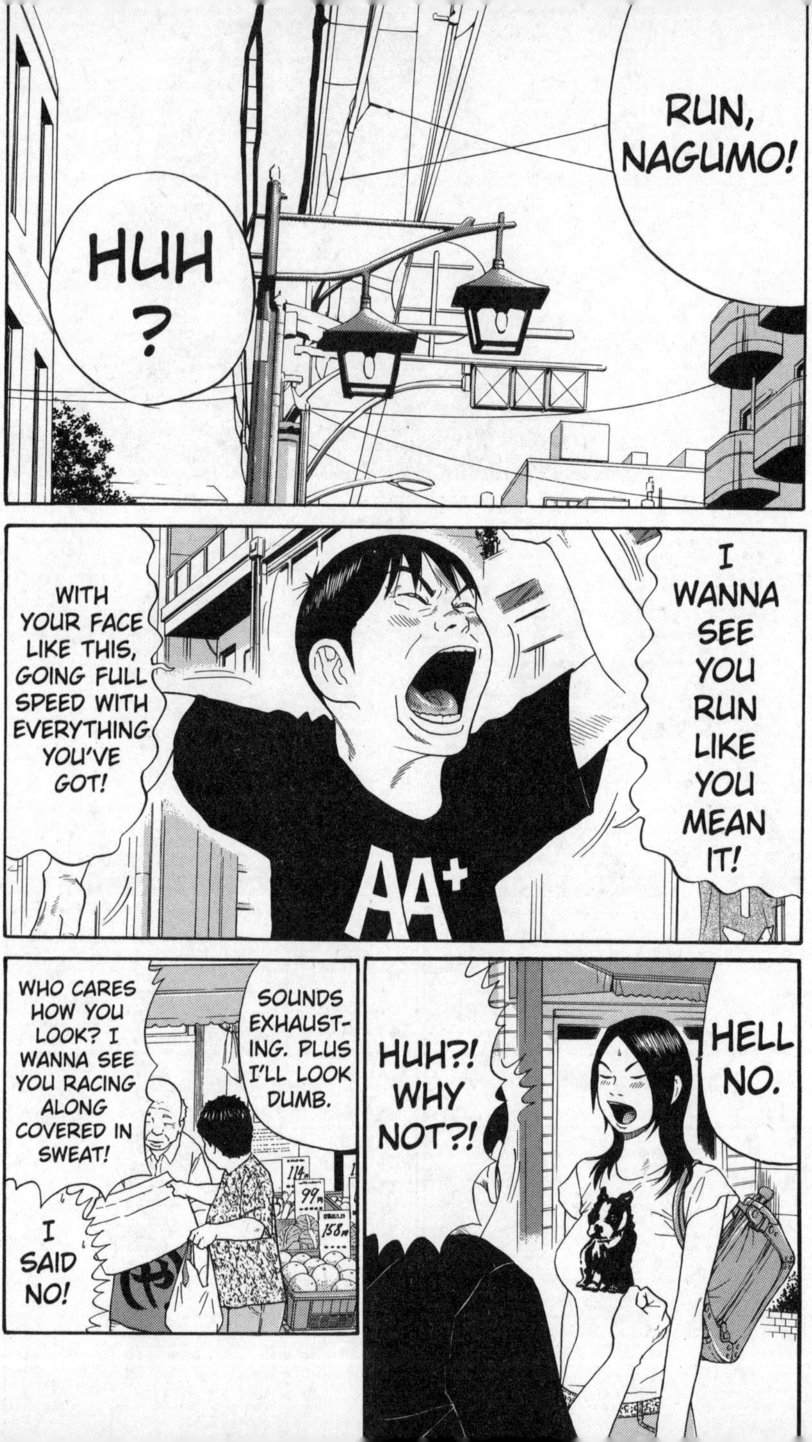
RUN, NAGUMO!
HUH ?
I WANNA SEE YOU RUN LIKE YOU MEAN IT!
WITH YOUR FACE LIKE THIS, GOING FULL SPEED WITH EVERYTHING YOU'VE GOT!
AA+
HELL NO.
HUH?! WHY NOT?!
SOUNDS EXHAUST-ING. PLUS I'LL LOOK DUMB.
WHO CARES HOW YOU LOOK? I WANNA SEE YOU RACING ALONG COVERED IN SWEAT!
I SAID NO!

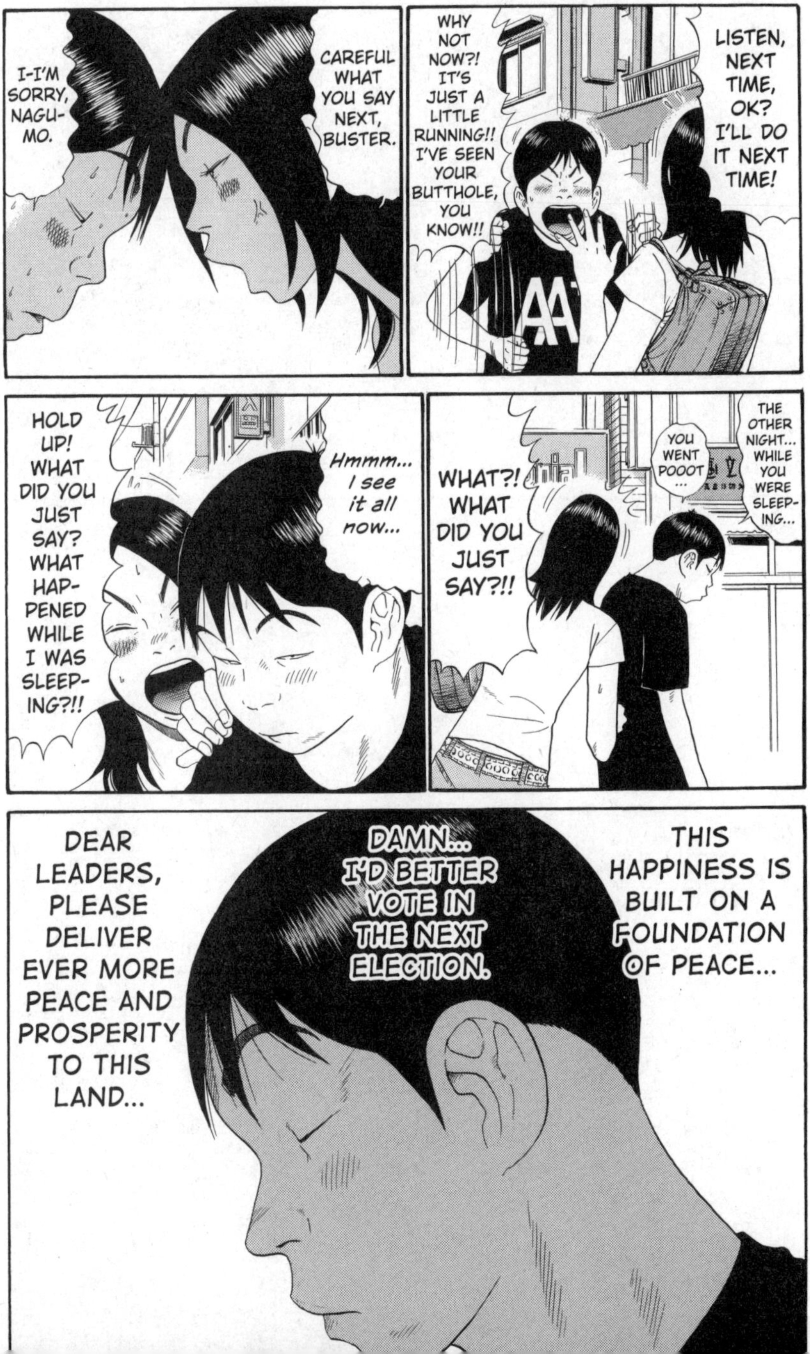

LISTEN, NEXT TIME, OK? I'LL DO IT NEXT TIME!
WHY NOT NOW?! IT'S JUST A LITTLE RUNNING!! I'VE SEEN YOUR BUTTHOLE, YOU KNOW!!
CAREFUL WHAT YOU SAY NEXT, BUSTER.
I-I'M SORRY, NAGUMO.
THE OTHER NIGHT... WHILE YOU WERE SLEEPING...
YOU WENT POOOT ...
WHAT?! WHAT DID YOU JUST SAY?!!
Hmmm... I see it all now...
HOLD UP! WHAT DID YOU JUST SAY? WHAT HAPPENED WHILE I WAS SLEEPING?!!
THIS HAPPINESS IS BUILT ON A FOUNDATION OF PEACE...
DAMN... I'D BETTER VOTE IN THE NEXT ELECTION.
DEAR LEADERS, PLEASE DELIVER EVER MORE PEACE AND PROSPERITY TO THIS LAND...

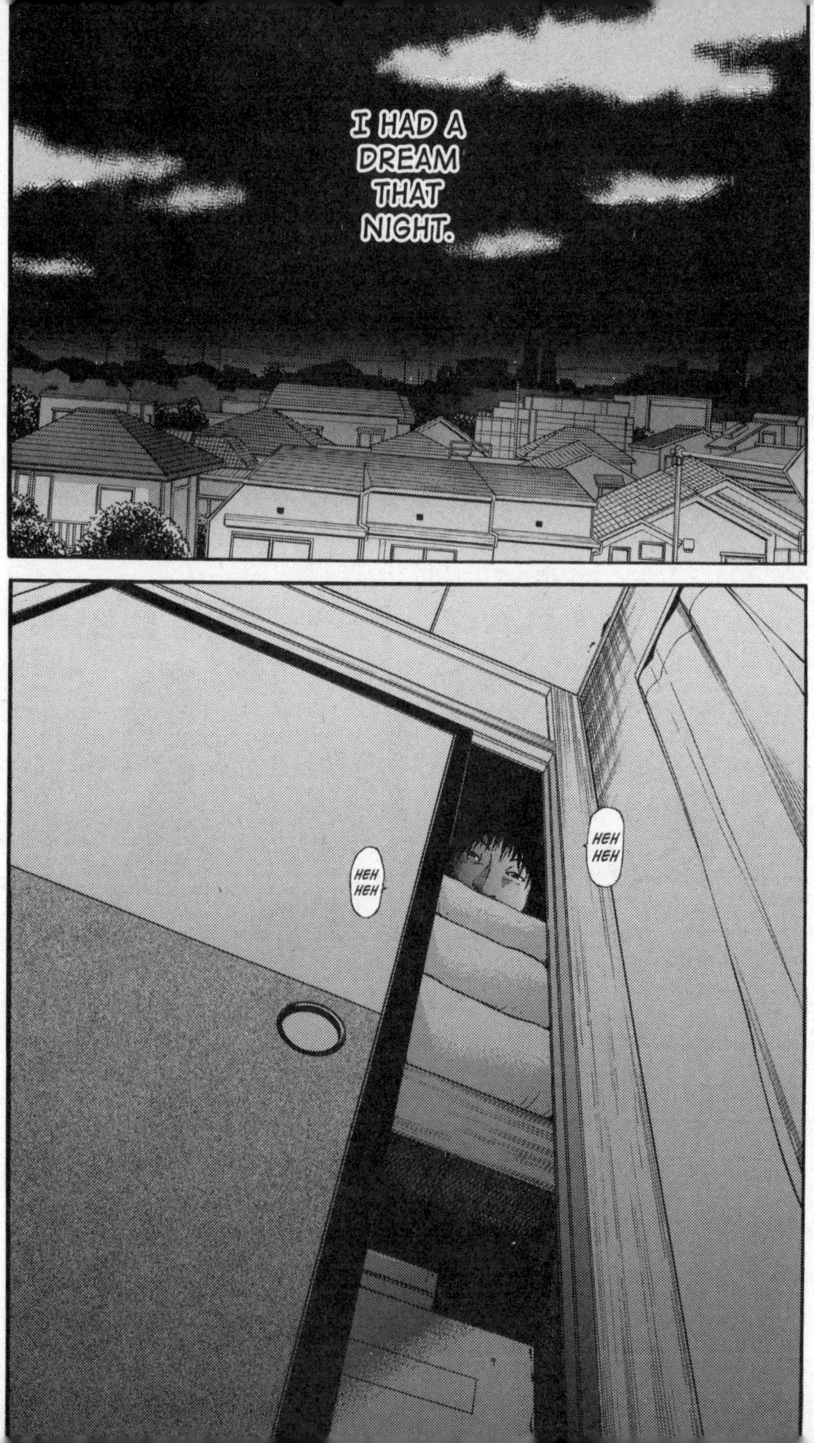
I HAD A DREAM THAT NIGHT.
HEH HEH
HEH HEH

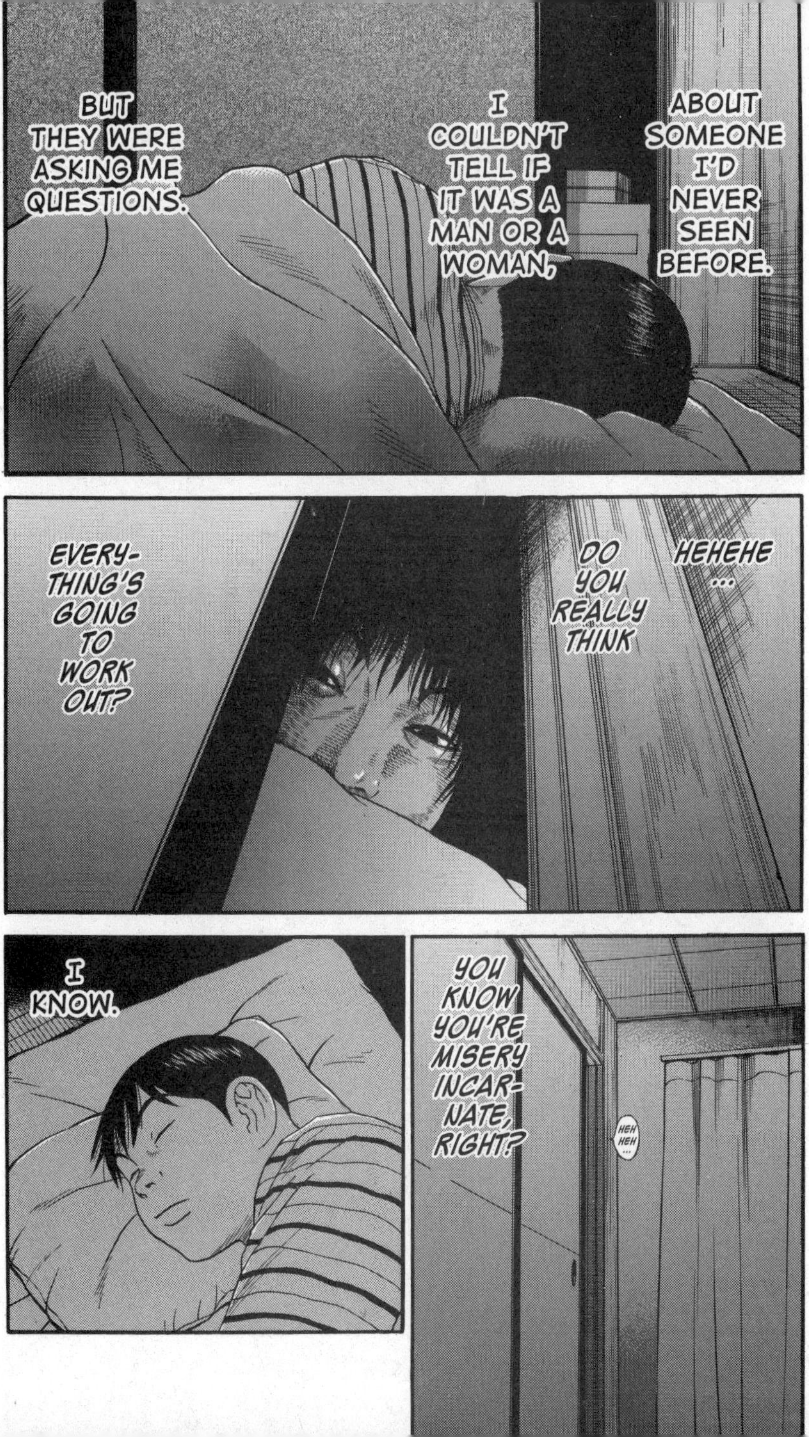
ABOUT SOMEONE I'D NEVER SEEN BEFORE.
I COULDN'T TELL IF IT WAS A MAN OR A WOMAN,
BUT THEY WERE ASKING ME QUESTIONS.
HEHEHE...
DO YOU REALLY THINK
EVERY-THING'S GOING TO WORK OUT?
YOU KNOW YOU'RE MISERY INCAR-NATE, RIGHT?
HEH HEH...
I KNOW.

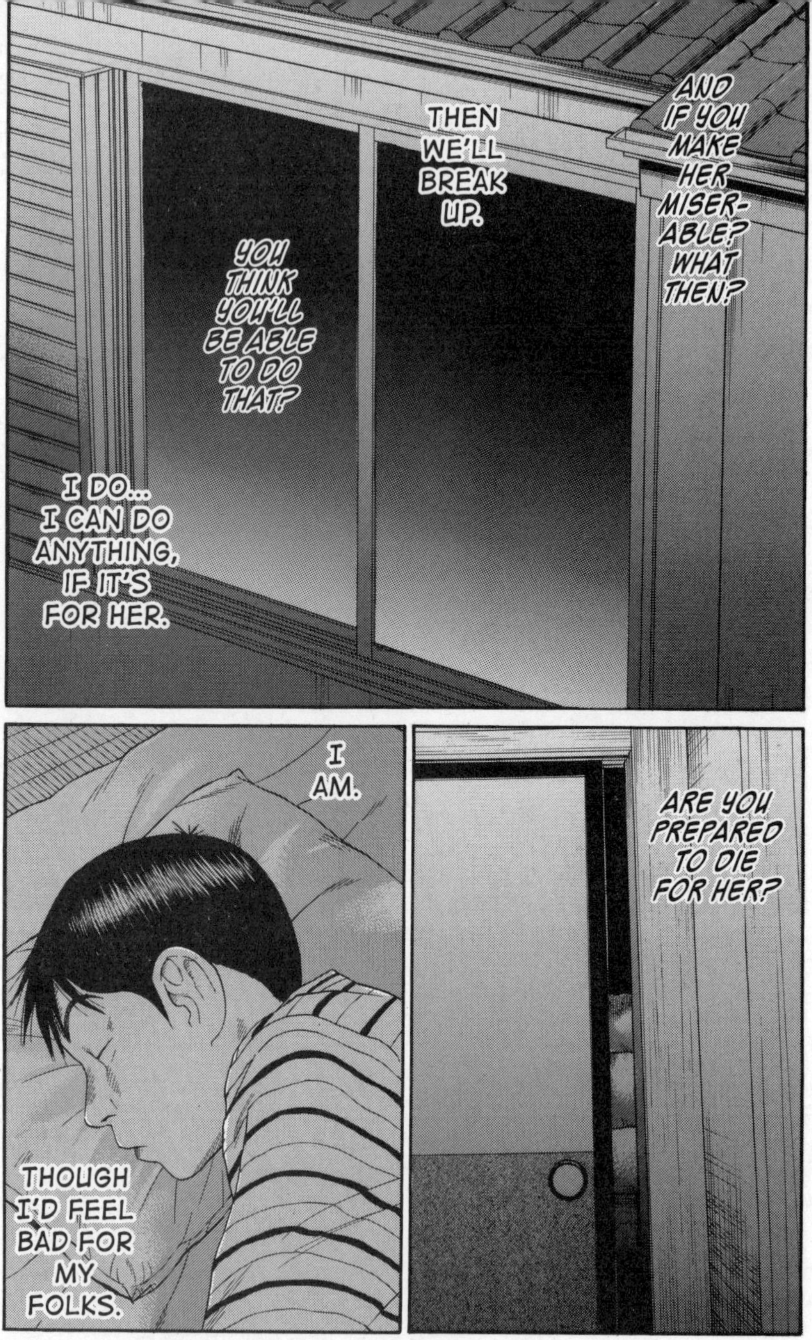
AND IF YOU MAKE HER MISER-ABLE? WHAT THEN?
THEN WE'LL BREAK UP.
YOU THINK YOU'LL BE ABLE TO DO THAT?
I DO... I CAN DO ANYTHING, IF IT'S FOR HER.
ARE YOU PREPARED TO DIE FOR HER?
I AM.
THOUGH I'D FEEL BAD FOR MY FOLKS.

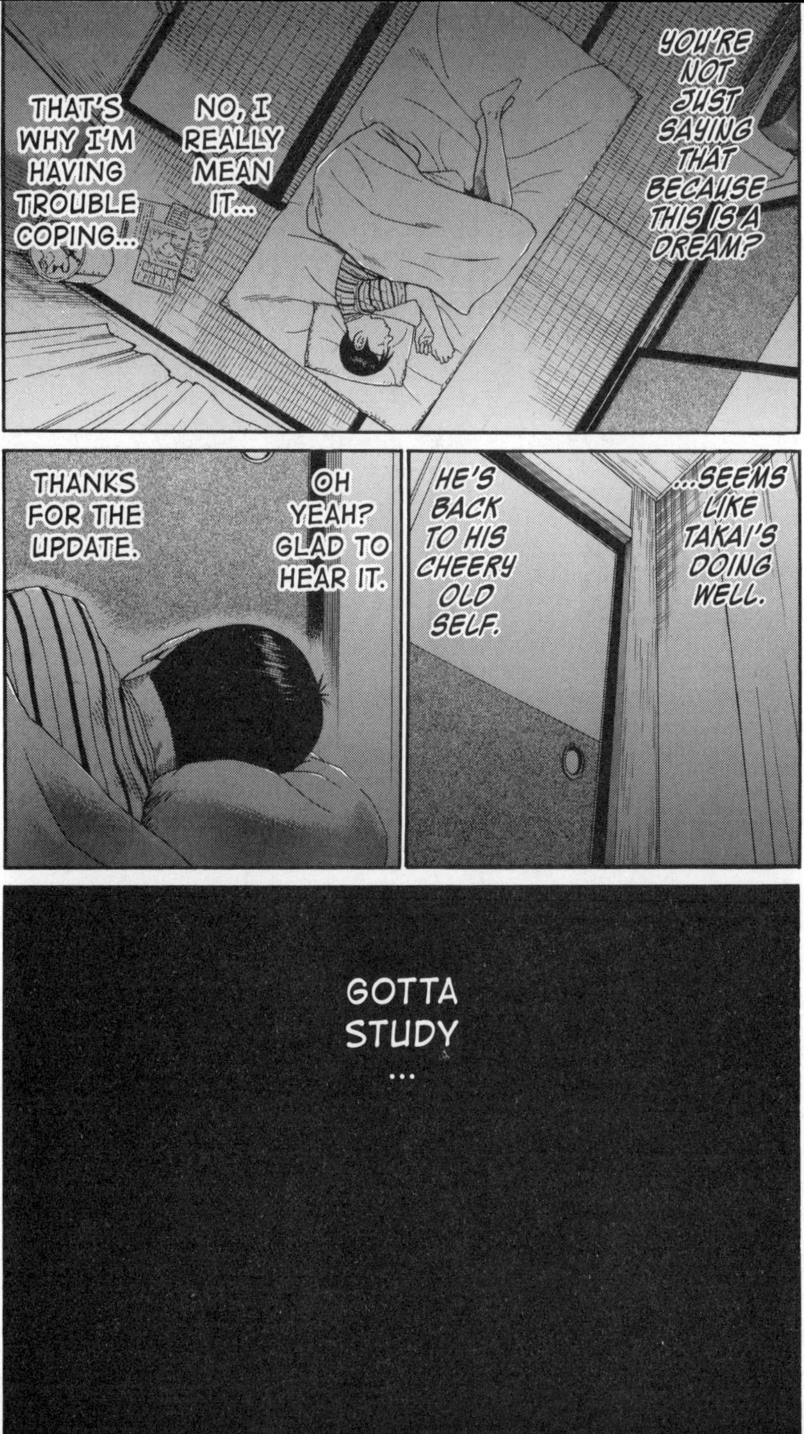
YOU'RE NOT JUST SAYING THAT BECAUSE THIS IS A DREAM?
NO, I REALLY MEAN IT...
THAT'S WHY I'M HAVING TROUBLE COPING...
...SEEMS LIKE TAKAI'S DOING WELL.
HE'S BACK TO HIS CHEERY OLD SELF.
OH YEAH? GLAD TO HEAR IT.
THANKS FOR THE UPDATE.
GOTTA STUDY ...

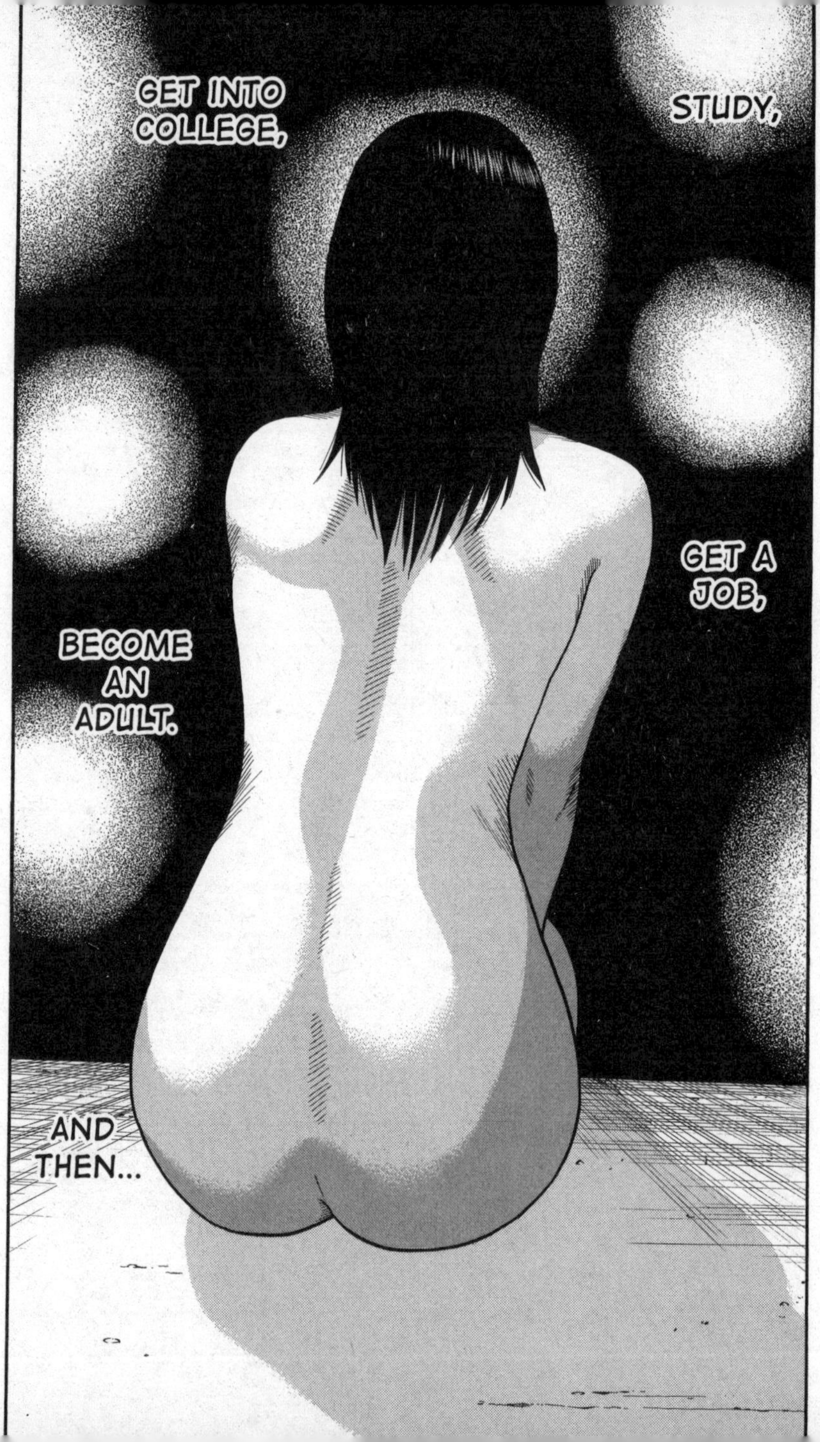
STUDY,
GET INTO COLLEGE,
GET A JOB,
BECOME AN ADULT.
AND THEN...

# Final Chapter: Adult

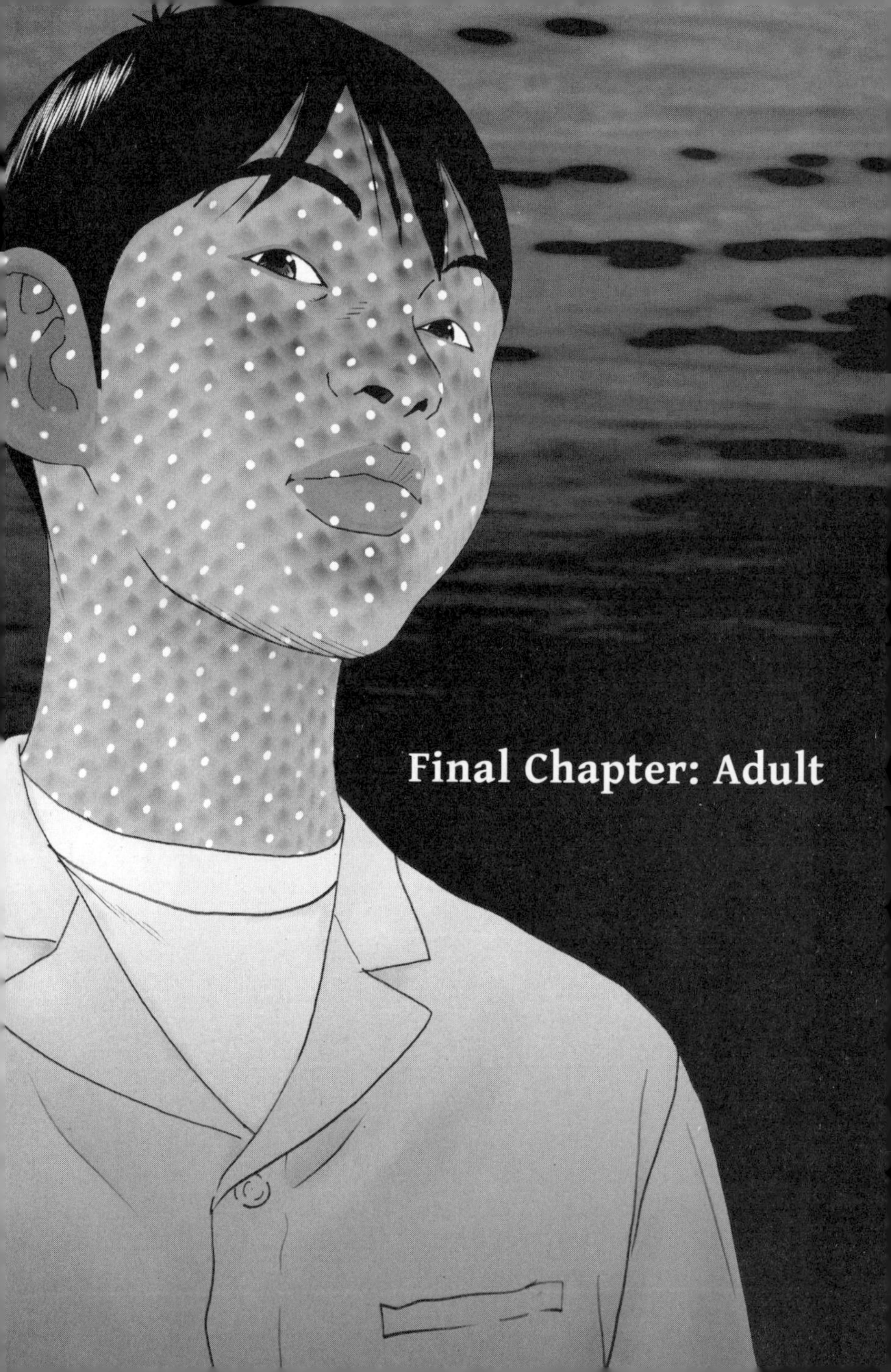

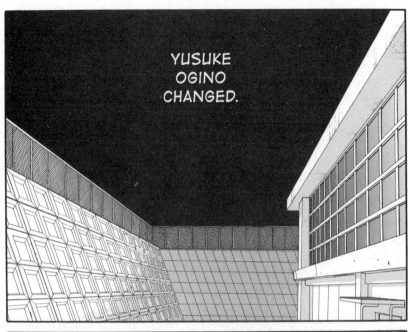

YUSUKE
OGINO
CHANGED.

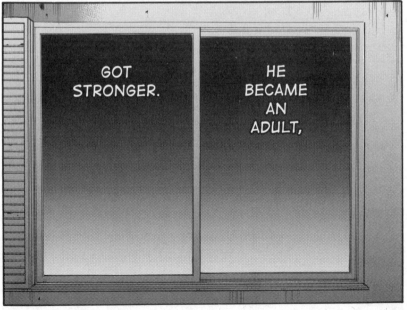

GOT
STRONGER.

HE
BECAME
AN
ADULT,

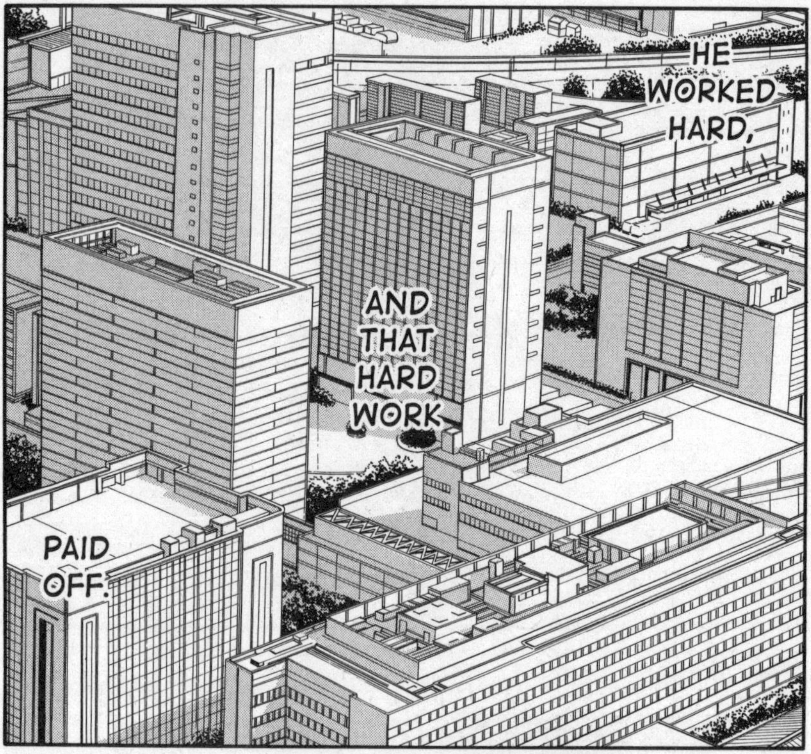
HE WORKED HARD,
AND THAT HARD WORK
PAID OFF.
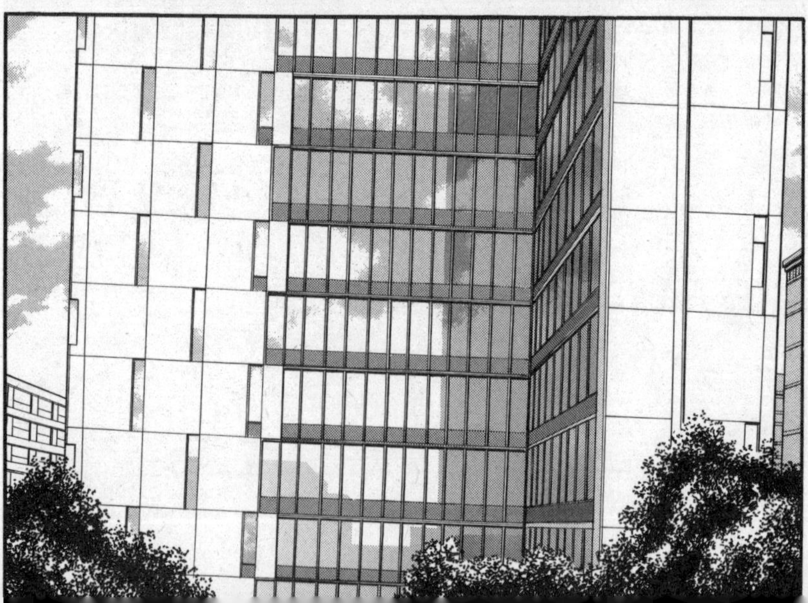

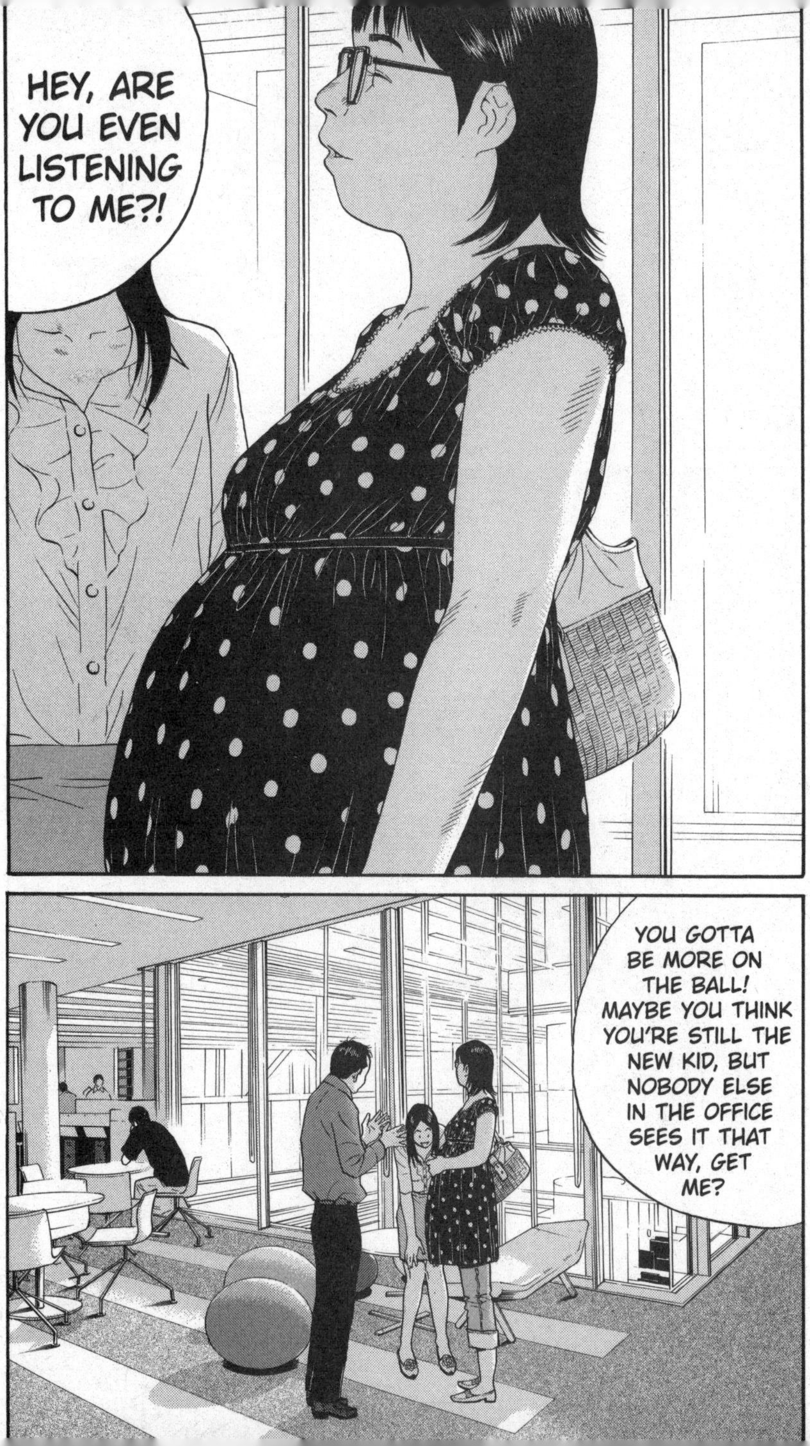
HEY, ARE YOU EVEN LISTENING TO ME?!
YOU GOTTA BE MORE ON THE BALL! MAYBE YOU THINK YOU'RE STILL THE NEW KID, BUT NOBODY ELSE IN THE OFFICE SEES IT THAT WAY, GET ME?

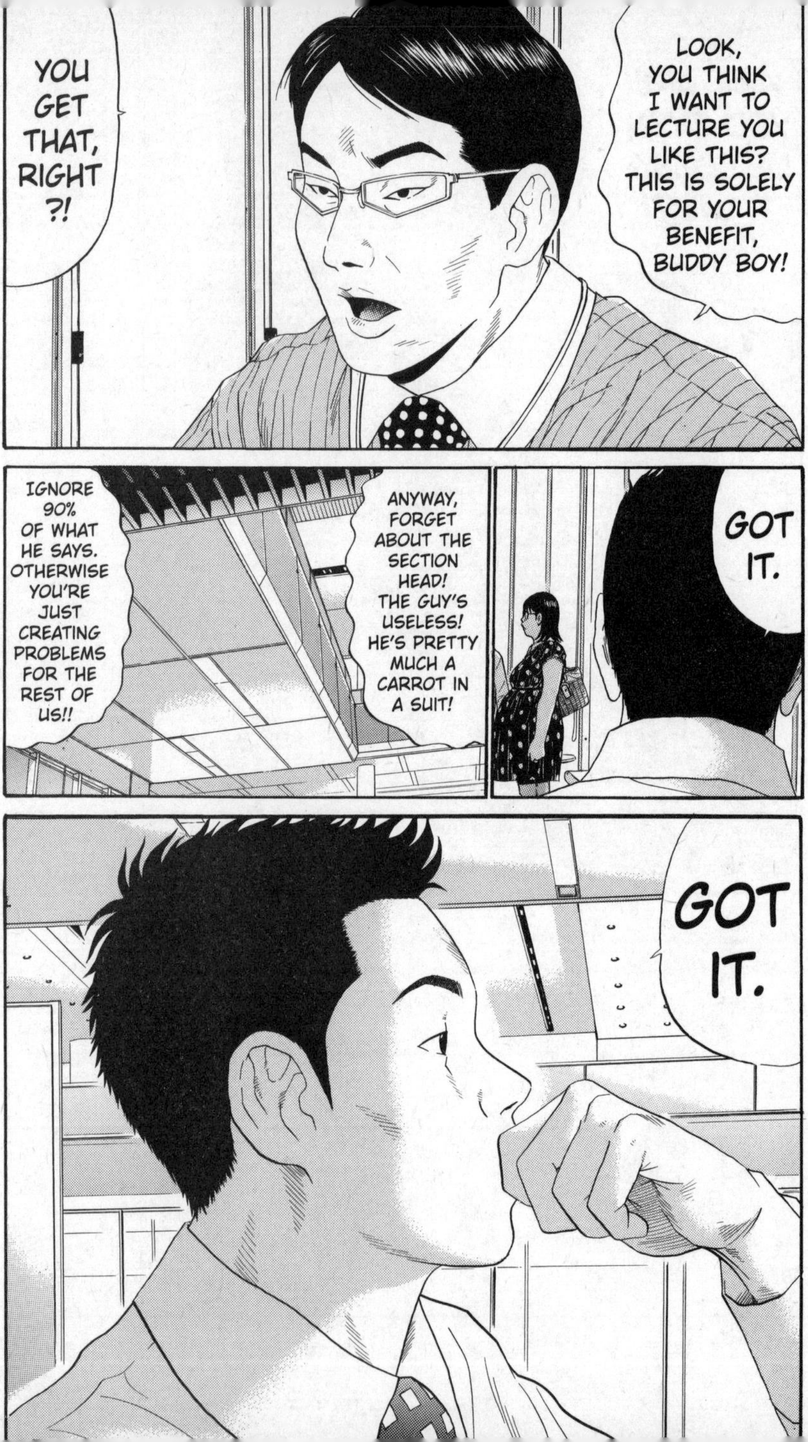
LOOK, YOU THINK I WANT TO LECTURE YOU LIKE THIS? THIS IS SOLELY FOR YOUR BENEFIT, BUDDY BOY!
YOU GET THAT, RIGHT?!
GOT IT.
ANYWAY, FORGET ABOUT THE SECTION HEAD! THE GUY'S USELESS! HE'S PRETTY MUCH A CARROT IN A SUIT!
IGNORE 90% OF WHAT HE SAYS. OTHERWISE YOU'RE JUST CREATING PROBLEMS FOR THE REST OF US!!
GOT IT.

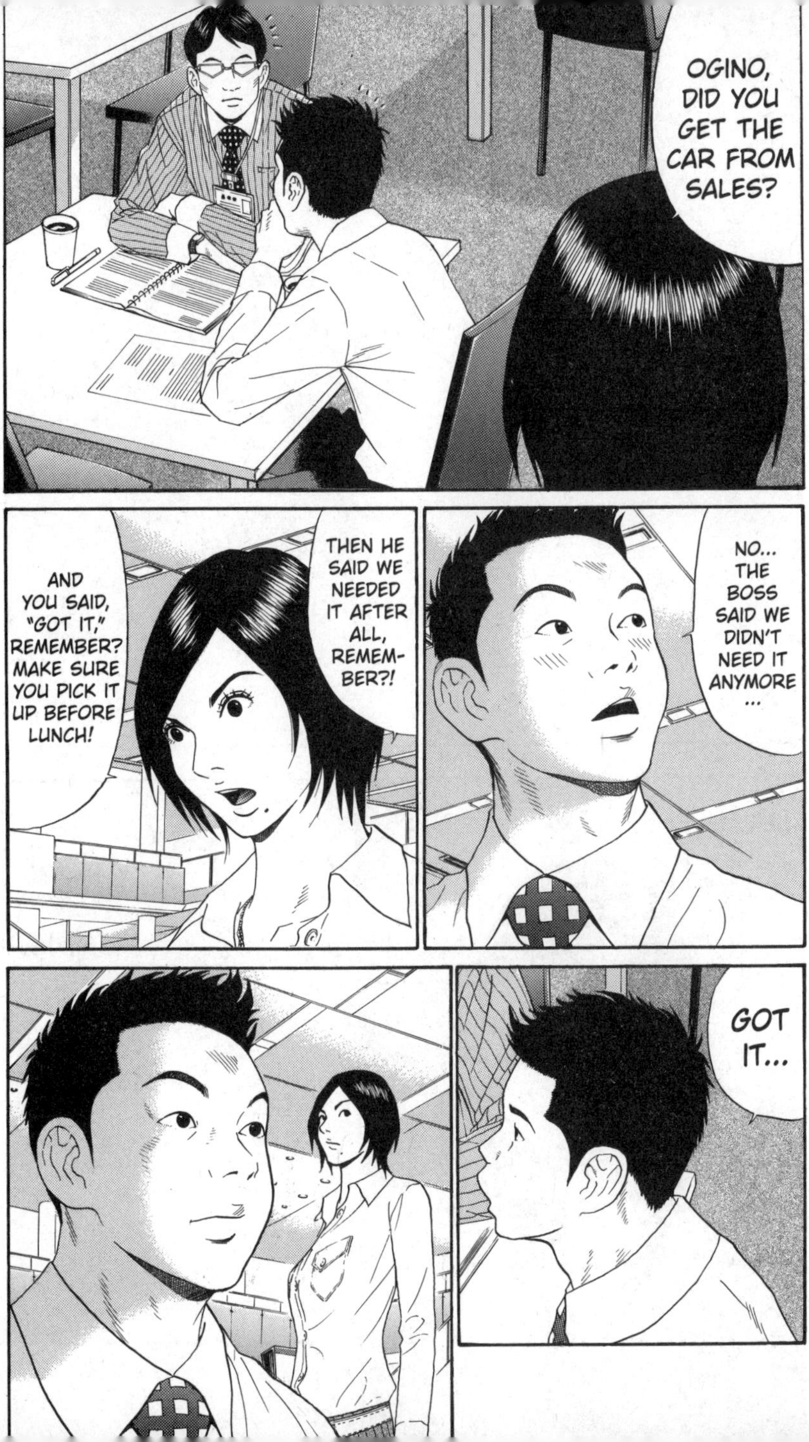
OGINO, DID YOU GET THE CAR FROM SALES?
NO... THE BOSS SAID WE DIDN'T NEED IT ANYMORE ...
THEN HE SAID WE NEEDED IT AFTER ALL, REMEMBER?!
AND YOU SAID, "GOT IT," REMEMBER? MAKE SURE YOU PICK IT UP BEFORE LUNCH!
GOT IT...

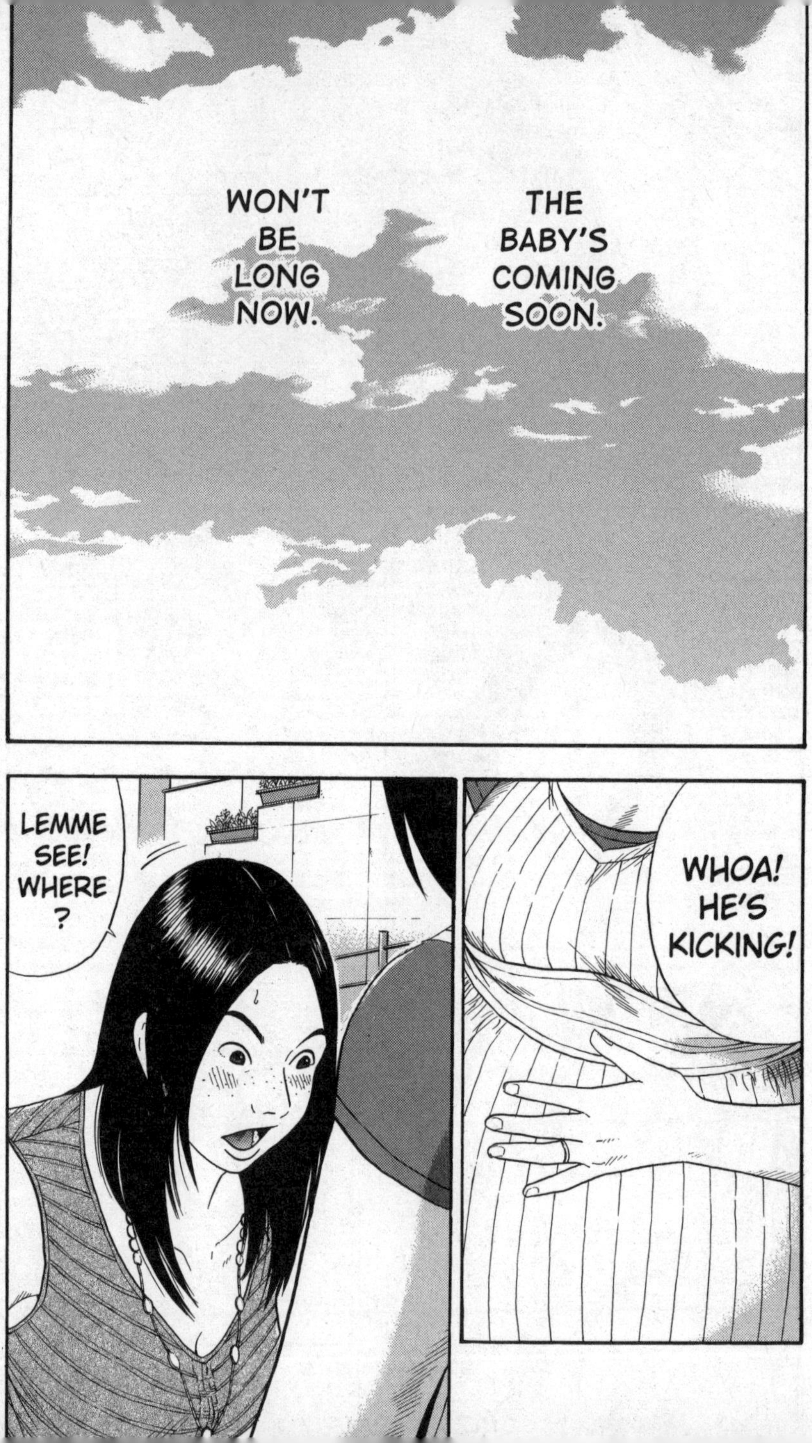
THE BABY'S COMING SOON.
WON'T BE LONG NOW.
WHOA! HE'S KICKING!
LEMME SEE! WHERE?

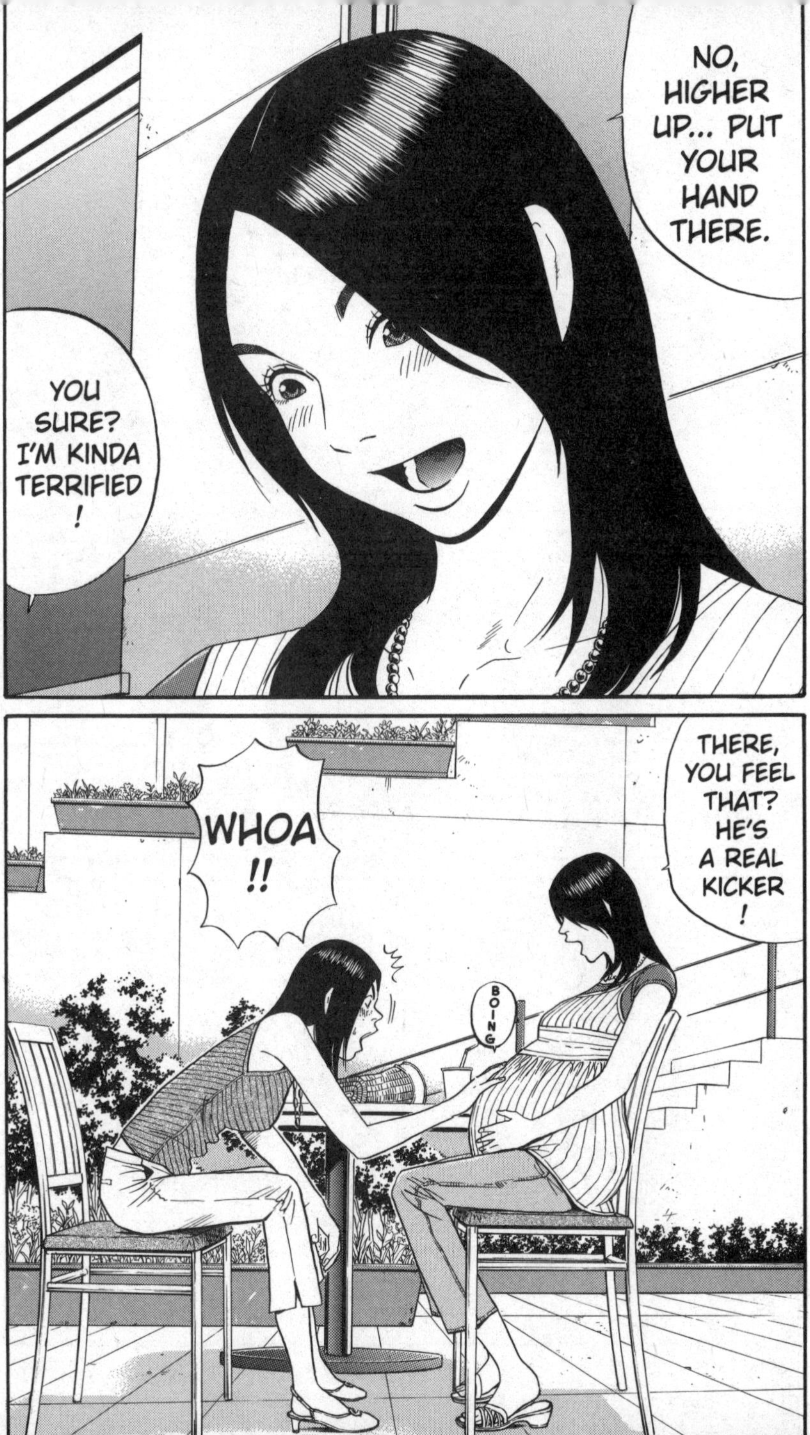
NO, HIGHER UP... PUT YOUR HAND THERE.
YOU SURE? I'M KINDA TERRIFIED!
THERE, YOU FEEL THAT? HE'S A REAL KICKER!
BOING
WHOA!!

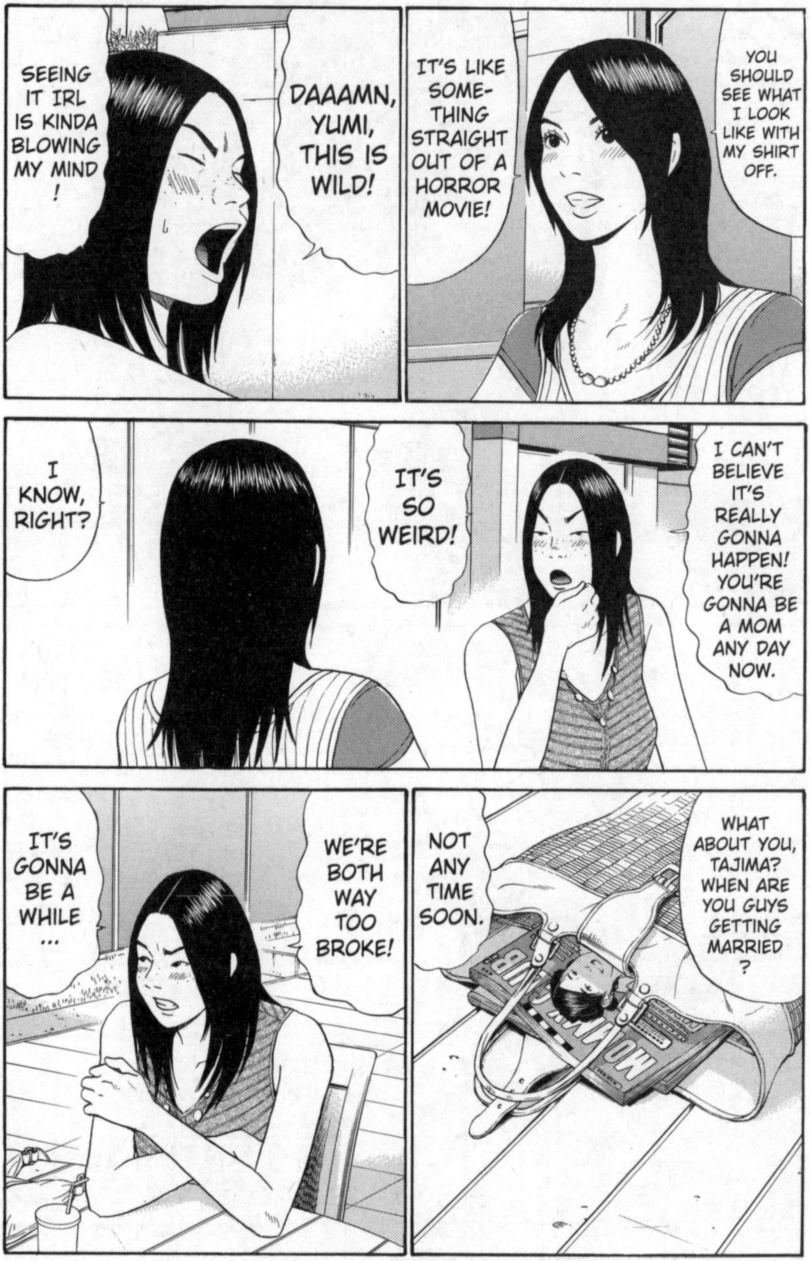
YOU SHOULD SEE WHAT I LOOK LIKE WITH MY SHIRT OFF.
IT'S LIKE SOME-THING STRAIGHT OUT OF A HORROR MOVIE!
DAAAMN, YUMI, THIS IS WILD!
SEEING IT IRL IS KINDA BLOWING MY MIND!
I CAN'T BELIEVE IT'S REALLY GONNA HAPPEN! YOU'RE GONNA BE A MOM ANY DAY NOW.
IT'S SO WEIRD!
I KNOW, RIGHT?
WHAT ABOUT YOU, TAJIMA? WHEN ARE YOU GUYS GETTING MARRIED?
NOT ANY TIME SOON.
WE'RE BOTH WAY TOO BROKE!
IT'S GONNA BE A WHILE...

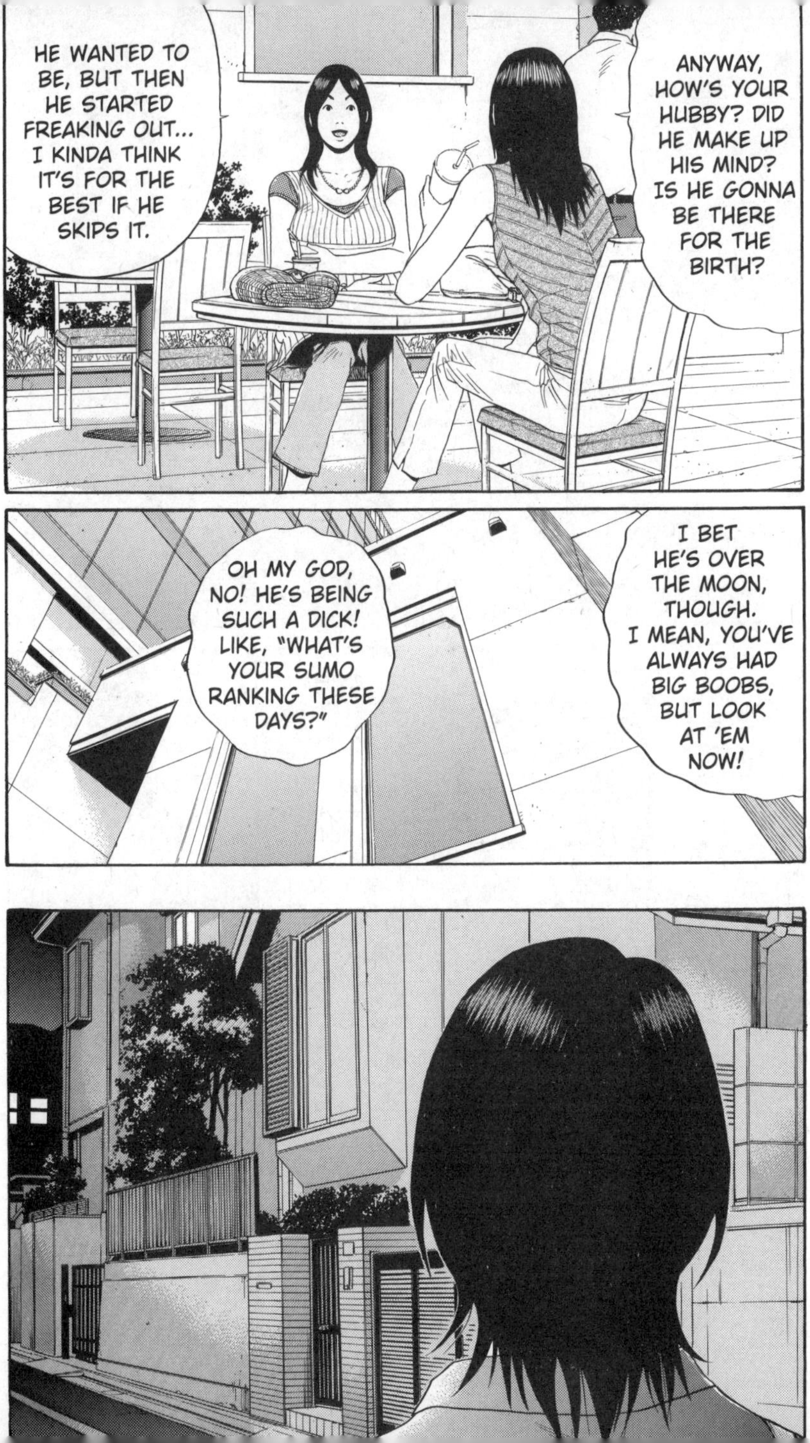
ANYWAY, HOW'S YOUR HUBBY? DID HE MAKE UP HIS MIND? IS HE GONNA BE THERE FOR THE BIRTH?
HE WANTED TO BE, BUT THEN HE STARTED FREAKING OUT... I KINDA THINK IT'S FOR THE BEST IF HE SKIPS IT.
I BET HE'S OVER THE MOON, THOUGH. I MEAN, YOU'VE ALWAYS HAD BIG BOOBS, BUT LOOK AT 'EM NOW!
OH MY GOD, NO! HE'S BEING SUCH A DICK! LIKE, "WHAT'S YOUR SUMO RANKING THESE DAYS?"

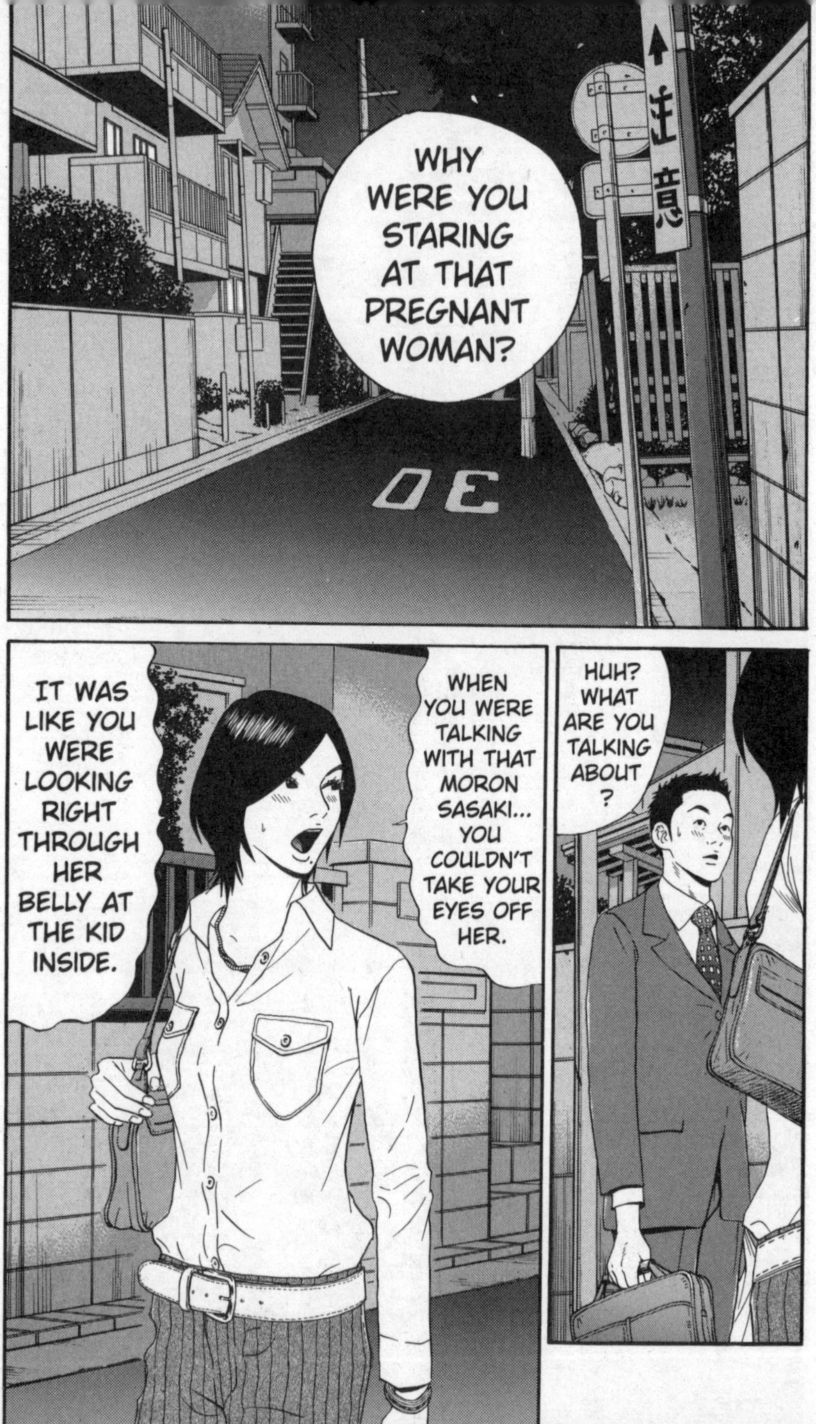
WHY WERE YOU STARING AT THAT PREGNANT WOMAN?
HUH? WHAT ARE YOU TALKING ABOUT ?
WHEN YOU WERE TALKING WITH THAT MORON SASAKI... YOU COULDN'T TAKE YOUR EYES OFF HER.
IT WAS LIKE YOU WERE LOOKING RIGHT THROUGH HER BELLY AT THE KID INSIDE.

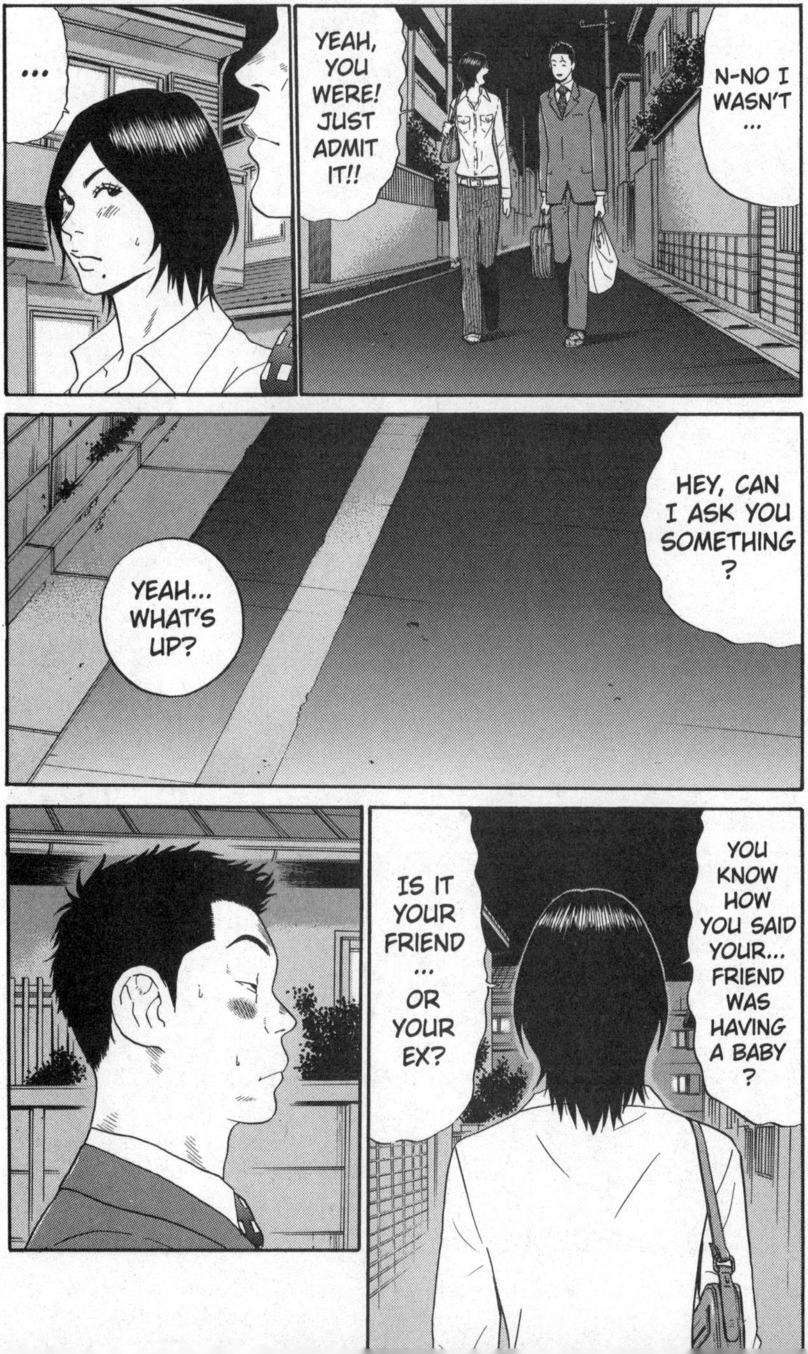
N-NO I WASN'T ...
YEAH, YOU WERE! JUST ADMIT IT!!
...
HEY, CAN I ASK YOU SOMETHING ?
YEAH... WHAT'S UP?
YOU KNOW HOW YOU SAID YOUR... FRIEND WAS HAVING A BABY ?
IS IT YOUR FRIEND ... OR YOUR EX?

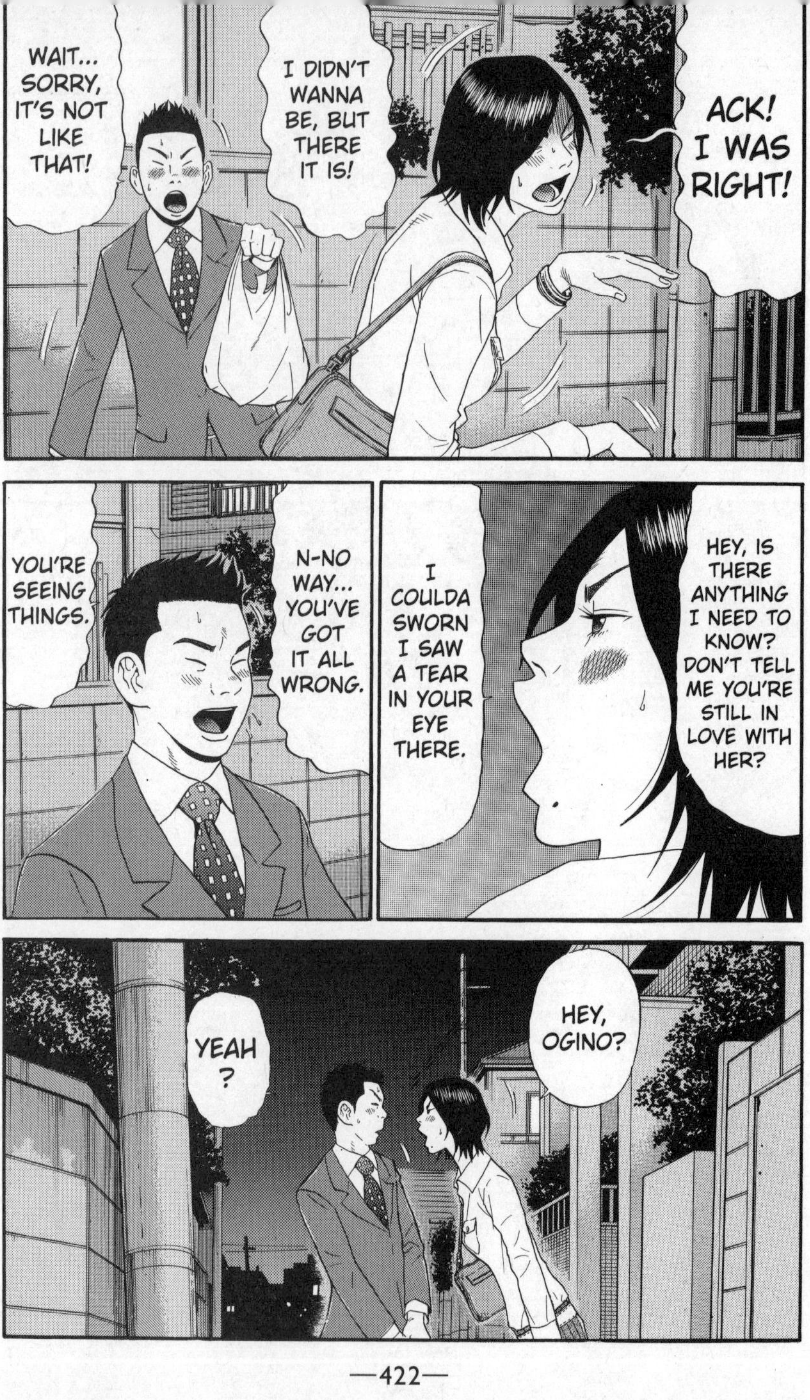
ACK! I WAS RIGHT!
I DIDN'T WANNA BE, BUT THERE IT IS!
WAIT... SORRY, IT'S NOT LIKE THAT!
HEY, IS THERE ANYTHING I NEED TO KNOW? DON'T TELL ME YOU'RE STILL IN LOVE WITH HER?
I COULDA SWORN I SAW A TEAR IN YOUR EYE THERE.
N-NO WAY... YOU'VE GOT IT ALL WRONG.
YOU'RE SEEING THINGS.
HEY, OGINO?
YEAH ?

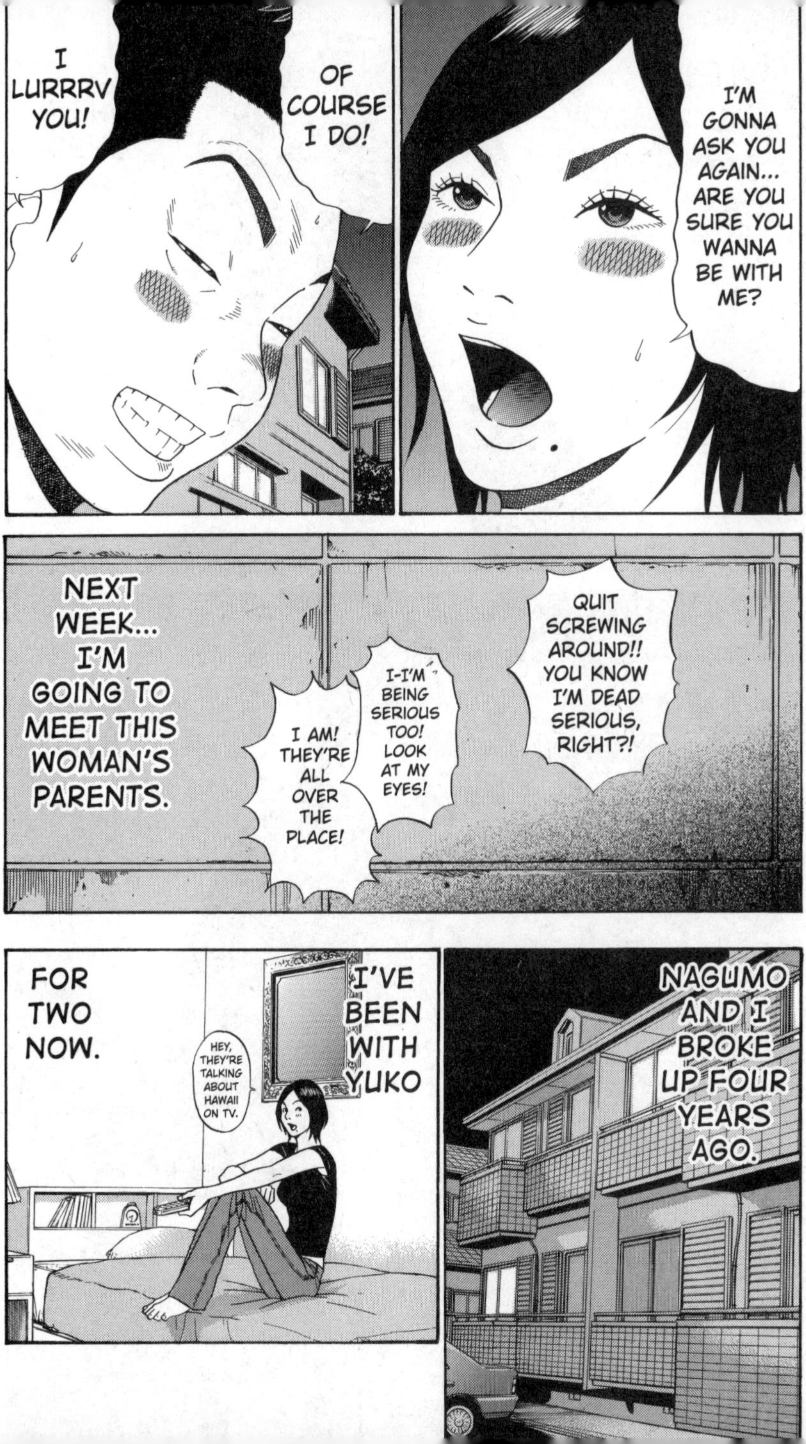
I'M GONNA ASK YOU AGAIN... ARE YOU SURE YOU WANNA BE WITH ME?
OF COURSE I DO!
I LURRRV YOU!
QUIT SCREWING AROUND!! YOU KNOW I'M DEAD SERIOUS, RIGHT?!
I-I'M BEING SERIOUS TOO! LOOK AT MY EYES!
I AM! THEY'RE ALL OVER THE PLACE!
NEXT WEEK... I'M GOING TO MEET THIS WOMAN'S PARENTS.
NAGUMO AND I BROKE UP FOUR YEARS AGO.
I'VE BEEN WITH YUKO
FOR TWO NOW.
HEY, THEY'RE TALKING ABOUT HAWAII ON TV.

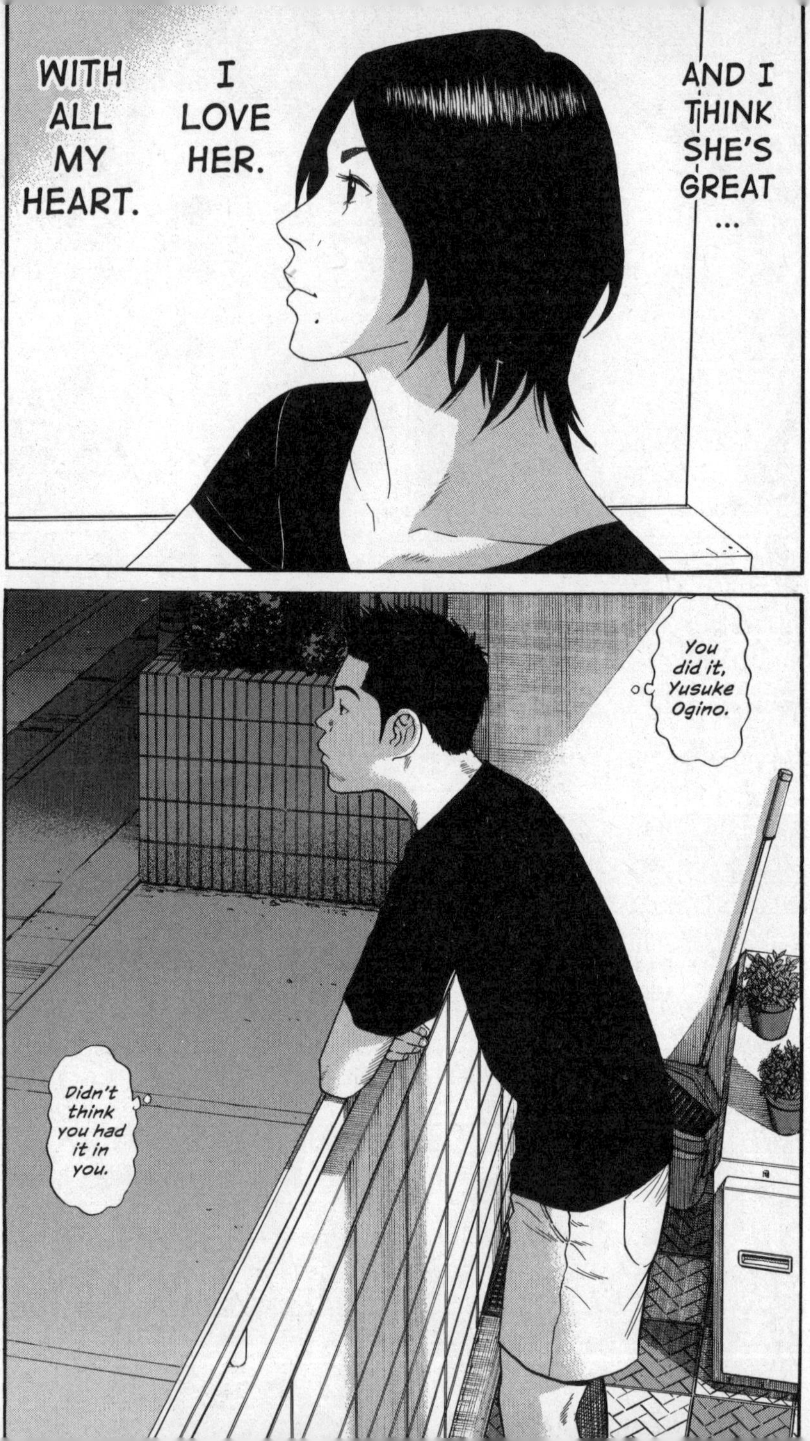
AND I THINK SHE'S GREAT ...
I LOVE HER.
WITH ALL MY HEART.
You did it, Yusuke Ogino.
Didn't think you had it in you.

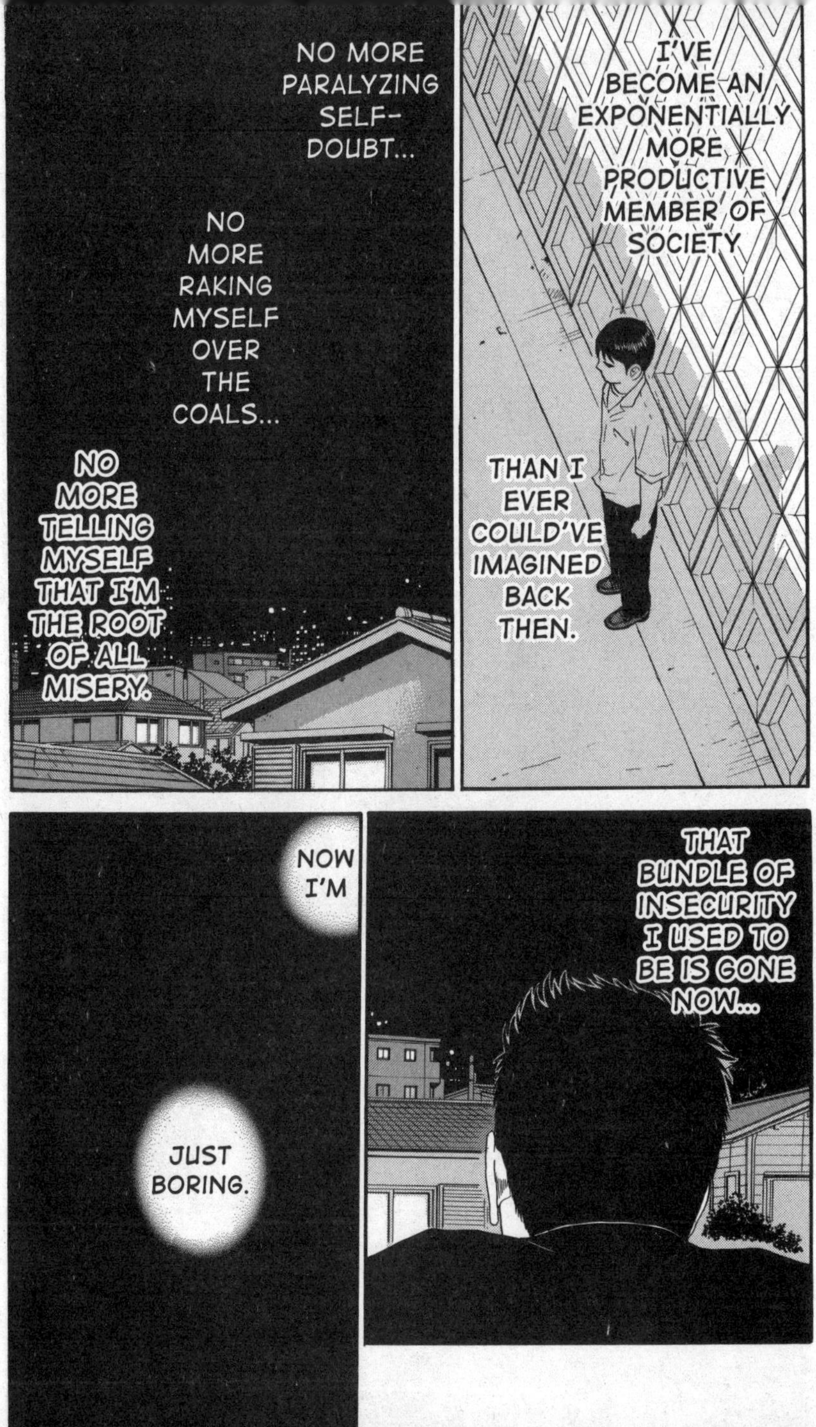
I'VE BECOME AN EXPONENTIALLY MORE PRODUCTIVE MEMBER OF SOCIETY
THAN I EVER COULD'VE IMAGINED BACK THEN.
NO MORE PARALYZING SELF-DOUBT...
NO MORE RAKING MYSELF OVER THE COALS...
NO MORE TELLING MYSELF THAT I'M THE ROOT OF ALL MISERY.
THAT BUNDLE OF INSECURITY I USED TO BE IS GONE NOW...
NOW I'M
JUST BORING.

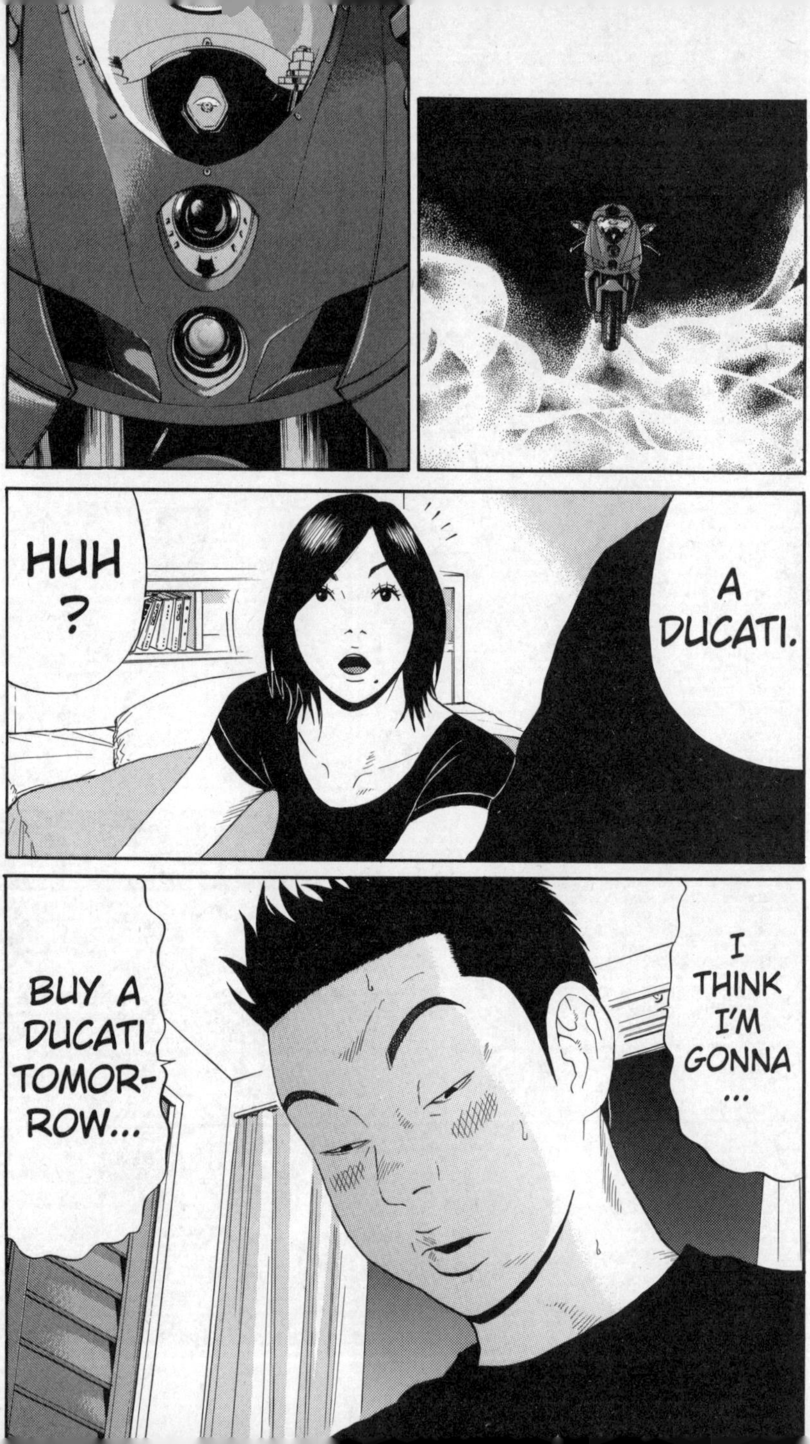
A DUCATI.
HUH ?
I THINK I'M GONNA ...
BUY A DUCATI TOMORROW...

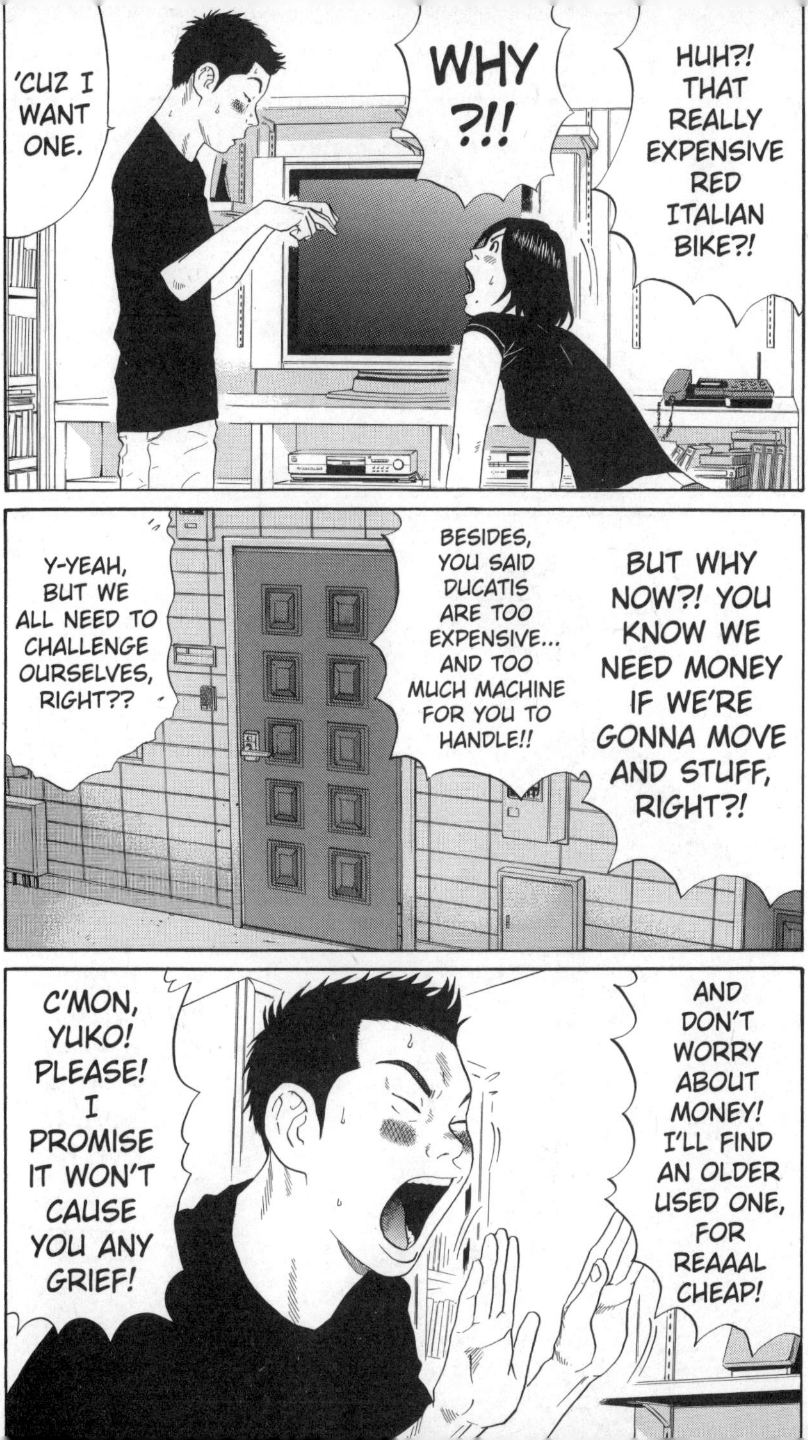
HUH?! THAT REALLY EXPENSIVE RED ITALIAN BIKE?!
WHY ?!!
'CUZ I WANT ONE.
BUT WHY NOW?! YOU KNOW WE NEED MONEY IF WE'RE GONNA MOVE AND STUFF, RIGHT?!
BESIDES, YOU SAID DUCATIS ARE TOO EXPENSIVE... AND TOO MUCH MACHINE FOR YOU TO HANDLE!!
Y-YEAH, BUT WE ALL NEED TO CHALLENGE OURSELVES, RIGHT??
AND DON'T WORRY ABOUT MONEY! I'LL FIND AN OLDER USED ONE, FOR REAAAL CHEAP!
C'MON, YUKO! PLEASE! I PROMISE IT WON'T CAUSE YOU ANY GRIEF!

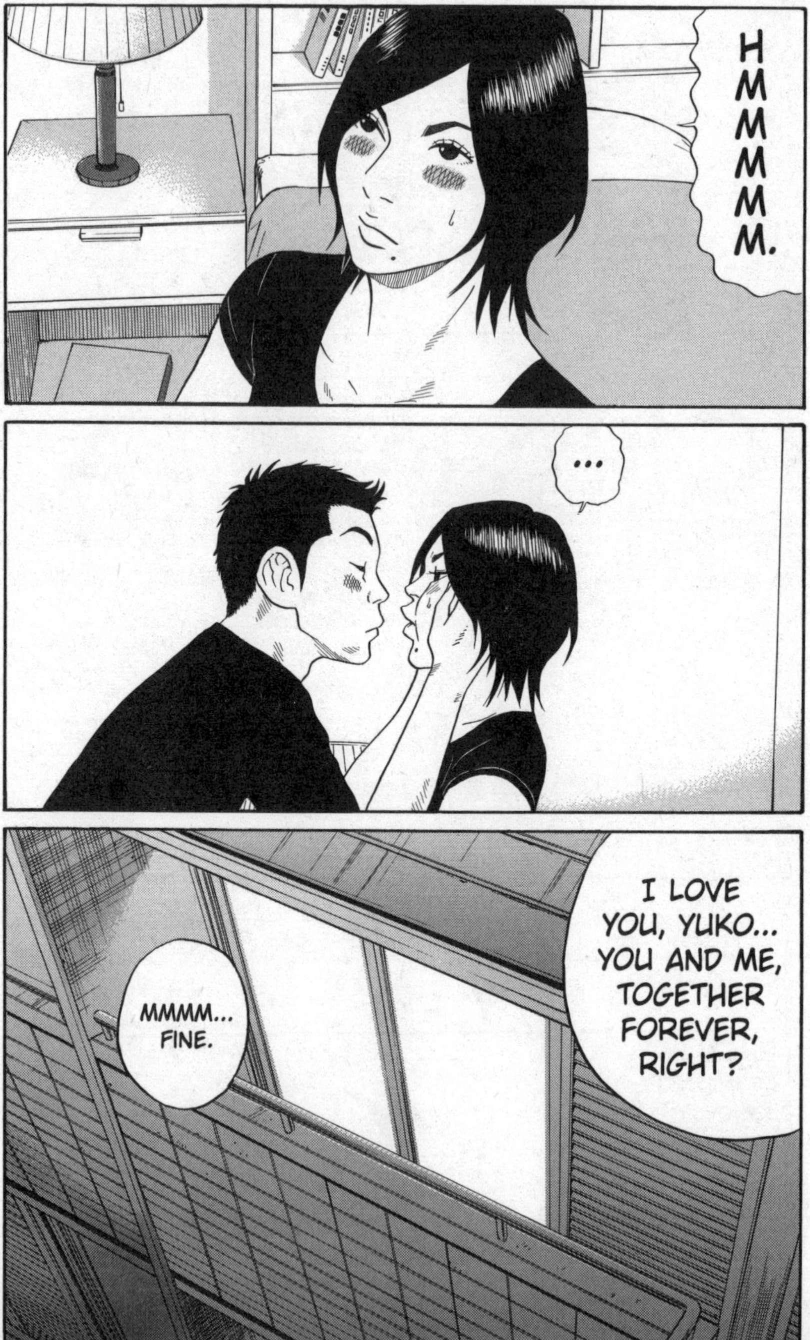
HMMMMM.
...
I LOVE YOU, YUKO... YOU AND ME, TOGETHER FOREVER, RIGHT?
MMMM... FINE.

# CIGUATERA

## vol·3 end

## not to be continued

The combined editions of this best-selling and acclaimed series, *The Flowers of Evil* follows the adventures of a lonely, bookish teen struggling to find his identity through Baudelaire's poetry, until two girls—a beauty and a bully— help him find true love and friendship.

Edgy, intense, and romantic, these new editions will give fans a chance to reconnect with Kasuga, Saeki, and Nakamura as they explore the issues of bullying, loneliness, individuality, and identity.

# Complete Series Now Available

www.kodansha.us

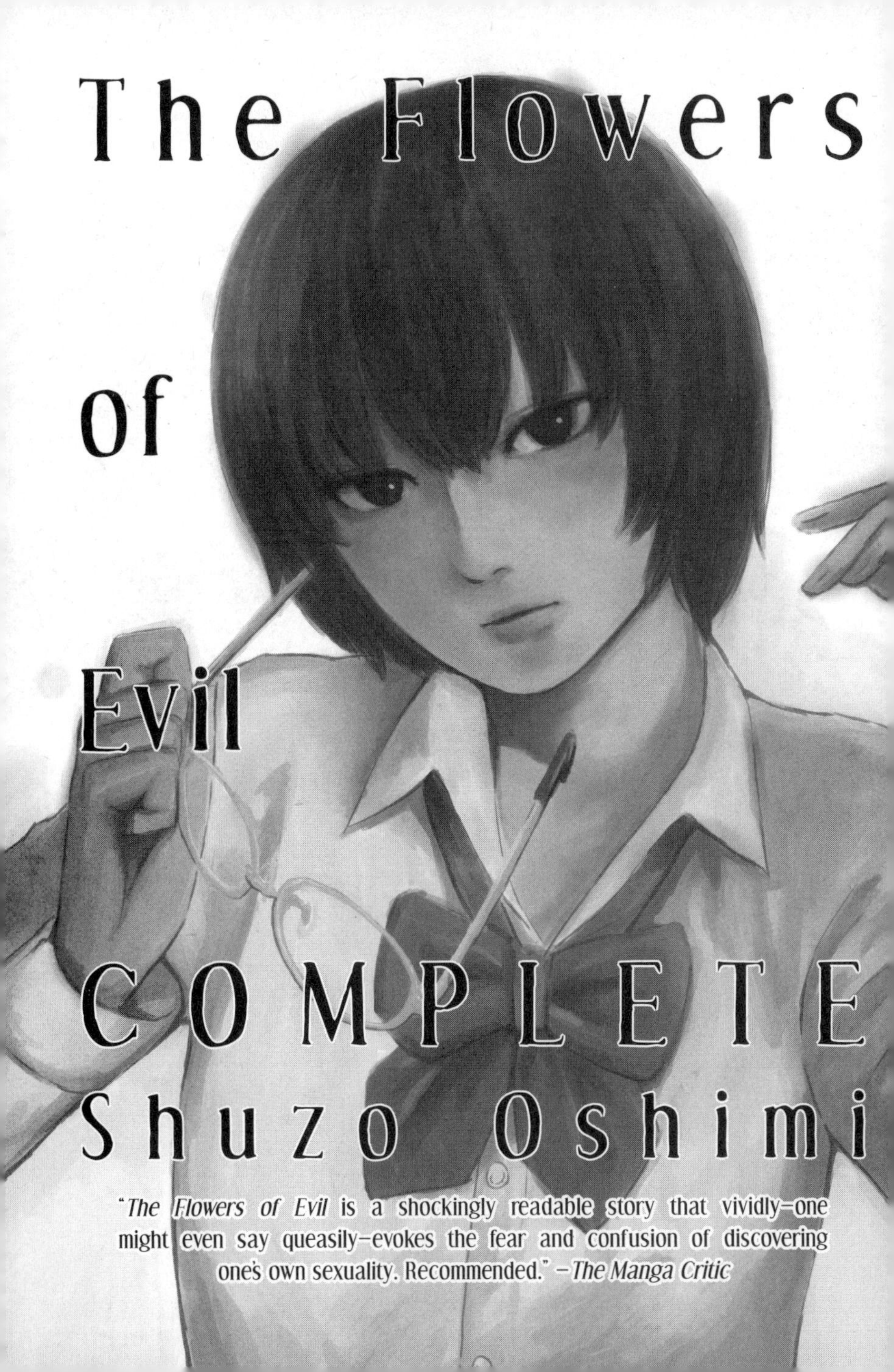
The Flowers
of
Evil
COMPLETE
Shuzo Oshimi
“*The Flowers of Evil* is a shockingly readable story that vividly—one might even say queasily—evokes the fear and confusion of discovering one’s own sexuality. Recommended.” —*The Manga Critic*

# Longing for Something Bigger

From the Eisner Award–nominated Inio Asano, creator of *Solanin* and *Nijigahara Holograph,* comes one of his most challenging works yet: an intense teen romance set in what may at first glance be one of the sleepiest places in Japan.

When Koume and Keisuke's relationship begins to take shape, it is apparent that they are both searching for something. Maybe Keisuke wants something more than a kiss from the fair Koume. Maybe Koume is looking for someone better than Misaki, the local playboy. But what they find in each other over the course of a summer might be far greater than anything they were expecting.

## Available Now!
© Inio Asano

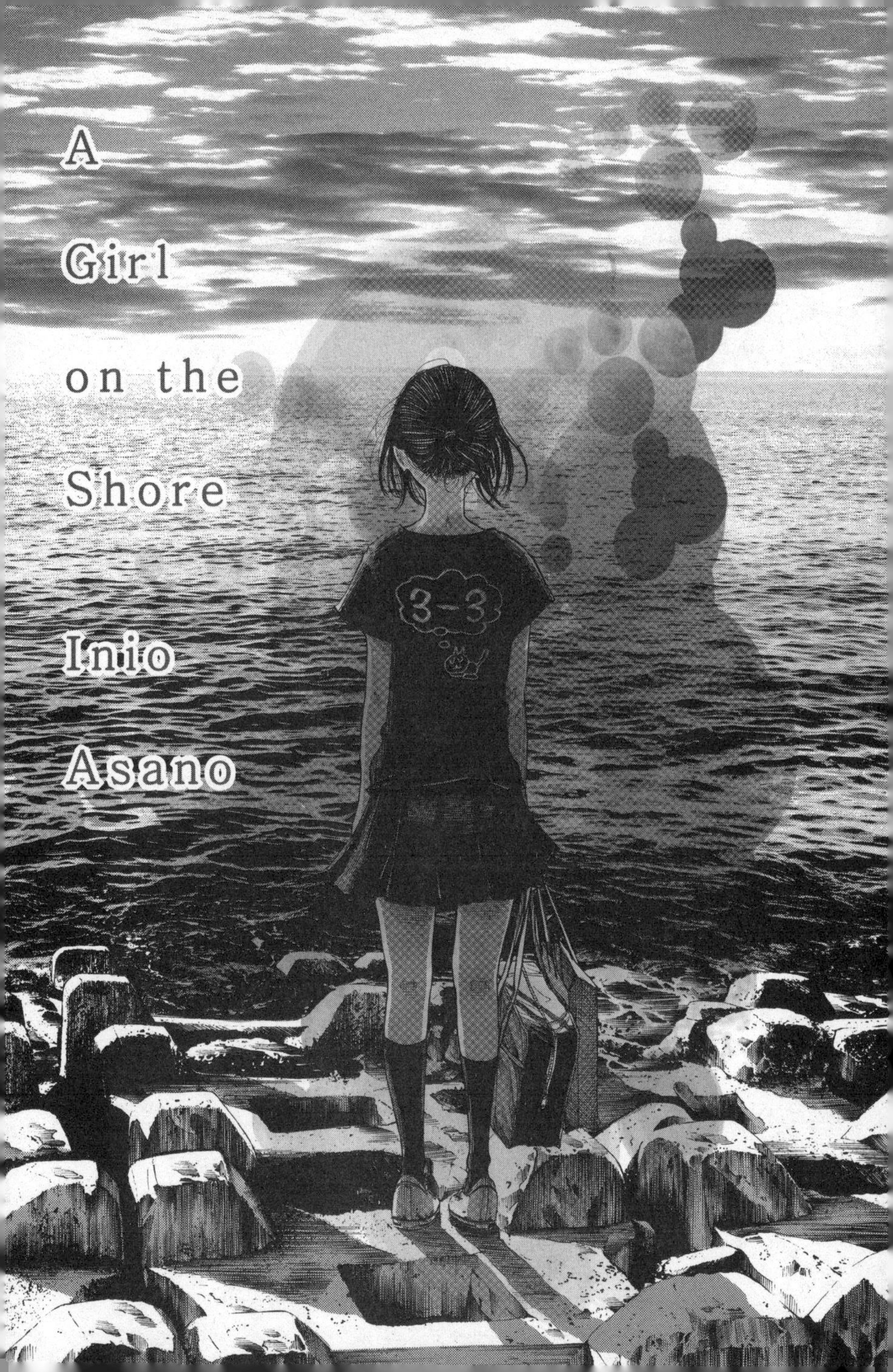
A
Girl
on the
Shore
Inio
Asano
3-3

# B U D D H A

A manga biography of the founder of one of the world's major religions.
8 volumes, $14.95 each.